IMPORTANT

D0086009

5fe2z-ticu-jtpp- un⊃к

REGISTRATION CODE
REGISTRATION CODE

Thank you, and welcome to your
McGraw-Hill Online Resources.

ISBN-13: 978-0-07-327444-7
ISBN-10: 0-07-327444-5 t/a
Bilhartz- Sacred Words:
A Source Book on the
Great Religions of the World, 1/e

The McGraw-Hill Companies

Higher Education

SACRED WORDS

SACRED

A Source Book on the Great Religions of the World

WORDS

Terry D. Bilhartz

Sam Houston State University

McGraw Hill

Boston   Burr Ridge, IL   Dubuque, IA   Madison, WI   New York   San Francisco   St. Louis
Bangkok   Bogotá   Caracas   Kuala Lumpur   Lisbon   London   Madrid   Mexico City
Milan   Montreal   New Delhi   Santiago   Seoul   Singapore   Sydney   Taipei   Toronto

The McGraw-Hill Companies

Higher Education

*A Division of the **McGraw-Hill** Companies*

1 2 3 4 5 6 7 8 9 0 QPD/QPD 0 9 8 7 6

ISBN 0-07-290098-9

Editor in Chief: *Emily Barrosse*
Publisher: *Lyn Uhl*
Senior Sponsoring Editor: *Jon-David Hague*
Editorial Coordinator: *Allison Rona*
Marketing Manager: *Susanna Ellison*
Managing Editor: *Jean Dal Porto*
Project Manager: *Jean R. Starr*
Art Director: *Jeanne Schreiber*
Senior Designer and Cover Design: *Kim Menning*
Interior Design: *Linda Robertson*
Art Editor: *Ayelet Arbel*
Maps: *Mapping Specialists*
Senior Photo Research Coordinator: *Alexandra Ambrose*
Photo Researcher: *David Tietz*
Cover Credit: © *Digital Vision*
Production Supervisor: *Tandra Jorgensen*
Composition: *10/12 pt Sabon, by Carlisle Publishing Services*
Printing: *45# Scholarly Matte Plus, Quebecor World Dubuque*

Credits: The credits section for this book begins on page C-1 and is considered an extension of the copyright page.

Library of Congress Cataloging-in-Publication Data
Bilhartz, Terry D.
  Sacred words : a source book on the great religions of the world/Terry D. Bilhartz.
    p. cm.
  Includes bib. references and index.
    ISBN 0-07-290098-9 (softcover : alk. paper)
    1. Religions--Textbooks. I. Title.
BL80.3.B55 2006
200--dc22   2005052201

To four generations of witnesses

Henry and Helen Coleman

Oscar and Louise Bilhartz

Skipper and Joy Coleman Bilhartz

Robert and Marietta Coleman

Lyman and Margaret Coleman

Paul and Ann Morell

James Morell

Linda Bilhartz Bannick and Harold Bannick

Skip and Janet Chalk Bilhartz

Lyman and Janet Leonard Bilhartz

Helen Bilhartz Marek and David Marek

Shana Morell Stadler and Lenny Stadler

Paula Morell Sarmast and Cyrus Sarmast

Rocky and Lindsey Barton Bilhartz

Teriann Noel Bilhartz

Table of Contents

Acknowledgments

My favorite Confucian quote from the *Analects* is this:

"The Master said:
'At fifteen, I had my mind bent on learning.
At thirty, I stood firm.
At forty, I had no doubts,
At fifty, I knew the decrees of Heaven.
At sixty, my ear was an obedient organ for the reception of truth.
At seventy, I could follow what my heart desired, without transgressing what was right.' "

The latter two lines I have not yet experienced, but I find much personal truth in the gist of this passage. In many ways my interest in this project dates to my teenage years, and since this distant time I have been influenced, inspired, and encouraged by scores of individuals, without whom *Sacred Words* would never have been started or completed.

I first wish to thank the family members to whom this work is dedicated. Although different in temperament and theological persuasion, across four generations each of these individuals has shaped my life in profound ways.

I also wish to thank the numerous teachers and mentors who have guided me throughout these years. I thank Dewey Wallace, my dissertation director at George Washington University, for introducing me to the academic study of religion. I also thank the instructors of the NEH Seminars that I have attended since the completion of my graduate studies. In particular, I thank Paul Conkin of Vanderbilt University for teaching me the importance of precision in language; Harry Stout of Yale University and Karen Kuppermann and Richard Brown of the University of Connecticut for demonstrating to me the benefits of using primary sources in the classroom; and Karen Offen of Stanford University for reminding me of the need to read texts through the lens of gender. Moreover, I especially want to thank Roger Ames, Elizabeth Buck, Eliot Deutsch, Lee Siegel, Barbara Metcalf, Peter Hershock, Henry Rosemont, Jr., Tu Weiming, Jonathan Spence and the other instructors at the various institutes offered at the University of Hawaii/East-West Center who introduced me to the wisdom of the East. I also am indebted to the coparticipants at these institutions, especially to David Jones, Ronnie Littlejohn, Virginia Jones, Carl Jackson, Shelton Woods, Kathleen Higgins, James Peterman, Sidney Pamela Brown, and Terry Mazurak, for sharing their insights into the thoughts of the world's great philosophers and sages.

I'd also like to thank the following reviewers, who helped in the development of the manuscript:

- David R. Bains, *Samford University*
- Gloria H. Dickinson, *The College of New Jersey*
- James E. Deitrick, *University of Central Arkansas*
- Paul Donnelly, *Northern Arizona University*
- Charles Farhadian, *Calvin College*
- Peter J. Judge, *Winthrop University*
- Ramdas Lamb, *University of Hawaii–Manoa*
- Richard A. Layton, *University of Illinois–Urbana-Champaign*
- Mark MacWilliams, *St. Lawrence University*
- Brian Malley, *University of Michigan*
- John T. Meadors, *Mississippi College*

- Eve Mullen, *Mississippi State University*
- Nathaniel S. Murrell, *University of North Carolina–Wilmington*
- Claude A. Perrotet, *University of Bridgeport*
- Richard B. Pilgrim, *Syracuse University*
- Rick Rogers, *Eastern Michigan University*
- Liyakat Takim, *University of Denver*
- Mark O. Webb, *Texas Tech University*
- Chun-Fang Yu, *Rutgers University*

Colleagues and friends closer to home also have assisted me greatly in this project. I thank Professors James Olson, Tracy Steele, and Bernadette Pruitt of Sam Houston State University for critiquing multi-ple drafts of *Sacred Words*. I also extend my thanks to the members of the New Beginnings Class at the First United Methodist Church, Huntsville, Texas, for piloting the early chapters of this work, and particularly to Joe Bon-Jorno for his careful reading of these chapters. Similarly, I thank the hundreds of undergraduate and graduate students at Sam Houston State University for piloting early drafts of this project. The errors that may remain in this volume would have been more numerous without the scrutiny of these astute colleagues, students, and friends.

Finally, I extend my heartfelt gratitude to Patty Ann Morell Bilhartz, my partner for life and friend, who has been with me not only through every step of this project, but also throughout my life's journey.

Introduction

It is unfortunate that the Internet with language translation software did not exist in the sixth century BCE. If it had, there may have been a moment when several of humanity's most profound and influential thinkers could have chatted with each other on Instant Messenger. Imagine if you will, the Hebrew prophets of second Isaiah[1] and Ezekiel chatting online with the Hindu reformers Gautama (The Buddha) and Mahavira (the founder of Jainism), only to be interrupted with additional comments by the Chinese sages Confucius and Lao-zi (the legendary Daoist founder and alleged author of the *Dao-de-jing*). Had these near contemporaries known each other, what common concerns and insights would they have shared? What would they have had to say to each other about humanity, the divine, ethics and the afterworld?

History, of course, cannot provide answers to hypothetical questions of this kind. Neither is there a "time machine" that can transport the religious giants of other eras into our classrooms in order to share their understandings of the mysteries of the universe. Imagining these possibilities, however, can help us to appreciate the value of examining and comparing the sacred words attributed to the world's most influential religious thinkers. This volume is based on the premise that there is much to be gained from studying these grand teachings that have given birth to the great world religions.

Most would agree that the study of how humans throughout time have struggled to understand their place in the universe is an inherently fascinating subject. It is true that contemporary observers stand far removed from the distant prophets and priests who articulated insights that fomented the great religions of the past. Yet, despite this distance in time and place, modern man and modern woman live in cultures largely shaped by the words of these mystics and theocrats. Their sacred stories, memorized and passed forward from generation to generation and eventually codified in form and print, have become a part of the everyday vocabulary that continues to be used to justify and/or to critique societal standards.

Most twenty-first century world citizens have at least a cursory knowledge of one religious tradition, as well as a fuzzy awareness of the existence of other religions. While few will claim to know the history or the Holy Scriptures of more than one tradition, most who observe the daily news will readily acknowledge that religion exerts a powerful influence on contemporary world events. At times, the news reported to us about the religious activities of others is heartwarming and life-affirming. At other times, the stories we hear about the religious practices of others sound strange, confusing, and perplexing. At still other times, the news presents religion in a decisively negative light. For example, when we hear about holy wars, about religious justifications of ethnic cleansings, and about the concerted efforts of those in one group to destroy the sacred artifacts of those in another, we are prone to question the worldviews that promote and justify such violent and destructive behaviors.

Perhaps there was a time when the various peoples on this planet were so separated that the ideas in one corner of the globe had little impact on the other peoples of the world. This time, if ever extant, no longer

---

[1]This reference is to the author of chapters 40–66 in the Book of Isaiah. Most scholars, although not all, believe that this writer lived during the sixth century BCE.

exists. In the twenty-first century, ideas crisscross the continents with amazing speed. Through the modern technologies of the World Wide Web and language translation software, it is possible for an American from the plains of North Dakota to instantaneously contact an Asian from the island of East Timor, an African from the hills of South Africa, and an Aussie from the deserts of Western Australia. Technology enables us to make immediate contact, but contact alone does not ensure communication. To truly communicate, we need more than a computer and a language translator. To fully connect with those in foreign places, we also need some understanding of who they are, what they believe, and what values they embrace. There is no better way to acquire this understanding than by examining the sacred texts that have profoundly influenced the development of these distant cultures.

Sacred Words is designed to provide readers with a concise overview of the central teachings that are contained in the Hebrew *Bible,* the *New Testament,* the *Qur'an,* the *Upanishads,* the Buddhist *Pali Canon,* the Confucian *Five Classics,* the *Dao-de-jing,* and the other classic texts that have shaped the courses of Western, Eastern, and traditional indigenous civilizations. Sometimes we are reluctant to approach these sacred texts, not because we believe them to be irrelevant, but because we fear that they will be incomprehensible to our modern eyes. It is true that readers without expertise in the original languages and without a specialized knowledge of the ancient cultures will not always be able to understand the depth and subtleties of these sacred texts. Nonetheless, this volume rests upon the premise that the central teachings of the ancients are approachable and can be comprehended by nonspecialized modern readers.

Current research on adult learning suggests that we learn best when we become our own teachers. Grounded in this educational theory, this source book is designed to equip adult learners to become their own teachers. Rather than simply providing authoritative statements about how humans at various times and places have answered questions about the meaning and purpose of life, *Sacred Words* provides readers with representative selections from core texts that have shaped the development of the major religious traditions. It presents sacred words that have been embraced, chanted, analyzed, and perhaps fiercely debated across the centuries, yet still remain cherished for large numbers of the faithful. By surveying the selections within *Sacred Words,* readers will become better able to understand the similarities and the differences among the major living religions and to comprehend and interpret those texts that have influenced world events since ancient times.

HINTS ON READING SACRED TEXTS

Readers should be aware that the sacred selections in this source book are more than haphazard statements made by individuals who claim personal knowledge of the absolute. In religious studies, it is common to label claims of divine insight "special revelation." Often, as with the cases of Moses and Mohammad, the claim of "special revelation" was made after the hearing of a voice. On other occasions, as with Gautama Buddha, the revelation of truth came as a sudden insight that did not require supernatural mediation. Although great differences exist between the forms and meanings of the received revelations, in religious traditions (both East and West) several steps had to occur before "special revelation" could be converted into "scripture." First, the oral teachings of the prophets and sages had to be received and memorized by their followers and eventually codified into some written form. Moreover, because "scripture" is not revelation itself but the reporting of a revelation that was received as authoritative not only by the prophet but also by his or her followers, the creation of scripture also required an official endorsement of a believing community. Thus, while "revelation" may have come to a single individual in a sudden divine moment, the formulation of scripture required the efforts and labors of many believers who "received," "remembered," "preserved," "codified," and formally "approved" a text before it was received into a sacred canon.

When reading any document, it is appropriate first to look for the surface content within it. Readers of sacred literature, however, also should be aware that perceived flashes of divine insight often can be read on more than one level. Sacred words often employ symbolism, metaphor, and parable to express realities that are too difficult to explain in simple language, so it also is appropriate to read sacred texts with an interpretive eye that seeks to understand the religious experience that is being communicated in the passage. Moreover, it is appropriate to ask this of each passage: How would this selection have been understood by those inside and outside of the tradition at the time it was received, in medieval times, and in modern times? Like most skills, these analytical abilities are not acquired overnight, but the interpretive art of discovering multiple meanings to a text is a skill that even novice readers can develop with practice.

This volume is based on the supposition that learning through the study of primary sources is the most intellectually stimulating and pedagogically sound method of appropriating knowledge about how humans have confronted the grand questions of life and death over the last four millennia. Its central purpose is to equip readers with the ability to construct for themselves from these ancient blueprints the essential value systems for each of the major world religions.

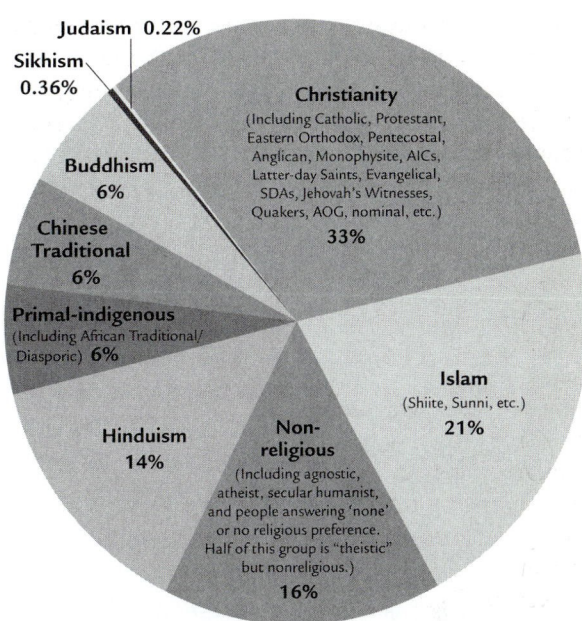

The relative sizes of the major religious groups.

CHAPTER CONTENT AND ORGANIZATION

Sacred Words is divided into three parts. Part 1: The Great Religions of the West, consists of three chapters that discuss, respectively, Judaism, Christianity, and Islam. Part 2: The Great Religions of the East, consists of three chapters that cover, respectively, Hinduism, Buddhism, and the Chinese religions of Daoism and Confucianism. Together, these religions with canonized sacred texts from the ancient world are embraced by almost 5 billion people, about 80 percent of the world's population. Part 3: Indigenous Oral Traditions, consists of three chapters that cover the great indigenous religious traditions without canonized sacred texts. The first chapter in this part covers the traditional religions of the Americas, while the final chapters treat the traditional religions of Africa and Oceania.

No single source book can include all of the world's religions. For reasons of economy, this work focuses primarily on the major living world. Smaller religious traditions (i.e., Jainism, Zoroastrianism), dead traditions (i.e., the religions of ancient Greece,

Mesopotamia, and Egypt), and religions with more recently acquired scriptures (i.e., Sikhism, Baha'i) may be mentioned in the discussion of the origins and historical developments of the other major world religions, but they are not represented in the anthology of sacred texts provided in this volume.

Each chapter opens with an introduction that is organized under six major headings, plus a Bibliography:

Setting

Sacred Stories and Beliefs

Scriptures (or Sacred Oral Traditions)

Subdivisions

Sacred Observances and Practices

Sources

Selected Bibliogrpahy

These compact introductions provide readers with a survey of a religious tradition's origins, defining characteristics, and sacred and secular histories. After perusing these introductions, readers will be equipped with the essential background material that will enable them to assess and interpret the sacred texts contained in this source book.

For each religious tradition, the anthology of scriptural passages in the Sources section is arranged into nine topical categories that have influenced major themes in world and religious history. Some of these thematic categories address philosophical and theological issues; others address sociological and psychological ones. The nine categories are listed here:

1. *Beginnings: God, Time, and the Universe*—descriptions and attributes of the Absolute; creation stories and accounts of the origins of the cosmos.
2. *Humanity: The Problem of Good and Evil*—descriptions of the nature of humankind; accounts of the origins of evil in the world.
3. *Sacred Stories: Divine Messengers, Prophets, and Priests*—accounts and claims of the founders of the faith during the formative years of the tradition.
4. *Divine Law: Justice, Reward, and Punishment*—divine expectations and demands; definitions of sin and its consequences.
5. *Gender: Women and Men in Society*—gender roles in the family and the community.
6. *Daily Living: Health, Etiquette, and Holy Days*—descriptions of the life-patterns and the rituals that define the tradition.
7. *The Human Quest: Paths to Salvation and Enlightenment*—statements on the purpose of human existence and the way of redemption.
8. *The Religious Life: Worship and Righteousness*—prescribed modes of public and private worship; descriptions of the ideal human.
9. *Endings: Death, Judgment, and the Afterlife*—eschatology; the journey after death; visions of heaven, hell, and nirvana.

TEXT SELECTION CRITERIA

Five criteria were used to determine the selections included in this anthology:

1. **Sacredness:** Are the passages considered to be sacred and worthy of serious reflection by large numbers of the faithful within the tradition?
2. **Historical importance:** Are the passages broadly known within the tradition? Have they had an impact upon the historical development of the religious tradition?
3. **Fairness and balance:** Are the selections representative of themes found within the whole canonized writings of the tradition and consistent with concepts presented in that particular section of scripture from which the passage was taken?
4. **Topical content:** Do the texts relate directly or indirectly to one of the nine thematic categories that frames the volume?
5. **Readability:** Will lay readers be able to comprehend and find meaning in the passages?

Only passages that passed all of these criteria were selected. To keep the volume to a reasonable length and to maintain its focus and readability, it was necessary to edit the passages to some degree. Efforts were made, however, to limit the use of the ellipsis and to present longer (complete passages or abridged selections of at least several hundred words in length) rather than shorter (single paragraph or less) passages. As far as possible, the texts are presented in the context in which they appear in the sacred writings and are allowed to speak for themselves without extensive commentary.

POWERWEB SUPPLEMENTS

At the end of the Sources section in each chapter is a list of recommended supplemental readings that students can access online via McGraw-Hill *PowerWeb*. These secondary readings include some scholarly and some popular articles about a wide variety of contemporary religious issues and controversies. Students will note that many of these modern pieces address themes that were introduced in the ancient scriptures of the various traditions. Although placed at the end of each chapter, these articles should not be read as final solutions to long debated religious conundrums. Like the other documents in this source book, however, these readings will shed additional light on the complexities of religious expression in the modern world. By focusing on contemporary religious thought and practices, these supplemental articles will illuminate more fully what it means to be a part of a living religious tradition.

To illustrate, after reading these introductory pages, some students may wish to know more about the scope and techniques of the discipline of comparative religion. To assist these students, four online articles available at http://www.dushkin.com/powerweb are recommended. A personal access code provided free with each new copy of this book is required to access the *PowerWeb* readings. Students who purchase a used copy may buy an access code at the website. The recommended selections include:

1. **The "Comparative" Study of Religion,** Ninian Smart, from *Worldviews: Crosscultural Explorations of Human Beliefs,* Prentice Hall, 1999.
2. **Each Religion Expresses an Important Part of the Truth,** Raimundo Panikkar, *The Intrareligious Dialogue,* Paulist Press, 1978.
3. **Religion; It Sounds Like Hate, but Is It?,** Teresa Watanabe, *Los Angeles Times,* February 16, 2002.
4. **Divine Intervention: Regional Reconciliation Through Faith.** David Smock, *Harvard International Review,* Winter 2004.

In the first recommended supplement, Ninian Smart encourages students of religion to suspend their presuppositions in order to learn how to view the world from a cross-cultural perspective. In the second piece, Raimundo Panikkar gives similar advice, asserting that just as good translators must understand a native speaker's insight into language, so too must students of comparative religion understand a tradition from a believer's point of view. The next two selections serve as a counterweight to the popular assertion that religion is a principle source of hatred and war. These supplemental readings, while acknowledging the association between religion and violence, also demonstrate the role that religion plays in promoting peace. In an insightful *Los Angeles Times* piece, Teresa Watanabe discusses how contemporary Jewish, Christian, and Islamic scholars are attempting to reconcile the diverse messages contained in their sacred scriptures. Similarly, David Smock in a *Harvard International Review* article explores how

the great world religions have played major roles in furthering peace and in exploring paths to reconciliation. Together these readings offer a variety of insights into the challenges and benefits of the study of religion.

ALTERNATIVE WAYS TO READ THIS SOURCE BOOK

Although the comparative questions in this volume assume that the source book is being read sequentially from Chapter 1 to Chapter 9, it also is possible to first read the Eastern religion units, Chapters 4–6, and then proceed with the remainder of the chapters. Another approach is to read the volume thematically rather than sequentially. Using this method, the pages in each chapter that address a common theme would be read as a unit. For instance, after examining the introductory sections for each tradition, readers would study, for all the traditions, the sacred texts in the first thematic category, "Beginnings: God, Time, and the Universe," and then proceed with the texts from all the traditions that discuss the remaining thematic categories 2 through 9.

A third approach that I have found to be effective for college classroom use is a mixture of these sequential and thematic methods. During the first half of the semester, I introduce each religious tradition one at a time, reading and discussing first the Setting, Sacred Stories and Beliefs, Scriptures, Subdivisions, and Sacred Observances and Practices sections for a given tradition, as well as the first three thematic categories in the Sources section. Midway into the semester, after spending about a week on each religious tradition, I assign for a week's readings the sacred texts from each of the traditions that address a single thematic category, beginning with category 4, "Divine Law: Justice, Reward, and Punishment," then category 5, "Gender: Women and Men in Society," and continuing with one category per week until we conclude the semester by examining the final topic, "Endings: Death, Judgment, and the Afterlife." This approach allows students first to gain confidence in understanding the history and core beliefs of a tradition before attempting to enter into the fascinating but more difficult task of comparative religious studies.

Examining, comparing, and reflecting upon the sacred words in this volume will not make us into spiritual masters of any religious tradition. However, it will start us on an intellectual journey that will take us into the heart of the enduring faiths that have shaped the world in which we live. In making this journey through the wisdoms of the East, West, North, and South, we not only will learn what the ancients believed to be sacred, but we also will come to a greater understanding of what it means to be human.

Judaism 1

Although one of the smaller living world religions with only about 15 million adherents, Judaism has had an enormous influence on world history for nearly 3 millennia. Founded by Hebrew-speaking tribes from the ancient Near East, Judaism is a monotheistic religion that embraces a high ethical code. This tradition not only has survived centuries of intense persecution and numerous pogroms, it has spawned the two largest religions of the Western world, Christianity and Islam. Together, these three Western religions claim about 3 billion adherents, about one-half of the world's population.

Like all traditions, Judaism emerged within a social context. A group of people living in a particular place and time blended unique spiritual insights with other religious elements common to their world. In doing so, they created a new tradition that differed in important ways from the religions that influenced it. Once born, the new tradition took on a life of its own—maturing, adapting, and evolving over time into the living religion that it is today. The people whose spiritual insights gave birth to Judaism were the ancient Hebrews. Neither great in numbers nor mighty in strength, they were pilgrims whose ancestors roamed across the stretches of the Near East from Mesopotamia to Egypt, only to congregate in the second millennium BCE[1] along the eastern Mediterranean in a land called Canaan.

---

[1]BCE stands for "Before the Common Era." Scholars use this terminology to designate the period that Christians label BC, which stands for "Before Christ." Similarly, the scholarly designation of the Christian era is CE, for "Common Era," rather than the traditional AD, which is an abbreviation for the Latin *Anno Domini* that means "In the Year of the Lord."

SETTING

For 3,000 years before the ascendancy of Greek culture in the fourth century BCE, two great river civilizations dominated the ancient Near East. The first of the great empires appeared along the banks of the Tigris and Euphrates Rivers. Later Greeks would call this region "Mesopotamia."

Mesopotamia: The Land between the Rivers

Mesopotamia included a semicircular fertile tract of land surrounded by the Mediterranean Sea to the west, the Anatolia and Zagros Mountains to the north and east, and the Arabian Desert to the south. Easily accessible from several directions, the land attracted wave after wave of invaders and immigrants from a variety of ethnic stocks. In many ways, the land was unappealing. It lacked timber, stone, and precious metals. Its climate was hot and humid, and the scarcity of rainfall in the winter months made even primitive agriculture impossible without irrigation. In the spring, rains and melting snow from the northern mountains swelled the river waters, producing terrifying and destructive flooding. Before humans learned to work together to blunt the harsh forces of nature with labor-intensive canal and irrigation projects, Mesopotamia was primarily a flat land of alternating whirling dust and stagnant mud that could support only small populations of marsh dwellers.

In the fourth millennium BCE, a racially mixed people known as the Sumerians transformed this perilous land into a land of milk and grain. The emerging agricultural civilization—successful because it was dependent on irrigation rather than rainfall—produced a surplus of food that made possible the settlement of urban communities. With urban life came specialized labor and craftsmen able to make finished goods that could be exported to obtain the copper, tin, and other raw materials not found along the rivers. Trade produced caravan merchants, who needed credit and the services of lenders, and bankers, who needed laws to protect them from creditors. At every level, the civilization depended on powerful rulers who were able to supervise the irrigation projects, establish the rule of law, and provide security and protection for the traders.

Perhaps the first real-life political rags-to-riches story was Sargon the Great (ca. 2350 BCE). Unlike the previous Sumerian rulers, Sargon was an Akkadian Semite; that is, he spoke the language of the seminomadic Semitic-speaking people who lived in Akkad of northern Mesopotamia. According to legend, Sargon was abandoned by his mother, set adrift in a reed basket on a river, rescued by a king's gardener, and raised in the palace. From these beginnings, Sargon became a king over Akkad and later unified under his rule all the city-states of both northern and southern Mesopotamia. Over the centuries the language of the early Sumerians was lost, but the tongue of Sargon lived to spawn several Semitic languages, including Assyrian, Aramaic, and Hebrew.

Sargon's story was repeated, albeit less dramatically, for the next two millennia, as successive conquerors rose to power, exercised dominance over the region, and established new dynasties that lasted a few centuries and then fell to even more powerful rivals. Each new dynasty brought new legends, heroes, and gods into Mesopotamia. Remembered among the greatest of these kings was Hammurabi of Babylon (1792–1750 BCE), a military master who codified and enforced a written law that provided some protection and justice for the poor, the widows, and the orphans.

Impressive cultural achievements accompanied the political advances of these Sumerians, Akkadians, and Babylonians. The Mesopotamian innovators created a calendar of 12 lunar months that stayed in cycle with the solar year with the addition of a leap month added every third year. They developed a system of writing—cuneiform—that used "wedge-shaped" signs impressed into clay. The signs represented words and syllabi sounds that, when grouped, could be used to communicate ideas in any spoken language. Originally cuneiform was used solely for economic documents. Written language, thus, was invented in the fourth millennium BCE as an accounting device to keep tract of Sumerian goods. In time, the Mesopotamians put their epic tales into written forms, thereby producing impressive works of literature. According to Sumerian mythology, the goddess Nisaba, wife of the air-god Enlil, invented the art of writing and revealed its secrets to humankind. In Mesopotamia, as in other places of antiquity that discovered written language, writing was a highly revered art that was associated with the gods.

One of the great literary works of the ancient world was the Epic of Gilgamesh. In this masterpiece, an assembly of gods became upset at humans for disturbing their sleep and decided to punish humanity by sending a great flood. Fortunately, one of the gods leaked news of the flood to a righteous man named Utnapishtim, who then survived the catastrophe by building a ship. Later, the repentant gods rewarded this Sumerian Noah for his ingenuity with the gift of

Image of a fragment and text of the Epic of Gilgamesh. The most complete version of the story comes from 12 clay tablets written in the "wedge-shaped" script known as cuneiform.

immortality. This gift, however, was not given to other humans, including the part man/part god legendary hero Gilgamesh. In the end, Gilgamesh faced his inevitable fate comforted only by the knowledge that he had achieved human greatness. For the ancient Mesopotamians, death could be protested, but not overcome.

The religion of Mesopotamia can best be characterized as naturalistic polytheism. Most of the deities (nearly 2,000 of which have been named) represented natural forces such as the sun, moon, and wind. These natural forces often took on human activities such as copulating and war making. The gods were immortal and had the power to direct worldly actions. Among the most important gods were An, the sky-god who was the father of the gods; Enlil, the air-god who presided over the assembly of the gods; Enki, the water-god who provided humans with wisdom and medicine; and Inanna, the mother-goddess of fertility. Alongside these benevolent deities were demons that brought terror and torment to humankind. To keep the deities happy, temples were built and staffed with specialists who performed magic and provided entertainment for the gods. Priests held sacrificial rituals and offered animals, vegetation, food, drink, and clothing to the gods. Kings consulted diviners who were skilled in reading omens by studying the livers of sacrificed animals and by investigating the movement of stars. Elaborate structures to serve hundreds of local deities and "national" gods were constructed. In the city of Babylon, a ziggurat (a great tower leading to a sanctuary for the god Marduk) was built, a monument so impressive that it was recognized by later Greeks as one of the great wonders of the ancient world. Notwithstanding these embellished sacred buildings and complex religious rituals, Mesopotamian religion was on the whole rather gloomy. It promised neither abundance in this life, nor eternal bliss in a world to come.

Egypt: The Gift of the Nile

The second great entity that influenced the cultures of the ancient Near East was Egypt, a land named after a Greek word meaning "the gift of the Nile." Environmental conditions in Egypt were similar to those in Sumer. Abundant life could not exist in the rainless African Sahara were it not for the Nile waters. Through cooperative irrigation projects, however, the land could produce ample food to support the peasant villages that dotted the Nile banks along a 600-mile stretch from the first cataract to the Mediterranean. Throughout antiquity, the Nile was the source of Egypt's food, wealth, and unity.

Like Mesopotamia, Egypt was a river civilization that was politically unified during the fourth millennium BCE. Similarly, it developed a written language, hieroglyphics, that was akin to Mesopotamian cuneiform. In many ways, however, Egypt developed very

The Marduk Ziggurat of Babylon. Although little is left of the base of this once massive structure, archeological findings and historical accounts put this tower at seven multicolored tiers, topped with a temple of exquisite proportions.

differently than Mesopotamia. Whereas Mesopotamia was easily approached by outsiders, and thus constantly challenged by invaders who embraced different gods and myths, Egypt was isolated by deserts and thereby largely protected from the political and cultural changes that accompany immigration and invasion. Moreover, with an abundance of stone and precious metals, Egypt had little need to rely upon the outside world for its natural resources. For 3 millennia, it remained comfortable in its own prosperity and security and reluctant to accept outside ideas from peoples it viewed as inferiors.

At the center of Egyptian life and culture was the divine ruler, the Pharaoh. With the exception of two periods of interruption, an Egyptian Pharaoh ruled over a unified Nile River kingdom for nearly 3,000 years. Viewing the Pharaoh as the incarnate son-god, the Egyptians did not find it necessary to seek the will of the gods. Justice was not based on codified law but on the Pharaoh's mandates. Those who resisted his authority received swift punishment. The Pharaoh also linked mortals with the eternal. In pictures on temple walls, only the Pharaoh is represented associating with other deities. He alone provided the gods with the offerings deemed necessary to ensure prosperity in this life and hope in the hereafter. The elaborate pyramid tombs of the Pharaohs were not so much a place to live after death as an ascent into the heavens where the deceased king would join the other gods. In death as in life, the Pharaoh helped his people. Modern thinkers may ask whether the capital and labor spent in building and furnishing the royal pyramids could have been devoted to more humane projects. From the perspective of the ancient Egyptians, however, work on the pyramids was more than a public relief project that kept the workers quiet and the economy stable. It also was a religious ritual assigned to the people by the gods that was believed to bring temporal and eternal benefits to all Egyptians.

In addition to the cult of the Pharaoh, ancient Egyptians embraced a great variety of local and national gods and goddesses. Many of these deities took on mixed human and animal forms. Anubis, for example, was a god of the cemetery who had a human body and the head of a jackal. His business was to escort the departed souls to a tribunal of deities. At the court of judgment, Anubis would weigh the hearts of the deceased on a scale of justice. Light hearts that

had been filled with virtue were admitted to another world where they could enjoy the articles that had been stored with them in their tombs. In contrast with the gloomy Mesopotamian views of the afterworld, this promise of reward or punishment in another life provided Egyptians with a more optimistic and less fatalistic view of life and death.

Throughout most of ancient Egypt's history, hundreds of hybrid deities shared power and respect. An exception to this rule occurred in the fourteenth century BCE when a Pharaoh who took the name Akhenaton singled out the sun god Aton to be revered above all others. At the Pharaoh's command, the names of less mighty gods were deleted from the registry of deities, and lofty psalms to Aton were etched into stone. For a generation, Egyptian religion tilted toward monotheism. In time, however, future Pharaohs reinstated the lesser gods. Although Egypt returned to its traditional polytheism, its brief flirtation with monotheism may have left a lingering impact upon the beliefs of Moses and the Hebrew people who lived along the Nile in the centuries following the reforms of Akhenaton.

The Peoples and Religions of the Levant

As political power oscillated between Egypt and Mesopotamia, the cultures of these two great rivals diffused into adjacent lands. Among the regions influenced by the superpowers was the main land route that connected Egypt and Mesopotamia. Throughout antiquity, the peoples of the Levant (the seaboard and hinterland of the eastern Mediterranean) faced challenges by their militarily ambitious neighbors. The Levant was not particularly fertile, nor rich in natural assets, but it did produce timber and was well positioned geographically to be a major player in interregional trade. Consequently, virtually every dynasty that emerged in Egypt and Mesopotamia tried to penetrate this important land bridge that linked the principal powers of the ancient world.

In the third millennium BCE, the population of the Levant began to grow. Most of the population centers were walled cities. At daybreak, large wooden gates opened and the farmers walked to their fields outside the inner city. At dusk, they returned to the interior that was protected by the walls. Common to

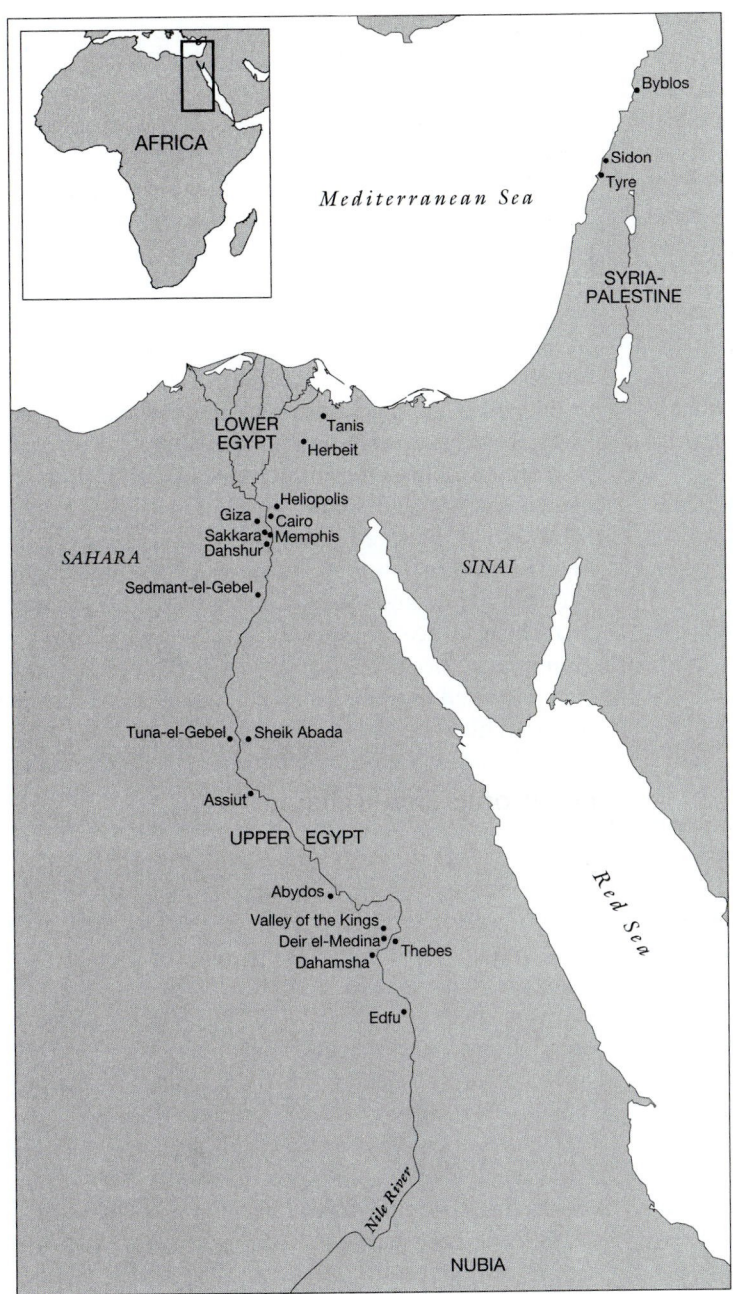

Ancient Egypt and the Levant.

most of these early cities was a three room religious shrine. Worshippers would enter the first room of the shrine, carrying with them small bowls filled with grain or wine. These gifts for the gods were placed on small benches in the middle chamber. In this second room, priests collected the offerings of the people, and brought them before the deities who resided in the innermost holy of holies. This third chamber typically was a square, dimly lit room with red paint on the walls.

The lack of rivers and irrigation possibilities in the Levant meant that the people were not bound to the riverbanks as in Mesopotamia and Egypt. Some towns, like Jericho, appeared inland from the coast near spring waters. Other population centers sprang up along the coastal plains. Among the greatest of these sea port centers was Byblos. This ancient city located 20 miles north of modern Beirut became Egypt's chief supplier of timber and papyrus. The word *Bible*, from the Greek *biblos*, meaning book, is derived from the name of this trading center.

Owing to the mountainous terrain, which roughly paralleled the eastern shores of the Mediterranean, and the deep gorges that separated the inland hills from the coast, the Levant was never politically united like Mesopotamia or Egypt. On rare occasions, groups of city-states formed confederations to protect themselves from invaders. More typically, however, the peoples of the Levant remained jealous of their own lands, and incessant local wars were endemic to the region.

By 2000 BCE, the population of the area was predominantly Semitic. Some of these people were Amorites, nomads who came to the interior and desert regions of the Levant from Mesopotamia. Other Semitic-speaking tribes, including the Canaanites, Arameans, and the Hebrews, settled in the narrow regions between the mountains and the Mediterranean Sea. Later Greeks called those who settled along the northern coastal plains Phoenicians. Although never a military giant, these Canaanites (or Phoenicians) were innovative ship builders and traders who established distant colonies as far away as Britain. Their cities of Sidon and Tyre were renowned in antiquity for their great wealth. These Semitic peoples also invented a script that radically altered the evolution of written languages. Unlike Mesopotamian cuneiform and Egyptian hieroglyphics—scripts that included hundreds of signs—the Semitic written language established one symbol for each consonant, thus reducing the number of signs to fewer than 300. The first two signs in the Semitic tongue were called *aleph* and *bet*, which in Greek became *alpha* and *beta*. This alphabet was the ancestor of all subsequent alphabetic scripts.

Much of our knowledge of the religion of the Canaanites comes from twentieth century excavations of the ancient city of Ugarit (modern Ras Shamra). The major Canaanite deities of Ugarit included El, the creator god; his wife Asherah, the lion lady and snake goddess who gave protection to sea travelers and to women in childbirth; Ba'al (mean-

> ## MAJOR CANAANITE DEITIES OF UGARIT
>
> **El:** creator god
> **Asherah:** snake goddess and protector of
>   women at childbirth
> **Ba'al:** storm god of fertility
> **Anat:** goddess of love and war
> **Mot:** lord of drought and death

ing "Master"), the storm-god and source of life-giving moisture; and Anat, a goddess of love and war. While El had dominion over all creation, Ba'al controlled fertility on the earth and thus was the most worshipped of the gods. Many Canaanite myths and rituals revolve around a perennial fight between Ba'al and Mot, the lord of the summer drought and death. Only if Ba'al wins will the region secure the winter rains that produce the vegetation needed for life. Ba'al is assisted in his battles by Anat, his sister and lover. At times, Ba'al is transformed into a bull and Anat into a heifer, and together they bring forth great progeny. Like many Near Eastern goddesses, Anat personifies a high level of energy that can find its outlet in the twin ecstasies of sex and war. While the Hebrews would borrow from the religion of these peoples, they also would react strongly against certain Canaanite practices that included sacred prostitution and human sacrifice. The Hebrew *Bible* portrays Canaanite religion in unflattering terms.

The southern region of the Levant was called Palestine by the Greeks, meaning "land of the Philistines." Unlike the Canaanites, the Philistines spoke an Indo-European rather than a Semitic language. A sea people, originally from somewhere in the Aegean (perhaps Crete or Cilicia [modern Turkey]), the Philistines raided Egypt in the twelfth century BCE. When repulsed, they settled into the coastal plains to the east and north of the Egyptian delta. A militant people armed with iron weapons and chariots, the Philistines built a strong confederation of city-states that included Gaza, Ashkelon, Ashdod, Ekron, and Gath. In time, the Philistines adopted the gods and religious fertility practices of Canaanite culture. Along with the Canaanites, the Philistines became bitter enemies with the Hebrew people during the Biblical period.

This stele discovered at Ugarit shows Ba'al as the storm god who "mounts the clouds."

SACRED STORIES AND BELIEFS

Ideas that alter history and shape civilizations are generally conceived by people who occupy positions of power. In India, for example, it was the powerful Brahmins who articulated the concepts of caste and karma that influenced Indian life for thousands of years. Likewise, in ancient China it was the literati who formulated the distinguishing characteristics that became the hallmarks of Chinese culture. Given these tendencies, it is surprising that so many of the central ideas that came to define Western culture originated from the Hebrews, an ancient people who left a far greater legacy than would be expected by their numbers or might.

The grand idea associated with Judaism is the concept of a single, personal, and moral god who reveals himself through both nature and history. Unlike the natural polytheistic religions of their neighbors, the religion of the Hebrews insisted that nature itself was an expression of one Lord who was the creator of all being. In Egypt and Mesopotamia, the gods and goddesses were immanent in nature. To the Hebrews, however, the heavens and the earth were not deities but testified to the glory of a single deity. Nature itself was not divine, but God created nature, declared it to be good, and gave humanity dominion over it. Consequently, the forces of nature were not rivals but subordinates to this single god that the Hebrews called Yahweh.[2] In contrast to most deities of antiquity, Yahweh was not given a visual image and was considered so holy that even speaking his name was to be avoided. Although he carried a male identity (perhaps to be distinguished from the common fertility goddesses of the Levant), Yahweh was a personal, transcendent spirit with no particular physical attributes.

The Hebraic concept of Yahweh also was unique in its characterization of the divine nature. Unlike the amoral and disinterested gods of most peoples of the ancient Near East, Yahweh was a demanding ethical deity who intervened directly into human affairs. In many ancient religious traditions, the world was viewed either as an illusory or corrupted world of matter from which the religious sought release or as a testing ground for the soul where unchanging amounts of good and evil existed together in relatively equal proportions. In such systems, attempts to change the world for the better found little appeal. Within Judaism, however, Yahweh stood as the god of history who called humans not to accept the status quo but to transform the world into what it ought to be.

Owing to Yahweh's peculiar ethical interests and involvement in world affairs, the ancient Hebrews had an intense interest in history. Although the various Mesopotamian and Egyptian peoples accomplished great deeds that were worth boasting about, their storytellers never attempted to narrate or describe the events of their past in a coherent form. They recorded historic deeds but discerned no pattern,

---

[2]The Hebrew alphabet does not contain vowels; thus the biblical name for the god of Judaism was the four consonants YHWH. These holy consonants, known by the Greek term *Tetragrammaton*, are translated throughout this work as Yahweh.

purpose, or plan in the flow of events. Most ancients lived in an almost timeless dimension in which people were born, matured, and died as they always had. The past carried no particular meaning, and the future of humanity had no particular goal. The ancient Hebrews, on the other hand, attached great importance to the events of human history. Unlike those who constructed cyclical theories of time, the Hebrews viewed time linearly and gave credence to the idea of progress. Humanity had a definite beginning and was moving in a direction guided by Yahweh toward a climatic conclusion. Yahweh's purposeful interventions in human time charged temporal events with ontological content. Every event testified to the will of their god. Thus, to a greater degree than most ancient peoples, the Hebrews presented their sacred stories as historical narratives that attempted to explain the saga of the relationship between their ancestors and Yahweh. The concept of linear time remains one of the great legacies that the Hebrews contributed to Western thought.

The sacred stories of the ancient Hebrews can be placed into six historic periods, the biblical traditions falling into the first five eras and the post-biblical traditions into the sixth. The first age opens with the story of Abram, later renamed Abraham, meaning in Hebrew "father is exalted." Abraham would become the father figure for each of the great Western religions: Judaism, Christianity, and Islam.

The Patriarchs and the Sojourn into Egypt

The setting for the story of Abraham is the Mesopotamian world of the early second millennium BCE. According to tradition, Abram came originally from Ur, once a great Sumerian city that lay along the Euphrates River near the head of the Persian Gulf. Abram moved with his father, wife, and relatives about 500 miles up the river to Haran, a trading center in northern Mesopotamia. Following his father's death, Abram was told by the Lord to leave Mesopotamia for "the land that I will show you." In this encounter, the Lord also promised to make a great nation from the descendants of Abraham, a nation that both would be blessed and would be used to bless all the families of the earth. Proclaiming allegiance to the Lord as his most high god, Abraham turned south, wondering first into Canaan and later into Egypt, before settling again into the promised

---

JACOB AND HIS DESCENDANTS

Jacob

Leah	*Zilpah*	*Bilhad*	*Rachel*
Reuben	Gad	Dan	Joseph
Simon	Asher	Naphtali	Benjamin
Levi			
Judah			
Issachar			
Zebulun			
Dinah			
(daughter)			

---

land of Canaan. After Abraham's death, his son Isaac, and then his grandson Jacob (also renamed Israel), took their places as patriarchs of the clan who claimed the Lord as their god.

During Jacob's life, a terrible famine in Canaan forced Jacob and his 12 sons to return to Egypt. For several centuries, the descendants of Abraham were treated well in Egypt. In time, however, a Pharaoh enslaved the growing masses of Hebrews, and to prevent their increase, ordered that all Hebrew male infants be killed. In response to these cruelties, the Hebrew people cried out to the Lord for deliverance.

Exodus and the Conquest

The man the Lord raised to bring deliverance was Moses. Like Sargon the Great, Moses was saved in his infancy by being placed in a basket near the river's edge. Discovered by the daughter of the Pharaoh, Moses grew up in the palace of the king. While a young man, Moses witnessed an Egyptian beating a Hebrew slave, killed the Egyptian, and fled for his life to the land of Midian. There he married the daughter of a Midianite priest and began a new life as a herdsman. One day while tending the flock, Moses experienced the divine in the presence of a flaming bush that burned but was not consumed. The deity, who identified himself as the God of Abraham, Isaac, and Jacob, told Moses to return to Egypt to liberate his kindred from bondage. Moses reluctantly agreed. When the Pharaoh refused Moses's demand to set the people free, the Lord directed Moses to unleash 10 terrible plagues against Egypt. Only after the last plague, the death of the first-born sons, did the Pharaoh relinquish and allow the Hebrews to leave.

Following their exodus from Egypt, the Hebrews wandered in the Sinai wilderness. At Mount Sinai, Yahweh renewed the covenant with the descendants of Abraham and provided Moses with the famous Ten Commandments, plus other laws considered necessary for communal living. The 12 tribes of Israel, however, grumbled against Moses and God. Owing to this rebellion, Yahweh determined that one generation would pass before the Israelites would be allowed to enter into the promised land of milk and honey. The conquest of Canaan would take place following Moses's death under the leadership of Joshua, Moses's successor. When victory was secured, each tribe (except the priestly tribe of Levi, for which special provisions were made) received a portion of land for its inheritance.

The Period of the Judges

The return to Canaan fulfilled Yahweh's promise of land that was made to Abraham. Entering Canaan, however, did not make the Israelites into an obedient people. According to the sacred stories, the 200-year period between the death of Joshua and the rise of the monarchy was characterized by a disheartening and recurring historic pattern. As the former Hebrew nomads settled into an agricultural lifestyle, many were drawn to the fertility deities of the Canaanites who specialized in providing an abundant harvest. Tempted by the appeal of the Canaanite religion, the Israelites ignored their covenant of allegiance with Yahweh and embraced the gods and religious practices of their neighbors. In response, Yahweh brought judgment upon the disobedient by allowing the enemies of the Israelites to gain dominance in the land. In the ensuing crisis, the people repented and cried to Yahweh to save them. God in return raised up a leader, known as a Judge, who—with divine aid—was able to throw off the oppressors and restore peace in the land. Unfortunately, the erring Israelites soon fell again to temptation and the cycle of apostasy, punishment, penitence, and peace started over again. This cycle appears 14 times in the book of Judges. Notwithstanding some heroic stories about flawed yet faithful men and women such as Gideon, Samson, and Deborah, the period of the Judges was remembered primarily as a time of political disarray and spiritual declension.

Statue of Astarte, used in Canaanite religious practices.

The United and Divided Kingdoms

By the end of the second millennium BCE, the military power of the nearby Philistine kings impressed the Israelites, who were unsatisfied living in a theocratic state with no monarch. The people cried to Samuel (the last of the Judges and first of the great prophets) to appoint for them a king so that they would be like other nations. Samuel reluctantly agreed and anointed Saul as King over all the tribes of Israel. Saul, followed by David and Solomon, ruled a United Kingdom for about a century. Future generations would look back to this era as the golden age of ancient Israel. King David captured Jerusalem and expanded the territory of the kingdom. King Solomon built a magnificent temple in Jerusalem as well as a majestic palace that made even the temple seem insignificant. Solomon's opulence, although known throughout the world, came at the high price of conscription, forced labor, and increased taxes. Rebellion was in the air.

Following Solomon's death, two of his sons struggled for power. The result was a division of the kingdom. The 10 northern tribes supported Jeroboam, called their kingdom Israel, and established Samaria as their capital. The 2 southern tribes supported Rehoboam, called their kingdom Judah, and maintained Jerusalem as the capital. The stories told about Jeroboam and Rehoboam and most of their successors are largely unflattering. None of the kings of Israel and less than one-half of the kings of Judah are portrayed as faithful monarchs.

The most heroic figures of the era of the Divided Kingdoms were not kings but prophets like Elijah, Hosea, Amos, and Isaiah. Without political or priestly authority, the prophets spoke boldly in the name of God, criticizing the disobedient kings for their lack of piety, their acceptance of foreign gods, and their toleration of social injustices. Their warn-

ings of impending doom came true, first in the northern kingdom when the Assyrians from the great city of Ninevah invaded Samaria. Israel's strongly fortified hill capital held out for two years, but in 721 BCE, Samaria fell to Sargon II's powerful army. The Assyrian king deported the leading citizens of Israel into exile and replaced them with imported foreigners who intermarried with the remaining Hebrews. The descendants of these mixed marriages would become known as Samaritans, a group later despised by Jews of "uncorrupted" lineage.

The southern kingdom of Judah survived a little longer, largely, according to the storytellers, because of the pious reforms of kings Hezekiah and Josiah. Hezekiah, king of Judah shortly after the fall of Israel, is remembered for closing the shrines to foreign deities and cleansing and then reconsecrating the Temple for Yahweh worship. Archeological data suggests that "good King" Hezekiah also was a friend to the poor and unprotected. During his reign, the population and enclosed territory of Jerusalem increased dramatically as refugees from the defeated northern tribes found sanctuary within the walled capital of Judea. A half century later, Josiah carried out a number of sweeping religious reforms, including purging the temple of all heathen altars and cult objects. Dur-

Chronology of the Hebrew peoples.

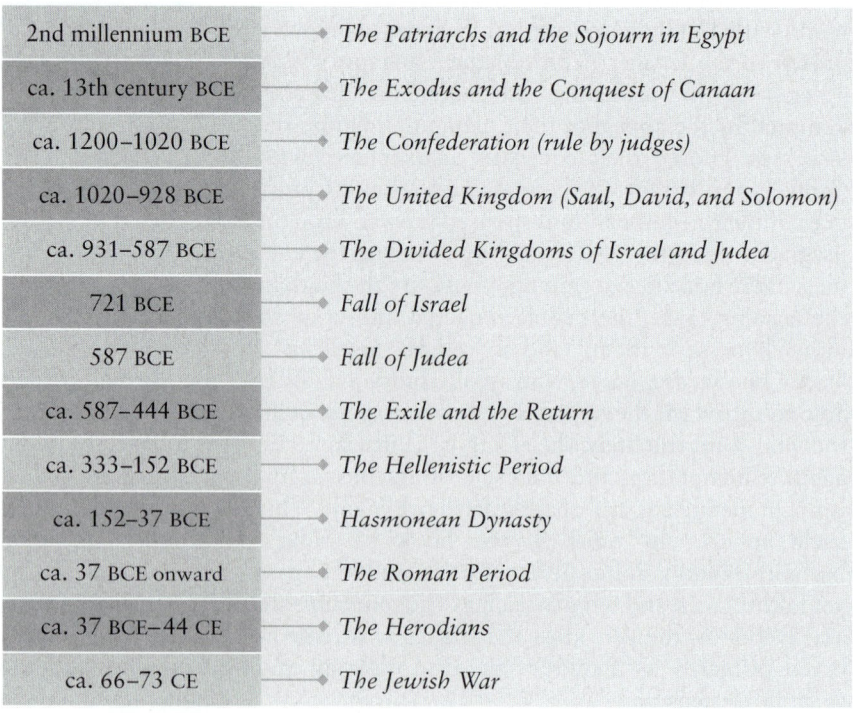

2nd millennium BCE	The Patriarchs and the Sojourn in Egypt
ca. 13th century BCE	The Exodus and the Conquest of Canaan
ca. 1200–1020 BCE	The Confederation (rule by judges)
ca. 1020–928 BCE	The United Kingdom (Saul, David, and Solomon)
ca. 931–587 BCE	The Divided Kingdoms of Israel and Judea
721 BCE	Fall of Israel
587 BCE	Fall of Judea
ca. 587–444 BCE	The Exile and the Return
ca. 333–152 BCE	The Hellenistic Period
ca. 152–37 BCE	Hasmonean Dynasty
ca. 37 BCE onward	The Roman Period
ca. 37 BCE–44 CE	The Herodians
ca. 66–73 CE	The Jewish War

ing Josiah's reign, Judah briefly rejoiced when the Babylonians captured Ninevah, the capital of the hated Assyrians. Their cheers turned to tears, however, when Judah's faithful king was killed while trying to frustrate an Egyptian attempt to aid the beleaguered Assyrians.

Following Josiah's death, Judah returned to its old ways. Rejecting the cries of the prophet Jeremiah to place trust in Yahweh rather in than diplomatic alliances, Judah choose to ally itself with Egypt against Babylon. In 597 BCE, Nebuchadnezar of Babylon invaded Judah, sent many of its noble members into exile, and appointed a new king to rule over the land. Again, Jeremiah implored the remnant in Judah to put their trust in Yahweh, and once more his pleas were ignored. Within a decade, the Babylonians returned. In 587 BCE, they ravaged Jerusalem, destroyed the temple, killed Judah's last king, and sent thousands of Judeans (from which comes the designation, Jews) into captivity in Babylon.

The Exile and Return

When the deported Judeans arrived in Babylon, they found two kindred groups already there: some of the great-grandchildren from Israel taken by the Assyrians and those taken from Judah in 597 BCE. These exiled peoples must have been impressed with the towering walls, massive palaces, domed temples, and hanging gardens of ancient Babylon—architectural accomplishments that made Jerusalem even in its glory appear simple and backward. Moreover, although the Babylonians had been cruel conquerors, they were lenient masters who provided those in exile with land and with some commercial opportunities. Under these circumstances, it would have been easy for the defeated Judeans to concede that the Babylonian god Marduk was the strongest of the gods and that it was now time to forsake their allegiance to Yahweh, embrace Babylonian culture, and begin a new life in this foreign land.

Inspired by words from the prophets of the Exile, however, the Jews in Babylon refused to reject Yahweh. The prophet Ezekiel laughed at the notion that the God of Israel had been defeated. To the contrary, Ezekiel proclaimed that the Lord of creation who ruled over all nations had used Babylon to punish the Hebrews for breaking their covenant with him. This punishment, however, would not last forever. Judah, indeed, was a heap of dry bones, but it would come

to life again. This affirmation of the power of one universal Lord who offered hope for the future also was expressed at this time in the beautiful poetry of an anonymous prophet known to us as Second Isaiah. Without a temple, a priestly class, or an anointed king, the religious life of those in exile changed during this time of captivity, but their allegiance to Yahweh remained inviolate.

Political developments of the sixth century BCE worked to the Jews' advantage. An alliance between two eastern kingdoms, the Medes and Persians, led to the fall of Babylon. To control the conquered Babylon, the Persian King Cyrus the Great decided to allow all exiled peoples to return to their original homelands in 537 BCE. His decree started a movement back to Canaan that would continue for a number of generations. Nearly a century after the original decree, two Babylonian Jews with close ties to Persia requested permission to go to Jerusalem to assist with the resettlement. Ezra, a priest by descent and scribe by profession, was most interested in reforming the religious life of the settlers. For this goal to be achieved, the Jerusalem temple had to be restored and temple worship reestablished. Meanwhile, Nehemiah, a layman with political expectations for Judea, wanted to rebuild the Jerusalem city walls and restore the population of this once-great city. Although supported with Persian funds, Ezra and Nehemiah met with many difficulties in completing their tasks, primarily because their leadership was not accepted by their kinsmen back home or in neighboring Samaria. In time, however, the city walls were raised, a temple rebuilt, and worship of Yahweh reestablished. In comparison to Solomon's temple, the new temple was small and ugly. Yet, after 70 years of absence, the returned exiles could again rejoice in hearing praises to Yahweh sung from the House of God in Jerusalem.[3]

The returning Jews had hoped to reestablish a Davidic monarchy, but Persian kings would not tolerate such action. Instead, the Persians appointed a governor over the Judean province, and placed high priests from the tribe of Levi in command. Governor Nehemiah thus joined with Ezra in establishing the written *Torah* as the constitution of the land, and Judea became a theocracy. On Rosh Hashahan (New Year's Day), 444 BCE, the people gathered to hear Ezra read

---

[3]The Samaritans in the north were not allowed to participate in the rebuilding of the temple. Consequently, they built for themselves a separate temple on Mount Gerizim.

the holy law that he had helped to codify while an exile in Babylon. Jews to this day see Ezra as the great Restorer of the Torah, and hold him second in importance only to Moses.

The Second Commonwealth

For two centuries following the rebuilding of the Temple, Judah was ruled as a Persian province. In 333 BCE, Greek armies under Alexander the Great defeated the Persians, and Palestine along with the rest of the empire came under Greek influence. Following Alexander's death, his kingdom was divided between two generals. Ptolemy received Egypt, and Seleucus, Asia. Although both laid claim to the Levant, Ptolemy seized it, and thus Palestine was joined with Egypt. Many Palestinian Jews were then brought into Egypt. Although most Jews in exile lived together in the same neighborhoods so that they could comply with Jewish dietary laws and continue the study of their traditions in the synagogues, they otherwise lived in a thoroughly Hellenized world. They learned to speak Greek, and most came to admire Greek culture. Meanwhile, in Ptolemaic Judea, Jerusalem became a trading center that offered lucrative commercial opportunities to those willing to assimilate into Hellenic culture. Jews of wealth generally favored adapting Greek dress, indulging in Greek games, and embracing a Greek constitution. Others, such as scribe Joshua ben Sirach, warned against falling into the hands of the wealth seekers. Bemoaning the growing division between rich and poor, these Jews insisted that contentment with one's lot and obedience to the Law were the proper recipes for the good life.

In the second century BCE, Judea became caught in a power struggle between Ptolemaic Egypt and Seleucid Syria. Some Jews supported the Seleucids; others insisted that Palestine remain with Egypt. During this crisis, the Seleucid king Antiochus IV gave himself the title Epiphanes (the visible god); replaced the high priest with someone of his choosing; prohibited Jews from practicing circumcision, owning copies of the *Torah,* or keeping the Sabbath day of rest; and bestowed upon Jerusalem a Greek constitution. Many pious Jews, known as *hasidim,* refused to accept these changes and were martyred. The situation deteriorated still further in 168 BCE when Antiochus' appointed high priest sold holy treasures from the temple, placed a statue of Jupiter in the holy of holies, and scarified a pig to the god Jupiter. These actions spurred a guerrilla-style revolt against the Seleucids. In 165, the rebels led by Ju-

Ancient Greek vase showing discus and javelin throwing. The nakedness of the athletes greatly offended Jewish sensibilities.

dah the Maccabee (meaning "hammer," short for "the hammer God used to smote the Syrians") entered Jerusalem and cleansed the temple. In a ceremony rededicating the temple to Yahweh, there was only enough oil to light the temple menorah for one day, but the oil burned for eight days until the priests could prepare more oil untouched by pagan hands. This event is still remembered by Jews in the eight-day winter Festival of Lights, known as Hanukkah.

Following the Maccabean victory over Syria, Judah enjoyed the status of an independent nation for about a century. These years were marred, however, by friction and ultimately civil war between divergent Jewish parties. In 63 BCE, the Roman general Pompey intervened, occupying Palestine and declaring it to be a Roman province. For another century Jewish parties argued over the benefits and cruelties that resulted from the Roman presence. In 66 CE, discontented Jews rebelled against Rome. Four years later the revolt was crushed when Rome razed Jerusalem and burned its temple. The destruction of Jerusalem ended the Second Commonwealth. Nearly 2,000 years would pass before Jewish people would again have a state of their own in Palestine.[4]

---

[4]This story is told in greater detail in Chapter 2.

SCRIPTURES

In a religious sense, the word *canon* (which was derived from the Sumerian word for "reed" and the Greek word for "rule" or "straight line") refers to a collection of writings that have been accepted as sacred and authoritative by a particular community of faith. It signifies the standard from which principles of practice and belief are judged. An authorized canon generally becomes necessary in troubled times when there exists in circulation other pieces of literature that are not deemed to be worthy of special reverence. Thus, the canonization process often involves the process of selecting, excluding, and editing sacred texts from a larger body of literature. According to some scholars, Judaism's sacred canon arose out of the ashes of the burnings of the two Jerusalem temples.

The holy scripture of Judaism is the Hebrew *Bible*. This collection of writings corresponds with the Old Testament of the Christian *Bible*. Except for a few passages written in Aramaic, which was the primary spoken language throughout Palestine after the period of captivity, the Jewish sacred canon was originally written in Hebrew. Until the invention of the printing press in modern times, all texts were manuscripts; that is, they were handwritten. Most ancient texts were written on a paperlike material that was made by soaking, pressing, and drying thin slices of a papyrus plant. Because papyrus decays over time, important documents considered worthy of preserving had to be recopied periodically by scribes. Jewish scribes took great care in reproducing the exact words of the master text, even counting and making lists of the letters in an attempt to ensure that no alterations crept into the text. Although the oldest copies of the Hebrew text of the *Bible,* known as the Masoretic Text, date back only to the tenth century CE, the quality of the 700 extant manuscript pieces is good. In fact, the words contained in the Dead Sea Scrolls, a library of ancient materials discovered only in 1947, are nearly identical with those in the Masoretic Text. This similarity is remarkable considering that the Dead Sea scrolls were written 1,000 years before the oldest Masoretic manuscripts were copied.

In addition to the Masoretic Text, the Hebrew *Bible* comes to us via the Greeks through a third-century BCE translation known as the Septuagint. The Septuagint, meaning Version of the Seventy, is named from the number of scholars allegedly involved in

THE BOOKS OF THE HEBREW BIBLE

Law (Torah, Pentateuch)
  Genesis
  Exodus
  Leviticus
  Numbers
  Deuteronomy

Prophets (Nevi'im)
  The Early Prophets
  Joshua
  Judges
  Samuel
  Kings
  The Later Prophets
  Isaiah
  Jeremiah
  Ezekiel
  The Twelve
    Hosea
    Joel
    Amos
    Obadiah
    Jonah
    Micah
    Nahum
    Habakkuk
    Zephaniah
    Haggai
    Zechariah
    Malachi

Writings (Ketubim)
  Psalms
  Proverbs
  Job
  Song of Songs
  Ruth
  Lamentations
  Ecclesiastes
  Esther
  Daniel
  Ezra-Nehemiah
  Chronicles

working on the translation. There are a number of differences in the wording of the Mesoretic Text and the Septuagint. Moreover, the Septuagint includes several additional Jewish works along with the Hebrew *Bible*. These works, called by some the Apocrypha (from a Greek word for "hidden" or "spurious"), contain some insightful information about Jewish life in the second and first centuries BCE, but are not considered part of Judaism's sacred canon.

The Hebrew *Bible* traditionally is contained in 24 books. The words in these books, ordered and arranged somewhat differently, comprise 39 books in the Christian Old Testament. Although the order of the works was not as important in an age when words were written on independent scrolls and not on separate pages in a bound volume, the Hebrews categorize their scriptures into three clearly defined groupings. Each collection was canonized in a different period. and possesses a different degree of holiness or authority. In Hebrew, the names of the three groups are *Torah, Nevi'im,* and *Ketuvim*. By drawing the first letter of each group and adding a vowel between each consonant, the acronym *Tanak* is formed. This is the name Jews commonly use to refer to their holy scriptures.

The most holy works in the *Tanak* are the Five Books of Moses, collectively called the Law (in Hebrew, Torah; in Greek, Pentateuch). These works contain stories of creation, the great flood, the age of the patriarchs, the sojourn in Egypt, the exodus, the wandering in the wilderness, and the death of Moses. These books also contain the entire range of civil and criminal law, and instructions concerning worship and religious life. Many scholars believe that the *Torah* reached its present form by combining four literary sources: a J document from the tenth century BCE that used the divine name Yahweh; an E document from the ninth century that used the divine name Elohim; a D document of the seventh century that includes most of the fifth book, Deuteronomy; and a P document of priestly writers of the sixth century or later who acted as editors of the collection. Tradition insists that Moses authored and Ezra edited the books of the Law. These books, the first to be accepted into the sacred canon, were recognized as authoritative texts at least as early as 400 BCE during the period of the Second Commonwealth. To this day, Jews view the *Torah* as the core of God's revelation. When the Law is read in public worship, everyone in the synagogue stands to pay respect and gives full attention to the primacy of the words of Moses.

The second category of writings is the Prophets (in Hebrew, *Nevi'im*). Traditionally this collection of eight books is subdivided into the Early Prophets and the Later Prophets. The four books of the Early Prophets include historical writings covering the period from the entry into Canaan to the Babylonian conquest of Jerusalem. The Later Prophets include the books of Isaiah, Jeremiah, Ezekiel, and the Twelve, the last of which is a collection of 12 writers called the Minor Prophets because of the shortness, not the lack of importance, of their works. The Later Prophets contain the words of those who claimed to speak for Yahweh. Although produced in different centuries by people of different classes, these prophets echoed several common themes: (1) Every human is a child of God and thereby possesses certain rights that even kings must respect; and (2) Yahweh has high standards and will not forever tolerate injustice, corruption, and religious hypocrisy. Their works were accepted into the sacred canon about 200 BCE.

The third category is the Writings (in Hebrew, *Ketuvim*). This collection of 11 books includes a wide range of literature. It contains history, romance, poetry, songs, proverbs, a philosophical discourse, and perhaps one work intended to be read as a fictional drama. As a rule, the writers of this collection seem more concerned with general human themes than with the peculiar concerns of the Jewish nation, and thus many of these works have universal appeal. The book of Proverbs, for example, includes a collection of maxims that wise readers desirous of a happy and prosperous life are encouraged to take to heart. The book of Psalms, sometimes called the Hymnbook of the Second Temple, contains 150 inspirational hymns of praise, penitence, and thanksgiving that can easily be put to liturgical use. Two books in this collection, Job and Ecclesiastes, appear to challenge the traditional Hebraic point of view that suggests that the righteous will prosper and the wicked will meet with calamity. Also included in the Writings are several works (Ruth, Lamentations, and Daniel) that Christian versions of the Old Testament generally place among the books of the Prophets.

The Writings, along with other Jewish works produced during the era of the Second Commonwealth, were read by Hellenistic and Palestinian Jews for several centuries during the periods of Persian, Greek, and Roman dominance. This third category of scripture, however, was not formally adopted into the sacred canon until the end of the first century of the Christian era. When Rome destroyed the Jerusalem temple in 70 CE, thus ending the sacrificial rites and thereby making scriptural study the new centerpiece of Jewish worship, it became imperative for Judaism to define the limits of its authoritative canon. Consequently, in 90 CE, a rabbinical council under the leadership of Rabbi Johanan ben Zakkai met at Jamnia, a town 30 miles west of Jerusalem, to determine the Jewish canon. After a long debate over the inclusion of Song of Songs, Esther, Ecclesiastes, and Ezekiel, the council agreed upon the 24 books that today comprise the *Tanak*. The council also declared the works of the Apocrypha and the Christian gospels nonscriptural. With these decisions, the sacred canon of Judaism was effectively closed.

Other cherished, but not canonized works, within Judaism are the *Mishnah* and the *Talmud*. The first of these great works was codified in the second century by a Palestinian rabbi known as Judah the Prince. At this time it was not written down but memorized and passed forward orally by rabbis instructed in Jewish academies. The *Mishnah* (meaning "to repeat [what was taught]") is the first written book of the Oral Law, and it contains the opinions and rulings of rabbinical scholars on a wide range of issues. Rather than a verse-by-verse commentary on the *Bible* (the Written Law), the *Mishnah* was arranged according to subject matter and divided into six topical orders, which were subdivided into 63 groups known as tractates. For example, one order in the *Mishnah* entitled "Festivals" contains tractates that detail Sabbath and holy day requirements; another order, "Women," consists of tractates on betrothal, marriage, and divorce rules. Produced in Hebrew during an age in which the spoken language of Palestine was Aramaic, the *Mishnah* played an influential role in reviving Hebrew speech among Jewish peoples.

The second noncanonical masterpiece within Judaism is the *Talmud*, literally meaning "study." There are two distinct works known as the Talmud. The Palestinian *Talmud*, although never finished, was a fourth-century compilation that included commentary on the first four orders of the *Mishnah*. The Babylonian *Talmud*, completed in the sixth century, includes within it the complete *Mishnah*; commentary on about one-half of the tractates in the *Mishnah*; and a wealth of miscellaneous legends, anecdotal materials, and wise sayings. Because the Babylonian *Talmud* is superior in quality and authority to the Palestinian *Talmud*, the generic term *Talmud* almost always refers to the Babylonian *Talmud*. Only on matters where the Babylonian *Talmud* is silent or unclear does the authority of the Palestinian *Talmud* prevail. As the supreme interpreter of the Law, the *Talmud* attempts to answer the basic question, What is required of Jews who wish to be loyal to the Law of Moses? In its modern, printed form, the Babylonian *Talmud* alone contains nearly 6,000 pages of text. When the *tosafot* or "additions" are included with it, the collection expands into a massive library of some 64 volumes. Next to the *Bible,* the *Talmud* is the most important work within the Jewish tradition.

SUBDIVISIONS

According to Jacob Neusner and Calvin Goldscheider, two noted authorities in Jewish studies, "There is not now, and never has been, a single Judaism. There have been only Judaisms, each with its distinctive system and new beginning. . . ."[5] This insight applies not only to Judaism but to all living religions which by nature are evolving organisms. Every religious system contains a received tradition, which, when passed forward across time and place, must interact with diverse environments. This interplay often produces tensions that are resolved through creative reinterpretations of the received tradition. Living religions are not fossils but living organisms that are forever responding to challenge and change.

All Judaic systems share an ancient tradition that includes a long, often painful history and a common canon of holy texts. For more than a millennium after the codification of the *Talmud,* the majority of Jews accepted the insights in the *Talmud* as the authoritative interpretation of holy scripture. Some Jewish peoples, however, rejected the authority of the rabbinic scholars and devised other ways to reconcile the traditions of their past with the circumstances of their life. While Judaism has experienced fewer schisms than many religions, the Jewish family tree includes several branches that have grown outward from the roots of sacred scripture and the trunk of Rabbinic Judaism.

Sectarian Divisions in the Middle Period

During the Middle Ages, three major Jewish groups emerged to challenge the authority of Rabbinic Judaism and the Talmudic interpretations of the sacred

---

[5]Calvin Goldscheider and Jacob Neusner, *Social Foundations of Judaism* (Englewood Cliffs, NJ: Prentice Hall, 1990), p. 7.

traditions. Perhaps the most radical of the three were the Karaites, a word literally meaning "readers of scriptures." Following the arguments of Anan ben David, an eighth-century critic of the Talmudic authorities, the Karaites insisted that the rabbis had misinterpreted the original intentions of the sacred text and built upon it unnecessary rules that made life excessively burdensome. Moreover, they announced that all Jews had a right to interpret for themselves the meaning of the holy text without regard to the official explanations offered by the scribes. Insisting upon the authority of scripture alone, the Karaites rejected the Oral Law, the *Talmud,* and the sacred calendar as formulated by the scribes. Some groups of Karaites still exist. According to the modern state of Israel, Karaites are Jews, but their positions are considered heretical.

A second group that viewed the rabbinic interpretations as too limiting were the Kabbalists. While not rejecting the Oral Tradition, the Kabbalists (from the Hebrew word meaning "to receive") insisted that God is beyond rational analysis and can only be known through revealed scripture. They primarily focused on the parts of the *Torah* that address the process of creation and the relationship that God maintains with creation. According to the Kabbalists, each of the 22 letters of the Hebrew alphabet has a number associated with it. When the letters are properly combined and added, the holy words release powerful creative energies. Only by learning the proper values of the letters can one decipher the deeper esoteric mysteries within the *Torah* that lead to reunion with God. The best-known work of the Kabbalists was a thirteenth-century piece known as *Zohar.* According to legend, the angels revealed to a Rabbi Simon the hidden meanings of scripture 1,000 years earlier. Simon disclosed these meanings in a commentary on the *Torah,* but this work was only known to a select few until distributed in the thirteenth century. *Zohar,* meaning "brilliance" (in reference to the heretofore unseen divine light), is an expression of Jewish mysticism that corresponds in many ways to the spiritual insights contained in the Eastern religious traditions.

Another brand of Jewish mysticism to challenge the Talmudists was Hasidism, a term derived from the same Hebrew word for "the pious" that had been applied to those ancient martyrs who had resisted Hellenization two millennia earlier. Hasidism developed in the eighteenth century as a vital, singing faith that taught that love and doing good works were more important than following the letter of the sacred law. Hasidic communities used music and dance to produce ecstatic states of piety—spiritual manifestations closely similar to the experiences of Christian Pentecostals and Islamic Sufi dervishes. Like many mystics, Hasids communicated with the divine directly, without the need of a priestly or rabbinic class. Today Hasidism is often remembered for its conservatism in dress and social mores. In the eighteenth century, however, its liberal attitude toward the role of Jewish law, its acceptance of ecstatic dancing and spontaneous prayers, and its profession that one could experience God in even profane activities such as eating, sleeping, and love making offended many orthodox Talmudists who opposed its emotional excesses and nontraditional leanings.

The Branches of Modern Judaism

Throughout medieval times, European Jews lived in a world of violence, segregation, and political insecurity. They lived in separate neighborhoods known as "ghettos," enjoyed few civil or legal rights, were forbidden to own land or join in craft guilds, and were without state citizenship. Ghetto life, however, had a few advantages. As a result of the forced segregation, Jewish institutions thrived. Synagogues opened thrice daily for prayer; shops were closed on the Sabbath and other holy days; marriages and bar mitzvah ceremonies became communitywide celebrations; and Jewish schools taught children to read and write and to remember their sacred heritage. Convinced that some day their sufferings would be ended, most medieval Jews looked forward to a time when a Messiah from the line of David would return, the Temple would be rebuilt, and peace and prosperity would encompass the world. The ghetto may have limited Jewish economic or political advancement, but it also fostered among Jews a sense of community, an appreciation for their past, and a hope for their future.

For Jewish history, the modern period really opens with the Jewish emancipation of the late eighteenth century. Beginning with reforms first initiated during the French Revolution, Jews across Europe slowly began to win new civil and political freedoms. Once emancipated from the ghetto, Jews faced new challenges that encouraged some to question the appropriateness of old Jewish forms and customs. Many began to seek ways to become fully integrated into society without losing their Jewish identity. Others insisted that all talk of integration was rank heresy. In this atmosphere of emancipation, reform, and orthodox opposition, several new forms of Judaism arose.

Modern Judaism can be divided into three major denominations and one more recently appearing minor one. The major groups include Orthodox, Reform, and Conservative Judaism. A significant yet smaller body is Reconstructionist Judaism.

The term *Orthodox Judaism* is applied to those traditionalist movements that resisted the influences of modernization that arose in response to emancipation. Of the major denominations, Orthodoxy is the least centralized. It does not have a single governing body but rather consists of several different movements that adhere to certain common principles. The fundamental principle that brings unity to the movements is the commitment to the *Torah*, both Written and Oral, as the exact word of God that was revealed without human creativity or influence. Viewing the revealed *Torah* as the inviolate standard, not a value system of a particular age, Orthodox bodies insist on retaining the traditional Jewish laws and customs. They observe the ancient dietary and dress regulations, prohibit women from leading in worship or counting toward a *minyon* (the quorum of 10 needed for public worship), segregate the sexes during worship, conduct all worship rituals in the Hebrew language, forbid the use of instrumental music in worship, and insist on the circumcision of Jewish males on the eighth day after birth by authorized mohels. Theologically, most Orthodox would embrace the statements within the 13 principles of faith written by Rabbi Moses Maimonides in the twelfth century. These principles include a belief in the coming of a Messiah and a final revival of the dead. Orthodox Jews comprise less than 10 percent of the Jewish community in America, but their numbers are much greater in other regions, including Israel where they comprise just under one-half of the population.

Reform Judaism originated in Germany in the early nineteenth century and spread to America in the second half of the century. The most liberal (meaning, "not bound by established forms") of the major Jewish denominations, Reform Judaism views the *Torah* as divinely inspired yet written in the language of the time in which it was given. While containing some important, even timeless truths, the words of the *Torah* are not eternal, but rather reflect the cultures of earlier human eras. The early reformers embraced five common principles:

1. Judaism is capable of continuous development and should adapt its teachings to the needs of the times.
2. Ancient rituals and dietary laws need not be observed.
3. Circumcision should be voluntary.
4. The *Talmud* is not the authoritative interpretation of the sacred tradition.
5. The coming of a personal Messiah to lead the Jews back to Palestine is no longer anticipated.

In the twentieth century, many Reform Jews felt that the early reformers had overreacted against the conservatism of the entrenched Orthodox and subsequently reclaimed some of the traditional customs of their heritage. Today, for instance, Reform Judaism maintains that Jews should participate fully in the Jewish life of the home and synagogue. This includes maintaining a prayer life, observing the Sabbath, and recognizing that the Written and Oral Law are important sources that should be adapted to the needs of each generation. In practice, Reform Judaism differs from the Orthodox in its insistence on the equality of the sexes; in its use of both Hebrew and vernacular languages in worship; and in its more liberal rules concerning Sabbath and holy day obligations, mourning practices, and marriage and divorce. Doctrinally, Reform Jews believe that the heart of Judaism lies in the doctrine of the One, living God who rules the world through law and love. Reform Jews look forward to the coming not of a personal Messiah, but of a Messianic age in which truth, justice, and peace will dwell among all peoples. Its leading seminary is Hebrew Union College, the oldest permanent rabbinical seminary in America. Currently, about 4 in 10 American Jews consider themselves within the Reform tradition.

The third major Jewish denomination is *Conservative Judaism*. This group is a hybrid tradition, a middle way between the Orthodox and Reform movements. The movement originated in the mid-nineteenth century and is often interpreted as a "counterreformation" necessitated by the alleged excesses of the Reform movement. Like the Orthodox, the Conservatives insist that the *Torah* and the *Talmud* are of divine origin. However, they also recognize the role played by humans in the formation of these texts and thus accept these works as historical documents that were influenced by other cultures. They embrace a number of reforms, such as the discarding of the ancient dress requirements, but keep other traditions, such as the use of Hebrew in the religious rituals and the traditional diet and Sabbath restrictions. In recent decades, the Conservatives have followed the pattern of the Reform in admitting women as rabbis. The educational center of Conservative Judaism is the Jewish Theological Seminary in New York. This body is the largest Jewish denomination in North America, although like the Reform tradition, its numbers remain small in modern Israel.

Reconstructionist Judaism was founded only in 1922 by Mordecai Kaplan, an American rabbi who argued for a naturalistic conception of God. According to Kaplan, Judaism was an evolving civilization that should be reconstructed in every generation. The cultural heritage of the Jews should be understood, but it was not a divine mandate. "The past," said Kaplan, "has a vote, not a veto." Kaplan personally did not believe in God, but he did believe in nature and in the possibility that people could better themselves. Despite the individual beliefs of its founder, today Reconstructionism has restored references in its liturgy to supernatural events that it once rejected as unbelievable myths. Although at the forefront of many modern trends within Judaism, especially its egalitarian liturgy, Reconstructionist Judaism remains small and encompasses only about 5 percent of the American Jewish community.

SACRED OBSERVANCES AND PRACTICES

For thousands of years, the descendants of Abraham have been identified by the religious practices they observe. A central Jewish custom is the tradition of maintaining the Sabbath (from a Hebrew word meaning "rest"), which is a designated weekly period of rest and worship that begins at sundown on Friday evening and continues until sundown on Saturday. On this day pious Jews refrain from work and gather together in a synagogue for prayer, singing, scripture reading, and worship. The Sabbath tradition is affirmed not only in the famous Decalogue allegedly given to Moses on Mount Sinai but also in the six-day creation story and seventh day of rest that is found in the opening chapter of Genesis.

Also embedded in the well-known Genesis story is the Lord's provision of heavenly lights to separate day from night and to indicate the set times of festivals, days, and years. Thus, not surprisingly, Jews also set aside a number of other special times throughout the year for sacred observances. Among the most holy days in the Jewish calendar is Rosh Hashanah (New Year), which, depending on the year, occurs in September or October. Jews celebrate their New Year with a traditional blowing of a ram's horn that ushers in a 10-day period of penitence. Many Jewish families eat apples dipped in honey on this day to anticipate an upcoming joyous year. The period of repentance following Rosh Hashanah culminates in Yom Kippur, the most holy Day of Atonement that is celebrated with rituals of prayer, fasting, and confessions. Five days after Yom Kippur and lasting for eight days (seven for Reformed Jews) is Sukkot, or the Feast of Tabernacles. In this harvest festival of thanksgiving, Jews remember how the ancient Hebrews lived in temporary huts while wandering in the desert wilderness. This festival ends with Simhat Torah, a day that celebrates the eternal continuity of the Torah. On this day, Jews end and begin the annual worship liturgy by reading together the last chapters of the book of Deuteronomy and the first chapter of the book of Genesis.

In December of each year, Jews observe Hanukkah, the eight day Festival of Lights that commemorates how the Lord miraculously kept a single day's supply of oil burning for eight days during the time of the Jewish struggle for freedom against the Greek-Syrian overlords. Jews recall another piece of their past by celebrating Purim, a February or March festival that commemorates Esther's triumph over the evil Haman who plotted to exterminate the Persian Jews. On this day, Jews read and reenact the story of Esther and often exchange gifts. Later in the spring Pesach or Passover is celebrated. This eight-day (seven for Reform Jews) festival commemorates the deliverance of the Jews from Egypt and centers on the *seder,* a kosher meal of wine and unleavened bread that is filled with sacred and symbolic meanings. Finally, 50 days later Jews celebrate Shavuot, the Festival of Weeks, which commemorates the Lord's giving of the Torah to Moses on Mount Sinai.

In addition to these annual holy days, Jews mark stages in individual life cycles with special sacred rites. Eight days after birth, Jewish boys are circumcised, an act embedded in Jewish tradition since the days of Abraham. Similarly, when boys reach age 13, they participate in a *bar mitzvah* (meaning "son of the commandment") ritual that signifies their maturity into manhood and their acceptance of the sacred commandments. In recent times, a similar ritual known as *bat mitzvah* (daughter of the commandment) has become common for preteen Jewish girls approaching maturity.

SOURCES

The following anthology of texts from the Hebrew *Bible* includes representative selections from the Law, the Prophets, and the Writings. Nineteen of the 24 books in the sacred canon are represented in this anthology. The texts are arranged into the nine thematic categories discussed in the Introduction to this volume.

SECTION 1: Beginnings: God, Time, and the Universe

One of the best-known lines in any sacred text is the opening statement in the book of Genesis. This simple statement affirms several faith assumptions: There was a beginning; before the beginning there was a god; and the cosmos, although the creation of this by god, is not god itself. These statements are among the central beliefs shared by each of the three great Western religions—Judaism, Christianity, and Islam.

As you read the first selection taken from the book of Genesis, use the following questions to help you find meaning in the passage: What is the relationship between the Creator and the created in the text? What attributes about the divine are suggested by this relationship? Note that the creation story is subdivided into six stages followed by a time of rest. What tradition within the Hebraic religious calendar does this story affirm? Does the seven-day narrative move toward a dramatic conclusion? If so, what is the climax?

THE CREATION FROM THE BOOK OF GENESIS

Chapter 1

¹In the beginning God created the heavens and the earth. ²Now the earth was formless and empty, darkness was over the surface of the deep, and the Spirit of God was hovering over the waters.

³And God said, "Let there be light," and there was light. ⁴God saw that the light was good, and He separated the light from the darkness. ⁵God called the light "day," and the darkness he called "night." And there was evening, and there was morning—the first day.

⁶And God said, "Let there be an expanse between the waters to separate water from water." ⁷So God made the expanse and separated the water under the expanse from the water above it. And it was so. ⁸God called the expanse "sky." And there was evening, and there was morning—the second day.

⁹And God said, "Let the water under the sky be gathered to one place, and let dry ground appear." And it was so. ¹⁰God called the dry ground "land," and the gathered waters he called "seas." And God saw that it was good.

¹¹Then God said, "Let the land produce vegetation: seed-bearing plants and trees on the land that bear fruit with seed in it, according to their various kinds." And it was so. ¹²The land produced vegetation: plants bearing seed according to their kinds and trees bearing fruit with seed in it according to their kinds. And God saw that it was good. ¹³And there was evening, and there was morning—the third day.

¹⁴And God said, "Let there be lights in the expanse of the sky to separate the day from the night, and let them serve as signs to mark seasons and days and years, ¹⁵and let them be lights in the expanse of the sky to give light on the earth." And it was so. ¹⁶God made two great lights—the greater light to govern the day and the lesser light to govern the night. He also made the stars. ¹⁷God set them in the expanse of the sky to give light on the earth, ¹⁸to govern the day and the night, and to separate light from darkness. And God saw that it was good. ¹⁹And there was evening, and there was morning—the fourth day.

²⁰And God said, "Let the water teem with living creatures, and let birds fly above the earth across the expanse of the sky." ²¹So God created the great creatures of the sea and every living and moving thing with which the water teems, according to their kinds, and every winged bird according to its kind. And God saw that it was good. ²²God blessed them and said, "Be fruitful and increase in number and fill the water in the seas, and let the birds increase on the earth." ²³And there was evening, and there was morning—the fifth day.

²⁴And God said, "Let the land produce living creatures according to their kinds: livestock, creatures that move along the ground, and wild animals, each according to its kind." And it was so. ²⁵God made the wild animals according to their kinds, the livestock according to their kinds, and all the creatures that move along the ground according to their kinds. And God saw that it was good.

²⁶Then God said, "Let us make man in our image, in our likeness, and let them rule over the fish of the sea and the birds of the air, over the livestock, over all the earth, and over all the creatures that move along the ground."

²⁷So God created man in his own image, in the image of God he created him; male and female he created them.

²⁸God blessed them and said to them, "Be fruitful and increase in number; fill the earth and subdue it. Rule over the fish of the sea and the birds of the air and over every living creature that moves on the ground."
²⁹Then God said, "I give you every seed-bearing plant on the face of the whole earth and every tree that has fruit with seed in it. They will be yours for food. ³⁰And to all the beasts of the earth and all the birds of the air and all the creatures that move on the ground—everything that has the breath of life in it—I give every green plant for food." And it was so.
³¹God saw all that he had made, and it was very good. And there was evening, and there was morning—the sixth day.

Chapter 2

¹Thus the heavens and the earth were completed in all their vast array. ²By the seventh day God had finished the work he had been doing; so on the seventh day he rested from all his work. ³And God blessed the seventh day and made it holy, because on it he rested from all the work of creating that he had done.

Both the Mesopotamians and Egyptians described the powers of nature as distinct deities. As the opening passage indicated, however, the Hebrews insisted that nature itself was the creation of a single Lord. The following selections from the book of Psalms and from the prophet Isaiah also describe this Lord of creation. As you read these selections, look for words and images the writers used to describe the divine. According to these passages, is the Hebrew god a personal deity, a divine principle, or both? What is the relationship between this god and humanity in general and the Hebrew people in particular?

IMAGES OF GOD FROM THE PSALMS AND THE PROPHETS

Psalm 19

¹The heavens declare the glory of God; the skies proclaim the work of his hands.
²Day after day they pour forth speech; night after night they display knowledge.
³There is no speech or language where their voice is not heard.
⁴Their voice goes out into all the earth, their words to the ends of the world. In the heavens he has pitched a tent for the sun,
⁵which is like a bridegroom coming forth from his pavilion, like a champion rejoicing to run his course.
⁶It rises at one end of the heavens and makes its circuit to the other; nothing is hidden from its heat.

⁷The law of the LORD is perfect, reviving the soul. The statutes of the LORD are trustworthy, making wise the simple.
⁸The precepts of the LORD are right, giving joy to the heart. The commands of the LORD are radiant, giving light to the eyes.
⁹The fear of the LORD is pure, enduring forever. The ordinances of the LORD are sure and altogether righteous.
¹⁰They are more precious than gold, than much pure gold; they are sweeter than honey, than honey from the comb.

Psalm 23

¹The LORD is my shepherd, I shall not be in want.
²He makes me lie down in green pastures, he leads me beside quiet waters,
³he restores my soul. He guides me in paths of righteousness for his name's sake.
⁴Even though I walk through the valley of the shadow of death, I will fear no evil, for you are with me; your rod and your staff, they comfort me.
⁵You prepare a table before me in the presence of my enemies. You anoint my head with oil; my cup overflows.
⁶Surely goodness and love will follow me all the days of my life, and I will dwell in the house of the LORD forever.

FROM THE BOOK OF ISAIAH

Chapter 40

¹⁸To whom, then, will you compare God? What image will you compare him to?
¹⁹As for an idol, a craftsman casts it, and a goldsmith overlays it with gold and fashions silver chains for it.
²⁰A man too poor to present such an offering selects wood that will not rot. He looks for a skilled craftsman to set up an idol that will not topple.
²¹Do you not know? Have you not heard? Has it not been told you from the beginning? Have you not understood since the earth was founded?
²²He sits enthroned above the circle of the earth, and its people are like grasshoppers. He stretches out the heavens like a canopy, and spreads them out like a tent to live in.
²³He brings princes to naught and reduces the rulers of this world to nothing.
²⁴No sooner are they planted, no sooner are they sown, no sooner do they take root in the ground, than he blows on them and they wither, and a whirlwind sweeps them away like chaff.
²⁵"To whom will you compare me? Or who is my equal?" says the Holy One.
²⁶Lift your eyes and look to the heavens: Who created all these? He who brings out the starry host one by one, and calls them each by name. Because of his great power and mighty strength, not one of them is missing.

²⁷Why do you say, O Jacob, and complain, O Israel, "My way is hidden from the LORD; my cause is disregarded by my God"?

²⁸Do you not know? Have you not heard? The LORD is the everlasting God, the Creator of the ends of the earth. He will not grow tired or weary, and his understanding no one can fathom.

²⁹He gives strength to the weary and increases the power of the weak.

³⁰Even youths grow tired and weary, and young men stumble and fall;

³¹but those who hope in the LORD will renew their strength. They will soar on wings like eagles; they will run and not grow weary, they will walk and not be faint.

SECTION 2: Humanity: The Problem of Good and Evil

Religions that affirm the goodness of creation must come to terms with the problem of evil in the universe. Similarly, systems that assert that matter is evil must confront the problem of goodness. The opening lines in Genesis affirm the goodness of creation. How then do the ancient Hebrews account for the presence of evil in the world?

Printed next is the familiar story of Adam and Eve, the parents of humanity. Some read this text as a story of the human quest for immortality; others see it as a story of human corruption. As you examine this text, speculate about what grand question this story attempts to answer and about why this piece may have been included in the Hebrew canon. What questions about the origins of evil does the story answer and what questions remain unanswered? According to this text, what is Yahweh's attitude toward sin? What does this tell us about the Hebraic understanding of the divine? Note that in the narrative, humanity is descended from one man and one woman. What are the social and gender implications of this assertion? To what degree, if any, is this text demeaning to women or to men?

THE STORY OF ADAM AND EVE
FROM THE BOOK OF GENESIS

Chapter 2

⁷The LORD God formed the man from the dust of the ground and breathed into his nostrils the breath of life, and the man became a living being.

⁸Now the LORD God had planted a garden in the east, in Eden; and there he put the man he had formed. ⁹And the LORD God made all kinds of trees grow out of the ground—trees that were pleasing to the eye and good for food. In the middle of the garden were the tree of life and the tree of the knowledge of good and evil.

¹⁰A river watering the garden flowed from Eden; from there it was separated into four headwaters. ¹¹The name of the first is the Pishon; it winds through the entire land of Havilah, where there is gold. ¹²(The gold of that land is good; aromatic resin and onyx are also there.) ¹³The name of the second river is the Gihon; it winds through the entire land of Cush. ¹⁴The name of the third river is the Tigris; it runs along the east side of Asshur. And the fourth river is the Euphrates.

¹⁵The LORD God took the man and put him in the Garden of Eden to work it and take care of it. ¹⁶And the LORD God commanded the man, "You are free to eat from any tree in the garden; ¹⁷but you must not eat from the tree of the knowledge of good and evil, for when you eat of it you will surely die."

¹⁸The LORD God said, "It is not good for the man to be alone. I will make a helper suitable for him."

¹⁹Now the LORD God had formed out of the ground all the beasts of the field and all the birds of the air. He brought them to the man to see what he would name them; and whatever the man called each living creature, that was its name. ²⁰So the man gave names to all the livestock, the birds of the air and all the beasts of the field. But for Adam no suitable helper was found. ²¹So the LORD God caused the man to fall into a deep sleep; and while he was sleeping, he took one of the man's ribs and closed up the place with flesh. ²²Then the LORD God made a woman from the rib he had taken out of the man, and he brought her to the man.

²³The man said, "This is now bone of my bones and flesh of my flesh; she shall be called 'woman,' for she was taken out of man."

²⁴For this reason a man will leave his father and mother and be united to his wife, and they will become one flesh.

²⁵The man and his wife were both naked, and they felt no shame.

Chapter 3

¹Now the serpent was more crafty than any of the wild animals the LORD God had made. He said to the woman, "Did God really say, 'You must not eat from any tree in the garden'?"

²The woman said to the serpent, "We may eat fruit from the trees in the garden, ³but God did say, 'You must not eat fruit from the tree that is in the middle of the garden, and you must not touch it, or you will die.'"

⁴"You will not surely die," the serpent said to the woman. ⁵"For God knows that when you eat of it your eyes will be opened, and you will be like God, knowing good and evil."

⁶When the woman saw that the fruit of the tree was good for food and pleasing to the eye, and also desirable for gaining wisdom, she took some and ate it. She also gave some to her husband, who was with her, and he ate it. ⁷Then the eyes of

both of them were opened, and they realized they were naked; so they sewed fig leaves together and made coverings for themselves.

[8]Then the man and his wife heard the sound of the LORD God as he was walking in the garden in the cool of the day, and they hid from the LORD God among the trees of the garden. [9]But the LORD God called to the man, "Where are you?" [10]He answered, "I heard you in the garden, and I was afraid because I was naked; so I hid."

[11]And he said, "Who told you that you were naked? Have you eaten from the tree that I commanded you not to eat from?" [12]The man said, "The woman you put here with me—she gave me some fruit from the tree, and I ate it."

[13]Then the LORD God said to the woman, "What is this you have done?" The woman said, "The serpent deceived me, and I ate."

[14]So the LORD God said to the serpent, "Because you have done this, Cursed are you above all the livestock and all the wild animals! You will crawl on your belly and you will eat dust all the days of your life.

[15]And I will put enmity between you and the woman, and between your offspring and hers; he will crush your head, and you will strike his heel."

[16]To the woman he said, "I will greatly increase your pains in childbearing; with pain you will give birth to children. Your desire will be for your husband, and he will rule over you."

[17]To Adam he said, "Because you listened to your wife and ate from the tree about which I commanded you, 'You must not eat of it,' "Cursed is the ground because of you; through painful toil you will eat of it all the days of your life.

[18]It will produce thorns and thistles for you, and you will eat the plants of the field.

[19]By the sweat of your brow you will eat your food until you return to the ground, since from it you were taken; for dust you are and to dust you will return."

[20]Adam named his wife Eve, because she would become the mother of all the living.

[21]The LORD God made garments of skin for Adam and his wife and clothed them. [22]And the LORD God said, "The man has now become like one of us, knowing good and evil. He must not be allowed to reach out his hand and take also from the tree of life and eat, and live forever." [23]So the LORD God banished him from the Garden of Eden to work the ground from which he had been taken. [24]After he drove the man out, he placed on the east side of the Garden of Eden cherubim and a flaming sword flashing back and forth to guard the way to the tree of life.

Are humans fundamentally good, bad, or neither? This question has been asked across time and place by inquiring minds of many cultures. The authors of the Hebrew canon, like those of many other sacred texts, do not attempt a systematic answer to this question but rather offer a variety of statements about the human condition. The Genesis creation stories provide some insights into how the ancient Hebrews viewed human nature. Similarly, the words of the psalmists and prophets offer further enlightenment. Examine the following passages from the Psalms and Isaiah. What assumptions about human nature are contained within these passages? To what degree are these statements compatible with each other and with the point of view of the author of the creation accounts?

IMAGES OF HUMANITY IN THE PSALMS AND THE PROPHETS

Psalm 8

[1]O LORD, our Lord, how majestic is your name in all the earth! You have set your glory above the heavens.
[2]From the lips of children and infants you have ordained praise because of your enemies, to silence the foe and the avenger.
[3]When I consider your heavens, the work of your fingers, the moon and the stars, which you have set in place,
[4]what is man that you are mindful of him, the son of man that you care for him?
[5]You made him a little lower than the heavenly beings and crowned him with glory and honor.
[6]You made him ruler over the works of your hands; you put everything under his feet:
[7]all flocks and herds, and the beasts of the field,
[8]the birds of the air, and the fish of the sea, all that swim the paths of the seas.
[9]O LORD, our Lord, how majestic is your name in all the earth!

Psalm 51

[1]Have mercy on me, O God, according to your unfailing love; according to your great compassion blot out my transgressions.
[2]Wash away all my iniquity and cleanse me from my sin.
[3]For I know my transgressions, and my sin is always before me.
[4]Against you, you only, have I sinned and done what is evil in your sight, so that you are proved right when you speak and justified when you judge.
[5]Surely I was sinful at birth, sinful from the time my mother conceived me.
[6]Surely you desire truth in the inner parts you teach me wisdom in the inmost place.
[7]Cleanse me with hyssop, and I will be clean; wash me, and I will be whiter than snow.

⁸Let me hear joy and gladness; let the bones you have crushed rejoice.

⁹Hide your face from my sins and blot out all my iniquity.

¹⁰Create in me a pure heart, O God, and renew a steadfast spirit within me.

¹¹Do not cast me from your presence or take your Holy Spirit from me.

¹²Restore to me the joy of your salvation and grant me a willing spirit, to sustain me.

¹³Then I will teach transgressors your ways, and sinners will turn back to you.

¹⁴Save me from bloodguilt, O God, the God who saves me, and my tongue will sing of your righteousness.

¹⁵O LORD, open my lips, and my mouth will declare your praise.

¹⁶You do not delight in sacrifice, or I would bring it; you do not take pleasure in burnt offerings.

¹⁷The sacrifices of God are a broken spirit; a broken and contrite heart, O God, you will not despise.

¹⁸In your good pleasure make Zion prosper; build up the walls of Jerusalem.

¹⁹Then there will be righteous sacrifices, whole burnt offerings to delight you; then bulls will be offered on your altar.

FROM THE BOOK OF ISAIAH

Chapter 59

¹Surely the arm of the LORD is not too short to save, nor his ear too dull to hear.

²But your iniquities have separated you from your God; your sins have hidden his face from you, so that he will not hear.

³For your hands are stained with blood, your fingers with guilt. Your lips have spoken lies, and your tongue mutters wicked things.

⁴No one calls for justice; no one pleads his case with integrity. They rely on empty arguments and speak lies; they conceive trouble and give birth to evil.

⁵They hatch the eggs of vipers and spin a spider's web. Whoever eats their eggs will die, and when one is broken, an adder is hatched.

⁶Their cobwebs are useless for clothing; they cannot cover themselves with what they make. Their deeds are evil deeds, and acts of violence are in their hands.

⁷Their feet rush into sin; they are swift to shed innocent blood. Their thoughts are evil thoughts; ruin and destruction mark their ways.

⁸The way of peace they do not know; there is no justice in their paths. They have turned them into crooked roads; no one who walks in them will know peace.

⁹So justice is far from us, and righteousness does not reach us. We look for light, but all is darkness; for brightness, but we walk in deep shadows.

SECTION 3: Sacred Stories: Divine Messengers, Prophets, and Priests

A central concept within Judaism is the idea that the One Lord of creation made a covenant with humankind in general and with the Hebrew people in particular. The covenant theme, which appears frequently in Hebrew scripture, assesses special privileges and responsibilities for those who accept its terms. The opening passages in this section tell two stories of God establishing covenant relationships. The first story describes God's promises to Noah. Preceding this encounter, God had become so angry with violence among humans that he sent a flood to destroy the wicked world. Only Noah and his family, who built an ark and remained within it during the flood, survived the catastrophe. The story of the flood continues with God establishing a covenant with Noah. The second set of passages describes the covenant God made with Abram, later renamed Abraham, the patriarch and father of the faith for Jews, Christians, and Muslims. In reading these stories, note the terms and the recipients of the covenants with Noah and Abram. How are the two covenants alike and different? What is promised and what is expected of those who accept the covenant relationships with God?

THE COVENANT WITH NOAH FROM THE BOOK OF GENESIS

Chapter 8

¹⁵Then God said to Noah, ¹⁶"Come out of the ark, you and your wife and your sons and their wives. ¹⁷Bring out every kind of living creature that is with you—the birds, the animals, and all the creatures that move along the ground—so they can multiply on the earth and be fruitful and increase in number upon it."

¹⁸So Noah came out, together with his sons and his wife and his sons' wives. ¹⁹All the animals and all the creatures that move along the ground and all the birds—everything that moves on the earth—came out of the ark, one kind after another.

²⁰Then Noah built an altar to the LORD and, taking some of all the clean animals and clean birds, he sacrificed burnt offerings on it. ²¹The LORD smelled the pleasing aroma and said in his heart: "Never again will I curse the ground because of man, even though every inclination of his heart is evil from childhood. And never again will I destroy all living creatures, as I have done.

[22]"As long as the earth endures, seedtime and harvest, cold and heat, summer and winter, day and night will never cease."

Chapter 9

[1]Then God blessed Noah and his sons, saying to them, "Be fruitful and increase in number and fill the earth. [2]The fear and dread of you will fall upon all the beasts of the earth and all the birds of the air, upon every creature that moves along the ground, and upon all the fish of the sea; they are given into your hands. [3]Everything that lives and moves will be food for you. Just as I gave you the green plants, I now give you everything.

[4]"But you must not eat meat that has its lifeblood still in it. [5]And for your lifeblood I will surely demand an accounting. I will demand an accounting from every animal. And from each man, too, I will demand an accounting for the life of his fellow man.

[6]"Whoever sheds the blood of man, by man shall his blood be shed; for in the image of God has God made man.

[7]As for you, be fruitful and increase in number; multiply on the earth and increase upon it."

[8]Then God said to Noah and to his sons with him: [9]"I now establish my covenant with you and with your descendants after you [10]and with every living creature that was with you—the birds, the livestock and all the wild animals, all those that came out of the ark with you—every living creature on earth. [11]I establish my covenant with you: Never again will all life be cut off by the waters of a flood; never again will there be a flood to destroy the earth."

[12]And God said, "This is the sign of the covenant I am making between me and you and every living creature with you, a covenant for all generations to come: [13]I have set my rainbow in the clouds, and it will be the sign of the covenant between me and the earth. [14]Whenever I bring clouds over the earth and the rainbow appears in the clouds, [15]I will remember my covenant between me and you and all living creatures of every kind. Never again will the waters become a flood to destroy all life. [16]Whenever the rainbow appears in the clouds, I will see it and remember the everlasting covenant between God and all living creatures of every kind on the earth."

[17]So God said to Noah, "This is the sign of the covenant I have established between me and all life on the earth."

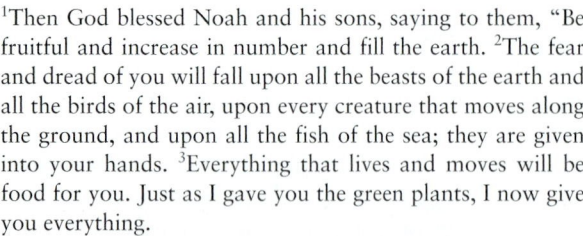

THE COVENANT WITH ABRAM
FROM THE BOOK OF GENESIS

Chapter 12

[1]The LORD had said to Abram, "Leave your country, your people and your father's household and go to the land I will show you.

[2]"I will make you into a great nation and I will bless you; I will make your name great, and you will be a blessing. [3]I will bless those who bless you, and whoever curses you I will curse; and all peoples on earth will be blessed through you."

[4]So Abram left, as the LORD had told him; and Lot went with him. Abram was seventy-five years old when he set out from Haran. [5]He took his wife Sarai, his nephew Lot, all the possessions they had accumulated and the people they had acquired in Haran, and they set out for the land of Canaan, and they arrived there.

[6]Abram traveled through the land as far as the site of the great tree of Moreh at Shechem. At that time the Canaanites were in the land. [7]The LORD appeared to Abram and said, "To your offspring I will give this land." So he built an altar there to the LORD, who had appeared to him.

In the ensuing chapters, Abram's barren wife Sarai tells Abram to have a child with Hagar, their Egyptian handmaid. Abram agrees, and Hagar gives birth to Abram's first son, Ishmael. The covenant story continues with the following encounter between God and Abram.

Chapter 17

[1]When Abram was ninety-nine years old, the LORD appeared to him and said, "I am God Almighty; walk before me and be blameless. [2]I will confirm my covenant between me and you and will greatly increase your numbers."

[3]Abram fell facedown, and God said to him, [4]"As for me, this is my covenant with you: You will be the father of many nations. [5]No longer will you be called Abram; your name will be Abraham, for I have made you a father of many nations. [6]I will make you very fruitful; I will make nations of you, and kings will come from you. [7]I will establish my covenant as an everlasting covenant between me and you and your descendants after you for the generations to come, to be your God and the God of your descendants after you. [8]The whole land of Canaan, where you are now an alien, I will give as an everlasting possession to you and your descendants after you; and I will be their God."

[9]Then God said to Abraham, "As for you, you must keep my covenant, you and your descendants after you for the generations to come. [10]This is my covenant with you and your descendants after you, the covenant you are to keep: Every male among you shall be circumcised. [11]You are to undergo circumcision, and it will be the sign of the covenant between me and you. [12]For the generations to come every male among you who is eight days old must be circumcised, including those born in your household or bought with money from a foreigner—those who are not your offspring. [13]Whether born in your household or bought with your money, they must be circumcised. My covenant in your flesh is to be an everlasting

covenant. [14]Any uncircumcised male, who has not been circumcised in the flesh, will be cut off from his people; he has broken my covenant."

[15]God also said to Abraham, "As for Sarai your wife, you are no longer to call her Sarai; her name will be Sarah. [16]I will bless her and will surely give you a son by her. I will bless her so that she will be the mother of nations; kings of peoples will come from her."

[17]Abraham fell facedown; he laughed and said to himself, "Will a son be born to a man a hundred years old? Will Sarah bear a child at the age of ninety?" [18]And Abraham said to God, "If only Ishmael might live under your blessing!"

[19]Then God said, "Yes, but your wife Sarah will bear you a son, and you will call him Isaac. I will establish my covenant with him as an everlasting covenant for his descendants after him. [20]And as for Ishmael, I have heard you: I will surely bless him; I will make him fruitful and will greatly increase his numbers. He will be the father of twelve rulers, and I will make him into a great nation. [21]But my covenant I will establish with Isaac, whom Sarah will bear to you by this time next year." [22]When he had finished speaking with Abraham, God went up from him.

The remaining chapters in Genesis tell stories of the special circumstances surrounding the birth of Isaac—a child of Abraham and Sarah—and theologically meaningful events in lives of Isaac, Isaac's son Jacob (also renamed Israel), and Jacob's 12 sons. The book ends with the children of Jacob living in prosperity in Egypt.

In the second book of Moses, Exodus, the descendants of the 12 sons of Jacob are made slaves under a cruel Egyptian Pharaoh. God responds by raising Moses to liberate his chosen people from bondage. Moses confronts the Pharaoh and demonstrates the power of Yahweh by performing a number of miracles. The first miracle involved turning a rod into a serpent that devoured other serpents produced by Egyptian magicians. Other miracles followed, including turning the waters of the Nile into blood; killing the fish that lived in the great river; sending frogs, and later lice and swarming flies to infest the dry land; destroying Egyptian cattle; and plummeting the land in a hail storm. Underlying each story is the subtle message that the formless Yahweh was more powerful than the Egyptian gods symbolized as serpents, frogs, and cattle. In the final supernatural act, Yahweh sent an angel of death to take the firstborn children and beasts from every Egyptian family. Only the Hebrews who marked their doorposts with blood from sacrificial lambs were spared from this terrible destruction.

The following selection from Exodus details the consequences of this last great plague. These events are still remembered by Jews in the celebration of Passover. This commemoration of deliverance from slavery remains the most important family festival in the religious calendar of modern Judaism.

THE PASSOVER FROM THE BOOK OF EXODUS

Chapter 12

[12]"On that same night I will pass through Egypt and strike down every firstborn—both men and animals—and I will bring judgment on all the gods of Egypt. I am the LORD. [13]The blood will be a sign for you on the houses where you are; and when I see the blood, I will pass over you. No destructive plague will touch you when I strike Egypt.

[14]"This is a day you are to commemorate; for the generations to come you shall celebrate it as a festival to the LORD—a lasting ordinance. [15]For seven days you are to eat bread made without yeast. On the first day remove the yeast from your houses, for whoever eats anything with yeast in it from the first day through the seventh must be cut off from Israel. [16]On the first day hold a sacred assembly, and another one on the seventh day. Do no work at all on these days, except to prepare food for everyone to eat—that is all you may do.

[17]"Celebrate the Feast of Unleavened Bread, because it was on this very day that I brought your divisions out of Egypt. Celebrate this day as a lasting ordinance for the generations to come. [18]In the first month you are to eat bread made without yeast, from the evening of the fourteenth day until the evening of the twenty-first day. [19]For seven days no yeast is to be found in your houses. And whoever eats anything with yeast in it must be cut off from the community of Israel, whether he is an alien or native-born. [20]Eat nothing made with yeast. Wherever you live, you must eat unleavened bread."

[21]Then Moses summoned all the elders of Israel and said to them, "Go at once and select the animals for your families and slaughter the Passover lamb. [22]Take a bunch of hyssop, dip it into the blood in the basin and put some of the blood on the top and on both sides of the doorframe. Not one of you shall go out the door of his house until morning. [23]When the LORD goes through the land to strike down the Egyptians, he will see the blood on the top and sides of the doorframe and will pass over that doorway, and he will not permit the destroyer to enter your houses and strike you down.

[24]"Obey these instructions as a lasting ordinance for you and your descendants. [25]When you enter the land that the LORD will give you as he promised, observe this ceremony. [26]And when your children ask you, 'What does this ceremony mean to you?' [27]then tell them, 'It is the Passover sacrifice to the LORD, who passed over the houses of the Israelites in Egypt

and spared our homes when he struck down the Egyptians.'" Then the people bowed down and worshiped. [28]The Israelites did just what the LORD commanded Moses and Aaron.

[29]At midnight the LORD struck down all the firstborn in Egypt, from the firstborn of Pharaoh, who sat on the throne, to the firstborn of the prisoner, who was in the dungeon, and the firstborn of all the livestock as well. [30]Pharaoh and all his officials and all the Egyptians got up during the night, and there was loud wailing in Egypt, for there was not a house without someone dead.

[31]During the night Pharaoh summoned Moses and Aaron and said, "Up! Leave my people, you and the Israelites! Go, worship the LORD as you have requested. [32]Take your flocks and herds, as you have said, and go. And also bless me."

After deliverance from Egypt, the Hebrew people wander in the desert for 40 years. These years in the wilderness are important, yet difficult years for the people of Israel. At Mount Sinai, God makes a special covenant with them, saying "If you obey me fully and keep my covenant, then out of all nations you will be my treasured possession." Deuteronomy, the last of the Five Books of Moses, ends with Moses transferring his leadership to Joshua and with his death on Mount Nebo.

The biblical narrative continues with several historical works (Joshua, Judges, Samuel, and Kings) that cover the periods of the Confederation, the United Kingdom, and the Divided Kingdom. The following selections include stories from each of these three eras in the political history of the ancient Hebrews. The first piece tells the legendary story of Samson, a corruptible man of God who lived during the period of Confederation. This dramatic story of disobedience, punishment, repentance, and deliverance illustrates a reoccurring theme contained in the Book of Judges. The second passage recounts a well-known episode in the life of David, the greatest ruler of the United Kingdom. The final selection in this section tells the story of Elijah, a prophet of the Divided Kingdom who confronts King Ahab and the prophets of Baal.

As you examine these texts, look for common threads that tie together the various accounts of these heroes of ancient Israel. Speculate about why these stories were included in the sacred canon. To what degree are these characters portrayed as saints, heroes, and villains? What can we learn from these stories about the religious beliefs, social values, and daily practices of the ancient Hebrews?

STORIES FROM THE PERIOD OF CONFEDERATION

The Life of Samson from the Book of Judges

Chapter 16

[1]One day Samson went to Gaza, where he saw a prostitute. He went in to spend the night with her. [2]The people of Gaza were told, "Samson is here!" So they surrounded the place and lay in wait for him all night at the city gate. They made no move during the night, saying, "At dawn we'll kill him."

[3]But Samson lay there only until the middle of the night. Then he got up and took hold of the doors of the city gate, together with the two posts, and tore them loose, bar and all. He lifted them to his shoulders and carried them to the top of the hill that faces Hebron.

[4]Some time later, he fell in love with a woman in the Valley of Sorek whose name was Delilah. [5]The rulers of the Philistines went to her and said, "See if you can lure him into showing you the secret of his great strength and how we can overpower him so we may tie him up and subdue him. Each one of us will give you eleven hundred shekels of silver."

[6]So Delilah said to Samson, "Tell me the secret of your great strength and how you can be tied up and subdued."

[7]Samson answered her, "If anyone ties me with seven fresh thongs that have not been dried, I'll become as weak as any other man."

[8]Then the rulers of the Philistines brought her seven fresh thongs that had not been dried, and she tied him with them. [9]With men hidden in the room, she called to him, "Samson, the Philistines are upon you!" But he snapped the thongs as easily as a piece of string snaps when it comes close to a flame. So the secret of his strength was not discovered.

[10]Then Delilah said to Samson, "You have made a fool of me; you lied to me. Come now, tell me how you can be tied."

[11]He said, "If anyone ties me securely with new ropes that have never been used, I'll become as weak as any other man."

[12]So Delilah took new ropes and tied him with them. Then, with men hidden in the room, she called to him, "Samson, the Philistines are upon you!" But he snapped the ropes off his arms as if they were threads.

[13]Delilah then said to Samson, "Until now, you have been making a fool of me and lying to me. Tell me how you can be tied." He replied, "If you weave the seven braids of my head into the fabric on the loom and tighten it with the pin, I'll become as weak as any other man." So while he was sleeping, Delilah took the seven braids of his head, wove them into the fabric [14]and tightened it with the pin. Again she called to him, "Samson, the Philistines are upon you!" He awoke from his sleep and pulled up the pin and the loom, with the fabric.

[15]Then she said to him, "How can you say, 'I love you,' when you won't confide in me? This is the third time you have made a fool of me and haven't told me the secret of your great strength." [16]With such nagging she prodded him day after day until he was tired to death.

¹⁷So he told her everything. "No razor has ever been used on my head," he said, "because I have been a Nazirite set apart to God since birth. If my head were shaved, my strength would leave me, and I would become as weak as any other man."

¹⁸When Delilah saw that he had told her everything, she sent word to the rulers of the Philistines, "Come back once more; he has told me everything." So the rulers of the Philistines returned with the silver in their hands. ¹⁹Having put him to sleep on her lap, she called a man to shave off the seven braids of his hair, and so began to subdue him. And his strength left him.

²⁰Then she called, "Samson, the Philistines are upon you!" He awoke from his sleep and thought, "I'll go out as before and shake myself free." But he did not know that the LORD had left him.

²¹Then the Philistines seized him, gouged out his eyes and took him down to Gaza. Binding him with bronze shackles, they set him to grinding in the prison. ²²But the hair on his head began to grow again after it had been shaved.

²³Now the rulers of the Philistines assembled to offer a great sacrifice to Dagon their god and to celebrate, saying, "Our god has delivered Samson, our enemy, into our hands."

²⁴When the people saw him, they praised their god, saying, "Our god has delivered our enemy into our hands, the one who laid waste our land and multiplied our slain."

²⁵While they were in high spirits, they shouted, "Bring out Samson to entertain us." So they called Samson out of the prison, and he performed for them. When they stood him among the pillars, ²⁶Samson said to the servant who held his hand, "Put me where I can feel the pillars that support the temple, so that I may lean against them." ²⁷Now the temple was crowded with men and women; all the rulers of the Philistines were there, and on the roof were about three thousand men and women watching Samson perform. ²⁸Then Samson prayed to the LORD, "O Sovereign LORD, remember me. O God, please strengthen me just once more, and let me with one blow get revenge on the Philistines for my two eyes." ²⁹Then Samson reached toward the two central pillars on which the temple stood. Bracing himself against them, his right hand on the one and his left hand on the other, ³⁰Samson said, "Let me die with the Philistines!" Then he pushed with all his might, and down came the temple on the rulers and all the people in it. Thus he killed many more when he died than while he lived.

STORIES FROM THE UNITED KINGDOM

David often is portrayed in Hebrew scripture as a courageous and heroic figure. For this characterization of his life read the famous story of David and Goliath that is contained in I Samuel, Chapter 17. The following selection, however, portrays David in less flattering terms. How is David presented in this text, and why do you think this story was included in the sacred Hebrew canon?

The Story of David and Bethsheba from the Book of II Samuel

Chapter 11

¹In the spring, at the time when kings go off to war, David sent Joab out with the king's men and the whole Israelite army. They destroyed the Ammonites and besieged Rabbah. But David remained in Jerusalem.

²One evening David got up from his bed and walked around on the roof of the palace. From the roof he saw a woman bathing. The woman was very beautiful, ³and David sent someone to find out about her. The man said, "Isn't this Bathsheba, the daughter of Eliam and the wife of Uriah the Hittite?" ⁴Then David sent messengers to get her. She came to him, and he slept with her. (She had purified herself from her uncleanness.) Then she went back home. ⁵The woman conceived and sent word to David, saying, "I am pregnant."

⁶So David sent this word to Joab: "Send me Uriah the Hittite." And Joab sent him to David. ⁷When Uriah came to him, David asked him how Joab was, how the soldiers were and how the war was going. ⁸Then David said to Uriah, "Go down to your house and wash your feet." So Uriah left the palace, and a gift from the king was sent after him.

⁹But Uriah slept at the entrance to the palace with all his master's servants and did not go down to his house.

¹⁰When David was told, "Uriah did not go home," he asked him, "Haven't you just come from a distance? Why didn't you go home?"

¹¹Uriah said to David, "The ark and Israel and Judah are staying in tents, and my master Joab and my lord's men are camped in the open fields. How could I go to my house to eat and drink and lie with my wife? As surely as you live, I will not do such a thing!"

¹²Then David said to him, "Stay here one more day, and tomorrow I will send you back." So Uriah remained in Jerusalem that day and the next. ¹³At David's invitation, he ate and drank with him, and David made him drunk. But in the evening Uriah went out to sleep on his mat among his master's servants; he did not go home.

¹⁴In the morning David wrote a letter to Joab and sent it with Uriah. ¹⁵In it he wrote, "Put Uriah in the front line where the fighting is fiercest. Then withdraw from him so he will be struck down and die."

¹⁶So while Joab had the city under siege, he put Uriah at a place where he knew the strongest defenders were. ¹⁷When the men of the city came out and fought against Joab, some of the men in David's army fell; moreover, Uriah the Hittite died.

¹⁸Joab sent David a full account of the battle. ¹⁹He instructed the messenger: "When you have finished giving the king this account of the battle, ²⁰the king's anger may flare up, and he

may ask you, 'Why did you get so close to the city to fight? Didn't you know they would shoot arrows from the wall? [21]Who killed Abimelech son of Jerub-Besheth? Didn't a woman throw an upper millstone on him from the wall, so that he died in Thebez? Why did you get so close to the wall?' If he asks you this, then say to him, 'Also, your servant Uriah the Hittite is dead.'"

[22]The messenger set out, and when he arrived he told David everything Joab had sent him to say. [23]The messenger said to David, "The men overpowered us and came out against us in the open, but we drove them back to the entrance to the city gate. [24]Then the archers shot arrows at your servants from the wall, and some of the king's men died. Moreover, your servant Uriah the Hittite is dead."

[25]David told the messenger, "Say this to Joab: 'Don't let this upset you; the sword devours one as well as another. Press the attack against the city and destroy it.' Say this to encourage Joab."

[26]When Uriah's wife heard that her husband was dead, she mourned for him. [27]After the time of mourning was over, David had her brought to his house, and she became his wife and bore him a son. But the thing David had done displeased the LORD.

STORIES FROM THE DIVIDED KINGDOM

The Life of Elijah from the Book of I Kings

Chapter 18

[17]When he [King Ahab] saw Elijah, he said to him, "Is that you, you troubler of Israel?"

[18]"I have not made trouble for Israel," Elijah replied. "But you and your father's family have. You have abandoned the LORD's commands and have followed the Baals. [19]Now summon the people from all over Israel to meet me on Mount Carmel. And bring the four hundred and fifty prophets of Baal and the four hundred prophets of Asherah, who eat at Jezebel's table."

[20]So Ahab sent word throughout all Israel and assembled the prophets on Mount Carmel. [21]Elijah went before the people and said, "How long will you waver between two opinions? If the LORD is God, follow him; but if Baal is God, follow him." But the people said nothing.

[22]Then Elijah said to them, "I am the only one of the LORD's prophets left, but Baal has four hundred and fifty prophets. [23]Get two bulls for us. Let them choose one for themselves, and let them cut it into pieces and put it on the wood but not set fire to it. I will prepare the other bull and put it on the wood but not set fire to it. [24]Then you call on the name of your god, and I will call on the name of the LORD. The god who answers by fire—he is God." Then all the people said, "What you say is good."

[25]Elijah said to the prophets of Baal, "Choose one of the bulls and prepare it first, since there are so many of you. Call on the name of your god, but do not light the fire." [26]So they took the bull given them and prepared it. Then they called on the name of Baal from morning till noon. "O Baal, answer us!" they shouted. But there was no response; no one answered. And they danced around the altar they had made.

[27]At noon Elijah began to taunt them. "Shout louder!" he said. "Surely he is a god! Perhaps he is deep in thought, or busy, or traveling. Maybe he is sleeping and must be awakened." [28]So they shouted louder and slashed themselves with swords and spears, as was their custom, until their blood flowed. [29]Midday passed, and they continued their frantic prophesying until the time for the evening sacrifice. But there was no response, no one answered, no one paid attention.

[30]Then Elijah said to all the people, "Come here to me." They came to him, and he repaired the altar of the LORD, which was in ruins. [31]Elijah took twelve stones, one for each of the tribes descended from Jacob, to whom the word of the LORD had come, saying, "Your name shall be Israel." [32]With the stones he built an altar in the name of the LORD, and he dug a trench around it large enough to hold two seahs of seed. [33]He arranged the wood, cut the bull into pieces and laid it on the wood. Then he said to them, "Fill four large jars with water and pour it on the offering and on the wood."

[34]"Do it again," he said, and they did it again. "Do it a third time," he ordered, and they did it the third time. [35]The water ran down around the altar and even filled the trench.

[36]At the time of sacrifice, the prophet Elijah stepped forward and prayed: "O LORD, God of Abraham, Isaac and Israel, let it be known today that you are God in Israel and that I am your servant and have done all these things at your command. [37]Answer me, O LORD, answer me, so these people will know that you, O LORD, are God, and that you are turning their hearts back again."

[38]Then the fire of the LORD fell and burned up the sacrifice, the wood, the stones and the soil, and also licked up the water in the trench. [39]When all the people saw this, they fell prostrate and cried, "The LORD—he is God! The LORD—he is God!"

[40]Then Elijah commanded them, "Seize the prophets of Baal. Don't let anyone get away!" They seized them, and Elijah had them brought down to the Kishon Valley and slaughtered there.

[41]And Elijah said to Ahab, "Go, eat and drink, for there is the sound of a heavy rain." [42]So Ahab went off to eat and drink, but Elijah climbed to the top of Carmel, bent down to the ground and put his face between his knees.

[43]"Go and look toward the sea," he told his servant. And he went up and looked. "There is nothing there," he said. Seven times Elijah said, "Go back."

[44]The seventh time the servant reported, "A cloud as small as a man's hand is rising from the sea." So Elijah said, "Go and tell Ahab, 'Hitch up your chariot and go down before the rain stops you.'"

[45]Meanwhile, the sky grew black with clouds, the wind rose, a heavy rain came on and Ahab rode off to Jezreel. [46]The

power of the LORD came upon Elijah and, tucking his cloak into his belt, he ran ahead of Ahab all the way to Jezreel.

Chapter 19

[1]Now Ahab told Jezebel everything Elijah had done and how he had killed all the prophets with the sword. [2]So Jezebel sent a messenger to Elijah to say, "May the gods deal with me, be it ever so severely, if by this time tomorrow I do not make your life like that of one of them."

[3]Elijah was afraid and ran for his life. When he came to Beersheba in Judah, he left his servant there, [4]while he himself went a day's journey into the desert. He came to a broom tree, sat down under it and prayed that he might die. "I have had enough, LORD," he said. "Take my life; I am no better than my ancestors." [5]Then he lay down under the tree and fell asleep. All at once an angel touched him and said, "Get up and eat." [6]He looked around, and there by his head was a cake of bread baked over hot coals, and a jar of water. He ate and drank and then lay down again.

[7]The angel of the LORD came back a second time and touched him and said, "Get up and eat, for the journey is too much for you." [8]So he got up and ate and drank. Strengthened by that food, he traveled forty days and forty nights until he reached Horeb, the mountain of God. [9]There he went into a cave and spent the night.

And the word of the LORD came to him: "What are you doing here, Elijah?"

[10]He replied, "I have been very zealous for the LORD God Almighty. The Israelites have rejected your covenant, broken down your altars, and put your prophets to death with the sword. I am the only one left, and now they are trying to kill me too."

[11]The LORD said, "Go out and stand on the mountain in the presence of the LORD, for the LORD is about to pass by." Then a great and powerful wind tore the mountains apart and shattered the rocks before the LORD, but the LORD was not in the wind. After the wind there was an earthquake, but the LORD was not in the earthquake. [12]After the earthquake came a fire, but the LORD was not in the fire. And after the fire came a gentle whisper. [13]When Elijah heard it, he pulled his cloak over his face and went out and stood at the mouth of the cave. Then a voice said to him, "What are you doing here, Elijah?"

[14]He replied, "I have been very zealous for the LORD God Almighty. The Israelites have rejected your covenant, broken down your altars, and put your prophets to death with the sword. I am the only one left, and now they are trying to kill me too."

[15]The LORD said to him, "Go back the way you came, and go to the Desert of Damascus. When you get there, anoint Hazael king over Aram. [16]Also, anoint Jehu son of Nimshi king over Israel, and anoint Elisha son of Shaphat from Abel Meholah to succeed you as prophet. [17]Jehu will put to death any who escape the sword of Hazael, and Elisha will put to

death any who escape the sword of Jehu. [18]Yet I reserve seven thousand in Israel—all whose knees have not bowed down to Baal and all whose mouths have not kissed him."

[19]So Elijah went from there and found Elisha son of Shaphat. He was plowing with twelve yoke of oxen, and he himself was driving the twelfth pair. Elijah went up to him and threw his cloak around him. [20]Elisha then left his oxen and ran after Elijah. "Let me kiss my father and mother good-by," he said, "and then I will come with you." "Go back," Elijah replied. "What have I done to you?"

[21]So Elisha left him and went back. He took his yoke of oxen and slaughtered them. He burned the plowing equipment to cook the meat and gave it to the people, and they ate. Then he set out to follow Elijah and became his attendant.

SECTION 4: Divine Law: Justice, Reward, and Punishment

Yahweh, the god of Judaism, is a moral god who expects humans to live according to high ethical standards. Yahweh also is portrayed as a jealous god who expects his people to worship him and him alone. The following selection from the book of Exodus tells the story of Yahweh revealing his moral code to Moses at Mount Sinai. Examine closely the Decalogue, the so-called Ten Commandments that are embraced by Jews, Christians, and Muslims alike. Later in this volume, sacred texts from other traditions will include some, but not all of these commands. Which of the commandments in the Decalogue do you expect to find among the divine laws that are expressed in the sacred texts of non-Western religious traditions? Be able to justify your speculations.

THE TEN COMMANDMENTS
FROM THE BOOK OF EXODUS

Chapter 20

[1]And God spoke all these words:

[2]"I am the LORD your God, who brought you out of Egypt, out of the land of slavery.

[3]"You shall have no other gods before me.

[4]"You shall not make for yourself an idol in the form of anything in heaven above or on the earth beneath or in the waters below. [5]You shall not bow down to them or worship them; for I, the LORD your God, am a jealous God, punishing the children for the sin of the fathers to the third and fourth generation of those who hate me, [6]but showing love to a thousand [generations] of those who love me and keep my commandments.

[7]"You shall not misuse the name of the LORD your God, for the LORD will not hold anyone guiltless who misuses his name.

⁸"Remember the Sabbath day by keeping it holy. ⁹Six days you shall labor and do all your work, ¹⁰but the seventh day is a Sabbath to the LORD your God. On it you shall not do any work, neither you, nor your son or daughter, nor your manservant or maidservant, nor your animals, nor the alien within your gates. ¹¹For in six days the LORD made the heavens and the earth, the sea, and all that is in them, but he rested on the seventh day. Therefore the LORD blessed the Sabbath day and made it holy.

¹²"Honor your father and your mother, so that you may live long in the land the LORD your God is giving you.

¹³"You shall not murder.

¹⁴"You shall not commit adultery.

¹⁵"You shall not steal.

¹⁶"You shall not give false testimony against your neighbor.

¹⁷"You shall not covet your neighbor's house. You shall not covet your neighbor's wife, or his manservant or maidservant, his ox or donkey, or anything that belongs to your neighbor."

¹⁸When the people saw the thunder and lightning and heard the trumpet and saw the mountain in smoke, they trembled with fear. They stayed at a distance ¹⁹and said to Moses, "Speak to us yourself and we will listen. But do not have God speak to us or we will die."

²⁰Moses said to the people, "Do not be afraid. God has come to test you, so that the fear of God will be with you to keep you from sinning."

²¹The people remained at a distance, while Moses approached the thick darkness where God was.

²²Then the LORD said to Moses, "Tell the Israelites this: 'You have seen for yourselves that I have spoken to you from heaven: ²³Do not make any gods to be alongside me; do not make for yourselves gods of silver or gods of gold.

²⁴"'Make an altar of earth for me and sacrifice on it your burnt offerings and fellowship offerings, your sheep and goats and your cattle. Wherever I cause my name to be honored, I will come to you and bless you. ²⁵If you make an altar of stones for me, do not build it with dressed stones, for you will defile it if you use a tool on it. ²⁶And do not go up to my altar on steps, lest your nakedness be exposed on it.'"

As a covenanted people, the Hebrews were expected to obey Yahweh's moral code. According to the following excerpts from Leviticus, what are the rewards for obedience and the consequences of disobedience?

REWARD AND PUNISHMENT FROM THE BOOK OF LEVITICUS

Chapter 26

¹"'Do not make idols or set up an image or a sacred stone for yourselves, and do not place a carved stone in your land to bow down before it. I am the LORD your God.

²"'Observe my Sabbaths and have reverence for my sanctuary. I am the LORD.

³"'If you follow my decrees and are careful to obey my commands, ⁴I will send you rain in its season, and the ground will yield its crops and the trees of the field their fruit. ⁵Your threshing will continue until grape harvest and the grape harvest will continue until planting, and you will eat all the food you want and live in safety in your land.

⁶"'I will grant peace in the land, and you will lie down and no one will make you afraid. I will remove savage beasts from the land, and the sword will not pass through your country. ⁷You will pursue your enemies, and they will fall by the sword before you. ⁸Five of you will chase a hundred, and a hundred of you will chase ten thousand, and your enemies will fall by the sword before you.

⁹"'I will look on you with favor and make you fruitful and increase your numbers, and I will keep my covenant with you. ¹⁰You will still be eating last year's harvest when you will have to move it out to make room for the new. ¹¹I will put my dwelling place among you, and I will not abhor you. ¹²I will walk among you and be your God, and you will be my people. ¹³I am the LORD your God, who brought you out of Egypt so that you would no longer be slaves to the Egyptians; I broke the bars of your yoke and enabled you to walk with heads held high.

¹⁴"'But if you will not listen to me and carry out all these commands, ¹⁵and if you reject my decrees and abhor my laws and fail to carry out all my commands and so violate my covenant, ¹⁶then I will do this to you: I will bring upon you sudden terror, wasting diseases and fever that will destroy your sight and drain away your life. You will plant seed in vain, because your enemies will eat it. ¹⁷I will set my face against you so that you will be defeated by your enemies; those who hate you will rule over you, and you will flee even when no one is pursuing you.'"

In addition to the Ten Commandments, the Hebrew Scriptures contain a number of other specific rules for living and worship. According to tradition, there are 613 specific laws for Jews to follow in their everyday life. For many rabbis, this number carries symbolic importance for it represents the sum of the number of parts of the body and the number of days of the year. Thus, according to this teaching, obeying the law means loving God with one's whole being at all times.

Several passages within the Hebrew canon attempt to summarize the Law in a single expression. One of these passages, known as the Shema, is repeated by pious Jews twice a day and placed in writing on the posts of their houses. Why do you think this text is important to Jews? How does it attempt to summarize the totality of the rabbinical law?

THE SHEMA FROM THE BOOK OF DEUTERONOMY

Chapter 6

⁴Hear, O Israel: The LORD our God, the LORD is one. ⁵Love the LORD your God with all your heart and with all your soul and with all your strength. ⁶These commandments that I give you today are to be upon your hearts. ⁷Impress them on your children. Talk about them when you sit at home and when you walk along the road, when you lie down and when you get up. ⁸Tie them as symbols on your hands and bind them on your foreheads. ⁹Write them on the doorframes of your houses and on your gates.

A large section of the Hebrew canon consists of the writings of the prophets. These individuals, often from poor, humble origins, confronted the politically powerful with warnings of the dire consequences of disobeying divine law. The following selections are taken from Jeremiah, Lamentations, and Ezekiel. Look for the central message of each passage. What common threads do you find running through each of the passages?

THE POTTER'S HOUSE FROM THE BOOK OF JEREMIAH

Chapter 18

¹This is the word that came to Jeremiah from the LORD: ²"Go down to the potter's house, and there I will give you my message." ³So I went down to the potter's house, and I saw him working at the wheel. ⁴But the pot he was shaping from the clay was marred in his hands; so the potter formed it into another pot, shaping it as seemed best to him.

⁵Then the word of the LORD came to me: ⁶"O house of Israel, can I not do with you as this potter does?" declares the LORD. "Like clay in the hand of the potter, so are you in my hand, O house of Israel. ⁷If at any time I announce that a nation or kingdom is to be uprooted, torn down and destroyed, ⁸and if that nation I warned repents of its evil, then I will relent and not inflict on it the disaster I had planned. ⁹And if at another time I announce that a nation or kingdom is to be built up and planted, ¹⁰and if it does evil in my sight and does not obey me, then I will reconsider the good I had intended to do for it.

¹¹"Now therefore say to the people of Judah and those living in Jerusalem, 'This is what the LORD says: Look! I am preparing a disaster for you and devising a plan against you. So turn from your evil ways, each one of you, and reform your ways and your actions.' ¹²But they will reply, 'It's no use. We will continue with our own plans; each of us will follow the stubbornness of his evil heart.'"

¹³Therefore this is what the LORD says: "Inquire among the nations: Who has ever heard anything like this? A most horrible thing has been done by Virgin Israel. ¹⁴Does the snow of Lebanon ever vanish from its rocky slopes? Do its cool waters from distant sources ever cease to flow? ¹⁵Yet my people have forgotten me; they burn incense to worthless idols, which made them stumble in their ways and in the ancient paths. They made them walk in bypaths and on roads not built up. ¹⁶Their land will be laid waste, an object of lasting scorn; all who pass by will be appalled and will shake their heads. ¹⁷Like a wind from the east, I will scatter them before their enemies; I will show them my back and not my face in the day of their disaster."

¹⁸They said, "Come, let's make plans against Jeremiah; for the teaching of the law by the priest will not be lost, nor will counsel from the wise, nor the word from the prophets. So come, let's attack him with our tongues and pay no attention to anything he says."

The following is a poem of 22 verses (the number of letters in the Hebrew alphabet) that contains a description of the sad conditions within the Jewish community. Note the attention given to the sufferings of women and children. Why do you think the author focuses on these particular social groups?

LAMENTS FROM LAMENTATIONS

Chapter 5

¹Remember, O LORD, what has happened to us; look, and see our disgrace. ²Our inheritance has been turned over to aliens, our homes to foreigners. ³We have become orphans and fatherless, our mothers like widows. ⁴We must buy the water we drink; our wood can be had only at a price. ⁵Those who pursue us are at our heels; we are weary and find no rest. ⁶We submitted to Egypt and Assyria to get enough bread. ⁷Our fathers sinned and are no more, and we bear their punishment. ⁸Slaves rule over us, and there is none to free us from their hands. ⁹We get our bread at the risk of our lives because of the sword in the desert. ¹⁰Our skin is hot as an oven, feverish from hunger. ¹¹Women have been ravished in Zion, and virgins in the towns of Judah. ¹²Princes have been hung up by their hands; elders are shown no respect.

¹³Young men toil at the millstones; boys stagger under loads of wood.

¹⁴The elders are gone from the city gate; the young men have stopped their music.

¹⁵Joy is gone from our hearts; our dancing has turned to mourning.

¹⁶The crown has fallen from our head. Woe to us, for we have sinned!

¹⁷Because of this our hearts are faint, because of these things our eyes grow dim

¹⁸for Mount Zion, which lies desolate, with jackals prowling over it.

¹⁹You, O LORD, reign forever; your throne endures from generation to generation.

²⁰Why do you always forget us? Why do you forsake us so long?

²¹Restore us to yourself, O LORD, that we may return; renew our days as of old

²²unless you have utterly rejected us and are angry with us beyond measure.

The following words from Ezekiel were proclaimed during a period when the Jews were in exile in Babylon. Many scholars have noted that Ezekiel placed a greater emphasis than the earlier prophets on individual rather than corporate responsibility. What in the text supports this assertion? Why would the concept of individual responsibility and reward hold special meaning to Jews living in exile?

THE SOUL WHO SINS WILL DIE
FROM THE BOOK OF EZEKIEL

Chapter 18

¹The word of the LORD came to me: ²"What do you people mean by quoting this proverb about the land of Israel: "'The fathers eat sour grapes, and the children's teeth are set on edge'?

³"As surely as I live, declares the Sovereign LORD, you will no longer quote this proverb in Israel. ⁴For every living soul belongs to me, the father as well as the son—both alike belong to me. The soul who sins is the one who will die.

⁵"Suppose there is a righteous man who does what is just and right.

⁶He does not eat at the mountain shrines or look to the idols of the house of Israel. He does not defile his neighbor's wife or lie with a woman during her period.

⁷He does not oppress anyone, but returns what he took in pledge for a loan. He does not commit robbery but gives his food to the hungry and provides clothing for the naked.

⁸He does not lend at usury or take excessive interest. He withholds his hand from doing wrong and judges fairly between man and man.

⁹He follows my decrees and faithfully keeps my laws. That man is righteous; he will surely live, declares the Sovereign LORD.

¹⁰"Suppose he has a violent son, who sheds blood or does any of these other things ¹¹ (though the father has done none of them): "He eats at the mountain shrines. He defiles his neighbor's wife. ¹²He oppresses the poor and needy. He commits robbery. He does not return what he took in pledge. He looks to the idols. He does detestable things. ¹³He lends at usury and takes excessive interest. Will such a man live? He will not! Because he has done all these detestable things, he will surely be put to death and his blood will be on his own head.

¹⁴"But suppose this son has a son who sees all the sins his father commits, and though he sees them, he does not do such things: ¹⁵"He does not eat at the mountain shrines or look to the idols of the house of Israel. He does not defile his neighbor's wife. ¹⁶He does not oppress anyone or require a pledge for a loan. He does not commit robbery but gives his food to the hungry and provides clothing for the naked. ¹⁷He withholds his hand from sin and takes no usury or excessive interest. He keeps my laws and follows my decrees. He will not die for his father's sin; he will surely live. ¹⁸But his father will die for his own sin, because he practiced extortion, robbed his brother and did what was wrong among his people.

¹⁹"Yet you ask, 'Why does the son not share the guilt of his father?' Since the son has done what is just and right and has been careful to keep all my decrees, he will surely live. ²⁰The soul who sins is the one who will die. The son will not share the guilt of the father, nor will the father share the guilt of the son. The righteousness of the righteous man will be credited to him, and the wickedness of the wicked will be charged against him.

²¹"But if a wicked man turns away from all the sins he has committed and keeps all my decrees and does what is just and right, he will surely live; he will not die. ²²None of the offenses he has committed will be remembered against him. Because of the righteous things he has done, he will live. ²³Do I take any pleasure in the death of the wicked? declares the Sovereign LORD. Rather, am I not pleased when they turn from their ways and live?

²⁴"But if a righteous man turns from his righteousness and commits sin and does the same detestable things the wicked man does, will he live? None of the righteous things he has done will be remembered. Because of the unfaithfulness he is guilty of and because of the sins he has committed, he will die. ²⁵Yet you say, 'The way of the Lord is not just.' Hear, O house of Israel: Is my way unjust? Is it not your ways that are unjust? ²⁶If a righteous man turns from his righteousness and commits sin, he will die for it; because of the sin he has committed he will die. ²⁷But if a wicked man turns away from the wickedness he has committed and does what is just and right, he will save his life. ²⁸Because he considers all the offenses he has committed and turns away from them, he will surely live; he will not die. ²⁹Yet the house of Israel says, 'The way of the

Lord is not just.' Are my ways unjust, O house of Israel? Is it not your ways that are unjust? ³⁰"Therefore, O house of Israel, I will judge you, each one according to his ways, declares the Sovereign LORD. Repent! Turn away from all your offenses; then sin will not be your downfall. ³¹Rid yourselves of all the offenses you have committed, and get a new heart and a new spirit. Why will you die, O house of Israel? ³²For I take no pleasure in the death of anyone, declares the Sovereign LORD. Repent and live!"

SECTION 5: Gender: Women and Men in Society

The status of Jewish women has fluctuated widely across time. In modern times, Jewish women, except in conservative groups, are active participants in business and politics and, in some synagogues, are eligible for rabbinical ordination. This recent spirit of gender equality represents a great shift from the Rabbinic Period when women were segregated behind a curtain in synagogue services and specifically barred from being judges, rabbis, and cantors. The authors of the *Talmud* insisted that women were not to be counted among the *minyan*, the quorum of 10 that was necessary for originating public worship. This Talmudic attitude of male superiority was also expressed in the traditional benediction commonly prayed by Jewish men: "Blessed are You, God . . . who has not made me a woman."

The Hebrew *Bible,* like the sacred texts of most traditions from the ancient world, contains ambiguous statements about the place of women in society. Some texts devalue women; other texts describe gory episodes of male violence against women. For many modern readers, these texts are doubly tragic because they portray God as a passive bystander who does not intervene to stop this violence. On the other hand, other passages affirm the worth of women and present God as an active agent protecting the defenseless, the widows, and the orphans. Still other texts portray women not as pawns of society but as powerful political leaders.

The following selections sample a variety of ways that women are treated in Hebrew scripture. The opening passages are taken from Numbers and Deuteronomy. The Numbers passage describes the religious/legal procedure known as the "jealousy offering." What is the occasion for this ritual, and what social and religious function does it serve? The Deuteronomy text includes a variety of instructions on how to resolve familial discord between husband and wife and parent and child. According to these passages, what rights does the law provide for men and women? How do you explain the gender discrepancies?

THE TEST FOR AN UNFAITHFUL WIFE FROM THE BOOK OF NUMBERS

Chapter 5

¹¹Then the LORD said to Moses, ¹²"Speak to the Israelites and say to them: 'If a man's wife goes astray and is unfaithful to him ¹³by sleeping with another man, and this is hidden from her husband and her impurity is undetected (since there is no witness against her and she has not been caught in the act), ¹⁴and if feelings of jealousy come over her husband and he suspects his wife and she is impure—or if he is jealous and suspects her even though she is not impure—¹⁵then he is to take his wife to the priest. He must also take an offering of a tenth of an ephah of barley flour on her behalf. He must not pour oil on it or put incense on it, because it is a grain offering for jealousy, a reminder offering to draw attention to guilt.

¹⁶"'The priest shall bring her and have her stand before the LORD. ¹⁷Then he shall take some holy water in a clay jar and put some dust from the tabernacle floor into the water. ¹⁸After the priest has had the woman stand before the LORD, he shall loosen her hair and place in her hands the reminder offering, the grain offering for jealousy, while he himself holds the bitter water that brings a curse. ¹⁹Then the priest shall put the woman under oath and say to her, "If no other man has slept with you and you have not gone astray and become impure while married to your husband, may this bitter water that brings a curse not harm you. ²⁰But if you have gone astray while married to your husband and you have defiled yourself by sleeping with a man other than your husband"— ²¹here the priest is to put the woman under this curse of the oath—"may the LORD cause your people to curse and denounce you when he causes your thigh to waste away and your abdomen to swell. ²²May this water that brings a curse enter your body so that your abdomen swells and your thigh wastes away." "'Then the woman is to say, "Amen. So be it."

²³"'The priest is to write these curses on a scroll and then wash them off into the bitter water. ²⁴He shall have the woman drink the bitter water that brings a curse, and this water will enter her and cause bitter suffering. ²⁵The priest is to take from her hands the grain offering for jealousy, wave it before the LORD and bring it to the altar. ²⁶The priest is then to take a handful of the grain offering as a memorial offering and burn it on the altar; after that, he is to have the woman drink the water. ²⁷If she has defiled herself and been unfaithful to her husband, then when she is made to drink the water that brings a curse, it will go into her and cause bitter suffering; her abdomen will swell and her thigh waste away, and she will become accursed among her people. ²⁸If, however, the woman

has not defiled herself and is free from impurity, she will be cleared of guilt and will be able to have children.

MARRIAGE AND INHERITANCE RIGHTS AND VARIOUS LAWS FROM THE BOOK OF DEUTERONOMY

Chapter 21

[15]If a man has two wives, and he loves one but not the other, and both bear him sons but the firstborn is the son of the wife he does not love, [16]when he wills his property to his sons, he must not give the rights of the firstborn to the son of the wife he loves in preference to his actual firstborn, the son of the wife he does not love. [17]He must acknowledge the son of his unloved wife as the firstborn by giving him a double share of all he has. That son is the first sign of his father's strength. The right of the firstborn belongs to him.

[18]If a man has a stubborn and rebellious son who does not obey his father and mother and will not listen to them when they discipline him, [19]his father and mother shall take hold of him and bring him to the elders at the gate of his town. [20]They shall say to the elders, "This son of ours is stubborn and rebellious. He will not obey us. He is a profligate and a drunkard." [21]Then all the men of his town shall stone him to death. You must purge the evil from among you. All Israel will hear of it and be afraid.

[22]If a man guilty of a capital offense is put to death and his body is hung on a tree, [23]you must not leave his body on the tree overnight. Be sure to bury him that same day, because anyone who is hung on a tree is under God's curse. You must not desecrate the land the LORD your God is giving you as an inheritance.

Chapter 22

[5]A woman must not wear men's clothing, nor a man wear women's clothing, for the LORD your God detests anyone who does this.

[6]If you come across a bird's nest beside the road, either in a tree or on the ground, and the mother is sitting on the young or on the eggs, do not take the mother with the young. [7]You may take the young, but be sure to let the mother go, so that it may go well with you and you may have a long life.

[8]When you build a new house, make a parapet around your roof so that you may not bring the guilt of bloodshed on your house if someone falls from the roof.

[9]Do not plant two kinds of seed in your vineyard; if you do, not only the crops you plant but also the fruit of the vineyard will be defiled.

[10]Do not plow with an ox and a donkey yoked together.

[11] Do not wear clothes of wool and linen woven together.

[12]Make tassels on the four corners of the cloak you wear.

[13]If a man takes a wife and, after lying with her, dislikes her [14]and slanders her and gives her a bad name, saying, "I mar-

ried this woman, but when I approached her, I did not find proof of her virginity," [15]then the girl's father and mother shall bring proof that she was a virgin to the town elders at the gate. [16]The girl's father will say to the elders, "I gave my daughter in marriage to this man, but he dislikes her. [17]Now he has slandered her and said, 'I did not find your daughter to be a virgin.' But here is the proof of my daughter's virginity." Then her parents shall display the cloth before the elders of the town, [18]and the elders shall take the man and punish him. [19]They shall fine him a hundred shekels of silver and give them to the girl's father, because this man has given an Israelite virgin a bad name. She shall continue to be his wife; he must not divorce her as long as he lives.

[20]If, however, the charge is true and no proof of the girl's virginity can be found, [21]she shall be brought to the door of her father's house and there the men of her town shall stone her to death. She has done a disgraceful thing in Israel by being promiscuous while still in her father's house. You must purge the evil from among you.

[22]If a man is found sleeping with another man's wife, both the man who slept with her and the woman must die. You must purge the evil from Israel

The next selection from Proverbs describes characteristics of the noble wife. To what degree does this passage affirm or challenge the Victorian era stereotype of women as passive housewives and mothers?

THE VIRTUOUS WOMAN FROM THE BOOK OF PROVERBS

Chapter 31

[10]A wife of noble character who can find? She is worth far more than rubies.

[11] Her husband has full confidence in her and lacks nothing of value.

[12]She brings him good, not harm, all the days of her life.

[13]She selects wool and flax and works with eager hands.

[14]She is like the merchant ships, bringing her food from afar.

[15]She gets up while it is still dark; she provides food for her family and portions for her servant girls.

[16]She considers a field and buys it; out of her earnings she plants a vineyard.

[17]She sets about her work vigorously; her arms are strong for her tasks.

[18]She sees that her trading is profitable, and her lamp does not go out at night.

[19]In her hand she holds the distaff and grasps the spindle with her fingers.

[20]She opens her arms to the poor and extends her hands to the needy.

²¹ When it snows, she has no fear for her household; for all of them are clothed in scarlet.

²²She makes coverings for her bed; she is clothed in fine linen and purple.

²³Her husband is respected at the city gate, where he takes his seat among the elders of the land.

²⁴She makes linen garments and sells them, and supplies the merchants with sashes.

²⁵She is clothed with strength and dignity; she can laugh at the days to come.

²⁶She speaks with wisdom, and faithful instruction is on her tongue.

²⁷She watches over the affairs of her household and does not eat the bread of idleness.

²⁸Her children arise and call her blessed; her husband also, and he praises her:

²⁹"Many women do noble things, but you surpass them all."

³⁰Charm is deceptive, and beauty is fleeting; but a woman who fears the LORD is to be praised.

³¹ Give her the reward she has earned, and let her works bring her praise at the city gate.

Two books in the Hebrew *Bible* are named after women. The book of Ruth tells the story of a loving and righteous Moabite woman who chooses to take a Hebrew husband and embrace the Hebrew God. This story goes to great lengths to trace the genealogy of King David through this Moabite woman. The inclusive nature of this statement is important for it runs counter to the prevailing opinion among Hebrews of the time that Moabite women were immoral and were to be avoided.

Another book depicting a heroine is Esther. This story is set in Persia during the era of captivity. It opens with King Ahasuerus (Xerxes) of Persia dethroning Queen Vashti for refusing to exhibit herself before the king's drunken advisors. After Ahasuerus banishes the queen, he selects from a harem of young women the beautiful Esther to be his new queen. Unbeknownst to the King, Esther is the niece of Mordecai, a faithful Jew who warns Esther not to reveal her Jewish identity to the king.

The story continues with Mordecai uncovering an assassination conspiracy against the king. He tells Esther of the plot, the King is warned, and the plot is foiled. Meanwhile, Haman, an evil advisor to the King, grows to despise Mordecai because this righteous Jew will not bow down and pay him honor. Haman advises the King to issue a decree to destroy all foreigners in the land who do not obey the king's laws. The king issues this edict, and by the casting of the *pur,* a day is set for the execution of Jews throughout the kingdom. When Mordecai discovers Haman's plot, he again asks Esther to intervene. The following excerpts detail how Esther courageously risks her life to stop the extermination of the Jewish people. Although the book of Esther includes no references to God, this story is still commemorated by modern Jews in their annual festival of Purim. As you examine this text, look for gender implications within the story. What words are used to describe Esther? Is Esther intended as a role model for other Hebrew women? Given the omission of references to God, why do you think the Bible includes this narrative?

READINGS FROM THE BOOK OF ESTHER

Chapter 5

¹On the third day Esther put on her royal robes and stood in the inner court of the palace, in front of the king's hall. The king was sitting on his royal throne in the hall, facing the entrance. ²When he saw Queen Esther standing in the court, he was pleased with her and held out to her the gold scepter that was in his hand. So Esther approached and touched the tip of the scepter.

³Then the king asked, "What is it, Queen Esther? What is your request? Even up to half the kingdom, it will be given you."

⁴"If it pleases the king," replied Esther, "let the king, together with Haman, come today to a banquet I have prepared for him."

⁵"Bring Haman at once," the king said, "so that we may do what Esther asks." So the king and Haman went to the banquet Esther had prepared. ⁶As they were drinking wine, the king again asked Esther, "Now what is your petition? It will be given you. And what is your request? Even up to half the kingdom, it will be granted."

⁷Esther replied, "My petition and my request is this: ⁸If the king regards me with favor and if it pleases the king to grant my petition and fulfill my request, let the king and Haman come tomorrow to the banquet I will prepare for them. Then I will answer the king's question."

⁹Haman went out that day happy and in high spirits. But when he saw Mordecai at the king's gate and observed that he neither rose nor showed fear in his presence, he was filled with rage against Mordecai. ¹⁰Nevertheless, Haman restrained himself and went home. Calling together his friends and Zeresh, his wife, ¹¹Haman boasted to them about his vast wealth, his many sons, and all the ways the king had honored him and how he had elevated him above the other nobles and officials. ¹²"And that's not all," Haman added. "I'm the only person Queen Esther invited to accompany the king to the banquet she gave. And she has invited me along with the king

tomorrow. ¹³But all this gives me no satisfaction as long as I see that Jew Mordecai sitting at the king's gate."

¹⁴His wife Zeresh and all his friends said to him, "Have a gallows built, seventy-five feet high, and ask the king in the morning to have Mordecai hanged on it. Then go with the king to the dinner and be happy." This suggestion delighted Haman, and he had the gallows built.

Chapter 6

¹ That night the king could not sleep; so he ordered the book of the chronicles, the record of his reign, to be brought in and read to him. ²It was found recorded there that Mordecai had exposed Bigthana and Teresh, two of the king's officers who guarded the doorway, who had conspired to assassinate King Xerxes.

³"What honor and recognition has Mordecai received for this?" the king asked. "Nothing has been done for him," his attendants answered.

⁴The king said, "Who is in the court?" Now Haman had just entered the outer court of the palace to speak to the king about hanging Mordecai on the gallows he had erected for him.

⁵His attendants answered, "Haman is standing in the court." "Bring him in," the king ordered.

⁶When Haman entered, the king asked him, "What should be done for the man the king delights to honor?" Now Haman thought to himself, "Who is there that the king would rather honor than me?" ⁷So he answered the king, "For the man the king delights to honor, ⁸have them bring a royal robe the king has worn and a horse the king has ridden, one with a royal crest placed on its head. ⁹Then let the robe and horse be entrusted to one of the king's most noble princes. Let them robe the man the king delights to honor, and lead him on the horse through the city streets, proclaiming before him, 'This is what is done for the man the king delights to honor!'"

¹⁰"Go at once," the king commanded Haman. "Get the robe and the horse and do just as you have suggested for Mordecai the Jew, who sits at the king's gate. Do not neglect anything you have recommended."

¹¹ So Haman got the robe and the horse. He robed Mordecai, and led him on horseback through the city streets, proclaiming before him, "This is what is done for the man the king delights to honor!"

¹²Afterward Mordecai returned to the king's gate. But Haman rushed home, with his head covered in grief, ¹³and told Zeresh his wife and all his friends everything that had happened to him. His advisers and his wife Zeresh said to him, "Since Mordecai, before whom your downfall has started, is of Jewish origin, you cannot stand against him— you will surely come to ruin!" ¹⁴While they were still talking with him, the king's eunuchs arrived and hurried Haman away to the banquet Esther had prepared.

Chapter 7

¹ So the king and Haman went to dine with Queen Esther, ²and as they were drinking wine on that second day, the king again asked, "Queen Esther, what is your petition? It will be given you. What is your request? Even up to half the kingdom, it will be granted." ³Then Queen Esther answered, "If I have found favor with you, O king, and if it pleases your majesty, grant me my life—this is my petition. And spare my people— this is my request. ⁴For I and my people have been sold for destruction and slaughter and annihilation. If we had merely been sold as male and female slaves, I would have kept quiet, because no such distress would justify disturbing the king."

⁵King Xerxes asked Queen Esther, "Who is he? Where is the man who has dared to do such a thing?"

⁶Esther said, "The adversary and enemy is this vile Haman." Then Haman was terrified before the king and queen. ⁷The king got up in a rage, left his wine and went out into the palace garden. But Haman, realizing that the king had already decided his fate, stayed behind to beg Queen Esther for his life.

⁸Just as the king returned from the palace garden to the banquet hall, Haman was falling on the couch where Esther was reclining. The king exclaimed, "Will he even molest the queen while she is with me in the house?" As soon as the word left the king's mouth, they covered Haman's face. ⁹Then Harbona, one of the eunuchs attending the king, said, "A gallows seventy-five feet high stands by Haman's house. He had it made for Mordecai, who spoke up to help the king." The king said, "Hang him on it!" ¹⁰So they hanged Haman on the gallows he had prepared for Mordecai. Then the king's fury subsided.

SECTION 6: Daily Living: Health, Etiquette, and Holy Days

For several millennia, Jews have distinguished themselves from others by observing certain dietary regulations and by celebrating special holidays or "holy days." The following passages from the Hebrew *Bible* detail the origins of some of these distinctive Jewish customs. The first selections from Deuteronomy provide instructions regarding clean and unclean food. To this day, Jews "keep kosher" by abiding by these and other dietary rules detailed in the Hebrew *Bible* and the *Talmud*. Throughout the centuries the maintenance of these traditions have enabled millions of Jews to preserve their identity in foreign and sometimes hostile environments. As you examine these detailed instructions, reflect upon their central meanings. Are these principally health instructions, or do these rituals serve other functions?

CLEAN AND UNCLEAN FOOD FROM THE BOOK OF DEUTERONOMY

Chapter 14

[3]Do not eat any detestable thing. [4]These are the animals you may eat: the ox, the sheep, the goat, [5]the deer, the gazelle, the roe deer, the wild goat, the ibex, the antelope and the mountain sheep. [6]You may eat any animal that has a split hoof divided in two and that chews the cud. [7]However, of those that chew the cud or that have a split hoof completely divided you may not eat the camel, the rabbit or the coney. Although they chew the cud, they do not have a split hoof; they are ceremonially unclean for you. [8]The pig is also unclean; although it has a split hoof, it does not chew the cud. You are not to eat their meat or touch their carcasses.

[9]Of all the creatures living in the water, you may eat any that has fins and scales. [10]But anything that does not have fins and scales you may not eat; for you it is unclean.

[11]You may eat any clean bird. [12]But these you may not eat: the eagle, the vulture, the black vulture, [13]the red kite, the black kite, any kind of falcon, [14]any kind of raven, [15]the horned owl, the screech owl, the gull, any kind of hawk, [16]the little owl, the great owl, the white owl, [17]the desert owl, the osprey, the cormorant, [18]the stork, any kind of heron, the hoopoe and the bat.

[19]All flying insects that swarm are unclean to you; do not eat them. [20]But any winged creature that is clean you may eat.

[21]Do not eat anything you find already dead. You may give it to an alien living in any of your towns, and he may eat it, or you may sell it to a foreigner. But you are a people holy to the LORD your God. Do not cook a young goat in its mother's milk.

The second passage, which is taken from the book of Exodus, offers instructions concerning the Sabbath. According to these and other texts describing the observations of "holy days" in the Jewish calendar, how important is public worship within the Jewish tradition? What insights about Judaism are contained in these passages? What do these texts tell us about how Jews understand the relationship between the descendants of Abraham and the divine?

THE SABBATH FROM THE BOOK OF EXODUS

Chapter 31

[12]Then the LORD said to Moses, [13]"Say to the Israelites, 'You must observe my Sabbaths. This will be a sign between me and you for the generations to come, so you may know that I am the LORD, who makes you holy.

[14]"'Observe the Sabbath, because it is holy to you. Anyone who desecrates it must be put to death; whoever does any work on that day must be cut off from his people. [15]For six days, work is to be done, but the seventh day is a Sabbath of rest, holy to the LORD. Whoever does any work on the Sabbath day must be put to death. [16]The Israelites are to observe the Sabbath, celebrating it for the generations to come as a lasting covenant. [17]It will be a sign between me and the Israelites forever, for in six days the LORD made the heavens and the earth, and on the seventh day he abstained from work and rested.'"

[18]When the LORD finished speaking to Moses on Mount Sinai, he gave him the two tablets of the Testimony, the tablets of stone inscribed by the finger of God.

The next selections in this section address Jewish attitudes toward sex. The sacred texts of Judaism, unlike those of some religious traditions, never infer that sex inside of marriage is in any way a hindrance to holiness or to spiritual purity. The Patriarchs, Moses, and the other heroes of scripture married and had children. In some passages, the sexual side of marriage is even referred to in the frankest terms, as when Jacob said to his father-in-law Laban: "Give me my wife, for my days are fulfilled, that I may go into her." Other passages, however, especially when discussing sex outside of marriage, are more purulent, and violations against sexual norms bring severe punishments.

The following selection from the Song of Solomon illustrates another view of sexuality in the Hebrew canon. This love story about a lover and his beloved affirms the sanctity of physical pleasure between a man and a woman. Like the book of Esther, this book makes few direct references to the divine. Some view this story as an allegory of the mystical union between humankind and God. On what level do you read this piece? Why do you think it was included in the Hebrew canon?

A LOVE STORY FROM THE SONG OF SONGS

Chapter 1

[2]Let him kiss me with the kisses of his mouth—for your love is more delightful than wine.

[3]Pleasing is the fragrance of your perfumes; your name is like perfume poured out. No wonder the maidens love you!

[4]Take me away with you—let us hurry! Let the king bring me into his chambers.

We rejoice and delight in you; we will praise your love more than wine.

How right they are to adore you!

[5]Dark am I, yet lovely, O daughters of Jerusalem, dark like the tents of Kedar, like the tent curtains of Solomon.

[6]Do not stare at me because I am dark, because I am darkened by the sun. My mother's sons were angry with me and made me take care of the vineyards; my own vineyard I have neglected.

[7]Tell me, you whom I love, where you graze your flock and where you rest your sheep at midday.

Why should I be like a veiled woman beside the flocks of your friends?

[8]If you do not know, most beautiful of women, follow the tracks of the sheep and graze your young goats by the tents of the shepherds.

[9]I liken you, my darling, to a mare harnessed to one of the chariots of Pharaoh.

[10]Your cheeks are beautiful with earrings, your neck with strings of jewels.

[11]We will make you earrings of gold, studded with silver.

[12]While the king was at his table, my perfume spread its fragrance.

[13]My lover is to me a sachet of myrrh resting between my breasts.

[14]My lover is to me a cluster of henna blossoms from the vineyards of En Gedi.

[15]How beautiful you are, my darling! Oh, how beautiful! Your eyes are doves.

[16]How handsome you are, my lover! Oh, how charming! And our bed is verdant.

[17]The beams of our house are cedars; our rafters are firs.

Chapter 2

[1]I am a rose of Sharon, a lily of the valleys.

[2]Like a lily among thorns is my darling among the maidens.

[3]Like an apple tree among the trees of the forest is my lover among the young men. I delight to sit in his shade, and his fruit is sweet to my taste.

[4]He has taken me to the banquet hall, and his banner over me is love.

[5]Strengthen me with raisins, refresh me with apples, for I am faint with love.

[6]His left arm is under my head, and his right arm embraces me. [7]Daughters of Jerusalem, I charge you by the gazelles and by the does of the field: Do not arouse or awaken love until it so desires.

[8]Listen! My lover! Look! Here he comes, leaping across the mountains, bounding over the hills.

[9]My lover is like a gazelle or a young stag. Look! There he stands behind our wall, gazing through the windows, peering through the lattice.

[10]My lover spoke and said to me, "Arise, my darling, my beautiful one, and come with me.

[11]See! The winter is past; the rains are over and gone.

[12]Flowers appear on the earth; the season of singing has come, the cooing of doves is heard in our land.

[13]The fig tree forms its early fruit; the blossoming vines spread their fragrance. Arise, come, my darling; my beautiful one, come with me."

[14]My dove in the clefts of the rock, in the hiding places on the mountainside, show me your face, let me hear your voice; for your voice is sweet, and your face is lovely. [15]Catch for us the foxes, the little foxes that ruin the vineyards, our vineyards that are in bloom.

[16]My lover is mine and I am his; he browses among the lilies.

[17]Until the day breaks and the shadows flee, turn, my lover, and be like a gazelle or like a young stag on the rugged hills.

Chapter 3

[1]All night long on my bed I looked for the one my heart loves; I looked for him but did not find him.

[2]I will get up now and go about the city, through its streets and squares; I will search for the one my heart loves. So I looked for him but did not find him.

[3]The watchmen found me as they made their rounds in the city. "Have you seen the one my heart loves?"

[4]Scarcely had I passed them when I found the one my heart loves. I held him and would not let him go till I had brought him to my mother's house, to the room of the one who conceived me.

[5]Daughters of Jerusalem, I charge you by the gazelles and by the does of the field: Do not arouse or awaken love until it so desires.

[6]Who is this coming up from the desert like a column of smoke, perfumed with myrrh and incense made from all the spices of the merchant?

[7]Look! It is Solomon's carriage, escorted by sixty warriors, the noblest of Israel,

[8]all of them wearing the sword, all experienced in battle, each with his sword at his side, prepared for the terrors of the night.

[9]King Solomon made for himself the carriage; he made it of wood from Lebanon.

[10]Its posts he made of silver, its base of gold. Its seat was upholstered with purple, its interior lovingly inlaid by the daughters of Jerusalem.

[11]Come out, you daughters of Zion, and look at King Solomon wearing the crown, the crown with which his mother crowned him on the day of his wedding, the day his heart rejoiced.

Chapter 4

[1]How beautiful you are, my darling! Oh, how beautiful! Your eyes behind your veil are doves. Your hair is like a flock of goats descending from Mount Gilead.

[2]Your teeth are like a flock of sheep just shorn, coming up from the washing. Each has its twin; not one of them is alone.

[3]Your lips are like a scarlet ribbon; your mouth is lovely. Your temples behind your veil are like the halves of a pomegranate.

[4]Your neck is like the tower of David, built with elegance; on it hang a thousand shields, all of them shields of warriors.
[5]Your two breasts are like two fawns, like twin fawns of a gazelle that browse among the lilies.
[6]Until the day breaks and the shadows flee, I will go to the mountain of myrrh and to the hill of incense.
[7]All beautiful you are, my darling; there is no flaw in you.

SECTION 7: The Human Quest: Paths to Salvation and Enlightenment

In modern times, most view the concept of "salvation" in individualistic ways. The cry "save me Lord" is a personalized expression of the more corporal prayer "deliver us from evil." Although the ancient Hebrews expressed human yearnings for both personal and corporate salvation, most scholars agree that the greater concern of the authors of the Hebrew *Bible* was upon national salvation. In ancient Israel, salvation was more generally viewed as a group rather than a personal achievement.

How was Israel to be saved? The selection from Deuteronomy provides a standard orthodox answer to these questions. The next passage, however, raises more questions than answers about the meaning of life. This selection from Ecclesiastes features the voice of a skeptic unconvinced by the promises of divine retribution.

RENEWAL OF THE COVENANT FROM THE BOOK OF DEUTERONOMY

Chapter 29

[9]Carefully follow the terms of this covenant, so that you may prosper in everything you do. . . .
[16]You yourselves know how we lived in Egypt and how we passed through the countries on the way here. [17]You saw among them their detestable images and idols of wood and stone, of silver and gold. [18]Make sure there is no man or woman, clan or tribe among you today whose heart turns away from the LORD our God to go and worship the gods of those nations; make sure there is no root among you that produces such bitter poison.
[19]When such a person hears the words of this oath, he invokes a blessing on himself and therefore thinks, "I will be safe, even though I persist in going my own way." This will bring disaster on the watered land as well as the dry. [20]The LORD will never be willing to forgive him; his wrath and zeal will burn against that man. All the curses written in this book will fall upon him, and the LORD will blot out his name from under heaven. [21]The LORD will single him out from all the tribes of Israel for disaster, according to all the curses of the covenant written in this Book of the Law.
[22]Your children who follow you in later generations and foreigners who come from distant lands will see the calamities that have fallen on the land and the diseases with which the LORD has afflicted it. [23]The whole land will be a burning waste of salt and sulfur—nothing planted, nothing sprouting, no vegetation growing on it. It will be like the destruction of Sodom and Gomorrah, Admah and Zeboiim, which the LORD overthrew in fierce anger. [24]All the nations will ask: "Why has the LORD done this to this land? Why this fierce, burning anger?"
[25]And the answer will be: "It is because this people abandoned the covenant of the LORD, the God of their fathers, the covenant he made with them when he brought them out of Egypt. [26]They went off and worshiped other gods and bowed down to them, gods they did not know, gods he had not given them. [27]Therefore the LORD's anger burned against this land, so that he brought on it all the curses written in this book. [28]In furious anger and in great wrath the LORD uprooted them from their land and thrust them into another land, as it is now."
[29]The secret things belong to the LORD our God, but the things revealed belong to us and to our children forever, that we may follow all the words of this law.

Chapter 30

[15]See, I set before you today life and prosperity, death and destruction. [16]For I command you today to love the LORD your God, to walk in his ways, and to keep his commands, decrees and laws; then you will live and increase, and the LORD your God will bless you in the land you are entering to possess.
[17]But if your heart turns away and you are not obedient, and if you are drawn away to bow down to other gods and worship them, [18]I declare to you this day that you will certainly be destroyed. You will not live long in the land you are crossing the Jordan to enter and possess.
[19]This day I call heaven and earth as witnesses against you that I have set before you life and death, blessings and curses. Now choose life, so that you and your children may live.

EVERYTHING IS MEANINGLESS FROM THE BOOK OF ECCLESIASTES

Chapter 1

[1]The words of the Teacher, son of David, king in Jerusalem:
[2]"Meaningless! Meaningless!" says the Teacher. "Utterly meaningless! Everything is meaningless."
[3]What does man gain from all his labor at which he toils under the sun?
[4]Generations come and generations go, but the earth remains forever.
[5]The sun rises and the sun sets, and hurries back to where it rises.

[6]The wind blows to the south and turns to the north; round and round it goes, ever returning on its course.

[7]All streams flow into the sea, yet the sea is never full. To the place the streams come from, there they return again.

[8]All things are wearisome, more than one can say. The eye never has enough of seeing, nor the ear its fill of hearing.

[9]What has been will be again, what has been done will be done again; there is nothing new under the sun.

[10]Is there anything of which one can say, "Look! This is something new"? It was here already, long ago; it was here before our time.

[11]There is no remembrance of men of old, and even those who are yet to come will not be remembered by those who follow.

[12]I, the Teacher, was king over Israel in Jerusalem. [13]I devoted myself to study and to explore by wisdom all that is done under heaven. What a heavy burden God has laid on men! [14]I have seen all the things that are done under the sun; all of them are meaningless, a chasing after the wind.

[15]What is twisted cannot be straightened; what is lacking cannot be counted.

[16]I thought to myself, "Look, I have grown and increased in wisdom more than anyone who has ruled over Jerusalem before me; I have experienced much of wisdom and knowledge." [17]Then I applied myself to the understanding of wisdom, and also of madness and folly, but I learned that this, too, is a chasing after the wind.

[18]For with much wisdom comes much sorrow; the more knowledge, the more grief.

Chapter 2

[1]I thought in my heart, "Come now, I will test you with pleasure to find out what is good." But that also proved to be meaningless. [2]"Laughter," I said, "is foolish. And what does pleasure accomplish?" [3]I tried cheering myself with wine, and embracing folly—my mind still guiding me with wisdom. I wanted to see what was worthwhile for men to do under heaven during the few days of their lives.'

[4]I undertook great projects: I built houses for myself and planted vineyards. [5]I made gardens and parks and planted all kinds of fruit trees in them. [6]I made reservoirs to water groves of flourishing trees. [7]I bought male and female slaves and had other slaves who were born in my house. I also owned more herds and flocks than anyone in Jerusalem before me. [8]I amassed silver and gold for myself, and the treasure of kings and provinces. I acquired men and women singers, and a harem as well—the delights of the heart of man. [9]I became greater by far than anyone in Jerusalem before me. In all this my wisdom stayed with me.

[10]I denied myself nothing my eyes desired; I refused my heart no pleasure. My heart took delight in all my work, and this was the reward for all my labor.

[11]Yet when I surveyed all that my hands had done and what I had toiled to achieve, everything was meaningless, a chasing after the wind; nothing was gained under the sun.

[12]Then I turned my thoughts to consider wisdom, and also madness and folly. What more can the king's successor do than what has already been done?

[13]I saw that wisdom is better than folly, just as light is better than darkness.

[14]The wise man has eyes in his head, while the fool walks in the darkness; but I came to realize that the same fate overtakes them both.

[15]Then I thought in my heart, "The fate of the fool will overtake me also. What then do I gain by being wise?" I said in my heart, "This too is meaningless."

[16]For the wise man, like the fool, will not be long remembered; in days to come both will be forgotten. Like the fool, the wise man too must die!

[17]So I hated life, because the work that is done under the sun was grievous to me. All of it is meaningless, a chasing after the wind. [18]I hated all the things I had toiled for under the sun, because I must leave them to the one who comes after me. [19]And who knows whether he will be a wise man or a fool? Yet he will have control over all the work into which I have poured my effort and skill under the sun. This too is meaningless. [20]So my heart began to despair over all my toilsome labor under the sun. [21]For a man may do his work with wisdom, knowledge and skill, and then he must leave all he owns to someone who has not worked for it. This too is meaningless and a great misfortune. [22]What does a man get for all the toil and anxious striving with which he labors under the sun? [23]All his days his work is pain and grief; even at night his mind does not rest. This too is meaningless.

[24]A man can do nothing better than to eat and drink and find satisfaction in his work. This too, I see, is from the hand of God, [25]for without him, who can eat or find enjoyment? [26]To the man who pleases him, God gives wisdom, knowledge and happiness, but to the sinner he gives the task of gathering and storing up wealth to hand it over to the one who pleases God. This too is meaningless, a chasing after the wind.

Chapter 12

[1]Remember your Creator in the days of your youth, before the days of trouble come and the years approach when you will say, "I find no pleasure in them"—

[2]before the sun and the light and the moon and the stars grow dark, and the clouds return after the rain;

[3]when the keepers of the house tremble, and the strong men stoop, when the grinders cease because they are few, and those looking through the windows grow dim;

[4]when the doors to the street are closed and the sound of grinding fades; when men rise up at the sound of birds, but all their songs grow faint;

[5]when men are afraid of heights and of dangers in the streets; when the almond tree blossoms and the grasshopper drags himself along and desire no longer is stirred. Then man goes to his eternal home and mourners go about the streets.

⁶Remember him—before the silver cord is severed, or the golden bowl is broken; before the pitcher is shattered at the spring, or the wheel broken at the well,

⁷and the dust returns to the ground it came from, and the spirit returns to God who gave it.

⁸"Meaningless! Meaningless!" says the Teacher. "Everything is meaningless!"

⁹Not only was the Teacher wise, but also he imparted knowledge to the people. He pondered and searched out and set in order many proverbs. ¹⁰The Teacher searched to find just the right words, and what he wrote was upright and true.

¹¹The words of the wise are like goads, their collected sayings like firmly embedded nails—given by one Shepherd. ¹²Be warned, my son, of anything in addition to them. Of making many books there is no end, and much study wearies the body.

¹³Now all has been heard; here is the conclusion of the matter: Fear God and keep his commandments, for this is the whole duty of man.

¹⁴For God will bring every deed into judgment, including every hidden thing, whether it is good or evil.

Some scholars argue that religions often evolve from an early cultic stage concerned with propitiating the gods through sacrificial rituals to a more advanced ethical stage that exalts good deeds, love and righteousness above sacrifices. Consider this premise as you examine the following texts taken from the prophetic books of Amos, Isaiah, and Micah. In what ways do these words support and/or challenge concepts of divine expectations presented in the books of the Pentateuch?

A CALL TO REPENTANCE FROM THE BOOK OF AMOS

Chapter 5

¹¹You trample on the poor and force him to give you grain. Therefore, though you have built stone mansions, you will not live in them; though you have planted lush vineyards, you will not drink their wine.

¹²For I know how many are your offenses and how great your sins. You oppress the righteous and take bribes and you deprive the poor of justice in the courts.

¹³Therefore the prudent man keeps quiet in such times, for the times are evil.

¹⁴Seek good, not evil, that you may live. Then the LORD God Almighty will be with you, just as you say he is.

¹⁵Hate evil, love good; maintain justice in the courts. Perhaps the LORD God Almighty will have mercy on the remnant of Joseph.

¹⁶Therefore this is what the Lord, the LORD God Almighty, says: "There will be wailing in all the streets and cries of an-guish in every public square. The farmers will be summoned to weep and the mourners to wail. ¹⁷There will be wailing in all the vineyards, for I will pass through your midst,"

¹⁸Woe to you who long for the day of the LORD! Why do you long for the day of the LORD? That day will be darkness, not light.

¹⁹It will be as though a man fled from a lion only to meet a bear, as though he entered his house and rested his hand on the wall only to have a snake bite him.

²⁰Will not the day of the LORD be darkness, not light—pitch-dark, without a ray of brightness?

²¹"I hate, I despise your religious feasts; I cannot stand your assemblies.

²²Even though you bring me burnt offerings and grain offerings, I will not accept them. Though you bring choice fellowship offerings, I will have no regard for them.

²³Away with the noise of your songs! I will not listen to the music of your harps.

²⁴But let justice roll on like a river, righteousness like a never-failing stream!

²⁵"Did you bring me sacrifices and offerings forty years in the desert, O house of Israel?

²⁶You have lifted up the shrine of your king, the pedestal of your idols, the star of your god which you made for yourselves.

²⁷Therefore I will send you into exile beyond Damascus," says the LORD, whose name is God Almighty.

TRUE FASTING FROM THE BOOK OF ISAIAH

Chapter 58

¹"Shout it aloud, do not hold back. Raise your voice like a trumpet. Declare to my people their rebellion and to the house of Jacob their sins.

²For day after day they seek me out; they seem eager to know my ways, as if they were a nation that does what is right and has not forsaken the commands of its God. They ask me for just decisions and seem eager for God to come near them.

³'Why have we fasted,' they say, 'and you have not seen it? Why have we humbled ourselves, and you have not noticed?'

"Yet on the day of your fasting, you do as you please and exploit all your workers.

⁴Your fasting ends in quarreling and strife, and in striking each other with wicked fists. You cannot fast as you do today and expect your voice to be heard on high.

⁵Is this the kind of fast I have chosen, only a day for a man to humble himself? Is it only for bowing one's head like a reed and for lying on sackcloth and ashes? Is that what you call a fast, a day acceptable to the LORD?

⁶"Is not this the kind of fasting I have chosen: to loose the chains of injustice and untie the cords of the yoke, to set the oppressed free and break every yoke?

⁷Is it not to share your food with the hungry and to provide the poor wanderer with shelter—when you see the naked, to clothe him, and not to turn away from your own flesh and blood?

[8]Then your light will break forth like the dawn, and your healing will quickly appear; then your righteousness will go before you, and the glory of the LORD will be your rear guard.

[9]Then you will call, and the LORD will answer; you will cry for help, and he will say: Here am I. "If you do away with the yoke of oppression, with the pointing finger and malicious talk,

[10]and if you spend yourselves in behalf of the hungry and satisfy the needs of the oppressed, then your light will rise in the darkness, and your night will become like the noonday.

[11]The LORD will guide you always; he will satisfy your needs in a sun-scorched land and will strengthen your frame. You will be like a well-watered garden, like a spring whose waters never fail.

[12]Your people will rebuild the ancient ruins and will raise up the age-old foundations; you will be called Repairer of Broken Walls, Restorer of Streets with Dwellings.

[13]"If you keep your feet from breaking the Sabbath and from doing as you please on my holy day, if you call the Sabbath a delight and the LORD's holy day honorable, and if you honor it by not going your own way and not doing as you please or speaking idle words,

[14]then you will find your joy in the LORD, and I will cause you to ride on the heights of the land and to feast on the inheritance of your father Jacob." The mouth of the LORD has spoken.

WHAT DOES THE LORD REQUIRE?

From the Book of Micah

Chapter 6

[1]Listen to what the LORD says: "Stand up, plead your case before the mountains; let the hills hear what you have to say.
[2]Hear, O mountains, the LORD's accusation; listen, you everlasting foundations of the earth. For the LORD has a case against his people; he is lodging a charge against Israel.
[3]"My people, what have I done to you? How have I burdened you? Answer me.
[4]I brought you up out of Egypt and redeemed you from the land of slavery. I sent Moses to lead you, also Aaron and Miriam.
[5]My people, remember what Balak king of Moab counseled and what Balaam son of Beor answered. Remember your journey from Shittim to Gilgal, that you may know the righteous acts of the LORD."
[6]With what shall I come before the LORD and bow down before the exalted God? Shall I come before him with burnt offerings, with calves a year old?
[7]Will the LORD be pleased with thousands of rams, with ten thousand rivers of oil? Shall I offer my firstborn for my transgression, the fruit of my body for the sin of my soul?
[8]He has showed you, O man, what is good. And what does the LORD require of you? To act justly and to love mercy and to walk humbly with your God.

SECTION 8: The Religious Life: Worship and Righteousness

The sacred texts of most religions provide examples of figures that tower above the rest of humanity in their purity and holiness. These saints are recognized within their traditions as models for imitation and objects of veneration. Sacred stories of the saints (hagiography) occupy a central place in most scriptural traditions. Judaism, however, differs from most world religions in that it refuses to designate a set of human beings as being worthy of special reverence. The Hebrew *Bible* and the *Talmud*, unlike most other sacred texts, depict human frailty even among the heroes of the faith. In the Hebrew *Bible*, Abraham lies, Sarah laughs at God, Jacob cheats his brother, Joseph boasts, and Moses and David murder. Although God accomplishes great things through these figures, the gulf between humanity and God is never bridged. Judaism embraces neither divine incarnation nor human apotheosis.

Despite the lack of a hagiographic tradition within Judaism, the Hebrew canon is filled with descriptive passages that define the ideal religious life. Jewish piety as depicted in the *Bible* and the *Talmud* consists of studying the *Torah* and living according to its commands, and observing the sacred calendar. The following selections from the Law and the Writings offer insights into Jewish attitudes toward worship and righteousness. The opening passage from the Book of Leviticus details instructions about proper worship rites on the Day of Atonement. Although these rituals have not been observed since the destruction of the temple in 70 CE, this day is still remembered as the most holy day of the year in the Jewish calendar. How do you explain the importance of the Day of Atonement among both ancient Hebrews and modern Jews?

THE DAY OF ATONEMENT FROM THE BOOK OF LEVITICUS

Chapter 16

[1]The LORD spoke to Moses after the death of the two sons of Aaron who died when they approached the LORD. [2]The LORD said to Moses: "Tell your brother Aaron not to come whenever he chooses into the Most Holy Place behind the curtain in front of the atonement cover on the ark, or else he will die, because I appear in the cloud over the atonement cover. [3]"This is how Aaron is to enter the sanctuary area: with a young bull for a sin offering and a ram for a burnt offering.

⁴He is to put on the sacred linen tunic, with linen undergarments next to his body; he is to tie the linen sash around him and put on the linen turban. These are sacred garments; so he must bathe himself with water before he puts them on. ⁵From the Israelite community he is to take two male goats for a sin offering and a ram for a burnt offering.

⁶"Aaron is to offer the bull for his own sin offering to make atonement for himself and his household. ⁷Then he is to take the two goats and present them before the LORD at the entrance to the Tent of Meeting. ⁸He is to cast lots for the two goats—one lot for the LORD and the other for the scapegoat. ⁹Aaron shall bring the goat whose lot falls to the LORD and sacrifice it for a sin offering. ¹⁰But the goat chosen by lot as the scapegoat shall be presented alive before the LORD to be used for making atonement by sending it into the desert as a scapegoat.

¹¹"Aaron shall bring the bull for his own sin offering to make atonement for himself and his household, and he is to slaughter the bull for his own sin offering. ¹²He is to take a censer full of burning coals from the altar before the LORD and two handfuls of finely ground fragrant incense and take them behind the curtain. ¹³He is to put the incense on the fire before the LORD, and the smoke of the incense will conceal the atonement cover above the Testimony, so that he will not die. ¹⁴He is to take some of the bull's blood and with his finger sprinkle it on the front of the atonement cover; then he shall sprinkle some of it with his finger seven times before the atonement cover.

¹⁵"He shall then slaughter the goat for the sin offering for the people and take its blood behind the curtain and do with it as he did with the bull's blood: He shall sprinkle it on the atonement cover and in front of it. ¹⁶In this way he will make atonement for the Most Holy Place because of the uncleanness and rebellion of the Israelites, whatever their sins have been. He is to do the same for the Tent of Meeting, which is among them in the midst of their uncleanness. ¹⁷No one is to be in the Tent of Meeting from the time Aaron goes in to make atonement in the Most Holy Place until he comes out, having made atonement for himself, his household and the whole community of Israel.

¹⁸"Then he shall come out to the altar that is before the LORD and make atonement for it. He shall take some of the bull's blood and some of the goat's blood and put it on all the horns of the altar. ¹⁹He shall sprinkle some of the blood on it with his finger seven times to cleanse it and to consecrate it from the uncleanness of the Israelites.

²⁰"When Aaron has finished making atonement for the Most Holy Place, the Tent of Meeting and the altar, he shall bring forward the live goat. ²¹He is to lay both hands on the head of the live goat and confess over it all the wickedness and rebellion of the Israelites—all their sins—and put them on the goat's head. He shall send the goat away into the desert in the care of a man appointed for the task. ²²The goat will carry on itself all their sins to a solitary place; and the man shall release it in the desert.

²³"Then Aaron is to go into the Tent of Meeting and take off the linen garments he put on before he entered the Most Holy Place, and he is to leave them there. ²⁴He shall bathe himself with water in a holy place and put on his regular garments. Then he shall come out and sacrifice the burnt offering for himself and the burnt offering for the people, to make atonement for himself and for the people. ²⁵He shall also burn the fat of the sin offering on the altar.

²⁶"The man who releases the goat as a scapegoat must wash his clothes and bathe himself with water; afterward he may come into the camp. ²⁷The bull and the goat for the sin offerings, whose blood was brought into the Most Holy Place to make atonement, must be taken outside the camp; their hides, flesh and offal are to be burned up. ²⁸The man who burns them must wash his clothes and bathe himself with water; afterward he may come into the camp.

²⁹"This is to be a lasting ordinance for you: On the tenth day of the seventh month you must deny yourselves and not do any work—whether native-born or an alien living among you—³⁰because on this day atonement will be made for you, to cleanse you. Then, before the LORD, you will be clean from all your sins. ³¹It is a sabbath of rest, and you must deny yourselves; it is a lasting ordinance. ³²The priest who is anointed and ordained to succeed his father as high priest is to make atonement. He is to put on the sacred linen garments ³³and make atonement for the Most Holy Place, for the Tent of Meeting and the altar, and for the priests and all the people of the community.

³⁴"This is to be a lasting ordinance for you: Atonement is to be made once a year for all the sins of the Israelites."
And it was done, as the LORD commanded Moses.

The following selections taken from the Writings describe the piety of the psalter. What ideas about worship, righteousness, and divine retribution are expressed in the passages? As you read these songs of praises, reflect about the public and private aspects of Judaism. Which were most important to the ancient Hebrews? What other texts in Hebrew scripture support your conclusions?

WORSHIP AND RIGHTEOUS IN THE PSALMS

Psalm 1

¹Blessed is the man who does not walk in the counsel of the wicked or stand in the way of sinners or sit in the seat of mockers.
²But his delight is in the law of the LORD, and on his law he meditates day and night.
³He is like a tree planted by streams of water, which yields its fruit in season and whose leaf does not wither. Whatever he does prospers.

⁴Not so the wicked! They are like chaff that the wind blows away.

⁵Therefore the wicked will not stand in the judgment, nor sinners in the assembly of the righteous.

⁶For the LORD watches over the way of the righteous, but the way of the wicked will perish.

Psalm 37

¹Do not fret because of evil men or be envious of those who do wrong;

²for like the grass they will soon wither, like green plants they will soon die away.

³Trust in the LORD and do good; dwell in the land and enjoy safe pasture.

⁴Delight yourself in the LORD and he will give you the desires of your heart.

⁵Commit your way to the LORD; trust in him and he will do this:

⁶He will make your righteousness shine like the dawn, the justice of your cause like the noonday sun.

⁷Be still before the LORD and wait patiently for him; do not fret when men succeed in their ways, when they carry out their wicked schemes.

⁸Refrain from anger and turn from wrath; do not fret—it leads only to evil.

⁹For evil men will be cut off, but those who hope in the LORD will inherit the land.

Psalm 100

¹Shout for joy to the LORD, all the earth.

²Worship the LORD with gladness; come before him with joyful songs.

³Know that the LORD is God. It is he who made us, and we are his; we are his people, the sheep of his pasture.

⁴Enter his gates with thanksgiving and his courts with praise; give thanks to him and praise his name.

⁵For the LORD is good and his love endures forever; his faithfulness continues through all generations.

Psalm 112

¹Praise the LORD. Blessed is the man who fears the LORD, who finds great delight in his commands.

²His children will be mighty in the land; the generation of the upright will be blessed.

³Wealth and riches are in his house, and his righteousness endures forever.

⁴Even in darkness light dawns for the upright, for the gracious and compassionate and righteous man.

⁵Good will come to him who is generous and lends freely, who conducts his affairs with justice.

⁶Surely he will never be shaken; a righteous man will be remembered forever.

⁷He will have no fear of bad news; his heart is steadfast, trusting in the LORD.

⁸His heart is secure, he will have no fear; in the end he will look in triumph on his foes.

⁹He has scattered abroad his gifts to the poor, his righteousness endures forever; his horn will be lifted high in honor.

¹⁰The wicked man will see and be vexed, he will gnash his teeth and waste away; the longings of the wicked will come to nothing.

The final selection is from the Book of Proverbs, a collection of wise Hebrews sayings gathered from early times to the return from exile in the fifth century. Many of the proverbs are poems written as couplets, with the second line repeating or expanding upon the idea presented in the first. The chapter presented below contains a number of comments about the righteous man. According to these texts, what are some characteristics and consequences of those who live a righteous life?

THE RIGHTEOUS MAN FROM THE BOOK OF PROVERBS

Chapter 10

¹The proverbs of Solomon: A wise son brings joy to his father, but a foolish son grief to his mother.

²Ill-gotten treasures are of no value, but righteousness delivers from death.

³The LORD does not let the righteous go hungry but he thwarts the craving of the wicked.

⁴Lazy hands make a man poor, but diligent hands bring wealth.

⁵He who gathers crops in summer is a wise son, but he who sleeps during harvest is a disgraceful son.

⁶Blessings crown the head of the righteous, but violence overwhelms the mouth of the wicked.

⁷The memory of the righteous will be a blessing, but the name of the wicked will rot.

⁸The wise in heart accept commands, but a chattering fool comes to ruin.

⁹The man of integrity walks securely, but he who takes crooked paths will be found out.

¹⁰He who winks maliciously causes grief, and a chattering fool comes to ruin.

¹¹The mouth of the righteous is a fountain of life, but violence overwhelms the mouth of the wicked.

¹²Hatred stirs up dissension, but love covers over all wrongs.

¹³Wisdom is found on the lips of the discerning, but a rod is for the back of him who lacks judgment.

¹⁴Wise men store up knowledge, but the mouth of a fool invites ruin.

[15]The wealth of the rich is their fortified city, but poverty is the ruin of the poor.

[16]The wages of the righteous bring them life, but the income of the wicked brings them punishment.

[17]He who heeds discipline shows the way to life, but whoever ignores correction leads others astray.

[18]He who conceals his hatred has lying lips, and whoever spreads slander is a fool.

[19]When words are many, sin is not absent, but he who holds his tongue is wise.

[20]The tongue of the righteous is choice silver, but the heart of the wicked is of little value.

[21]The lips of the righteous nourish many, but fools die for lack of judgment.

[22]The blessing of the LORD brings wealth, and he adds no trouble to it.

[23]A fool finds pleasure in evil conduct, but a man of understanding delights in wisdom.

[24]What the wicked dreads will overtake him; what the righteous desire will be granted.

[25]When the storm has swept by, the wicked are gone, but the righteous stand firm forever.

[26]As vinegar to the teeth and smoke to the eyes, so is a sluggard to those who send him.

[27]The fear of the LORD adds length to life, but the years of the wicked are cut short.

[28]The prospect of the righteous is joy, but the hopes of the wicked come to nothing.

[29]The way of the LORD is a refuge for the righteous, but it is the ruin of those who do evil.

[30]The righteous will never be uprooted, but the wicked will not remain in the land.

SECTION 9: Endings: Death, Judgment, and the Afterlife

Most religious traditions include sacred stories of the beginning and ending of the world. Often these accounts are described as cosmic events unrelated to human activity. In these stories, the time between cosmic beginning and ending is not characterized by human change, variation, or development. Rather, human history is more generally viewed as a changeless continuum wherein people are born, live as their ancestors lived, die, and are either reborn back into the changeless cosmic order or enter an afterlife of reward or punishment.

The ancient Hebrews differed from many ancients in their understanding of time and history. Viewing time as linear rather than cyclical, they attached great importance to human actions. Remembering human events were important to the Hebrews because they viewed Yahweh as the god over history who intervened in human time to establish a covenant relationship with Israel. As a watcher over human affairs, Yahweh promised retribution either in this life or in the hereafter. History seems to be moving toward a climactic ending when all will be judged, a corrupted creation will be redeemed, and God's kingdom again will reign.

Hebrew scripture describes the drama of the end times in a variety of ways. Some prophets suggest that the promised new heaven and earth will follow the establishment of a just and righteous society. Others suggest that humanity will evolve deeper and deeper into sin until the world explodes from excessive inequity. Some view divine retribution in nationalistic ways; others expect an individualized resurrection of the body or an eternal merging of the soul with the immortal. The following selections from Isaiah, Ezekiel, Malachi, and Daniel present a variety of prophetic insights about end times and the world to come. As you examine these passages, look for ideas shared by all the prophets, and ideas unique to each. Based on these readings, would you say that Judaism is primarily a this-worldly or an other-worldly religion?

A NEW HEAVEN AND A NEW EARTH FROM THE BOOK OF ISAIAH

Chapter 65

[17]"Behold, I will create new heavens and a new earth. The former things will not be remembered, nor will they come to mind.

[18]But be glad and rejoice forever in what I will create, for I will create Jerusalem to be a delight and its people a joy.

[19]I will rejoice over Jerusalem and take delight in my people; the sound of weeping and of crying will be heard in it no more.

[20]"Never again will there be in it an infant who lives but a few days, or an old man who does not live out his years; he who dies at a hundred will be thought a mere youth; he who fails to reach a hundred will be considered accursed.

[21]They will build houses and dwell in them; they will plant vineyards and eat their fruit.

[22]No longer will they build houses and others live in them, or plant and others eat. For as the days of a tree, so will be the days of my people; my chosen ones will long enjoy the works of their hands.

[23]They will not toil in vain or bear children doomed to misfortune; for they will be a people blessed by the LORD, they and their descendants with them.

[24]Before they call I will answer; while they are still speaking I will hear.

[25]The wolf and the lamb will feed together, and the lion will eat straw like the ox, but dust will be the serpent's food. They will neither harm nor destroy on all my holy mountain," says the LORD.

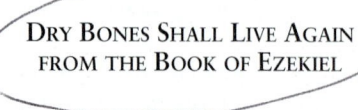

DRY BONES SHALL LIVE AGAIN
FROM THE BOOK OF EZEKIEL

Chapter 36

[33]" 'This is what the Sovereign LORD says: On the day I cleanse you from all your sins, I will resettle your towns, and the ruins will be rebuilt. [34]The desolate land will be cultivated instead of lying desolate in the sight of all who pass through it. [35]They will say, "This land that was laid waste has become like the garden of Eden; the cities that were lying in ruins, desolate and destroyed, are now fortified and inhabited." [36]Then the nations around you that remain will know that I the LORD have rebuilt what was destroyed and have replanted what was desolate. I the LORD have spoken, and I will do it.'

[37]"This is what the Sovereign LORD says: Once again I will yield to the plea of the house of Israel and do this for them: I will make their people as numerous as sheep, [38]as numerous as the flocks for offerings at Jerusalem during her appointed feasts. So will the ruined cities be filled with flocks of people. Then they will know that I am the LORD."

Chapter 37

[1]The hand of the LORD was upon me, and he brought me out by the Spirit of the LORD and set me in the middle of a valley; it was full of bones. [2]He led me back and forth among them, and I saw a great many bones on the floor of the valley, bones that were very dry. [3]He asked me, "Son of man, can these bones live?" I said, "O Sovereign LORD, you alone know."

[4]Then he said to me, "Prophesy to these bones and say to them, 'Dry bones, hear the word of the LORD ! [5]This is what the Sovereign LORD says to these bones: I will make breath enter you, and you will come to life. [6]I will attach tendons to you and make flesh come upon you and cover you with skin; I will put breath in you, and you will come to life. Then you will know that I am the LORD.' "

[7]So I prophesied as I was commanded. And as I was prophesying, there was a noise, a rattling sound, and the bones came together, bone to bone. [8]I looked, and tendons and flesh appeared on them and skin covered them, but there was no breath in them.

[9]Then he said to me, "Prophesy to the breath; prophesy, son of man, and say to it, 'This is what the Sovereign LORD says: Come from the four winds, O breath, and breathe into these slain, that they may live.' " [10]So I prophesied as he com-

manded me, and breath entered them; they came to life and stood up on their feet—a vast army.

[11]Then he said to me: "Son of man, these bones are the whole house of Israel. They say, 'Our bones are dried up and our hope is gone; we are cut off.' [12]Therefore prophesy and say to them: 'This is what the Sovereign LORD says: O my people, I am going to open your graves and bring you up from them; I will bring you back to the land of Israel. [13]Then you, my people, will know that I am the LORD, when I open your graves and bring you up from them. [14]I will put my Spirit in you and you will live, and I will settle you in your own land. Then you will know that I the LORD have spoken, and I have done it, declares the LORD.' "

THE DAY OF THE LORD
FROM THE BOOK OF MALACHI

Chapter 2

[17]You have wearied the LORD with your words. "How have we wearied him?" you ask. By saying, "All who do evil are good in the eyes of the LORD, and he is pleased with them" or "Where is the God of justice?"

Chapter 3

[1]"See, I will send my messenger, who will prepare the way before me. Then suddenly the Lord you are seeking will come to his temple; the messenger of the covenant, whom you desire, will come," says the LORD Almighty.

[2]But who can endure the day of his coming? Who can stand when he appears? For he will be like a refiner's fire or a launderer's soap. [3]He will sit as a refiner and purifier of silver; he will purify the Levites and refine them like gold and silver. Then the LORD will have men who will bring offerings in righteousness, [4]and the offerings of Judah and Jerusalem will be acceptable to the LORD, as in days gone by, as in former years.

[5]"So I will come near to you for judgment. I will be quick to testify against sorcerers, adulterers and perjurers, against those who defraud laborers of their wages, who oppress the widows and the fatherless, and deprive aliens of justice, but do not fear me," says the LORD Almighty.

[6]"I the LORD do not change. So you, O descendants of Jacob, are not destroyed. [7]Ever since the time of your forefathers you have turned away from my decrees and have not kept them. Return to me, and I will return to you," says the LORD Almighty. "But you ask, 'How are we to return?'

[8]"Will a man rob God? Yet you rob me. "But you ask, 'How do we rob you?' "In tithes and offerings. [9]You are under a curse—the whole nation of you—because you are robbing me. [10]Bring the whole tithe into the storehouse, that there may be food in my house. Test me in this," says the LORD Almighty, "and see if I will not throw open the floodgates of heaven and pour out so much blessing that you will not have

room enough for it. [11]I will prevent pests from devouring your crops, and the vines in your fields will not cast their fruit," says the LORD Almighty. [12]"Then all the nations will call you blessed, for yours will be a delightful land," says the LORD Almighty.

[13]"You have said harsh things against me," says the LORD. "Yet you ask, 'What have we said against you?'

[14]"You have said, 'It is futile to serve God. What did we gain by carrying out his requirements and going about like mourners before the LORD Almighty? [15]But now we call the arrogant blessed. Certainly the evildoers prosper, and even those who challenge God escape.'"

[16]Then those who feared the LORD talked with each other, and the LORD listened and heard. A scroll of remembrance was written in his presence concerning those who feared the LORD and honored his name.

[17]"They will be mine," says the LORD Almighty, "in the day when I make up my treasured possession. I will spare them, just as in compassion a man spares his son who serves him. [18]And you will again see the distinction between the righteous and the wicked, between those who serve God and those who do not.

Chapter 4

[1]"Surely the day is coming; it will burn like a furnace. All the arrogant and every evildoer will be stubble, and that day that is coming will set them on fire," says the LORD Almighty. "Not a root or a branch will be left to them. [2]But for you who revere my name, the sun of righteousness will rise with healing in its wings. And you will go out and leap like calves released from the stall. [3]Then you will trample down the wicked; they will be ashes under the soles of your feet on the day when I do these things," says the LORD Almighty.

[4]"Remember the law of my servant Moses, the decrees and laws I gave him at Horeb for all Israel.

[5]"See, I will send you the prophet Elijah before that great and dreadful day of the LORD comes. [6]He will turn the hearts of the fathers to their children, and the hearts of the children to their fathers; or else I will come and strike the land with a curse."

THE END TIMES FROM THE BOOK OF DANIEL

Chapter 12

[1]"At that time Michael, the great prince who protects your people, will arise. There will be a time of distress such as has not happened from the beginning of nations until then. But at that time your people—everyone whose name is found written in the book—will be delivered. [2]Multitudes who sleep in the dust of the earth will awake: some to everlasting life, others to shame and everlasting contempt. [3]Those who are wise will shine like the brightness of the heavens, and those who lead many to righteousness, like the stars for ever and ever.

[4]But you, Daniel, close up and seal the words of the scroll until the time of the end. Many will go here and there to increase knowledge."

[5]Then I, Daniel, looked, and there before me stood two others, one on this bank of the river and one on the opposite bank. [6]One of them said to the man clothed in linen, who was above the waters of the river, "How long will it be before these astonishing things are fulfilled?"

[7]The man clothed in linen, who was above the waters of the river, lifted his right hand and his left hand toward heaven, and I heard him swear by him who lives forever, saying, "It will be for a time, times and half a time. When the power of the holy people has been finally broken, all these things will be completed."

[8]I heard, but I did not understand. So I asked, "My lord, what will the outcome of all this be?"

[9]He replied, "Go your way, Daniel, because the words are closed up and sealed until the time of the end. [10]Many will be purified, made spotless and refined, but the wicked will continue to be wicked. None of the wicked will understand, but those who are wise will understand.

[11]"From the time that the daily sacrifice is abolished and the abomination that causes desolation is set up, there will be 1,290 days. [12]Blessed is the one who waits for and reaches the end of the 1,335 days.

PowerWeb SUPPLEMENTS

1. **Sayings of Rabbi Nachman,** Maurice Friedman, from *The Tales of Rabbi Nachman,* Humanities Press International, 1956.
2. **He Who Was Caught in His Own Trap,** Andrew Handler, from *Rabbi Eizik: Hasidic Stories About the Zaddik of Kallo,* Fairleigh Dickinson University Press, 1978.
3. **The Sacred Space of Judaism,** Irving Friedman, *Parabola,* 1978.
4. **Holocaust Remembrance Day Brings Memories of Evil, Courage,** Anne Bahr, *The Brookings Register,* February 21, 2002.

Like the faithful within many world religions, Jews throughout the ages have grappled with ideas of truth and justice, have consecrated sacred space, and have designated remembrance as a sacred duty. How these concerns and actions have contributed to the emergence of modern Judaism is a major theme that runs through the recommended *PowerWeb* supplements for this chapter. In the opening selections, Maurice Friedman explores how the inspirational ideas of a revered early nineteenth-century Jewish thinker, Rabbi Nachman, have influenced the development of the age-old question, "Why do good people suffer?" Next, in a cogent article originally written for *Parabola,* Irving Friedman examines how

early attitudes toward sacred space have impacted modern Judaism, and Anne Bahr underscores the importance "Yom ha-Shoad" (Holocaust Remembrance Day) within contemporary Jewry. Together these selections offer numerous insights into the relationships between ancient Jewish concepts of goodness, truth, and life and modern Jewish thought and practices.

Readings from *PowerWeb: Religion* are available at the McGraw-Hill *PowerWeb* website http://www.dushkin.com/ powerweb. A personal access code to *PowerWeb: Religion* is provided free with each new copy of this book. Those who purchase a used copy may buy an access code at the website.

SELECTED BIBLIOGRAPHY

Albright, W. F. *Yahweh and the Gods of Canaan.* Garden City, NY: Doubleday, 1968.

Barnavi, Eli, ed. *A Historical Atlas of the Jewish People: From the Time of the Patriarchs to the Present.* New York: Schocken Books, 2002.

Ben-Sasson, H. H. *A History of the Jewish People.* Cambridge: Harvard University Press, 1976.

Berlin, Adele, and Marc Zvi Brettler, eds. *The Jewish Study Bible.* New York: Oxford University Press, 2004.

Biale, David. *Cultures of the Jews.* New York: Schocken Books, 2002.

Diamond, Eliezer. *Holy Men and Hunger Artists: Fasting and Asceticism in Rabbinic Culture.* New York: Oxford University Press, 2004.

Efros, Israel I. *Ancient Jewish Philosophy.* New York: Block Publishing, 1964.

Flanders, Henry Jackson, Robert Wilson, and David Anthony Smith. *People of the Covenant: An Introduction to the Hebrew Bible.* New York: Oxford University Press, 1996.

Fleming, James. *Archaeology and the Bible.* Jerusalem: Biblical Resources, 2001.

Goldscheider, C., and J. Neusner, eds. *Social Foundations of Judaism.* Englewood Cliffs, NJ: Prentice-Hall, 1990.

Grayzel, S. *A History of the Jews.* New York: Meridan, 1968.

Gruen, Erich S. *Diaspora: Jews amidst Greeks and Romans.* Cambridge: Harvard University Press, 2002.

Holz, Barry W., ed. *Back to the Sources.* New York: Simon and Schuster, 1986.

Jaffee, Martin S. *Torah in the Mouth: Writing and Oral Tradition in Palestinian Judaism, 200 BCE–400 CE.* New York: Oxford University Press, 2000.

Johnson, Paul. *A History of the Jews.* New York: Harper & Row, 1987.

Kirsch, Jonathan. *Moses: A Life.* New York: Ballantine, 1998.

Neusner, Jacob. *The Way of Torah.* Belmont, CA: Wadsworth, 1988.

Potok, Chaim. *Wanderings.* New York: Fawcett, 1987.

The Fertile Crescent.

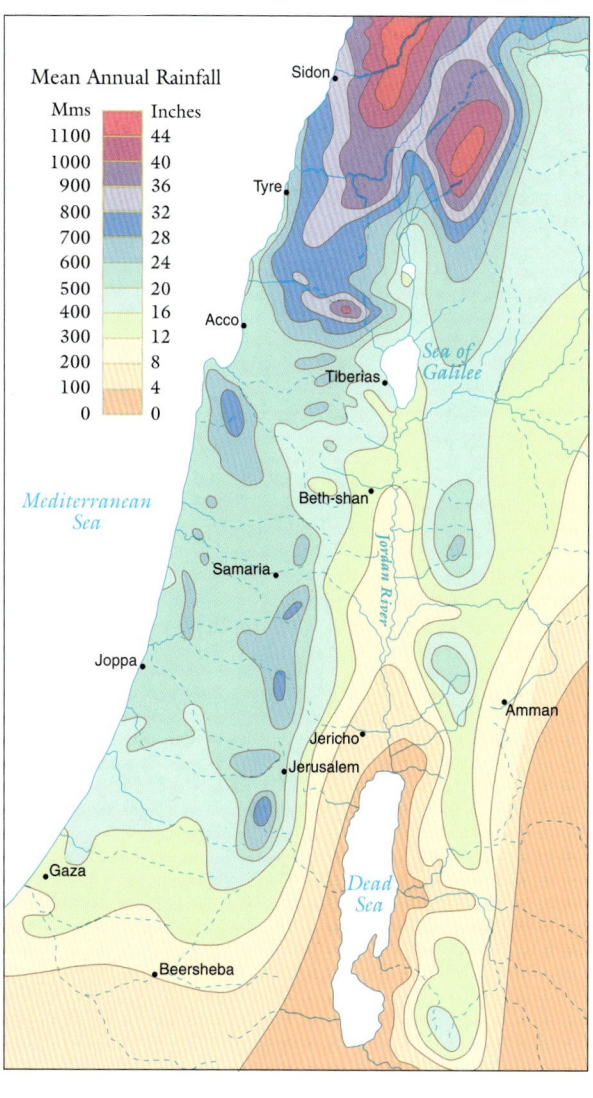

Rainfall in the Holy Land.

Population locations of the world's major religions.

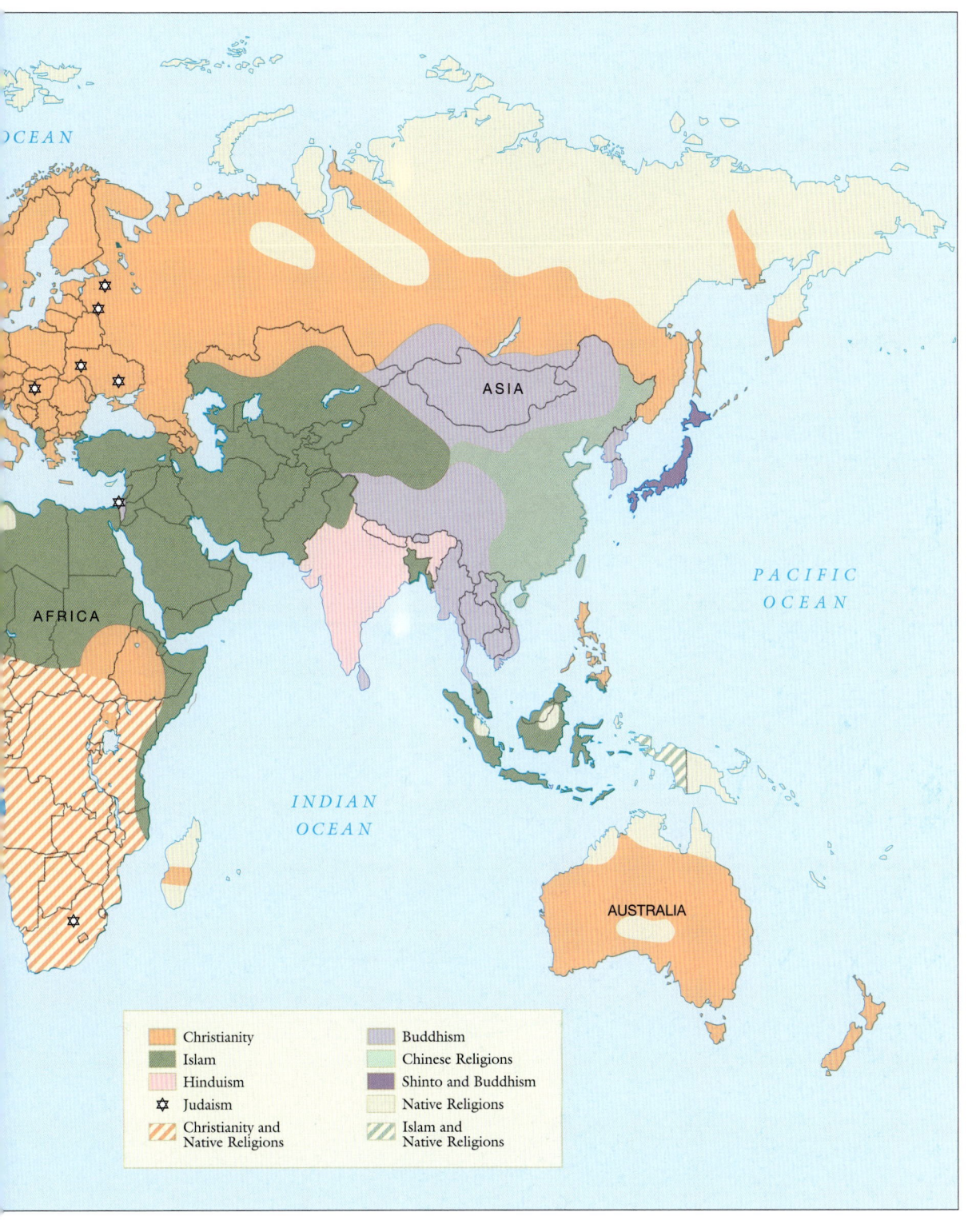

■	Christianity	■	Buddhism
■	Islam	■	Chinese Religions
■	Hinduism	■	Shinto and Buddhism
✡	Judaism	■	Native Religions
▨	Christianity and Native Religions	▨	Islam and Native Religions

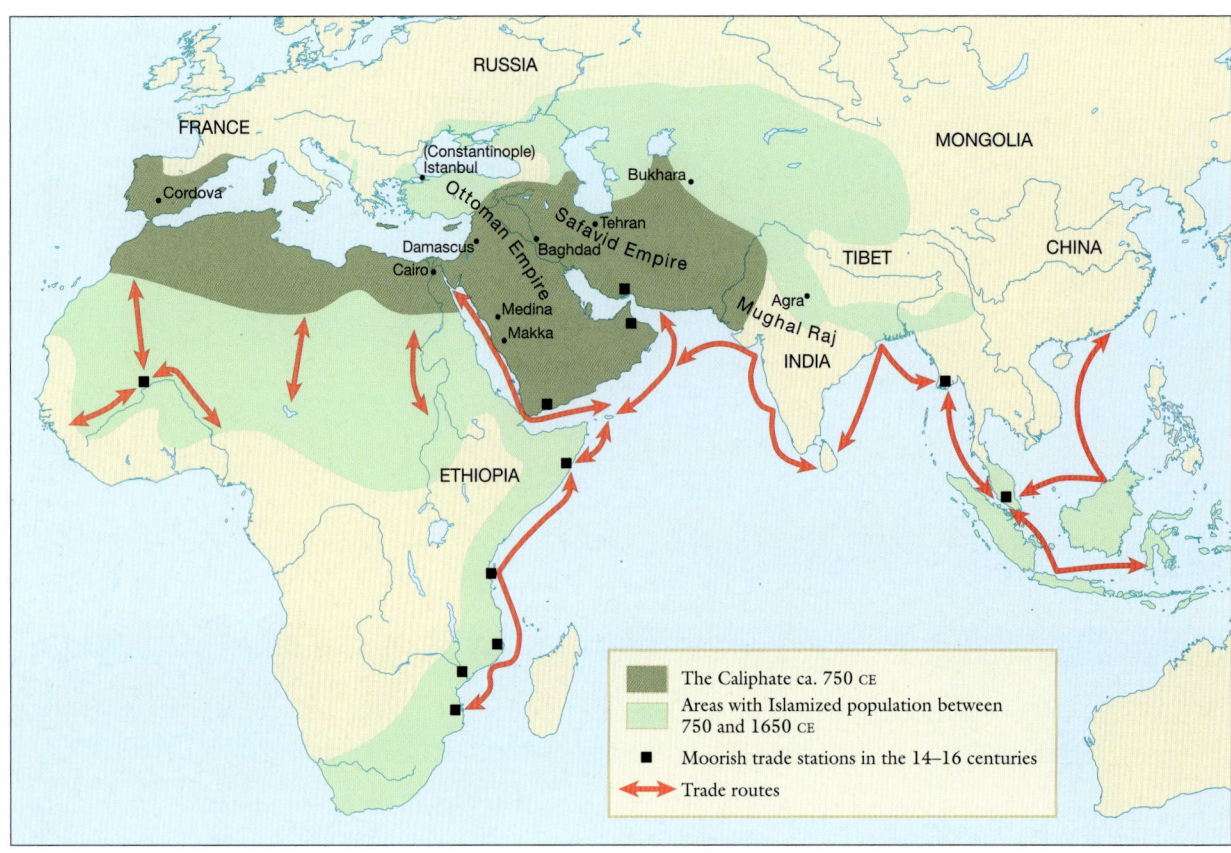

Expansion of the Islamic world.

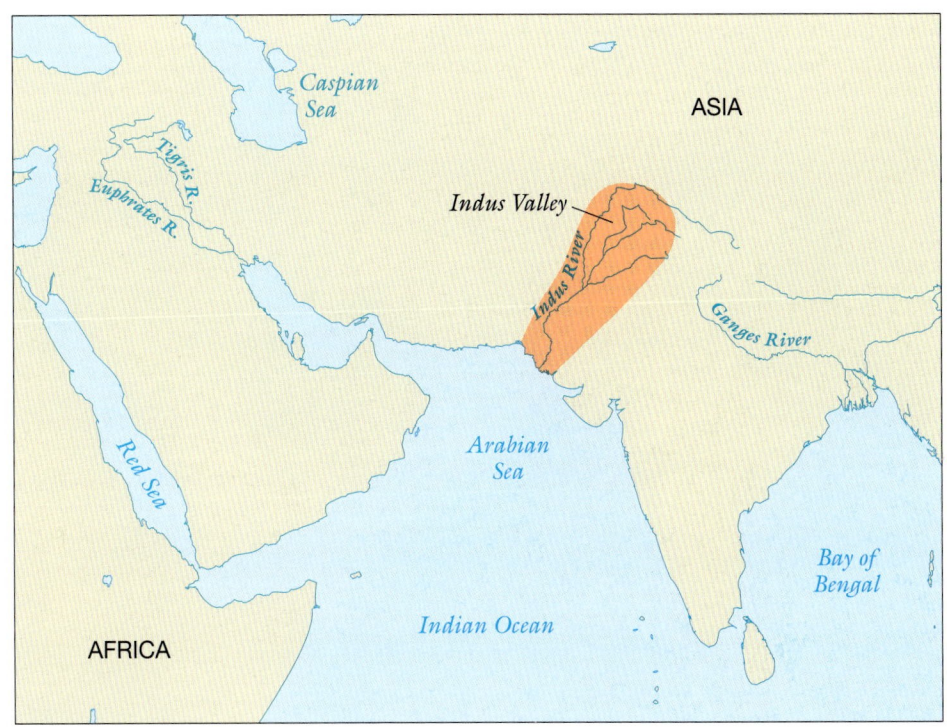

The Indus Valley.

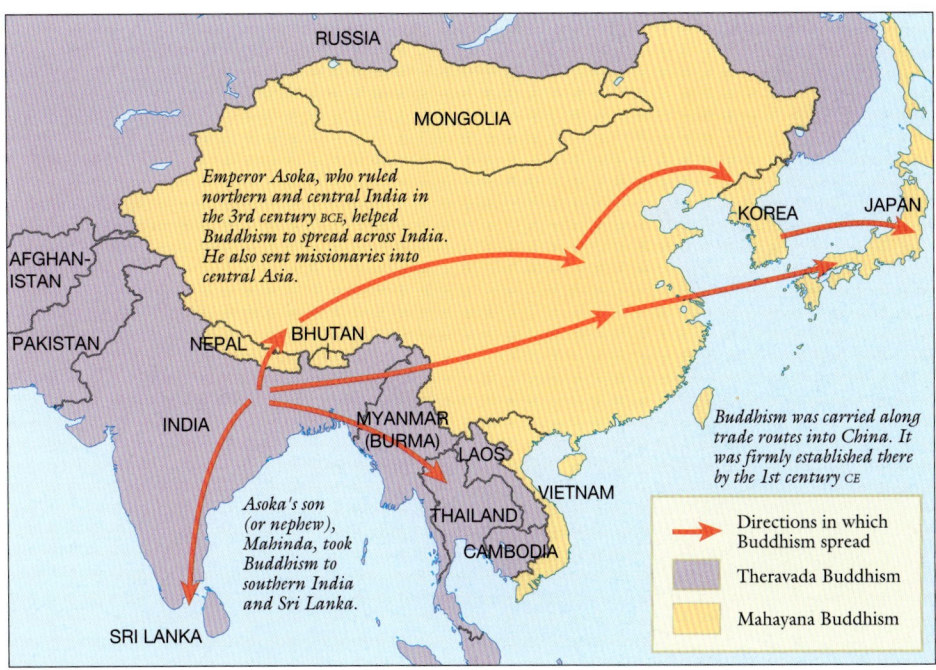

The expansion of Buddhism.

Ancient China.

Cultural Areas

- Arctic
- Subarctic
- Northwest Coast
- Plateau
- Great Basin
- California
- Southwest
- Plains
- Eastern Woodlands–Northeast
- Eastern Woodlands–Southeast
- Mexico and Central America
- Caribbean

Inupiaq

Aleut

Ingalik
Tanaina

Kutchin

Dogrib

Yellowknife

Inuit

Kaska

Chipewyan

Slave

Tlingit

Beaver

Tsimshian

Haida

Cree

Hudson Bay

Inuit

Montagnais
Naskapi

Micmac

Kwakiutl

Nootka

Sarsee

Shuswap
Thompson
Kalispel

Blackfoot

Gros
Ventre

Assiniboine

Ojibwa

Huron

Abenaki

Chinook

Cowlitz
Nez Perce

Klamath

Crow

Mandan

Menominee

Potawatomi
Sauk

Mohawk
Oneida
Onondaga
Cayuga
Seneca
Erie

Mahican

Massachusett

Wampanoag
Narragansett
Pequot

Shoshone

Cheyenne

Arikara

Miami

Shawnee

Susquehannock

Delaware

Yurok

Pomo

Yokut

Washoe

Gosiute

Pawnee

Arapaho

Illinois

Powhatan

Chumash

Paiute

Ute

Osage

Tuscarora

Luiseño

Walapai
Mohave

Hopi
Navajo
Zuni
Rio Grande
Pueblo
Apache

Kiowa

Cherokee

Catawba

Yuma
Papago
Piman

Wichita

Creek

Guale

Chickasaw
Choctaw

Caddo

Natchez

Mobile

Pacific
Ocean

Calusa

Atlantic
Ocean

Coahuiltec

Gulf of Mexico

Ciboney

Sub Taino

Tamaulipec

Otomi

Tarascan

Totonac

Caribbean
Sea

Aztec
Mixtec
Zapotec

Zoquen

Maya

Miskito

Lencan

Native American cultures.

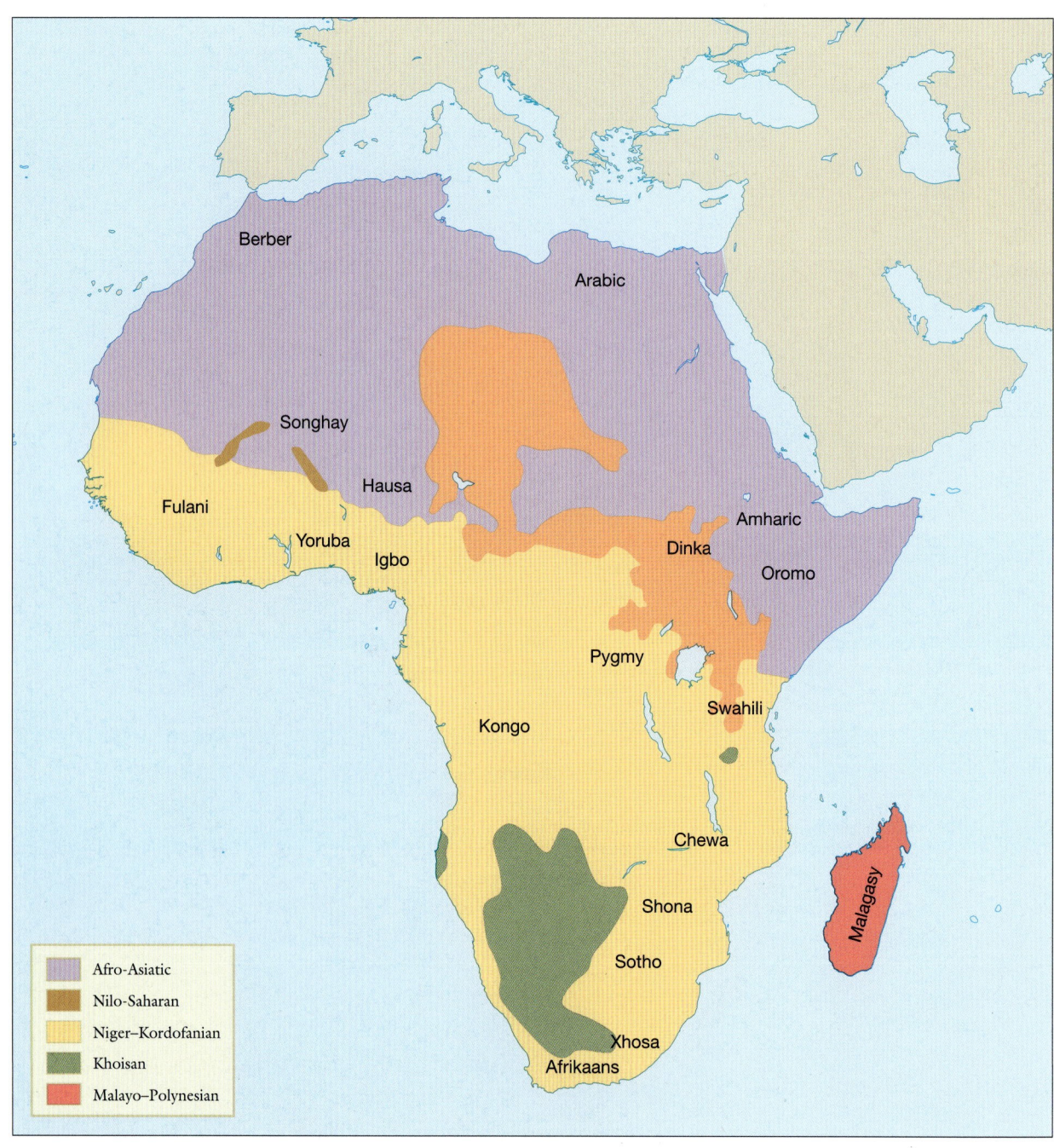

Afro-Asiatic	
Nilo-Saharan	
Niger–Kordofanian	
Khoisan	
Malayo–Polynesian	

African language families and selected ethnic groups.

Christianity 2

A popular devotional tract describes the life of Jesus in the following words:

> *He was born in an obscure village, the child of a peasant. He grew up in another village, where he worked in a carpenter shop until he was 30. Then, for three years, he was an itinerant preacher.*
>
> *He never wrote a book. He never held an office. He never had a family or owned a home. He didn't go to college. He never lived in a big city. He never traveled 200 miles from the place where he was born. He did none of the things that usually accompany greatness. He had no credentials but himself.*
>
> *He was only 33 when the tide of public opinion turned against him. His friends ran away. One of them denied him. He was turned over to his enemies and went through the mockery of a trial. He was nailed to a cross between two thieves. While he was dying, his executioners gambled for his garments, the only property he had on earth.*
>
> *When he was dead, he was laid in a borrowed grave, through the pity of a friend. Nineteen centuries have come and gone, and today he is the central figure of the human race.*
>
> *All the armies that ever marched, all the navies that ever sailed, all the parliaments that ever sat, all the kings that ever reigned—put together—have not affected the life of man on this earth as much as that one, solitary life.*

Although filled with sentimentality, this pious polemic captures the sense of irony that surrounds a faith that grew from lowly and obscure origins into the world's largest religion.

SETTING

Like Judaism, Christianity emerged from a small, yet geographically diverse piece of the planet. Ninety-five percent of the stories described in the Christian Old and New Testaments took place on a small piece of rugged land about 50 miles wide and 150 miles long that lies to the east of the Mediterranean Sea. Although not as fertile as the irrigated plains in Mesopotamia or as rich in natural resources as the areas around the Nile, as the only place on earth where three continents touch, this land bridge that connects Africa, Asia, and Europe served as highways for the great armies of the ancient world. In biblical times, war and the threat of invasion were ever-present realities for the peoples who lived in these lands.

This so-called promised land also was touched by two of the driest deserts on earth, the Sahara Desert to the south and the Arabian Desert to the east. If Jerusalem is viewed as the center of a clock, the driest section of the region would be the quarter of the clock from about 3 to 7 o'clock that faces these deserts. Life near the deserts was fragile, isolated, and unpredictable. With little available wealth, this land also was largely egalitarian. The Bible refers to this area as the land of Milk, which infers a land suitable only for the herdsmen of sheep and goats. The wetter northwestern quarter, from about 9 to 1 o'clock, is known as the land of Honey. This land of farmers and large cities enjoyed more wealth but also more class distinctions. Among the mighty indigenous deities worshipped in this region were the Philistine *Dagon*, the Phoenician *Astarte*, and the Canannite *Ba'al*. This fertile region that stretched from Galilee to the Mediterranean coastal plains supported temples for these fertility deities that took care of the economy, the weather, and the produce of the fields. The remaining regions from, about 1 to 3 and 7 to 9 o'clock, are known as the land of Milk and Honey. On these lands, farming was plentiful in the wetter, higher regions, while herding was the means for survival in the lower, drier regions.

The religious legacy that emerged from this region was the overriding conviction that the cosmos was created and controlled by a single, invisible, moral god. As meta-historian Arnold Toynbee argued throughout his classic multivolume series *The History of Civilization*, the great and powerful river cultures that flourished on the Tigris and Euphrates, the Nile, the Amazon, and the Indus rivers produced religious traditions that marveled at the predictability of the cycles of nature.[1] These areas, however, did not produce monotheistic religions. This legacy was left to Judaism, Christianity, and Islam, traditions that arose from a common land that was noted more for its hardship than its ease, for its unpredictability than its predictability, and for its political vulnerability than its strength.

The Inter-Testament Period: The Hasmonean Century, 165–63 BCE

History as well as geography influenced the religious innovations that would become associated with the rise of Christianity. As outlined in Chapter 1, after the Temple in Jerusalem was rebuilt in the fifth century BCE, the Jews remained under foreign control, first by the Persians and later under the Hellenistic successors to Alexander the Great. However, when the hated Seleucid king Antiochus IV attempted to force the Jews to offer a sacrifice to an alien god (168 BCE), the Jews revolted. Leadership of the rebellion fell into the hands of an elderly priest named Mattathias (also called Hashmonay) and his five sons. In time, each of Mattathias' five sons would die in battle, but not before achieving stunning military and political successes. The adventures of Mattathias and his sons are recorded in 1 and 2 Maccabees, pre-Christian era works that are accepted by some Christian bodies as part of the holy canon.

Under Judah the Maccabee, the most heroic of the Hasmoneans, Jerusalem was reclaimed and the

Temple cleansed and reconsecrated. Judah's brother Jonathan replaced Judah following his death, securing for himself both the high priesthood and the governorship of Judea. When Jonathan died, the only surviving son of Mattathias, Simon, called for a gathering of "The Great Assembly." This council of Jewish elders later would become known as the Sanhedrin. The council elected Simon as the hereditary "Ruler and High Priest." Simon and his son and successor, John Hyrcanus, had great aspirations for Judea. To achieve their secular dreams, they designed ambitious policies of territorial expansion, hired foreign mercenary soldiers who often offended the religious sensibilities of many Jews, and ruthlessly suppressed the religious freedoms of the conquered foes who refused to convert to Judaism. In an ironic twist of fate, the dynasty that was birthed in a struggle to achieve religious freedom and to arrest the Hellenization of Judea was itself acting like the Hellenizers it hated and was violating the very principles that had ignited the holy rebellion.

Many aristocratic Jews and governing officials who profited commercially from Judea's aggressive foreign policies supported the ambitions of the Hasmonean kings. Others who paid the price of expansion in heavy taxes and conscription concluded that war produced only more wealth for the aristocrats and less piety for the people. Class tensions in Judea fostered the rise of competing political parties. Those who opposed expansion became known as the Pharisees, perhaps from a Hebrew word meaning "the separated" or "the opposition." In contrast, those who favored the Hasmonean rulers, foreign expansion, and rule by the aristocrats became known as the Sadducees.

The Sadducees and Pharisees differed in many ways: socially, politically, and religiously. The Sadducees represented the upper crust of society; the Pharisees the more middling classes. The Sadducees controlled a majority in the Sanhedrin and a near monopoly of the religious offices in the Temple. They applauded the forcible conversion of the pagans and insisted that a powerful nation was needed to save both the Jewish people and their religion. The Pharisees also wanted to spread Judaism but not through the use of the state, as the Hellenizers had spread paganism, but through example and persuasion. They insisted that it was Judaism that had saved the state, not the other way around.

---

[1]Arnold Toynbee, *The History of Civilizations* (12 volumes, 1934–1961).

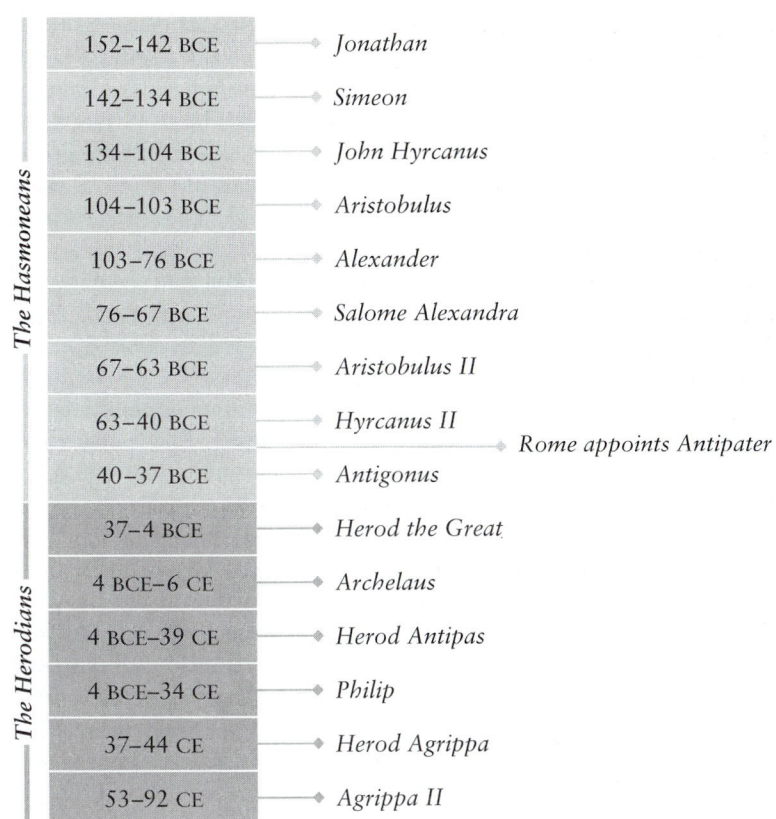

Chronology of Jewish rulers.

The Hasmoneans	152–142 BCE	Jonathan
	142–134 BCE	Simeon
	134–104 BCE	John Hyrcanus
	104–103 BCE	Aristobulus
	103–76 BCE	Alexander
	76–67 BCE	Salome Alexandra
	67–63 BCE	Aristobulus II
	63–40 BCE	Hyrcanus II — Rome appoints Antipater
	40–37 BCE	Antigonus
The Herodians	37–4 BCE	Herod the Great
	4 BCE–6 CE	Archelaus
	4 BCE–39 CE	Herod Antipas
	4 BCE–34 CE	Philip
	37–44 CE	Herod Agrippa
	53–92 CE	Agrippa II

The parties also differed in their understanding of scripture. The Sadducees accepted only the Written Law, nothing more, nothing less. Because there was little in the Torah to support the doctrines of resurrection, angels, mediating spirits, or a coming day of judgment, the conservative Sadducees rejected these ideas as unscriptural innovations. The Pharisees, in contrast, interpreted the Torah more liberally. They insisted that the Torah was a body of principles that needed to be applied to every phase of life. They claimed that an Oral Law had been handed down since Moses along with the Written Law, and that this equally sacred tradition affirmed the existence of angel intermediaries, the prospects of a coming day of judgment, and an eventual resurrection of the dead. In one sense, the Pharisees made Judaism easier by accepting the Written Law as principles that could be adapted to the changing needs of the people. In other ways, however, Pharisaic Judaism was more difficult for it insisted upon proper behavior in every conceivable human circumstance.

Following the death of John Hyrcanus in 104 BCE, the state of affairs in Judea became even more decadent when his son and successor, Aristobulus, imprisoned and executed three of his brothers. Such actions to ensure the throne may have been common in pagan lands, but they were shocking to the Judean Jews. Many rejoiced when Aristobulus died after only a one-year reign. Unfortunately, however, his successor Alexander proved to be no better. When a Pharisean plot against him was discovered, Alexander invited his Sadducean friends to a banquet, and in their presence had 800 Pharisees crucified. Gruesome actions such as this made reconciliation between the Pharisees and Sadducees untenable. Some Jews, like the Essenes, became so disillusioned at Alexander's impieties that they withdrew from society and gathered together in communities to study the scriptures and pray for a deliverer who would come to purify Israel and destroy the enemies of God.

Following the death of Alexander (76 BCE) and Salome (67 BCE), the wife of Alexander who became

Queen after Alexander's death, the children of the former king and queen fought for control of the kingdom. The Pharisees supported John Hyrcanus II, the eldest son of Alexander and Salome who had served as high priest during his mother's reign. The Sadducees, in contrast, rallied to the younger son, Aristobulus II, an ambitious general favored by the army. When war erupted, both sides appealed to the Roman general Pompey for assistance. As neither contender impressed Pompey, his decision favored neither Jewish party, only Rome. Pompey forced Judea to relinquish the land it had captured in previous wars, annexed the former Hasmonean kingdom to Syria, sent Aristobulus II and his sons into exile in Rome and made Hyrcanus II a high priest, thus eliminating the Jewish monarchy altogether. Later Rome installed its own pawn, Antipater, as a procurator to oversee the newly created Roman province of Judea. After a century of self-rule, Judea once again was under foreign domination.

The Era of Roman Domination

Even as the Sadducees and Pharisees were fighting among themselves in the third-rate kingdom of Judea, rival factions were competing for control of Rome, the great superpower of the era that appeared to be collapsing under its own weight. Reformers who desired a more efficient administration supported Julius Caesar. For senatorial aristocrats, however, the ambitions of the reformers seemed more dangerous to Rome than the inefficiencies in governing its distant frontiers. The resulting power struggles in Rome produced shock waves felt throughout the world.

The sordid history of Rome during this era is too complex to treat in this cursory overview. Ultimately, however, after Antipater shrewdly sent Jewish troops to assist Julius Caesar in putting down a revolt in Egypt, Caesar displayed his gratitude by bestowing a number of favors upon the Jews. He restored Hyrcanus II as ruler over Judea, reduced taxes on Jewish cities, excused certain Jewish territories from furnishing troops to the Roman armies, and allowed Jewish priests to increase taxes to support their shrines. Moreover, he conferred Roman citizenship on his new friend Antipater; made Antipater procurator of all Jewish territory in Syria; and appointed Antipater's two sons, Phasael and Herod, as local military governors over Jerusalem and Galilee, respectively.

In 44 BCE, senatorial conspirators assassinated Caesar. The assassins had hoped that Caesar's death would bring about a return to Senate domination. This hope proved to be only a fantasy as Caesar's ambitious subordinates moved quickly to fill the power vacuum. A Triumvirate consisting of two of Caesar's generals and his grandnephew Octavian was formed, but ultimately Octavian outmaneuvered his rivals and was left alone to reorganize Rome to his liking. The old Roman Republic was dead. In its place Octavian—who soon would be called Augustus, a religious title meaning "the Majestic One"—built the Principate, a new form of government characterized by the personal rule of an emperor. The Principate of Augustus and his successors would dominate the world for the next three centuries.

The Period of Herod's Dictatorship

The grinding gears of the Roman Civil War not only chewed human flesh in its teeth, it also turned wheels of change in Roman provinces throughout the world, including distant Judea. For a moment following the assassination of Caesar, the eastern part of the Roman Empire was in the hands of Caesar's murderers, Brutus and Cassius. Desperate for money, Cassius imposed a high tax on Judea and ordered Antipater and his sons to collect it. Without a Caesar to protect him, Antipater soon was murdered by his enemies at home. At this time Antigonus, the youngest son of the former Jewish king Aristobulus II, saw an opportunity to restore the Hasmonean dynasty in Judea. Securing an alliance with the Parthians (peoples from the other side of the Euphrates), Antigonus raised an army and invaded Judea. Meeting only token Roman resistance, Antigonus entered Jerusalem triumphantly and assumed the royal title and the high priesthood. The Sadducees again could celebrate with a Hasmonean king on the throne.

Meanwhile, Herod, the son of the murdered Antipater, fled to Rome and secured the backing of the empire. In 40 BCE, Rome agreed to remove Antigonus and proclaimed Herod as "King of Judea." At this time, however, Herod was merely a ruler in exile, a king without a country. For three years, Antigonus held on to the throne. Ultimately, however, following a siege on Jerusalem that resulted in the slaughtering of 12,000 Jews, the Roman legions prevailed. Antigonus was captured and, at Herod's request, executed. To further secure his position, Herod also had 40 prominent Sadducees condemned. This act not only eliminated his competitors, it also filled his pockets with the confiscated wealth of the executed men. In time, Herod also would execute one of his wives and two of his sons. Paranoid and brutal, Herod secured total control over his people by keeping them in a constant state of mortal fear.

For more than three decades, Herod the Great ruled ruthlessly over Judea. The son of a shrewd politician who was forcibly converted to Judaism by the Hasmoneans, Herod considered himself a Jew who had great sympathy for Hellenistic culture. A great builder, Herod engaged thousands of workers to enlarge the Temple in Jerusalem. Jews could look upon Herod's Temple with pride for it was broader, taller, and more elaborate even than Solomon's. Over the gate of the new Temple, however, Herod placed a huge Roman eagle, an ever-present reminder of the limitations of Jewish freedoms.

In addition to the Jerusalem Temple, Herod constructed a Greek theater and hippodrome in Jerusalem, numerous pagan temples and amphitheaters in Greek cities scattered across his kingdom, and several personal palaces and fortifications for his legions. To complete these tasks, Herod spent more than he could afford. Taxes were high and tax collectors, almost everywhere. For every tax collector there also were scores of Jews who hated Herod and the Roman eagle that supported his throne.

Although a small group called the Herodians gave their allegiance to the king, most Jews simply tried to make the best of what they considered to be a bad situation. Neither the Sadducees nor the Pharisees played a major role in the Herodean government, although the more accommodating Sadducees did enjoy some benefits stemming from their control of the high priesthood and the revenues of the Temple. However, throughout the period of Roman domination, members of the Sanhedrin were not elected but appointed by the king, and their powers were restricted to minor civil and religious decisions. They were more like scholars than politicians. Similarly, the high priests were little more than puppets of Roman authorities. Some Jews, the so-called Zealots, became so embittered against Herod and Rome that they pledged themselves to a violent overthrow of the government. Other less violent Jews withdrew into the desert to live in purity and to await the coming of a Messiah, a promised King who would bring deliverance to the people of Israel. Given the prevalence of widespread anti-Herodean sentiment, it is hardly surprising that when Herod died in 4 BCE, the so-called King of Judea was mourned not by the Jews but by the pagans within his kingdom.

The Rule of Herod's Successors

After Herod's death, his kingdom was divided among his three surviving sons. The eldest survivor, Herod Archelaus, received half of his father's kingdom, including the regions of Judea, Samaria, and Idumea. A man of little talent or integrity, Archelaus

Among the projects of Herod the Great was the building of the four-towered palace that he named "Herodium." This palace-fortress also served as his tomb.

ruled for 10 years before Rome charged him with mismanagement and banished him to Gaul. Between 6 and 41 CE, these regions were not governed by Jews but by appointed Roman procurators. Pontius Pilate was the fifth of six procurators who governed during this era.

The second surviving son of Herod the Great was Herod Antipas. He was declared tetrarch (literally, "ruler of a quarter" of his father's kingdom) of Galilee and Perea. Antipas also was corrupt but survived longer than his older brother, keeping his inheritance until he was banished by the Roman Emperor Caligula in the year 39 CE. Antipas is remembered in the New Testament for having John the Baptist executed and for being in Jerusalem at the time of Jesus's trial.

The youngest and most efficient of the sons of Herod the Great was Herod Philip, tetrarch of Iturea, Gaulanitis, and Trachonitis. Philip held his position until his death in 34 CE. On his death, this region was given to his nephew Herod Agrippa. In time, Agrippa would receive the royal title and all three areas once governed by Herod the Great. The New Testament identifies Agrippa I as king during the time of the first royal persecution of the church.[2] Upon his death, the kingdom was passed to his son, Agrippa II, who would rule between 50–92 CE. About the year 60, Paul of Tarsus appeared before Agrippa II at the request of a Roman procurator who wished to draw up charges against Paul before sending him to trial in Rome. Agrippa II also was king at the time of the Jewish revolt of 66–70 that ended with Roman soldiers destroying the Jerusalem Temple. Agrippa II survived the disastrous revolt and retired to Rome. With his death in 92, the Herodean dynasty came to an end.

As this cursory summary suggests, powerful and power-hungry Roman authorities dominated the world into which Jesus was born. Friends of Rome governed the provinces, but only so long as they remained in good standing with the Emperor. In Jerusalem, Herod's Temple was magnificent, but Judea was sorely divided among parties that despised the Jewish authorities almost as much as they hated the Romans who placed them in power. It was an era characterized by terror, violence, and intrigue. Memories produced cries for revenge. Blood feuds and racial hostilities were commonplace. Excepting the wealthy

Sadducees and the politically positioned Herodeans, few Palestinian Jews enjoyed the good life. Sectarian groups—Pharisees, Essenes, Zealots, plus dozens of lesser known bodies—dreamed and schemed for better days, perhaps for a Messiah who would bring deliverance to a people in trouble. Into this dark and violent world, Jesus of Nazareth was born.

SACRED STORIES AND BELIEFS

Jesus, the Greek form of the common Hebrew name Joshua, means "God is salvation." Most Christians believe that Jesus was born in Bethlehem under special, miraculous circumstances. According to traditional accounts, a young woman from Nazareth named Mary was engaged but not yet married to a Galilean carpenter named Joseph. An angel came to Mary and told her that the Holy Spirit would come upon her and that she would conceive a son who would be named Jesus. About this time, Roman authorities announced that all families must return to the town of their ancestors in order to register for a census. Because Joseph was a descendent of David, the couple traveled about 200 miles to Bethlehem, the town of David. While in Bethlehem, Mary gave birth to Jesus. Like all Jewish boys, Jesus was circumcised and dedicated to God eight days after birth. Little is told in New Testament sources about the youth of Jesus, except for one episode when he traveled with his parents at age 12 to Jerusalem. According to this story, even as a child Jesus was an inquisitive scholar with an impressive understanding of Jewish law.

At age 30, Jesus is found among the followers of John the Baptist, a Jewish ascetic who predicted an imminent end of historic time and urged sinners to repent and be cleansed through a ritual of water baptism. Although the New Testament does not give the name of John's sect, his teachings are similar to the views of the Essenes, an ancient Jewish group whose holy writings were discovered in 1947 in the Dead Sea Scrolls. All four Gospel writers identify John the Baptist as the one that the prophet Isaiah promised would cry out from the desert, proclaiming "Prepare the way for the Lord."

Jesus was baptized by John in the Jordan River. As Jesus came out of the water, a voice was heard from heaven saying, "This is my son, whom I love;

---

[2] This story is told in the 12th chapter of the Book of Acts.

Early portrait of Jesus in the Catacomb of Domitilla, Rome. Mid-fourth century CE.

with him I am well pleased." Following baptism, Jesus retired into the wilderness, where he was tempted by Satan three times. Each time Jesus rejected the wiles of the tempter with a quotation from Hebrew scripture. Overcoming these temptations, Jesus left the wilderness for Galilee, where he learned that John the Baptist had been imprisoned by Herod Antipas. Feeling that it was now time to begin his ministry, Jesus recruited a group of 12 male disciples who traveled with him from place to place proclaiming "good news" about the Kingdom of God. The 12 shared little in common except a willingness to drop what they were doing to follow Jesus. They displayed few obvious talents or special qualifications. One was a hated Roman tax collector; another was known as a "Zealot," an uncompromising enemy of Rome. The inner circle of disciples closest to Jesus consisted of Peter, James, and John, three simple Galilean fishermen.

Jesus traveled around the countryside teaching, healing, and working wonders. Years later when Peter attempted to explain what Jesus did, his partial answer was "He went about doing good." Jesus was the personification of goodness, and everywhere he went crowds flocked to him. People were amazed at his teachings, not so much because of what he said—which was not particularly new—but because of how he said it. He spoke in parables that common folk could understand, not in the scholarly legal jargon of the scribes. He made points by the use of hyperbole—speaking of logs protruding from one's eyes, of camels going through the eye of a needle, of cutting off one's

hands to prevent falling into sin, of forgiving others not seven times but seventy times seven. He shocked audiences with almost absurd statements like it will be the meek, not the powerful, who will inherit the earth. He crafted stories with unlikely heroes, such as the parable of a Good Samaritan—one who, although despised by Jews for being racially impure, illustrated the meaning of true neighborliness. The masses that heard such teachings marveled at his words, saying, "No man ever spoke like this."

Jesus's words, however, produced enemies as well as followers. His warnings about the dangers of wealth upset the Sadducees. His command to turn the other cheek and to love your enemies offended the Zealots. His association with prostitutes, tax collectors, and Samaritans disturbed many who regarded such groups as social outcasts whom respectable Jews were supposed to avoid. Moreover, his popularity with the masses frightened the Roman authorities whose foremost concern was to maintain order in the province.

The Jewish sect most often challenging Jesus in the gospel accounts was the Pharisees. Actually, Jesus shared more in common with this group than the other major Jewish parties. Unlike the Sadducees, both Jesus and the Pharisees embraced the Oral Tradition and with it a belief in a spirit world, in angels, and in a final resurrection. Unlike the Zealots, both Jesus and the Pharisees rejected military violence as a means for establishing the Kingdom of God. Unlike the Essenes, both refused to withdraw from society and passively await the coming end. Public

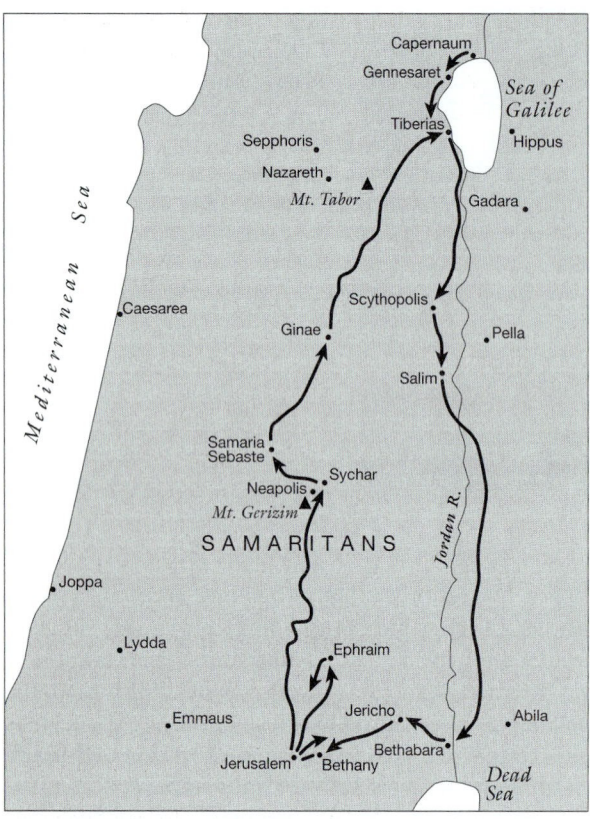

Map of Jesus's journeys in Galilee and Jerusalem.

encounters between Jesus and the Pharisees did occur, however, primarily because the two parties differed in their understanding of the essential nature of God. Although each insisted that Yahweh was both a righteous and a merciful God, the Pharisees placed a greater emphasis on God's holiness, while Jesus stressed God's compassion.

For many Pharisees, the centerpiece of religion was the divine command, "Ye shall be holy, for I, the Lord your God, am holy." To achieve holiness, they formulated rules of appropriate conduct touching upon every conceivable circumstance in life and often scolded those who failed to live according to these righteous standards. Jesus, following the line of some Pharisees, summarized the commandments with two positive principles: love God and love your neighbor. He also condemned the ostentatious public displays of piety for which many Pharisees were well known and insisted that the Pharisaic willingness to erect barriers to separate the clean from the unclean and

the Jew from the Gentile ran counter to the will of a forgiving and compassionate God who was a Father to all peoples.

In the final week of his life, Jesus traveled with his followers to Jerusalem to celebrate the Jewish Passover. According to New Testament sources, after Jesus confronted the religious authorities in the Temple, Jewish leaders plotted his demise. Judas Iscariot, 1 of the 12 disciples, cooperated with Jesus's enemies in the conspiracy. After holding a Passover seder with his disciples (known in Christian parlance as the Last Supper), Jesus was arrested and brought before the Jewish Sanhedrin, which, in turn, handed him over to the Roman procurator Pontius Pilate. Although Pilate announced that he found nothing illegal in the actions or words of Jesus, in order to appease those who demanded Jesus's death, Pilate sentenced Jesus to be executed through crucifixion. On a Friday, Jesus was crucified, pronounced dead, and buried in a borrowed tomb. The ensuing Sunday morning, several women approached the tomb and were told by an angel that Jesus had risen. Jesus subsequently appeared to some of his followers on several occasions. Forty days after his resurrection, in the midst of a band of followers, Jesus ascended into heaven.

Ten days after the ascension, on the morning of the Jewish festival of Pentecost, the timid disciples were transformed into fearless preachers. While gathered together in seclusion, they heard the noise of a great wind and saw the Holy Spirit appear among them as "tongues of fire." A crowd of God-fearing Jews who had come to Jerusalem for Pentecost quickly gathered. Miraculously, peoples of various language groupings were able to communicate with each other about the wonders of God in their own tongue. In the midst of the excitement, Peter boldly came forward and proclaimed that the crucified Jesus had been raised from the dead to sit at the right hand of the heavenly Father. Death could not contain him. Jesus was the Risen Lord. Following the message, 3,000 joined the movement. Christians look to this Pentecost event as the birthday of the church.

As the church grew, however, opponents of the movement attempted to arrest its growth. Among the leaders of the opposition was a Pharisee named Saul. After participating in the stoning of Stephen, Saul secured permission from the high priest to imprison the followers of Jesus who had fled to the Syrian city of Damascus. While en route to Damascus, Saul fell from his horse, was temporarily blinded, and heard

This fifth century ivory casket depicts both the crucifixion of Jesus and the hanging of Judas.

the voice of Jesus ask him, "Why do you persecute me?" This event changed Saul's life and the future of the Christian movement. Saul, later to be known as Paul, became the great missionary of the early church. His labors helped transform a small Jewish sect into a world religion of Gentiles and Jews alike.

At the center of Paul's message was the concept of the Lordship of Christ.[3] To redeem sinful humanity from its fallen state, Paul asserted that Jesus the Christ paid the penalty of sin through his death on the cross and that God demonstrated his power over sin and death by raising Christ from the dead. This triumph was to be shared by those who in faith bound themselves to the Risen Lord. For Paul, it was no longer necessary to become righteous in God's sight through the observance of Jewish rituals. Instead, the path to righteousness was through faith in the person and work of Jesus the Christ.

This message was widely embraced among the Gentiles, in part because it was so congenial with the belief system of the Hellenistic world. By the beginning of the Christian era, the idea that a god could die and be revived for the good of the world was not a novel concept. One rendition of this ancient story was the Isis-Osiris myth. Osiris, the god of the Nile, was dismembered by the evil Typhon, only to be reunited and brought back to life by the loving goddess Isis. Jesus Christ, of course, differed from Osiris in that he was a historic person, not a distant mythological being. The popular ancient motif, however, helped the non-Jewish populations of the Empire to take seriously Paul's proclamations concerning a Cosmic Christ who humbled himself by taking human form in order to bring redemption to a corrupted world.

Paul's determination to take the gospel to the Gentiles and to demote the importance of adhering to Jewish law created tensions within the early church, but in the end his ideas largely prevailed. By focusing on such themes as sin, redemption, justification, and reconciliation, Paul created the vocabulary that would shape the development of Christian theology in the centuries following the end of the New Testament era.

SCRIPTURES

Most Christians accept as Holy Scripture the Old Testament (the Hebrew Bible) and the New Testament, an additional 27 books written in the century following the death of Jesus. The Old Testament includes the same words that were contained in the 24 books of Jewish scripture. However, Christians subdivide a number

---

[3] The word *Christ* is Greek for the Hebrew word for *Messiah*, which means "God's anointed one."

of these books into smaller units, so there are 39 rather than 24 books in the Christian Old Testament.

In addition to these 39 books, some groups of Christians accept as scripture other collections of Jewish books that were written between about 200 BCE and 100 CE. Most of these works were written in Greek or Aramaic, the primary written and spoken languages of the era. Protestant Christians, who generally do not accept this literature as sacred, refer to these books as the Apocrypha, meaning "hidden or spurious things." Roman Catholic Christians, in contrast, prefer the term Deuterocanonical, meaning second canon. Although these works were never adopted into the Hebrew canon, most were included in the Septuagint, an early translation of Jewish works into the Greek language. Since the Septuagint was the version of the Hebrew Bible read by the early Christian community, these works were read and quoted by church fathers during the early centuries of the Christian era. Excepting vague references to these works in the books of II Peter and Jude, however, New Testament writers did not quote from the deuterocanonical works.

The 27 books of the New Testament include four gospel narratives of the life of Jesus (Matthew, Mark, Luke, and John); a companion volume to the Gospel of Luke that narrates select events in the history of the early church (Acts of the Apostles); 13 letters ascribed to Paul, 9 of which are written to churches and 4 to individuals (Romans, 1 and 2 Corinthians, Galatians, Ephesians, Philippians, Colossians, 1 and 2 Thessalonians, 1 and 2 Timothy, Titus, and Philemon); a letter addressed to the Hebrews written by an unnamed author; 7 general letters ascribed to James, Peter, John, and Jude; and a piece of apocalyptic literature known as Revelation. The narrative portions of the New Testament (the four gospels and Acts) comprise about 60 percent of the volume, and the Letters and Revelation, the remaining 40 percent.

The Writing of the Gospels and Acts

Following the life of Jesus, the early Christians preached the central message that "Christ had risen from the dead" and would return soon to establish his kingdom. As the years passed and the eyewitnesses to the life, death, and resurrection of Jesus were growing older, a written record of the life and teachings of Jesus became essential. The need for such an authoritative record became greater after 64 CE, when Emperor Nero's persecution of Chris-

tians resulted in the probable death of the two principal Christian apostles, Peter and Paul.

The first narrative of Jesus's life probably written was the Gospel of Mark. Mark's account recorded few references to the teachings of Jesus, perhaps because there was in circulation at this time another source that contained a collection of the remembered sayings of Jesus. This nonextant document is sometimes called Q, from the German word Quelle, meaning "source." The demand for an enlarged gospel account that incorporated both narrative and teaching may have prompted the writing of the gospels of Matthew and Luke. Because nearly all of the passages in Mark (almost 95 percent) are contained in either Matthew or Luke, many believe that Matthew and Luke made extensive use of Mark's gospel, as well as the Q source of Jesus's teachings. Matthew appears to be written for an audience familiar with Old Testament scripture; Luke's gospel seems more directed to Gentiles reared in a Hellenized world. Owing to their similarities in substance, language, and order, the three gospels—Matthew, Mark, and Luke—are commonly called the "Synoptic Gospels," from a Greek word meaning "from the same point of view."

The fourth gospel differs from the synoptic gospels in order and style. The Gospel of John, probably written after the first three accounts, offers more interpretation than the synoptic gospels. John attempts to explain to a Greek world the role that was played by a Jewish Messiah in God's universal plan of salvation. A central message of John is that Jesus is the Way, the Truth, and the Life for all humanity, not simply for those of Jewish heritage.

The author of the Gospel of Luke also wrote the Book of Acts. The central characters in this work are Peter and Paul, although the hero is Jesus and the power behind the activities of the evangelists is the Holy Spirit. The book covers a period of about three decades, from the ascension of Jesus to the imprisonment of Paul in Rome.

The Epistles and the Apocalypse

Although placed after the narrative sections of the New Testament, most of the 21 epistles (from a Greek word meaning "message" or "letter") were written before the gospel accounts. Paul wrote (or dictated) the earliest letters about two decades after the life of Jesus, around the year 50 CE. With the exception of the Epistle to the Hebrews and 1 John, the epistles began with a customary introduction that included the name or title of the alleged writer and the person or church to whom the let-

THE DIVISIONS AND ORDER OF THE NEW TESTAMENT

Narrative Accounts
  The Gospels
    Matthew
    Mark
    Luke
    John

    The Book of Acts

Epistles
  Letters Attributed to Paul
    Romans
    1 Corinthians
    2 Corinthians
    Galatians
    Ephesians
    Philippians
    Colossians
    1 Thessalonians
    2 Thessalonians
    1 Timothy
    2 Timothy
    Titus
    Philemon

    The Book of Hebrews

  The Catholic or General Epistles
    James
    1 Peter
    2 Peter
    1 John
    2 John
    3 John
    Jude

The Apocalypse
    The Book of Revelation

The final book of the New Testament is the Revelation of John (also called the Apocalypse). The name is taken from a Latin word meaning "unveiling," suggesting the revealing of divine truths previously unknown. The book claims to be a disclosure of the future. It includes seven visions of highly symbolic character that the author asserts were communicated from God to Jesus Christ, to an angel, and to himself. The author received these visions after being banished for his Christian faith to the island of Patmos. Written during a time of persecution (perhaps during Emperor Domitian's reign of terror against the Christians in 96 CE), the purpose of the work was to encourage Christians to remain faithful even unto death. Its central message expressed the hope that spiritual, not material, forces will prevail in the end.

The Canonization of the New Testament

First-century Christians regarded the Old Testament and the remembered words of Jesus as their authoritative guides. By the second century, most Christian communities had accepted the four gospels as authoritative documents that captured the essence of the oral tradition of Jesus's life and teachings. Meanwhile, churches also were collecting, circulating, preserving, and using in worship the text of letters ascribed to Paul and the apostles. Questions concerning what texts held apostolic authority took on greater importance when a second-century philosopher-theologian named Marcion asserted that Yahweh, the Jewish god of creation, was antithetical to Abba, the god and Father of Jesus Christ. Rejecting the Old Testament and three of the gospels, Marcion accepted as authoritative only an abbreviated Gospel of Luke and 10 Pauline letters addressed to the churches. Although Marcion and his list of sacred books were denounced by the larger Christian community, his efforts drew attention to the need for Christians to establish a canon of scripture that could be used to answer the basic question, What is authentic Christianity?

Late second- and third-century lists of authoritative texts generally included approximately 20 of the works later accepted in the New Testament canon. At this time the Epistle to the Hebrews, James, 2 Peter, 2 and 3 John, and Jude, as well as the Revelation of John lacked general recognition, while other works such as the Epistle of Barnabas, the Shepherd of

ter was addressed. Some were general letters of instruction written to the church at large; others were replies to specific requests for answers to questions concerning doctrine or behavior. Like all ancient texts, the letters were more likely to be read aloud than in silence. Their general aim was to inspire, edify, and control groups of Christians, many of whom could not read.

Hermas, and the Didache made some lists of authoritative texts. The first known statement listing the exact 27 works of the New Testament was contained in a 367 CE Easter Letter of Bishop Athanasius of Alexandria. Various church councils at Hippo in 393 and at Carthage in 397 and 419 subsequently approved this list. Although this canon was widely accepted, a few regions rejected the definitions of these councils. The Syrian Church, for example, accepted a shorter canon of 22 books, excluding Revelation and the four general epistles. The Coptic Church and the Ethiopian Church, in contrast, embraced a slightly enlarged canon that included the standard 27 plus some additional works known as the Apostolic Constitutions. By the fifth century, however, most of Christendom was satisfied that the New Testament canon consisted of 27 books, the same works that had appeared on Anthanasius' list.

From Manuscript to Publication

The original copies written on papyrus with ink are not extant, but there are more than 5,000 ancient Greek manuscripts of portions of New Testament books. In 405, Saint Jerome completed a Latin translation of the Old and New Testaments. After an initial round of criticism, Jerome's work became the authoritative text for more than 1,000 years. The books of the Bible were divided into chapters in the thirteenth century and subdivided into verses in the sixteenth century. Since its publication in 1455, more copies of the Bible have been printed than any work of literature. Likewise, more books have been written about the Bible than any literary collection. Today the Bible can be read in more than 1,000 world languages.

SUBDIVISIONS

It is ironic that the ideas of an obscure Galilean, who taught that all people share the same heavenly Father, would develop over the centuries into the world's largest and most fragmented religion. Irony, however, suggests the unexpected, not the unexplainable. The triumph of Christianity, while remarkable, is understandable given the advantages it possessed over its rivals. Likewise, its division into hundreds of bodies is a function of its size and multicultural appeal, the di-

versity and richness of its scriptures and perhaps the universal tendency of an imperfect human race to make absolute the relative. The family tree of Christianity is an enormously complex organism. Our task here is simply to describe the formation of Christianity's main trunk and the characteristics of its three major modern branches: Roman Catholicism, Eastern Orthodoxy, and Protestantism.

The Emergence of Christian Dogma

During the first four centuries of the Christian era, the early church transformed itself from a parochial Jewish sect into a global world religion. This transformation was not the result of a strategic plan designed by a human board of directors who set world dominance as its foremost goal. Rather, the church evolved in reaction to external and internal pressures that shaped its character and mission.

Externally, the early church was initially challenged by state persecution. Although Romans prided themselves on allowing a diversity of religious beliefs, their tolerance did not apply to atheists who refused to treat the gods of the Empire with proper respect. Because Christians stubbornly refused to worship the state gods, local mobs and occasionally Roman officials viewed them as social outcasts deserving of death. Misunderstood Christian parlance about loving one another and eating the body of Christ also made Christians suspect to charges of immoral conduct. To defend themselves against such attacks, second-century apologists wrote polemics to inform the authorities that Christians were not guilty of atheism, incest, and cannibalism.

For nearly three centuries, Christians suffered from periodic waves of persecution. Troubled times, however, produced heroes of the faith, and the heroes produced more followers. Isolation from Rome also brought some competitive advantage. Because the official pagan gods essentially were hired to protect the state, as Rome experienced decay in the third century, the status of state gods declined with Rome. Meanwhile, a number of oriental mystery cults promising salvation through secret initiation rituals gained popularity, but the limited appeal of these cults never equaled the universal appeal of Christianity. For example, the largest of these groups, Mithraism, attracted great numbers of Roman soldiers, but as a male-only religion, it eliminated one-half the human race from its membership. By the end of the third cen-

Mithras slaying the sacred bull. Like Christianity, Mithraism was a religion that promised its followers an immortal rebirth.

tury, a quarter of the Roman world was Christian, even though the church was still a persecuted faith. In 313, a Christian emperor, Constantine, brought an official end to the persecution. By the end of the fourth century, when future Christian emperors declared war on paganism, most of the Roman world was at least nominally Christian.

The transition from a persecuted to a persecuting faith aggravated rather than ended the internal tensions that were disrupting Christian communities during the early centuries of the Christian era. At this time, the Roman world was flirting with dualistic notions that held that the human soul tragically had become separated from the eternal spirit and entrapped in a corrupted material body. Humans while living in the body could not find God, thus humans were in need of divine revelation and redemption. To some extent, the popularity of these Hellenistic ideas worked to the benefit of the Christian church. Some, however, concluded that because Jesus was perfect, he could not have been human. For many Christians, this was heresy. Hence, to stamp out the heretical

fires, the developing church produced anti-Gnostic creeds, canonized a narrow canon of scripture that distanced itself from the Gnostic writings, and recognized as clergy only those individuals ordained by those with apostolic authority. The rise of creeds, canon, and clergy brought some degree of unity to the church, but it did not fully resolve all questions concerning the nature of God and Christ.

When Constantine embraced Christianity, his foremost goal was to consolidate and bring harmony to the church. In the year 325 CE, Constantine called 318 church leaders to Nicea to end the theological bickering. Many of the bishops came with disfigured bodies, having paid a heavy price for their faith during the torturous reign of Emperor Diocletian. Now they were asked to define what they had been willing to die for.

Present at the Council of Nicea was Arius, the leader of a party that believed that Christ was the Logos (the Reason or Word of God) but not of the same substance as the Father. Arius taught that as a son is a creation of a father, so the divine Logos is something less than and separate from God. At the other extreme were the Monarchians, who placed an emphasis on the unity of God. For these Christians, the Father, Son, and Spirit were only names used to express the one eternal being known as God. The church fathers at this first ecumenical council ultimately rejected both of these extreme positions. According to the Nicene Creed, the Son was "begotten, not made, of one substance with the Father." Several decades later, in 381 CE, another 150 bishops gathered at Constantinople at the second ecumenical council. This group amplified the Nicene Creed with language that affirmed the full deity of the Holy Spirit as well as the Son. With these declarations, the Christian church defined the godhead as a Holy Trinity, three divine persons of one essence.

Ecumenical councils met twice again in the fifth century. In 431 CE at Ephesus, the church solved a dispute over the nature of Christ and his mother Mary. Here the church defined Christ as the Incarnate Word of God, and Mary as *theotokos*, literally the "mother of God." Two decades later, at the fourth ecumenical council in Chalcedon the church produced still another creed that declared Christ to be 100 percent God and 100 percent human. Although some may view such formulas as theological hairsplitting, the creeds of the ecumenical councils demonstrate the unwillingness of Christians to reject either the human

Built in the late first century, the Roman Coliseum was an entertainment facility for blood sports that included fights between exotic animals, the mutilation and execution of prisoners, and gladiatorial contests. Early Christians were among the criminals thrown into the arena to face the hungry wild beasts. Following emperor Constantine's military victory over his rival in 312, the first Christian emperor ordered the end of government-sanctioned religious persecution. In 325, Constantine also outlawed gladiatorial games, although some contests continued throughout the empire until the mid-fifth century.

or the divine nature of Christ. Christian dogma insists upon a mysterious union of opposites: Jesus was fully human, yet absolutely and eternally divine.

Roman Catholic Christianity

Almost all Christians would agree with the notion that God came to the world in the person of Jesus Christ to teach men and women how they should live in this life in order to enjoy happiness in the next life. Most Christians also would agree that all knowledge necessary for salvation has been preserved in the words of the Bible. To whom, however, does one turn for definitive responses to important questions with seemingly multiple scriptural answers? The Roman Catholic Church answers this question differently than the other two major families within Christianity. Catholics believe not only that Christ established the Church to adjudicate between truth and error but also that the pope (the bishop of Rome), as the apostolic successor to St. Peter, is the earthly head of the Church. According to Catholic doctrine, the Holy Spirit protects the pope from communicating errors in select spiritual matters. Hence Catholics, unlike other Christians,

accept official statements of the pope as the definitive and infallible answers to questions of faith and morals.

A second notion central to Catholicism is the idea that God uses the sacraments of the church to empower the followers of Jesus to rise above those selfish instincts that inhibit them from holy living. At least since the twelfth century, the Roman Catholic Church has recognized seven sacraments. Each sacrament corresponds with either a great event in the life cycle or one of humanity's basic needs. Humans, for instance, are born, come of age, marry or dedicate themselves to some life purpose, and die. Meanwhile, they continuously are in need of being reconciled with those they offend and in need of physical nourishment. The sacraments parallel these natural events. Just as in birth a human enters the natural world, in *baptism* God envelops him or her in divine grace. After the baptized reaches maturity, he or she affirms his/her understanding of the faith in *confirmation,* and the baptism into God's grace is made complete. As an adult, he/she makes a life commitment to be joined with a spouse, *Holy Matrimony,* or dedicates himself entirely to God in priestly ministry, *Holy Orders.* As she or he nears death, the sacrament of healing, *The Anointing of the Sick,* prepares the soul for eternity.

Throughout all stages of life, humans rely on two sacraments for spiritual nourishment. When humans sin, they confess their sins to one of God's priests, and if the penitence is genuine, the sacrament of *Reconciliation* brings forgiveness. Finally, just as humans partake of food and drink for physical health, they must partake of the body and blood of Jesus for spiritual health. In the sacrament of the *Holy Eucharist,* the priest reenacts the Last Supper, when Christ gave his disciples bread and wine and said, "This is my body that is broken for you; . . . this is my blood that is shed for you." For Catholics, this sacrament is not simply a memorial of Christ's death. As the priest utters the words of consecration, a miracle occurs and the elements of the bread and wine are "transubstantiated" into the real body and blood of Christ. Through eating Christ's body and drinking his blood, Catholic souls are infused with God's supernatural grace that joins them with Christ and prepares them for eternity.

There are almost 1 billion Roman Catholics worldwide, including 75 million (about 30 percent of the Christian community) in North America.

The Eastern Orthodox Tradition

Regional tensions between Christians existed for centuries before the formal split between the Roman Catholic Church and the Eastern Orthodox Church took place in 1054 CE. The causes of the divide were numerous. Geographical and political rivalries and differences in language and culture contributed to the final break as much as religious and theological matters. In many ways, the two Christian families are very much alike. Both accept the definitions of the Godhead determined by the ecumenical councils. Both honor the same seven sacraments as the vehicles for the dispensation of God's grace. Both acknowledge that the Church has the responsibility to ensure that matters of faith do not disintegrate into conflicting claims of private interpretation.

The Eastern Church, however, differs from Roman Catholicism in polity and focus. Orthodox Christians consider ecumenical councils, not the pope, as the ultimate earthly authority of the Church and do not insist that the regular clergy be celibate. The Orthodox tradition also demands unanimity in belief on a more narrow range of issues than Roman Catholicism. According to the Orthodox, the Church can interpret doctrines contained in scripture, but it cannot initiate them. Consequently, while the Roman Catholic Church has issued dogmatic pronouncements on such matters as purgatory, indulgences, and the Immaculate Conception, the Eastern Church does not accept the validity of such suprascriptural doctrines.

Another distinctive attribute of the Eastern Church is the importance it places upon the use of holy icons as an aid to worship. The Eastern Church has long argued that because the Word of God came in the flesh, it is biblical and proper for Christians to venerate material objects that depict the incarnate deity. Worshipful Orthodox enter churches embellished with iconic murals and prostrate themselves before the holy icons, kissing them and burning candles before them. For the Orthodox, the sacred icons express the Word of God to the illiterate masses just as scripture depicts the Word to the literate. Perhaps to a greater degree than other Christians, the Orthodox encourage the faithful to experience the supernatural life while here on earth. The aim of life for Orthodox laity and clergy alike is to achieve a mystical union with God, to be deified by grace with the Divine.

Worldwide there are about 250 million communicants within the Eastern Orthodox connection. Major branches within the tradition include the Churches of Albania, Bulgaria, Georgia, Greece, Romania, Russia, Serbia, and Sinai. In North America, about 3 percent of the Christian community considers themselves Orthodox.

The Dynamics and Divisions of Protestantism

About a half millennium after the schism between the East and the West, the Catholic West again was divided by a religious revolution known as the Protestant Reformation. Like Christendom's first great schism, the Protestant Reformation was long in the making and a consequence of political as well as religious tensions. The uproar began on Halloween Day, 1517 CE, when a Catholic monk named Martin Luther nailed on the door of a cathedral in Wittenberg a list of 95 complaints against his beloved, yet corrupted church. Although not the first to register these complaints, Luther and his famous Ninety-Five Theses set in motion a reform movement that would fragment the Western church into numerous doctrinally diverse smaller bodies.

The major branches of Christianity emerged from Judaic roots in Hellenistic soil.

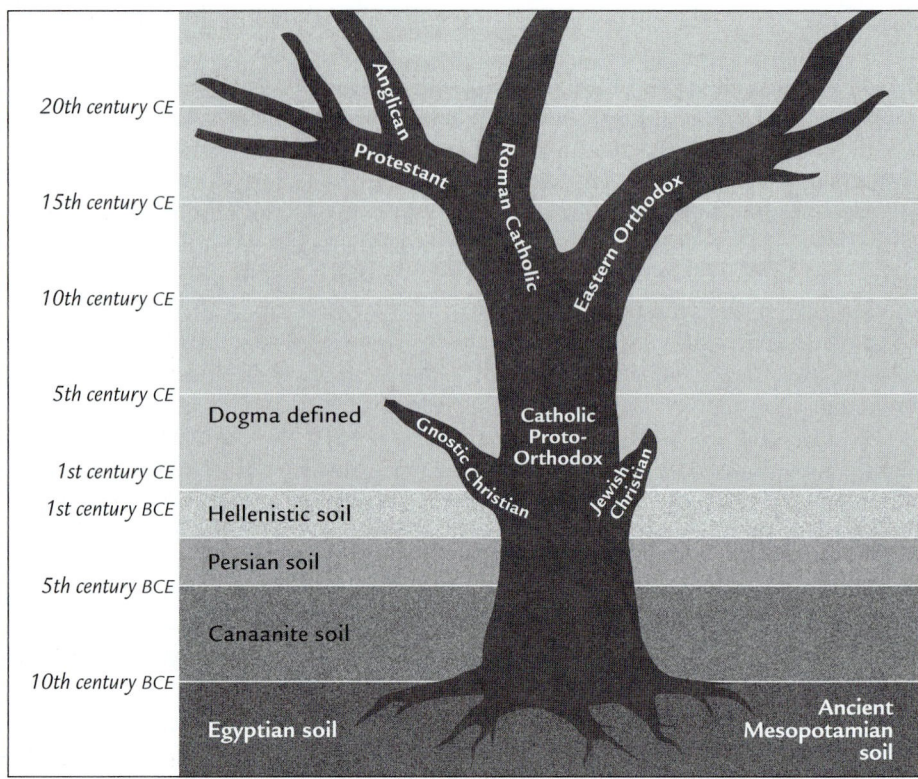

What began as an isolated challenge to the church's sale of indulgences (certificates that promised to reduce the time a soul must spend in purgatory) grew within a generation into a massive rebellion against the authority of the pope and against the sacramental system of the Roman Church. Two catch phrases of the Reformation were *sola scriptura* and *sola fides*. By the first phrase, the protesters or Protestants insisted that ultimate authority in the church rested on the words of scripture alone—not in the decisions of a pope or in the creeds of the ecumenical councils. The second phrase emphasized the Protestant idea that humans were incapable of meriting salvation through an accumulation of good deeds. No number of religious observances or righteous acts could earn sinful men and women a ticket to heaven. Salvation came only by God's gracious gift and only by faith in the saving grace of God.

The Protestant emphasis on an individual's responsibility to find truth in scripture and secure salvation through faith has led to the creation of almost 1,000 different Protestant denominations. More than 85 percent of all Protestants, however, belong to one of 12 larger denominations. There are some 750 million Protestants worldwide. In North America, nearly two in three Christians (more than 150 million) belong to some Protestant group.

SACRED OBSERVANCES AND PRACTICES

Like Jews, Christians affirm the tradition of a weekly Sabbath, although for most Christian denominations, this day of rest and worship is not the Jewish Sabbath but Sunday, the day of the week on which Christians believe Jesus was resurrected. Every week on this day Christians gather in churches to pray, sing, receive spiritual instructions from lay or ordained ministers, and on some occasions, remember the passion and death of Jesus by partaking in the sacrament of Holy Communion. Since the early nineteenth century, many Christians also attend "Sunday School," a weekly class of religious instruction. Most Christians initiate members into the faith through a rite known as water baptism, a tradition that corresponds with the Jewish practice of male circumcision but is offered to females and males alike. Within most Christian denominations, baptism occurs in infancy, but in other Christian groups, this sacrament is reserved only for more mature "believers" who have experienced "the saving grace" of life in Christ.

The liturgical calendar of most Christians focuses around two great seasons, Christmas and Easter. Christmas is the day that Christians commemorate the birth of Jesus. Most Christians in the West celebrate this event on December 25, while Eastern Orthodox churches celebrate the manifestation of Jesus Christ on January 6. Before Christmas is the season of Advent, a time of spiritual preparation for the coming of Christ. Following Christmas, many Christians observe a brief season of Epiphany that commemorates the baptism of Jesus and the visit of the Magi to Bethlehem.

The holiest day of the year for most Christians is Easter, the day that the resurrection of Christ is celebrated. For Western Christians, this day is observed on the first Sunday after the first full moon following the vernal equinox (March 21), although Eastern Christians use a different dating method and celebrate Easter on a different date, usually several weeks later. Preceding Easter is a season of fasting and prayer known as Lent. Following Easter, most Christian liturgies celebrate two feast days, Ascension Day, which commemorates the ascension of Jesus into the heavens, and Pentecost Sunday, the day that celebrates the coming of the Holy Spirit.

SOURCES

Most of the passages in this anthology of Christian writings come from the New Testament. No selections are included from the deuterocanon books. Twenty-four of the 27 New Testament books are represented.

SECTION 1: Beginnings: God, Time, and the Universe

Christianity embraces the creation accounts contained in the Hebrew Bible. In addition to these creation texts, the Christian New Testament includes a number of statements about cosmic beginnings and about the nature of God and the person of Jesus the Christ. In the fourth century, church councils formulated dogmas that defined the Godhead as a Trinity of Father, Son, and Holy Spirit. Later councils addressed and answered other speculative questions about the relationship between the human and divine natures of Christ. Although there have always been Christians who have rejected these "orthodox" teachings, Christian majorities throughout the centuries have affirmed the work of the ecumenical councils as summations of the biblical teachings concerning the nature of God.

The following New Testament texts are among the biblical sources that influenced the wording of the ecumenical creeds drafted in the fourth and fifth centuries. Based on these texts, how do you think first-century Christians would have answered questions about the nature of God and the nature of Christ?

DEPICTIONS OF CHRIST AS LOGOS IN THE PROLOGUE TO THE GOSPEL OF JOHN

Chapter 1

[1]In the beginning was the Word, and the Word was with God, and the Word was God. [2]He was with God in the beginning. [3]Through him all things were made; without him nothing was made that has been made. [4]In him was life, and that life was the light of men. [5]The light shines in the darkness, but the darkness has not understood it.
[6]There came a man who was sent from God; his name was John. [7]He came as a witness to testify concerning that light, so that through him all men might believe. [8]He himself was not the light; he came only as a witness to the light. [9]The true light that gives light to every man was coming into the world. [10]He was in the world, and though the world was made through him, the world did not recognize him. [11]He came to that which was his own, but his own did not receive him. [12]Yet to all who received him, to those who believed in his name, he gave the right to become children of God—[13]children born not of natural descent, nor of human decision or a husband's will, but born of God.
[14]The Word became flesh and made his dwelling among us. We have seen his glory, the glory of the One and Only who came from the Father, full of grace and truth.
[15]John testifies concerning him. He cries out, saying, "This was he of whom I said, 'He who comes after me has surpassed me because he was before me.'" [16]From the fullness of his grace we have all received one blessing after another. [17]For the law was given through Moses; grace and truth came through Jesus Christ. [18]No one has ever seen God, but God the One and Only, who is at the Father's side, has made him known.

Depictions of Christ in the Writings of Paul from the Book of Colossians

Chapter 1

¹⁵He is the image of the invisible God, the firstborn over all creation. ¹⁶For by him all things were created: things in heaven and on earth, visible and invisible, whether thrones or powers or rulers or authorities; all things were created by him and for him. ¹⁷He is before all things, and in him all things hold together. ¹⁸And he is the head of the body, the church; he is the beginning and the firstborn from among the dead, so that in everything he might have the supremacy. ¹⁹For God was pleased to have all his fullness dwell in him, ²⁰and through him to reconcile to himself all things, whether things on earth or things in heaven, by making peace through his blood, shed on the cross.

²¹Once you were alienated from God and were enemies in your minds because of your evil behavior. ²²But now he has reconciled you by Christ's physical body through death to present you holy in his sight, without blemish and free from accusation— ²³if you continue in your faith, established and firm, not moved from the hope held out in the gospel. This is the gospel that you heard and that has been proclaimed to every creature under heaven, and of which I, Paul, have become a servant.

Depictions of Christ in the Writings of Paul from the Book of Philippians

Chapter 2

⁵Your attitude should be the same as that of Christ Jesus: ⁶Who, being in very nature God, did not consider equality with God something to be grasped, ⁷but made himself nothing, taking the very nature of a servant, being made in human likeness. ⁸And being found in appearance as a man, he humbled himself and became obedient to death—even death on a cross! ⁹ Therefore God exalted him to the highest place and gave him the name that is above every name, ¹⁰that at the name of Jesus every knee should bow, in heaven and on earth and under the earth, ¹¹and every tongue confess that Jesus Christ is Lord, to the glory of God the Father.

Jesus Portrayed as the Great High Priest in the Epistle to the Hebrews

Chapter 4

¹⁴Therefore, since we have a great high priest who has gone through the heavens, Jesus the Son of God, let us hold firmly to the faith we profess. ¹⁵For we do not have a high priest who is unable to sympathize with our weaknesses, but we have one who has been tempted in every way, just as we are— yet was without sin. ¹⁶Let us then approach the throne of grace with confidence, so that we may receive mercy and find grace to help us in our time of need.

Chapter 5

¹Every high priest is selected from among men and is appointed to represent them in matters related to God, to offer gifts and sacrifices for sins. ²He is able to deal gently with those who are ignorant and are going astray, since he himself is subject to weakness.

³This is why he has to offer sacrifices for his own sins, as well as for the sins of the people.

⁴No one takes this honor upon himself; he must be called by God, just as Aaron was. ⁵So Christ also did not take upon himself the glory of becoming a high priest. But God said to him, "You are my Son; today I have become your Father." ⁶And he says in another place, "You are a priest forever, in the order of Melchizedek."

⁷During the days of Jesus' life on earth, he offered up prayers and petitions with loud cries and tears to the one who could save him from death, and he was heard because of his reverent submission. ⁸Although he was a son, he learned obedience from what he suffered ⁹and, once made perfect, he became the source of eternal salvation for all who obey him ¹⁰and was designated by God to be high priest in the order of Melchizedek.

The Loving Nature of God as Depicted in 1 John

Chapter 4

⁷Dear friends, let us love one another, for love comes from God. Everyone who loves has been born of God and knows God. ⁸Whoever does not love does not know God, because God is love. ⁹This is how God showed his love among us: He sent his one and only Son into the world that we might live through him. ¹⁰This is love: not that we loved God, but that he loved us and sent his Son as an atoning sacrifice for our sins. ¹¹Dear friends, since God so loved us, we also ought to love one another. ¹²No one has ever seen God; but if we love one another, God lives in us and his love is made complete in us.

¹³We know that we live in him and he in us, because he has given us of his Spirit. ¹⁴And we have seen and testify that the Father has sent his Son to be the Savior of the world. ¹⁵If anyone acknowledges that Jesus is the Son of God, God lives in him and he in God. ¹⁶And so we know and rely on the love God has for us. God is love. Whoever lives in love lives in God, and God in him. ¹⁷In this way, love is made complete among us so that we will have confidence on the day of judgment, because in this world we are like him. ¹⁸There is no fear in love. But perfect love drives out fear, because fear has to do with punishment. The one who fears is not made perfect in love.

¹⁹We love because he first loved us. ²⁰If anyone says, "I love God," yet hates his brother, he is a liar. For anyone who does

not love his brother, whom he has seen, cannot love God, whom he has not seen. ²¹And he has given us this command: Whoever loves God must also love his brother.

SECTION 2: Humanity: The Problem of Good and Evil

The Christian Old Testament presents humanity as a mixture of dust and divinity. Although humans are portrayed as made in the image of God, just a little lower than the angels, they also are depicted as frail and morally corruptible. Created for noble purposes, but given the freedom to make moral choices, humans often use this freedom to make selfish rather than righteous decisions. For these misdeeds, which the Judeo-Christian scriptures label as sins, humans stand in need of forgiveness from a creator God who is both just and merciful.

Some New Testament writers seem to reflect this Jewish understanding of the human condition. Other New Testament authors, most notably the apostle Paul, place a greater emphasis on total human depravity. For Paul, since the time of Adam humans have inherited a sin nature that taints them even before birth with the sins of their ancestors. Goodness by choice is not possibility. Without grace through faith in Christ, humans are incapable of performing good works and must face the penalty of sin, which is declared to be death.

The following selections from the Gospels, the works of Paul, and the epistles of John provide glimpses of New Testament understandings of the human predicament. Compare how each writer depicts the human condition. To what degree are humans free to make moral choices? Can these various points of view be reconciled?

DEPICTIONS OF THE HUMAN
CONDITION IN THE GOSPELS

From the Gospel of Matthew

Chapter 7

¹³"Enter through the narrow gate. For wide is the gate and broad is the road that leads to destruction, and many enter through it. ¹⁴But small is the gate and narrow the road that leads to life, and only a few find it.

¹⁵"Watch out for false prophets. They come to you in sheep's clothing, but inwardly they are ferocious wolves. ¹⁶By their fruit you will recognize them. Do people pick grapes from thornbushes, or figs from thistles? ¹⁷Likewise every good tree bears good fruit, but a bad tree bears bad fruit. ¹⁸A good tree cannot bear bad fruit, and a bad tree cannot bear good fruit. ¹⁹Every tree that does not bear good fruit is cut down and thrown into the fire. ²⁰Thus, by their fruit you will recognize them.

²¹"Not everyone who says to me, 'Lord, Lord,' will enter the kingdom of heaven, but only he who does the will of my Father who is in heaven. ²²Many will say to me on that day, 'Lord, Lord, did we not prophesy in your name, and in your name drive out demons and perform many miracles?' ²³Then I will tell them plainly, 'I never knew you. Away from me, you evildoers!'

²⁴"Therefore everyone who hears these words of mine and puts them into practice is like a wise man who built his house on the rock. ²⁵The rain came down, the streams rose, and the winds blew and beat against that house; yet it did not fall, because it had its foundation on the rock. ²⁶But everyone who hears these words of mine and does not put them into practice is like a foolish man who built his house on sand. ²⁷The rain came down, the streams rose, and the winds blew and beat against that house, and it fell with a great crash." ²⁸When Jesus had finished saying these things, the crowds were amazed at his teaching, ²⁹because he taught as one who had authority, and not as their teachers of the law.

FROM THE GOSPEL OF LUKE

Chapter 8

⁴While a large crowd was gathering and people were coming to Jesus from town after town, he told this parable: ⁵"A farmer went out to sow his seed. As he was scattering the seed, some fell along the path; it was trampled on, and the birds of the air ate it up. ⁶Some fell on rock, and when it came up, the plants withered because they had no moisture. ⁷Other seed fell among thorns, which grew up with it and choked the plants. ⁸Still other seed fell on good soil. It came up and yielded a crop, a hundred times more than was sown." When he said this, he called out, "He who has ears to hear, let him hear."

⁹His disciples asked him what this parable meant. ¹⁰He said, "The knowledge of the secrets of the kingdom of God has been given to you, but to others I speak in parables, so that, " 'though seeing, they may not see; though hearing, they may not understand.'

¹¹"This is the meaning of the parable: The seed is the word of God. ¹²Those along the path are the ones who hear, and then the devil comes and takes away the word from their hearts, so that they may not believe and be saved. ¹³Those on the rock are the ones who receive the word with joy when they hear it, but they have no root. They believe for a while, but in the time of testing they fall away. ¹⁴The seed that fell among thorns stands for those who hear, but as they go on

their way they are choked by life's worries, riches and pleasures, and they do not mature. [15]But the seed on good soil stands for those with a noble and good heart, who hear the word, retain it, and by persevering produce a crop.

DESCRIPTIONS OF THE HUMAN CONDITION IN THE WRITINGS OF PAUL

From the Book of Romans
Chapter 1

[18]The wrath of God is being revealed from heaven against all the godlessness and wickedness of men who suppress the truth by their wickedness, [19]since what may be known about God is plain to them, because God has made it plain to them. [20]For since the creation of the world God's invisible qualities—his eternal power and divine nature—have been clearly seen, being understood from what has been made, so that men are without excuse.

[21]For although they knew God, they neither glorified him as God nor gave thanks to him, but their thinking became futile and their foolish hearts were darkened. [22]Although they claimed to be wise, they became fools [23]and exchanged the glory of the immortal God for images made to look like mortal man and birds and animals and reptiles. [24]Therefore God gave them over in the sinful desires of their hearts to sexual impurity for the degrading of their bodies with one another. [25]They exchanged the truth of God for a lie, and worshiped and served created things rather than the Creator—who is forever praised. Amen.

[26]Because of this, God gave them over to shameful lusts. Even their women exchanged natural relations for unnatural ones. [27]In the same way the men also abandoned natural relations with women and were inflamed with lust for one another. Men committed indecent acts with other men, and received in themselves the due penalty for their perversion. [28]Furthermore, since they did not think it worthwhile to retain the knowledge of God, he gave them over to a depraved mind, to do what ought not to be done. [29]They have become filled with every kind of wickedness, evil, greed and depravity. They are full of envy, murder, strife, deceit and malice. They are gossips, [30]slanderers, Godhaters, insolent, arrogant and boastful; they invent ways of doing evil; they disobey their parents; [31]they are senseless, faithless, heartless, ruthless. [32]Although they know God's righteous decree that those who do such things deserve death, they not only continue to do these very things but also approve of those who practice them.

Chapter 3

[9]What shall we conclude then? Are we any better? Not at all! We have already made the charge that Jews and Gentiles alike are all under sin. [10]As it is written: "There is no one righteous,

not even one; [11]there is no one who understands, no one who seeks God. [12]All have turned away, they have together become worthless; there is no one who does good, not even one." [13]"Their throats are open graves; their tongues practice deceit." "The poison of vipers is on their lips." [14]"Their mouths are full of cursing and bitterness." [15]"Their feet are swift to shed blood; [16]ruin and misery mark their ways, [17]and the way of peace they do not know." [18]"There is no fear of God before their eyes."

[19]Now we know that whatever the law says, it says to those who are under the law, so that every mouth may be silenced and the whole world held accountable to God. [20]Therefore no one will be declared righteous in his sight by observing the law; rather, through the law we become conscious of sin. [21]But now a righteousness from God, apart from law, has been made known, to which the Law and the Prophets testify. [22]This righteousness from God comes through faith in Jesus Christ to all who believe. There is no difference, [23]for all have sinned and fall short of the glory of God,

DEPICTIONS OF THE HUMAN CONDITION IN 1 JOHN

Chapter 3

[1]How great is the love the Father has lavished on us, that we should be called children of God! And that is what we are! The reason the world does not know us is that it did not know him. [2]Dear friends, now we are children of God, and what we will be has not yet been made known. But we know that when he appears, we shall be like him, for we shall see him as he is. [3]Everyone who has this hope in him purifies himself, just as he is pure. [4]Everyone who sins breaks the law; in fact, sin is lawlessness. [5]But you know that he appeared so that he might take away our sins. And in him is no sin. [6]No one who lives in him keeps on sinning. No one who continues to sin has either seen him or known him. [7]Dear children, do not let anyone lead you astray. He who does what is right is righteous, just as he is righteous. [8]He who does what is sinful is of the devil, because the devil has been sinning from the beginning. The reason the Son of God appeared was to destroy the devil's work. [9]No one who is born of God will continue to sin, because God's seed remains in him; he cannot go on sinning, because he has been born of God. [10]This is how we know who the children of God are and who the children of the devil are: Anyone who does not do what is right is not a child of God; nor is anyone who does not love his brother. [11]This is the message you heard from the beginning: We should love one another. [12]Do not be like Cain, who belonged to the evil one and murdered his brother. And why did he murder him? Because his own actions were evil and his brother's were righteous. [13]Do not be surprised, my brothers, if the world hates you. [14]We know that we have passed from

death to life, because we love our brothers. Anyone who does not love remains in death. [15]Anyone who hates his brother is a murderer, and you know that no murderer has eternal life in him.

[16]This is how we know what love is: Jesus Christ laid down his life for us. And we ought to lay down our lives for our brothers. [17]If anyone has material possessions and sees his brother in need but has no pity on him, how can the love of God be in him? [18]Dear children, let us not love with words or tongue but with actions and in truth. [19]This then is how we know that we belong to the truth, and how we set our hearts at rest in his presence [20]whenever our hearts condemn us. For God is greater than our hearts, and he knows everything. [21]Dear friends, if our hearts do not condemn us, we have confidence before God [22]and receive from him anything we ask, because we obey his commands and do what pleases him. [23]And this is his command: to believe in the name of his Son, Jesus Christ, and to love one another as he commanded us. [24]Those who obey his commands live in him, and he in them. And this is how we know that he lives in us: We know it by the Spirit he gave us.

SECTION 3: Sacred Stories: Divine Messengers, Prophets, and Priests

The New Testament writers portrayed Jesus both as the Messiah (meaning "God's anointed one"—the coming King who would bring deliverance for his people) and as the Suffering Servant of the Lord whose vicarious suffering would bring healing and forgiveness. Although both of these concepts were introduced by the ancient Hebrew prophets and were well-known images among first-century Jews, the disciples of Jesus were the first to identify the vicarious death of the Suffering Servant with the promised Messiah. The first selection includes passages from the Old Testament Book of Isaiah. Most Jews consider the opening verses to be a reference to the "good king" Hezekiah. Since the early days of the church, however, Christians have interpreted these words to be prophecies of the birth and life of Jesus.

OLD TESTAMENT PROPHECIES FROM THE BOOK OF ISAIAH

Chapter 9

[6]For to us a child is born, to us a son is given, and the government will be on his shoulders. And he will be called Wonderful Counselor, Mighty God, Everlasting Father, Prince of Peace. [7] Of the increase of his government and peace there

will be no end. He will reign on David's throne and over his kingdom, establishing and upholding it with justice and righteousness from that time on and forever. The zeal of the LORD Almighty will accomplish this.

Chapter 52

[13]See, my servant will act wisely; he will be raised and lifted up and highly exalted. [14]Just as there were many who were appalled at him—his appearance was so disfigured beyond that of any man and his form marred beyond human likeness— [15]so will he sprinkle many nations, and kings will shut their mouths because of him. For what they were not told, they will see, and what they have not heard, they will understand.

Chapter 53

[1]Who has believed our message and to whom has the arm of the LORD been revealed?
[2]He grew up before him like a tender shoot, and like a root out of dry ground. He had no beauty or majesty to attract us to him, nothing in his appearance that we should desire him. [3]He was despised and rejected by men, a man of sorrows, and familiar with suffering. Like one from whom men hide their faces he was despised, and we esteemed him not. [4] Surely he took up our infirmities and carried our sorrows, yet we considered him stricken by God, smitten by him, and afflicted. [5] But he was pierced for our transgressions, he was crushed for our iniquities; the punishment that brought us peace was upon him, and by his wounds we are healed. [6]We all, like sheep, have gone astray, each of us has turned to his own way; and the LORD has laid on him the iniquity of us all. [7] He was oppressed and afflicted, yet he did not open his mouth; he was led like a lamb to the slaughter, and as a sheep before her shearers is silent, so he did not open his mouth. [8]By oppression and judgment he was taken away. And who can speak of his descendants? For he was cut off from the land of the living; for the transgression of my people he was stricken. [9]He was assigned a grave with the wicked, and with the rich in his death, though he had done no violence, nor was any deceit in his mouth. [10]Yet it was the LORD's will to crush him and cause him to suffer, and though the LORD makes his life a guilt offering, he will see his offspring and prolong his days, and the will of the LORD will prosper in his hand. [11]After the suffering of his soul, he will see the light of life and be satisfied; by his knowledge my righteous servant will justify many, and he will bear their iniquities.

The following selections from the Gospels and the Book of Acts recount well-known stories about Jesus and his followers. As you read these accounts, try to identify areas of similarity and diversity between the emerging Christian sect and the Jewish tradition of which Jesus was a part. In addition, ask yourself why these stories were important to the early church. How have these accounts influenced the development of the religion of Christianity?

THE BIRTH AND CHILDHOOD OF JESUS FROM THE GOSPEL OF LUKE

Chapter 2

[1]In those days Caesar Augustus issued a decree that a census should be taken of the entire Roman world. [2](This was the first census that took place while Quirinius was governor of Syria.) [3]And everyone went to his own town to register. [4]So Joseph also went up from the town of Nazareth in Galilee to Judea, to Bethlehem the town of David, because he belonged to the house and line of David. [5]He went there to register with Mary, who was pledged to be married to him and was expecting a child. [6]While they were there, the time came for the baby to be born, [7]and she gave birth to her firstborn, a son. She wrapped him in cloths and placed him in a manger, because there was no room for them in the inn.

[8]And there were shepherds living out in the fields nearby, keeping watch over their flocks at night. [9]An angel of the Lord appeared to them, and the glory of the Lord shone around them, and they were terrified. [10]But the angel said to them, "Do not be afraid. I bring you good news of great joy that will be for all the people. [11]Today in the town of David a Savior has been born to you; he is Christ the Lord. [12]This will be a sign to you: You will find a baby wrapped in cloths and lying in a manger." [13]Suddenly a great company of the heavenly host appeared with the angel, praising God and saying, [14]"Glory to God in the highest, and on earth peace to men on whom his favor rests."

[15]When the angels had left them and gone into heaven, the shepherds said to one another, "Let's go to Bethlehem and see this thing that has happened, which the Lord has told us about." [16]So they hurried off and found Mary and Joseph, and the baby, who was lying in the manger. [17]When they had seen him, they spread the word concerning what had been told them about this child, [18]and all who heard it were amazed at what the shepherds said to them. [19]But Mary treasured up all these things and pondered them in her heart. [20]The shepherds returned, glorifying and praising God for all the things they had heard and seen, which were just as they had been told.

[21]On the eighth day, when it was time to circumcise him, he was named Jesus, the name the angel had given him before he had been conceived. . . .

[40]And the child grew and became strong; he was filled with wisdom, and the grace of God was upon him.

[41]Every year his parents went to Jerusalem for the Feast of the Passover. [42]When he was twelve years old, they went up to the Feast, according to the custom. [43]After the Feast was over, while his parents were returning home, the boy Jesus stayed behind in Jerusalem, but they were unaware of it. [44]Thinking he was in their company, they traveled on for a day. Then they began looking for him among their relatives and friends. [45]When they did not find him, they went back to Jerusalem to look for him. [46]After three days they found him in the temple courts, sitting among the teachers, listening to them and asking them questions. [47]Everyone who heard him was amazed at his understanding and his answers. [48]When his parents saw him, they were astonished. His mother said to him, "Son, why have you treated us like this? Your father and I have been anxiously searching for you." [49]"Why were you searching for me?" he asked. "Didn't you know I had to be in my Father's house?" [50]But they did not understand what he was saying to them. [51]Then he went down to Nazareth with them and was obedient to them. But his mother treasured all these things in her heart. [52]And Jesus grew in wisdom and stature, and in favor with God and men.

THE BAPTISM AND TEMPTATION OF JESUS FROM THE GOSPEL OF MATTHEW

Chapter 3

[13]Then Jesus came from Galilee to the Jordan to be baptized by John. [14]But John tried to deter him, saying, "I need to be baptized by you, and do you come to me?" [15]Jesus replied, "Let it be so now; it is proper for us to do this to fulfill all righteousness." Then John consented.

[16]As soon as Jesus was baptized, he went up out of the water. At that moment heaven was opened, and he saw the Spirit of God descending like a dove and lighting on him. [17]And a voice from heaven said, "This is my Son, whom I love; with him I am well pleased."

Chapter 4

[1]Then Jesus was led by the Spirit into the desert to be tempted by the devil. [2]After fasting forty days and forty nights, he was hungry. [3]The tempter came to him and said, "If you are the Son of God, tell these stones to become bread." [4]Jesus answered, "It is written: 'Man does not live on bread alone, but on every word that comes from the mouth of God.' "

[5]Then the devil took him to the holy city and had him stand on the highest point of the temple. [6]"If you are the Son of God," he said, "throw yourself down. For it is written: " 'He will command his angels concerning you, and they will lift you up in their hands, so that you will not strike your foot against a stone.' " [7]Jesus answered him, "It is also written: 'Do not put the Lord your God to the test.' "

[8]Again, the devil took him to a very high mountain and showed him all the kingdoms of the world and their splendor. [9]"All this I will give you," he said, "if you will bow down and worship me." [10]Jesus said to him, "Away from me, Satan! For

it is written: 'Worship the Lord your God, and serve him only.' " [11]Then the devil left him, and angels came and attended him.

THE CRUCIFIXION AND RESURRECTION FROM THE GOSPEL OF JOHN

Chapter 19

[1]Then Pilate took Jesus and had him flogged. [2]The soldiers twisted together a crown of thorns and put it on his head. They clothed him in a purple robe [3]and went up to him again and again, saying, "Hail, king of the Jews!" And they struck him in the face.

[4]Once more Pilate came out and said to the Jews, "Look, I am bringing him out to you to let you know that I find no basis for a charge against him." [5]When Jesus came out wearing the crown of thorns and the purple robe, Pilate said to them, "Here is the man!" [6]As soon as the chief priests and their officials saw him, they shouted, "Crucify! Crucify!" But Pilate answered, "You take him and crucify him. As for me, I find no basis for a charge against him." [7]The Jews insisted, "We have a law, and according to that law he must die, because he claimed to be the Son of God." [8]When Pilate heard this, he was even more afraid, [9]and he went back inside the palace. "Where do you come from?" he asked Jesus, but Jesus gave him no answer. [10]"Do you refuse to speak to me?" Pilate said. "Don't you realize I have power either to free you or to crucify you?" [11]Jesus answered, "You would have no power over me if it were not given to you from above. Therefore the one who handed me over to you is guilty of a greater sin." [12]From then on, Pilate tried to set Jesus free, but the Jews kept shouting, "If you let this man go, you are no friend of Caesar. Anyone who claims to be a king opposes Caesar."

[13]When Pilate heard this, he brought Jesus out and sat down on the judge's seat at a place known as the Stone Pavement (which in Aramaic is Gabbatha). [14]It was the day of Preparation of Passover Week, about the sixth hour. "Here is your king," Pilate said to the Jews. [15]But they shouted, "Take him away! Take him away! Crucify him!" "Shall I crucify your king?" Pilate asked. "We have no king but Caesar," the chief priests answered. [16]Finally Pilate handed him over to them to be crucified. So the soldiers took charge of Jesus. [17]Carrying his own cross, he went out to the place of the Skull (which in Aramaic is called Golgotha). [18]Here they crucified him, and with him two others—one on each side and Jesus in the middle.

[19]Pilate had a notice prepared and fastened to the cross. It read: JESUS OF NAZARETH, THE KING OF THE JEWS. [20]Many of the Jews read this sign, for the place where Jesus was crucified was near the city, and the sign was written in Aramaic, Latin and Greek. [21]The chief priests of the Jews protested to Pilate, "Do not write 'The King of the Jews,' but that this man claimed to be king of the Jews." [22]Pilate answered, "What I have written, I have written."

[23]When the soldiers crucified Jesus, they took his clothes, dividing them into four shares, one for each of them, with the undergarment remaining. This garment was seamless, woven in one piece from top to bottom. [24]"Let's not tear it," they said to one another. "Let's decide by lot who will get it." This happened that the scripture might be fulfilled which said, "They divided my garments among them and cast lots for my clothing." So this is what the soldiers did.

[25]Near the cross of Jesus stood his mother, his mother's sister, Mary the wife of Clopas, and Mary Magdalene. [26]When Jesus saw his mother there, and the disciple whom he loved standing nearby, he said to his mother, "Dear woman, here is your son," [27]and to the disciple, "Here is your mother." From that time on, this disciple took her into his home.

[28]Later, knowing that all was now completed, and so that the Scripture would be fulfilled, Jesus said, "I am thirsty." [29]A jar of wine vinegar was there, so they soaked a sponge in it, put the sponge on a stalk of the hyssop plant, and lifted it to Jesus' lips. [30]When he had received the drink, Jesus said, "It is finished." With that, he bowed his head and gave up his spirit.

[31]Now it was the day of Preparation, and the next day was to be a special Sabbath. Because the Jews did not want the bodies left on the crosses during the Sabbath, they asked Pilate to have the legs broken and the bodies taken down. [32]The soldiers therefore came and broke the legs of the first man who had been crucified with Jesus, and then those of the other. [33]But when they came to Jesus and found that he was already dead, they did not break his legs. [34]Instead, one of the soldiers pierced Jesus' side with a spear, bringing a sudden flow of blood and water. [35]The man who saw it has given testimony, and his testimony is true. He knows that he tells the truth, and he testifies so that you also may believe. [36]These things happened so that the scripture would be fulfilled: "Not one of his bones will be broken," [37]and, as another scripture says, "They will look on the one they have pierced."

[38]Later, Joseph of Arimathea asked Pilate for the body of Jesus. Now Joseph was a disciple of Jesus, but secretly because he feared the Jews. With Pilate's permission, he came and took the body away. [39]He was accompanied by Nicodemus, the man who earlier had visited Jesus at night. Nicodemus brought a mixture of myrrh and aloes, about seventy-five pounds. [40]Taking Jesus' body, the two of them wrapped it, with the spices, in strips of linen. This was in accordance with Jewish burial customs. [41]At the place where Jesus was crucified, there was a garden, and in the garden a new tomb, in which no one had ever been laid. [42]Because it was the Jewish day of Preparation and since the tomb was nearby, they laid Jesus there.

Chapter 20

[1]Early on the first day of the week, while it was still dark, Mary Magdalene went to the tomb and saw that the stone had been removed from the entrance. [2]So she came running

to Simon Peter and the other disciple, the one Jesus loved, and said, "They have taken the Lord out of the tomb, and we don't know where they have put him!" [3]So Peter and the other disciple started for the tomb. [4]Both were running, but the other disciple outran Peter and reached the tomb first. [5]He bent over and looked in at the strips of linen lying there but did not go in. [6]Then Simon Peter, who was behind him, arrived and went into the tomb. He saw the strips of linen lying there, [7]as well as the burial cloth that had been around Jesus' head. The cloth was folded up by itself, separate from the linen. [8]Finally the other disciple, who had reached the tomb first, also went inside. He saw and believed. [9](They still did not understand from Scripture that Jesus had to rise from the dead.)

[10]Then the disciples went back to their homes, [11]but Mary stood outside the tomb crying. As she wept, she bent over to look into the tomb [12]and saw two angels in white, seated where Jesus' body had been, one at the head and the other at the foot. [13]They asked her, "Woman, why are you crying?" "They have taken my Lord away," she said, "and I don't know where they have put him." [14]At this, she turned around and saw Jesus standing there, but she did not realize that it was Jesus. [15]"Woman," he said, "why are you crying? Who is it you are looking for?" Thinking he was the gardener, she said, "Sir, if you have carried him away, tell me where you have put him, and I will get him." [16]Jesus said to her, "Mary." She turned toward him and cried out in Aramaic, "Rabboni!" (which means Teacher). [17]Jesus said, "Do not hold on to me, for I have not yet returned to the Father. Go instead to my brothers and tell them, 'I am returning to my Father and your Father, to my God and your God.'" [18]Mary Magdalene went to the disciples with the news: "I have seen the Lord!" And she told them that he had said these things to her.

[19]On the evening of that first day of the week, when the disciples were together, with the doors locked for fear of the Jews, Jesus came and stood among them and said, "Peace be with you!" [20]After he said this, he showed them his hands and side. The disciples were overjoyed when they saw the Lord. [21]Again Jesus said, "Peace be with you! As the Father has sent me, I am sending you." [22]And with that he breathed on them and said, "Receive the Holy Spirit. [23]If you forgive anyone his sins, they are forgiven; if you do not forgive them, they are not forgiven."

[24]Now Thomas (called Didymus), one of the Twelve, was not with the disciples when Jesus came. [25]So the other disciples told him, "We have seen the Lord!" But he said to them, "Unless I see the nail marks in his hands and put my finger where the nails were, and put my hand into his side, I will not believe it." [26]A week later his disciples were in the house again, and Thomas was with them. Though the doors were locked, Jesus came and stood among them and said, "Peace be with you!" [27]Then he said to Thomas, "Put your finger here; see my hands. Reach out your hand and put it into my side. Stop doubting and believe." [28]Thomas said to him, "My Lord and my God!" [29]Then Jesus told him, "Because you have seen me, you have believed; blessed are those who have not seen and yet have believed."

[30]Jesus did many other miraculous signs in the presence of his disciples, which are not recorded in this book. [31]But these are written that you may believe that Jesus is the Christ, the Son of God, and that by believing you may have life in his name.

FROM THE ASCENSION TO PENTECOST FROM THE BOOK OF ACTS

Chapter 1

[1]In my former book, Theophilus, I wrote about all that Jesus began to do and to teach [2]until the day he was taken up to heaven, after giving instructions through the Holy Spirit to the apostles he had chosen. [3]After his suffering, he showed himself to these men and gave many convincing proofs that he was alive. He appeared to them over a period of forty days and spoke about the kingdom of God. [4]On one occasion, while he was eating with them, he gave them this command: "Do not leave Jerusalem, but wait for the gift my Father promised, which you have heard me speak about. [5]For John baptized with water, but in a few days you will be baptized with the Holy Spirit."

[6]So when they met together, they asked him, "Lord, are you at this time going to restore the kingdom to Israel?" [7]He said to them: "It is not for you to know the times or dates the Father has set by his own authority. [8]But you will receive power when the Holy Spirit comes on you; and you will be my witnesses in Jerusalem, and in all Judea and Samaria, and to the ends of the earth." [9]After he said this, he was taken up before their very eyes, and a cloud hid him from their sight. [10]They were looking intently up into the sky as he was going, when suddenly two men dressed in white stood beside them. [11]"Men of Galilee," they said, "why do you stand here looking into the sky? This same Jesus, who has been taken from you into heaven, will come back in the same way you have seen him go into heaven."

[12]Then they returned to Jerusalem from the hill called the Mount of Olives, a Sabbath day's walk from the city. [13]When they arrived, they went upstairs to the room where they were staying. Those present were Peter, John, James and Andrew; Philip and Thomas, Bartholomew and Matthew; James son of Alphaeus and Simon the Zealot, and Judas son of James. [14]They all joined together constantly in prayer, along with the women and Mary the mother of Jesus, and with his brothers.

Chapter 2

[1]When the day of Pentecost came, they were all together in one place. [2]Suddenly a sound like the blowing of a violent wind came from heaven and filled the whole house where

they were sitting. ³They saw what seemed to be tongues of fire that separated and came to rest on each of them. ⁴All of them were filled with the Holy Spirit and began to speak in other tongues as the Spirit enabled them.

⁵Now there were staying in Jerusalem Godfearing Jews from every nation under heaven. ⁶When they heard this sound, a crowd came together in bewilderment, because each one heard them speaking in his own language. ⁷Utterly amazed, they asked: "Are not all these men who are speaking Galileans? ⁸Then how is it that each of us hears them in his own native language? ⁹Parthians, Medes and Elamites; residents of Mesopotamia, Judea and Cappadocia, Pontus and Asia, ¹⁰Phrygia and Pamphylia, Egypt and the parts of Libya near Cyrene; visitors from Rome ¹¹(both Jews and converts to Judaism) Cretans and Arabs—we hear them declaring the wonders of God in our own tongues!" ¹²Amazed and perplexed, they asked one another, "What does this mean?" ¹³Some, however, made fun of them and said, "They have had too much wine."

¹⁴Then Peter stood up with the Eleven, raised his voice and addressed the crowd: "Fellow Jews and all of you who live in Jerusalem, let me explain this to you; listen carefully to what I say. ¹⁵These men are not drunk, as you suppose. It's only nine in the morning! ¹⁶No, this is what was spoken by the prophet Joel: ¹⁷" 'In the last days, God says, I will pour out my Spirit on all people. Your sons and daughters will prophesy, your young men will see visions, your old men will dream dreams. ¹⁸Even on my servants, both men and women, I will pour out my Spirit in those days, and they will prophesy. ¹⁹I will show wonders in the heaven above and signs on the earth below, blood and fire and billows of smoke. ²⁰The sun will be turned to darkness and the moon to blood before the coming of the great and glorious day of the Lord. ²¹And everyone who calls on the name of the Lord will be saved.' " . . .

³⁷When the people heard this, they were cut to the heart and said to Peter and the other apostles, "Brothers, what shall we do?" ³⁸Peter replied, "Repent and be baptized, every one of you, in the name of Jesus Christ for the forgiveness of your sins. And you will receive the gift of the Holy Spirit. ³⁹The promise is for you and your children and for all who are far off—for all whom the Lord our God will call."

⁴⁰With many other words he warned them; and he pleaded with them, "Save yourselves from this corrupt generation." ⁴¹Those who accepted his message were baptized, and about three thousand were added to their number that day.

⁴²They devoted themselves to the apostles' teaching and to the fellowship, to the breaking of bread and to prayer. ⁴³Everyone was filled with awe, and many wonders and miraculous signs were done by the apostles. ⁴⁴All the believers were together and had everything in common. ⁴⁵Selling their possessions and goods, they gave to anyone as he had need. ⁴⁶Every day they continued to meet together in the temple courts. They broke bread in their homes and ate together

with glad and sincere hearts, ⁴⁷praising God and enjoying the favor of all the people. And the Lord added to their number daily those who were being saved.

THE CONVERSION OF PAUL FROM THE BOOK OF ACTS

Chapter 9

¹Meanwhile, Saul was still breathing out murderous threats against the Lord's disciples. He went to the high priest ²and asked him for letters to the synagogues in Damascus, so that if he found any there who belonged to the Way, whether men or women, he might take them as prisoners to Jerusalem. ³As he neared Damascus on his journey, suddenly a light from heaven flashed around him. ⁴He fell to the ground and heard a voice say to him, "Saul, Saul, why do you persecute me?" ⁵"Who are you, Lord?" Saul asked. "I am Jesus, whom you are persecuting," he replied. ⁶"Now get up and go into the city, and you will be told what you must do."

⁷The men traveling with Saul stood there speechless; they heard the sound but did not see anyone. ⁸Saul got up from the ground, but when he opened his eyes he could see nothing. So they led him by the hand into Damascus. ⁹For three days he was blind, and did not eat or drink anything.

¹⁰In Damascus there was a disciple named Ananias. The Lord called to him in a vision, "Ananias!" "Yes, Lord," he answered. ¹¹The Lord told him, "Go to the house of Judas on Straight Street and ask for a man from Tarsus named Saul, for he is praying. ¹²In a vision he has seen a man named Ananias come and place his hands on him to restore his sight." ¹³"Lord," Ananias answered, "I have heard many reports about this man and all the harm he has done to your saints in Jerusalem. ¹⁴And he has come here with authority from the chief priests to arrest all who call on your name." ¹⁵But the Lord said to Ananias, "Go! This man is my chosen instrument to carry my name before the Gentiles and their kings and before the people of Israel. ¹⁶I will show him how much he must suffer for my name."

¹⁷Then Ananias went to the house and entered it. Placing his hands on Saul, he said, "Brother Saul, the Lord—Jesus, who appeared to you on the road as you were coming here—has sent me so that you may see again and be filled with the Holy Spirit." ¹⁸Immediately, something like scales fell from Saul's eyes, and he could see again. He got up and was baptized, ¹⁹and after taking some food, he regained his strength. Saul spent several days with the disciples in Damascus. ²⁰At once he began to preach in the synagogues that Jesus is the Son of God. ²¹All those who heard him were astonished and asked, "Isn't he the man who raised havoc in Jerusalem among those who call on this name? And hasn't he come here to take them as prisoners to the chief priests?" ²²Yet Saul grew more and more powerful and baffled the Jews living in Damascus by proving that Jesus is the Christ.

SECTION 4: Divine Law: Justice, Reward, and Punishment

The opening selection contains passages from Matthew's account of Jesus's famous Sermon on the Mount. This sermon provides the most complete summary we have of Jesus's ethical expectations for his followers. In this discourse, Jesus insists that he is not presenting a new law, but rather, is pointing his hearers to the spiritual values that buttress the Jewish legal requirements. He reprimands "the teachers of the law" not because he views the law of Moses as evil, but because he believes the law was being interpreted in cruel and oppressive ways. The sermon opens with eight "Beatitudes" or qualities that are present within those who are citizens of the "kingdom of heaven." What standards of right and wrong does Jesus offer in this sermon? In what ways are these teachings consistent with those contained in the Hebrew Bible? What new insights about murder, adultery, divorce, oaths, and social justice does Jesus offer?

THE SERMON ON THE MOUNT
FROM THE GOSPEL OF MATTHEW

Chapter 5

[1]Now when he saw the crowds, he went up on a mountainside and sat down. His disciples came to him, [2]and he began to teach them saying: [3]"Blessed are the poor in spirit, for theirs is the kingdom of heaven. [4]Blessed are those who mourn, for they will be comforted. [5]Blessed are the meek, for they will inherit the earth. [6]Blessed are those who hunger and thirst for righteousness, for they will be filled. [7]Blessed are the merciful, for they will be shown mercy. [8]Blessed are the pure in heart, for they will see God. [9]Blessed are the peacemakers, for they will be called sons of God. [10]Blessed are those who are persecuted because of righteousness, for theirs is the kingdom of heaven. [11]Blessed are you when people insult you, persecute you and falsely say all kinds of evil against you because of me. [12]Rejoice and be glad, because great is your reward in heaven, for in the same way they persecuted the prophets who were before you.

[13]"You are the salt of the earth. But if the salt loses its saltiness, how can it be made salty again? It is no longer good for anything, except to be thrown out and trampled by men.

[14]"You are the light of the world. A city on a hill cannot be hidden. [15]Neither do people light a lamp and put it under a bowl. Instead they put it on its stand, and it gives light to everyone in the house. [16]In the same way, let your light shine before men, that they may see your good deeds and praise your Father in heaven.

[17]"Do not think that I have come to abolish the Law or the Prophets; I have not come to abolish them but to fulfill them. [18]I tell you the truth, until heaven and earth disappear, not the smallest letter, not the least stroke of a pen, will by any means disappear from the Law until everything is accomplished. [19]Anyone who breaks one of the least of these commandments and teaches others to do the same will be called least in the kingdom of heaven, but whoever practices and teaches these commands will be called great in the kingdom of heaven. [20]For I tell you that unless your righteousness surpasses that of the Pharisees and the teachers of the law, you will certainly not enter the kingdom of heaven.

[21]"You have heard that it was said to the people long ago, 'Do not murder, and anyone who murders will be subject to judgment.' [22]But I tell you that anyone who is angry with his brother will be subject to judgment. Again, anyone who says to his brother, 'Raca,' is answerable to the Sanhedrin. But anyone who says, 'You fool!' will be in danger of the fire of hell. [23]"Therefore, if you are offering your gift at the altar and there remember that your brother has something against you, [24]leave your gift there in front of the altar. First go and be reconciled to your brother; then come and offer your gift. [25]"Settle matters quickly with your adversary who is taking you to court. Do it while you are still with him on the way, or he may hand you over to the judge, and the judge may hand you over to the officer, and you may be thrown into prison. [26]I tell you the truth, you will not get out until you have paid the last penny.

[27]"You have heard that it was said, 'Do not commit adultery.' [28]But I tell you that anyone who looks at a woman lustfully has already committed adultery with her in his heart. [29]If your right eye causes you to sin, gouge it out and throw it away. It is better for you to lose one part of your body than for your whole body to be thrown into hell. [30]And if your right hand causes you to sin, cut it off and throw it away. It is better for you to lose one part of your body than for your whole body to go into hell.

[31]"It has been said, 'Anyone who divorces his wife must give her a certificate of divorce.' [32]But I tell you that anyone who divorces his wife, except for marital unfaithfulness, causes her to become an adulteress, and anyone who marries the divorced woman commits adultery.

[33]"Again, you have heard that it was said to the people long ago, 'Do not break your oath, but keep the oaths you have made to the Lord.' [34]But I tell you, Do not swear at all: either by heaven, for it is God's throne; [35]or by the earth, for it is his footstool; or by Jerusalem, for it is the city of the Great King. [36]And do not swear by your head, for you cannot make even one hair white or black. [37]Simply let your 'Yes' be 'Yes,' and your 'No,' 'No'; anything beyond this comes from the evil one.

[38]"You have heard that it was said, 'Eye for eye, and tooth for tooth.' [39]But I tell you, Do not resist an evil person. If someone strikes you on the right cheek, turn to him the other also. [40]And if someone wants to sue you and take your tunic, let

him have your cloak as well. ⁴¹If someone forces you to go one mile, go with him two miles. ⁴²Give to the one who asks you, and do not turn away from the one who wants to borrow from you.

⁴³"You have heard that it was said, 'Love your neighbor and hate your enemy.' ⁴⁴But I tell you: Love your enemies and pray for those who persecute you, ⁴⁵that you may be sons of your Father in heaven. He causes his sun to rise on the evil and the good, and sends rain on the righteous and the unrighteous. ⁴⁶If you love those who love you, what reward will you get? Are not even the tax collectors doing that? ⁴⁷And if you greet only your brothers, what are you doing more than others? Do not even pagans do that? ⁴⁸Be perfect, therefore, as your heavenly Father is perfect."

Chapter 6

¹⁹"Do not store up for yourselves treasures on earth, where moth and rust destroy, and where thieves break in and steal. ²⁰But store up for yourselves treasures in heaven, where moth and rust do not destroy, and where thieves do not break in and steal. ²¹For where your treasure is, there your heart will be also.

²²"The eye is the lamp of the body. If your eyes are good, your whole body will be full of light. ²³But if your eyes are bad, your whole body will be full of darkness. If then the light within you is darkness, how great is that darkness!

²⁴"No one can serve two masters. Either he will hate the one and love the other, or he will be devoted to the one and despise the other. You cannot serve both God and Money.

²⁵"Therefore I tell you, do not worry about your life, what you will eat or drink; or about your body, what you will wear. Is not life more important than food, and the body more important than clothes? ²⁶Look at the birds of the air; they do not sow or reap or store away in barns, and yet your heavenly Father feeds them. Are you not much more valuable than they? ²⁷Who of you by worrying can add a single hour to his life? ²⁸And why do you worry about clothes? See how the lilies of the field grow. They do not labor or spin. ²⁹Yet I tell you that not even Solomon in all his splendor was dressed like one of these. ³⁰If that is how God clothes the grass of the field, which is here today and tomorrow is thrown into the fire, will he not much more clothe you, O you of little faith? ³¹So do not worry, saying, 'What shall we eat?' or 'What shall we drink?' or 'What shall we wear?' ³²For the pagans run after all these things, and your heavenly Father knows that you need them. ³³But seek first his kingdom and his righteousness, and all these things will be given to you as well. ³⁴Therefore do not worry about tomorrow, for tomorrow will worry about itself. Each day has enough trouble of its own."

Perhaps the New Testament writer most interested in offering a reinterpretation of the Jewish law was the apostle Paul. The following passage from the Letter to the Galatians illustrates Paul's contempt toward those who would have Christians submit to the legal requirements of Jewish law and customs. The next passage from Paul's letter to the Romans outlines how Christians freed from the Law should live in response to God's grace. According to Paul, what is the purpose of the Mosaic Law? What is expected of those who live under grace in Christ?

> PAUL'S INTERPRETATION OF THE PURPOSE OF THE
> JEWISH LAW FROM THE BOOK OF GALATIANS

Chapter 3

¹You foolish Galatians! Who has bewitched you? Before your very eyes Jesus Christ was clearly portrayed as crucified. ²I would like to learn just one thing from you: Did you receive the Spirit by observing the law, or by believing what you heard? ³Are you so foolish? After beginning with the Spirit, are you now trying to attain your goal by human effort? ⁴Have you suffered so much for nothing—if it really was for nothing? ⁵Does God give you his Spirit and work miracles among you because you observe the law, or because you believe what you heard?

⁶Consider Abraham: "He believed God, and it was credited to him as righteousness."

⁷ Understand, then, that those who believe are children of Abraham. ⁸The Scripture foresaw that God would justify the Gentiles by faith, and announced the gospel in advance to Abraham: "All nations will be blessed through you." ⁹So those who have faith are blessed along with Abraham, the man of faith.

¹⁰All who rely on observing the law are under a curse, for it is written: "Cursed is everyone who does not continue to do everything written in the Book of the Law." ¹¹Clearly no one is justified before God by the law, because, "The righteous will live by faith." ¹²The law is not based on faith; on the contrary, "The man who does these things will live by them." ¹³Christ redeemed us from the curse of the law by becoming a curse for us, for it is written: "Cursed is everyone who is hung on a tree." ¹⁴He redeemed us in order that the blessing given to Abraham might come to the Gentiles through Christ Jesus, so that by faith we might receive the promise of the Spirit.

¹⁵Brothers, let me take an example from everyday life. Just as no one can set aside or add to a human covenant that has been duly established, so it is in this case. ¹⁶The promises were spoken to Abraham and to his seed. The Scripture does not say "and to seeds," meaning many people, but "and to your seed," meaning one person, who is Christ. ¹⁷What I mean is this: The law, introduced 430 years later, does not set aside the covenant previously established by God and thus do away with the promise. ¹⁸For if the inheritance depends on the law, then it no longer depends on a promise; but God in his grace gave it to Abraham through a promise.

[19]What, then, was the purpose of the law? It was added because of transgressions until the Seed to whom the promise referred had come. The law was put into effect through angels by a mediator. [20]A mediator, however, does not represent just one party; but God is one. [21]Is the law, therefore, opposed to the promises of God? Absolutely not! For if a law had been given that could impart life, then righteousness would certainly have come by the law. [22]But the Scripture declares that the whole world is a prisoner of sin, so that what was promised, being given through faith in Jesus Christ, might be given to those who believe.

[23]Before this faith came, we were held prisoners by the law, locked up until faith should be revealed. [24]So the law was put in charge to lead us to Christ that we might be justified by faith. [25]Now that faith has come, we are no longer under the supervision of the law. [26]You are all sons of God through faith in Christ Jesus, [27]for all of you who were baptized into Christ have clothed yourselves with Christ. [28]There is neither Jew nor Greek, slave nor free, male nor female, for you are all one in Christ Jesus. [29]If you belong to Christ, then you are Abraham's seed, and heirs according to the promise.

A CHRISTIAN CODE OF CONDUCT FROM THE BOOK OF ROMANS

Chapter 12

[1]Therefore, I urge you, brothers, in view of God's mercy, to offer your bodies as living sacrifices, holy and pleasing to God—this is your spiritual act of worship. [2]Do not conform any longer to the pattern of this world, but be transformed by the renewing of your mind. Then you will be able to test and approve what God's will is—his good, pleasing and perfect will. [3]For by the grace given me I say to every one of you: Do not think of yourself more highly than you ought, but rather think of yourself with sober judgment, in accordance with the measure of faith God has given you. [4]Just as each of us has one body with many members, and these members do not all have the same function, [5]so in Christ we who are many form one body, and each member belongs to all the others. [6]We have different gifts, according to the grace given us. If a man's gift is prophesying, let him use it in proportion to his faith. [7]If it is serving, let him serve; if it is teaching, let him teach; [8]if it is encouraging, let him encourage; if it is contributing to the needs of others, let him give generously; if it is leadership, let him govern diligently; if it is showing mercy, let him do it cheerfully.

[9]Love must be sincere. Hate what is evil; cling to what is good. [10]Be devoted to one another in brotherly love. Honor one another above yourselves. [11]Never be lacking in zeal, but keep your spiritual fervor, serving the Lord. [12]Be joyful in hope, patient in affliction, faithful in prayer. [13]Share with God's people who are in need. Practice hospitality. [14]Bless those who persecute you; bless and do not curse. [15]Rejoice with those who rejoice; mourn with those who mourn. [16]Live in harmony with one another. Do not be proud, but be willing to associate with people of low position. Do not be conceited. [17]Do not repay anyone evil for evil. Be careful to do what is right in the eyes of everybody. [18]If it is possible, as far as it depends on you, live at peace with everyone. [19]Do not take revenge, my friends, but leave room for God's wrath, for it is written: "It is mine to avenge; I will repay," says the Lord. [20]On the contrary: "If your enemy is hungry, feed him; if he is thirsty, give him something to drink. In doing this, you will heap burning coals on his head." [21]Do not be overcome by evil, but overcome evil with good.

SECTION 5: Gender: Women and Men in Society

Some view Christian scripture as an abominable leash that has chained women to inferior social conditions for thousands of years. Others consider the Bible as a liberating source book that has inspired reformers of many generations to challenge those traditional dehumanizing customs that brutalize or marginalize women. In truth, for many centuries people have used the Bible to justify both the enslavement and the liberation of women. This paradox, no doubt, is in part the result of ignorance and selfishness. It also may be a result of ambiguities within Christian scriptures about the place of women in society.

The selections in this section include stories from the gospels that involve Jesus and his ministry among women and passages from several epistles containing familial instructions that the early church believed were written by Paul and Peter. As you read each text, try to determine the degree to which the message embraces and/or challenges the gender mores of the first century. Do the authors always agree? If so, what is that central teaching? If not, how do you account for the differences?

LUKE'S ACCOUNTS OF JESUS'S MINISTRY AMONG WOMEN

Chapter 7

[36]Now one of the Pharisees invited Jesus to have dinner with him, so he went to the Pharisee's house and reclined at the table. [37]When a woman who had lived a sinful life in that town learned that Jesus was eating at the Pharisee's house, she brought an alabaster jar of perfume, [38]and as she stood

behind him at his feet weeping, she began to wet his feet with her tears. Then she wiped them with her hair, kissed them and poured perfume on them. [39]When the Pharisee who had invited him saw this, he said to himself, "If this man were a prophet, he would know who is touching him and what kind of woman she is—that she is a sinner." [40]Jesus answered him, "Simon, I have something to tell you." "Tell me, teacher," he said. [41]"Two men owed money to a certain moneylender. One owed him five hundred denarii, and the other fifty. [42]Neither of them had the money to pay him back, so he canceled the debts of both. Now which of them will love him more?" [43]Simon replied, "I suppose the one who had the bigger debt canceled." "You have judged correctly," Jesus said. [44]Then he turned toward the woman and said to Simon, "Do you see this woman? I came into your house. You did not give me any water for my feet, but she wet my feet with her tears and wiped them with her hair. [45]You did not give me a kiss, but this woman, from the time I entered, has not stopped kissing my feet. [46]You did not put oil on my head, but she has poured perfume on my feet. [47]Therefore, I tell you, her many sins have been forgiven—for she loved much. But he who has been forgiven little loves little." [48]Then Jesus said to her, "Your sins are forgiven." [49]The other guests began to say among themselves, "Who is this who even forgives sins?" [50]Jesus said to the woman, "Your faith has saved you; go in peace."

Chapter 8

[1]After this, Jesus traveled about from one town and village to another, proclaiming the good news of the kingdom of God. The Twelve were with him, [2]and also some women who had been cured of evil spirits and diseases: Mary (called Magdalene) from whom seven demons had come out; [3]Joanna the wife of Cuza, the manager of Herod's household; Susanna; and many others. These women were helping to support them out of their own means.

Chapter 20

[45]While all the people were listening, Jesus said to his disciples, [46]"Beware of the teachers of the law. They like to walk around in flowing robes and love to be greeted in the marketplaces and have the most important seats in the synagogues and the places of honor at banquets. [47]They devour widows' houses and for a show make lengthy prayers. Such men will be punished most severely."

Chapter 21

[1]As he looked up, Jesus saw the rich putting their gifts into the temple treasury. [2]He also saw a poor widow put in two very small copper coins. [3]"I tell you the truth," he said, "this poor widow has put in more than all the others. [4]All these people gave their gifts out of their wealth; but she out of her poverty put in all she had to live on."

Chapter 23

[55]The women who had come with Jesus from Galilee followed Joseph and saw the tomb and how his body was laid in it. [56]Then they went home and prepared spices and perfumes. But they rested on the Sabbath in obedience to the commandment.

Chapter 24

[1]On the first day of the week, very early in the morning, the women took the spices they had prepared and went to the tomb. [2]They found the stone rolled away from the tomb, [3]but when they entered, they did not find the body of the Lord Jesus. [4]While they were wondering about this, suddenly two men in clothes that gleamed like lightning stood beside them. [5]In their fright the women bowed down with their faces to the ground, but the men said to them, "Why do you look for the living among the dead? [6]He is not here; he has risen! Remember how he told you, while he was still with you in Galilee: [7]'The Son of Man must be delivered into the hands of sinful men, be crucified and on the third day be raised again.'" [8]Then they remembered his words. [9]When they came back from the tomb, they told all these things to the Eleven and to all the others. [10]It was Mary Magdalene, Joanna, Mary the mother of James, and the others with them who told this to the apostles. [11]But they did not believe the women, because their words seemed to them like nonsense.

JESUS AND THE SAMARITAN WOMAN FROM THE GOSPEL OF JOHN

Chapter 4

[1]The Pharisees heard that Jesus was gaining and baptizing more disciples than John, [2]although in fact it was not Jesus who baptized, but his disciples. [3]When the Lord learned of this, he left Judea and went back once more to Galilee. [4]Now he had to go through Samaria. [5]So he came to a town in Samaria called Sychar, near the plot of ground Jacob had given to his son Joseph. [6]Jacob's well was there, and Jesus, tired as he was from the journey, sat down by the well. It was about the sixth hour.

[7]When a Samaritan woman came to draw water, Jesus said to her, "Will you give me a drink?" [8](His disciples had gone into the town to buy food.) [9]The Samaritan woman said to him, "You are a Jew and I am a Samaritan woman. How can you ask me for a drink?" (For Jews do not associate with Samaritans.)

[10]Jesus answered her, "If you knew the gift of God and who it is that asks you for a drink, you would have asked him and he would have given you living water." [11]"Sir," the woman said, "you have nothing to draw with and the well is deep. Where can you get this living water? [12]Are you greater than our father Jacob, who gave us the well and

drank from it himself, as did also his sons and his flocks and herds?" [13]Jesus answered, "Everyone who drinks this water will be thirsty again, [14]but whoever drinks the water I give him will never thirst. Indeed, the water I give him will become in him a spring of water welling up to eternal life." [15]The woman said to him, "Sir, give me this water so that I won't get thirsty and have to keep coming here to draw water." [16]He told her, "Go, call your husband and come back." [17]"I have no husband," she replied. Jesus said to her, "You are right when you say you have no husband. [18]The fact is, you have had five husbands, and the man you now have is not your husband. What you have just said is quite true." [19]"Sir," the woman said, "I can see that you are a prophet. [20]Our fathers worshiped on this mountain, but you Jews claim that the place where we must worship is in Jerusalem." [21]Jesus declared, "Believe me, woman, a time is coming when you will worship the Father neither on this mountain nor in Jerusalem. [22]You Samaritans worship what you do not know; we worship what we do know, for salvation is from the Jews. [23]Yet a time is coming and has now come when the true worshipers will worship the Father in spirit and truth, for they are the kind of worshipers the Father seeks. [24]God is spirit, and his worshipers must worship in spirit and in truth." [25]The woman said, "I know that Messiah" (called Christ) "is coming. When he comes, he will explain everything to us." [26]Then Jesus declared, "I who speak to you am he."

[27]Just then his disciples returned and were surprised to find him talking with a woman. But no one asked, "What do you want?" or "Why are you talking with her?" [28]Then, leaving her water jar, the woman went back to the town and said to the people, [29]"Come, see a man who told me everything I ever did. Could this be the Christ?" [30]They came out of the town and made their way toward him. [31]Meanwhile his disciples urged him, "Rabbi, eat something." [32]But he said to them, "I have food to eat that you know nothing about." [33]Then his disciples said to each other, "Could someone have brought him food?" [34]"My food," said Jesus, "is to do the will of him who sent me and to finish his work.[35]Do you not say, 'Four months more and then the harvest'? I tell you, open your eyes and look at the fields! They are ripe for harvest. [36]Even now the reaper draws his wages, even now he harvests the crop for eternal life, so that the sower and the reaper may be glad together. [37]Thus the saying 'One sows and another reaps' is true. [38]I sent you to reap what you have not worked for. Others have done the hard work, and you have reaped the benefits of their labor."

[39]Many of the Samaritans from that town believed in him because of the woman's testimony, "He told me everything I ever did." [40]So when the Samaritans came to him, they urged him to stay with them, and he stayed two days. [41]And because of his words many more became believers. [42]They said to the woman, "We no longer believe just because of what you said; now we have heard for ourselves, and we know that this man really is the Savior of the world."

JESUS AND THE ADULTEROUS WOMAN FROM THE GOSPEL OF JOHN

Chapter 8

[1]But Jesus went to the Mount of Olives. [2]At dawn he appeared again in the temple courts, where all the people gathered around him, and he sat down to teach them. [3]The teachers of the law and the Pharisees brought in a woman caught in adultery. They made her stand before the group [4]and said to Jesus, "Teacher, this woman was caught in the act of adultery. [5]In the Law Moses commanded us to stone such women. Now what do you say?" [6]They were using this question as a trap, in order to have a basis for accusing him. But Jesus bent down and started to write on the ground with his finger. [7]When they kept on questioning him, he straightened up and said to them, "If any one of you is without sin, let him be the first to throw a stone at her." [8]Again he stooped down and wrote on the ground.

[9]At this, those who heard began to go away one at a time, the older ones first, until only Jesus was left, with the woman still standing there. [10]Jesus straightened up and asked her, "Woman, where are they? Has no one condemned you?" [11]"No one, sir," she said. "Then neither do I condemn you," Jesus declared. "Go now and leave your life of sin."

JESUS'S TEACHINGS ABOUT MARRIAGE, CHILDREN, AND DIVORCE FROM THE GOSPEL OF MARK

Chapter 10

[1]Jesus then left that place and went into the region of Judea and across the Jordan. Again crowds of people came to him, and as was his custom, he taught them. [2]Some Pharisees came and tested him by asking, "Is it lawful for a man to divorce his wife?" [3]"What did Moses command you?" he replied. [4]They said, "Moses permitted a man to write a certificate of divorce and send her away." [5]"It was because your hearts were hard that Moses wrote you this law," Jesus replied. [6]"But at the beginning of creation God 'made them male and female.' [7]For this reason a man will leave his father and mother and be united to his wife, [8]and the two will become one flesh.' So they are no longer two, but one. [9]Therefore what God has joined together, let man not separate." [10]When they were in the house again, the disciples asked Jesus about this. [11]He answered, "Anyone who divorces his wife and marries another woman commits adultery against her. [12]And if she divorces her husband and marries another man, she commits adultery."

[13]People were bringing little children to Jesus to have him touch them, but the disciples rebuked them. [14]When Jesus saw this, he was indignant. He said to them, "Let the little children come to me, and do not hinder them, for the kingdom of God belongs to such as these. [15]I tell you the truth,

anyone who will not receive the kingdom of God like a little child will never enter it." [16]And he took the children in his arms, put his hands on them and blessed them.

FAMILIAL INSTRUCTIONS IN EPISTLES ATTRIBUTED TO PAUL[4]

From the Letter to the Romans

Chapter 16

[1]I commend to you our sister Phoebe, a servant of the church in Cenchrea. [2]I ask you to receive her in the Lord in a way worthy of the saints and to give her any help she may need from you, for she has been a great help to many people, including me. [3]Greet Priscilla and Aquila, my fellow workers in Christ Jesus. [4]They risked their lives for me. Not only I but all the churches of the Gentiles are grateful to them. [5]Greet also the church that meets at their house. Greet my dear friend Epenetus, who was the first convert to Christ in the province of Asia. [6]Greet Mary, who worked very hard for you.

From 1 Corinthians

Chapter 11

[3]Now I want you to realize that the head of every man is Christ, and the head of the woman is man, and the head of Christ is God. [4]Every man who prays or prophesies with his head covered dishonors his head. [5]And every woman who prays or prophesies with her head uncovered dishonors her head—it is just as though her head were shaved. [6]If a woman does not cover her head, she should have her hair cut off; and if it is a disgrace for a woman to have her hair cut or shaved off, she should cover her head. [7]A man ought not to cover his head, since he is the image and glory of God; but the woman is the glory of man. [8]For man did not come from woman, but woman from man; [9]neither was man created for woman, but woman for man. [10]For this reason, and because of the angels, the woman ought to have a sign of authority on her head. [11]In the Lord, however, woman is not independent of man, nor is man independent of woman. [12]For as woman came from man, so also man is born of woman. But everything comes from God. [13]Judge for yourselves: Is it proper for a woman to pray to God with her head uncovered? [14]Does not the very nature of things teach you that if a man has long hair, it is a disgrace to him, [15]but that if a woman has long hair, it is her glory? For long hair is given to her as a covering. [16]If anyone wants to be contentious about this, we have no other practice—nor do the churches of God.

---

[4] Most scholars attest that Paul was the author of Romans and 1 Corinthians, although many scholars question the Pauline authenticity of Ephesians and 1 Timothy.

From 1 Timothy

Chapter 2

[8]I want men everywhere to lift up holy hands in prayer, without anger or disputing. [9]I also want women to dress modestly, with decency and propriety, not with braided hair or gold or pearls or expensive clothes, [10]but with good deeds, appropriate for women who profess to worship God. [11]A woman should learn in quietness and full submission. [12]I do not permit a woman to teach or to have authority over a man; she must be silent. [13]For Adam was formed first, then Eve. [14]And Adam was not the one deceived; it was the woman who was deceived and became a sinner. [15]But women will be saved through childbearing—if they continue in faith, love and holiness with propriety.

From the Letter to the Ephesians

Chapter 5

[21]Submit to one another out of reverence for Christ. [22]Wives, submit to your husbands as to the Lord. [23]For the husband is the head of the wife as Christ is the head of the church, his body, of which he is the Savior. [24]Now as the church submits to Christ, so also wives should submit to their husbands in everything. [25]Husbands, love your wives, just as Christ loved the church and gave himself up for her [26]to make her holy, cleansing her by the washing with water through the word, [27]and to present her to himself as a radiant church, without stain or wrinkle or any other blemish, but holy and blameless. [28]In this same way, husbands ought to love their wives as their own bodies. He who loves his wife loves himself. [29]After all, no one ever hated his own body, but he feeds and cares for it, just as Christ does the church— [30]for we are members of his body. [31]"For this reason a man will leave his father and mother and be united to his wife, and the two will become one flesh." [32]This is a profound mystery—but I am talking about Christ and the church. [33]However, each one of you also must love his wife as he loves himself, and the wife must respect her husband.

Chapter 6

[1]Children, obey your parents in the Lord, for this is right. [2]"Honor your father and mother"—which is the first commandment with a promise— [3]"that it may go well with you and that you may enjoy long life on the earth." [4]Fathers, do not exasperate your children; instead, bring them up in the training and instruction of the Lord. [5]Slaves, obey your earthly masters with respect and fear, and with sincerity of heart, just as you would obey Christ. [6]Obey them not only to win their favor when their eye is on you, but like slaves of Christ, doing the will of God from your heart. [7]Serve wholeheartedly, as if you were serving the Lord, not men, [8]because you know that the Lord will reward everyone for whatever good he does, whether he is slave or free. [9]And masters, treat

your slaves in the same way. Do not threaten them, since you know that he who is both their Master and yours is in heaven, and there is no favoritism with him.

FAMILIAL INSTRUCTIONS IN THE BOOK OF 1 PETER

Chapter 3

[1]Wives, in the same way be submissive to your husbands so that, if any of them do not believe the word, they may be won over without words by the behavior of their wives, [2]when they see the purity and reverence of your lives. [3]Your beauty should not come from outward adornment, such as braided hair and the wearing of gold jewelry and fine clothes. [4]Instead, it should be that of your inner self, the unfading beauty of a gentle and quiet spirit, which is of great worth in God's sight. [5]For this is the way the holy women of the past who put their hope in God used to make themselves beautiful. They were submissive to their own husbands, [6]like Sarah, who obeyed Abraham and called him her master. You are her daughters if you do what is right and do not give way to fear. [7]Husbands, in the same way be considerate as you live with your wives, and treat them with respect as the weaker partner and as heirs with you of the gracious gift of life, so that nothing will hinder your prayers. [8]Finally, all of you, live in harmony with one another; be sympathetic, love as brothers, be compassionate and humble. [9]Do not repay evil with evil or insult with insult, but with blessing, because to this you were called so that you may inherit a blessing.

SECTION 6: Daily Living: Health, Etiquette, and Holy Days

Most ancient cultures set side special holy days during the year to honor the gods and to commemorate important religious events. During the period of Roman ascendancy, for instance, state authorities designated more than 100 days a year for Roman religious ceremonies. In first-century Palestine, however, it was the Hebrew sacred calendar, not the Roman calendar, that influenced everyday activities. Of great importance to the Jews was the weekly Sabbath, the only Jewish holiday whose observance was mandated in the Ten Commandments. Also important were seasonal festivals such as Passover, *Shavuot* (Pentecost), and *Sukkot* (the Feast of Tabernacles).

Jesus understood these holy occasions differently than many of his contemporaries and, as a result, often found himself in conflict with the Pharisees who insisted upon a strict observance of the holy days. The following passages from the Gospels contain some of Jesus's comments about Jewish ritual observances. What is the central message in these teachings? In what ways did this message differ from the teachings of the Pharisees? From the point of view of the Pharisees, in what ways did Jesus threaten sacred customs that were grounded in the Hebrew Bible?

JESUS'S TEACHINGS ON THE MEANING OF THE SABBATH FROM THE GOSPEL OF MARK

Chapter 2

[23]One Sabbath Jesus was going through the grainfields, and as his disciples walked along, they began to pick some heads of grain. [24]The Pharisees said to him, "Look, why are they doing what is unlawful on the Sabbath?" [25]He answered, "Have you never read what David did when he and his companions were hungry and in need? [26]In the days of Abiathar the high priest, he entered the house of God and ate the consecrated bread, which is lawful only for priests to eat. And he also gave some to his companions." [27]Then he said to them, "The Sabbath was made for man, not man for the Sabbath. [28]So the Son of Man is Lord even of the Sabbath."

Chapter 3

[1]Another time he went into the synagogue, and a man with a shriveled hand was there. [2]Some of them were looking for a reason to accuse Jesus, so they watched him closely to see if he would heal him on the Sabbath. [3]Jesus said to the man with the shriveled hand, "Stand up in front of everyone." [4]Then Jesus asked them, "Which is lawful on the Sabbath: to do good or to do evil, to save life or to kill?" But they remained silent. [5]He looked around at them in anger and, deeply distressed at their stubborn hearts, said to the man, "Stretch out your hand." He stretched it out, and his hand was completely restored.

JESUS CONFRONTS THE PHARISEES REGARDING RITUAL OBSERVANCES FROM THE GOSPEL OF MARK

Chapter 7

[1]The Pharisees and some of the teachers of the law who had come from Jerusalem gathered around Jesus and [2]saw some of his disciples eating food with hands that were "unclean," that is, unwashed. [3](The Pharisees and all the Jews do not eat unless they give their hands a ceremonial washing, holding to the tradition of the elders. [4]When they come from the marketplace they do not eat unless they wash. And they observe many other traditions, such as the washing of cups, pitchers

and kettles.) [5]So the Pharisees and teachers of the law asked Jesus, "Why don't your disciples live according to the tradition of the elders instead of eating their food with 'unclean' hands?" [6]He replied, "Isaiah was right when he prophesied about you hypocrites; as it is written: " 'These people honor me with their lips, but their hearts are far from me. [7]They worship me in vain; their teachings are but rules taught by men.' [8]You have let go of the commands of God and are holding on to the traditions of men." [9]And he said to them: "You have a fine way of setting aside the commands of God in order to observe your own traditions! [10]For Moses said, 'Honor your father and your mother,' and, 'Anyone who curses his father or mother must be put to death.' [11]But you say that if a man says to his father or mother: 'Whatever help you might otherwise have received from me is Corban' (that is, a gift devoted to God), [12]then you no longer let him do anything for his father or mother. [13]Thus you nullify the word of God by your tradition that you have handed down. And you do many things like that." [14]Again Jesus called the crowd to him and said, "Listen to me, everyone, and understand this. [15]Nothing outside a man can make him 'unclean' by going into him. Rather, it is what comes out of a man that makes him 'unclean.' "

[17]After he had left the crowd and entered the house, his disciples asked him about this parable. [18]"Are you so dull?" he asked. "Don't you see that nothing that enters a man from the outside can make him 'unclean'? [19]For it doesn't go into his heart but into his stomach, and then out of his body." (In saying this, Jesus declared all foods "clean.") [20]He went on: "What comes out of a man is what makes him 'unclean.' [21]For from within, out of men's hearts, come evil thoughts, sexual immorality, theft, murder, adultery, [22]greed, malice, deceit, lewdness, envy, slander, arrogance and folly. [23]All these evils come from inside and make a man 'unclean.' "

The Jewish Sabbath (from the Hebrew *shavat*, "to rest") was observed on the seventh day of the week, or Saturday. Throughout most of the first century, followers of Jesus retained the Jewish practice of keeping the Saturday Sabbath holy. As the church became predominantly Gentile, however, more Christians considered the day of Resurrection, Sunday, as the most holy day of the week. When the Roman Empire formally embraced the Christian religion in the fourth century, Sunday officially replaced Saturday as the proper day for Christian assembly and worship.

The following excerpts contain New Testament references to Sabbath (Saturday) and Lord's Day (Sunday) practices. What activities typically took place during New Testament times on the seventh and first days of the week?

THE DAY OF RESURRECTION FROM THE GOSPEL OF MARK

Chapter 16

[1]When the Sabbath was over, Mary Magdalene, Mary the mother of James, and Salome bought spices so that they might go to anoint Jesus' body. [2]Very early on the first day of the week, just after sunrise, they were on their way to the tomb [3]and they asked each other, "Who will roll the stone away from the entrance of the tomb?" [4]But when they looked up, they saw that the stone, which was very large, had been rolled away. [5]As they entered the tomb, they saw a young man dressed in a white robe sitting on the right side, and they were alarmed. [6]"Don't be alarmed," he said. "You are looking for Jesus the Nazarene, who was crucified. He has risen! He is not here. See the place where they laid him. [7]But go, tell his disciples and Peter, 'He is going ahead of you into Galilee. There you will see him, just as he told you.' " [8]Trembling and bewildered, the women went out and fled from the tomb. They said nothing to anyone, because they were afraid.

SABBATH DAY ACTIVITIES FROM THE BOOK OF ACTS

Chapter 13

[42]As Paul and Barnabas were leaving the synagogue, the people invited them to speak further about these things on the next Sabbath. [43]When the congregation was dismissed, many of the Jews and devout converts to Judaism followed Paul and Barnabas, who talked with them and urged them to continue in the grace of God. [44]On the next Sabbath almost the whole city gathered to hear the word of the Lord. [45]When the Jews saw the crowds, they were filled with jealousy and talked abusively against what Paul was saying. [46]Then Paul and Barnabas answered them boldly: "We had to speak the word of God to you first. Since you reject it and do not consider yourselves worthy of eternal life, we now turn to the Gentiles. [47]For this is what the Lord has commanded us: " 'I have made you a light for the Gentiles, that you may bring salvation to the ends of the earth.' " [48]When the Gentiles heard this, they were glad and honored the word of the Lord; and all who were appointed for eternal life believed.

Chapter 18

[1]After this, Paul left Athens and went to Corinth. [2]There he met a Jew named Aquila, a native of Pontus, who had recently come from Italy with his wife Priscilla, because Claudius had ordered all the Jews to leave Rome. Paul went to see them, [3]and because he was a tentmaker as they were, he stayed and worked with them. [4]Every Sabbath he reasoned in the synagogue, trying to persuade Jews and Greeks.

[5]When Silas and Timothy came from Macedonia, Paul devoted himself exclusively to preaching, testifying to the Jews that Jesus was the Christ.[6]But when the Jews opposed Paul and became abusive, he shook out his clothes in protest and said to them, "Your blood be on your own heads! I am clear of my responsibility. From now on I will go to the Gentiles." [7]Then Paul left the synagogue and went next door to the house of Titius Justus, a worshiper of God. [8]Crispus, the synagogue ruler, and his entire household believed in the Lord; and many of the Corinthians who heard him believed and were baptized.

For Paul, the observance of Jewish holy days and dietary rituals was not necessary for salvation. Paul, nonetheless, insisted that Christians should not offend those who embraced certain sacred traditions. The following passage contains Paul's instructions to the Christians in Rome. Summarize the essential points of this teaching.

PAUL'S INSTRUCTIONS ON OBSERVING THE DIETARY RITUALS FROM THE BOOK OF ROMANS

Chapter 14

[1]Accept him whose faith is weak, without passing judgment on disputable matters. [2]One man's faith allows him to eat everything, but another man, whose faith is weak, eats only vegetables. [3]The man who eats everything must not look down on him who does not, and the man who does not eat everything must not condemn the man who does, for God has accepted him. [4]Who are you to judge someone else's servant? To his own master he stands or falls. And he will stand, for the Lord is able to make him stand.

[5]One man considers one day more sacred than another; another man considers every day alike. Each one should be fully convinced in his own mind. [6]He who regards one day as special, does so to the Lord. He who eats meat, eats to the Lord, for he gives thanks to God; and he who abstains, does so to the Lord and gives thanks to God. [7]For none of us lives to himself alone and none of us dies to himself alone. [8]If we live, we live to the Lord; and if we die, we die to the Lord. So, whether we live or die, we belong to the Lord.

[9]For this very reason, Christ died and returned to life so that he might be the Lord of both the dead and the living. [10]You, then, why do you judge your brother? Or why do you look down on your brother? For we will all stand before God's judgment seat. [11]It is written: " 'As surely as I live,' says the Lord, 'every knee will bow before me; every tongue will confess to God.' " [12]So then, each of us will give an account of himself to God.

[13]Therefore let us stop passing judgment on one another. Instead, make up your mind not to put any stumbling block or obstacle in your brother's way. [14]As one who is in the Lord Jesus, I am fully convinced that no food is unclean in itself. But if anyone regards something as unclean, then for him it is unclean. [15]If your brother is distressed because of what you eat, you are no longer acting in love. Do not by your eating destroy your brother for whom Christ died. [16]Do not allow what you consider good to be spoken of as evil. [17]For the kingdom of God is not a matter of eating and drinking, but of righteousness, peace and joy in the Holy Spirit, [18]because anyone who serves Christ in this way is pleasing to God and approved by men.

[19]Let us therefore make every effort to do what leads to peace and to mutual edification. [20]Do not destroy the work of God for the sake of food. All food is clean, but it is wrong for a man to eat anything that causes someone else to stumble. [21]It is better not to eat meat or drink wine or to do anything else that will cause your brother to fall. [22]So whatever you believe about these things keep between yourself and God. Blessed is the man who does not condemn himself by what he approves.

The final piece in this section is from the Book of Titus. This letter appears to serve as a reminder for Christians to live in ways that will make the Christian gospel attractive to all. What rules of social decorum are contained in this passage?

SOCIAL DECORUM IN THE PAULINE LETTERS FROM THE BOOK OF TITUS

Chapter 2

[1]You must teach what is in accord with sound doctrine. [2]Teach the older men to be temperate, worthy of respect, self-controlled, and sound in faith, in love and in endurance. [3]Likewise, teach the older women to be reverent in the way they live, not to be slanderers or addicted to much wine, but to teach what is good. [4]Then they can train the younger women to love their husbands and children, [5]to be self-controlled and pure, to be busy at home, to be kind, and to be subject to their husbands, so that no one will malign the word of God. [6]Similarly, encourage the young men to be self-controlled. [7]In everything set them an example by doing what is good. In your teaching show integrity, seriousness [8]and soundness of speech that cannot be condemned, so that those who oppose you may be ashamed because they have nothing bad to say about us. [9]Teach slaves to be subject to their masters in everything, to try to please them, not to talk back to them, [10]and not to steal from them, but to show that they can be fully trusted, so that in every way they will make the teaching about God our Savior attractive. [11]For the grace of God that brings salvation has appeared to all men. [12]It teaches us to say "No" to ungodliness and worldly passions, and to live self-controlled, upright and godly lives in this present age,

¹³while we wait for the blessed hope—the glorious appearing of our great God and Savior, Jesus Christ, ¹⁴who gave himself for us to redeem us from all wickedness and to purify for himself a people that are his very own, eager to do what is good. ¹⁵These, then, are the things you should teach. Encourage and rebuke with all authority. Do not let anyone despise you.

Chapter 3

¹Remind the people to be subject to rulers and authorities, to be obedient, to be ready to do whatever is good, ²to slander no one, to be peaceable and considerate, and to show true humility toward all men. ³At one time we too were foolish, disobedient, deceived and enslaved by all kinds of passions and pleasures. We lived in malice and envy, being hated and hating one another. ⁴But when the kindness and love of God our Savior appeared, ⁵he saved us, not because of righteous things we had done, but because of his mercy. He saved us through the washing of rebirth and renewal by the Holy Spirit, ⁶whom he poured out on us generously through Jesus Christ our Savior, ⁷so that, having been justified by his grace, we might become heirs having the hope of eternal life.

SECTION 7: The Human Quest: Paths to Salvation and Enlightenment

God's plan of salvation is a theme that appears frequently throughout the books of the New Testament. The opening selections taken from the Gospels and from the Book of Acts include stories of how Jesus and his disciples responded to those who approached them with questions about eternal life. According to these texts, what does the concept "salvation" mean for Christians? From what and for what are Christians "saved"? How is this salvation realized?

NEW TESTAMENT ANSWERS TO ETERNAL QUESTIONS

Jesus and the Rich, Young Ruler from the Gospel of Luke
Chapter 18

¹⁸A certain ruler asked him, "Good teacher, what must I do to inherit eternal life?" ¹⁹"Why do you call me good?" Jesus answered. "No one is good—except God alone. ²⁰You know the commandments: 'Do not commit adultery, do not murder, do not steal, do not give false testimony, honor your father and mother.'" ²¹"All these I have kept since I was a boy," he said. ²²When Jesus heard this, he said to him, "You still lack one thing. Sell everything you have and give to the poor, and you will have treasure in heaven. Then, come, follow me." ²³When he heard this, he became very sad, because he was a

man of great wealth. ²⁴Jesus looked at him and said, "How hard it is for the rich to enter the kingdom of God! ²⁵Indeed, it is easier for a camel to go through the eye of a needle than for a rich man to enter the kingdom of God." ²⁶Those who heard this asked, "Who then can be saved?" ²⁷Jesus replied, "What is impossible with men is possible with God." ²⁸Peter said to him, "We have left all we had to follow you!" ²⁹"I tell you the truth," Jesus said to them, "no one who has left home or wife or brothers or parents or children for the sake of the kingdom of God ³⁰will fail to receive many times as much in this age and, in the age to come, eternal life."

Jesus and Nicodemus from the Gospel of John
Chapter 3

¹Now there was a man of the Pharisees named Nicodemus, a member of the Jewish ruling council. ²He came to Jesus at night and said, "Rabbi, we know you are a teacher who has come from God. For no one could perform the miraculous signs you are doing if God were not with him."
³In reply Jesus declared, "I tell you the truth, no one can see the kingdom of God unless he is born again." ⁴"How can a man be born when he is old?" Nicodemus asked. "Surely he cannot enter a second time into his mother's womb to be born!" ⁵Jesus answered, "I tell you the truth, no one can enter the kingdom of God unless he is born of water and the Spirit. ⁶Flesh gives birth to flesh, but the Spirit gives birth to spirit. ⁷You should not be surprised at my saying, 'You must be born again.' ⁸The wind blows wherever it pleases. You hear its sound, but you cannot tell where it comes from or where it is going. So it is with everyone born of the Spirit."
⁹"How can this be?" Nicodemus asked. ¹⁰"You are Israel's teacher," said Jesus, "and do you not understand these things? ¹¹I tell you the truth, we speak of what we know, and we testify to what we have seen, but still you people do not accept our testimony. ¹²I have spoken to you of earthly things and you do not believe; how then will you believe if I speak of heavenly things? ¹³No one has ever gone into heaven except the one who came from heaven—the Son of Man. ¹⁴Just as Moses lifted up the snake in the desert, so the Son of Man must be lifted up, ¹⁵that everyone who believes in him may have eternal life. ¹⁶"For God so loved the world that he gave his one and only Son, that whoever believes in him shall not perish but have eternal life. ¹⁷For God did not send his Son into the world to condemn the world, but to save the world through him. ¹⁸Whoever believes in him is not condemned, but whoever does not believe stands condemned already because he has not believed in the name of God's one and only Son. ¹⁹This is the verdict: Light has come into the world, but men loved darkness instead of light because their deeds were evil. ²⁰Everyone who does evil hates the light, and will not come into the light for fear that his deeds will be exposed. ²¹But whoever lives by the truth comes into the light, so that it may be seen plainly that what he has done has been done through God."

Jesus's Farewell Discourses
from the Gospel of John

Chapter 14

[1]"Do not let your hearts be troubled. Trust in God; trust also in me. [2]In my Father's house are many rooms; if it were not so, I would have told you. I am going there to prepare a place for you. [3]And if I go and prepare a place for you, I will come back and take you to be with me that you also may be where I am. [4]You know the way to the place where I am going." [5]Thomas said to him, "Lord, we don't know where you are going, so how can we know the way?" [6]Jesus answered, "I am the way and the truth and the life. No one comes to the Father except through me. [7]If you really knew me, you would know my Father as well. From now on, you do know him and have seen him."

[8]Philip said, "Lord, show us the Father and that will be enough for us." [9]Jesus answered: "Don't you know me, Philip, even after I have been among you such a long time? Anyone who has seen me has seen the Father. How can you say, 'Show us the Father'? [10]Don't you believe that I am in the Father, and that the Father is in me? The words I say to you are not just my own. Rather, it is the Father, living in me, who is doing his work. [11]Believe me when I say that I am in the Father and the Father is in me; or at least believe on the evidence of the miracles themselves. [12]I tell you the truth, anyone who has faith in me will do what I have been doing. He will do even greater things than these, because I am going to the Father. [13]And I will do whatever you ask in my name, so that the Son may bring glory to the Father. [14]You may ask me for anything in my name, and I will do it.

[15]"If you love me, you will obey what I command. [16]And I will ask the Father, and he will give you another Counselor to be with you forever— [17]the Spirit of truth. The world cannot accept him, because it neither sees him nor knows him. But you know him, for he lives with you and will be in you. [18]I will not leave you as orphans; I will come to you. [19]Before long, the world will not see me anymore, but you will see me. Because I live, you also will live. [20]On that day you will realize that I am in my Father, and you are in me, and I am in you. [21]Whoever has my commands and obeys them, he is the one who loves me. He who loves me will be loved by my Father, and I too will love him and show myself to him."

The Necessity of Circumcision Rejected
from the Book of Acts

Chapter 15

[1]Some men came down from Judea to Antioch and were teaching the brothers: "Unless you are circumcised, according to the custom taught by Moses, you cannot be saved." [2]This brought Paul and Barnabas into sharp dispute and debate with them. So Paul and Barnabas were appointed, along with some other believers, to go up to Jerusalem to see the apostles and elders about this question. [3]The church sent them on their way, and as they traveled through Phoenicia and Samaria, they told how the Gentiles had been converted. This news made all the brothers very glad. [4]When they came to Jerusalem, they were welcomed by the church and the apostles and elders, to whom they reported everything God had done through them.

[5]Then some of the believers who belonged to the party of the Pharisees stood up and said, "The Gentiles must be circumcised and required to obey the law of Moses." [6]The apostles and elders met to consider this question. [7]After much discussion, Peter got up and addressed them: "Brothers, you know that some time ago God made a choice among you that the Gentiles might hear from my lips the message of the gospel and believe. [8]God, who knows the heart, showed that he accepted them by giving the Holy Spirit to them, just as he did to us. [9]He made no distinction between us and them, for he purified their hearts by faith. [10]Now then, why do you try to test God by putting on the necks of the disciples a yoke that neither we nor our fathers have been able to bear? [11]No! We believe it is through the grace of our Lord Jesus that we are saved, just as they are."

[12]The whole assembly became silent as they listened to Barnabas and Paul telling about the miraculous signs and wonders God had done among the Gentiles through them. [13]When they finished, James spoke up: "Brothers, listen to me. [14]Simon has described to us how God at first showed his concern by taking from the Gentiles a people for himself. [15]The words of the prophets are in agreement with this, as it is written: [16]" 'After this I will return and rebuild David's fallen tent. Its ruins I will rebuild, and I will restore it, [17]that the remnant of men may seek the Lord, and all the Gentiles who bear my name, says the Lord, who does these things' [18]that have been known for ages. [19]"It is my judgment, therefore, that we should not make it difficult for the Gentiles who are turning to God. [20]Instead we should write to them, telling them to abstain from food polluted by idols, from sexual immorality, from the meat of strangled animals and from blood. [21]For Moses has been preached in every city from the earliest times and is read in the synagogues on every Sabbath."

[22]Then the apostles and elders, with the whole church, decided to choose some of their own men and send them to Antioch with Paul and Barnabas. They chose Judas (called Barsabbas) and Silas, two men who were leaders among the brothers. [23]With them they sent the following letter: The apostles and elders, your brothers, To the Gentile believers in Antioch, Syria and Cilicia: Greetings. [24]We have heard that some went out from us without our authorization and disturbed you, troubling your minds by what they said. [25]So we all agreed to choose some men and send them to you with our dear friends Barnabas and Paul— [26]men who have risked their lives for the name of our Lord Jesus Christ. [27]Therefore we are sending Judas and Silas to confirm by word of mouth what we are writing. [28]It seemed good to the Holy Spirit and to us not to

burden you with anything beyond the following requirements: [29]You are to abstain from food sacrificed to idols, from blood, from the meat of strangled animals and from sexual immorality. You will do well to avoid these things. Farewell.

The following selections from the epistles contain comments by Paul, John, and James about the plan of salvation. What common themes appear in each of these passages? In what ways do the teachings of the three authors differ? Contrast these texts with the Old Testament selections contained in Section 7 in the chapter on Judaism. To what degree are the New Testament passages compatible with the teachings of the Old Testament? Be able to explain your answer.

PATHS TO SALVATION IN THE WRITINGS OF PAUL FROM THE BOOK OF ROMANS

Chapter 4

[1]What then shall we say that Abraham, our forefather, discovered in this matter? [2]If, in fact, Abraham was justified by works, he had something to boast about—but not before God. [3]What does the Scripture say? "Abraham believed God, and it was credited to him as righteousness."

[4]Now when a man works, his wages are not credited to him as a gift, but as an obligation. [5]However, to the man who does not work but trusts God who justifies the wicked, his faith is credited as righteousness. [6]David says the same thing when he speaks of the blessedness of the man to whom God credits righteousness apart from works: [7]"Blessed are they whose transgressions are forgiven, whose sins are covered. [8]Blessed is the man whose sin the Lord will never count against him."

[9]Is this blessedness only for the circumcised, or also for the uncircumcised? We have been saying that Abraham's faith was credited to him as righteousness. [10]Under what circumstances was it credited? Was it after he was circumcised, or before? It was not after, but before! [11]And he received the sign of circumcision, a seal of the righteousness that he had by faith while he was still uncircumcised. So then, he is the father of all who believe but have not been circumcised, in order that righteousness might be credited to them. [12]And he is also the father of the circumcised who not only are circumcised but who also walk in the footsteps of the faith that our father Abraham had before he was circumcised.

[13]It was not through law that Abraham and his offspring received the promise that he would be heir of the world, but through the righteousness that comes by faith. [14]For if those who live by law are heirs, faith has no value and the promise is worthless, [15]because law brings wrath. And where there is no law there is no transgression.

[16]Therefore, the promise comes by faith, so that it may be by grace and may be guaranteed to all Abraham's offspring—not only to those who are of the law but also to those who are of the faith of Abraham. He is the father of us all. [17]As it is written: "I have made you a father of many nations." He is our father in the sight of God, in whom he believed—the God who gives life to the dead and calls things that are not as though they were.

PATHS TO SALVATION IN THE WRITINGS OF PAUL FROM THE BOOK OF II CORINTHIANS

Chapter 5

[1]Now we know that if the earthly tent we live in is destroyed, we have a building from God, an eternal house in heaven, not built by human hands. [2]Meanwhile we groan, longing to be clothed with our heavenly dwelling, [3]because when we are clothed, we will not be found naked. [4]For while we are in this tent, we groan and are burdened, because we do not wish to be unclothed but to be clothed with our heavenly dwelling, so that what is mortal may be swallowed up by life. [5]Now it is God who has made us for this very purpose and has given us the Spirit as a deposit, guaranteeing what is to come.

[6]Therefore we are always confident and know that as long as we are at home in the body we are away from the Lord. [7]We live by faith, not by sight. [8]We are confident, I say, and would prefer to be away from the body and at home with the Lord. [9]So we make it our goal to please him, whether we are at home in the body or away from it. [10]For we must all appear before the judgment seat of Christ, that each one may receive what is due him for the things done while in the body, whether good or bad.

[11]Since, then, we know what it is to fear the Lord, we try to persuade men. What we are is plain to God, and I hope it is also plain to your conscience. [12]We are not trying to commend ourselves to you again, but are giving you an opportunity to take pride in us, so that you can answer those who take pride in what is seen rather than in what is in the heart. [13]If we are out of our mind, it is for the sake of God; if we are in our right mind, it is for you. [14]For Christ's love compels us, because we are convinced that one died for all, and therefore all died. [15]And he died for all, that those who live should no longer live for themselves but for him who died for them and was raised again.

[16]So from now on we regard no one from a worldly point of view. Though we once regarded Christ in this way, we do so no longer. [17]Therefore, if anyone is in Christ, he is a new creation; the old has gone, the new has come! [18]All this is from God, who reconciled us to himself through Christ and gave us the ministry of reconciliation: [19]that God was reconciling the world to himself in Christ, not counting men's sins against them. And he has committed to us the message of

reconciliation. [20]We are therefore Christ's ambassadors, as though God were making his appeal through us. We implore you on Christ's behalf: Be reconciled to God. [21]God made him who had no sin to be sin for us, so that in him we might become the righteousness of God.

PATHS TO SALVATION IN THE BOOK OF 1 JOHN

Chapter 5

[1]Everyone who believes that Jesus is the Christ is born of God, and everyone who loves the father loves his child as well. [2]This is how we know that we love the children of God: by loving God and carrying out his commands. [3]This is love for God: to obey his commands. And his commands are not burdensome, [4]for everyone born of God overcomes the world. This is the victory that has overcome the world, even our faith. [5]Who is it that overcomes the world? Only he who believes that Jesus is the Son of God.

[6]This is the one who came by water and blood—Jesus Christ. He did not come by water only, but by water and blood. And it is the Spirit who testifies, because the Spirit is the truth. [7]For there are three that testify: [8]the Spirit, the water and the blood; and the three are in agreement. [9]We accept man's testimony, but God's testimony is greater because it is the testimony of God, which he has given about his Son. [10]Anyone who believes in the Son of God has this testimony in his heart. Anyone who does not believe God has made him out to be a liar, because he has not believed the testimony God has given about his Son. [11]And this is the testimony: God has given us eternal life, and this life is in his Son. [12]He who has the Son has life; he who does not have the Son of God does not have life.

[13]I write these things to you who believe in the name of the Son of God so that you may know that you have eternal life. [14]This is the confidence we have in approaching God: that if we ask anything according to his will, he hears us. [15]And if we know that he hears us—whatever we ask—we know that we have what we asked of him.

[16]If anyone sees his brother commit a sin that does not lead to death, he should pray and God will give him life. I refer to those whose sin does not lead to death. There is a sin that leads to death. I am not saying that he should pray about that. [17]All wrongdoing is sin, and there is sin that does not lead to death.

[18]We know that anyone born of God does not continue to sin; the one who was born of God keeps him safe, and the evil one cannot harm him. [19]We know that we are children of God, and that the whole world is under the control of the evil one. [20]We know also that the Son of God has come and has given us understanding, so that we may know him who is true. And we are in him who is true—even in his Son Jesus Christ. He is the true God and eternal life. [21]Dear children, keep yourselves from idols.

PATHS TO SALVATION IN THE BOOK OF JAMES

Chapter 1

[1]Consider it pure joy, my brothers, whenever you face trials of many kinds, [3]because you know that the testing of your faith develops perseverance. [4]Perseverance must finish its work so that you may be mature and complete, not lacking anything. [5]If any of you lacks wisdom, he should ask God, who gives generously to all without finding fault, and it will be given to him. [6]But when he asks, he must believe and not doubt, because he who doubts is like a wave of the sea, blown and tossed by the wind. [7]That man should not think he will receive anything from the Lord; [8]he is a doubleminded man, unstable in all he does.

[9]The brother in humble circumstances ought to take pride in his high position. [10]But the one who is rich should take pride in his low position, because he will pass away like a wild flower. [11]For the sun rises with scorching heat and withers the plant; its blossom falls and its beauty is destroyed. In the same way, the rich man will fade away even while he goes about his business.

[12]Blessed is the man who perseveres under trial, because when he has stood the test, he will receive the crown of life that God has promised to those who love him.

[13]When tempted, no one should say, "God is tempting me." For God cannot be tempted by evil, nor does he tempt anyone; [14]but each one is tempted when, by his own evil desire, he is dragged away and enticed. [15]Then, after desire has conceived, it gives birth to sin; and sin, when it is fullgrown, gives birth to death.

[16]Don't be deceived, my dear brothers. [17]Every good and perfect gift is from above, coming down from the Father of the heavenly lights, who does not change like shifting shadows. [18]He chose to give us birth through the word of truth, that we might be a kind of firstfruits of all he created.

[19]My dear brothers, take note of this: Everyone should be quick to listen, slow to speak and slow to become angry, [20]for man's anger does not bring about the righteous life that God desires. [21]Therefore, get rid of all moral filth and the evil that is so prevalent and humbly accept the word planted in you, which can save you.

[22]Do not merely listen to the word, and so deceive yourselves. Do what it says. [23]Anyone who listens to the word but does not do what it says is like a man who looks at his face in a mirror [24]and, after looking at himself, goes away and immediately forgets what he looks like. [25]But the man who looks intently into the perfect law that gives freedom, and continues to do this, not forgetting what he has heard, but doing it—he will be blessed in what he does.

[26]If anyone considers himself religious and yet does not keep a tight rein on his tongue, he deceives himself and his religion is worthless. [27]Religion that God our Father accepts as pure and faultless is this: to look after orphans and widows in their distress and to keep oneself from being polluted by the world.

SECTION 8: The Religious Life: Worship and Righteousness

The New Testament both affirms and critiques Jewish patterns of worship and piety. The first selection drawn from Matthew's account of Jesus' Sermon on the Mount provides one definition of godly living. According to this text, what does Jesus appreciate about first century Jewish piety? What specific shortcomings does Jesus identify among those who claim to be the people of God?

NEW TESTAMENT CRITIQUES OF JEWISH PIETY AND WORSHIP FROM THE GOSPEL OF MATTHEW

Chapter 6

[1]"Be careful not to do your 'acts of righteousness' before men, to be seen by them. If you do, you will have no reward from your Father in heaven. [2]So when you give to the needy, do not announce it with trumpets, as the hypocrites do in the synagogues and on the streets, to be honored by men. I tell you the truth, they have received their reward in full. [3]But when you give to the needy, do not let your left hand know what your right hand is doing, [4]so that your giving may be in secret. Then your Father, who sees what is done in secret, will reward you.

[5]"And when you pray, do not be like the hypocrites, for they love to pray standing in the synagogues and on the street corners to be seen by men. I tell you the truth, they have received their reward in full. [6]But when you pray, go into your room, close the door and pray to your Father, who is unseen. Then your Father, who sees what is done in secret, will reward you. [7]And when you pray, do not keep on babbling like pagans, for they think they will be heard because of their many words. [8]Do not be like them, for your Father knows what you need before you ask him.

[9]"This, then, is how you should pray: "'Our Father in heaven, hallowed be your name, [10]your kingdom come, your will be done on earth as it is in heaven. [11]Give us today our daily bread. [12]Forgive us our debts, as we also have forgiven our debtors. [13]And lead us not into temptation, but deliver us from the evil one.' [14]For if you forgive men when they sin against you, your heavenly Father will also forgive you. [15]But if you do not forgive men their sins, your Father will not forgive your sins.

[16]"When you fast, do not look somber as the hypocrites do, for they disfigure their faces to show men they are fasting. I tell you the truth, they have received their reward in full. [17]But when you fast, put oil on your head and wash your face, [18]so that it will not be obvious to men that you are fasting, but only to your Father, who is unseen; and your Father, who sees what is done in secret, will reward you.

[19]"Do not store up for yourselves treasures on earth, where moth and rust destroy, and where thieves break in and steal.

[20]But store up for yourselves treasures in heaven, where moth and rust do not destroy, and where thieves do not break in and steal. [21]For where your treasure is, there your heart will be also. [22]"The eye is the lamp of the body. If your eyes are good, your whole body will be full of light. [23]But if your eyes are bad, your whole body will be full of darkness. If then the light within you is darkness, how great is that darkness! [24]"No one can serve two masters. Either he will hate the one and love the other, or he will be devoted to the one and despise the other. You cannot serve both God and Money. [25]"Therefore I tell you, do not worry about your life, what you will eat or drink; or about your body, what you will wear. Is not life more important than food, and the body more important than clothes? [26]Look at the birds of the air; they do not sow or reap or store away in barns, and yet your heavenly Father feeds them. Are you not much more valuable than they? [27]Who of you by worrying can add a single hour to his life? [28]"And why do you worry about clothes? See how the lilies of the field grow. They do not labor or spin. [29]Yet I tell you that not even Solomon in all his splendor was dressed like one of these. [30]If that is how God clothes the grass of the field, which is here today and tomorrow is thrown into the fire, will he not much more clothe you, O you of little faith? [31]So do not worry, saying, 'What shall we eat?' or 'What shall we drink?' or 'What shall we wear?' [32]For the pagans run after all these things, and your heavenly Father knows that you need them. [33]But seek first his kingdom and his righteousness, and all these things will be given to you as well. [34]Therefore do not worry about tomorrow, for tomorrow will worry about itself. Each day has enough trouble of its own.

Chapter 7

[1]"Do not judge, or you too will be judged. [2]For in the same way you judge others, you will be judged, and with the measure you use, it will be measured to you. [3]"Why do you look at the speck of sawdust in your brother's eye and pay no attention to the plank in your own eye? [4]How can you say to your brother, 'Let me take the speck out of your eye,' when all the time there is a plank in your own eye? [5]You hypocrite, first take the plank out of your own eye, and then you will see clearly to remove the speck from your brother's eye.

The author of the Book of Hebrews contrasts the limitations of the sacrificial system of the Old Testament with the finality of the sacrifice of Christ. According to this text, what was the purpose of the animal sacrifices described in the Hebrew Bible? Why are future sacrifices no longer needed? What arguments does the author use to support these assertions? What is the central point of this teaching, and why do you think this passage was included in the Christian canon?

SACRIFICIAL PIETY IN THE EPISTLE
TO THE HEBREWS

Chapter 10

[1]The law is only a shadow of the good things that are coming—not the realities themselves. For this reason it can never, by the same sacrifices repeated endlessly year after year, make perfect those who draw near to worship. [2]If it could, would they not have stopped being offered? For the worshipers would have been cleansed once for all, and would no longer have felt guilty for their sins. [3]But those sacrifices are an annual reminder of sins, [4]because it is impossible for the blood of bulls and goats to take away sins.

[5]Therefore, when Christ came into the world, he said: "Sacrifice and offering you did not desire, but a body you prepared for me; [6]with burnt offerings and sin offerings you were not pleased. [7]Then I said, 'Here I am—it is written about me in the scroll—I have come to do your will, O God.' " [8]First he said, "Sacrifices and offerings, burnt offerings and sin offerings you did not desire, nor were you pleased with them" (although the law required them to be made). [9]Then he said, "Here I am, I have come to do your will." He sets aside the first to establish the second. [10]And by that will, we have been made holy through the sacrifice of the body of Jesus Christ once for all.

[11]Day after day every priest stands and performs his religious duties; again and again he offers the same sacrifices, which can never take away sins. [12]But when this priest had offered for all time one sacrifice for sins, he sat down at the right hand of God. [13]Since that time he waits for his enemies to be made his footstool, [14]because by one sacrifice he has made perfect forever those who are being made holy.

[15]The Holy Spirit also testifies to us about this. First he says: [16]"This is the covenant I will make with them after that time, says the Lord. I will put my laws in their hearts, and I will write them on their minds." [17]Then he adds: "Their sins and lawless acts I will remember no more." [18]And where these have been forgiven, there is no longer any sacrifice for sin. [19]Therefore, brothers, since we have confidence to enter the Most Holy Place by the blood of Jesus, [20]by a new and living way opened for us through the curtain, that is, his body, [21]and since we have a great priest over the house of God, [22]let us draw near to God with a sincere heart in full assurance of faith, having our hearts sprinkled to cleanse us from a guilty conscience and having our bodies washed with pure water. [23]Let us hold unswervingly to the hope we profess, for he who promised is faithful. [24]And let us consider how we may spur one another on toward love and good deeds. [25]Let us not give up meeting together, as some are in the habit of doing, but let us encourage one another—and all the more as you see the Day approaching.

For many Christians, the sacrament of the Lord's Supper is the centerpiece of Christian worship. Scriptural sources for this Christian rite are found in both the gospels and the epistles. Below are two such passages. The event described in Luke's gospel took place during the Passover meal that Jesus ate with his disciples on the night that he was betrayed and arrested. Paul refers to this incident while scolding the Christians at Corinth for their selfish and ungodly behavior. Why do you think this story remains so important to Christians around the world?

THE LAST SUPPER AS DESCRIBED
IN LUKE AND IN 1 CORINTHIANS

Luke

Chapter 22

[7]Then came the day of Unleavened Bread on which the Passover lamb had to be sacrificed. [8]Jesus sent Peter and John, saying, "Go and make preparations for us to eat the Passover." [9]"Where do you want us to prepare for it?" they asked. [10]He replied, "As you enter the city, a man carrying a jar of water will meet you. Follow him to the house that he enters, [11]and say to the owner of the house, 'The Teacher asks: Where is the guest room, where I may eat the Passover with my disciples?' [12]He will show you a large upper room, all furnished. Make preparations there." [13]They left and found things just as Jesus had told them. So they prepared the Passover.

[14]When the hour came, Jesus and his apostles reclined at the table. [15]And he said to them, "I have eagerly desired to eat this Passover with you before I suffer. [16]For I tell you, I will not eat it again until it finds fulfillment in the kingdom of God." [17]After taking the cup, he gave thanks and said, "Take this and divide it among you. [18]For I tell you I will not drink again of the fruit of the vine until the kingdom of God comes." [19]And he took bread, gave thanks and broke it, and gave it to them, saying, "This is my body given for you; do this in remembrance of me." [20]In the same way, after the supper he took the cup, saying, "This cup is the new covenant in my blood, which is poured out for you. [21]But the hand of him who is going to betray me is with mine on the table. [22]The Son of Man will go as it has been decreed, but woe to that man who betrays him." [23]They began to question among themselves which of them it might be who would do this.

1 Corinthians

Chapter 11

[23]The Lord Jesus, on the night he was betrayed, took bread, [24]and when he had given thanks, he broke it and said, "This is my body, which is for you; do this in remembrance of me." [25]In the same way, after supper he took the cup, saying, "This cup is the new covenant in my blood; do this, whenever you drink it, in remembrance of me." [26]For whenever you eat this bread and drink this cup, you proclaim the Lord's death until he comes.

²⁷Therefore, whoever eats the bread or drinks the cup of the Lord in an unworthy manner will be guilty of sinning against the body and blood of the Lord. ²⁸A man ought to examine himself before he eats of the bread and drinks of the cup. ²⁹For anyone who eats and drinks without recognizing the body of the Lord eats and drinks judgment on himself. ³⁰That is why many among you are weak and sick, and a number of you have fallen asleep. ³¹But if we judged ourselves, we would not come under judgment. ³²When we are judged by the Lord, we are being disciplined so that we will not be condemned with the world.

³³So then, my brothers, when you come together to eat, wait for each other. ³⁴If anyone is hungry, he should eat at home, so that when you meet together it may not result in judgment. And when I come I will give further directions.

Among the most beautiful passages within the New Testament is the following hymn of love that is contained in Paul's first letter to the church at Corinth. According to Paul, what qualities define a person filled with divine love? To what degree do the sacred texts of other traditions echo the themes found in this famous text?

DEFINITIONS OF DIVINE LOVE FROM THE BOOK OF 1 CORINTHIANS

Chapter 13

¹If I speak in the tongues of men and of angels, but have not love, I am only a resounding gong or a clanging cymbal. ²If I have the gift of prophecy and can fathom all mysteries and all knowledge, and if I have a faith that can move mountains, but have not love, I am nothing. ³If I give all I possess to the poor and surrender my body to the flames, but have not love, I gain nothing.

⁴Love is patient, love is kind. It does not envy, it does not boast, it is not proud. ⁵It is not rude, it is not selfseeking, it is not easily angered, it keeps no record of wrongs. ⁶Love does not delight in evil but rejoices with the truth. ⁷It always protects, always trusts, always hopes, always perseveres. ⁸Love never fails. But where there are prophecies, they will cease; where there are tongues, they will be stilled; where there is knowledge, it will pass away. ⁹For we know in part and we prophesy in part, ¹⁰but when perfection comes, the imperfect disappears. ¹¹When I was a child, I talked like a child, I thought like a child, I reasoned like a child. When I became a man, I put childish ways behind me. ¹²Now we see but a poor reflection as in a mirror; then we shall see face to face. Now I know in part; then I shall know fully, even as I am fully known. ¹³And now these three remain: faith, hope and love. But the greatest of these is love.

Although all Christians were expected to abide by the rule of love, the early church set apart certain individuals for special ministerial roles. The following passages are taken from two letters that the early church believed were sent from Paul to his younger assistant Timothy. These letters detail some of the additional characteristics expected from those chosen to fulfill these leadership positions. According to tradition, Paul was beheaded shortly after writing the second passage.

SPECIAL REQUIREMENTS FOR CHURCH LEADERS FROM THE BOOK OF 1 TIMOTHY

Chapter 3

¹Here is a trustworthy saying: If anyone sets his heart on being an overseer, he desires a noble task. ²Now the overseer must be above reproach, the husband of but one wife, temperate, self-controlled, respectable, hospitable, able to teach, ³not given to drunkenness, not violent but gentle, not quarrelsome, not a lover of money. ⁴He must manage his own family well and see that his children obey him with proper respect. ⁵(If anyone does not know how to manage his own family, how can he take care of God's church?) ⁶He must not be a recent convert, or he may become conceited and fall under the same judgment as the devil. ⁷He must also have a good reputation with outsiders, so that he will not fall into disgrace and into the devil's trap.

⁸Deacons, likewise, are to be men worthy of respect, sincere, not indulging in much wine, and not pursuing dishonest gain. ⁹They must keep hold of the deep truths of the faith with a clear conscience. ¹⁰They must first be tested; and then if there is nothing against them, let them serve as deacons.

¹¹In the same way, their wives are to be women worthy of respect, not malicious talkers but temperate and trustworthy in everything. ¹²A deacon must be the husband of but one wife and must manage his children and his household well. ¹³Those who have served well gain an excellent standing and great assurance in their faith in Christ Jesus.

FROM THE BOOK OF 2 TIMOTHY

Chapter 4

¹In the presence of God and of Christ Jesus, who will judge the living and the dead, and in view of his appearing and his kingdom, I give you this charge: ²Preach the Word; be prepared in season and out of season; correct, rebuke and encourage—with great patience and careful instruction. ³For the time will come when men will not put up with sound doctrine. Instead, to suit their own desires, they will gather around them a great number of teachers to say what their

itching ears want to hear. ⁴They will turn their ears away from the truth and turn aside to myths. ⁵But you, keep your head in all situations, endure hardship, do the work of an evangelist, discharge all the duties of your ministry.

⁶For I am already being poured out like a drink offering, and the time has come for my departure. ⁷I have fought the good fight, I have finished the race, I have kept the faith. ⁸Now there is in store for me the crown of righteousness, which the Lord, the righteous Judge, will award to me on that day—and not only to me, but also to all who have longed for his appearing.

SECTION 9: Endings: Death, Judgment, and the Afterlife

The New Testament is filled with eschatological statements about the end of human history. The following selections illustrate the range of New Testament comments regarding matters of death, judgment, and the afterlife. Why do you think these themes appear so frequently in the New Testament? According to these texts, what can you say about what early Christians believed about the future of humanity?

ESCHATOLOGY IN THE BOOK OF MARK

Chapter 13

¹As he was leaving the temple, one of his disciples said to him, "Look, Teacher! What massive stones! What magnificent buildings!" ²"Do you see all these great buildings?" replied Jesus. "Not one stone here will be left on another; every one will be thrown down."

³As Jesus was sitting on the Mount of Olives opposite the temple, Peter, James, John and Andrew asked him privately, ⁴"Tell us, when will these things happen? And what will be the sign that they are all about to be fulfilled?"

⁵Jesus said to them: "Watch out that no one deceives you. ⁶Many will come in my name, claiming, 'I am he,' and will deceive many. ⁷When you hear of wars and rumors of wars, do not be alarmed. Such things must happen, but the end is still to come. ⁸Nation will rise against nation, and kingdom against kingdom. There will be earthquakes in various places, and famines. These are the beginning of birth pains.

⁹"You must be on your guard. You will be handed over to the local councils and flogged in the synagogues. On account of me you will stand before governors and kings as witnesses to them. ¹⁰And the gospel must first be preached to all nations. ¹¹Whenever you are arrested and brought to trial, do not worry beforehand about what to say. Just say whatever is given you at the time, for it is not you speaking, but the Holy Spirit.

¹²"Brother will betray brother to death, and a father his child. Children will rebel against their parents and have them put to death. ¹³All men will hate you because of me, but he who stands firm to the end will be saved.

¹⁴"When you see 'the abomination that causes desolation' standing where it does not belong—let the reader understand—then let those who are in Judea flee to the mountains. ¹⁵Let no one on the roof of his house go down or enter the house to take anything out. ¹⁶Let no one in the field go back to get his cloak. ¹⁷How dreadful it will be in those days for pregnant women and nursing mothers! ¹⁸Pray that this will not take place in winter, ¹⁹because those will be days of distress unequaled from the beginning, when God created the world, until now—and never to be equaled again. ²⁰If the Lord had not cut short those days, no one would survive. But for the sake of the elect, whom he has chosen, he has shortened them. ²¹At that time if anyone says to you, 'Look, here is the Christ!' or, 'Look, there he is!' do not believe it. ²²For false Christs and false prophets will appear and perform signs and miracles to deceive the elect—if that were possible. ²³So be on your guard; I have told you everything ahead of time.

²⁴"But in those days, following that distress, " 'the sun will be darkened, and the moon will not give its light; ²⁵the stars will fall from the sky, and the heavenly bodies will be shaken.'

²⁶"At that time men will see the Son of Man coming in clouds with great power and glory. ²⁷And he will send his angels and gather his elect from the four winds, from the ends of the earth to the ends of the heavens.

²⁸Now learn this lesson from the fig tree: As soon as its twigs get tender and its leaves come out, you know that summer is near. ²⁹Even so, when you see these things happening, you know that it is near, right at the door. ³⁰I tell you the truth, this generation will certainly not pass away until all these things have happened. ³¹Heaven and earth will pass away, but my words will never pass away.

³²"No one knows about that day or hour, not even the angels in heaven, nor the Son, but only the Father. ³³Be on guard! Be alert! You do not know when that time will come. ³⁴It's like a man going away: He leaves his house and puts his servants in charge, each with his assigned task, and tells the one at the door to keep watch. ³⁵Therefore keep watch because you do not know when the owner of the house will come back—whether in the evening, or at midnight, or when the rooster crows, or at dawn. ³⁶If he comes suddenly, do not let him find you sleeping. ³⁷What I say to you, I say to everyone: 'Watch!' "

ESCHATOLOGY IN THE WRITINGS OF PAUL FROM THE BOOK OF 1 THESSALONIANS

Chapter 4

¹³Brothers, we do not want you to be ignorant about those who fall asleep, or to grieve like the rest of men, who have no hope. ¹⁴We believe that Jesus died and rose again and so we

believe that God will bring with Jesus those who have fallen asleep in him. [15]According to the Lord's own word, we tell you that we who are still alive, who are left till the coming of the Lord, will certainly not precede those who have fallen asleep. [16]For the Lord himself will come down from heaven, with a loud command, with the voice of the archangel and with the trumpet call of God, and the dead in Christ will rise first. [17]After that, we who are still alive and are left will be caught up together with them in the clouds to meet the Lord in the air. And so we will be with the Lord forever. [18]Therefore encourage each other with these words.

Chapter 5

[1]Now, brothers, about times and dates we do not need to write to you, [2]for you know very well that the day of the Lord will come like a thief in the night. [3]While people are saying, "Peace and safety," destruction will come on them suddenly, as labor pains on a pregnant woman, and they will not escape. [4]But you, brothers, are not in darkness so that this day should surprise you like a thief. [5]You are all sons of the light and sons of the day. We do not belong to the night or to the darkness. [6]So then, let us not be like others, who are asleep, but let us be alert and self-controlled. [7]For those who sleep, sleep at night, and those who get drunk, get drunk at night. [8]But since we belong to the day, let us be self-controlled, putting on faith and love as a breastplate, and the hope of salvation as a helmet. [9]For God did not appoint us to suffer wrath but to receive salvation through our Lord Jesus Christ. [10]He died for us so that, whether we are awake or asleep, we may live together with him. [11]Therefore encourage one another and build each other up, just as in fact you are doing.

ESCHATOLOGY IN THE WRITINGS OF PAUL FROM THE BOOK OF 2 THESSALONIANS

Chapter 2

[1]Concerning the coming of our Lord Jesus Christ and our being gathered to him, we ask you, brothers, [2]not to become easily unsettled or alarmed by some prophecy, report or letter supposed to have come from us, saying that the day of the Lord has already come. [3]Don't let anyone deceive you in any way, for (that day will not come) until the rebellion occurs and the man of lawlessness is revealed, the man doomed to destruction. [4]He will oppose and will exalt himself over everything that is called God or is worshiped, so that he sets himself up in God's temple, proclaiming himself to be God. [5]Don't you remember that when I was with you I used to tell you these things? [6]And now you know what is holding him back, so that he may be revealed at the proper time. [7]For the secret power of lawlessness is already at work; but the one who now holds it back will continue to do so till he is taken out of the way. [8]And then the lawless one will be revealed, whom the Lord Jesus will overthrow with the breath of his mouth and destroy by the splendor of his coming. [9]The coming of the lawless one will be in accordance with the work of Satan displayed in all kinds of counterfeit miracles, signs and wonders, [10]and in every sort of evil that deceives those who are perishing. They perish because they refused to love the truth and so be saved. [11]For this reason God sends them a powerful delusion so that they will believe the lie [12]and so that all will be condemned who have not believed the truth but have delighted in wickedness.

ESCHATOLOGY IN THE BOOK OF 2 PETER

Chapter 3

[1]Dear friends, this is now my second letter to you. I have written both of them as reminders to stimulate you to wholesome thinking. [2]I want you to recall the words spoken in the past by the holy prophets and the command given by our Lord and Savior through your apostles.

[3]First of all, you must understand that in the last days scoffers will come, scoffing and following their own evil desires. [4]They will say, "Where is this 'coming' he promised? Ever since our fathers died, everything goes on as it has since the beginning of creation." [5]But they deliberately forget that long ago by God's word the heavens existed and the earth was formed out of water and by water. [6]By these waters also the world of that time was deluged and destroyed. [7]By the same word the present heavens and earth are reserved for fire, being kept for the day of judgment and destruction of ungodly men.

[8]But do not forget this one thing, dear friends: With the Lord a day is like a thousand years, and a thousand years are like a day. [9]The Lord is not slow in keeping his promise, as some understand slowness. He is patient with you, not wanting anyone to perish, but everyone to come to repentance.

[10]But the day of the Lord will come like a thief. The heavens will disappear with a roar; the elements will be destroyed by fire, and the earth and everything in it will be laid bare.

[11]Since everything will be destroyed in this way, what kind of people ought you to be? You ought to live holy and godly lives [12]as you look forward to the day of God and speed its coming. That day will bring about the destruction of the heavens by fire, and the elements will melt in the heat. [13]But in keeping with his promise we are looking forward to a new heaven and a new earth, the home of righteousness.

[14]So then, dear friends, since you are looking forward to this, make every effort to be found spotless, blameless and at peace with him. [15]Bear in mind that our Lord's patience means salvation, just as our dear brother Paul also wrote you with the wisdom that God gave him. [16]He writes the same way in all his letters, speaking in them of these matters. His letters contain some things that are hard to understand, which ignorant and unstable people distort, as they do the other Scriptures, to their own destruction.

¹⁷Therefore, dear friends, since you already know this, be on your guard so that you may not be carried away by the error of lawless men and fall from your secure position. ¹⁸But grow in the grace and knowledge of our Lord and Savior Jesus Christ. To him be glory both now and forever! Amen.

ESCHATOLOGY IN THE BOOK OF JUDE

⁵Though you already know all this, I want to remind you that the Lord delivered his people out of Egypt, but later destroyed those who did not believe. ⁶And the angels who did not keep their positions of authority but abandoned their own home—these he has kept in darkness, bound with everlasting chains for judgment on the great Day. ⁷In a similar way, Sodom and Gomorrah and the surrounding towns gave themselves up to sexual immorality and perversion. They serve as an example of those who suffer the punishment of eternal fire.

⁸In the very same way, these dreamers pollute their own bodies, reject authority and slander celestial beings. ⁹But even the archangel Michael, when he was disputing with the devil about the body of Moses, did not dare to bring a slanderous accusation against him, but said, "The Lord rebuke you!" ¹⁰Yet these men speak abusively against whatever they do not understand; and what things they do understand by instinct, like unreasoning animals—these are the very things that destroy them.

¹¹Woe to them! They have taken the way of Cain; they have rushed for profit into Balaam's error; they have been destroyed in Korah's rebellion.

¹²These men are blemishes at your love feasts, eating with you without the slightest qualm—shepherds who feed only themselves. They are clouds without rain, blown along by the wind; autumn trees, without fruit and uprooted—twice dead. ¹³They are wild waves of the sea, foaming up their shame; wandering stars, for whom blackest darkness has been reserved forever.

¹⁴Enoch, the seventh from Adam, prophesied about these men: "See, the Lord is coming with thousands upon thousands of his holy ones ¹⁵to judge everyone, and to convict all the ungodly of all the ungodly acts they have done in the ungodly way, and of all the harsh words ungodly sinners have spoken against him." ¹⁶These men are grumblers and faultfinders; they follow their own evil desires; they boast about themselves and flatter others for their own advantage.

¹⁷But, dear friends, remember what the apostles of our Lord Jesus Christ foretold. ¹⁸They said to you, "In the last times there will be scoffers who will follow their own ungodly desires." ¹⁹These are the men who divide you, who follow mere natural instincts and do not have the Spirit.

²⁰But you, dear friends, build yourselves up in your most holy faith and pray in the Holy Spirit. ²¹Keep yourselves in God's love as you wait for the mercy of our Lord Jesus Christ to bring you to eternal life.

²²Be merciful to those who doubt; ²³snatch others from the fire and save them; to others show mercy, mixed with fear—hating even the clothing stained by corrupted flesh.

²⁴To him who is able to keep you from falling and to present you before his glorious presence without fault and with great joy— ²⁵to the only God our Savior be glory, majesty, power and authority, through Jesus Christ our Lord, before all ages, now and forevermore! Amen.

ESCHATOLOGY IN THE BOOK OF REVELATION

Chapter 20

¹And I saw an angel coming down out of heaven, having the key to the Abyss and holding in his hand a great chain. ²He seized the dragon, that ancient serpent, who is the devil, or Satan, and bound him for a thousand years. ³He threw him into the Abyss, and locked and sealed it over him, to keep him from deceiving the nations anymore until the thousand years were ended. After that, he must be set free for a short time.

⁴I saw thrones on which were seated those who had been given authority to judge. And I saw the souls of those who had been beheaded because of their testimony for Jesus and because of the word of God. They had not worshiped the beast or his image and had not received his mark on their foreheads or their hands. They came to life and reigned with Christ a thousand years. ⁵(The rest of the dead did not come to life until the thousand years were ended.) This is the first resurrection. ⁶Blessed and holy are those who have part in the first resurrection. The second death has no power over them, but they will be priests of God and of Christ and will reign with him for a thousand years.

⁷When the thousand years are over, Satan will be released from his prison ⁸and will go out to deceive the nations in the four corners of the earth—Gog and Magog—to gather them for battle. In number they are like the sand on the seashore. ⁹They marched across the breadth of the earth and surrounded the camp of God's people, the city he loves. But fire came down from heaven and devoured them. ¹⁰And the devil, who deceived them, was thrown into the lake of burning sulfur, where the beast and the false prophet had been thrown. They will be tormented day and night for ever and ever.

¹¹Then I saw a great white throne and him who was seated on it. Earth and sky fled from his presence, and there was no place for them. ¹²And I saw the dead, great and small, standing before the throne, and books were opened. Another book was opened, which is the book of life. The dead were judged according to what they had done as recorded in the books. ¹³The sea gave up the dead that were in it, and death and Hades gave up the dead that were in them, and each person was judged according to what he had done. ¹⁴Then death and Hades were thrown into the lake of fire. The lake of fire is the

second death. ¹⁵If anyone's name was not found written in the book of life, he was thrown into the lake of fire.

Chapter 21

¹Then I saw a new heaven and a new earth, for the first heaven and the first earth had passed away, and there was no longer any sea. ²I saw the Holy City, the new Jerusalem, coming down out of heaven from God, prepared as a bride beautifully dressed for her husband. ³And I heard a loud voice from the throne saying, "Now the dwelling of God is with men, and he will live with them. They will be his people, and God himself will be with them and be their God. ⁴He will wipe every tear from their eyes. There will be no more death or mourning or crying or pain, for the old order of things has passed away."

⁵He who was seated on the throne said, "I am making everything new!" Then he said, "Write this down, for these words are trustworthy and true."

⁶He said to me: "It is done. I am the Alpha and the Omega, the Beginning and the End. To him who is thirsty I will give to drink without cost from the spring of the water of life. ⁷He who overcomes will inherit all this, and I will be his God and he will be my son. ⁸But the cowardly, the unbelieving, the vile, the murderers, the sexually immoral, those who practice magic arts, the idolaters and all liars—their place will be in the fiery lake of burning sulfur. This is the second death."

Among the best-known passages in the New Testament are the following two selections from Paul's writings. In these texts, Paul affirms hope in a final triumph over sin and death. How important to Paul is the doctrine of the Resurrection? According to Paul, how should belief in this doctrine affect our daily life?

BEATIFIC VISIONS IN THE EPISTLES OF PAUL FROM THE BOOK OF ROMANS

Chapter 8

¹Therefore, there is now no condemnation for those who are in Christ Jesus, ²because through Christ Jesus the law of the Spirit of life set me free from the law of sin and death. ³For what the law was powerless to do in that it was weakened by the sinful nature, God did by sending his own Son in the likeness of sinful man to be a sin offering. And so he condemned sin in sinful man, ⁴in order that the righteous requirements of the law might be fully met in us, who do not live according to the sinful nature but according to the Spirit.

⁵Those who live according to the sinful nature have their minds set on what that nature desires; but those who live in accordance with the Spirit have their minds set on what the

Spirit desires. ⁶The mind of sinful man is death, but the mind controlled by the Spirit is life and peace; ⁷the sinful mind is hostile to God. It does not submit to God's law, nor can it do so. ⁸Those controlled by the sinful nature cannot please God.

⁹You, however, are controlled not by the sinful nature but by the Spirit, if the Spirit of God lives in you. And if anyone does not have the Spirit of Christ, he does not belong to Christ. ¹⁰But if Christ is in you, your body is dead because of sin, yet your spirit is alive because of righteousness. ¹¹And if the Spirit of him who raised Jesus from the dead is living in you, he who raised Christ from the dead will also give life to your mortal bodies through his Spirit, who lives in you.

¹²Therefore, brothers, we have an obligation—but it is not to the sinful nature, to live according to it. ¹³For if you live according to the sinful nature, you will die; but if by the Spirit you put to death the misdeeds of the body, you will live, ¹⁴because those who are led by the Spirit of God are sons of God. ¹⁵For you did not receive a spirit that makes you a slave again to fear, but you received the Spirit of sonship. And by him we cry, "Abba, Father." ¹⁶The Spirit himself testifies with our spirit that we are God's children. ¹⁷Now if we are children, then we are heirs—heirs of God and coheirs with Christ, if indeed we share in his sufferings in order that we may also share in his glory.

¹⁸I consider that our present sufferings are not worth comparing with the glory that will be revealed in us. ¹⁹The creation waits in eager expectation for the sons of God to be revealed. ²⁰For the creation was subjected to frustration, not by its own choice, but by the will of the one who subjected it, in hope ²¹that the creation itself will be liberated from its bondage to decay and brought into the glorious freedom of the children of God.

²²We know that the whole creation has been groaning as in the pains of childbirth right up to the present time. ²³Not only so, but we ourselves, who have the firstfruits of the Spirit, groan inwardly as we wait eagerly for our adoption as sons, the redemption of our bodies. ²⁴For in this hope we were saved. But hope that is seen is no hope at all. Who hopes for what he already has? ²⁵But if we hope for what we do not yet have, we wait for it patiently.

²⁶In the same way, the Spirit helps us in our weakness. We do not know what we ought to pray for, but the Spirit himself intercedes for us with groans that words cannot express. ²⁷And he who searches our hearts knows the mind of the Spirit, because the Spirit intercedes for the saints in accordance with God's will.

²⁸And we know that in all things God works for the good of those who love him, who have been called according to his purpose. ²⁹For those God foreknew he also predestined to be conformed to the likeness of his Son, that he might be the firstborn among many brothers. ³⁰And those he predestined, he also called; those he called, he also justified; those he justified, he also glorified.

³¹What, then, shall we say in response to this? If God is for us, who can be against us? ³²He who did not spare his own Son, but gave him up for us all—how will he not also, along with him, graciously give us all things? ³³Who will bring any charge against those whom God has chosen? It is God who justifies. ³⁴Who is he that condemns? Christ Jesus, who died—more than that, who was raised to life—is at the right hand of God and is also interceding for us. ³⁵Who shall separate us from the love of Christ? Shall trouble or hardship or persecution or famine or nakedness or danger or sword? ³⁶As it is written: "For your sake we face death all day long; we are considered as sheep to be slaughtered." ³⁷No, in all these things we are more than conquerors through him who loved us. ³⁸For I am convinced that neither death nor life, neither angels nor demons, neither the present nor the future, nor any powers, ³⁹neither height nor depth, nor anything else in all creation, will be able to separate us from the love of God that is in Christ Jesus our Lord.

FROM THE BOOK OF 1 CORINTHIANS

Chapter 15

¹Now, brothers, I want to remind you of the gospel I preached to you, which you received and on which you have taken your stand. ²By this gospel you are saved, if you hold firmly to the word I preached to you. Otherwise, you have believed in vain.

³For what I received I passed on to you as of first importance: that Christ died for our sins according to the Scriptures, ⁴that he was buried, that he was raised on the third day according to the Scriptures, ⁵and that he appeared to Peter, and then to the Twelve. ⁶After that, he appeared to more than five hundred of the brothers at the same time, most of whom are still living, though some have fallen asleep. ⁷Then he appeared to James, then to all the apostles, ⁸and last of all he appeared to me also, as to one abnormally born.

⁹For I am the least of the apostles and do not even deserve to be called an apostle, because I persecuted the church of God. ¹⁰But by the grace of God I am what I am, and his grace to me was not without effect. No, I worked harder than all of them—yet not I, but the grace of God that was with me. ¹¹Whether, then, it was I or they, this is what we preach, and this is what you believed.

¹²But if it is preached that Christ has been raised from the dead, how can some of you say that there is no resurrection of the dead? ¹³If there is no resurrection of the dead, then not even Christ has been raised. ¹⁴And if Christ has not been raised, our preaching is useless and so is your faith. ¹⁵More than that, we are then found to be false witnesses about God, for we have testified about God that he raised Christ from the dead. But he did not raise him if in fact the dead are not raised. ¹⁶For if the dead are not raised, then Christ has not been raised either. ¹⁷And if Christ has not been raised, your faith is futile; you are still in your sins. ¹⁸Then those also who have fallen asleep in Christ are lost. ¹⁹If only for this life we have hope in Christ, we are to be pitied more than all men.

²⁰But Christ has indeed been raised from the dead, the first-fruits of those who have fallen asleep. ²¹For since death came through a man, the resurrection of the dead comes also through a man. ²²For as in Adam all die, so in Christ all will be made alive. ²³But each in his own turn: Christ, the first-fruits; then, when he comes, those who belong to him. ²⁴Then the end will come, when he hands over the kingdom to God the Father after he has destroyed all dominion, authority and power. ²⁵For he must reign until he has put all his enemies under his feet. ²⁶The last enemy to be destroyed is death. ²⁷For he "has put everything under his feet." Now when it says that "everything" has been put under him, it is clear that this does not include God himself, who put everything under Christ. ²⁸When he has done this, then the Son himself will be made subject to him who put everything under him, so that God may be all in all.

²⁹Now if there is no resurrection, what will those do who are baptized for the dead? If the dead are not raised at all, why are people baptized for them? ³⁰And as for us, why do we endanger ourselves every hour? ³¹I die every day—I mean that, brothers—just as surely as I glory over you in Christ Jesus our Lord. ³²If I fought wild beasts in Ephesus for merely human reasons, what have I gained? If the dead are not raised, "Let us eat and drink, for tomorrow we die." ³³Do not be misled: "Bad company corrupts good character." ³⁴Come back to your senses as you ought, and stop sinning; for there are some who are ignorant of God—I say this to your shame.

³⁵But someone may ask, "How are the dead raised? With what kind of body will they come?" ³⁶How foolish! What you sow does not come to life unless it dies. ³⁷When you sow, you do not plant the body that will be, but just a seed, perhaps of wheat or of something else. ³⁸But God gives it a body as he has determined, and to each kind of seed he gives its own body. ³⁹All flesh is not the same: Men have one kind of flesh, animals have another, birds another and fish another. ⁴⁰There are also heavenly bodies and there are earthly bodies; but the splendor of the heavenly bodies is one kind, and the splendor of the earthly bodies is another. ⁴¹The sun has one kind of splendor, the moon another and the stars another; and star differs from star in splendor.

⁴²So will it be with the resurrection of the dead. The body that is sown is perishable, it is raised imperishable; ⁴³it is sown in dishonor, it is raised in glory; it is sown in weakness, it is raised in power; ⁴⁴it is sown a natural body, it is raised a spiritual body. If there is a natural body, there is also a spiritual body. ⁴⁵So it is written: "The first man Adam became a living being"; the last Adam, a lifegiving spirit. ⁴⁶The spiritual did not come first, but the natural, and after that the spiritual. ⁴⁷The first man was of the dust of the earth, the second man from heaven. ⁴⁸As was the earthly man, so are those who are

of the earth; and as is the man from heaven, so also are those who are of heaven. [49]And just as we have borne the likeness of the earthly man, so shall we bear the likeness of the man from heaven.

[50]I declare to you, brothers, that flesh and blood cannot inherit the kingdom of God, nor does the perishable inherit the imperishable. [51]Listen, I tell you a mystery: We will not all sleep, but we will all be changed— [52]in a flash, in the twinkling of an eye, at the last trumpet. For the trumpet will sound, the dead will be raised imperishable, and we will be changed. [53]For the perishable must clothe itself with the imperishable, and the mortal with immortality. [54]When the perishable has been clothed with the imperishable, and the mortal with immortality, then the saying that is written will come true: "Death has been swallowed up in victory." [55]"Where, O death, is your victory? Where, O death, is your sting?" [56]The sting of death is sin, and the power of sin is the law. [57]But thanks be to God! He gives us the victory through our Lord Jesus Christ. [58]Therefore, my dear brothers, stand firm. Let nothing move you. Always give yourselves fully to the work of the Lord, because you know that your labor in the Lord is not in vain.

PowerWeb SUPPLEMENTS

1. **The Bible's Lost Stories,** Barbara Kantrowitz and Anne Underwood, *Newsweek,* December 8, 2003.
2. **The Real Jesus: How a Jewish Reformer Lost his Jewish Identity,** Jay Tolson and Linda Kulman, *U.S. News & World Report,* March 8, 2004.
3. **The Changing Face of the Church,** Kenneth L. Woodward, *Newsweek,* April 16, 2001.
4. **A Matter of Faith,** Karen Armstrong, *Harvard International Review,* Winter, 2004.

Books and movies with religious themes are ubiquitous, but rarely do works with such themes achieve blockbuster status. Two recent exceptions to this rule, however, were Dan Brown's 2003 novel *The Da Vinci Code* and Mel Gibson's 2004 movie *The Passion of the Christ.* The media coverage given to these masterpieces directed public interest toward religious topics that scholars have been studying for decades. Brown's novel, for example, inspired a rethinking of the place of Mary Magdalene in particular and women in general in Christian history, while Gibson's movie renewed the debate on the relationship between Jews, Jesus, and Christianity. Two thoughtful articles written during the uproar that surrounded these commercial hits are available in the *PowerWeb* resources. In the first article, Barbara Kantrowitz and Anne Underwood discuss how modern scholars are challenging the traditional minimization of the roles of biblical women in the history of both Judaism and Christianity. In the second piece, Jay Tolson and Linda

Kulman remind readers of the anti-Semitic outbreaks that have plagued the history of Christianity since its early attempt to distance itself from Jesus's Jewish origins.

Also highly recommended are two articles that call to our attention the simple fact that all spiritual traditions must meet the challenges of every age in order to survive as living religions. Confronting and overcoming these challenges often produce painful inner tensions and controversies. The third supplemental reading, a *Newsweek* article by Kenneth L. Woodward, describes the consequences of the dramatic transitions that have taken place within Christianity during the twentieth century when it was transformed from a predominately Caucasian to a predominately non-Caucasian religion with major centers in Asia, Africa, and Latin America. In a final *PowerWeb* selection taken from the *Harvard International Review,* Karen Armstrong comments on the history and meanings of "fundamentalism." Examining these articles about Christianity's recent past will prime readers to ponder questions about its future and to speculate about what scholars a century from now will be writing about the history of Christianity in the twenty-first century.

Readings from *PowerWeb: Religion* are available at the McGraw-Hill *PowerWeb* website http://www.dushkin.com/powerweb. A personal access code to *PowerWeb: Religion* is provided free with each new copy of this book. Those who purchase a used copy may buy an access code at the website.

SELECTED BIBLIOGRAPHY

Akenson, Donald Harman. *Saint Saul: A Skeleton Key to the Historical Jesus.* New York: Oxford University Press, 2000.

Bettenson, Henry, and Chris Maunder, ed., *Documents of the Christian Church.* Oxford: Oxford University Press, 1999.

Borg, Marcus. *Jesus: A New Vision.* San Francisco: Harper and Row, 1988.

Brownrigg, Ronald, *Who's Who in the New Testament.* New York: Holt, Rinehart and Wilson, 1971.

Buss, Andreas E. *The Russian-Orthodox Tradition and Modernity.* Boston: Brill, 2003.

Carmody, Denise, and John Carmody. *Christianity: An Introduction.* Belmont, CA: Wadsworth, 1983.

Chadwick, Henry. *The Early Church.* New York: Penguin, 1993.

Charlesworth, James, and Walter P. Weaver, ed. *Jesus Two Thousand Years Later.* Valley Forge, PA: Trinity Press International, 2000.

Dawes, Gregory W. *The Historical Jesus Question: The Challenge of History to Religious Authority.* London: Westminster John Knox Press, 2001.

Fleming, James. *The God Present During Difficulty.* Jerusalem: Biblical Resources, 2001.

Ehrman, Bart D. *The Orthodox Corruption of Scripture: The Effect of Early Christological Controversies on the Text of the New Testament.* New York: Oxford University Press, 1993.

Jenkins, Phillip. *Hidden Gospels: How the Search for Jesus Lost Its Way.* New York: Oxford University Press, 2001.

Johnson, Paul. *A History of Christianity.* New York: Atheneum, 1976.

Metzger, Bruce. *The Canon of the New Testament.* Oxford: Clarendon, 1987.

Perrin, Norman, and Dennis Duling. *The New Testament: An Introduction.* New York: Harcourt Brace Jovanovich, 1982.

Sanders, E. P. *The Historical Figure of Jesus.* New York: Penguin Books, 1993.

Schillebeeckx, Edward. *Jesus.* New York: Crossroad, 1981.

Stark, Rodney. *The Rise of Christianity.* New York: HarperCollins, 1997.

Wiggins, James B., and Robert S. Ellwood. *Christianity: A Cultural Perspective.* Englewood Cliffs, NJ: Prentice Hall, 1988.

Young, Frances M. *Biblical Exegesis and the Formation of Christian Culture.* Cambridge: Cambridge University Press, 1997.

Islam 3

With more than 1 billion followers, Islam is now the second largest religion in the world, superseded in size only by Christianity. Despite its immensity, however, Islam remains one of the world's most misunderstood religious traditions. Some still incorrectly refer to it as Muhammadanism. This term is offensive to Muslims because it focuses on a man rather than on God and because it implies that Muhammad was the creator of the tradition. Faithful Muslims vehemently deny this assertion and insist that Muhammad was only the mouthpiece God used to call people back to the pure faith earlier delivered to Abraham, Jesus, and the other prophets. The correct name of this tradition is Islam. The Arabic letters *s-l-m* form the root for the English words "surrender" and "peace." Hence, Islam can carry a double meaning. In its fullest sense, Islam refers to the peace that comes when a person's life is surrendered to God. One who knows the peace that proceeds from submitting to God's will is known as a Muslim.[1]

Many Westerners also mistakenly equate Islam with the Arab world. Although Islam grew out of Arabia and remains the preferred religion of most Arabic-speaking peoples, not all Arabs are Muslims, and less than one in four Muslims worldwide are Arabs. The four nations with the largest Islamic populations—Indonesia, Pakistan, Bangladesh, and India—are located in South Asia, not in the Middle East. In the West, Muslims are more numerous than Methodists in England and Episcopalians in the

United States. Muslim, in sum, is a religious, not an ethnic term, and Islam, far from being a regional religion, is one of the world's most diffused religions.

SETTING

Muhammad was born around 570 CE in Mecca, a small Arabian town located about 50 miles east of the Red Sea. At the time of his birth, the Roman and the Persian empires that had dominated the ancient world for more than a millennium were in decline. Although the demise of these powers did not produce the religion of the prophet Muhammad, the disintegration of these powers did allow for its rapid expansion. The story of the birth of Islam (or the story of the restoration of true monotheistic religion) is intricately linked with the social and cultural history of the Arabian peninsula during the early seventh century. The larger story of the remarkable rise of Islam to a position of world dominance is a chapter in the complex history of the decline of the Roman and the Persian empires.

About two centuries before the birth of Muhammad, Germanic peoples penetrated the frontiers of the Roman Empire. Over the next century, the so-called barbarians overran the Roman provinces from Britain to Asia Minor. The city of Rome itself was sacked by the Visigoths in 410 and pillaged again by the Vandals in 455. After the assassination of Romulus Augustulus in 476, no Roman emperor ever again ruled the western half of the empire. Romans, or at least Greek speakers who called themselves Romans, would continue to command the eastern empire for another 1,000 years. On occasions these Eastern Roman (or

---

[1]There are a number of variant English spellings for the name of the prophet (Mohammed, Mahomet, Muhammad) and of the followers of Islam (Moslems, Muslims). Muhammad and Muslim are the spellings used in this text.

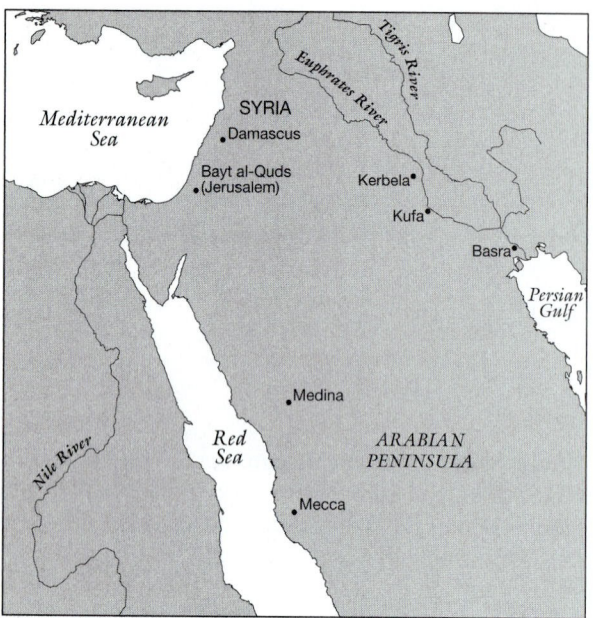

The Arabian peninsula.

Byzantine) emperors aspired to restore Rome's former greatness. At one point in the sixth century during the reign of Emperor Justinian I, it looked as if the Eastern Empire would regain the lost provinces of the West. This moment of glory, however, soon faded. Within a generation following Justinian's death, the Lombards invaded Italy, the Visigoths reconquered Spain, and the Slavs overran most of the Balkan provinces. Sensing the weakness of the teetering Byzantine regime, the Sassanid Persians attacked their ancient adversary's southern frontiers. The ensuing Byzantine-Persian War was fought between two evenly matched powers, both of which had long passed their prime. This prolonged and bitter conflict exhausted the reserves of both parties and encouraged the empires to levy greater taxes on the subjects under their control. Both consequences of the war—the weakening of the imperial powers and the growing distaste of subjected peoples to the policies of these powers—worked to the advantage of a new empire that would rise from the sands of Arabia to challenge the former imperial giants for control of the Mediterranean world.

Arabia was an unlikely place to give birth to an empire that within a century would extend from the Atlantic Ocean to China—a geographic region larger than the Roman Empire at the height of its power. Be-

fore the time of Muhammad, the Arabian peninsula had never achieved political unity. The peninsula, roughly the size of the United States east of the Mississippi River, was mostly a desert wilderness. Traditionally, its most populated and prosperous area was the well-watered highlands of Yemen. Known in biblical times as the Land of Sheba, this irrigated region in southern Arabia supported a settled farming population and was known throughout the Mediterranean as a source for frankincense, myrrh, and other spices. In the sixth century, however, Yemen was invaded and occupied first by the Christian kingdom of Ethiopia and later by the Sassanid Persians. By the time of Muhammad's birth, central Arabia was replacing Yemen as the cultural center of the peninsula.

The cradle of Islam was not Yemen, but the Hejaz (an Arabic word meaning the "barrier"). The Hejaz was a hot, arid, and rugged region between the Red Sea coastline and the desert interior of central Arabia. It was settled by tribes that lived on oases and by nomadic peoples known as Bedouins[2] who survived on the herding of animals. In this harsh environment, physical strength and courage were highly esteemed virtues. The peoples of the Hejaz were divided into clans and placed a premium on clan honor. If a member of one clan was killed or dishonored, there would be a vendetta placed against the kin group of the one who committed the wrong. Consequently, chronic feuding was commonplace. According to Islamic sources, the age before Muhammad was an age of ignorance ("Jahiliah"), a time when irrational violence characterized life in the Hejaz.

The two primary towns of the Hejaz were Mecca and Yathrib (renamed Medinatul-Nabi, or "city of the Prophet," which later was shortened to simply Medina). Mecca was located near a famous spring, "Zamzam," in a rocky valley between a range of mountains paralleling the coast.[3] The town grew up around a religious shrine known as the Kaaba, which means "cube." The box-shaped Kaaba housed a sacred black stone, perhaps a meteorite, which accord-

---

[2]The term *Bedouin* is derived from the Arabic word for primitiveness, and it often is used to describe the nomads of the Arabian, Syrian, and North African deserts.

[3]Muslims believe that the story of the Zamzam well is referenced in Genesis 21:19 in the familiar account of Hagar and Ishmael. The verse reads: "And God opened her eyes, and she saw a well of water; and she went, and filled the bottle with water, and gave the lad drink."

ing to Islamic tradition was delivered by the angel Gabriel to Abraham. This holy site was considered so important that Bedouins observed a four-month annual truce to allow pilgrims to go to the shrine to worship. The area around the shrine was recognized as a sanctuary where neither the taking of life nor the apprehension of criminals was permitted. Yathrib (Medina) was located 250 miles to the north of Mecca on a large oasis in the midst of an otherwise barren desert. This city consisted of a group of fortified farming villages that produced palm dates and grains for export. Its population included Jews who were the descendants of refugees escaping Babylonian or Roman persecution. Although the Jews adopted the Arabic language and many features of Arab culture, they maintained a strict monotheistic faith that separated them from their polytheistic Arabian neighbors.

By the seventh century, Mecca was emerging as the most important trading center in Arabia. Situated at the junction of a north/south caravan route linking Palestine with Yemen and an east/west road connecting the Red Sea with the Persian Gulf, the city attracted a large merchant class that not only supplied the local pilgrims visiting the Kaaba with their wares but also acted as middlemen for interregional trade between Africa and the Fertile Crescent. When the Byzantine-Persian war broke out and disrupted competing trade arteries, the merchants of Mecca enjoyed both increased traffic and profits. According to some historians, the new prosperity and the greater contact with the distant world strained the social fabric of Arabian society. The gradual transition in Mecca toward a mercantile economy created class tensions that undermined traditional folkways. As a result, power shifted from tribal leaders to people of wealth, drunken orgies and gambling became commonplace, orphans were sold into slavery, women were sexually exploited, and the rich oppressed the poor. Simply stated, old pastoral rules no longer provided adequate solutions for the problems of an increasingly cosmopolitan society. For many scholars, Muhammad's forceful teachings on the virtues of almsgiving and dependence on God rather than wealth describe an environment in which neglect for the poor and an excessive attachment to wealth were commonplace vices. Muhammad's Mecca had become a thriving economic center, but its progress brought with it great social hardships as well as great prosperity.

According to Islamic sources, pre-Islamic religion provided few incentives for noble living. There was no concept of an afterlife that rewarded selflessness or punished selfishness. Death was final; making the most of life was considered the best path to happiness. To receive earthly benefits from the supernatural powers, Arabs paid homage to their tribal deities, making periodic visits to sacred sites that often were located near springs, trees, or unusual rock formations. The Kaaba in Mecca contained 360 idols representing the various spirits of the Hejaz. Mecca's chief god was Hubal, represented as a man with a body made of red precious stones and with arms made of solid gold. Mecca was also a center for the worship of three goddesses: al-Lat, al-Uzza, and Manat. Al-Lat and al-Uzza were manifestations of the planet Venus, the evening and morning star. Manat was a goddess of destiny, suggesting the importance of fatalism in Arabic culture.

Between the gods and humankind were the jinns, supernatural beings who took on earthly form to harass or, on occasion, to assist human mortals. The jinns communicated with mortals through soothsayers who interpreted dreams, made prophecies, and performed miracles under the empowerment of the spirits. These supernatural messages often were communicated through the seers in short, staccato-rhymed prose, punctuated with repeated oaths calling upon the names of the various deities. Soothsayers with these special prophetic gifts were held in high esteem and were often consulted as advisers in both private and public matters.

In pre-Islamic Arabia, there also was a belief in a deity called Allah. The name is a contraction of the Arabic words "al-" meaning "the" and "ilah" meaning "god." Allah, thus, literally means "The God." Before the time of Muhammad, Allah was not worshipped as the one and only god, but He still was viewed as a god of enormous power and wonder. He was the creator, provider, and determiner of human destiny. Although too abstract for most Arabs, some of the more contemplative types focused on Allah to the exclusion of the lesser deities. Later Muslims would call these ascetics who yearned for a higher god as Hanifs, meaning "rightly inclined" but sometimes translated as "monotheists." Modern scholars disagree on whether or not the Hanifs were indeed monotheists, and on the extent, if any, that Jewish or Christian teachings influenced Hanif beliefs. Most would agree, however, that in the seventh century there were growing numbers of Arabs who were rejecting traditional polytheism for new forms of ethical monotheism.

In the century before Muhammad, a militant anti-Byzantine convert to Judaism gained power over the south Arabian kingdom of Himyar. In an attempt to consolidate his control, the Jewish king burned Christian churches and massacred Christian civilians throughout the region. When the neighboring Christian state of Ethiopia learned of the atrocities, Ethiopian forces invaded Himyar, secured dominance over the region, and replaced the Jewish king with a Christian prince. Himyar survived as a nominally Christian kingdom until it was conquered in 570 by an army of the Sassanid Persians.

Although there were relatively few Christians in central Arabia during the seventh century, some knowledge of Christianity penetrated the region via trade with the two neighboring states north of the Hejaz. These states included Ghassanid, a Byzantine buffer state, and Lakhmid, a state largely controlled by the Sassanid Persians. The peoples of both kingdoms spoke Arabic and, for the most part, were Christian, although the brand of Christianity they practiced was not the Orthodox faith of the Byzantine Empire. The Ghassanid Christians were Monophysites, from a word meaning "one nature." Unlike the Christian Orthodox, the Monophysites rejected the statements approved in 451 at the Council of Chalcedon that asserted that Jesus was both fully divine and fully human. The Monophysites instead emphasized the single divine nature of Christ, insisting that Jesus had a human body but that his mind was divine. At the opposite end of the theological spectrum were the Lakhmid Christians who embraced a brand of Christianity known as Nestorianism. The Nestorians emphasized the humanity of Christ over his divinity and specifically rejected the Orthodox use of the term "mother of God" to describe the Virgin Mary. Orthodox Christians condemned both the Ghassanid Monophysites and the Lakhmid Nestorians as heretics. Although few common folk of the region would have understood the subtle theological differences between the various sects, many were aware of the bitter divisions among those who called themselves Christian. The Christianity that entered seventh-century central Arabia via the caravan traders of the northern kingdoms or through the military conquests of the southern ones would have appeared to the people of Bedouin culture as militant, sectarian, and enormously complex.

In sum, by the early seventh century Arabia was in a state of transition. Interregional trade was bringing new money and new ideas into a region that for centuries had been isolated from the power centers of the Mediterranean world. Economic change created new wealth, but it also produced a moral crisis. Old mores and pagan religious traditions seemed to be dissolving. Both Judaism and Christianity had penetrated the peninsula to some degree, but neither one was able to gain dominance over the region. The land was ripe for change, but it needed an innovator who could fuse together the pagan, Jewish, and Christian religions in a way that would connect the old traditions of the desert with the new requirements of a more complex commercial society. It was into this world that Muhammad was born.

SACRED STORIES AND BELIEFS

The sacred history of Islam begins not with Muhammad, but with Adam, the first man; Noah, a prophet at the time of a great flood; and Abraham, the father of all Semitic peoples. Accounts of these men are found in the book of Genesis, which is accepted as scripture by Jews and Christians as well as Muslims, and in the Qur'an, a work singularly within the holy canon of Islam.

Abraham and His Sons

Two important stories within Islam are those concerning the patriarch Abraham and his two sons, Isaac and Ishmael. The word *Islam*, meaning "surrendering," conjures memories of the story in which Abraham offers his son as a sacrifice to God. Although God intervenes and prevents the slaughter, the willingness of Abraham to sacrifice his son in obedience to God demonstrates his complete surrender to God's will. In submitting himself totally to God, Abraham acted as a Muslim, one who finds peace through submission to God.

A second story central to Islam involves Abraham and his son Ishmael (or Ismail). Ishmael was the son of Abraham and Hagar, the Egyptian handmaid of Abraham's wife Sarah. After Sarah gave birth to Isaac, she became jealous of Hagar and Ishmael and asked that they be banished from the tribe. Here a divergence between the biblical and quranic accounts

The Dome of the Rock. Muslims believe that two sacred events took place at this holy site: (1) Abraham prepared to sacrifice his son at this location before Allah intervened to stop the slaughter, and (2) Muhammad began his night journey from this Jerusalem location.

In the Hajj ritual, pilgrims run back and forth between Safa and Marwa, the two points that Hagar is believed to have run between seven times in search of water.

exists. According to the Qur'an, Hagar and Ishmael settled in the Becca Valley along the ancient trade route between Canaan and Yemen, the site of the future city of Mecca. Upon arriving in this barren valley, Ishmael became desperately ill and in need of water. While searching for assistance, Hagar ran back and forth seven times between two promontories. In response to her cry for help, God provided the spring of Zamzam to supply Ishmael's needs. Ishmael survived and became the father of the Arab peoples. Abraham later visited his son, and at the visit God showed Abraham where he should build a place of worship, the Kaaba. The angel Gabriel then gave Abraham a black celestial stone that was placed in the southeast corner of the Kaaba. God instructed Abraham to begin a rite of pilgrimage to the Kaaba. In the rite, pilgrims were told to circle the stone in a counterclockwise direction seven times before they approached and kissed the stone. According to Islamic belief, Arabs have been making pilgrimages to the Kaaba since the age of Abraham. Over time, however, the worship of the true God at the Kaaba was corrupted by the importation of pagan idols. In the pre-Islamic age of ignorance, the originally holy shrine erected to the God without form was filled with 360 idols of various pagan deities.

Islamic Stories of Jesus

Muslims embrace a number of sacred stories about the life of Jesus. The Qur'an speaks of angels appearing to a virgin woman, Mary, the future mother of Jesus. The angels told Mary that she would be impregnated by God and would give birth to a child who would be the Messiah. His name was to be Jesus. He would be an apostle of God, and, being filled with the Holy Spirit, he would do wondrous signs and lead a righteous life.

Unlike orthodox Christians, Muslims deny that Jesus was God in the flesh. They also insist that Jesus did not die on a cross, but was taken by God into Paradise. Many Muslims believe in the Second Coming of Jesus and that in the final Day of Resurrection, Jesus will testify against the evil doers and those who claim that he was a deity and not God's prophet.

Muhammad's Ancestry, Birth, and Childhood

The year of Muhammad's birth, according to Islamic sources, was a special year in the memory of the people of Arabia. In this year, remembered by Muslims as the Year of the Elephant, the Christian ruler of Yemen planned to destroy the Kaaba and divert the pilgrims and their money to a church recently constructed in southern Arabia. When he approached the Kaaba with a large army supported by a herd of elephants, his army and elephants were attacked by a swarm of birds that dropped pea-sized pellets. An epidemic of death followed the attack, and the survivors were forced into retreat. Muslims believe that God sent the birds to protect the Kaaba from destruction.

Many stories abound describing Muhammad's ancestry, birth, and childhood. According to these accounts, Muhammad's great-grandfather pioneered the caravan trade that connected Mecca with the outside empires. His grandfather secured for the Quaraish tribe of Mecca the privilege of serving the pilgrims who visited the Kaaba with food and water. He also was the man responsible for restoring the sacred Zamzam well that centuries earlier had provided water to Ishmael. Muhammad's father, Abd-allah (meaning "servant of God") had a mysterious "white light" between his eyes on the day that Muhammad was conceived. His mother, Amina, at the time of her delivery, heard a voice tell her that her child was "the

lord of the people" and that he was to be named Muhammad, meaning "the praised one." Although a child of the city, Muhammad was nursed by a Bedouin woman and thus received through her the strength of the desert nomads. At age five, Muhammad received a vision in which two men dressed in white opened his chest and removed a black clot from his heart. They then placed him on scales against the weight of 1,000 men and found that Muhammad outweighed the whole community of men.

Muhammad's father died before his son was born, and his mother died when Muhammad was only six years old. Muhammad then lived for two years with his grandfather, the keeper of the Kaaba. When his grandfather died, he was raised by his uncle, Abu Talib, who also was a prominent merchant involved in the caravan trade. According to legend, at age 12 Muhammad went with his uncle to Syria, where he met a Christian monk who recognized his special qualities and warned those in his party to protect Muhammad from those who would try to harm him.

Muhammad's Early Prophetic Career

At age 25, Muhammad became the business manager of Khadija, a wealthy widow involved in the caravan trade. Although she was 15 years his senior, Muhammad and Khadija married and together had four daughters, each of whom lived to adulthood, and two or three sons, each of whom died in infancy. Muhammad, however, adopted into his household two boys: his cousin, Ali, a son of Abu Talib, and a slave, Zayd, whom his wife purchased and Muhammad freed and adopted into the family. Muhammad's marriage to Khadija was said to be a happy one. Contrary to the custom of his day, Muhammad never married other wives until after Khadija's death in 619.

By mid-life, Muhammad already had experienced both great joys and sorrows. Born into a prestigious family, he nonetheless was orphaned as a child and consequently received no fatherly inheritance. His marriage to Khadija supplied him with wealth and with a family of daughters, but the deaths of his infant sons brought him personal sorrow if not community shame. Although prosperous and respected throughout Mecca, Muhammad was not fully satisfied. He became more contemplative and spent quiet times in meditation in the nearby caves around Mount Hira.

When Muhammad was approaching 40 years of age, an angel appeared to him in a cave and commanded him to "recite." Muhammad at first delayed, insisting that he was illiterate and not prepared for the task. The angel, however, repeated the command. After three warnings, Muhammad began to recite what he was told: "Recite in the name of your Lord who created—created man from clots of blood. Recite! Your Lord is the Most Bountiful One, who by the pen taught man what he did not know." Muhammad received this first revelation in the year 610. The words of this famous revelation later would be codified in Surah 96 of the Qur'an.

Upon leaving the cave, Muhammad heard a voice telling him, "You are the messenger of Allah, and I am Gabriel." He promptly returned home and told his wife his experience. Khadija encouraged him to continue to proclaim the truth. His wife, thus, became the first believer in the genuineness of Muhammad's call. Other early believers who would play a role in the later history of Islam included Muhammad's adopted sons, Ali and Zayd, and Abu Bakr, a close friend and, according to the majority of Muslims, his subsequent successor.

Converts to Islam, however, came slowly, largely because the central message "no god but Allah" threatened the lucrative Meccan economy. Local merchants feared that this teaching would bring an end to the traditional annual pilgrimages to the Kaaba. They also disliked the tenor of his social teachings, which condemned the pursuit of wealth without regard to the conditions of the weak and which called for an end to alcohol consumption and to promiscuous sex. Although some Meccans secretly came to Muhammad to receive his teachings, the leadership of the city ridiculed Muhammad and those who embraced his radical vision of ethical monotheism.

Owing to the prestige of Muhammad's family, the Prophet was protected from those who wanted to see him eliminated. Some of the less influential converts, however, enjoyed no such protection. Muhammad sent a few families across the Red Sea to the more tolerant kingdom of Ethiopia, where the Christian king granted them asylum and protected them from the Meccan leaders who sought their capture and return. Other followers who remained in Mecca were stoned, beaten, or thrown into prison by the politically powerful polytheists. For a brief period, even Muhammad was forced to seek refuge in a mountain fortress of his uncle, Abu Talib. The hostile local climate convinced Muhammad that a location outside Mecca, desirably one less removed from Arabian culture than the African kingdom of Ethiopia, was needed to serve as a base of operation for those who chose to submit to God's will.

Islamic tradition informs us that around the year 620 Muhammad experienced either an extraordinary vision or a miraculous physical journey in which he was taken from Mecca to Jerusalem, making stops along the way at Mount Sinai and Bethlehem. While on this journey, Muhammad prayed with Abraham, Moses, and Jesus and then ascended a celestial ladder to a seventh heaven to speak with God. According to one version of the story, while in the seventh heaven God told him to have his people offer 50 prayers daily. Upon hearing the command, Moses urged Muhammad to negotiate a more reasonable deal for humanity. Muhammad agreed, and after several intercessions, God agreed to reduce the number of daily prayers to five, thus explaining the number of daily prayers required in Islamic law.

The Medina Years

Muslims remember 619 as the Year of Sadness. In this year, Khadija, Muhammad's beloved wife, and Abu Talib, Muhammad's uncle who protected the Prophet from his archenemies, died within a few days of each other. With their deaths, Muhammad and the Muslims of Mecca became more vulnerable to the plots of those who wished to eliminate the growing influence of the Prophet and his teachings.

In 622 a delegation from Yathrib came to Mecca to speak with Muhammad. At this time Yathrib was embroiled in a three-way struggle between two warring Arab tribes and a party of Yathrib Jews. The mission of the delegation was to convince Muhammad to return with them to Yathrib to arbitrate a settlement between the competing parties. Muhammad and the delegation negotiated a pact. Muhammad and all interested Muslims would emigrate to Yathrib, and the natives of that city would submit to God and respect Muhammad as the Prophet of God. In July 622, Mecca Muslims quietly began moving to Yathrib, leaving in small groups at different times in order to avoid being noticed. When

This sixteenth century Turkish miniature depicts Muhammad's vision of ascension into the heavens. Note that in Islamic art, Muhammad is portrayed with a veiled face.

their exodus was noticed, however, the enemies of Islam plotted Muhammad's assassination. Muhammad and his close associate Abu Bukr spent the last night before their departure hiding in a cave. Legend tells us that a spider spun a web over the cave's entrance, making the cave look unoccupied and thereby protecting Muhammad and Abu Bakr from being discovered. Muhammad safely arrived in Yathrib on September 22, 622. Muslims call the journey from Mecca to Yathrib the *Hegira,* a word that means "emigration." This event marks the beginning of the Islamic calendar. Muslims view the Christian year 622 as AH1, which means Anno He-

gira, or Year of the Hegira. The Hegira also came to mark the transition in Islam from the old community based on blood ties to the new worldwide community, known as the Umma, based on adherence to the eternal laws of God.[4]

In time, Yathrib became known as Medinat-al-Nabi, meaning "the city of the Prophet," or simply, Medina, "the city." Muhammad was not the ruler of "the city," but as the Prophet of God he had considerable political and military authority. An immediate task before him was to provide a livelihood for those who had made the Hegira. One attractive option—attractive because it would both strengthen the friends and weaken the enemies of Islam—was to send out parties to raid the caravans traveling to Mecca. Thus, when Muhammad learned of a large caravan traveling from Gaza to Mecca, he sent a force to overtake it. In 624, Muhammad's force met the Meccan army at a site near the wells of Badr. Although outnumbered three to one, the Muslims won the day, killing large numbers of the Meccan leaders while suffering few losses themselves. Remembered by Muslims as the "Day of Distinction," the military victory at Badr provided Muhammad with a harvest of booty and prisoners who could be held for ransom. Viewed as a providential sign of God's special favor, the victory bonded the Muslim community even more tightly together and increased the prestige and power of its leader.

The battle at Badr also triggered a war with Mecca that would drag on for several years. In 627 (AH 5), the Meccans sent a large army against Medina but failed to take the city. During the siege, they convinced a Jewish tribe in Medina to turn against Muhammad. After the crisis passed, Muhammad confronted the disloyal Jews who had betrayed him. Muhammad allowed a mortally wounded Arab soldier to decide how the traitors should be punished. The dying soldier sentenced the Jewish men to death and the women and children to slavery.

---

[4]Unlike the solar calendars of the West, the Muslim year consists of 12 lunar months, or about 354 days. Hence, a Christian century is equivalent to 103 Muslim years. The Qur'an forbids adding extra days periodically to make up for the discrepancies between the lunar and solar years. Most Muslims, however, do not consider it impious to make reference to the dating system used in the West. When using documents produced by Muslim authors, students should be aware of the different dating systems and consult conversion charts to correlate Muslim and Western historical timelines.

Muhammad's Return to Mecca

As news of Muhammad's strength spread across Arabia, many tribal peoples became convinced that Muhammad was the messenger of God and flocked to his side. Fearing Islam's power, in 628 (AH 6) the Meccans agreed to sign a 10-year truce with the Muslims. Two years later, however, when some Meccan allies broke the truce, Muhammad marched with a large force toward Mecca. Outside the city, a delegation of Meccans met Muhammad. There they submitted themselves to God, accepted the Prophet's authority, and pleaded for mercy. Graciously granting amnesty to those who submitted, in January 630 (AH 8) Muhammad triumphantly entered the city, cleansed the Kaaba of its pagan idols, and dedicated the ancient shrine to Islam.

Although Medina remained the political capital for some time, following the cleansing of the Kaaba, Mecca became the religious center of Islam. To this day Muslims turn toward this site during their times of prayer. Pilgrimages to Mecca continued, but after the cleansing, pilgrims came to the Kaaba to worship Allah, the one living God. According to Islamic belief, by the time of Muhammad's death in 632 (AH 10), the Prophet had succeeded in restoring the primeval Arabian monotheism that had been brought to the peninsula more than 2 millennia earlier by Abraham and his son Ishmael.

The Articles of Faith

Muslims embrace six fundamental statements of belief. One summary that contains five of these core articles of faith is the quranic text: "True piety is this: to believe in God, and the Last Day, the Angels, the Book, and the Prophets" (Qur'an 2.176). As this passage suggests, the foremost tenet of Islam is faith in God. For Muslims, this means an acknowledgment of God's divine unity. Although it is generally believed that God has 99 names or attributes, the God of Islam is viewed as one omnipotent, formless being who has existed throughout all eternity. A second faith assumption is a belief in the Last Day, that is, the day of resurrection when all humans will give an account of their actions on earth. Following this day of judgment, those who obeyed God and his messengers will enter Paradise, while the evil doers and rejecters of God will be condemned to Hell. A third fundamental tenet of Islam is belief in intermediary beings called angels. In Islamic tradition, among the more important are Gabriel, the one who communicated God's will to the prophets; Michael, the angel in charge of the natural world; Israfil, the angel who trumpets in the Last Judgment; and Azrael, the angel of death. A fourth statement of faith is belief in God's sacred books. The last of these sacred works, the Qur'an, contains God's final revelation, and thereby supersedes all previous revelations. A fifth article of faith is a belief in the Prophets. From Adam, the first of God's messengers, to Muhammad, the "seal of the prophets," the prophets of God have instructed humankind in matters of faith and practice. Muslims believe that their words of truth provide humans with all that is necessary for salvation. Finally, although not referenced in the preceding passage, another article of faith, at least for the largest body of Muslims known as Sunni, is a belief in destiny. Sunnis teach that everything that happens is controlled by God and is a part of His eternal plan. Nothing happens by chance; all events are for the ultimate benefit of humankind. Muslims insist, however, that this positive affirmation in God's power does not exonerate humans from punishment for immoral actions or from passive resignation in the face of evil.

SCRIPTURES

The Qur'an teaches that God speaks to humans in three ways. The simplest form of revelation (in Arabic, *wahy*) comes to humans as sudden flashes of insight. These messages are not given in words but in the form of ideas that bring immediate enlightenment and clear up doubt. A second form of revelation is through visions or dreams. In this mode, people hear words, but, in the language of the Qur'an, the words are heard as if "from behind a veil." These two forms of revelation can come to all righteous individuals who seek to know God. A third form of revelation, known within Islam as "revelation that is recited" (in Arabic, *wahy matluww*), comes to Prophets only. In this highest form of revelation, God uses a divine messenger—sometimes called the angel Gabriel, sometimes called the Holy Spirit—to communicate directly to humankind through a human mouthpiece known as a prophet. These messages, literally the words of God, provide instruction and guidance intended for the welfare of humankind.

The Qur'an.

Muslims accept as scripture several pieces of revelation that were recited to prophets and later placed into written forms. They, for instance, accept as sacred the Torah, which is God's revelation to Moses on Mount Sinai; the book of Psalms, which was delivered to David; and the Gospels as revealed to Jesus. Islamic law provides certain privileges to Jews and Christians specifically because they are a "people of the book"—that is, because God has spoken to them through prophets and provided them with Holy Scriptures. Muslims also believe that on special occasions God has produced scriptures in other languages for other peoples. According to Islamic belief, however, over time the pure sacred words originally delivered to these peoples became corrupted. Hence, for the benefit of humankind, God sent a final revelation, the Qur'an. The purpose of the Qur'an, which literally means the "recitation," was to correct the imperfections that had crept into the previous holy books. Muslims believe that the Qur'an is the only revealed writing that has not been altered since its original revelation.

The Miracle of the Qur'an

For Muslims, the Qur'an is the infallible Word of God. It is considered an "eternal book," the transcript of a tablet preserved in heaven and later revealed to Muhammad by the angel Gabriel. Unlike Jewish and Christian scriptures, which are largely narrative and only occasionally punctuated with quotations from God, the Qur'an is written as the direct words of God. God sometimes speaks in the first person, sometimes in the third person, and sometimes through the mouths of Gabriel or Muhammad. The voice of the speaker changes frequently, occasionally even in mid-sentence, thus sometimes making the text appear jumbled, obscure, and almost indecipherable. To quote from one prominent Muslim authority, it was as if "the language of mortal man were, under the formidable pressure of the Heavenly Word, broken into a thousand fragments."[5]

The words delivered to Muhammad were recited in rhymed prose, in a form that follows in the tradition of the poets and soothsayers of Arabia. When asked how the message was received, Muhammad said that sometimes it was harsh like the ringing of a bell, and that after the angel left he remembered what was said. On these occasions, the revelation transported Muhammad into a trancelike state that caused him to shake and groan and left him with headaches and severe muscle spasms. At other times, Muhammad said that the angel came to him less violently in the shape of a man who spoke to him, and afterward he remembered what was said. Sometimes companions were with Muhammad at the time of the revelations, but they did not see the angel or hear the voice. Muslims, thus, believe that the message was received with other-than-normal senses and that Muhammad, an uneducated, illiterate man, could not have produced such a work. Muslims insist that the Qur'an was miraculously received, and miraculously remembered, for while Muhammad may have forgotten other things, he never forgot any part of the Qur'an. Muslims, who accept the miracles of Jesus as a proof of his prophet status, also consider the miracle of the Qur'an as a "sign of proof" to its authenticity as God's final word to humankind.

✤ From Revelation to Text

Muhammad received the revelations over a 22-year period between about 610 and his death in 632. Early in his ministry, Muhammad recited the passages to professional remembrancers until they knew them by heart. Later, the memorized words were written down on palm leaves, stones, or other miscellaneous materials at hand. While Muhammad lived in Mecca, his amanuenses were Abu Bakr, his close associate, Ali, his cousin, and Khajidah, his wife. After 622, when

---

[5]Frithjof Schuon, *Understanding Islam* (New York: Penguin Books, 1972), p. 45.

the Prophet moved to Medina, Muhammad's adopted son Zayd did most of the scribal work.

About two-thirds of the quranic verses were received at Mecca and the remainder at Medina. Generally speaking, the larger collection of the earlier Meccan revelations consists of shorter verses that focus primarily on matters of faith and doctrine. They are clothed in vivid and passionate language that often is punctuated with dramatic oaths and bold metaphors. These passages warn of a coming day of judgment, when the righteous will be rewarded and sinners will be punished with hellfire. In comparison, the later Medina revelations are longer instructions that attempt to translate Islamic faith into community actions. More practical and community oriented, these surahs define the difference between good and evil. To sum, the Meccan texts primarily call Muslims to a vertical relationship with an Omnipotent God who promises to requite every deed, while the Medinan verses provide greater details regarding how humans should treat and relate to one another in this world.

During Muhammad's life, there was little need to codify into writing a standardized copy of the revelations. God's command to Muhammad, after all, was "to recite," not to write. Arabian culture was largely an oral culture where the normal mode of transmitting knowledge was via recitation and memorization. Moreover, as long as Muhammad lived, older revelations could be abrogated or expanded upon by newer divine commands. However, following the Prophet's death—after the source of revelation was exhausted, there arose a need to compile and to arrange the memorized and miscellaneous written accounts of the revealed words. Most Muslims hold that the ultimate arrangement as well as the content of the Qur'an is part of the divine plan, although there is some disagreement regarding the role that Muhammad played in the organization of these materials.[6]

The Qur'an is divided into 114 chapters known as *surahs*. The chapters are arranged largely by length, not subject matter or chronological order. After an opening chapter that consists of a short prayer, the chapters are generally arranged from longest to shortest. Chapter 2, for example, contains 286 verses and Chapter 3, 200 verses, while the final 10 chapters contain only about five verses each.[7] Hence, the Qur'an intermingles the Meccan and Medina revelations, although most of the shorter Mecca revelations appear in the second half of the work. The total length of the Qur'an is about 78,000 words, or roughly about 400 pages of text. More than half of these words are contained in the first 19 chapters.

Within a decade after Muhammad's death, Umar (the second caliph or successor to Muhammad) asked Zayd, Muhammad's adopted son and scribe, to produce a copy of the entire Qur'an from the miscellaneous written sources that had been collected. Zayd completed the work and entrusted it with Hafsa, a widow of Muhammad. In addition to Zayd's manuscript, however, several other copies were in circulation. These copies generally had the same surahs as Zayd's copy, but the surahs were arranged in different orders and contained a number of word variations that generally resulted from the use of different Arabic dialects. Several years later, Muslim warriors in distant Armenia complained to the third Caliph Uthman that different versions of the Qur'an were being recited. To prevent a repeat of the Jewish and Christian corruptions of their sacred texts, Uthman instructed Hafsa to send him the copy of the Qur'an that she had in her possession. Uthman then gave the copy to Zayd, who lived in Medina, and to three members of the Quarish tribe from Mecca and instructed them to draft copies from the original. In places where variant wording appeared, the Quraishi form was to be used, since this was the dialect that God used to speak to Muhammad. This task consisted primarily of recopying Zayd's earlier draft. Copies of this text were then sent to the major Islamic centers of Kufa, Basra, Damascus, and perhaps Mecca. Uthman then ordered the destruction of all other copies. This version, the Uthman Authorized Version, is regarded by most Muslims as the authoritative Word of God.

---

[6]Both Sunni and Shi'ite Muslims believe that the words of the Qur'an are the authentic words that were recited to Muhammad, although the Shi'ites suspect that Umar and the Ummiyad rulers arranged the quranic verses in a confusing order in order to make it easier for them to rule over their subjects.

[7]A verse essentially consists of the words written in prose between the rhymed passages. In Arabic, the word *ayats* ("verse") also means "signs" or "proofs." Each verse in the Qur'an, thus, is a sign or proof of God. Because verse designations were not included in the original copy of the Uthman Authorized Version, there are slight variations in the way that the Qur'an has been divided into verses. There are approximately 6,240 verses in the Qur'an, plus the often repeated verse "In the Name of God, the Compassionate, the Merciful," which introduces all but 1 of the 114 chapters.

Quranic Content and Controversy

The oral form of the Qur'an remains of great importance within Islam. Muslim children from diverse nationalities begin their education by learning how to recite this ancient Arabic text properly with correct enunciation and intonation. For more than a millennium, the Qur'an has been the world's most memorized and recited book. Muslims worldwide look to this book much like Christians look to the person of Jesus, as the living Word of God. It regulates every phase of Islamic life—law, faith, and culture.

Although the Qur'an continues themes found in Jewish and Christian scriptures and includes references to 21 biblical characters, unlike the Old and the New Testaments the Qur'an does not ground its theology in historical epics. Biblical references are inserted without commentary and without regard for chronological order, not to tell the history of the relationship between an ethnic group and its god but to illustrate God's character and purpose. The Qur'an gives God 99 names or attributes. Over and over again, it proclaims God's unity and omnipotence. The stern God of the Qur'an is a god of both judgment and mercy. All surahs but one open with the assertion, "In the name of God, the Compassionate, the Merciful." In comparison with the Old and New Testaments (texts that were written by multiple authors over a period in excess of 1,000 years), the Qur'an (a product of one mind, delivered over a period of scarcely more than two decades) appears more uniform, dogmatic, and, to some, more wearisome and redundant. Yet for Muslims, it is not simply a book about truth. It is the divine truth in its final and infallible form.

Even devout Muslims agree that the Qur'an contains some obscure statements and still other passages that are open to more than one interpretation. Moreover, at the beginning of 29 chapters are placed some cryptic Arabic letters. Muslim scholars have offered a number of theories concerning the meanings of these insertions, but none of the interpretations have found universal agreement. Most traditional quranic commentaries dismiss the headings by saying that "God alone knows what He means by these letters." Another controversy surrounding the Qur'an that has divided Islam concerns which quranic verses were abrogated by subsequent revelations and therefore are no longer considered binding. Some scholars place this number at upward of 500 verses. Other students

of the Qur'an reduce the number to five. Still other conservatives consider all verses binding and insist that the quranic references to the abrogation of former scriptures apply only to the Jewish and Christian texts and not the Qur'an itself.

Other Sources of Islamic Teachings

While the Qur'an spells out principles for Muslims to follow, these principles are not always fully explained in the holy text. For example, the Qur'an commands Muslims to pray and to give to charities, but it does not provide details about how to pray or about how much and to whom one should give. To find answers to these and to hundreds of other matters referenced in the Qur'an, Muslims look to the practices and sayings of Muhammad, the one they regard as the most competent interpreter of the Qur'an. Since the Prophet, however, never wrote a book of his sayings or an autobiographical narrative of his life, it was left to a succession of his associates to tell stories of his customs and teachings. These stories, first told and memorized, and much later put down in writing, come to us in large collections known as the Hadith, or The Tradition. Next to the Qur'an, The Tradition is the most important piece of Islamic literature.

There are six major collections of Hadith, which together total hundreds of thousands of stories about the life of Muhammad. Probably the most revered of the collections for Sunni Muslims was compiled by Bukhari, an Islamic scholar who lived two centuries

---

MAJOR ISLAMIC SACRED WRITINGS

The Qur'an ("recitation")
The Word of God revealed to Muhammad by the angel Gabriel
Divided into 114 surahs which are composed of verses called "ayats."

The Hadith ("tradition")
The remembered sayings of Muhammad and his companions
No absolutely canonical edition exists, although there are six major collections that include hundreds of thousands of stories about the life of Muhammad

after the Prophet.[8] Bukhari allegedly examined 600,000 reports about Muhammad, and after scrutinizing each assertion, selected for his collection some 7,400 traditions that he considered most trustworthy. Each tradition is introduced with a statement that links the testimony about Muhammad with a chain of trustworthy reporters dating back to someone who knew the Prophet. In other words, each hadith opens with a comment that says so-and-so said that he heard so-and-so say that he once heard the Prophet make the following statement. Given the vast volumes of reported sayings, it is not surprising that there are numerous discrepancies within the various traditions. Although not claimed by Muslims to be the words of God, the Hadiths make for enjoyable reading and shed considerable light upon the values and culture of early Islamic societies.

SUBDIVISIONS

Succession and the Seeds of Disunity

Shortly after returning to Medina from a pilgrimage to Mecca, Muhammad died in June 632 in the hut of his wife Aisha, the daughter of Abu Bakr. Rumors of the Prophet's death sent shock waves across the city. Umar, one of Muhammad's closest companions and the father of Hafsah, another wife of the Prophet, wept bitterly as he cried: "By God, the Messenger of God will return and will cut off the hands and feet of those who allege that he is dead." Abu Bakr, however, came to Umar and asked him to be silent. At this point, Abu Bakr quoted the quranic verse: "Muhammad is only a messenger; and many a messenger has gone before him. So if he dies or is killed, will you turn back on your heels?" According to tradition, Abu Bakr then placed the passing of the Prophet in perspective, saying, "If you worship Muhammad, know that he is dead; but if you worship God, know that God is living."

At least according to Sunni historiography, since Muhammad had not designated a successor, the Muslim community turned to tribal precedent to elect a new leader—a man who would hold the title

---

CHRONOLOGY OF THE CALIPHS

Muhammad and his Early Successors

Muhammad (d. 632 CE)
Abu Bakr (d. 634 CE)
Umar (d. 644 CE)
Uthman (d. 656 CE)
Ali (d. 661 CE)

"caliph," meaning "successor" of the messenger of God.[9] This was not an easy decision. Many of those who had emigrated with Muhammad from Mecca believed that the caliph should be someone who had been with the Prophet from the beginning. Others who lived in Medina wanted one from their numbers to be selected. Still others believed that someone from Muhammad's family should be chosen. Members of this party supported Ali, the cousin and adopted son of the Prophet and the husband of Fatima, one of Muhammad's daughters.

Ultimately, the electors decided upon Abu Bakr. This elder statesman was perhaps the first male convert to the faith. He also was Muhammad's father-in-law and the sole companion who stood at the Prophet's side during Muhammad's flight from Mecca to Medina. Disappointed and offended at the decision, Ali delayed his recognition of Abu Bakr's authority. Six months later, after his wife Fatima died, Ali acquiesced. Some of his partisan followers, however, who were known throughout Islam as the "party of Ali" or "Shi'ites," never acknowledged the legitimacy of the new caliph's authority.

Abu Bakr survived two years and was succeeded by his preferred successor, Umar. During Umar's 10-year rule, Islam emerged as a world phenomenon, sending Muslim armies into Egypt and forcing Byzantine and Persian troops out of Syria and Iraq. In 644, a Christian slave assassinated Umar, and a council of elders, appointed by Umar on his deathbed, selected Uthman as the third caliph. Uthman was a member of the wealthy Meccan Umayyad family. At least early in his tenure as caliph, Uthman continued in the policies set by Umar. He enlarged the boundaries of Islam,

---

[8]Unlike the Sunni, Shi'ite Muslims revere only those collections that can be linked in narration to Muhammad's family. Consequently, Sunnis have many more sources for these stories than the Shi'ite.

[9]Shi'ites contend, however, that spiritual rulers are not elected but receive their authority from Allah. Moreover, Shi'ites insist that Muhammad at Ghadir appointed Ali to be his successor.

conquering the remainder of Persia in the east and expanding in the west as far as Tripoli on the African coast.

Despite his accomplishments, however, Uthman was hated by many Muslims, in part because of his willingness to award members of his own family with lucrative positions. His decision to establish a standardized, written version of the Qur'an also probably cost him support among the class of professional reciters who heretofore held responsibility for preserving God's holy words. Like his predecessor, Uthman died at the hands of assassins. In 656 (AH 32), his home and headquarters were attacked by a delegation of disgruntled Egyptian Muslims. During the siege, Ali did not rally the Medinans to Uthman's defense. The resulting death of Uthman was a watershed event in Islamic history. After 656 (AH 34), Islam was divided both politically and spiritually along party lines.

After being passed over twice before, Ali finally was selected as Uthman's successor, becoming the fourth caliph of Islam. A number of Muslims, however, rejected his authority. At first he was opposed by an army led by Aisha, the popular wife of Muhammad. An even stronger foe of Ali was Muawiya, a governor of Syria and relative of Uthman who was incensed by Ali's refusal to seek blood revenge against the assassins of the former caliph. When the armies of Ali and Muawiya met at the Plain of Siffin, Muawiya's soldiers placed copies of the Qur'an—the symbol of divine judgment—on their lances. This tactic intimidated Ali's army and forced Ali to accept Muawiya's offer to allow arbitrators to rule on whether Uthman's murderers should be avenged. The resulting arbitration decided in Muawiya's favor.

This episode was a double defeat for Ali. Following the decision, a number of Muslims declared Muawiya to be the rightful caliph of Islam. Moreover, even some of Ali's former supporters broke from him for showing weakness in sending the issue to arbitration. These men, known as the Kharijites or "Seceders," consisted of the bitter enemies of the aristocratic Umayyad family. Viewing *jihad* as the sixth Pillar of the Faith, the Kharijites boldly justified the elimination of grave sinners, such as Uthman, who breached the mandates of the Islamic community. Although never a majority party, this militant puritan sect survived to influence Muslim reformers on several occasions throughout the centuries. Some Kharijite communities remain to this day in parts of the Islamic world, most notably in the nations of northern and eastern Africa.

During Ali's five-year rule, Islam was fragmented into the Shia, Umayyad, and Kharijite parties. Like his two predecessors, in 661 (AH 39) Ali was assassinated, probably by a member of the Kharijite sect. His death marked the end of the era of "rightly guided" caliphs. Upon his death, the powerful Umayyad family installed Muawiya as caliph. When Muawiya died, Hussein, a son of Ali, challenged Yazid, a son of Muawiya, for authority over Islam. In the ensuing conflict, Hussein and his followers were captured and mutilated at Karbala. The anniversary of this tragic event is an important day of mourning for Shite Muslims to this day. From the days of Muawiya onward, members of the Umayyad family ruled as hereditary caliphs from their capital in Damascus until 750, when a Shite-inspired revolution toppled the Umayyad dynasty and replaced it with an Abbasid dynastic line. The Abbasid dynasty survived with only minor territorial losses until the Mongols sacked its capital of Baghdad in 1258.

Islamic Orthodoxy— The Path of the Sunni

Even though there are smaller Islamic sects, the major division within Islam is between the Sunni and the Shi'ite groups. Sunni Islam, which encompasses more than 8 in 10 Muslims worldwide, was originally called "The People of the Path and the Congregation." Historically, the Sunnis are the faithful followers of the *Sunna* (meaning the "path" or "custom") of the Muslim community. The Sunna of the community is derived from several sources: the Qur'an, the traditions contained in the Hadith, and the precedents set by the first four caliphs. During the early centuries of Islam, Sunni scholars developed a number of schools for interpreting the Qur'an and the Sunna. Four of these schools survive in Sunni Islam. The purpose of each of these legal schools was to clarify how to apply the teachings of the Qur'an to all aspects of daily living. To illustrate, the Qur'an commands Muslims to perform daily prayers in a state of purity. What, however, constitutes defilement between the time of washing and the moment of prayer? The four schools provide different sets of answers to such questions. Sunnis consider any of the answers contained in the four legal traditions as acceptable. Another distinguishing principle of Sunni Islam is the principle of community consensus. Sunnis insist that when the scholars of sacred law (*ulama*) reach a consensus, the consensus is never wrong. Hence, according to the Sunnis, ultimate authority rests not in the decisions of a single leader, but in the agreements reached by a consensus of the learned scholars of Islamic law.

Shi'ite Muslims

The largest minority group within Islam is Shi'ite, a group that includes about 15 percent of the worldwide Muslim population. Polity disagreements over questions concerning the line of succession and the ultimate source of religious authority separated the Shi'ite from the Sunni majorities during the first century of Islamic development, and this break has never been fully mended. Shi'ites insist that Muhammad, in obedience to God, appointed his son-in-law Ali as his successor and as the first "Imam," the leader of prayers. Hence, unlike the Sunnis who believe in the validity of the elected caliphs, Shi'ites view the caliphs as usurpers of the rights of Imams, the true spiritual leaders of Islam.

Within Sunni parlance, *Imam* is a term that simply refers to the one who leads the congregation in prayers. For Shi'ites, however, the Imam is the divinely designated leader of Islam, superior to the angels and equal in rank to the Prophets; he is born circumcised and, being immune to sin, is immaculate and infallible. As an intercessor between mortals and God, the Imam reveals to the faithful the esoteric inner meanings of the Qur'an, thus leading them from darkness into light. According to Shi'ite beliefs, Imams are not elected by men, but they are chosen by God from the descendants of Ali and his wife Fatima, Muhammad's daughter. Shi'ites also are convinced that the Umayyad family conspired to eliminate the descendants of Ali by poisoning his eldest son Hassan and by murdering his younger son Hussein. The annual reenactment of Hussein's murder, which took place in 680 in Karbala (a city in modern Iraq), is among the most holy events in the Shi'ite religious calendar. The concept of the Imamate is so important within this tradition that the Shi'ites have expanded the confession of faith to read: "I bear witness that there is no god but God and that Muhammad is His Servant and Messenger and that Ali is the designated Imam and trustee of God."

Shi'ite Subsects: The Twelvers and the Seveners

Most Shi'ites belong to a subgroup known as the Twelvers, named because of their belief that God sent 12 Imams, the first of which was Ali and the last of which was Muhammad al-Muntazzar, meaning Muhammad the "expected." The father of Muhammad al-Muntazzar announced that his son was the "Mahdi," the expected messiah. When the child was five years old, however, he disappeared. Twelvers believe that Muhammad al-Muntazzar did not die but was hidden for a time and will return with Jesus as the Mahdi at the end of time. Twelvers constitute the majority of Muslims in Iran and a substantial minority in the states of Iraq, Lebanon, Pakistan, and India.

A smaller subgroup within the Shi'ite tradition is the Seveners, also known as the Ismailis. The Seveners insist that the true seventh Imam Ismail, was unjustly passed over by the Twelvers, who after falsely accusing him of drunkenness, accepted his younger brother as Imam. Seveners affirm Ismail as the seventh Imam, and assert that his descendant was the hidden Imam who will someday return as the Mahdi.

The Sufi Tradition

As Islam grew in power and wealth, some Muslims longed for a simpler form of piety that focused on prayer and devotion, not military conquest and the pursuit of personal gain. Many of these ascetics adopted the custom of wearing austere garments made of *suuf*, the Arabic word for wool. This practice may explain the origins of the term *Sufi*, a word widely used to describe the mystics of Islam.

Technically, Sufism was not and is not a separate Islamic sect, for most Sufis also view themselves as Sunni or Shi'ite Muslims. Like others in Islam, they follow the Five Pillars of Islam and find spiritual solace by reciting the 99 beautiful names of God. Their ascetic lifestyles and spiritual intensity, however, distinguish them from most other mainstream Muslims. Sufis traditionally read their scriptures on several levels, always looking for the interior, often hidden or subtle spiritual truths that undergird the sacred words. In comparison with non-Sufi Sunnis or non-Sufi Shi'ites, the Sufis generally are more tolerant of other religious traditions and more willing to promote concepts of gender equity. Their spiritual leaders, known as *shaykhs*, serve as guides for spiritual exercises designed to bring seekers into union with God. This Islamic tradition with its emphasis upon emotion and personal experience with God shares many similarities with the mystical traditions that are found within most of the world's great religions.

SACRED OBSERVANCES AND PRACTICES

The Pillars of Islam

Five principles regulate the lives of Muslims in their dealings with God. Muslims refer to these principles as the Five Pillars of Islam. Although there are many other recommended acts of worship, according to the Sunni, these five activities are (1) the witness, (2) the prayers, (3) the alms, (4) the fasting, and (5) the pilgrimage.[10] They are obligatory for all Muslims. The following is a brief description of each of these five pillars of faith.

- *The Witness (Shahada)*   The first duty of a Muslim is to recite the confession of faith, "There is no other god but God, and Muhammad is the Prophet of God." This concise, twofold statement is repeated numerous times each day by devout Muslims.

- *The Prayers (Salat)*   After the confession has been uttered, the next appropriate action is to participate in the prayer services held five times daily: just before dawn, just after noon, in mid-afternoon, just after sunset, and after nightfall. This act of worship, known as *Salat,* is a highly formalized ritual. Before performing the Salat, individuals must first ritually purify themselves by washing their face, head, ears, mouth, nose, hands and arms to the elbow, feet, and ankles. If no water is available, it is permissible to wash with fine sand, earth, or dirt. The purification ritual is important, because if the

Muslims at prayer.

Salat is practiced while impure, worship is considered invalid.

Following purification, worshippers face toward the Kaaba in Mecca. If congregated with others, they form straight rows behind the imam, a prayer leader who establishes the pace for the reciting of the prayers. All prayers are recited in Arabic, no matter which native tongue the worshippers speak. While delivering the prayers, the worshippers lower their palms to their knees, bow their head, straighten up, then prostate themselves on their toes, knees, palms, and forehead, and finally come to a sitting position with their hands on their knees for the final prayer. This sequence is repeated two to four times, depending on the time of day. On Friday, most commonly at the noon hour, Muslims gather for communal prayers at a special place of worship that Muslims call *Masjid* and Westerners call a mosque (literally, a "place of prostration"). In respect to Allah, worshippers leave their shoes at the entrance of the mosque, proceed to the pool or fountain to perform their ablutions, and then listen to a sermon delivered by an Imam before they perform the Salat.

- *The Alms*   The third pillar of faith rests upon the quranic warnings that personal property can be justified only if the owner is generous to others. Muslims recognize that they are stewards, not owners, of God's possessions, and thus should use their worldly goods for God's purposes. There are two forms of

---

[10]Shi'ites also acknowledge the importance of these activities, although they call these actions the "branches" rather than the "pillars" of faith. To Shi'ites, the "pillars of faith" are principles, not actions, and these pillars consists of five faith assertions: (1) the oneness of God, (2) the justice of God, (3) God's communication via prophets, (4) God's appointment of divine leaders known as "Imams," and (5) the Coming Day of Judgment.

almsgiving, the voluntary gift (*sadaqa*) and the mandatory poor tax (*zakat*). According to tradition, all Muslims are expected to give a fixed one-fortieth portion of their assets to the Muslim community. In addition to this poor tax, they are encouraged to give free will offerings to those in need. Pious Muslims are taught never to refuse a beggar.

- *The Fasting*   Muslims are expected to fast (in Arabic, *sawm*) from before sunrise to sunset each day during the lunar month of Ramadan. This month was the month of two important events in Islamic history: Muhammad's first revelation and the victory at Badr. During the fast, nothing is to enter the body. Pious Muslims avoid food, drink (even the swallowing of one's saliva), tobacco, and sexual intercourse. Exceptions are allowed for travelers, the ill, children and the elderly, and pregnant or nursing mothers. During Ramadan, the devout will spend as much time as is possible in prayer and will hear or recite the Qur'an at least once in its entirety. At the end of month, preparations are made for *Eid*, a joyous feast that breaks the time of fasting.

- *The Pilgrimage*   The fifth pillar of the faith is the pilgrimage, known in Arabic as the *Hajj*. All Muslim men and women, whose health and financial circumstances permit, are to make this pilgrimage to Mecca at least once during their life. Those unable to make the journey can fulfill this obligation by assisting substitute pilgrims to go in their stead. Before the pilgrims enter Mecca, they must first purify themselves. For men, this includes replacing their normal clothing, which reflects differences in income and social status, with a two-piece, sheetlike garment, which symbolizes equality before God. All pilgrims must abstain from sexual relations and go without bathing or cutting their hair or nails during the pilgrimage. Total concentration is to be focused on religious duties, not physical appearances.

  When inside the holy city, the pilgrims encircle the Kaaba in a counterclockwise manner seven times, three times quickly and four times slowly. As they encircle the Kaaba, if the crowds allow, they touch or kiss the black stone. They also drink water from the well of Zamzam and move rapidly between two small hills just outside the Kaaba, just as Hagar did when she was seeking assistance for Ishmael. Pilgrims also visit and conduct symbolic rites at other holy sites in the area, including a site remembered as the place where Adam and Eve were reunited after being expelled from the Garden of Eden, and Mount Arafat, where Muhammad delivered a final sermon to pilgrims during the last year of his life.

  Another important event is a standing ceremony on the Plain of Arafat. Here the pilgrims ask God to forgive their sins, and resolve to spend the remainder of their lives in service to Him. The climatic event of the Hajj is the stoning of the pillars of Satan in Mina, which takes place on what Muslims call *Eidul-Akbar*, or "the big Eid." After stoning the pillars, the male pilgrims shave their head, and all pilgrims have an animal slaughtered, whose meat is then distributed to the poor. Those who complete the pilgrimage receive an honorific title, *Hajji*, which may be included in their name for the rest of their life.

Jihad: The Sixth Pillar of Faith

The Five Pillars establish only the minimum standards of Islamic piety. Besides the five pillars, there are numerous other actions that Muslims should and should not do. All Muslims, for example, are expected to refrain from gambling, having sexual relations outside of marriage, eating pork and consuming alcoholic drink, even as they aspire to serve God through noble living. One form of service to God is known as *jihad*. This Arabic word, although often translated "holy war," technically means "exertion [for God]." Jihad can involve a willingness to go to war on God's behalf, that is, to fight against sin, oppression, and the enemies of Islam. Another aspect of jihad, however, is to struggle against and overcome corruption within one's own soul. This concept is so important within Islam that it is sometimes called the sixth pillar of faith. For a thorough discussion of the concept and practice of Jihad, see the *PowerWeb* supplemental article by Michael Knapp. This reading from *PowerWeb: Religion* is available at the McGraw-Hill *PowerWeb* website http://www.duskin.com/powerweb.

SOURCES

The following anthology includes selections from more than 1,000 verses from the *Qur'an*[11] as well as a brief sampling of stories contained in the *Bakhari Hadith*. About one-half of the 114 surahs in the sacred canon are represented in this anthology.

SECTION 1: Beginnings: God, Time, and the Universe

Like Judaism and Christianity, Islam accepts the creation accounts in the Hebrew Bible. In addition, the Qur'an contains several references to the creative activities of Allah. The opening selections in this section include some of these creation texts. As you read these selections, look for the central message within the passages. What do these texts tell us about Allah? Why do you think these teachings are included in the Qur'an?

ALLAH AS CREATOR OF THE HEAVENS AND THE EARTH

Surah 7

54. Your guardian-Lord is Allah Who created the heavens and the earth in six days and is firmly established on the throne (of authority): He draweth the night as a veil O'er the day each seeking the other in rapid succession: He created the sun the moon and the stars (all) governed by laws under His command. Is it not His to create and to govern? Blessed be Allah the cherisher and sustainer of the worlds!

Surah 16

1. (Inevitable) cometh (to pass) the Command of Allah. seek ye not then to hasten it: Glory to Him, and far is He above having the partners they ascribe unto Him!
2. He doth send down His angels with inspiration of His Command, to such of His servants as He pleaseth, (saying): "Warn (Man) that there is no god but I: so do your duty unto Me."
3. He has created the heavens and the earth for just ends: Far is He above having the partners they ascribe to Him!
4. He has created man from a sperm-drop; and behold this same (man) becomes an open disputer!

---

[11]The translation used in this volume is taken from *The Meaning of the Holy Qur'an*, translated by Abdullah Yusuf Ali (Beltsville, MD: Amana Publications, 1997).

5. And cattle He has created for you (men): from them ye derive warmth, and numerous benefits, and of their (meat) ye eat.
6. And ye have a sense of pride and beauty in them as ye drive them home in the evening, and as ye lead them forth to pasture in the morning.
7. And they carry your heavy loads to lands that ye could not (otherwise) reach except with souls distressed: for your Lord is indeed Most Kind, Most Merciful,
8. And (He has created) horses, mules, and donkeys, for you to ride and use for show; and He has created (other) things of which ye have no knowledge.
9. And unto Allah leads straight the Way, but there are ways that turn aside: if Allah had willed, He could have guided all of you.
10. It is He who sends down rain from the sky: from it ye drink, and out of it (grows) the vegetation on which ye feed your cattle.
11. With it He produces for you corn, olives, date-palms, grapes and every kind of fruit: verily in this is a sign for those who give thought.
12. He has made subject to you the Night and the Day; the sun and the moon; and the stars are in subjection by His Command: verily in this are Signs for men who are wise.
13. And the things on this earth which He has multiplied in varying colours (and qualities): verily in this is a sign for men who celebrate the praises of Allah (in gratitude).
14. It is He Who has made the sea subject, that ye may eat thereof flesh that is fresh and tender, and that ye may extract therefrom ornaments to wear; and thou seest the ships therein that plough the waves, that ye may seek (thus) of the bounty of Allah and that ye may be grateful.
15. And He has set up on the earth mountains standing firm, lest it should shake with you; and rivers and roads; that ye may guide yourselves;
16. And marks and sign-posts; and by the stars (men) guide themselves.
17. Is then He Who creates like one that creates not? Will ye not receive admonition?
18. If ye would count up the favours of Allah, never would ye be able to number them: for Allah is Oft-Forgiving, Most Merciful.

Surah 57

1. Whatever is in the heavens and on earth let it declare the Praises and Glory of Allah: for He is the Exalted in Might the Wise.
2. To Him belongs the dominion of the heavens and the earth; it is He Who gives life and Death; and He has Power over all things.
3. He is the First and the Last the Evident and the immanent: and He has full knowledge of all things.
4. He it is Who created the heavens and the earth in six Days and is moreover firmly established on the Throne (of author-

ity). He knows what enters within the earth and what comes forth out of it what comes down from heaven and what mounts up to it. And He is with you wheresoever ye may be. And Allah sees well all that ye do.

5. To Him belongs the dominion of the heavens and the earth: and all affairs are referred back to Allah.

6. He merges Night into Day and He merges Day into Night; and He has full knowledge of the secrets of (all) hearts.

7. Believe in Allah and His Apostle and spend (in charity) out of the (substance) whereof He has made you heirs. For those of you who believe and spend (in charity) for them is a great Reward.

In addition to being a god of creation, Allah is described in the Qur'an as being a god of judgment, compassion, mercy, and generosity. According to tradition, the Qur'an includes 99 different names of God. Identify some of the divine characteristics attributed to Allah in the following passages. To what degree are these divine attributes also descriptive of the characteristics of God contained in the Hebrew and Christian Bibles?

CHARACTERISTICS OF ALLAH

Surah 1

1. In the name of Allah, Most Gracious, Most Merciful.
2. Praise be to Allah, the Cherisher and Sustainer of the worlds;
3. Most Gracious, Most Merciful;
4. Master of the Day of Judgment.
5. Thee do we worship, and Thine aid we seek.
6. Show us the straight way,
7. The way of those on whom Thou hast bestowed Thy Grace, those whose (portion) is not wrath, and who go not astray.

Surah 2

255. Allah! there is no Allah but He the living the Self-subsisting Eternal. No slumber can seize him nor sleep. His are all things in the heavens and on earth. Who is there can intercede in His presence except as He permitteth? He knoweth what (appeareth to his creatures as) before or after or behind them. Nor shall they compass aught of his knowledge except as He willeth. His throne doth extend over the heavens and the earth and He feeleth no fatigue in guarding and preserving them. For He is the Most High the Supreme (in glory).

256. Let there be no compulsion in religion. Truth stands out clear from error; whoever rejects evil and believes in Allah hath grasped the most trustworthy hand-hold that never breaks. And Allah heareth and knoweth all things.

257. Allah is the Protector of those who have faith: from the depths of darkness He will lead them forth into light.

Of those who reject faith the patrons are the Evil Ones: from light they will lead them forth into the depths of darkness. They will be companions of the fire to dwell therein (for ever).

Surah 42

49. To Allah belongs the dominion of the heavens and the earth. He creates what He wills (and plans). He bestows (children) male or female according to His Will (and Plan),

50. Or He bestows both males and females, and He leaves barren whom He will: for He is full of Knowledge and Power.

51. It is not fitting for a man that Allah should speak to him except by inspiration, or from behind a veil, or by the sending of a messenger to reveal, with Allah's permission, what Allah wills: for He is Most High, Most Wise.

52. And thus have We, by Our Command, sent inspiration to thee: thou knewest not (before) what was Revelation, and what was Faith; but We have made the (Qur'an) a Light, wherewith We guide such of Our servants as We will; and verily thou dost guide (men) to the Straight Way,—

53. The Way of Allah, to Whom belongs whatever is in the heavens and whatever is on earth. Behold (how) all affairs tend towards Allah.

Surah 56

57. It is We Who have created you: why will ye not witness the Truth?

58. Do ye then see? The (human seed) that ye throw out,

59. Is it ye who create it or are We the Creators?

60. We have decreed Death to be your common lot and We are not to be frustrated

61. From changing your Forms and creating you (again) in (Forms) that ye know not.

62. And ye certainly know already the first form of creation: why then do ye not celebrate His praises?

63. See ye the seed that ye sow in the ground?

64. Is it ye that cause it to grow or are We the Cause?

65. Were it Our Will we could crumble it to dry powder and ye would be left in wonderment

66. (Saying) "We are indeed left with debts (for nothing):

67. "Indeed are we shut out (of the fruits of our labor)."

68. See ye the water which ye drink?

69. Do ye bring it Down (in rain) from the Cloud or do We?

70. Were it Our Will We could make it salt (and unpalatable): then why do ye not give thanks?

71. See ye the Fire which ye kindle?

72. Is it ye who grow the tree which feeds the fire or do We grow it?

73. We have made it a memorial (of our handiwork) and an article of comfort and convenience for the denizens of deserts.

74. Then celebrate with praises the name of the Lord the Supreme:

SECTION 2: Humanity: The Problem of Good and Evil

Islamic scriptures teach that if creation is the handiwork of Allah, who is perfect goodness, the material world and humanity itself also must be good. Evil as personified in Iblis or Satan, however, also is real and is able to seduce humans who are often prone to forget their divine origins. The first selections in this section contain passages that recount the biblical story of Adam, the first human. According to these texts, what is the divine purpose of humankind? How important are humans in relation to Allah and to the angels? What sin did Satan commit that resulted in his fall? Compare these passages with the accounts in Genesis. How are the stories alike? What additional details are contained in the Qur'an? How do you account for these additions?

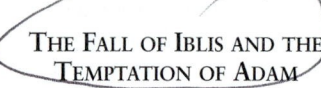

THE FALL OF IBLIS AND THE TEMPTATION OF ADAM

Surah 2

30. Behold thy Lord said to the angels: "I will create a vicegerent on earth." They said "Wilt thou place therein one who will make mischief therein and shed blood? Whilst we do celebrate Thy praises and glorify Thy holy (name)?" He said: "I know what ye know not."

31. And He taught Adam the nature of all things; then He placed them before the angels and said: "Tell Me the nature of these if ye are right."

32. They said: "Glory to Thee of knowledge we have none save that Thou hast taught us: in truth it is Thou who art perfect in knowledge and wisdom."

33. He said: "O Adam! tell them their natures." When he had told them Allah said: "Did I not tell you that I know the secrets of heaven and earth and I know what ye reveal and what ye conceal?"

34. And behold We said to the angels: "Bow down to Adam"; and they bowed down not so Iblis he refused and was haughty he was of those who reject Faith.

35. We said: "O Adam! dwell thou and thy wife in the garden and eat of the bountiful things therein as (where and when) ye will but approach not this tree or ye run into harm and transgression."

36. Then did Satan make them slip from the (garden) and get them out of the state (of felicity) in which they had been. We said: "Get ye down all (ye people) with enmity between yourselves. On earth will be your dwelling place and your means of livelihood for a time."

37. Then learnt Adam from his Lord words of inspiration and his Lord turned toward him; for He is Oft-Returning Most Merciful.

38. We said: "Get ye down all from here; and if as is sure there comes to you guidance from Me" whosoever follows My guidance on them shall be no fear nor shall they grieve.

39. "But those who reject Faith and belie Our Signs they shall be Companions of the Fire; they shall abide therein."

Surah 7

11. It is We Who created you and gave you shape; then We bade the angels bow down to Adam, and they bowed down; not so Iblis; He refused to be of those who bow down.

12. ((Allah)) said: "What prevented thee from bowing down when I commanded thee?" He said: "I am better than he: Thou didst create me from fire, and him from clay."

13. ((Allah)) said: "Get thee down from this: it is not for thee to be arrogant here: get out, for thou art of the meanest (of creatures)."

14. He said: "Give me respite till the day they are raised up."

15. ((Allah)) said: "Be thou among those who have respite."

16. He said: "Because thou hast thrown me out of the way, lo! I will lie in wait for them on thy straight way:

17. "Then will I assault them from before them and behind them, from their right and their left: Nor wilt thou find, in most of them, gratitude (for thy mercies)."

18. ((Allah)) said: "Get out from this, disgraced and expelled. If any of them follow thee,—Hell will I fill with you all.

19. "O Adam! dwell thou and thy wife in the Garden, and enjoy (its good things) as ye wish: but approach not this tree, or ye run into harm and transgression."

20. Then began Satan to whisper suggestions to them, bringing openly before their minds all their shame that was hidden from them (before): he said: "Your Lord only forbade you this tree, lest ye should become angels or such beings as live for ever."

21. And he swore to them both, that he was their sincere adviser.

22. So by deceit he brought about their fall: when they tasted of the tree, their shame became manifest to them, and they began to sew together the leaves of the garden over their bodies. And their Lord called unto them: "Did I not forbid you that tree, and tell you that Satan was an avowed enemy unto you?"

23. They said: "Our Lord! We have wronged our own souls: If thou forgive us not and bestow not upon us Thy Mercy, we shall certainly be lost."

24. ((Allah)) said: "Get ye down. With enmity between yourselves. On earth will be your dwelling-place and your means of livelihood,—for a time."

25. He said: "Therein shall ye live, and therein shall ye die; but from it shall ye be taken out (at last)."

26. O ye Children of Adam! We have bestowed raiment upon you to cover your shame, as well as to be an adornment to you. But the raiment of righteousness,—that is the best. Such are among the Signs of Allah, that they may receive admonition!

27. O ye Children of Adam! Let not Satan seduce you, in the same manner as He got your parents out of the Garden, stripping them of their raiment, to expose their shame: for he and his tribe watch you from a position where ye cannot see them: We made the evil ones friends (only) to those without faith.

28. When they do aught that is shameful, they say: "We found our fathers doing so"; and "(Allah) commanded us thus": Say: "Nay, Allah never commands what is shameful: do ye say of Allah what ye know not?"

29. Say: "My Lord hath commanded justice; and that ye set your whole selves (to Him) at every time and place of prayer, and call upon Him, making your devotion sincere as in His sight: such as He created you in the beginning, so shall ye return."

30. Some He hath guided: Others have (by their choice) deserved the loss of their way; in that they took the evil ones, in preference to Allah, for their friends and protectors, and think that they receive guidance.

From the following excerpts, how would you describe human nature from an Islamic point of view? What within human nature enables us to know divine truth, and why do many still live in ignorance?

DEPICTIONS OF HUMAN NATURE

Surah 67

1. Blessed be He in Whose hands is Dominion: and He over all things Hath Power

2. He Who created Death and Life that He may try which of you is best in deed: and He is the Exalted in Might Oft-Forgiving

3. He Who created the seven heavens one above another; no want of proportion wilt thou see in the Creation of (Allah) Most Gracious so turn thy vision again: Seest thou any flaw?

4. Again turn thy vision a second time; (thy) vision will come back to thee dull and discomfited in a state worn out.

5. And We have (from of old) adorned the lowest heaven with Lamps and We have made such (Lamps) (as) missiles to drive away the Evil Ones and have prepared for them the Penalty of the Blazing Fire.

6. For those who reject their Lord (and Cherisher) is the Penalty of Hell: and evil is (such) destination.

7. When they are cast therein they will hear the (terrible) drawing in of its breath even as it blazes forth.

8. Almost bursting with fury: every time a Group is cast therein its Keepers will ask "Did no Warner come to you?"

9. They will say: "Yes indeed: a Warner did come to us but we rejected him and said 'Allah never sent down any (Message): ye are in nothing but an egregious delusion!'"

10. They will further say: "Had we but listened or used our intelligence we should not (now) be among the Companions of the Blazing Fire!"

11. They will then confess their sins: but far will be (Forgiveness) from the Companions of the Blazing Fire!

12. As for those who fear their Lord unseen for them is Forgiveness and a great Reward.

13. And whether ye hide your word or publish it He certainly has (full) knowledge of the secrets of (all) hearts.

14. Should He not know He that created? And He is the One that understands the finest mysteries (and) is well-acquainted (with them).

Surah 70

19. Truly man was created very impatient

20. Fretful when evil touches him;

21. And niggardly when good reaches him

22. Not so those devoted to Prayer

23. Those who remain steadfast to their prayer;

24. And those in whose wealth is a recognized right

25. For the (needy) who asks and him who is prevented (for some reason from asking);

26. And those who hold to the truth of the Day of Judgment;

27. And those who fear the displeasure of their Lord

28. For their Lord's displeasure is the opposite of Peace and Tranquillity

29. And those who guard their chastity

30. Except with their wives and the (captives) whom their right hands possess for (then) they are not to be blamed

31. But those who trespass beyond this are transgressors

32. And those who respect their trusts and covenants;

33. And those who stand firm in their testimonies;

34. And those who guard (the sacredness) of their worship

35. Such will be the honored ones in the Gardens of (Bliss).

Surah 76

1. Has there not been over Man a long period of Time when he was nothing—(not even) mentioned?

2. Verily We created Man from a drop of mingled sperm in order to try him: so We gave him (the gifts) of Hearing and Sight.

3. We showed him the Way: whether he be grateful or ungrateful (rests on his will).

4. For the Rejecters We have prepared Chains Yokes and a Blazing Fire.

5. As to the Righteous they shall drink of a Cup (of Wine) mixed with Kafur

6. A Fountain where the Devotees of Allah do drink making it flow in unstinted abundance.

7. They perform (their) vows and they fear a Day whose evil flies far and wide.

8. And they feed for the love of Allah the indigent the orphan and the captive

9. (Saying) "We feed you for the sake of Allah alone: No reward do we desire from you nor thanks.

10. "We only fear a Day of distressful Wrath from the side of our Lord."

11. But Allah will deliver them from the evil of that Day and will shed over them a light of Beauty and a (blissful) Joy.

Surah 95. The Fig, The Figtree

1. By the Fig and the Olive,

2. And the Mount of Sinai,

3. And this City of security,—

4. We have indeed created man in the best of moulds,

5. Then do We abase him (to be) the lowest of the low,—

6. Except such as believe and do righteous deeds: For they shall have a reward unfailing.

7. Then what can, after this, contradict thee, as to the judgment (to come)?

8. Is not Allah the wisest of judges?

SECTION 3: Sacred Stories: Divine Messengers, Prophets, and Priests

Historical narratives occupy a primary place in the sacred writings of the Hebrews and Christians. Within Judaism, God is identified as a god of history who reveals his purposes through human prophets and sinners who act and speak in specific times and places. Similarly, within Christianity the doctrine of the Incarnation presents Jesus as God in human form, a historic being who is at once the Message and the messenger of God. Sacred truths are often presented in the Hebrew and Christian Bibles indirectly through stories told as historical narratives. The Qur'an, in contrast, contains few historical narratives. In this sacred book, Allah often speaks directly in the first person rather than indirectly through interpreted history. Biblical characters and historical occurrences are sometimes cited, but they are usually presented without reference to chronology and in an abbreviated, matter-of-fact manner.

The following selections contain a number of quranic passages about important biblical characters. Compare these accounts with the stories of these personalities found in the Hebrew and Christian scrip-

tures. How are the accounts alike and unlike? How do you explain the differences? What is the primary purpose of the inclusion of this information in the Qur'an?

SELECTED ACCOUNTS OF BIBLICAL CHARACTERS IN THE QUR'AN

Surah 4

153. The people of the Book ask thee to cause a book to descend to them from heaven: Indeed they asked Moses for an even greater (miracle), for they said: "Show us Allah in public," but they were dazed for their presumption, with thunder and lightning. Yet they worshipped the calf even after clear signs had come to them; even so we forgave them; and gave Moses manifest proofs of authority.

154. And for their covenant we raised over them (the towering height) of Mount (Sinai); and (on another occasion) we said: "Enter the gate with humility"; and (once again) we commanded them: "Transgress not in the matter of the sabbath." And we took from them a solemn covenant.

155. (They have incurred divine displeasure): In that they broke their covenant; that they rejected the signs of Allah that they slew the Messengers in defiance of right; that they said, "Our hearts are the wrappings (which preserve Allah's Word; We need no more)";—Nay, Allah hath set the seal on their hearts for their blasphemy, and little is it they believe;—

156. That they rejected Faith; that they uttered against Mary a grave false charge;

157. That they said (in boast), "We killed Christ Jesus the son of Mary, the Messenger of Allah;—but they killed him not, nor crucified him, but so it was made to appear to them, and those who differ therein are full of doubts, with no (certain) knowledge, but only conjecture to follow, for of a surety they killed him not:—

158. Nay, Allah raised him up unto Himself; and Allah is Exalted in Power, Wise;—

159. And there is none of the People of the Book but must believe in him before his death; and on the Day of Judgment he will be a witness against them. . . .

171. O People of the Book! Commit no excesses in your religion: Nor say of Allah aught but the truth. Christ Jesus the son of Mary was (no more than) an apostle of Allah, and His Word, which He bestowed on Mary, and a spirit proceeding from Him: so believe in Allah and His apostles. Say not "Trinity": desist: it will be better for you: for Allah is one Allah. Glory be to Him: (far exalted is He) above having a son. To Him belong all things in the heavens and on earth. And enough is Allah as a Disposer of affairs.

172. Christ disdaineth nor to serve and worship Allah, nor do the angels, those nearest (to Allah: those who disdain His worship and are arrogant,—He will gather them all together unto Himself to (answer).

173. But to those who believe and do deeds of righteousness, He will give their (due) rewards,—and more, out of His bounty: But those who are disdainful and arrogant, He will punish with a grievous penalty; Nor will they find, besides Allah, any to protect or help them.

Surah 10

66. Behold! verily to Allah belong all creatures, in the heavens and on earth. What do they follow who worship as His "partners" other than Allah. They follow nothing but fancy, and they do nothing but lie.

67. He it is That hath made you the night that ye may rest therein, and the day to make things visible (to you). Verily in this are signs for those who listen (to His Message).

68. They say: "(Allah) hath begotten a son!"—Glory be to Him! He is self-sufficient! His are all things in the heavens and on earth! No warrant have ye for this! say ye about Allah what ye know not?

69. Say: "Those who invent a lie against Allah will never prosper."

70. A little enjoyment in this world!—and then, to Us will be their return, then shall We make them taste the severest penalty for their blasphemies.

71. Relate to them the story of Noah. Behold! he said to his people: "O my people, if it be hard on your (mind) that I should stay (with you) and commemorate the signs of Allah,—yet I put my trust in Allah. Get ye then an agreement about your plan and among your partners, so your plan be on to you dark and dubious. Then pass your sentence on me, and give me no respite.

72. "But if ye turn back, (consider): no reward have I asked of you: my reward is only due from Allah, and I have been commanded to be of those who submit to Allah's will (in Islam)."

73. They rejected Him, but We delivered him, and those with him, in the Ark, and We made them inherit (the earth), while We overwhelmed in the flood those who rejected Our Signs. Then see what was the end of those who were warned (but heeded not)!

74. Then after him We sent (many) apostles to their peoples: they brought them Clear Signs, but they would not believe what they had already rejected beforehand. Thus do We seal the hearts of the transgressors.

75. Then after them sent We Moses and Aaron to Pharaoh and his chiefs with Our Signs. But they were arrogant: they were a people in sin.

76. When the Truth did come to them from Us, they said: "This is indeed evident sorcery!"

77. Said Moses: "Say ye (this) about the truth when it hath (actually) reached you? Is sorcery (like) this? But sorcerers will not prosper."

78. They said: "Hast thou come to us to turn us away from the ways we found our fathers following,—in order that thou and thy brother may have greatness in the land? But not we shall believe in you!"

79. Said Pharaoh: "Bring me every sorcerer well versed."

80. When the sorcerers came, Moses said to them: "Throw ye what ye (wish) to throw!"

81. When they had had their throw, Moses said: "What ye have brought is sorcery: Allah will surely make it of no effect: for Allah prospereth not the work of those who make mischief.

82. "And Allah by His words doth prove and establish His truth, however much the sinners may hate it!"

83. But none believed in Moses except some children of his people, because of the fear of Pharaoh and his chiefs, lest they should persecute them; and certainly Pharaoh was mighty on the earth and one who transgressed all bounds.

84. Moses said: "O my people! If ye do (really) believe in Allah, then in Him put your trust if ye submit (your will to His)."

85. They said: "In Allah do we put out trust. Our Lord! make us not a trial for those who practise oppression;

86. "And deliver us by Thy Mercy from those who reject (Thee)."

87. We inspired Moses and his brother with this Message: "Provide dwellings for your people in Egypt, make your dwellings into places of worship, and establish regular prayers: and give glad tidings to those who believe!"

88. Moses prayed: "Our Lord! Thou hast indeed bestowed on Pharaoh and his chiefs splendour and wealth in the life of the present, and so, Our Lord, they mislead (men) from Thy Path. Deface our Lord, the features of their wealth, and send hardness to their hearts, so they will not believe until they see the grievous penalty."

89. Allah said: "Accepted is your prayer (O Moses and Aaron)! So stand ye straight, and follow not the path of those who know not."

90. We took the Children of Israel across the sea: Pharaoh and his hosts followed them in insolence and spite. At length, when overwhelmed with the flood, he said: "I believe that there is no god except Him Whom the Children of Israel believe in: I am of those who submit (to Allah in Islam)."

Surah 19

16. Relate in the Book (the story of) Mary, when she withdrew from her family to a place in the East.

17. She placed a screen (to screen herself) from them; then We sent her our angel, and he appeared before her as a man in all respects.

18. She said: "I seek refuge from thee to ((Allah)) Most Gracious: (come not near) if thou dost fear Allah."

19. He said: "Nay, I am only a messenger from thy Lord, (to announce) to thee the gift of a holy son.

20. She said: "How shall I have a son, seeing that no man has touched me, and I am not unchaste?"

21. He said: "So (it will be): Thy Lord saith, 'that is easy for Me: and (We wish) to appoint him as a Sign unto men and a Mercy from Us': It is a matter (so) decreed."

22. So she conceived him, and she retired with him to a remote place.

23. And the pains of childbirth drove her to the trunk of a palm-tree: She cried (in her anguish): "Ah! would that I had died before this! would that I had been a thing forgotten and out of sight!"

24. But (a voice) cried to her from beneath the (palm-tree): "Grieve not! for thy Lord hath provided a rivulet beneath thee;

25. "And shake towards thyself the trunk of the palm-tree: It will let fall fresh ripe dates upon thee.

26. "So eat and drink and cool (thine) eye. And if thou dost see any man, say, 'I have vowed a fast to ((Allah)) Most Gracious, and this day will I enter into not talk with any human being'"

27. At length she brought the (babe) to her people, carrying him (in her arms). They said: "O Mary! truly an amazing thing hast thou brought!

28. "O sister of Aaron! Thy father was not a man of evil, nor thy mother a woman unchaste!"

29. But she pointed to the babe. They said: "How can we talk to one who is a child in the cradle?"

30. He said: "I am indeed a servant of Allah. He hath given me revelation and made me a prophet;

31. "And He hath made me blessed wheresoever I be, and hath enjoined on me Prayer and Charity as long as I live;

32. "(He) hath made me kind to my mother, and not overbearing or miserable;

33. "So peace is on me the day I was born, the day that I die, and the day that I shall be raised up to life (again)"!

34. Such (was) Jesus the son of Mary: (it is) a statement of truth, about which they (vainly) dispute.

35. It is not befitting to (the majesty of) Allah that He should beget a son. Glory be to Him! when He determines a matter, He only says to it, "Be," and it is.

36. Verily Allah is my Lord and your Lord: Him therefore serve ye: this is a Way that is straight. . . .

41. Also mention in the Book (the story of) Abraham: He was a man of Truth, a prophet.

42. Behold, he said to his father: "O my father! why worship that which heareth not and seeth not, and can profit thee nothing?

43. "O my father! to me hath come knowledge which hath not reached thee: so follow me: I will guide thee to a way that is even and straight.

44. "O my father! serve not Satan: for Satan is a rebel against ((Allah)) Most Gracious.

45. "O my father! I fear lest a Penalty afflict thee from ((Allah)) Most Gracious, so that thou become to Satan a friend."

46. (The father) replied: "Dost thou hate my gods, O Abraham? If thou forbear not, I will indeed stone thee: Now get away from me for a good long while!"

47. Abraham said: "Peace be on thee: I will pray to my Lord for thy forgiveness: for He is to me Most Gracious.

48. "And I will turn away from you (all) and from those whom ye invoke besides Allah. I will call on my Lord: perhaps, by my prayer to my Lord, I shall be not unblest."

49. When he had turned away from them and from those whom they worshipped besides Allah, We bestowed on him Isaac and Jacob, and each one of them We made a prophet.

50. And We bestowed of Our Mercy on them, and We granted them lofty honour on the tongue of truth. . . .

88. They say: "((Allah)) Most Gracious has begotten a son!"

89. Indeed ye have put forth a thing most monstrous!

90. At it the skies are ready to burst, the earth to split asunder, and the mountains to fall down in utter ruin,

91. That they should invoke a son for ((Allah)) Most Gracious.

92. For it is not consonant with the majesty of ((Allah)) Most Gracious that He should beget a son.

93. Not one of the beings in the heavens and the earth but must come to ((Allah)) Most Gracious as a servant.

94. He does take an account of them (all), and hath numbered them (all) exactly.

95. And everyone of them will come to Him singly on the Day of Judgment.

96. On those who believe and work deeds of righteousness, will ((Allah)) Most Gracious bestow love.

97. So have We made the (Qur'an) easy in thine own tongue, that with it thou mayest give Glad Tidings to the righteous, and warnings to people given to contention.

98. But how many (countless) generations before them have We destroyed? Canst thou find a single one of them (now) or hear (so much as) a whisper of them?

Because Muslims believe that Allah, not Muhammad, was the author of the Qur'an, it is not surprising that this sacred text does not include a biography of Muhammad. It does, however, include some isolated bits of material on the prophet. After Muhammad's death, his followers wanted to preserve a more detailed memory of the prophet's life and teachings. To fill this need, collections of writings known as the Hadith (Tradition) emerged. Next to the Qur'an, the Hadith is the most important piece of literature within Islam.

This section includes some of the isolated pieces of information in the Qur'an on Muhammad's life and a sampling of the details on his life contained in the Hadith. What facts about Muhammad are presented in the Qur'an itself? Why do these themes appear? Based upon the Hadith selections, what type of a man did the followers of Islam consider Muhammad to be? Compare these descriptions of Muhammad with the New Testament accounts of

Jesus, the stories of the Buddha contained in the Tripitaka, and the accounts of Confucius in the Analects. Do you find any similarities in the way these figures are remembered by their followers?

REFERENCES TO MUHAMMAD IN THE QUR'AN

Surah 3

144. Muhammad is no more than an Apostle: many were the Apostles that passed away before him. If he died or were slain will ye then turn back on your heels? If any did turn back on his heels not the least harm will he do to Allah; but Allah (on the other hand) will swiftly reward those who (serve him) with gratitude.

Surah 7

188. Say: (O Muhammad) "I have no power over any good or harm to myself except as Allah willeth. If I had knowledge of the unseen I should have multiplied all good and no evil should have touched me I am but a warner and a bringer of glad tidings to those who have faith."

Surah 17

1. Glory to ((Allah)) Who did take His servant (Muhammad) for a Journey by night from the Sacred Mosque to the farthest Mosque, whose precincts We did bless,—in order that We might show him some of Our Signs: for He is the One Who heareth and seeth (all things). . . .
72. But those who were blind in this world will be blind in the Hereafter and most astray from the Path.
73. And their purpose was to tempt thee (Muhammad) away from that which We had revealed unto thee to substitute in Our name something quite different: (in that case) behold! they would certainly have made thee (their) friend!
74. And had We not given thee (Muhammad) strength thou wouldst nearly have inclined to them a little.
75. In that case We should have made thee taste an equal portion (of punishment) in this life and an equal portion in death: and moreover thou wouldst have found none to help thee against Us!
76. Their purpose was to scare thee off the land in order to expel thee (Muhammad); but in that case they would not have stayed (therein) after thee except for a little while.
77. (This was Our) way with the apostles We sent before thee: thou wilt find no change in Our ways.

Surah 25

4. But the Misbelievers say: "Naught is this (the Qur'an) but a lie which he (Muhammad) has forged and others have helped him at it." In truth it is they who have put forward an iniquity and a falsehood.

5. And they say: "Tales of the ancients which he has caused to be written: and they are dictated before him morning and evening."
6. Say: "The (Qur'an) was sent down by Him Who knows the Mystery (that is) in the heavens and the earth: verily He is Oft-Forgiving Most Merciful."
7. And they say: "What sort of an apostle is this who eats food and walks through the streets? Why has not an angel been sent down to him to give admonition with him?
8. "Or (why) has not a treasure been bestowed on him or why has he (not) a garden for enjoyment?" The wicked say: "Ye follow none other than a man bewitched."
9. See what kinds of companions they make for thee! But they have gone astray and never a way will they be able to find!

Sarah 29

47. And thus (it is) that We have sent down the Book to thee (Muhammad). So the People of the Book believe therein as also do some of these (pagan Arabs): and none but Unbelievers reject Our Signs.
48. And thou (Muhammad) wast not (able) to recite a Book before this (Book came) nor art thou (able) to transcribe it with thy righthand: in that case indeed would the talkers of vanities have doubted.

Surah 33

28. O Prophet! Say to thy Consorts: "If it be that ye desire the life of this World, and its glitter,—then come! I will provide for your enjoyment and set you free in a handsome manner.
29. But if ye seek Allah and His Messenger, and the Home of the Hereafter, verily Allah has prepared for the well-doers amongst you a great reward.
30. O Consorts of the Prophet! If any of you were guilty of evident unseemly conduct, the Punishment would be doubled to her, and that is easy for Allah.
31. But any of you that is devout in the service of Allah and His Messenger, and works righteousness,—to her shall We grant her reward twice: and We have prepared for her a generous Sustenance.
32. O Consorts of the Prophet! Ye are not like any of the (other) women: if ye do fear ((Allah)), be not too complacent of speech, lest one in whose heart is a disease should be moved with desire: but speak ye a speech (that is) just.
33. And stay quietly in your houses, and make not a dazzling display, like that of the former Times of Ignorance; and establish regular Prayer, and give regular Charity; and obey Allah and His Messenger. And Allah only wishes to remove all abomination from you, ye members of the Family, and to make you pure and spotless.
34. And recite what is rehearsed to you in your homes, of the Signs of Allah and His Wisdom: for Allah understands the finest mysteries and is well-acquainted (with them).

35. For Muslim men and women,—for believing men and women, for devout men and women, for true men and women, for men and women who are patient and constant, for men and women who humble themselves, for men and women who give in Charity, for men and women who fast (and deny themselves), for men and women who guard their chastity, and for men and women who engage much in Allah's praise,—for them has Allah prepared forgiveness and great reward.

36. It is not fitting for a Believer, man or woman, when a matter has been decided by Allah and His Messenger to have any option about their decision: if any one disobeys Allah and His Messenger, he is indeed on a clearly wrong Path.

37. Behold! Thou didst say to one who had received the grace of Allah and thy favour: "Retain thou (in wedlock) thy wife, and fear Allah." But thou didst hide in thy heart that which Allah was about to make manifest: thou didst fear the people, but it is more fitting that thou shouldst fear Allah. Then when Zaid had dissolved (his marriage) with her, with the necessary (formality), We joined her in marriage to thee: in order that (in future) there may be no difficulty to the Believers in (the matter of) marriage with the wives of their adopted sons, when the latter have dissolved with the necessary (formality) (their marriage) with them. And Allah's command must be fulfilled.

38. There can be no difficulty to the Prophet in what Allah has indicated to him as a duty. It was the practice (approved) of Allah amongst those of old that have passed away. And the command of Allah is a decree determined.

39. (It is the practice of those) who preach the Messages of Allah, and fear Him, and fear none but Allah. And enough is Allah to call (men) to account.

40. Muhammad is not the father of any of your men, but (he is) the Messenger of Allah, and the Seal of the Prophets: and Allah has full knowledge of all things.

Surah 41

2. A revelation from (Allah) Most Gracious Most Merciful

3. A Book whereof the verses are explained in detail a Qur'an in Arabic for people who understand

4. Giving Good News and Admonition: yet most of them turn away and so they hear not.

5. They say: "Our hearts are under veils (concealed) from that to which thou dost invite us and in ours ears in a deafness and between us and thee is a screen: so do thou (what thou wilt); for us we shall do (what we will!)."

6. Say thou (Muhammad): "I am but a man like you: it is revealed to me by inspiration that your Allah is One Allah: so stand true to Him and ask for His forgiveness." And woe to those who join gods with Allah

Surah 44

2. By the Book that makes things clear;—

3. We sent it down during a Blessed Night: for We (ever) wish to warn (against Evil). . . .

13. How shall the message be (effectual) for them, seeing that a Messenger explaining things clearly has (already) come to them,—

14. Yet they turn away from him and say: "Tutored (by others), a man possessed!"

Surah 53

1. By the Star when it goes down,—

2. Your Companion (Muhammad) is neither astray nor being misled.

3. Nor does he say (aught) of (his own) Desire.

4. It is no less than inspiration sent down to him:

5. He was taught by one Mighty in Power,

6. Endued with Wisdom: for he appeared (in stately form);

7. While he was in the highest part of the horizon:

8. Then he approached and came closer,

9. And was at a distance of but two bow-lengths or (even) nearer;

10. So did ((Allah)) convey the inspiration to His Servant—(conveyed) what He (meant) to convey.

11. The (Prophet's) (mind and) heart in no way falsified that which he saw.

12. Will ye then dispute with him concerning what he saw?

13. For indeed he saw him at a second descent,

14. Near the Lote-tree beyond which none may pass:

15. Near it is the Garden of Abode.

16. Behold, the Lote-tree was shrouded (in mystery unspeakable!)

17. (His) sight never swerved, nor did it go wrong!

18. For truly did he see, of the Signs of his Lord, the Greatest!

Surah 61

6. And remember, Jesus, the son of Mary, said: "O Children of Israel! I am the apostle of Allah (sent) to you, confirming the Law (which came) before me, and giving Glad Tidings of a Messenger to come after me, whose name shall be Ahmad." But when he came to them with Clear Signs, they said, "this is evident sorcery!"

Surah 93

2. And by the Night when it is still,—

3. Thy Guardian-Lord hath not forsaken thee (Muhammad), nor is He displeased.

4. And verily the Hereafter will be better for thee than the present.

5. And soon will thy Guardian-Lord give thee (that wherewith) thou shalt be well-pleased.

6. Did He not find thee (Muhammad) an orphan and give thee shelter (and care)?

7. And He found thee wandering, and He gave thee guidance.

8. And He found thee in need, and made thee independent.

Selections on Muhammad's Life and Teachings from the Hadith[12]

Sahih Bukhari Hadith: Book 1

2) Narrated 'Aisha: (the mother of the faithful believers) Al-Harith bin Hisham asked Allah's Apostle "O Allah's Apostle! How is the Divine Inspiration revealed to you?" Allah's Apostle replied, "Sometimes it is (revealed) like the ringing of a bell, this form of Inspiration is the hardest of all and then this state passes off after I have grasped what is inspired. Sometimes the Angel comes in the form of a man and talks to me and I grasp whatever he says." 'Aisha added: Verily I saw the Prophet being inspired Divinely on a very cold day and noticed the sweat dropping from his forehead (as the Inspiration was over).

3) Narrated 'Aisha: (the mother of the faithful believers) The commencement of the Divine Inspiration to Allah's Apostle was in the form of good dreams which came true like bright daylight, and then the love of seclusion was bestowed upon him. He used to go in seclusion in the cave of Hira where he used to worship (Allah alone) continuously for many days before his desire to see his family. He used to take with him the journey food for the stay and then come back to (his wife) Khadija to take his food likewise again till suddenly the Truth descended upon him while he was in the cave of Hira. The angel came to him and asked him to read. The Prophet replied, "I do not know how to read."

The Prophet added, "The angel caught me (forcefully) and pressed me so hard that I could not bear it any more. He then released me and again asked me to read and I replied, 'I do not know how to read.' Thereupon he caught me again and pressed me a second time till I could not bear it any more. He then released me and again asked me to read but again I replied, 'I do not know how to read (or what shall I read)?' Thereupon he caught me for the third time and pressed me, and then released me and said, 'Read in the name of your Lord, who has created (all that exists) has created man from a clot. Read! And your Lord is the Most Generous." Then Allah's Apostle returned with the Inspiration and with his heart beating severely. Then he went to Khadija bint Khuwailid and said, "Cover me! Cover me!" They covered him till his fear was over and after that he told her everything that had happened and said, "I fear that something may happen to me." Khadija replied, "Never! By Allah, Allah will never disgrace you. You keep good relations with your kith and kin, help the poor and the destitute, serve your guests generously and assist the deserving calamity-afflicted ones."

5) Narrated Ibn 'Abbas: Allah's Apostle was the most generous of all the people, and he used to reach the peak in generosity in the month of Ramadan when Gabriel met him. Gabriel used to meet him every night of Ramadan to teach him the Qur'an. Allah's Apostle was the most generous person, even more generous than the strong uncontrollable wind (in readiness and haste to do charitable deeds).

6) Narrated 'Abdullah bin 'Abbas: Abu Sufyan bin Harb informed me that Heraclius had sent a messenger to him while he had been accompanying a caravan from Quraish. They were merchants doing business in Sham (Syria, Palestine, Lebanon and Jordan), at the time when Allah's Apostle had truce with Abu Sufyan and Quraish infidels. So Abu Sufyan and his companions went to Heraclius at Ilya (Jerusalem). Heraclius called them in the court and he had all the senior Roman dignitaries around him. He called for his translator who, translating Heraclius's question said to them, "Who amongst you is closely related to that man who claims to be a Prophet?" Abu Sufyan replied, "I am the nearest relative to him (amongst the group)."

Heraclius said, "Bring him (Abu Sufyan) close to me and make his companions stand behind him." Abu Sufyan added, Heraclius told his translator to tell my companions that he wanted to put some questions to me regarding that man (The Prophet) and that if I told a lie they (my companions) should contradict me." Abu Sufyan added, "By Allah! Had I not been afraid of my companions labeling me a liar, I would not have spoken the truth about the Prophet. The first question he asked me about him was:

'What is his family status amongst you?'
I replied, 'He belongs to a good (noble) family amongst us.'
Heraclius further asked, 'Has anybody amongst you ever claimed the same (i.e., to be a Prophet) before him?'
I replied, 'No.'
He said, 'Was anybody amongst his ancestors a king?'
I replied, 'No.'
Heraclius asked, 'Do the nobles or the poor follow him?'
I replied, 'It is the poor who follow him.'
He said, 'Are his followers increasing decreasing (day by day)?'
I replied, 'They are increasing.'
He then asked, 'Does anybody amongst those who embrace his religion become displeased and renounce the religion afterwards?'
I replied, 'No.'
Heraclius said, 'Have you ever accused him of telling lies before his claim (to be a Prophet)?'
I replied, 'No. '
Heraclius said, 'Does he break his promises?'
I replied, 'No. We are at truce with him but we do not know what he will do in it.' I could not find opportunity to say anything against him except that.
Heraclius asked, 'Have you ever had a war with him?'
I replied, 'Yes.'
Then he said, 'What was the outcome of the battles?'

---

[12]This selection is taken from *Sahih Bukhari Hadith, Book 1*, translated by M. Muhsin Khan, which is available at www.usc.edu/dept/MSA/fundamentals/hadithsunnah/bukhari/sbtintro.html.

I replied, 'Sometimes he was victorious and sometimes we.' Heraclius said, 'What does he order you to do?'

I said, 'He tells us to worship Allah and Allah alone and not to worship anything along with Him, and to renounce all that our ancestors had said. He orders us to pray, to speak the truth, to be chaste and to keep good relations with our kith and kin.' . . .

10) Narrated Abu Musa: Some people asked Allah's Apostle, "Whose Islam is the best? i.e. (Who is a very good Muslim)?" He replied, "One who avoids harming the Muslims with his tongue and hands."

11) Narrated 'Abdullah bin 'Amr: A man asked the Prophet, "What sort of deeds or (what qualities of) Islam are good?" The Prophet replied, 'To feed (the poor) and greet those whom you know and those whom you do not know

12) Narrated Anas: The Prophet said, "None of you will have faith till he wishes for his (Muslim) brother what he likes for himself."

14) Narrated Anas: The Prophet said "None of you will have faith till he loves me more than his father, his children and all mankind."

15) Narrated Anas: The Prophet said, "Whoever possesses the following three qualities will have the sweetness (delight) of faith:

1. The one to whom Allah and His Apostle becomes dearer than anything else.
2. Who loves a person and he loves him only for Allah's sake.
3. Who hates to revert to Atheism (disbelief) as he hates to be thrown into the fire."

SECTION 4: Divine Law: Justice, Reward, and Punishment

A line from the Qur'an reads:

> *If you avoid the great sins which you are forbidden to do, We shall remit from you your (small) sins, and admit you to a Noble Entrance (into paradise).* [Surah 4:31]

Commentators disagree about the number of great sins. Some see 7 grave sins, while others list closer to 700. Most agree, however, that the gravest sin is that of associating other gods with Allah.

The following selections are quranic passages that detail some of the commandments of Allah. Based on a reading of these selections, what types of sins does the Qur'an most emphatically condemn? What inferences about pre-Islamic Arabian society can be drawn from these passages? In what ways were these laws intended to transform this culture? Finally, compare Is-

lamic law with the ethical teachings of other religious traditions. In what ways are these instructions similar and unique?

DIVINE EXPECTATIONS IN THE QUR'AN

Surah 17

22. Take not with Allah another object of worship; or thou (O man!) wilt sit in disgrace and destitution.

23. Thy Lord hath decreed that ye worship none but Him and that ye be kind to parents. Whether one or both of them attain old age in thy life say not to them a word of contempt nor repel them but address them in terms of honor.

24. And out of kindness lower to them the wing of humility and say: "My Lord! bestow on them Thy Mercy even as they cherished me in childhood."

25. Your Lord knoweth best what is in your hearts: if ye do deeds of righteousness verily He is Most Forgiving to those who turn to Him again and again (in true penitence).

26. And render to the kindred their due rights as (also) to those in want and to the wayfarer: but squander not (your wealth) in the manner of a spendthrift.

27. Verily spendthrifts are brothers of the Evil Ones; and the Evil One is to his Lord (Himself) ungrateful.

28. And even if thou hast to turn away from them in pursuit of the Mercy from thy Lord which thou dost expect yet speak to them a word of easy kindness.

29. Make not thy hand tied (like a niggard's) to thy neck nor stretch it forth to its utmost reach so that thou become blameworthy and destitute.

30. Verily thy Lord doth provide sustenance in abundance for whom He pleaseth and He provideth in a just measure: for He doth know and regard all His servants.

31. Kill not your children for fear of want: We shall provide sustenance for them as well as for you: verily the killing of them is a great sin.

32. Nor come nigh to adultery: for it is a shameful (deed) and an evil opening the road (to other evils).

33. Nor take life which Allah has made sacred except for just cause. And if anyone is slain wrongfully We have given his heir authority (to demand Qisas or to forgive): but let him not exceed bounds in the matter of taking life: for he is helped (by the Law).

34. Come not nigh to the orphan's property except to improve it until he attains the age of full strength; and fulfil (every) engagement for (every) engagement will be enquired into (on the Day of Reckoning).

35. Give full measure when ye measure and weigh with a balance that is straight: that is the most fitting and the most advantageous in the final determination.

36. And pursue not that of which thou hast no knowledge; for every act of hearing or of seeing or of (feeling in) the heart will be enquired into (on the Day of Reckoning).

37. Nor walk on the earth with insolence: for thou canst not rend the earth asunder nor reach the mountains in height.

38. Of all such things the evil is hateful in the sight of thy Lord.

39. These are among the (precepts of) wisdom which thy Lord Has revealed to thee. Take not with Allah another object of worship lest thou shouldst be thrown into Hell blameworthy and rejected.

Surah 5

Allah punishes [those] who all against Mohammed

33. The punishment of those who wage war against Allah and His Apostle and strive with might and main for mischief through the land is: execution or crucifixion of the cutting off of hands and feet from opposite sides or exile from the land: that is their disgrace in this world and a heavy punishment is theirs in the Hereafter.

34. Except for those who repent before they fall into your power: in that case know that Allah is Oft-Forgiving Most Merciful.

35. O ye who believe! do your duty to Allah seek the means of approach unto Him and strive with might and main in His cause: that ye may prosper.

36. As to those who reject faith if they had everything on earth and twice repeated to give as ransom for the penalty of the Day of Judgment it would never be accepted of them. Theirs would be a grievous penalty.

37. Their wish will be to get out of the fire but never will they get out therefrom: their penalty will be one that endures.

38. As to the thief male or female cut off his or her hands: a punishment by way of example from Allah for their crime: and Allah is Exalted in Power.

39. But if the thief repent after his crime and amend his conduct Allah turneth to him in forgiveness; for Allah is Oft-Forgiving Most Merciful.

40. Knowest thou not that to Allah (alone) belongeth the dominion of the heavens and the earth? He punisheth whom He pleaseth and He forgiveth whom He pleaseth: and Allah hath power over all things.

Surah 6

150. Say: "Bring forward your witnesses to prove that Allah did forbid so and so." If they bring such witnesses be not thou amongst them: nor follow thou the vain desires of such as treat Our Signs as falsehoods and such as believe not in the Hereafter: for they hold others as equal with their Guardian-Lord.

151. Say: "Come I will rehearse what Allah hath (really) prohibited you from": join not anything as equal with Him; be good to your parents: kill not your children on a plea of want; We provide sustenance for you and for them; come not nigh to shameful deeds whether open or secret; take not life which Allah hath made sacred except by way of justice and law: thus doth He command you that ye may learn wisdom.

152. And come not nigh to the orphan's property except to improve it until he attain the age of full strength; give measure and weight with (full) justice; no burden do We place on any soul but that which it can bear; whenever ye speak speak justly even if a near relative is concerned; and fulfil the Covenant of Allah: thus doth He command you that ye may remember.

153. Verily this is My Way leading straight: follow it: follow not (other) paths: they will scatter you about from His (great) path: thus doth He command you that ye may be righteous.

154. Moreover We gave Moses the Book completing (Our favor) to those who would do right and explaining all things in detail and a guide and a mercy that they might believe in the meeting with their Lord.

155. And this is a Book which We have revealed as a blessing: so follow it and be righteous that ye may receive mercy:

156. Lest ye should say: "The Book was sent down to two peoples before us and for our part we remained unacquainted with all that they learned by assiduous study."

157. Or lest ye should say: "If the Book had only been sent down to us we should have followed its guidance better than they." Now then hath come unto you a Clear (sign) from your Lord and a guide and a mercy: then who could do more wrong than one who rejecteth Allah's signs and turneth away therefrom? In good time shall We requite those who turn away from Our Signs with a dreadful penalty for their turning away.

158. Are they waiting to see if the angels come to them or thy Lord (Himself) or certain of the signs of thy Lord! the day that certain of the signs of thy Lord do come no good will it do to a soul to believe in them then if it believed not before nor earned righteousness through its Faith. Say: "Wait ye: we too are waiting."

159. As for those who divide their religion and break up into sects thou hast no part in them in the least: their affair is with Allah: He will in the end tell them the truth of all that they did.

160. He that doeth good shall have ten times as much to his credit: he that doeth evil shall only be recompensed according to his evil. No wrong shall be done unto (any of) them.

Surah 64

12. So obey Allah and obey His Apostle; but if ye turn back the duty of Our Apostle is but to proclaim (the Message) clearly and openly.

13. Allah! there is no god but He: and on Allah therefore let the Believers put their trust.

14. O ye who believe! truly among your wives and your children are (some that are) enemies to yourselves: so beware of them! But if ye forgive and overlook and cover up (their faults) verily Allah is Oft-Forgiving Most Merciful.

15. Your riches and your children may be but a trial: but in the Presence of Allah is the highest Reward.

16. So fear Allah as much as ye can; listen and obey; and spend in charity for the benefit of your own souls: and those saved from the covetousness of their own souls they are the ones that achieve prosperity.

17. If ye loan to Allah a beautiful loan He will double it to your (credit) and He will grant you Forgiveness: for Allah is most Ready to appreciate (service) Most Forbearing

18. Knower of what is hidden and what is open exalted in Might Full of Wisdom.

Surah 107

1. Seest thou one who denies the Judgment (to come)?
2. Then such is the (man) who repulses the orphan (with harshness)
3. And encourages not the feeding of the indigent.
4. So woe to the worshippers
5. Who are neglectful of their Prayers
6. Those who (want but) to be seen (of men)
7. But refuse (to supply) (Even) neighborly needs.

Like other sacred texts, the Qur'an discusses the temporal and eternal consequences of obedience and disobedience to divine law. According to the following passages, what motivation is there to adhere to the commandments of Allah? To what degree are these promises similar to those of the other traditions?

REWARDS AND PUNISHMENTS

Surah 2

2. This is the Book; in it is guidance sure without doubt to those who fear Allah.

3. Who believe in the Unseen are steadfast in prayer and spend out of what We have provided for them.

4. And who believe in the Revelation sent to thee and sent before thy time and (in their hearts) have the assurance of the Hereafter.

5. They are on (true) guidance from their Lord and it is these who will prosper.

6. As to those who reject Faith it is the same to them whether thou warn them or do not warn them; they will not believe.

7. Allah hath set a seal on their hearts and on their hearing and on their eyes is a veil; great is the penalty they (incur).

Surah 18

27. And recite (and teach) what has been revealed to thee of the Book of thy Lord: none can change His Words and none wilt thou find as a refuge other than Him.

28. And keep thy soul content with those who call on their Lord morning and evening seeking his Face; and let not thine eyes pass beyond them seeking the pomp and glitter of this Life; nor obey any whose heart We have permitted to neglect the remembrance of Us one who follows his own desires whose case has gone beyond all bounds.

29. Say "The Truth is from your Lord": let him who will believe and let him who will reject (it): for the wrongdoers We have prepared a Fire whose (smoke and flames) like the wall and roof of a tent will hem them in: if they implore relief they will be granted water like melted brass that will scald their faces. How dreadful the drink! How uncomfortable a couch to recline on!

30. As to those who believe and work righteousness verily We shall not suffer to perish the reward of any who do a (single) righteous deed.

31. For them will be Gardens of Eternity; beneath them rivers will flow; they will be adorned therein with bracelets of gold and they will wear green garments of fine silk and heavy brocade; they will recline therein on raised thrones. How good the recompense! How beautiful a couch to recline on!

32. Set forth to them the parable of two men: for one of them We provided two gardens of grapevines and surrounded them with date-palms: in between the two We placed corn-fields.

33. Each of those gardens brought forth its produce and failed not in the least therein: in the midst of them We caused a river to flow.

34. (Abundant) was the produce this man had: he said to his companion in the course of a mutual argument: "More wealth have I than you and more honor and power in (my following of) men."

35. He went into his garden in a state (of mind) unjust to his soul: He said "I deem not that this will ever perish.

36. "Nor do I deem that the Hour (of Judgment) will (ever) come: even if I am brought back to my Lord I shall surely find (there) something better in exchange."

37. His companion said to him in the course of the argument with him: "Dost thou deny Him Who created thee out of dust then out of a sperm-drop then fashioned thee into a man?

38. "But (I think) for my part that He is Allah my Lord and none shall I associate with my Lord.

39. "Why didst thou not as thou wentest into thy garden say: 'Allah's Will (be done)! There is no power but with Allah!' If thou dost see me less than thee in wealth and sons

40. "It may be that my Lord will give me something better than thy garden and that He will send on thy garden thunderbolts (by way of reckoning) from heaven making it (but) slippery sand!

41. "Or the water of the garden will run off underground so that thou wilt never be able to find it."

42. So his fruits (and enjoyment) were encompassed (with ruin) and he remained twisting and turning his hands over what he had spent on his property which had (now) tumbled to pieces to its very foundations and he could only say "Woe is me! would I had never ascribed partners to my Lord and Cherisher!"

43. Nor had he numbers to help him against Allah nor was he able to deliver himself.

44. There the (only) protection comes from Allah the True One. He is the Best to reward and the Best to give success.

Surah 57

17. Know ye (all) that Allah giveth life to the earth after its death! already have We shown the Signs plainly to you that ye may learn wisdom.

18. For those who give in Charity men and women and loan to Allah a Beautiful Loan it shall be increased manifold (to their credit) and they shall have (besides) a liberal reward.

19. And those who believe in Allah and His apostles they are the Sincere (Lovers of truth) and the witnesses (who testify) in the eyes of their Lord: they shall have their Reward and their Light but those who reject Allah and deny Our Signs they are the Companions of Hell-Fire.

20. Know ye (all) that the life of this world is but play and amusement pomp and mutual boasting and multiplying (in rivalry) among yourselves riches and children: Here is a similitude: How rain and the growth which it brings forth delight (the hearts of) the tillers; soon it withers; thou wilt see it grow yellow; then it becomes dry and crumbles away. But in the Hereafter is a Penalty severe (for the devotees of wrong) and Forgiveness from Allah and (His) Good Pleasure (for the devotees of Allah). And what is the life of this world but goods and chattels of deception?

21. Be ye foremost (in seeking) forgiveness from your Lord and a Garden (of Bliss) the width whereof is as the width of heaven and earth prepared for those who believe in Allah and His apostles: that is the Grace of Allah which He bestows on whom He pleases: and Allah is the Lord of Grace abounding.

Surah 83

1. Woe to those that deal in fraud

2. Those who when they have to receive by measure from men exact full measure.

3. But when they have to give by measure or weight to men give less than due.

4. Do they not think that they will be called to account?

5. On a Mighty Day

6. A Day when (all) mankind will stand before the Lord of the Worlds?

7. Nay! Surely the Record of the Wicked is (preserved) in Sijjin

8. And what will explain to thee what Sijjin is?

9. (There is) a Register (fully) inscribed.

10. Woe that Day to those that deny

11. Those that deny the Day of Judgment.

12. And none can deny it but the Transgressor beyond bounds the Sinner!

13. When Our Signs are rehearsed to him he says "Tales of the Ancients!"

14. By no means! but on their hearts is the stain of the (ill) which they do!

15. Verily from (the Light of) their Lord that Day will they be veiled.

16. Further they will enter the Fire of Hell.

SECTION 5: Gender: Women and Men in Society

According to Islamic theology and law, women and men are equal before Allah. This equality before Allah, however, does not necessarily result in equality within human society. In modern times, the status of women in predominantly Islamic nations is one characteristic that distinguishes the world of Islam from many other Western cultures. The following passages reflect quranic attitudes concerning the role of women in the family and in society. Compare these Islamic regulations concerning marriage, inheritance, divorce, and adultery with similar passages contained in the sacred texts of other ancient religious traditions. To what degree would these rules have protected women in seventh-century Arabia? In what ways do these customs restrict female activities in the modern world?

MARRIAGE AND INHERITANCE REGULATIONS

Surah 4

1. O mankind! reverence your Guardian-Lord Who created you from a single person created of like nature his mate and from them twain scattered (like seeds) countless men and women; reverence Allah through Whom ye demand your mutual (rights) and (reverence) the wombs (that bore you): for Allah ever watches over you.

2. To orphans restore their property (when they reach their age) nor substitute (your) worthless things for (their) good ones; and devour not their substance (by mixing it up) with your own. For this is indeed a great sin.

3. If ye fear that ye shall not be able to deal justly with the orphans marry women of your choice two or three or four; but if ye fear that ye shall not be able to deal justly (with them) then only one or (a captive) that your right hands possess. That will be more suitable to prevent you from doing injustice.

4. And give the women (on marriage) their dower as a free gift; but if they of their own good pleasure remit any part of it to you take it and enjoy it with right good cheer.

5. To those weak of understanding make not over your property which Allah hath made a means of support for you

but feed and clothe them therewith and speak to them words of kindness and justice.

6. Make trial of orphans until they reach the age of marriage; if then ye find sound judgment in them release their property to them; but consume it not wastefully nor in haste against their growing up. If the guardian is well-off let him claim no remuneration but if he is poor let him have for himself what is just and reasonable. When ye release their property to them take witnesses in their presence: but all-sufficient is Allah in taking account.

7. From what is left by parents and those nearest related there is a share for men and a share for women whether the property be small or large a determinate share.

8. But if at the time of division other relatives of orphans or poor are present feed them out of the (property) and speak to them words of kindness and justice.

9. Let those (disposing of an estate) have the same fear in their minds as they would have for their own if they had left a helpless family behind: let them fear Allah and speak words of appropriate (comfort).

10. Those who unjustly eat up the property of orphans eat up a fire into their own bodies: they will soon be enduring a blazing fire!

11. Allah (thus) directs you as regards your children's (inheritance): to the male a portion equal to that of two females: if only daughters two or more their share is two-thirds of the inheritance; if only one her share is a half. For parents a sixth share of the inheritance to each if the deceased left children; if no children and the parents are the (only) heirs the mother has a third; if the deceased left brothers (or sisters) the mother has a sixth. (The distribution in all cases is) after the payment of legacies and debts. Ye know not whether your parents or your children are nearest to you in benefit. These are settled portions ordained by Allah and Allah is All-Knowing All-Wise.

12. In what your wives leave your share is a half if they leave no child; but if they leave a child ye get a fourth; after payment of legacies and debts. In what ye leave their share is a fourth if ye leave no child; but if ye leave a child they get an eighth; after payment of legacies and debts. If the man or woman whose inheritance is in question has left neither ascendants nor descendants but has left a brother or a sister each one of the two gets a sixth; but if more than two they share in a third; after payment of legacies and debts; so that no loss is caused (to anyone). Thus is it ordained by Allah and Allah is All-Knowing Most Forbearing.

13. Those are limits set by Allah: those who obey Allah and His Apostle will be admitted to Gardens with rivers flowing beneath to abide therein (for ever) and that will be the Supreme achievement.

14. But those who disobey Allah and His Apostle and transgress His limits will be admitted to a fire to abide therein: and they shall have a humiliating punishment.

15. If any of your women are guilty of lewdness take the evidence of four (reliable) witnesses from amongst you against them; and if they testify confine them to houses until death do claim them or Allah ordain for them some (other) way.

16. If two men among you are guilty of lewdness punish them both. If they repent and amend leave them alone; for Allah is Oft-returning Most Merciful.

17. Allah accepts the repentance of those who do evil in ignorance and repent soon afterwards; to them will Allah turn in mercy; for Allah is full of knowledge and wisdom.

18. Of no effect is the repentance of those who continue to do evil until death faces one of them and he says "Now have I repented indeed"; nor of those who die rejecting faith: for them have We prepared a punishment most grievous.

19. O ye who believe! ye are forbidden to inherit women against their will. Nor should ye treat them with harshness that ye may take away part of the dower ye have given them except where they have been guilty of open lewdness; on the contrary live with them on a footing of kindness and equity. If ye take a dislike to them it may be that ye dislike a thing and Allah brings about through it a great deal of good.

20. But if ye decide to take one wife in place of another even if ye had given the latter a whole treasure for dower take not the least bit of it back: would ye take it by slander and a manifest wrong?

21. And how could ye take it when ye have gone in unto each other and they have taken from you a solemn covenant?

22. And marry not women whom your fathers married except what is past: it was shameful and odious and abominable custom indeed.

23. Prohibited to you (for marriage) are: your mother daughters sisters father's sisters mother's sisters; brother's daughters sister's daughters foster-mothers (who gave you suck) foster-sisters; your wives' mothers; your step-daughters under your guardianship born of your wives to whom ye have gone in no prohibition if ye have not gone in; (those who have been) wives of your sons proceeding from your loins; and two sisters in wedlock at one and the same time except for what is past; for Allah is Oft-Forgiving Most Merciful.

24. Also (prohibited are) women already married except those whom your right hands possess. Thus hath Allah ordained (prohibitions) against you: except for these all others are lawful provided ye seek (them in marriage) with gifts from your property desiring chastity not lust. Seeing that ye derive benefit from them give them their dowers (at least) as prescribed; but if after a dower is prescribed ye agree mutually (to vary it) there is no blame on you and Allah is All-Knowing All-Wise.

25. If any of you have not the means wherewith to wed free believing women they may wed believing girls from among those whom your right hands possess: and Allah hath full knowledge about your faith. Ye are one from another: wed them with the leave of their owners and give them their dowers according to what is reasonable: they should be chaste not lustful nor taking paramours: when they are taken in wedlock if they fall into shame their punishment is half that for free

women. This (permission) is for those among you who fear sin; but it is better for you that ye practice self-restraint: and Allah is Oft-forgiving Most Merciful.

34. Men are the protectors and maintainers of women because Allah has given the one more (strength) than the other and because they support them from their means. Therefore the righteous women are devoutly obedient and guard in (the husband's) absence what Allah would have them guard. As to those women on whose part ye fear disloyalty and ill-conduct admonish them (first) (next) refuse to share their beds (and last) beat them (lightly); but if they return to obedience seek not against them means (of annoyance): for Allah is Most High Great (above you all).

35. If ye fear a breach between them twain appoint (two) arbiters one from his family and the other from hers; if they wish for peace Allah will cause their reconciliation: for Allah hath full knowledge and is acquainted with all things.

36. Serve Allah and join not any partners with Him: and do good to parents kinsfolk orphans those in need neighbors who are near neighbors who are strangers the companion by your side the wayfarer (ye meet) and what your right hands possess: for Allah loveth not the arrogant the vainglorious. . . .

127. They ask thy instruction concerning the women. Say: Allah doth instruct you about them: and (remember) what hath been rehearsed unto you in the Book concerning the orphans of women to whom ye give not the portions prescribed and yet whom ye desire to marry as also concerning the children who are weak and oppressed: that ye stand firm for justice to orphans. There is not a good deed which ye do but Allah is well-acquainted therewith.

128. If a wife fears cruelty or desertion on her husband's part there is no blame on them if they arrange an amicable settlement between themselves; and such settlement is best; even though men's souls are swayed by greed. But if ye do good and practice self-restraint Allah is well-acquainted with all that ye do.

129. Ye are never able to be fair and just as between women even if it is your ardent desire: but turn not away (from a woman) altogether so as to leave her (as it were) hanging (in the air). If ye come to a friendly understanding and practice self-restraint Allah is Oft-Forgiving Most Merciful.

130. But if they disagree (and must part) Allah will provide abundance for all from His all-reaching bounty: for Allah is He that careth for all and is Wise.

RULES CONCERNING DIVORCE

Surah 2

226. For those who take an oath for abstention from their wives a waiting for four months is ordained; if then they return Allah is Oft-Forgiving Most Merciful.

227. But if their intention is firm for divorce Allah heareth and knoweth all things.

228. Divorced women shall wait concerning themselves for three monthly periods nor is it lawful for them to hide what Allah hath created in their wombs if they have faith in Allah and the Last Day. And their husbands have the better right to take them back in that period if they wish for reconciliation. And women shall have rights similar to the rights against them according to what is equitable; but men have a degree (of advantage) over them and Allah is Exalted in Power Wise.

232. When ye divorce women and they fulfil the term of their ('Iddat) do not prevent them from marrying their (former) husbands if they mutually agree on equitable terms. This instruction is for all amongst you who believe in Allah and the Last Day. That is (the course making for) most virtue and purity amongst you and Allah knows and ye know not.

233. The mothers shall give suck to their offspring for two whole years if the father desires to complete the term. But he shall bear the cost of their food and clothing on equitable terms. No soul shall have a burden laid on it greater than it can bear. No mother shall be treated unfairly on account of her child nor father on account of his child. An heir shall be chargeable in the same way if they both decide on weaning by mutual consent and after due consultation there is no blame on them. If ye decide on a foster-mother for your offspring there is no blame on you provided ye pay (the mother) what ye offered on equitable terms. But fear Allah and know that Allah sees well what ye do.

234. If any of you die and leave widows behind they shall wait concerning themselves four months and ten days: when they have fulfilled their term there is no blame on you if they dispose of themselves in a just and reasonable manner. And Allah is well acquainted with what ye do.

235. There is no blame on you if ye make an offer of betrothal or hold it in your hearts. Allah knows that ye cherish them in your hearts: but do not make a secret contract with them except in terms honorable nor resolve on the tie of marriage till the term prescribed is fulfilled. And know that Allah knoweth what is in your hearts and take heed of Him; and know that Allah is Oft-Forgiving Most Forbearing.

236. There is no blame on you if ye divorce women before consummation or the fixation of their dower; but bestow on them (a suitable gift) the wealthy according to his means and the poor according to his means; a gift of a reasonable amount is due from those who wish to do the right thing.

237. And if ye divorce them before consummation but after the fixation of a dower for them then the half of the dower (is due to them) unless they remit it. Or (the man's half) is remitted by him in whose hands is the marriage tie; and the remission (of the man's half) is the nearest to righteousness. And do not forget liberality between yourselves. For Allah sees well all that ye do.

Surah 65

1. O Prophet! when ye do divorce women divorce them at their prescribed periods and count (accurately) their prescribed periods: and fear Allah your Lord: and turn them

not out of their houses nor shall they (themselves) leave except in case they are guilty of some open lewdness. Those are limits set by Allah: and any who transgresses the limits of Allah does verily wrong his (own) soul: thou knowest not if perchance Allah will bring about thereafter some new situation.

2. Thus when they fulfil their term appointed either take them back on equitable terms or part with them on equitable terms; and take for witness two persons from among you endued with justice and establish the evidence (as) before Allah. Such is the admonition given to him who believes in Allah and the Last Day. And for those who fear Allah He (ever) prepares a way out

3. And He provides for him from (sources) he never could imagine. And if anyone puts his trust in Allah sufficient is (Allah) for him. For Allah will surely accomplish His purpose: verily for all things has Allah appointed a due proportion.

4. Such of your women as have passed the age of monthly courses for them the prescribed period if ye have any doubt is three months and for those who have no courses (it is the same): for those who carry (life within their wombs) their period is until they deliver their burdens: and for those who fear Allah He will make their path easy.

5. That is the Command of Allah which He has sent down to you: and if anyone fears Allah He will remove his ills from him and will enlarge His reward.

6. Let the women live (in 'iddah) in the same style as ye live according to your means: annoy them not so as to restrict them. And if they carry (life in their wombs) then spend (your substance) on them until they deliver their burden: and if they suckle your (offspring) give them their recompense: and take mutual counsel together according to what is just and reasonable. And if ye find yourselves in difficulties let another woman suckle (the child) on the (father's) behalf.

7. Let the man of means spend according to his means: and the man whose resources are restricted let him spend according to what Allah has given him. Allah puts no burden on any person beyond what He has given him. After a difficulty Allah will soon grant relief.

Rules Concerning Adultery and Modesty

Surah 24

1. A Surah which We have sent down and which We have ordained: in it have We sent down Clear Signs in order that ye may receive admonition.

2. The woman and the man guilty of adultery or fornication flog each of them with a hundred stripes: let not compassion move you in their case in a matter prescribed by Allah if ye believe in Allah and the Last Day: and let a party of the Believers witness their punishment.

3. Let no man guilty of adultery or fornication marry any but a woman similarly guilty or an Unbeliever nor let any but such a man or an Unbeliever marry such a woman: to the Believers such a thing is forbidden.

4. And those who launch a charge against chaste women and produce not four witnesses (to support their allegation) flog them with eighty stripes: and reject their evidence ever after: for such men are wicked transgressors

5. Unless they repent thereafter and mend (their conduct): for Allah is Oft-Forgiving Most Merciful.

6. And for those who launch a charge against their spouses and have (in support) no evidence but their own their solitary evidence (can be received) if they bear witness four times (with an oath) by Allah that they are solemnly telling the truth;

7. And the fifth (oath) (should be) that they solemnly invoke the curse of Allah on themselves if they tell a lie.

8. But it would avert the punishment from the wife if she bears witness four times (with an oath) by Allah that (her husband) is telling a lie;

9. And the fifth (oath) should be that she solemnly invokes the wrath of Allah on herself if (her accuser) is telling the truth. . . .

23. Those who slander chaste women indiscreet but believing are cursed in this life and in the Hereafter: for them is a grievous Penalty

24. On the Day when their tongues their hands and their feet will bear witness against them as to their actions.

25. On that Day Allah will pay them back (all) their just dues and they will realize that Allah is the (very) Truth that makes all things manifest.

26. Women impure are for men impure and men impure are for women impure; and women of purity are for men of purity and men of purity are for women of purity: these are not affected by what people say: for them there is forgiveness and a provision honorable.

27. O ye who believe! enter not houses other than your own until ye have asked permission and saluted those in them: that is best for you in order that ye may heed (what is seemly).

28. If ye find no one in the house enter not until permission is given to you: if ye are asked to go back go back: that makes for greater purity for yourselves: and Allah knows well all that ye do.

29. It is no fault on your part to enter houses not used for living in which serve some (other) use for you: and Allah has knowledge of what ye reveal and what ye conceal.

30. Say to the believing men that they should lower their gaze and guard their modesty: that will make for greater purity for them: and Allah is well acquainted with all that they do.

31. And say to the believing women that they should lower their gaze and guard their modesty; that they should not display their beauty and ornaments except what (must ordinarily) appear thereof; that they should draw their veils over their bosoms and not display their beauty except to their husbands their fathers their husbands' fathers their sons their husbands' sons their brothers or their brothers' sons or their

sisters' sons or their women or the slaves whom their right hands possess or male servants free of physical needs or small children who have no sense of the shame of sex; and that they should not strike their feet in order to draw attention to their hidden ornaments. And O ye Believers! turn ye all together towards Allah that ye may attain Bliss.

32. Marry those among you who are single or the virtuous ones among your slaves male or female: if they are in poverty Allah will give them means out of His grace: for Allah encompasseth all and He knoweth all things.

33. Let those who find not the wherewithal for marriage keep themselves chaste until Allah gives them means out of His grace. And if any of your slaves ask for a deed in writing (to enable them to earn their freedom for a certain sum) give them such a deed if ye know any good in them; yea give them something yourselves out of the means which Allah has given to you. But force not your maids to prostitution when they desire chastity in order that ye may make a gain in the goods of this life. But if anyone compels them yet after such compulsion is Allah Oft-Forgiving Most Merciful (to them).

34. We have already sent down to you verses making things clear an illustration from (the story of) people who passed away before you and an admonition for those who fear (Allah).

SECTION 6: Daily Living: Health, Etiquette, and Holy Days

Islam is a complete way of life, and its scriptures provide definitive instructions about a wide range of possible human activities. To a greater degree than the sacred texts of many traditions, the Qur'an joins together religion, politics, and culture. The scope of Islamic law is large, and its prescriptions are often specific. Muslims, for example, believe that Allah sent Jesus to teach the divine principle "love thy neighbor" and later provided the prophet Muhammad with more detailed answers as to how we should love our neighbor. The Qur'an, consequently, is a legal compendium for its followers as well as a spiritual guide.

The selections in this section sample the wide variety of daily activities discussed in the Qur'an. These passages address everyday issues such as diet and appropriate sexual conduct and special occasion instructions such as combat etiquette. As you read these selections, try to identify commands that are common to the Jews and to the Christians, and those that are peculiar to Islam. Based on these readings, what should be some of the distinguishing traits of those who embrace the teachings of the Qur'an?

INSTRUCTIONS ON DIET, SEX, AND COMBAT

Surah 2

168. O ye people! eat of what is on earth lawful and good; and do not follow the footsteps of the evil one for he is to you an avowed enemy.

169. For he commands you what is evil and shameful and that ye should say of Allah that of which ye have no knowledge.

170. When it is said to them: "Follow what Allah hath revealed" they say: "Nay! we shall follow the ways of our fathers." What! even though their fathers were void of wisdom and guidance?

171. The parable of those who reject faith is as if one were to shout like a goat-herd to things that listen to nothing but calls and cries; deaf dumb and blind they are void of wisdom.

172. O ye who believe! eat of the good things that We have provided for you and be grateful to Allah if it is Him ye worship.

173. He hath only forbidden you dead meat and blood and the flesh of swine and that on which any other name hath been invoked besides that of Allah but if one is forced by necessity without wilful disobedience nor transgressing due limits then is he guiltless. For Allah is Oft-Forgiving Most Merciful. . . .

216. Fighting is prescribed for you and ye dislike it. But it is possible that ye dislike a thing which is good for you and that ye love a thing which is bad for you. But Allah knoweth and ye know not.

217. They ask thee concerning fighting in the Prohibited Month. Say: "Fighting therein is a grave (offence); but graver is it in the sight of Allah to prevent access to the path of Allah to deny Him to prevent access to the Sacred Mosque and drive out its members. Tumult and oppression are worse than slaughter. Nor will they cease fighting you until they turn you back from your faith if they can. And if any of you turn back from their faith and die in unbelief their works will bear no fruit in this life and in the Hereafter; they will be Companions of the Fire and will abide therein.

218. Those who believed and those who suffered exile and fought (and strove and struggled) in the path of Allah they have the hope of the Mercy of Allah; and Allah is Oft-Forgiving Most Merciful.

219. They ask thee concerning wine and gambling. Say: "In them is great sin and some profit for men; but the sin is greater than the profit." They ask thee how much they are to spend; say: "What is beyond your needs." Thus doth Allah make clear to you His Signs: in order that ye may consider.

220. (Their bearings) on this life and the Hereafter. They ask thee concerning orphans. Say: "The best thing to do is what is for their good; if ye mix their affairs with yours they are your brethren; but Allah knows the man who means mischief from the man who means good. And if Allah had wished He could have put you into difficulties: He is indeed Exalted in Power Wise."

221. Do not marry unbelieving women (idolaters) until they believe; a slave woman who believes is better than an unbelieving woman even though she allure you. Nor marry (your girls) to unbelievers until they believe: a man slave who believes is better than un unbeliever even though he allure you. Unbelievers do (but) beckon you to the fire. But Allah beckons by His grace to the Garden (of Bliss) and forgiveness and makes His Signs clear to mankind: that they may celebrate His praise.

222. They ask thee concerning women's courses. Say: They are a hurt and a pollution; so keep away from women in their courses and do not approach them until they are clean. But when they have purified themselves ye may approach them in any manner time or place ordained for you by Allah. For Allah loves those who turn to Him constantly and He loves those who keep themselves pure and clean.

223. Your wives are as a tilth unto you; so approach your tilth when or how ye will. But do some good act for your souls beforehand; and fear Allah and know that ye are to meet Him (in the Hereafter) and give (these) good tidings to those who believe.

224. And make not Allah's (name) an excuse in your oaths against doing good or acting rightly or making peace between persons; for Allah is one who heareth and knoweth all things.

225. Allah will not call you to account for thoughtlessness in your oaths but for the intention in your hearts; and He is Oft-Forgiving Most Forbearing.

Surah 5

1. O ye who believe! fulfil (all) obligations. Lawful unto you (for food) are all four-footed animals with the exceptions named: but animals of the chase are forbidden while ye are in the Sacred Precincts or in pilgrim garb: for Allah doth command according to His Will and Plan.

2. O ye who believe! violate not the sanctity of the Symbols of Allah nor of the Sacred Month nor of the animals brought for sacrifice nor the garlands that mark out such animals nor the people resorting to the Sacred House seeking of the bounty and good pleasure of their Lord. But when ye are clear of the Sacred Precincts and of pilgrim garb ye may hunt and let not the hatred of some people in (once) shutting you out of the Sacred Mosque lead you to transgression (and hostility on your part). Help ye one another in righteousness and piety but help ye not one another in sin and rancor: fear Allah: for Allah is strict in punishment.

3. Forbidden to you (for food) are: dead meat blood the flesh of swine and that on which hath been invoked the name of other than Allah that which hath been killed by strangling or by a violent blow or by a headlong fall or by being gored to death; that which hath been (partly) eaten by a wild animal; unless ye are able to slaughter it (in due form); that which is sacrificed on stone (altars); (forbidden) also is the division (of meat) by raffling with arrows: that is impiety. This day have those who reject faith given up all hope of your religion: yet fear them not

but fear Me. This day have I perfected your religion for you completed my favor upon you and have chosen for you Islam as your religion. But if any forced by hunger with no inclination to transgression Allah is indeed Oft-Forgiving Most Merciful.

4. They ask thee what is lawful to them (as food): say: Lawful unto you are (all) things good and pure: and what ye have taught your trained hunting animals (to catch) in the manner directed to you by Allah; eat what they catch for you but pronounce the name of Allah over it: and fear Allah; for Allah is swift in taking account. . . .

74. Let those fight in the cause of Allah who sell the life of this world for the Hereafter. To him who fighteth in the cause of Allah whether he is slain or gets victory soon shall We give him a reward of great (value).

75. And why should ye not fight in the cause of Allah and of those who being weak are ill-treated (and oppressed)? Men women and children whose cry is: "Our Lord! rescue us from this town whose people are oppressors; and raise for us from Thee one who will protect; and raise for us from Thee one who will help!"

76. Those who believe fight in the cause of Allah and those who reject faith fight in the cause of evil: so fight ye against the friends of Satan: feeble indeed is the cunning of Satan.

77. Hast thou not turned thy vision to those who were told to hold back their hands (from fight) but establish regular prayers and spend in regular charity? When (at length) the order for fighting was issued to them behold! a section of them feared men as or even more than they should have feared Allah: they say: "Our Lord! why hast Thou ordered us to fight? Wouldst Thou not grant us respite to our (natural) term near (enough)?" Say: "Short is the enjoyment of this world: the Hereafter is the best for those who do right: never will ye be dealt with unjustly in the very least!

78. "Wherever ye are death will find you out even if ye are in towers built up strong and high!" If some good befalls them they say "This is from Allah"; but if evil they say "this is from thee" (O Prophet). Say: "All things are from Allah. But what hath come to these people that they fail to understand a single fact? . . .

87. O ye who believe! make not unlawful the good things which Allah hath made lawful for you but commit no excess: for Allah loveth not those given to excess.

88. Eat of the things which Allah hath provided for you lawful and good: but fear Allah in Whom ye believe.

89. Allah will not call you to account for what is futile in your oaths but He will call you to account for your deliberate oaths: for expiation feed ten indigent persons on a scale of the average for the food of your families; or clothe them; or give a slave his freedom. If that is beyond your means fast for three days. That is the expiation for the oaths ye have sworn. But keep to your oaths. Thus doth Allah make clear to you His Signs that ye may be grateful.

90. O ye who believe! intoxicants and gambling (dedication of) stones and (divination by) arrows are an abomination of Satan's handiwork: eschew such (abomination) that ye may prosper.

91. Satan's plan is (but) to excite enmity and hatred between you with intoxicants and gambling and hinder you from the remembrance of Allah and from prayer: will ye not then abstain?

92. Obey Allah and obey the Apostle and beware (of evil): if ye do turn back know ye that it is Our Apostle's duty to proclaim (the Message) in the clearest manner.

93. On those who believe and do deeds of righteousness there is no blame for what they ate (in the past) when they guard themselves from evil and believe and do deeds of righteousness (or) again guard themselves from evil and do good. For Allah loveth those who do good. . . .

101. O ye who believe! ask not questions about things which if made plain to you may cause you trouble. But if ye ask about things when the Qur'an is being revealed they will be made plain to you: Allah will forgive those: for Allah is Oft-Forgiving Most Forbearing.

102. Some people before you did ask such questions and on that account lost their faith.

103. It was not Allah Who instituted (superstitions like those of) a slit-ear she-camel or a she-camel let loose for free pasture or idol sacrifices for twin-births in animals or stallion-camels freed from work; it is blasphemers who invent a lie against Allah but most of them lack wisdom.

Surah 9

18. The mosques of Allah shall be visited and maintained by such as believe in Allah and the Last Day establish regular prayers and practice regular charity and fear none (at all) except Allah. It is they who are expected to be on true guidance.

19. Do ye make the giving of drink to pilgrims or the maintenance of the Sacred Mosque equal to (the pious service of) those who believe in Allah and the Last Day and strive with might and main in the cause of Allah? They are not comparable in the sight of Allah: and Allah guides not those who do wrong.

20. Those who believe and suffer exile and strive with might and main in Allah's cause with their goods and their persons have the highest rank in the sight of Allah: They are the people who will achieve (salvation).

21. Their Lord doth give them Glad tidings of a Mercy from Himself of His good pleasure and of gardens for them wherein are delights that endure.

22. They will dwell therein forever. Verily in Allah's presence is a reward the greatest (of all).

23. O ye who believe! take not for protectors your fathers and your brothers if they love infidelity above faith: if any of you do so they do wrong.

24. Say: If it be that your fathers your sons your brothers your mates or your kindred; the wealth that ye have gained; the commerce in which ye fear a decline; or the dwellings in which ye delight are dearer to you than Allah or His apostle or the striving in his cause; then wait until Allah brings about His decision: and Allah guides not the rebellious.

25. Assuredly Allah did help you in many battle-fields and on the day of Hunain: Behold! your great numbers elated you but they availed you naught: the land for all that it is wide did constrain you and ye turned back in retreat.

26. But Allah did pour His calm on the apostle and on the believers and sent down forces which ye saw not: He punished the unbelievers: thus doth He reward those without faith. . . .

36. The number of months in the sight of Allah is twelve (in a year) so ordained by Him the day He created the heavens and the earth; of them four are sacred; that is the straight usage. So wrong not yourselves therein and fight the pagans all together as they fight you all together. But know that Allah is with those who restrain themselves. . . .

113. It is not fitting for the prophet and those who believe that they should pray for forgiveness for pagans even though they be of kin after it is clear to them that they are companions of the Fire.

114. And Abraham prayed for his father's forgiveness only because of a promise he had made to him. But when it became clear to him that he was an enemy to Allah he dissociated himself from him: for Abraham was most tender-hearted forbearing.

115. And Allah will not mislead a people after He hath Guided them in order that He may make clear to them what to fear (and avoid) for Allah hath knowledge of all things.

116. Unto Allah belongeth the dominion of the heavens and the earth. He giveth life and He taketh it. Except for Him ye have no protector nor helper.

Surah 23

1. The Believers must (eventually) win through

2. Those who humble themselves in their prayers;

3. Who avoid vain talk;

4. Who are active in deeds of charity;

5. Who abstain from sex

6. Except with those joined to them in the marriage bond or (the captives) whom their right hands possess for (in their case) they are free from blame

7. But those whose desires exceed those limits are transgressors

8. Those who faithfully observe their trust and their covenants;

9. And who (strictly) guard their prayers

10. Those will be the heirs

11. Who will inherit Paradise: they will dwell therein (forever).

SECTION 7: The Human Quest: Paths to Salvation and Enlightenment

The opening Surah of the Qur'an summarizes the human quest as follows:

> *Guide us in the straight path, the path of those on whom Thou hast poured forth Thy grace. Not the path of those who have incurred Thy wrath and gone astray.*

Much of the remainder of the Qur'an is devoted to describing this "straight path," which is the way of Allah. According to Islamic beliefs, these words originated with Allah himself. Muhammad was simply the one Allah chose to deliver the message. For Muslims, the message of the Qur'an was not new. Instead, it confirmed the truth that Allah earlier had revealed to Jewish prophets from Abraham to Jesus. Within this message was a promise that those who followed the straight path would be admitted into a heavenly kingdom. Decisions made in this life, therefore, carry eternal consequences. No intercessors will stand between Allah and his creatures on the coming day of judgment. Allah alone will determine those worthy to enter his kingdom.

For Muslims, every passage in the Qur'an is offered to provide insight into the expectations of the All-powerful and All-merciful Allah. According to the following selections, what will determine one's ultimate fate on that day of judgment? To what degree is the path to salvation within Islam similar to and different from the way presented in the Jewish and Christian scriptures?

PATHS TO SALVATION WITHIN ISLAM

Surah 4

105. We have sent down to thee the Book in truth that thou mightest judge between men as guided by Allah: so be not (used) as an advocate by those who betray their trust.

106. But seek the forgiveness of Allah; for Allah is Oft-Forgiving Most Merciful.

107. Contend not on behalf of such as betray their own souls: for Allah loveth not one given to perfidy and crime.

108. They may hide (their crimes) from men but they cannot hide (them) from Allah seeing that He is in their midst when they plot by night in words that He cannot approve: and Allah doth compass round all that they do.

109. Ah! these are the sort of men on whose behalf ye may contend in this world; but who will contend with Allah on their behalf on the Day of Judgment or who will carry their affairs through?

110. If anyone does evil or wrongs his own soul but afterwards seeks Allah's forgiveness he will find Allah Oft-Forgiving Most Merciful.

111. And if anyone earns sin he earns it against his own soul: for Allah is full of knowledge and wisdom.

112. But if anyone earns a fault or a sin and throws it on to one that is innocent He carries (on himself) (both) a falsehood and a flagrant sin.

113. But for the Grace of Allah to thee and His Mercy a party of them would certainly have plotted to lead thee astray. But (in fact) they will only lead their own souls astray and to thee they can do no harm in the least. For Allah hath sent down to thee the Book and wisdom and taught thee what thou knewest not (before); and great is the grace of Allah unto thee.

114. In most of their secret talks there is no good: but if one exhorts to a deed of charity or justice or conciliation between men (secrecy is permissible): to him who does this seeking the good pleasure of Allah We shall soon give a reward of the highest (value).

115. If anyone contends with the Apostle even after guidance has been plainly conveyed to him and follows a path other than that becoming to men of faith We shall leave him in the path he has chosen and land him in Hell—what an evil refuge! . . .

135. O ye who believe! stand out firmly for justice as witnesses to Allah even as against yourselves or your parents or your kin and whether it be (against) rich or poor: for Allah can best protect both. Follow not the lusts (of your hearts) lest ye swerve and if ye distort (justice) or decline to do justice verily Allah is well-acquainted with all that ye do.

136. O ye who believe! believe in Allah and his Apostle and the scripture which He hath sent to His Apostle and the scripture which He sent to those before (him). And who denieth Allah His angels His Books His Apostles and the Day of Judgment hath gone far far astray.

137. Those who believe then reject faith then believe (again) and (again) reject faith and go on increasing in unbelief Allah will not forgive them nor guide them on the way.

138. To the hypocrites give the glad tidings that there is for them (but) a grievous penalty.

139. Yea to those who take for friends unbelievers rather than believers: is it honor they seek among them? Nay all honor is with Allah.

140. Already has He sent you word in the Book that when ye hear the signs of Allah held in defiance and ridicule ye are not to sit with them unless they turn to a different theme: if ye did ye would be like them. For Allah will collect the Hypocrites and those who defy faith all in hell. . . .

170. O mankind! the Apostle hath come to you in truth from Allah: believe in him: it is best for you. But if ye reject faith to Allah belong all things in the heavens and on earth: and Allah is All-Knowing All-Wise.

171. O people of the Book! commit no excesses in your religion: nor say of Allah aught but truth. Christ Jesus the son of Mary was (no more than) an Apostle of Allah and His Word which He bestowed on Mary and a Spirit proceeding from Him: so believe in Allah and His Apostles. Say not "Trinity": desist: it will be better for you: for Allah is One Allah: glory be to him: (for Exalted is He) above having a son. To Him belong all things in the heavens and on earth. And enough is Allah as a Disposer of affairs.

172. Christ disdaineth not to serve and worship Allah nor do the angels those nearest (to Allah): those who disdain His worship and are arrogant He will gather them all together unto himself to (answer).

173. But those who believe and do deeds of righteousness He will give their (due) rewards and more out of His bounty: but those who are disdainful and arrogant He will punish with a grievous penalty; nor will they find besides Allah any to protect or help them.

174. O mankind! verily there hath come to you a convincing proof from your Lord: for We have sent unto you a light (that is) manifest.

Surah 24

55. Allah has promised to those among you who believe and work righteous deeds that He will of a surety grant them in the land inheritance (of power) as He granted it to those before them; that He will establish in authority their religion the one which He has chosen for them; and that He will change (their state) after the fear in which they (lived) to one of security and peace: 'They will worship Me (alone) and not associate aught with Me.' If any do reject faith after this they are rebellious and wicked.

56. So establish regular Prayer and give regular Charity: and obey the Apostle; that ye may receive mercy.

Surah 31

2. These are Verses of the Wise Book,
3. A Guide and a Mercy to the Doers of Good,
4. Those who establish regular Prayer and give regular Charity and have (in their hearts) the assurance of the Hereafter.
5. These are on (true) guidance from their Lord; and these are the ones who will prosper.
6. But there are among men those who purchase idle tales without knowledge (or meaning) to mislead (men) from the Path of Allah and throw ridicule (on the Path): for such there will be a humiliating Penalty.
7. When Our Signs are rehearsed to such a one he turns away in arrogance as if he heard them not as if there were deafness in both his ears: announce to him a grievous Penalty.
8. For those who believe and work righteous deeds there will be Gardens of Bliss.
9. To dwell therein. The promise of Allah is true: and He is Exalted in power Wise. . . .
13. Behold Luqman said to his son by way of instruction: "O my son! Join not in worship (others) with Allah: for false worship is indeed the highest wrong-doing."

Surah 53

24. Nay shall man have (just) anything he hankers after?
25. But it is to Allah that the End and the Beginning (of all things) belong.

26. How many so ever be the angels in the heavens their intercession will avail nothing except after Allah has given leave for whom He pleases and that he is acceptable to Him.

27. Those who believe not in the Hereafter name the angels with female names.

28. But they have no knowledge therein. They follow nothing but conjecture; and conjecture avails nothing against Truth.

29. Therefore shun those who turn away from Our Message and desire nothing but the life of this world.

30. That is as far as knowledge will reach them. Verily thy Lord knoweth best those who stray from His path and He knoweth best those who receive guidance.

31. Yea to Allah belongs all that is in the heavens and on earth; so that He rewards those who do evil according to their deeds and He rewards those who do good with what is best.

32. Those who avoid great sins and shameful deeds, Only (falling into) small faults—verily thy Lord is ample in forgiveness. He knows you well when He brings you out of the earth and when ye are hidden in your mother's wombs therefore justify not yourselves. He knows best who it is that guards against evil.

Surah 92

1. By the Night as it conceals (the light);
2. By the Day as it appears in glory;
3. By (the mystery of) the creation of male and female
4. Verily (the ends) ye strive for are diverse.
5. So he who gives (in charity) and fears (Allah)
6. And (in all sincerity) testifies to the Best
7. We will indeed make smooth for him the path to Bliss.
8. But he who is a greedy miser and thinks himself self-sufficient.
9. And gives the lie to the Best
10. We will indeed make smooth for him the Path to Misery;
11. Nor will his wealth profit him when he falls headlong (into the Pit).
12. Verily We take upon Ourselves to guide.
13. And verily unto Us (belong) the End and the Beginning.
14. Therefore do I warn you of a Fire blazing fiercely;
15. None shall reach it but those most unfortunate ones
16. Who give the lie to Truth and turn their backs.
17. But those most devoted to Allah shall be removed far from it
18. Those who spend their wealth for increase in self-purification
19. And have in their minds no favor from anyone for which a reward is expected in return
20. But only the desire to seek for the countenance of their Lord Most High.
21. And soon will they attain (complete) satisfaction.

Surah 98

1. Those who reject (Truth) among the People of the Book and among the Polytheists were not going to depart (from their ways) until there should come to them Clear Evidence

2. An apostle from Allah rehearsing scriptures kept pure and holy:

3. Wherein are laws (or decrees) right and straight.

4. Nor did the people of the Book make schisms until after there came to them Clear Evidence.

5. And they have been commanded no more than this: to worship Allah offering Him sincere devotion being True (in faith); to establish regular Prayer; and to practice regular Charity; and that is the Religion Right and Straight.

6. Those who reject (Truth) among the People of the Book and among the Polytheists will be in hell-fire to dwell therein (for aye). They are the worst of creatures.

7. Those who have faith and do righteous deeds they are the best of creatures.

8. Their reward is with Allah: Gardens of Eternity Beneath which rivers flow; They will dwell therein for ever; Allah well pleased with them and they with Him: all this for such as fear their Lord and Cherisher.

Surah 103. *The Declining Day, Eventide, The Epoch*

1. By (the Token of) Time (through the ages),

2. Verily Man is in loss,

3. Except such as have Faith, and do righteous deeds, and (join together) in the mutual teaching of Truth, and of Patience and Constancy.

SECTION 8: The Religious Life: Worship and Righteousness

Muslims believe that every action that is performed to fulfill the will of Allah and to seek his pleasure is an act of worship. Consequently, everyday activities such as earning a living and parenting children are forms of worship. In addition, there are five obligatory acts of worship that followers of Allah are instructed to perform. These include professing faith in Allah and his prophet Muhammad, offering prayers five times daily, giving charitably to the needy, fasting during the holy month of Ramadan, and making a once-in-a-lifetime pilgrimage to Mecca.

The Qur'an provides instructions concerning each of the five pillars of Islam. These comments, however, are not grouped together and no single Surah focuses exclusively on these five acts of worship. The following selections bring together selected passages scattered throughout the Qur'an that pertain to the fulfillment of these special religious obligations. According to these passages, what religious obligations are required of those who embrace Islam? What benefits come to those who faithfully meet their obligations?

PLACES, TIMES, AND ETIQUETTE OF PRAYER AND FASTING

Surah 2

43. And be steadfast in prayer; practice regular charity; and bow down your heads with those who bow down (in worship).

44. Do ye enjoin right conduct on the people and forget (to practice it) yourselves and yet ye study the Scripture? Will ye not understand?

45. Nay seek (Allah's) help with patient perseverance and prayer: it is indeed hard except to those who bring a lowly spirit.

46. Who bear in mind the certainty that they are to meet their Lord and that they are to return to Him. . . .

125. Remember We made the house (the Ka'bah at Mecca) a place of assembly for men and a place of safety; and take ye the station of Abraham as a place of prayer; and We covenanted with Abraham and Isma'il that they should sanctify My House for those who compass it round or use it as a retreat or bow or prostrate themselves (therein in prayer).

126. And remember Abraham said: "My Lord make this a City of Peace and feed its people with fruits such of them as believe in Allah and the Last Day." He said: "(Yea) and such as reject faith for a while will I grant them their pleasure but will soon drive them to the torment of fire an evil destination (indeed)!"

127. And remember Abraham and Isma'il raised the foundations of the House (with this prayer): "Our Lord! accept (this service) from us for thou art the All-Hearing the All-Knowing.

128. "Our Lord! make of us Muslims bowing to Thy (Will) and of our progeny a people Muslim bowing to Thy (Will) and show us our places for the celebration of (due) rites; and turn unto us (in mercy); for Thou art the Oft-Returning Most-Merciful. . . .

142. The fools among the people will say: "What hath turned them from the Qiblah [prayer directed toward Jerusalem] to which they were used?" Say: To Allah belong both East and West; He guideth whom He will to a Way that is straight.

143. Thus have We made of you an Ummah justly balanced that ye might be witnesses over the nations and the Apostle a witness over yourselves; and We appointed the Qiblah to which thou wast used only to test those who followed the Apostle from those who would turn on their heels (from the faith). Indeed it was (a change) momentous except to those guided by Allah. And never would Allah make your faith of no effect. For Allah is to all people most surely full of kindness Most Merciful.

144. We see the turning of thy face (for guidance) to the heavens; now shall We turn thee to a Qiblah that shall please thee. Turn then thy face in the direction of the Sacred Mosque [at

Mecca]; wherever ye are turn your faces in that direction. The people of the book know well that that is the truth from their Lord nor is Allah unmindful of what they do.

145. Even if thou wert to bring to the people of the Book all the signs (together) they would not follow thy Qiblah; nor art thou going to follow their Qiblah; nor indeed will they follow each other's Qiblah. If thou after the knowledge hath reached thee wert to follow their (vain) desires then wert thou indeed (clearly) in the wrong.

146. The people of the Book know this as they know their own sons; but some of them conceal the truth which they themselves know.

147. The truth is from thy Lord so be not at all in doubt.

148. To each is a goal to which Allah turns him; then strive together (as in a race) toward all that is good. Wheresoever ye are Allah will bring you together. For Allah hath power over all things.

149. From whencesoever thou startest forth turn thy face in the direction of the Sacred Mosque; that is indeed the truth from thy Lord. And Allah is not unmindful of what ye do.

150. So from whencesoever thou startest forth turn thy face in the direction of the Sacred Mosque; among wheresoever ye are turn your face thither that there be no ground of dispute against you among the people except those of them that are bent on wickedness; so fear them not but fear Me; and that I may complete My favors on you and ye may (consent to) be guided.

151. A similar (favor have ye already received) in that We have sent among you an Apostle of your own rehearsing to you Our signs and sanctifying you and instructing you in Scripture and wisdom and in new Knowledge.

152. Then do ye remember Me; I will remember you. Be grateful to Me and reject not faith.

153. O ye who believe! seek help with patient perseverance and prayer: for Allah is with those who patiently persevere. . . .

177. It is not righteousness that ye turn your faces toward East or West; but it is righteousness to believe in Allah and the Last Day and the Angels and the Book and the Messengers; to spend of your substance out of love for Him for your kin for orphans for the needy for the wayfarer for those who ask and for the ransom of slaves; to be steadfast in prayer and practice regular charity; to fulfil the contracts which ye have made; and to be firm and patient in pain (or suffering) and adversity and throughout all periods of panic. Such are the people of truth the Allah-fearing. . . .

183. O ye who believe! fasting is prescribed to you as it was prescribed to those before you that ye may (learn) self-restraint.

184. (Fasting) for a fixed number of days; but if any of you is ill or on a journey the prescribed number (should be made up) from days later. For those who can do it (with hardship) is a ransom the feeding of one that is indigent. But he that will give more of his own free will it is better for him and it is better for you that ye fast if ye only knew.

185. Ramadan is the (month) in which was sent down the Qur'an as a guide to mankind also clear (Signs) for guidance

and judgment (between right and wrong). So everyone of you who is present (at his home) during that month should spend it in fasting but if anyone is ill or on a journey the prescribed period (should be made up) by days later. Allah intends every facility for you He does not want to put you to difficulties. (He wants you) to complete the prescribed period and to glorify Him in that He has guided you; and perchance ye shall be grateful.

186. When my servants ask thee concerning Me I am indeed close (to them); I listen to the prayer of every suppliant when he calleth on Me; let them also with a will listen to My call and believe in Me; that they may walk in the right way.

187. Permitted to you on the night of the fasts is the approach to your wives. They are your garments. And ye are their garments. Allah knoweth what ye used to do secretly among yourselves; but He turned to you and forgave you; so now associate with them and seek what Allah hath ordained for you and eat and drink until the white thread of dawn appear to you distinct from its black thread; then complete your fast till the night appears; but do not associate with your wives while ye are in retreat in the mosques. Those are limits (set by) Allah; approach not nigh thereto. Thus doth Allah make clear His signs to men that they may learn self-restraint.

Surah 5

6. O ye who believe! when ye prepare for prayer wash your faces and your hands (and arms) to the elbows; rub your heads (with water); and (wash) your feet to the ankles. If ye are in a state of ceremonial impurity bathe your whole body. But if ye are ill or on a journey or one of you cometh from offices of nature or ye have been in contact with women and ye find no water then take for yourselves clean sand or earth and rub therewith your faces and hands. Allah doth not wish to place you in a difficulty but to make you clean and to complete His favor to you that ye may be grateful.

7. And call in remembrance the favor of Allah unto you and His Covenant which He ratified with you when ye said: "We hear and we obey": and fear Allah for Allah knoweth well the secrets of your hearts.

Surah 7

31. O children of Adam! wear your beautiful apparel at every time and place of prayer: eat and drink: but waste not by excess for Allah loveth not the wasters.

Surah 11

114. And establish regular prayers at the two ends of the day and at the approaches of the night: for those things that are good remove those that are evil: be that the word of remembrance to those who remember (their Lord):

115. And be steadfast in patience; for verily Allah will not suffer the reward of the righteous to perish.

Surah 17

78. Establish regular prayers at the sun's decline till the darkness of the night and the morning prayer and reading: for the prayer and reading in the morning carry their testimony.
79. And pray in the small watches of the morning: (it would be) an additional prayer (or spiritual profit) for thee: soon will thy Lord raise thee to a station of Praise and Glory!

Surah 62

9. O ye who believe! when the call is proclaimed to prayer on Friday (the Day of Assembly) hasten earnestly to the Remembrance of Allah and leave off business (and traffic): that is best for you if ye but knew!
10. And when the Prayer is finished then may ye disperse through the land and seek of the Bounty of Allah: and celebrate the Praises of Allah often (and without stint): that ye may prosper.
11. But when they see some bargain or some amusement they disperse headlong to it and leave thee standing. Say: "The (blessing) from the Presence of Allah is better than any amusement or bargain! And Allah is the Best to provide (for all needs)."

INSTRUCTIONS ON TAKING PILGRIMAGES

Surah 5

95. O ye who believe! kill not game while in the Sacred Precincts or in pilgrim garb. If any of you doth so intentionally the compensation is an offering brought to the Ka'ba of a domestic animal equivalent to the one he killed as adjudged by two just men among you; or by way of atonement the feeding of the indigent; or its equivalent in fasts: that he may taste of the penalty of his deed. Allah forgives what is past: for repetition Allah will exact from him the penalty: for Allah is Exalted and Lord of Retribution.
96. Lawful to you is the pursuit of water-game and its use for food for the benefit of yourselves and those who travel; but forbidden is the pursuit of land-game: as long as ye are in the Sacred Precincts or in pilgrim garb. And fear Allah to whom ye shall be gathered back.
97. Allah made the Ka'ba the Sacred House an asylum of security for men as also the Sacred Months the animals for offerings and the garlands that mark them: that ye may know that Allah hath knowledge of what is in the heavens and on earth and that Allah is well acquainted with all things.
98. Know ye that Allah is strict in punishment and that Allah is Oft-Forgiving Most Merciful.

Surah 22

26. Behold! We gave the site to Abraham of the (Sacred) House (saying): "Associate not any thing (in worship) with Me; and sanctify My House for those who compass it round or stand up or bow or prostrate themselves (therein in prayer).
27. "And proclaim the Pilgrimage among men: they will come to thee on foot and (mounted) on every kind of camel lean on account of journeys through deep and distant mountain highways;
28. "That they may witness the benefits (provided) for them and celebrate the name of Allah through the Days appointed over the cattle which He has provided for them (for sacrifice): then eat ye thereof and feed the distressed ones in want.
29. "Then let them complete the rites prescribed for them perform their vows and (again) circumambulate the Ancient House."
30. Such (is the Pilgrimage): whoever honors the sacred rites of Allah for him it is good in the sight of his Lord. Lawful to you (for food in pilgrimage) are cattle except those mentioned to you (as exceptions): but shun the abomination of idols and shun the word that is false. . . .
34. To every people did We appoint rites (of sacrifice) that they might celebrate the name of Allah over the sustenance He gave them from animals (fit for food) but your Allah is one Allah: submit then your wills to Him (in Islam) and give thou the Good News to those who humble themselves
35. To those whose hearts when Allah is mentioned are filled with fear who show patient perseverance over their afflictions keep up regular prayer and spend (in charity) out of what we have bestowed upon them.
36. The sacrificial camels we have made for you as among the Symbols from Allah: in them is (much) good for you: then pronounce the name of Allah over them as they line up (for sacrifice): when they are down on their sides (after slaughter) eat ye thereof and feed such as (beg not but) live in contentment and such as beg with due humility: thus have we made animals subject to you that ye may be grateful.
37. It is not their meat nor their blood that reaches Allah: it is your piety that reaches Him: He has thus made them subject to you that ye may glorify Allah for His guidance to you: and proclaim the Good News to all who do right.
38. Verily Allah will defend (from ill) those who believe: verily Allah loveth not any that is a traitor to faith or shows ingratitude. . . .
76. He knows what is before them and what is behind them: and to Allah go back all questions (for decision).
77. O ye who believe! bow down prostrate yourselves and adore your Lord; and do good; that ye may prosper.
78. And strive in His cause as ye ought to strive (with sincerity and under discipline): He has chosen you and has imposed no difficulties on you in religion; it is the cult of your father Abraham. It is He Who has named you Muslims both before and in this (Revelation); that the Apostle may be a witness for you and ye be witnesses for mankind! So establish regular Prayer give regular Charity and hold fast to Allah! He is your Protector the Best to protect and the Best to help!

ADMONITIONS ON CHARITABLE GIVING

Surah 2

261. The parable of those who spend their substance in the way of Allah is that of a grain of corn: it groweth seven ears and each ear hath a hundred grains. Allah giveth manifold increase to whom He pleaseth; and Allah careth for all and He knoweth all things.

262. Those who spend their substance in the cause of Allah and follow not up their gifts with reminders of their generosity or with injury for them their reward is with their Lord; on them shall be no fear nor shall they grieve.

263. Kind words and the covering of faults are better than charity followed by injury. Allah is free of all wants and he is Most Forbearing.

264. O ye who believe! cancel not your charity by reminders of your generosity or by injury like those who spend their substance to be seen of men but believe neither in Allah nor in the last day. They are in Parable like a hard barren rock on which is a little soil; on it falls heavy rain which leaves it (just) a bare stone. They will be able to do nothing with aught they have earned. And Allah guideth not those who reject faith.

265. And the likeness of those who spend their substance seeking to please Allah and to strengthen their souls is as a garden high and fertile: heavy rain falls on it but makes it yield a double increase of harvest and if it receives not heavy rain light moisture sufficeth it. Allah seeth well whatever ye do.

266. Does any of you wish that he should have a garden with date-palms and vines and streams flowing underneath and all kinds of fruit while he is stricken with old age and his children are not strong (enough to look after themselves) that it should be caught in a whirlwind with fire therein and be burnt up? Thus doth Allah make clear to you (His) signs; that ye may consider.

267. O ye who believe! give of the good things which ye have (honorably) earned and of the fruits of the earth which We have produced for you and do not even aim at getting anything which is bad in order that out of it ye may give away something when ye yourselves would not receive it except with closed eyes. And know that Allah is free of all wants and worthy of all praise.

268. The Evil One threatens you with poverty and bids you to conduct unseemly. Allah promiseth you His forgiveness and bounties and Allah careth for all and He knoweth all things.

269. He granteth wisdom to whom He pleaseth; and he to whom wisdom is granted receiveth indeed a benefit overflowing; but none will grasp the message but men of understanding.

270. And whatever ye spend in charity or devotion be sure Allah knows it all. But the wrong-doers have no helpers.

271. If ye disclose (acts of) charity even so it is well but if ye conceal them and make them reach those (really) in need that

is best for you: it will remove from you some of your (stains of) evil. And Allah is well acquainted with what ye do.

272. It is not required of thee (O Apostles) to set them on the right path but Allah sets on the right path whom He pleaseth. Whatever of good ye give benefits your own souls and ye shall only do so seeking the "Face" of Allah. Whatever good ye give, shall be rendered back to you and ye shall not bedealt with unjustly.

273. (Charity is) for those in need who in Allah's cause are restricted (from travel) and cannot move about in the land seeking (for trade or work). The ignorant man thinks because of their modesty that they are free from want. Thou shalt know them by their (unfailing) mark: they beg not importunately from all and sundry. And whatever of good ye give be assured Allah knoweth it well.

274. Those who (in charity) spend of their goods by night and by day in secret and in public have their reward with their Lord: on them shall be no fear nor shall they grieve.

275. Those who devour usury will not stand except as stands one whom the Evil One by his touch hath driven to madness. That is because they say: "Trade is like usury but Allah hath permitted trade and forbidden usury. Those who after receiving direction from their Lord desist shall be pardoned for the past; their case is for Allah (to judge); but those who repeat (the offence) are companions of the fire: they will abide therein (for ever).

276. Allah will deprive usury of all blessing but will give increase for deeds of charity: for He loveth not creatures ungrateful and wicked.

277. Those who believe and do deeds of righteousness and establish regular prayers and regular charity will have their reward with their Lord: on them shall be no fear nor shall they grieve.

Surah 27

1. Ta Sin. These are verses of the Qur'an a Book that makes (things) clear;

2. A Guide; and Glad Tidings for the Believers

3. Those who establish regular prayers and give in regular charity and also have (full) assurance of the Hereafter.

4. As to those who believe not in the Hereafter We have made their deeds pleasing in their eyes; and so they wander about in distraction.

5. Such are they for whom a grievous Penalty is (waiting): and in the Hereafter theirs will be the greatest loss.

Surah 31

2. These are Verses of the Wise Book,

3. A Guide and a Mercy to the Doers of Good,

4. Those who establish regular Prayer and give regular Charity and have (in their hearts) the assurance of the Hereafter.

5. These are on (true) guidance from their Lord; and these are the ones who will prosper.

6. But there are among men those who purchase idle tales without knowledge (or meaning) to mislead (men) from the Path of Allah and throw ridicule (on the Path): for such there will be a humiliating Penalty.

Surah 57

7. Believe in Allah and His Apostle and spend (in charity) out of the (substance) whereof He has made you heirs. For those of you who believe and spend (in charity) for them is a great Reward.

Surah 58

12. O ye who believe! When ye consult the Apostle in private spend something in charity before your private consultation. That will be best for you and most conducive to purity (of conduct). But if ye find not (the wherewithal) Allah is Oft-Forgiving Most Merciful.

13. Is it that ye are afraid of spending sums in charity before your private consultation (with him)? If then ye do not so and Allah forgives you then (at least) establish regular prayer; practice regular charity; and obey Allah and His Apostle: and Allah is well-acquainted will all that ye do.

Surah 73

20. . . . Read ye therefore as much of the Qur'an as may be easy (for you); and establish regular Prayer and give regular Charity; and loan to Allah a Beautiful Loan. And whatever good ye send forth for your souls Ye shall find it in Allah's presence yea better and greater in Reward. And seek ye the Grace of Allah: for Allah is Oft-Forgiving Most Merciful.

Surah 92

5. So he who gives (in charity) and fears (Allah)
6. And (in all sincerity) testifies to the Best
7. We will indeed make smooth for him the path to Bliss.
8. But he who is a greedy miser and thinks himself self-sufficient.
9. And gives the lie to the Best
10. We will indeed make smooth for him the Path to Misery;
11. Nor will his wealth profit him when he falls headlong (into the Pit).

SECTION 9: Endings: Death, Judgment, and the Afterlife

Islam embraces five fundamental articles of faith. The first four articles affirm God and his messengers of revelation. These articles of faith include the belief in Allah, in the Angels, in the prophets, and in the sacredness of the Qur'an. The fifth tenet of faith in Islam affirms belief in the Last Day. On this day all

beings will be resurrected and called to account for their record on earth. After judgment comes the bliss of heaven or the punishment of hell. Muslims embrace this fifth article of faith, just as they affirm that there is no other god but Allah.

The Qur'an is filled with references to the Last Day and with vivid descriptions of heaven and hell. The following selections are but a small sampling of these moving passages. As you read these selections, note the sharpness of the contrast between heaven and hell. What is the purpose of these passages? To what degree is the doctrine of the Last Day central to the religion of Islam?

THE LAST DAY

Surah 3

185. Every soul shall have a taste of death: and only on the Day of Judgment shall you be paid your full recompense. Only he who is saved far from the fire and admitted to the garden will have attained the object (of life): for the life of this world is but goods and chattels of deception.

186. Ye shall certainly be tried and tested in your possessions and in your personal selves; and ye shall certainly hear much that will grieve you from those who received the Book before you and from those who worship many gods. But if ye persevere patiently and guard against evil then that will be a determining factor in all affairs.

187. And remember Allah took a Covenant from the People of the Book to make it known and clear to mankind and not to hide it; but they threw it away behind their backs and purchased with it some miserable gain! and vile was the bargain they made!

188. Think not that those who exult in what they have brought about and love to be praised for what they have not done think not that they can escape the penalty. For them is a penalty grievous indeed.

189. To Allah belongeth the dominion of the heavens and the earth; and Allah hath power over all things.

190. Behold! in the creation of the heavens and the earth and the alternation of night and day there are indeed Signs for men of understanding.

191. Men who celebrate the praises of Allah standing sitting and lying down on their sides and contemplate the (wonders of) creation in the heavens and the earth (with the thought): "Our Lord! not for naught hast thou created (all) this! Glory to thee! give us salvation from the penalty of the fire.

192. "Our Lord! any whom thou dost admit to the fire truly thou coverest with shame and never will wrong-doers find any helpers!

193. "Our Lord! we have heard the call of one calling (us) to faith 'Believe ye in the Lord' and we have believed. Our Lord! forgive us our sins blot out from us our iniquities and take to thyself our souls in the company of the righteous.

194. "Our Lord! grant us what Thou didst promise unto us through thine Apostles and save us from shame on the Day of Judgment: for thou never breakest Thy promise."

195. And their Lord hath accepted of them and answered them: "Never will I suffer to be lost the work of any of you be he male or female: ye are members one of another; those who have left their homes or been driven out therefrom or suffered harm in My cause or fought or been slain verily I will blot out from them their iniquities and admit them into gardens with rivers flowing beneath; a reward from the presence of Allah and from His presence is the best of rewards."

196. Let not the strutting about of the unbelievers through the land deceive thee:

197. Little is it for enjoyment; their ultimate abode is Hell: what an evil bed (to lie on)!

198. On the other hand for those who fear their Lord are gardens with rivers flowing beneath therein are they to dwell (for ever) a gift from the presence of Allah and that which is in the presence of Allah is the best (bliss) for the righteous.

199. And there are certainly among the people of the Book those who believe in Allah in the revelation to you and in the revelation to them bowing in humility to Allah: they will not sell the signs of Allah for a miserable gain! for them is a reward with their Lord and Allah is swift in account.

200. O ye who believe! persevere in patience and constancy: vie in such perseverance; strengthen each other; and fear Allah; that ye may prosper.

Surah 40

15. Raised high above ranks (or degrees) (He is) the Lord of the Throne (of authority): by his command doth He send the spirit (of inspiration) to any of His servants He pleases that it may warn (men) of the Day of Mutual Meeting

16. The Day whereon they will (all) come forth: Not a single thing concerning them is hidden from Allah. Whose will be the dominion that Day? That of Allah the One the Irresistible!

17. That Day will every soul be requited for what it earned; no injustice will there be that Day for Allah is Swift in taking account.

18. Warn them of the Day that is (ever) drawing near when the Hearts will (come) right up to the Throats to choke (them); no intimate friend nor intercessor will the wrongdoers have who could be listened to.

19. (Allah) knows of (the tricks) that deceive with the eyes and all that hearts (of men) conceal.

20. And Allah will judge with (Justice and) Truth: but those whom (men) invoke besides Him will not (be in a position) to judge at all. Verily it is Allah (alone) Who hears and sees (all things).

59. The Hour will certainly come: therein is no doubt: yet most men believe not.

Surah 47

14. Is then one who is on a clear (Path) from his Lord no better than one to whom the evil of his conduct seems pleasing and such as follow their own lusts?

15. (Here is) a Parable of the Garden which the righteous are promised: in it are rivers of water incorruptible: rivers of milk of which the taste never changes; rivers of wine a joy to those who drink; and rivers of honey pure and clear. In it there are for them all kinds of fruits and Grace from their Lord. (Can those in such Bliss) be compared to such as shall dwell for ever in the Fire and be given to drink boiling water so that it cuts up their bowels (to pieces)?

Surah 52

1. By the Mount (of Revelation);
2. By a Decree Inscribed
3. In a Scroll unfolded;
4. By the much-frequented House;
5. By the Canopy Raised High;
6. And by the Ocean filled with Swell
7. Verily the Doom of thy Lord will indeed come to pass
8. There is none can avert it
9. On the day when the firmament will be in dreadful commotion.
10. And the mountain will fly hither and thither.
11. Then woe that Day to those that treat (truth) as Falsehood
12. That play (and paddle) in shallow trifles.
13. That Day shall they be thrust down to the Fire of Hell irresistibly.
14. "This" it will be said "is the Fire which ye were wont to deny!
15. "Is this then a fake or is it ye that do not see?
16. "Burn ye therein: the same is it to you whether ye bear it with patience or not: Ye but receive the recompense of your (own) deeds."
17. As to the Righteous they will be in Gardens and in Happiness
18. Enjoying the (Bliss) which their Lord hath bestowed on them and their Lord shall deliver them from the Penalty of the Fire.
19. (To them will be said:) "Eat and drink ye with profit and health because of your (good) deeds."
20. They will recline (with ease) on Thrones (of dignity) arranged in ranks; and We shall join them to Companions with beautiful big and lustrous eyes.
21. And those who believe and whose families follow them in Faith to them shall We join their families: nor shall We deprive them (of the fruit) of aught of their works: (Yet) is each individual in pledge for his deeds.
22. And We shall bestow on them of fruit and meat anything they shall desire.

23. They shall there exchange one with another a (loving) cup free of frivolity free of all taint of ill.

24. Round about them will serve (devoted) to them youths (handsome) as Pearls well-guarded.

25. They will advance to each other engaging in mutual enquiry.

26. They will say: "Aforetime We were not without fear for the sake of our people.

27. "But Allah has been good to us and has delivered us from the Penalty of the Scorching Wind.

28. "Truly we did call unto Him from of old: truly it is He the Beneficent the Merciful"

Surah 56

1. When the event inevitable cometh to pass.

2. Then will no (soul) entertain falsehood concerning its coming.

3. (Many) will it bring low (many) will it exalt;

4. When the earth shall be shaken to its depths

5. And the mountains shall be crumbled to atoms

6. Becoming dust scattered abroad

7. And ye shall be sorted out into three classes.

8. Then (there will be) the Companions of the Right Hand what will be the Companions of the Right Hand?

9. And the Companions of the left hand what will be the Companions of the Left Hand?

10. And those Foremost (in Faith) will be Foremost (in the Hereafter).

11. These will be those Nearest to Allah:

12. In Gardens of Bliss:

13. A number of people from those of old

14. And a few from those of later times.

15. (They will be) on Thrones encrusted (with gold and precious stones).

16. Reclining on them facing each other.

17. Round about them will (serve) youths of perpetual (freshness).

18. With goblets (shining) beakers and cups (filled) out of clear-flowing fountains:

19. No after-ache will they receive therefrom nor will they suffer intoxication:

20. And with fruits any that they may select;

21. And the flesh of fowls any that they may desire.

22. And (there will be) Companions with beautiful big and lustrous eyes—

23. Like unto Pearls well-guarded.

24. A Reward for the Deeds of their past (Life).

25. No frivolity will they hear therein nor any taint of ill

26. Only the saying "Peace! Peace."

27. The Companions of the Right Hand what will be the Companions of the Right Hand?

28. (They will be) among lote trees without thorns

29. Among Talh trees with flowers (or fruits) piled one above another

30. In shade long-extended

31. By water flowing constantly

32. And fruit in abundance

33. Whose season is not limited nor (supply) forbidden

34. And on Thrones (of Dignity) raised high.

35. We have created (their Companions) of special creation.

36. And made them virgin-pure (and undefiled)

37. Beloved (by nature) equal in age

38. For the companions of the Right Hand.

39. A (goodly) number from those of old

40. And a (goodly) number from those of later times.

41. The Companions of the Left Hand—what will be the Companions of the Left Hand?

42. (They will be) in the midst of a fierce Blast of Fire and in Boiling Water

43. And in the shades of Black Smoke:

44. Nothing (will there be) to refresh nor to please:

45. For that they were wont to be indulged before that in wealth (and luxury).

46. And persisted obstinately in wickedness supreme!

47. And they used to say "what! when we die and become dust and bones shall we then indeed be raised up again?

48. "(We) and our fathers of old?"

49. Say: "Yea those of old and those of later times

50. "All will certainly be gathered together for the meeting appointed for a Day Well-known.

51. "Then will ye truly o ye that go wrong and treat (Truth) as Falsehood!

52. "Ye will surely taste of the Tree of Zaqqum.

53. "Then will ye fill your insides therewith

54. "And drink Boiling Water on top of it:

55. "Indeed ye shall drink like diseased camels raging with thirst!

56. Such will be their entertainment on the Day of Requital!

Surah 75

1. I do call to witness the Resurrection Day;

2. And I do call to witness the self-reproaching spirit; (eschew Evil).

3. Does man think that We cannot assemble his bones?

4. Nay We are able to put together in perfect order the very tips of his fingers.

5. But man wishes to do wrong (even) in the time in front of him.

6. He questions: "When is the Day of Resurrection?"

7. At length when the Sight is dazed

8. And the moon is buried in darkness.

9. And the sun and moon are joined together

10. That Day will Man say "Where is the refuge?"

11. By no means! No place of safety!

12. Before thy Lord (alone) that Day will be the place of rest.

13. That Day will man be told (all) that he put forward and all that he put back.

14. Nay man will be evidence against himself

15. Even though he were to put up his excuses.

Surah 82

1. When the Sky is cleft asunder;

2. When the Stars are scattered;

3. When the Oceans are suffered to burst forth;

4. And when the Graves are turned upside down

5. (Then) shall each soul know what it hath sent forward and (what it hath) kept back.

6. O man! what has seduced thee from thy Lord Most Beneficent?

7. Him Who created thee. Fashioned thee in due proportion and gave thee a just bias;

8. In whatever Form He wills does He put thee together.

9. Nay! but ye do Reject Right and Judgment!

10. But verily over you (are appointed angels) to protect you

11. Kind and honorable writing down (your deeds):

12. They know (and understand) all that ye do.

13. As for the Righteous they will be in Bliss;

14. And the Wicked they will be in the Fire

15. Which they will enter on the Day of Judgment.

16. And they will not be Able to keep away therefrom.

17. And what will explain to thee what the Day of Judgment is?

18. Again what will explain to thee what the Day of Judgment is?

19. (It will be) the Day when no soul shall have power (to do) aught for another: for the Command that Day will be (wholly) with Allah.

Surah 88

1. Has the story reached thee of the Overwhelming (Event)?

2. Some faces that Day will be humiliated

3. Laboring (hard) weary

4. The while they enter the Blazing Fire

5. The while they are given to drink of a boiling hot spring.

6. No food will there be for them but a bitter Dhari

7. Which will neither nourish nor satisfy hunger.

8. Other faces that Day will be joyful.

9. Pleased with their Striving

10. In a Garden on high

11. Where they shall hear no (word) of vanity:

12. Therein will be a bubbling spring:

13. Therein will be Thrones (of dignity) raised on high.

14. Goblets placed (ready).

15. And Cushions set in rows

16. And rich carpets (All) spread out.

17. Do they not look at the Camels how they are made?

18. And at the Sky how it is raised high?

19. And at the Mountains How they are fixed firm?

20. And at the Earth how it is spread out?

21. Therefore do thou give admonition for thou art one to admonish.

22. Thou art not one to manage (men's) affairs.

23. But if any turn away and reject Allah

24. Allah will punish him with a mighty Punishment.

25. For to Us will be their Return;

26. Then it will be for Us to call them to account.

PowerWeb SUPPLEMENTS

1. **Arab and Muslim America: A Snapshot,** Shibley Telhami, *Brookings Review,* Winter 2002.

2. **The Concept and Practice of Jihad in Islam,** Michael G. Knapp, *Parameters,* Spring 2003.

3. **In the Beginning, There Were the Holy Books,** Kenneth L. Woodward, *Newsweek,* February 11, 2002.

4. **What is the Koran?,** Toby Lester, *The Atlantic Monthly,* January 1999.

Like the violence that took place at Pearl Harbor 60 years earlier, the events of September 11, 2001 instantaneously transformed the lives of millions. No peoples arguably were more impacted by this tragedy than Arab Americans and Muslim Americans. In the first recommended selection taken from the *Brookings Review,* Shibley Telhami discusses numerous Western misconceptions about each of these groups, including the erroneous belief that the two groups are one and the same. In a related piece from *Parameters,* Michael G. Knapp describes and traces the development of the much-feared and little-understood Islamic concept of "jihad." Noting that holy wars and crusades have a long history, Kenneth L. Woodward in the third reading discusses how the religions of the God of Abraham have historically justified wars against nonbelievers. Finally, in a selection entitled "What is the Koran?," Toby Lester seeks to explain why some Muslims feel threatened by modern scholarship about their holy book. Each of these thoughtful selections offers insights into the sources of tensions that have caused divisions among diverse Islamic groups and between orthodox Muslim and non-Mulsim populations.

Readings from *PowerWeb: Religion* are available at the McGraw-Hill *PowerWeb* website http://www.duskin.com/powerweb. A personal access code to *PowerWeb: Religion* is provided free with each new copy of this book. Those who purchase a used copy may buy an access code at the website.

SELECTED BIBLIOGRAPHY

Al-Azmeh, Aziz. *Islams and Modernities.* London: Verso, 1996.

Aslan, Reza. *No god but God: The Origins, Evolution and Future of Islam.* New York: Random House, 2005.

Ayoub, Mahmond. *Islam: Faith and History.* Oxford: Oneworld, 2004.

Ayoub, Mahmond M. *The Crisis of Muslim History: Religion and Politics in Early Islam.* Oxford: Oneworld Publications, 2003.

Cole, Juan R. *Sacred Space and Holy War: The Politics, Culture and History of Shi'ite Islam.* New York: I. B. Tauris, 2002.

Cook, David. *Understanding Jihad.* Berkeley, CA: University of California Press, 2005.

Denny, Frederick M. *An Introduction to Islam.* New York: Macmillan, 1994.

Esack, Farid. *The Qur'an: A User's Guide.* Oxford: Oneworld Publications, 2005.

Haddad, Yvonne Yazbeck. *Islamic Values in the United States.* New York: Oxford University Press, 1987.

Jackson, Sherman A. *Islam and the Black American: Looking Toward the Third Resurrection.* Oxford, New York: Oxford University Press, 2005.

Kepel, Gilles. *Jihad: The Trail of Political Islam.* Cambridge: Harvard University Press, 2002.

Moaddel, Mansoor. *Islamic Modernism, Nationalism and Fundamentalism: Episode and Discourse.* Chicago: University of Chicago Press, 2005.

Nakash, Yitzhak. *The Shi'is of Iraq.* Princeton, NJ: Princeton University Press, 1994.

Peters, F. E. *Islam: A Guide for Jews and Christians.* Princeton, NJ: Princeton University Press, 2003.

Renard, John. *Seven Doors to Islam: Spirituality and the Religious Life of Muslims.* Berkeley, CA: University of California Press, 1996.

Watt, William Montgomery. *The Formative Period of Islamic Thought.* Oxford: Oneworld Publications, 1998.

Watt, William Montgomery. *Muhammad: Statesman and Prophet.* New York: Oxford University Press, 1990.

Williams, John Alden. *The World of Islam.* Austin, TX: University of Texas Press, 1994.

Modern Jewish sacred practices. Jewish people gather in a synagogue to worship, read their holy scriptures, and pray. Except in progressive synagogues, men and women sit separately, and men and boys cover their heads during worship.

Modern Christian sacred practices. Thousands of Christians gather in St. Peter's Square at the Vatican to pray and to hear words from the pope.

The Kaaba in Mecca is a small, cube-shaped building that Muslims believe was built by Abraham and sits on the site where Adam and Eve originally worshipped God. In the corner of the Kaaba is a silver frame containing the Black Stone, which modern pilgrims touch or kiss as they pass the sacred structure.

Modern Hindu sacred practices. Hindu pilgrims wade into the waters of the sacred rivers to cleanse and purify themselves.

Buddhist monk in meditation.

Amitabha Buddha, whose name means "infinite light" is believed to pervade the universe with his presence and power. According to Pure Land Buddhists, a long time ago, a bodhisattva named Dharmakara made forty-eight vows in order to save all sentient beings. After eons of practice, he fulfilled them, became Amitbha Buddha, and created the Pure Land as a part of his vows. Amitabha Buddha is believed to still continue his preaching in his Pure Land in the West.

The modern Chinese Dragon Boat festival commemorates the life and death of the ancient poet Qu Yuan.

Modern Native American sacred practices. The peace pipe ceremony is a sacred ritual for many contemporary Native American peoples.

Modern African marriage ceremony.

Modern Melaneasian sacred practices.

Hinduism 4

The ancient Persians called the land beyond the Indus River "Hind" and the people who lived in this region, "Hindus." *Hinduism*, hence, is the term used to describe the religion that was practiced by the ancient Hindu people and by their modern spiritual descendants. Until about 150 years ago, it was common to define a Hindu in two ways:

1. A Hindu accepted as sacred a collection of ancient writings known as the *Vedas*.
2. A Hindu embraced a particular cosmological social order known as the caste system.

To reject the *Vedas* or to ignore the caste system was to place oneself outside the bounds of Hinduism. During the past 150 years, however, this rigid formula has largely been discarded. Some scholars, noting the great variations in the religious practices of the inhabitants of the Indian subcontinent, question the utility of the term *Hinduism*. Others argue that there are sufficient similarities in the beliefs of the ancient and modern inhabitants of the region to warrant the use of the descriptive noun. Almost all scholars agree that defining the essential characteristics of this religion and assessing the circumstances of its origins are difficult tasks surrounded with controversy.

Many Hindus prefer to call their religion *Sanatana Dharma*, meaning Eternal Religion. This term, which carries a timeless, nonhistorical overtone, captures an aspect of this tradition that separates it from many other world religions. Unlike Judaism, Christianity, Islam, Buddhism, and Confucianism, for instance, Hinduism does not claim a central human founder. To the contrary, Hindus hold that *Sanatana Dharma* is the timeless, eternal truth that is without human ori-

gins. The *Sanatana Dharma* is the sustaining power that keeps things forever the way they are.

Within this tradition, historic time itself is a concept with little value. Time is like a revolving wheel that spins but does not move forward. As the discipline of history involves keeping records of human actions over time, it is not surprising that the ancient Hindus, who attached no great importance to temporal time or to societal changes, failed to produce the type of chronicles that were produced by many other peoples. The ancient inhabitants of India accomplished many great deeds, but they did not generate histories that recorded these accomplishments. Our difficulty in telling the story of the origins of this tradition is at least in part because the Indians have regarded the practice of keeping records of historical events as being relatively unimportant.

SETTING

Among the basic questions of where, when, and among whom did Hindu concepts originate, the only question with an uncontested answer is the one concerning its place of origins. Hinduism, as its name implies, is related to the land of India, a region often characterized in the West as a land of mystery, wonder, and enchantment.

The Land of India

The kite-shaped Indian subcontinent is bounded in the north by the Hindu Kush and the Himalayan mountain ranges and in the south by the Indian Ocean. Its 1.5 million square miles of land (about

151

one-third the size of the continental United States) encompasses virtually every sort of topography and climate. In its most northern region, eternal snow covers the world's highest peaks. The Himalayan glaciers provide the water source for India's three great river systems: the Indus, the Yamuna-Ganga, and the Brahmaputra. The northern mountains also serve as a natural barrier that protects the alluvial plains from both invading armies and Arctic winds, thereby contributing to the cultural isolation and the warm climate of India's great river valleys. The southern portion of the subcontinent that lies below the alluvial plains depends more on rain than on rivers for its water supply. Summer monsoons provide upward of 200 inches of annual precipitation to the tropical rain forests of the peninsula's western coastal regions. These western steppes, which tower 3,000 feet above sea level, capture most of the moisture drawn from the Arabian Sea, thereby turning the eastern portions of the peninsula into barren, waterless badlands. The desert wilderness and a rugged mountain range that lie below the Tropic of Cancer separate the southern peninsular from India's northern alluvial regions. For thousands of years, these natural barriers have weakened communication lines between the north and the south. To this day, there are significant language and cultural differences separating the peoples of northern and southern India.

Geography does not predetermine religious form, but it often does influence it. India is a land of mighty mountains, powerful rivers, brilliant stars, massive plains, suffering heat, and violent rainstorms. Some observers suggest a correlation between these climatic and geological characteristics and the sacred interests of the ancient Hindus—a people who deified both fire and the sun; washed themselves in holy rivers; greeted the summer monsoons with ritual dance and ecstatic worship; and venerated astrological objects, sacred trees, cows, snakes, rats, and vultures. For the Hindus, India is a holy land flooded with spiritual entities, a testing ground for souls in transit.

The Peoples of India

Although there is much debate over the timing of the settlement of India, it is generally agreed that at least three separate peoples influenced the development of the tradition we call Hinduism. Archeological evidence traces human life on the Indian subcontinent back to the Early Stone Age, perhaps 500,000 years ago. The Paleolithic natives of India included people from several racial groupings: Negrito, Proto-Australoid, Mediterranean, Mongolian, and Alpine. For thousands of years, they survived as seminomadic hunters and gatherers. About the ninth millennium BCE, agriculture was discovered and village life began to appear. As these settlements grew, the inhabitants developed the use of copper and bronze utensils, made pottery, domesticated animals, and began trade activities. Little is known about the religion of these ancient people, although the survival of figurines of women and cattle from this era suggest probable religious attitudes.

The ruins of a Harappan urban village.

By the third millennium BCE, a uniform culture had spread across nearly 0.5 million square miles of the region. When this civilization was discovered in the 1920s, scholars first thought that it was confined to the valley of the river Indus; hence, it was named the Indus Valley civilization. Today, we generally refer to it as the Harappa Civilization, a name taken from one of the great cities representing the high-water mark of this ancient civilization. Harappa culture, which flourished for nearly 1,000 years, was a highly developed and urbanized civilization that was noted for its well-planned cities built with regular-shaped, baked bricks. The great cities included public buildings, vast granaries, covered drains, and streets laid at right angles. The houses of these peoples were nearly of equal size, a fact suggesting a more egalitarian social structure than was common in other ancient civilizations.

The Harappans were advanced in many ways. They domesticated goats, camels, and water buffaloes; cultivated barley, peas, and wheat; and wore clothing made from cotton. They were active traders who exchanged goods throughout the Indus Valley, trading even with peoples in the distant lands of Sumer (modern Iraq) and the Persian Gulf. Among the religious artifacts found among these people include animal and mother goddess statues, figurines of a naked dancing girl with her hand on her hip, a male god in a yoga posture depicted with three faces and two horns, and phallic- and ring-shaped stones. These artifacts suggest the worship of a variety of gods and goddesses in both animal and human forms, including forms that later would be associated in India with Shakti and Shiva worship. Many believe that the idea of reincarnation also was indigenous with these people. Scholars disagree as to how or when these people arrived in the region. Later Indo-European invaders to the subcontinent labeled them "Dravidians" and described them as being a darked-skinned, curly-haired, snub-nosed people. In modern times, the Tamils and Telgus are considered to be descendants of these ancient peoples.

Owing to ecological changes that resulted in a drop in the food supply to the region, the Harappan culture began to decline during the early centuries of the second millennium BCE. Some historians believe that invasions by barbarian tribes from the northwest also contributed to this demise. By 1500 BCE, when a new wave of Aryan migrants began to flood over the Himalayan passes into India, the Harappan culture was only a shadow of its once great past. The larger and fairer-skinned new arrivals, who arrogantly called themselves Aryans or "the noble ones," brought three important commodities to the region: the horse, the Sanskrit language, and the religion of Brahmanism. With the horse and its corollary, "cavalry warfare," the invaders gained control over vast regions of northwestern India. Political dominance led also to cultural domination. Sanskrit became the language of the elite. Local tribal deities were transformed into Brahman deities, although in the process of this transformation the Brahman deities took on pre-Aryan forms. Meanwhile, the different tribes and professional groups of the local civilizations were incorporated into the hierarchical socioreligious caste system of the new arrivals. Although not the city builders of their Dravidian predecessors, the conquering Aryans with their military prowess, their highly developed language, their rich pantheon of gods and goddesses, and their hierarchical social organizations produced a vigorous Sanskrit civilization that would dominate the region for the next 1,000 years.

SACRED STORIES AND BELIEFS

The Hindu tradition that flourished during the first millennium BCE was a mixture of the Vedic religion of the Aryans (a this-worldly religion that emphasized animal sacrifices and ritual purity) and the spiritual leanings of the indigenous Dravidian and aboriginal populations (peoples who valued asceticism and nonviolence and embraced a notion of reincarnation). The tradition that emerged was a conglomeration of these ancient beliefs, practices, and institutions, which were remarkable both for their richness and complexity. The Hindu tradition, thus, has grown to contain within it many doctrines about the nature of Reality and many paths of search for this Reality. Other traditions may label such divergent tendencies as inconsistencies. The Hindu mind, however, celebrates unboundedness and seeks to push all thoughts to their furthest limits. Consequently, the Hindu religion does not consider competing ideas such as monotheism and polytheism to be mutually exclusive. Indeed, for the Hindu, the profundity of the tradition lies precisely in its recognition that the divine cannot be limited to a single form.

The chariot wheel from a temple in Konarak, India, symbolizes the cycle of birth, death, and rebirth.

What, then, are the core beliefs within Hinduism? If pressed to condense Hindu thought into a few words, perhaps two simple affirmations come closest to capturing the essence of this vast and enduring tradition. First, Hinduism is a religion that teaches that the divine is within us and can be realized in direct experience. Second, the religion promises that we can have what we want, but we always get what we deserve.

Getting What You Want

Before attempting to penetrate into the depths of Hindu understandings of ultimate Reality, let us first examine some basic Hindu affirmations about the four goals, the four stations and the four stages of life.

The Four Goals

According to the ancient Indian sages, humans desire four things from life. First, people seek that which is pleasurable. Enjoying the pleasures of the senses (in Sanskrit, *kama*) is not wicked, but because it is too trivial to be fully satisfying, individuals in time will replace the mere desire for pleasure with a second life goal: worldly success, or *artha*. Like the pursuit of sensual pleasures, the ambition to attain wealth,

fame, and power is a natural and worthy goal that should not be repressed as long as it is what a person desires. However, both *kama* and *artha*, which together are known as the "path of desire," are like children's toys that are appropriate for the immature but are ultimately unsatisfying for the more enlightened. Consequently, according to the Hindu schema, a time will come—either in this life or in another future incarnation—when people will recognize that living for the community is more satisfying than living for themselves. At this point, they will abandon the "path of desire" for the "path of renunciation" and seek after the third goal of life: *dharma*, or doing your social duty. To be duty-bound does not mean to follow a single set of moral rules, but instead, it means to live in a manner that is appropriate to your particular sex, age, caste, and profession. When individuals fulfill their *dharma*, it is believed that they fulfill the purpose for which they were created, and in so doing, they uphold the sacred cosmic order of Reality.

Doing your social duty, however, is still not humankind's highest attainment. Ultimately, what humans really want is to be infinite, that is, to have infinite knowledge and to experience infinite bliss. The Sanskrit word for this is *moksha*, meaning liberation from the finite. Although there is disagreement as to how liberation is obtained, all orthodox Hindus accept *moksha* as the final goal of life that is to be pursued after recognizing the limitations of the lower goals of pleasure, success, and service.[1]

Just as there are four ends of life, there also are four major stations of life (known as *varnas* or castes) and four stages of life (known as *ashramas*). Although there is not a rigid connection between the life goals, stages, and stations, the life goals are associated to some degree with the various life stages and life stations.

The Four Stations

The four stations (castes) into which Hindus are born include the priestly caste (*brahman*), the warrior-ruler caste (*kshatriya*), the merchant caste (*vaishya*), and the servant caste (*shudra*). The *brahman* priests and the *kshatriya* rulers are the social elites who perform

---

[1]For more than a 1,000 years, nonbrahmanical Hindu *bhakti* cults have challenged this orthodox view by suggesting that the highest goal is not liberation. For these devotees, liberation is simply the first step that prepares the soul for the highest goal, which is to fully experience the love of God.

priestly functions and protect the social order from invasion and decay. In the middle of the social order are the producing *vaishyas,* a group that includes farmers, artisans, merchants, and free peasants. Individuals born as *shudras* include the servants and other unskilled laborers who perform society's most menial tasks. The only people lower than the *shudras* are the untouchables, people who are excluded from full participation in society because their ancestral occupations are considered by the orthodox to be inherently impure.

The Four Stages

According to the ancient brahmanical teachings, the life cycle of males born into one of the higher castes is divided into four life stages. These life stages include an individual's years as a student, a householder, a hermit, and a wandering mendicant. The student stage is the time for higher caste boys to learn the *dharma* appropriate for their station. After learning their *dharma,* the young men marry and enter the householder stage. During this stage, the householders are encouraged to enjoy life's earthly pleasures, strive for worldly success, and carry out their familial and community responsibilities, including the fathering of a son to continue the family name. After fulfilling these duties, which ideally is accomplished about the time a male becomes a grandfather, the men of advancing age may choose to enter the hermit stage of life. During this stage, they are permitted to retire with their wives from their village to the forests. Here, in the secluded forests, they can devote their time to meditation and spiritual development. The final idealized stage of life begins when the hermit abandons his wife and all his earthly possessions, except his staff and begging bowl, and seeks the final goal of liberation.

Classical Hinduism attempts to integrate the four religious goals with the natural life cycle. In youth, a boy from the upper castes learns his dharma; in midlife, he pursues the path of desire and does his community duty; and in old age, he seeks to obtain life's ultimate spiritual goal. Within this schema, the supreme goal of liberation is usually adopted after living a normal life and after all debts have been paid to the gods, ancestors, family members, and society. Of course, in Hinduism as in all religions, the "idealized" life has always been more honored than practiced. Few Hindu males actually organize and live out their

A devotee of Vishnu. This is a "sadhu" or holy man who is in the last of the four life stages. He devotes his life to prayer and meditation and survives solely off alms.

lives according to the life cycle prescribed in these ancient brahmanical ideals.

Getting What You Deserve

It has been said that the Hindu universe is like a great wishing tree with branches that reach into every soul. In time, every wish we desire can be granted. However, this universe also is fundamentally just, and what we get is precisely what we deserve. The mechanism that delivers our just reward is known as *karma,* the moral law of cause and effect that connects today's good or bad actions with good or bad fruits to be reaped in the future. Chance or accident does not exist in the Hindu universe. The impersonal, binding law of *karma* decrees that every decision will have its determinate consequence: good works are always rewarded; evil deeds, always punished. According to the law of *karma,* the consequences for all actions may be delayed but never lost. Hence, fortune and misfortune are viewed as the results of actions taken either in this life or in previous lives. Proper conduct today may not produce an immediate favorable tune of events tomorrow, but it will result in a higher birth in the next incarnation. According to classical brahman orthodoxy (which growing numbers of modern Hindus reject), the reward for carrying out your *dharma* is to be reborn as a male in a high caste, or perhaps even to be reborn as a lower god. Likewise, failure to live according to your *dharma* in this life will result in a lower rebirth, perhaps even to rebirth as an animal or insect.

Realizing the Godhead Within

In the Hindu view, carrying out your *dharma* produces good *karma*, which, in turn, guarantees a more favored rebirth. However, if life's ultimate goal is not rebirth but liberation from the endless birth/death cycle, the best *karma* is not good *karma* but no *karma* at all. In other words, because desire produces actions, and actions create good or bad *karma*, and *karma* leads to rebirth, then to be liberated from rebirth a person must be completely freed from desire itself. Eliminating all desire is not an easy task, but it is possible after realizing the truth of another fundamental Hindu affirmation: All is self, and whoever knows himself, knows ultimate Reality. To see the self not as an "I" with individual needs and desires but as the essence of ultimate Reality is to soar from the finite into the infinite.

This mystery, one of the core beliefs within Hinduism, is often expressed by the phrase, "*Atman* is *Brahman*." The word *Brahman*, from *br*, "to breathe" and *brih*, "to expand," is without gender, an "it" or a "that" rather than a "he" or a "she." *Brahman* has been translated into English in various ways, including "the Absolute Reality," "pure Being and pure Consciousness," "the Unlimited," and "the Godhead." The word attempts to define the indefinable and to label that which transcends time and space. It designates that which pervades the universe and yet is still beyond it. *Atman*, on the other hand, is a masculine noun that expresses the human correlate of the Absolute. Often translated as self or soul, *Atman* is the infinite center of every life, the imperishable divinity within each of us that death cannot touch. The *Brahman-Atman* doctrine, hence, is an affirmation that the immanent *Atman* is identical to the transcendent *Brahman*. The doctrine insists that the "I" within and the "That" of the universe are one.

In the sacred Hindu literature, this mystery is described in several ways. As honey is produced from the juices of many flowers, so *Brahman* is the *Atman* of every being. As the moisture of rivers originates from and returns to the sea, so does the individual *Atman* originate from and return to the universal *Brahman*, its source and destination. As salt dissolved in a jar of water can be tasted but not found in the bottom, middle, or top of the jar, so is *Brahman* present in everything that exists. These analogies suggest an indivisible association between the outer world and the inner self. Everything that has true value is within you. The Godhead is not to be found somewhere "up there," but within.

If *Atman*, the infinite center of every life, is no less than *Brahman*, the Godhead, then why is this reality not self-evident to all? The answer is because of human ignorance. Hindus insist that humans often are like kings with amnesia, wandering across our kingdoms, without realizing our true identity. The final goal of life, *moksha*, is to overcome this ignorance and recognize our oneness with the Godhead.

The Four Paths to Moksha

Hindus recognize that humans have vastly different personalities and temperaments. Some are highly reflective. Others are doers rather than thinkers. Some are deeply emotional. Still others are experimentally inclined. Owing to these differences, not all humans will come to realize their oneness with *Brahman* in the same way. *Moksha* is everyone's final destination, but the path to *moksha* will vary depending on spiritual inclinations.

Classical Hinduism acknowledges four disciplines or *yogas* that lead to liberation from the finite. Reflective thinkers may choose the path of knowledge (*jnana yoga*), a path to the Godhead that demands rigorous intellectual analysis, heightened concentration powers, and the ability to discriminate between the unreal and the real, between the changing and the changeless. This approach to the realization that all beings are one with *Brahman* is arduous and requires both long preparation and strenuous self-discipline. Few outside the professional classes choose this path to the goal. Greater numbers are attracted to the path of works (*karma yoga*), a path that demands a methodical commitment to the observance of the rites, ceremonies, and social obligations that are appropriate to a person's station in life. This path of work promises that a person may reach god by performing selfless actions that are not concerned with the fruits of his or her work. A third, and still more popular path is the way of devotion (*bhakti yoga*). Those who follow this path are passionately committed to a chosen deity who they believe is worthy of their love, service, and adoration. This path involves honoring the chosen god or goddess with private meditations and communal celebrations that often include singing, chanting, and dancing. Finally, a fourth path to liberation is *raja yoga*, a path that has been described as the way to self-realization through "psychological experiments." This path involves mastering mind and body control techniques through psychophysical postures, movements, and meditations. Although rivalry may exist between the followers of the various *yogas*, most Hindus agree that each path to the divine is valid. It is common, in fact, for Hindus to select and choose among the paths at various times and for various reasons. Just as there are diverse rivers that flow into the same sea, there are multiple paths that lead to the same final destination.

SCRIPTURES

The sacred literature of classical orthodox Hinduism is divided into two groups of writings: *sruti* (revelation) and *smriti* (tradition). *Sruti*, literally "what was heard," refers to the sacred words that were heard by the *rishis*, the ancient poet-priests. Hindus do not consider these words to be of human origin. *Sruti is* Revelation in the most literal sense, words that were directly revealed to the seers. Although many moderns find much of this literature difficult to compre-

hend, a careful reading of these texts (some of which date back nearly 4,000 years) provide us with rich insights into the most ancient manifestations of Aryan culture. The religion of these distant peoples is often called Vedic Religion.

Although many of the forms associated with Vedic Religion are no longer practiced, contemporary Hindus treat *sruti* scripture with great reverence. A *sruti* text can be discussed for the purpose of clarifying its meaning, but it is not to be questioned. Rules strictly govern the time, place, and external circumstances of recitation of *sruti* texts. Care also is given to the proper pronunciation of these words, which Hindus considered to be sacred in sound as well as in meaning.

The second group of sacred writings is called *smriti*, which means that which "is remembered." These sacred stories and commentaries hold secondary authority within Hinduism and represent the Tradition that has been remembered and passed down from generation to generation. The *smriti* canon is larger and less rigorously defined than *sruti* literature, but because these books are written in a more popular style, they probably exert a greater influence on the everyday lives of Hindus than any other literature.

Vedic Religion

Sruti literature consists of four collections of hymns and incantations known as the *Vedas* (from a Sanskrit word meaning "sacred knowledge"), plus three additional collections of commentaries on the *Vedas* known as the *Brahmanas*, the *Aranyakas*, and the

ca. 2500 BCE	Indus Valley (Harappa) Civilization–Dravidian Culture
ca. 1500 BCE	Aryan entrance into India–The Vedic Age begins
ca. 1500–600 BCE	The Vedas
ca. 1000–700 BCE	The Brahmanas
ca. 6th century BCE	Reforms of Mahavira and Gautama (the Buddha)
ca. 800–300 BCE	The Aranyakas and Upanishads
ca. 200 BCE–200 CE	The Law of Manu
ca. 400 BCE–300 CE	The Great Epics–Ramayana and Mahabharata
ca. 300–800 CE	The Puranas

Timeline of ancient Indian spirituality.

Upanishads. According to the worldview of the Aryans who embraced Vedic religion, the universe consisted of three tiers (the earth, atmosphere, and heavens) and was governed by 33 divine beings or *devas.* Solid objects were of no value to these noncorporeal beings, so sacrificial fires were employed to carry the offerings of earthlings to the *devas* or gods above. Priests, who were highly trained in the art of ritual, chanted praises to the gods as they cast offerings of grain, butter, and meat into the sacrificial fires. The fire-god Agni served as the intermediary who ushered the human gifts into the heavenly realms. When the sacred rites were properly performed, the ancient Aryans believed that energies were unleashed that compelled the gods to act. Perfectly performed rituals propitiated the gods and maintained universal harmony.

The Four Vedas *and the* Brahmanas

The Vedas are divided into four collections: *Rig Veda, Sama Veda, Yajur Veda,* and *Atharva Veda.* The oldest of the four is the *Rig Veda.* This collection consists of 1,028 hymns (about five times the length of the Hebrew Book of Psalms) that are commonly organized into 10 *mandalas* or circles. Scholars believe that most of these hymns were composed between about 1500 and 900 BCE, although some Hindu schools insist that the Vedas were not composed but are authorless, eternal sounds that are channeled to humans through seers at the start of each creation cycle. In ancient times the hymns were chanted at agricultural and animal sacrificial rituals that honored the 33 gods who were credited with providing the Aryans with military victories, wealth, health, and long life. A number of the hymns refer to the intoxicating *soma* juice that was squeezed from a mysterious *soma* plant and used in worship. Most scholars view the hymns as embracing a polytheistic cosmos, but some Hindus interpret the hymns to the different deities as manifestations of different faces of one Reality and thus support a monistic rather than a polytheistic world view.

The *Sama Veda,* a hymnal for the religious rites, contains the music for the chants that were used in the agricultural offerings to the gods. Its function was to help train the musicians who performed these sacred rites. The *Yajur Veda* is a collection of ritual formulas that were used by other priests in the fire sacrifices. Its verses explain how to construct the fire

altars for the moon sacrifices and other sacred ceremonies. Its last chapter expresses the mystical idea that the supreme spirit pervades everything. The fourth collection, the *Atharva Veda,* is considerably longer than and deviates more from the *Rig Veda* than the *Sama* and *Yajur Vedas.* It primarily consists of collections of magical spells and incantations that could be used to heal disease, to ward off demons, and to harm enemies.

During the Vedic period, the caste system became fully established. The lighter-skinned Aryans served as *Brahman* priests, *Kshatriya* warriors, and *Vaisya* artisans, while the darker-skinned Dravidians were the *Shudra* servants. Power and wealth were placed in the hands of the warriors who ruled and the priests who supervised a religion that none but themselves fully understood. Because it was believed that the sacred rites sustained social stability and that the *Brahman* priests alone could perform these rites, the authority of the priests corresponded directly with the complexity of the rituals. The more elaborate the rituals, the greater the power and prestige allotted to the priests.

Between about 900 and 700 BCE, prose commentaries on the four *Vedas* were written to guide the sacrificial rituals and to explain in mythological language the sacred customs. These books, known as the *Brahmanas,* describe the mysteries and the symbolism of the increasingly elaborate rituals. The *Brahmanas* contain a number of stories in which the hero discovers a new chant or rite that is needed to solve a pressing problem. These works, which attempt to rationalize Vedic religious practices, can be read as justifications for the actions of the priestly class. The *Brahmanas* together with the four *Vedas* comprise that body of Vedic literature that places a priority on the value of rituals and the work of the fire sacrifices.

The Aranyakas *and the* Upanishads

Around the seventh century BCE, Vedic religion entered into a period of decline. This decline was likely spurred by the abuse of power of the priestly caste. As the sole keepers of Vedic knowledge, the priests charged high fees for their services, which the other castes depended on for their success in this life and the next. Moreover, the priestly assertion that the gods were compelled to respond to properly performed rituals led to the notion that the priests were superior to the gods themselves. This subordination of the other castes and degradation of the gods provoked a reaction against the priestly caste. The ensuing reform would result in the transformation of Vedic religion into what we now think of as Hinduism.

Appearing in the sacred literature at the end of the *Brahmanas* is a collection of writings known as the *Aranyakas,* or "forest-treatises." Three *Aranyakas* are extant, two of which are associated with the *Rig Veda* and one with the *Yajur Veda.* These "forest" texts are composed for religious ascetics who retire to the forests to study spiritual doctrines with their students. These ascetics can be members from any of the higher castes. The texts discuss many of the sacrificial rites and magical formulas that are discussed in the Vedas and the *Brahmanas.* The *Aranyakas,* however, are transitional texts that lead us away from a religion grounded in sacrifices toward a more reflective religion that is centered on the attainment of truth and knowledge.

Following the *Aranyakas* are the beautiful *Upanishads,* sometimes called *Vedanta,* meaning the "end of the Veda." For many Westerners, the *Upanishads* represent the high mark of Hindu spirituality. The word *Upanishads* literally means "those who sit beneath" and it refers to seekers who wish to sit at the feet of their *guru* or spiritual teacher in order to learn the mystical secrets of the universe. Tradition holds that there are 108 *Upanishads,* a number that is considered sacred within Hinduism. However, more than 200 *Upanishads* exist, although only about 15 are considered Vedic and of primary importance to Hindus of all sects. Most of the *Upanishads* are short, but if all were collected into a single volume, they would produce a book about the size of the Christian Bible. The older *Upanishads* were composed between about 700 and 300 BCE. Like other *sruti* texts considered to be "revealed" literature, the names of the authors of these texts are not known.

The primary message of the *Upanishads* is that *Atman* is *Brahman* and that when we realize this Truth, we discover that we have nothing to fear. This teaching carries within it revolutionary overtones. The *Upanishads* subordinate the Vedic rituals and even the caste duties to the supreme goal of self-realization. Some verses support the priestly system of sacrificial observances, but the main tendencies of the *Upanishads* run counter to them. These texts insist that the individual self discovers ultimate Reality by an inward journey. The ascent to the divine is an inner journey that does not require priestly formulas.

Smrti: The Sacred Tradition

Aside from the *sruti* texts that are not considered to be of human origin, the Hindus hold a second corpus of literature to be sacred. Although not considered as "Vedic wisdom," this literature, which consists of scores of lengthy volumes, includes some of the most well-known and revered texts within Hinduism. These texts reinterpret the central Hindu beliefs in popular forms. The most ancient divisions of *smriti* texts include the law books (*Dharma Sastras*) and the epics (*Itihasas*).

The Law of Manu

In the evolution of many world religions, innovative periods marked by heightened philosophical speculation are often followed by a more legalistic era during which the insights of the previous era become institutionalized. Within Hinduism, a legalistic movement appeared at the close of the *Upanishad* era during the third century BCE. Among the great literary works produced during the ensuing centuries were the *Dharma Sastras,* a genre of law books that detailed civil, moral, and religious codes.

The most important of the *Dharma Sastras* is the *Law of Manu,* a metrical work of 2,685 verses that deals with religion, politics, marriage, sex, food preparation, and hundreds of other everyday human activities. The laws are ascribed to Manu, the mythical progenitor of the human race. Manu is to the Hindu what the Adam of Genesis is to the West. The main concern of the Manu code is the conservation of the social order. The code upholds traditional Hindu beliefs in the four stations, stages, and goals of life. This text, which glorifies custom and convention, was composed at a time when the traditional social order was being undermined by forces of reform.

The Great Epics

Itihasas, which often is translated as "history" but literally means "that which was," is the a genre that encompasses the two greatest literary masterpieces that India has produced, the *Mahabharata* and the *Ramayana.* Every Hindu knows by heart the storylines of both of these epic tales. These works, along with the 18 principle *Puranas* or "ancient narratives," are sometimes called the Fifth Veda because together they provide for all Hindus the spiritual insights that the Four Vedas provided for the Brahman caste.

The *Mahabharata* is the story of the Lunar dynasty, which culminates in the birth of the five Pandava brothers; the *Ramayana* is the story of the career of Rama, the great king and hero of the Solar dynasty. Both stories take place in sacred time, before the beginning of the present cosmic epoch when the gods receded and the line between the spiritual and material realms became distinct. In this distant past the divines interacted daily with mortals. No curtain separated the sacred from the profane. By reflecting upon the tales from this spiritual golden age, Hindus hope to retrieve a sense of this sacred time.

The shorter, more unified, and more popular of the two epics is the *Ramayana*, or "The Adventures of *Rama*." *Rama* is the seventh avatar[2] of *Vishnu*, although throughout most of the work he is not aware of his divine identity. Whether human or divine, *Rama* is the prototype of perfect man. He is the ideal son, sibling, husband, citizen, king, and deity who always puts the interests of others above his own. The story line includes *Rama's* extraordinary birth and heroic childhood which culminates with his marriage to the beautiful *Sita*; *Rama's* endurance of a 13-year banishment from his kingdom and the abduction of his wife by a 10-headed demon; *Rama's* rescue of *Sita* with the help of an army of monkeys; *Sita's* ordeal by fire that proves that she was a faithful wife; and *Sita's* final banishment to the forest, notwithstanding her marital faithfulness. *Rama* and *Sita* are portrayed as the perfect couple because they put the good of the community ahead of their personal happiness and love. The story exalts the virtue of doing your duty, even if following your *dharma* produces short-term unhappiness.

The second epic, the *Mahabharata*, is the longest poem ever written. About 100,000 stanzas in length, this single work is about four times the size of the Old and the New Testaments combined. Its name is taken from *maha* meaning great, and *bharata* meaning the descendants of King Bharata, the legendary founder of India. It is likely that the basic plot of the story is based on true historical events that took place during the second or first millennium BCE. This story of the conflict between two rival claimants to the throne can be read symbolically as the struggle between good and evil. Its complex plot is made more complicated by its numerous digressions into matters of politics, religion, mythologies, and customs. The *Mahabharata* is a treasure house of Indian lore that was composed by many authors over perhaps 1,000-year period. It was finally codified in its present form in the fifth century of the Common Era.

Inserted within the *Mahabharata* is the most popular sacred text within Hinduism, the *Bhagavad-Gita.* The title of this 700-stanza poem means "Song of God." The poem is in the form of a dialogue between Lord Krishna and his disciple, Arjuna. The scene of the poem is the battlefield of Kuruksetra (near present day Delhi) just before the onset of a great civil war between the Pandus, who were descendants of King Bharata, and the Kuauravas, who were descendants of the rival patriarch Kuru. Because Lord Krishna, an avatar of Vishnu, was related to both the Pandus and Kurus, he could not take sides in the battle. He, however, offered his army to one side and himself to the other. The greedy leader of the Kurus foolishly chose Lord Krishna's army, thus allowing the Pandavas to select the incarnate god himself as their deliverer. The great truth revealed in this dialogue is that God (Vishnu) has incarnated himself in human form as Krishna to teach people divine truth.

The *Puranas, Tantras,* and Non-Sanskrit Texts

A more recently composed collection of writings important to the daily lives of Hindus are the *Puranas,* a term meaning "ancient narratives." Codified during the fourth to the eighth centuries of the modern era, these works move us beyond the *Brahman-Atman* doctrine found in the *Upanishads* toward a more personalized conception of the Absolute that is manifested in Vishnu, Shiva, and other chosen deities. Although the *Puranas* are different in structure and content, each *Purana* addresses several common themes: the stages of creation; the genealogies of the gods, sages, and kings; the cyclical epochs of history; and the histories of the Solar and Lunar dynasties. Throughout these sacred stories, supreme deities personally direct the flow of history, interacting with heroic kings and sages who provide us with austerities, prayers, and devotions that are worthy of our at-

---

[2]An avatar is a human or animal incarnation of a god. The word literally means "descent of Vishnu."

tention. Just as the *Bhagavad Gita* attempts to reconcile the path of knowledge with the path of action, so do the *Puranas* attempt to reconcile the path of knowledge with the path of devotion. These poetic narratives, which detail the nature, appearances, and attributes of the supreme God—no matter what His or Her particular form—are intended to arouse the reader to greater devotion toward the Absolute Being, who is personal as well as all-powerful.

Puranas have become the scriptures of the common folk, largely because they are accessible to men and women of all castes. Eighteen major and 18 minor *Puranas* are generally held to be authoritative. The *Puranas* are incredibly long, so it is common for Hindus to be familiar only with the *Puranas* associated with their favorite deities. The most important single *Purana* revered by Hindus of all sects is the *Bhagavata Purana*, a lengthy text of 18,000 stanzas. While this work describes and speaks with affection about each of the 10 principle incarnations of Vishnu, the *Bhagavata Purana* exalts Krishna as the most complete transcendental manifestation of the Godhead. Lord Krishna is portrayed as the quintessential avatar who surpasses all others in popularity, sweetness, splendor, and beauty.

Similarly, the *Tantras* (literally, "looms") are popular texts composed between 500 and 1800 CE that provide the masses with techniques for the worship of Vishnu, Shiva, and Shakti. Many of these texts focus on temple rituals and the use of *mantras* (chants), and *mandalas* (symbols used in meditation), although some also provide descriptions of sacred sexual techniques that entail ritual intercourse with semen retention. A basic theme within the *Tantras* is the idea that the individual is a microcosm of the universe and that the goal of spiritual fulfillment may be achieved by learning to unite the pairs of opposites that reside within each being.

In more recent centuries, many Hindus find spiritual direction in collections of non-Sanskrit sacred texts written in a variety of regional languages by poet-saints devoted to the gods Vishnu and Shiva. Of particular importance is Tulsi Das, a seventeenth-century author of a Hindi language version of the *Ramayana*. His text is not simply a translation of the ancient Sanskrit epic; Tulsi Das refashions the story to emphasize that Rama is God incarnate and that the only way to access the divine is through devotion to the true God. This version of the story is the most popular scripture that is recited among Hindus in contemporary northern India.

SUBDIVISIONS

Hinduism is a pluralistic religion that acknowledges that there are many paths to truth. Accordingly, most Hindus embrace the well-known *Rig Veda* verse: "Truth is one; the wise call it by different names." This intellectual openness, however, does not mean that Hindus refrain from passionate arguments over matters of faith and doctrine. To the contrary, since ancient times fierce debate and verbal combat between rival claimants to the truth have been an integral part of the Hindu tradition.

One consequence of this tradition of rigorous debate has been the emergence within Hinduism of six major metaphysical systems. The Sanskrit word for these schools is *darshanas*, a word that means "viewpoints" or "visions of reality." Although all six *darshanas* accept the authority of the Vedas and thereby are considered "orthodox," they hold widely different philosophical, theological, and ethical positions.

Historians of Hindu thought often divide the development of Indian philosophy into four overlapping chronological periods. The Vedic period, which dates from distance antiquity to about 600 BCE, was the era that produced Hinduism's most sacred literature, the Vedas and the *Upanishads*. The second period was the Epic Period (circa 600 BCE–200 CE), an era characterized by the indirect presentation of philosophical ideas through nonsystematic literature such as the *Ramayana* and the *Mahabharata*. It was during this era that the outlines for Hinduism's six metaphysical systems or *darshanas* first appeared in their most primitive forms. In the next period, which overlaps to a large degree with the Epic Period, the basic teachings of each *darshana* were condensed into pithy statements known as *sutras* (literally, "threads"). Each *sutra* was associated with an historic or legendary figure considered to be the founder of that philosophical school. During this Sutra Period, the doctrines of the six schools took their classical forms. While the *sutras* were easy to memorize, their brevity made them almost unintelligible without additional explanations. Consequently, in subsequent centuries disciples within each school produced elaborate commentaries to explain the tenets

NAMES, FOUNDERS AND DATES OF THE SIX PHILOSOPHICAL SCHOOLS		
School	*Founder*	*Approximate Date*
Nyaya	Gautama	Sixth century BCE
Vaisheshika	Kanada	Third century BCE
Samkhya	Kapila	Sixth century BCE
Yoga	Patanjali	Second century BCE
Mimamsa	Jaimini	Second century BCE
Vedanta	Badarayana	Fifth century BCE

that were succinctly contained in the *sutras*. The age that produced these commentaries is often called the Scholastic Period.

Classical Hinduism commonly groups the six philosophical schools into three sets that are paired thematically rather than chronologically.

Nyaya and *Vaisheshika*: Schools of Logic and Physics

The *Nyaya* and *Vaisheshika* schools are more concerned with questions of epistemology (how do we know what we know?) than with matters of ethics and theology. *Nyaya* (whose founder Akshapada Guatama should not be confused with Siddhartha Guatama, the Buddha) literally means "that which leads to a conclusion." As its name suggests, the primary concern of this system is to define the canons of proof that lead to correct knowledge. According to Guatama, there are four legitimate means to true knowledge: sense perception, inference (knowledge that follows other knowledge), comparisons (knowledge acquired by understanding the similarity of something to another well-known thing), and reliable testimony (Vedic scripture). This school teaches that all misery comes from false notions. Correspondingly, release or freedom from suffering is achieved only when we obtain the true knowledge that dispels our ignorance.

Like the *Nyaya* school, the *Vaisheshika* school teaches that knowledge of ultimate truth brings prosperity and salvation. A distinguishing mark of this philosophical system is the teaching that reality consists of an infinite number of indestructible atomlike particles that are forever combining and recombining. According to Kanada, atoms are eternal and interact

according to an unknown invisible cause. Later commentators, however, insisted that an all-knowing and all-powerful divine force is responsible for the order and movements of atoms. The *Vaisheshika* god, thus, is much like the clock-maker god of the Western deists—an eternal power that gives laws to the universe and sets the universe into motion yet never interferes with it subsequently. When we realize that all objects that seem attractive or repulsive to us are, in fact, merely compounds of atoms, then we can overcome our desire for them and obtain absolute freedom from pain.

Samkhya and *Yoga*: Schools of Psychology and Metaphysics

Kapila, the legendary founder of the *Samkhya* school, is said to be have been an incarnation of Vishnu who took pity on humans by teaching them the means to terminate their sufferings. In many ways, this system is in sharp contrast to the "all is one" teaching that pervades the *Upanishads*. *Samkhya* is a dualistic system that teaches that there are two realities: *prakriti* (matter) and *purusha* (self). Ideally, before the creation of existences, these female and male principles existed separately in polarity. *Prakriti* (matter) consisted of three qualities (goodness, passion, and darkness), and when these qualities were in equilibrium, *prakriti* was static. However, a disturbance of the equilibrium initiated an evolutionary process that first produced intellect and ultimately the elements of the material world. In this world of existence, *prakrit* (matter) and *purusha* (self) combined, and owing to this interaction the Self appears to be bound to matter. This union is compared to a lame man with good vision resting on the shoulders of a blind man with able legs. In saintly people, goodness dominates, while in ordinary people and the animals, passion and darkness dominate. The Self needs to be liberated from its association with matter, but this is not possible until intellect destroys the illusion of bondage. With this insight, the Self realizes its eternal existence and becomes free from torment. Although early versions of *Samkhya* may have been theistic, classical *Samkhya* does not include the concept of god among its elements of reality.

The *Yoga* school expounded by Patanjali accepts the psychology and metaphysics of *Samkhya*. Although it is a theistic philosophy that adds the category of God to *Samkhya*'s descriptions of reality,

Yoga's main concern is not metaphysical speculation but practical instruction on to how to achieve enlightenment through *yoga*, or "disciplined activity." According to Patanjali, the human ego is different from the Self, for the ego suffers from ignorance of eternal realities, attachment to pleasant things, repulsion to unpleasant things, and instinctive love of life and dread of death. Patanjali teaches that these afflictions can be overcome by following an eight-stage discipline of self-control and meditation. The eight steps of *Yoga* include restraint, observances, posture, breath control, withdrawal of the senses, attention, concentration, and meditation. The first two steps, restraint and observances, are ethical ones and include not injuring, stealing, lying, or lusting and being clean, content, disciplined, studious, and pious. Proper posture, breath control, and sublimation of the senses help to release tension and to prepare the mind for the final three steps that lead to enlightenment. These steps—attention, concentration, and meditation—are the same as the last three steps in Buddhism's eightfold path to nirvana.

Mimamsa and *Vedanta*: Schools of Vedic and Upanishadic Theology

The schools of classical Hinduism that are the most filled with theological speculations are the *Mimamsa* and *Vedanta* systems. The central concern of *Mimamsa* is to demonstrate the validity and eternality of the Vedas. According to Jaimini, the Vedas are not a creation of God but are uncreated eternal words that are sacred in sound as well as in meanings. These words promise rewards to those who follow the Vedic injunctions and live according to their *dharma*. The school teaches that a good or bad act is held in the form of an unseen force, *apurva*, until the act receives its reward at some later time. Unlike most of the other Hindu systems, liberation for the *Mimamsa* is described as life in heaven rather than release from torment. Jaimini accepts the Vedic deities but does not mention the existence of a Supreme God. Later commentators react to this silence, some arguing in favor of this Supreme Being and others arguing against the necessity of God's existence.

While the *Mimamsa* school is a defense of the theology of the four Vedas, the *Vedanta* school celebrates the religious and philosophical speculations of the *Upanishads*. The *Vedanta Sutra*, also called the *Brahma Sutra* because it deals with the doctrine of *Brahman*, attempts to systematize in 555 verses the teachings of the *Upanishads*. Each line consists of only two or three words, so the meaning of the *Sutra* is ambiguous and has been interpreted in various ways through the centuries by commentators. The three greatest commentators who have attempted to explain this book are Samkara, Ramanuja, and Madhva.

Samkara, considered by many Western philosophers to represent *Vedanta* in its purest form, lived in the eighth century CE during a time when the influence of Buddhism was strong in India. The central concern of his teaching, which is often called *Advaita* or Non-Dualism, is that ultimate Reality, *brahman*, is unitary and that all apparent differences that are perceived in the universe are mere illusions. Samkara insisted that all human knowledge is distorted by our preconceived misconceptions. Consequently, we can doubt all perceptions. We, however, cannot doubt the reality of Self since every perception, whether true or false, presupposes a perceiver. Thus, Self (Atman) is pure existence; it exists independently from all objects and remains after the body and mind perish. Samkara admitted that the world of matter and mind also is real, but he insisted that it is not ultimate Reality because it is limited by space, time, and cause. To Samkara, the changing condition of the world points us toward something unalterable, something beyond the finite empirical world. That something is *brahman*. *Brahman* is not the world, but the world cannot exist without *brahman*. The most controversial teaching of Samkara is his distinction between the eternal *brahman*, which being infinite is beyond descriptive attributes, and the temporal manifestation of *brahman* (which Samkara called *Isvara* or Lord God), a personal god who is the creator and preserver of the universe for as long as creation lasts. Samkara wrote beautiful hymns to the traditional lords of Hindu religion and encouraged devotion to the Lord of the universe as a stage in an individual's spiritual process. The ultimate human goal, however, is to realize *brahman* not with attributes as a personal Lord but as infinite ultimate Reality. According to Samkara, the existence of *brahman* can be known because *Brahman* is *Atman*, the imperishable Self that is within everyone.

Ramanuja, the second of the great commentators, wrote in the twelfth century CE after Buddhism had all but disappeared from India. Ramanuja's main opponents were the *Saivites*, members of a Hindu sect that worships the god of destruction Shiva, and the *Advaitas,* who taught Non-Dualism. Unlike Samkara, Ramanuja rejected the doctrine that all differences are a result of ignorance. To Ramanuja, God, Self, and Matter are three different kinds of reality, although the latter two have no existence or purpose apart from God. Moreover, for Ramanuja the ultimate human goal is not to be dissolved into an undifferentiated *brahman* but to enjoy the bliss of knowing the personal Lord God who is eternally endowed with all desirable attributes. Ramanuja's doctrine is sometimes called Qualified Non-Dualism.

The third commentator, Madhva, founded a system known as *Dvaita Vedanta* in the thirteenth century CE. Like Ramanuja, Madhva taught that the *brahman* of Vedic literature was identified with the personal Lord Vishnu. Madhva took Ramanuja's theism one step further, however, teaching an unqualified dualism that detailed fundamental differences between God and self, God and matter, matter and self, and individual selves. Opening the worship of Vishnu to all castes, Madhva taught four steps to liberation: detachment from material comforts; devotion to God; meditation on God as the only independent reality; and earning the grace of God through consistent works. Although many philosophically minded Hindus are attracted to Samkara's Non-Dualism, the teachings of Ramanuja and Madhva that place a greater emphasis on devotion to the popular gods hold greater sway among the masses.

Hindu Gods, Sects, and Cults

Hindus also are divided into several major sects that are aligned in varying degrees with the Hindu pantheon of gods. The greatest of the deities include Brahma, Vishnu, and Shiva, the triumvirate of Hindu male deities, and Shakti, the female manifestations of the gods. Generally, each god and goddess is associated with a consort, a family, a symbol, a color, an animal, and a mission.

The first god of the Hindu trinity is Brahma the creator. Brahma is often depicted as an old man with four faces. He is the supreme sage from whom the other gods seek wisdom. His duty is to create the cosmos and to attribute a form for each soul. His sign is the lotus, a beautiful water lily that floats above the muck of swamps, symbolizing that which is able to live in the world without being corrupted by it. His consort is Sarasvati, the goddess of speech and learning. Brahma is worshipped by the other gods, but because He is beyond comprehension, humans generally do not worship him. Few temples honor him, and no sect bears his name.

The second god of the trinity is Vishnu the preserver. Vishnu's consort is Lakshmi, the model wife and the goddess of wealth and prosperity. Vishnu is often depicted with four arms that carry his four symbols: a shell (to spread the divine sound *OM*), a discus (to remind us of the wheel of time), a lotus (to remind us of his glorious existence), and a sword (to indicate his power to punish those who ignore life's disciplines). His vehicle is a swift-flying bird that spreads Vedic knowledge. His color is blue. The followers of Vishnu are known as Vaishnavaities.

As the protector of the cosmos, Vishnu comes to the earth as an *avatar* in times of great human need. Although Hindus generally acknowledge 10 *avatars,* Vishnu's two most popular incarnations are as Rama and Krishna.

Rama is a more conventional character than the unpredictable Krishna. Always noble and virtuous, Rama is the son of Kausalya, the paragon of motherhood, the elder brother of his obedient younger sibling Lakshmana, and the husband of his loyal and beloved wife Sita. Rama is defended by the monkey god Hanuman, whose devotion to Him serves as a model for appropriate human devotion to God. Rama cults focus more on moral conduct and duty than the more ecstatic cults of Krishna, but a common teaching among Rama devotees is that salvation can come simply by uttering the name of God.

Krishna appears more human and complex than Rama. As a boy Krishna often did naughty deeds. Although His divine nature is fully revealed in the *Bhagavad Gita,* in the *Puranas* He is presented not as the master teacher but as the handsome lover of humanity who beguiles our soul with the sweet melodies of his flute. His favorite mistress is Radha, although He also is the lover of many women, including on one occasion 16,000 cowgirls (gopis). The many love affairs of Krishna symbolize God's eternal love affair with us. Krishna devotees insist that God is in love with the soul and the soul is in love with God. In this love affair, God is male and the soul is female. Consequently, to receive God's inflowing grace, the soul must become female and abandon itself completely to the divine. Approximately 580 million or about 60 percent of modern-day Hindus are Vaishavaities.

THE TEN AVATARS OR INCARNATIONS OF VISHNU.

The ten traditional incarnations or avatars of Vishnu.

Another enormously popular god is Shiva the destroyer. Hindus view the cosmos to be in a continuous state of creation/destruction/re-creation; thus, Shiva's role as destroyer complements that of Brahma the creator. He is, in a sense, the great recycler, whose destructive powers pave the way for new life. Shiva has a complex character. He is the god of disease, death, and destruction, yet he also is the god of the dance and reproduction. He is both terrible and mild. He is portrayed as the great yoga disciplinarian with three eyes and matted hair who stands with one leg raised, ever ready to unleash his fierceness. In two of his four hands he holds a drum to beat the rhythm of life and a pot of fire to destroy it, yet his two empty hands are extended with gestures of friendship and liberation. One of His sons is Ganesha, the elephant-headed, pot-bellied patron god of good fortune and wisdom who devotees invoke before any important undertaking. Shiva's sign is the erect penis (lingam) and the vagina (yoni). His vehicle is the bull, a symbol of happiness and strength. As the most feared of the gods, great kings of India have worshipped Him and built temples to appease him. In sacred rituals, some of the so-called left-hand devotees make sacramental use of the normally forbidden, eating meat, drinking wine, and having sexual intercourse, a sacred act that symbolizes the eternal union of Shiva with his shakti or creative power. His followers, known as Shaivites, number about 220 million and represent about one-fourth of those in the larger Hindu tradition.

A third large sect within Hinduism is Shaktism. The devotees within this sect, known as Shaktas, believe that Shiva is too immersed in a yogic trance to hear the prayers of humans; consequently, worship should be directed to the feminine manifestations of Shiva ("shakti") rather than Shiva himself. Shakti is the energy force of nature personified in the form of Devi, the Mother Goddess. Devi is represented as the yoni, the female principle that surrounds the male lingam.

Like the avatars of the male deities, Devi is believed to have appeared throughout cosmic time in various forms. She has many manifestations, some of which are benevolent and others, malignant. As Parvati and Uma, she is a benign goddess who is turned to for boons for health and children. As Kali and Durga, she is the destroyer goddess who devours and drinks the blood of the demons of ignorance. In Hindu iconography, Kali is depicted with black skin and a hideous tusked face, who like her consort Shiva, has a third eye on her forehead and four arms, two of which hold a weapon and a skull and the other two are raised to bless her worshippers. Similarly, Durga is presented as a multiarmed woman who stands on the buffalo demon she has killed. In her many hands are weapons and the head of the slain demon. With one of her hands, however, she blesses her faithful worshippers, reassuring them that they have nothing to fear. More than 50 million contemporary Hindus give their highest allegiance to some form of Mother Goddess worship.

The fourth major Hindu sect is an ecumenical group that worships all gods without any exclusive preference to any particular deity. Members of this group are known as Smartas. They represent about 2 percent of modern-day Hindus.

The Heterodox Systems

During India's fertile Epic Period in the middle centuries of the first millennium BCE, several additional metaphysical systems grew up alongside the six orthodox schools within Hinduism. Unlike the orthodox schools, however, these systems rejected the efficacy of the Vedas and thereby are labeled as heterodox. From the insights of these heretical systems emerged one school of philosophical skepticism, three significant new religious traditions, and a number of reform movements that have altered popular expressions of modern Hinduism.

The radical philosophical school that challenged Hindu orthodoxy is known as Charvaka. This system holds that matter alone is real and that the soul has no existence apart from the body. Because the Charvakas insist that nothing exists beyond this world, they view the gods and the concept of soul immortality as mere illusions. Moreover, because nature does not respond to good or evil action, the central premise of life is simply to secure pleasure and avoid pain. This system attracted few followers and has been extinct in India since ancient times.

Kali, the consort of Shiva the Destroyer.

The first of the new religions to challenge traditional brahmanical orthodoxy is Jainism. This religion is derived from doctrines taught by the ancient *jinas* or "spiritual conquerors" that achieved soul purity. The greatest of the jinas was Mahavira (599–525 BCE), who was born about a generation before Siddharta Gautama, the Buddha. What Mahavira and the other "pure soul" jinas conquered was their passion. According to Jain cosmology, the cosmos consists of soul and matter. Humans in their imperfect state are a mixture of these two realities. It is possible, however, to purify the soul through the three "jewels" of right faith, right knowledge, and right conduct. Right conduct means practicing the five virtues, which consist of nonviolence, truth-speaking, nonstealing, chastity, and nonattachment to worldly things. Jains take nonviolence and the renunciation of worldly things seriously. They are vegetarians who go to great lengths not to harm any living thing, including insects. One sect within Jainism rejects even the wearing of clothing. Although only about 5 million strong, the Jains remain a respected minority within modern India.

The second great religion to grow out of ancient Hindu teaching is Buddhism. With 350 million followers, Buddhism is the world's fourth largest religion and is the subject of Chapter 5.

In the sixteenth century CE, another schism within Hinduism produced yet another major religious system, Sikhism. Some scholars view Sikhism as a reform movement within Hinduism, while others consider it to be a blend of Hinduism and Islam. Sikhs embrace the teachings Guru Nanak (1469–1539) and his nine guru successors who served as the channels through which the divine truth was interpreted to the devotees. The utterances of the gurus were compiled into a canonized collection known as the *Adi Granth*, a phrase that means "The Original Book." After the 10th guru prepared a final version of the collection and announced the *Adi Granth* as Guru, the book itself became the mouthpiece of the divine. The *Adi Granth* is housed in a special room, placed on a cushion, and wrapped in special cloths, and it is ritually awakened every morning by ceremonially pure and shoeless devotees. For Sikhs, viewing the holy book is a means of receiving God's grace.

The essential message of the *Adi Granth* is that there is only one God, *Sat Nam* (meaning the True Name). *Sat Nam* is the uncreated creator, the indweller of all things, whose voice is the *Adi Granth* speaking as Guru to the world. Just as others look to living gurus for spiritual direction, Sikhs look to the *Adi Granth*, ritually opening it at random and reading to discover God's word for any given occasion. Sikhs teach that the individual soul will develop through many rebirths until it is absorbed into the infinite One. With 18 million followers, this schismatic sect within Hinduism is also one of the world's 10 largest religions.

Reform Movements within Modern Hinduism

If Hindu-Muslim encounters in medieval and early modern times laid the foundation for the rise of Sikhism, in more recent centuries contact between Christians and Hindus has contributed to the rise in a number of reform movements that have transformed aspects of modern Hinduism. The first significant Hindu reformer was Ram Mohan Roy (1772–1833), who fought against the ancient practice of burning widows on their husbands' funeral pyres by insisting that this custom was not part of the original Hindu dharma. In 1828, Roy launched the Brahmo Samaj movement, an attempt to combine Hinduism and Christianity by denouncing all forms of polytheism and idolatry. Another reformer, Swami Dayananda (1824–1883), sought a return to orthodox Vedic religion by rejecting as corruptions the later religious teachings in the epics and the *Puranas*. In 1875, he founded the Arya Samaj, a movement that advocated persuasion or even violence to convert Muslims and Christians into the ancient Vedic religion.

More liberal reformers, including Sri Paramahamsa Ramakrishna (1836–1886) and his disciple Swami Vivekananda (1862–1902), laid the foundation for the Ramakrishna Mission, a nonsectarian movement that taught that "all religions were different paths to God." While these Hindu reformers opposed the need for seekers to convert to other religious traditions, they did insist that "each religion must assimilate the spirit of the others and yet preserve its individuality and grow according to its own law of growth." Other modern thinkers that have greatly influenced Hinduism include Sarvepalli Radhakrishnan (1888–1975), a President of India who espoused a spiritualized, nonsectarian Hinduism as the "world religion of the future," and Mahatama Gandhi (1869–1948), who transformed both India and Hinduism through the preaching of the doctrine of passive resistance to oppressors.

SACRED OBSERVANCES AND PRACTICES

In Vedic times, the peoples of India relied on Brahmin priests to perform the sacred rites deemed necessary to activate the gods and to maintain the cosmic order. Although the forms of the rituals have evolved over the last 3 millennia, the observation of sacred practices remains of great importance to modern Hindus. Popular daily private devotional practices include tending a household sacred fire; reciting mantras and passages from holy writings; calming the mind through meditation and yoga exercises; and offering gifts to humans in need, to animals, to their ancestors, and to their favorite gods.

Millions of Hindus also visit at least once a week a temple where they pay respect to their chosen deity. Generally within each temple resides a representation of the honored deity that the faithful treat with great respect. In the morning, the image is greeted with a ceremonial awakening, bathed, and then presented with garlands and water. During the day, worshippers visiting the temple approach the image and ask it for special favors and grace, honoring it with the lighting and waving of candles and the chanting of mantras. Before departing, worshippers often present gifts of grain, ghee, rice, spices, flowers, or incense—offerings that the deity graciously shares with the other temple guests. On special occasions the image is entertained by musicians or dancing girls or taken on a procession around the temple area. At bedtime every night, the image is ceremonially laid to rest with an end of day sacred rite.

In addition to observing sacred duties at household shrines and in public temples, devout Hindus go on pilgrimages to visit the thousands of holy sites that dot the landscape of India. Great rivers and the junctions of these rivers attract large numbers of pilgrims who come to purify themselves in the sacred flowing waters. Bathing at these sacred sites, especially at specific times, is considered to be an auspicious act that brings cleansing, favor, and spiritual bliss to the participating pilgrims.

Modern Hindus also celebrate a number of sacred festivals. Each of the four major sects has special occasions for religious celebrations that commemorate auspicious events like the birthday of a god. Huge numbers of sectarians gather seasonally at holy sites to honor their favorite deity. In Bengal, for instance, Durga worship provides the occasion for one of Hinduism's most popular modern day festivities. During this nine-day celebration, Shaktas come together to sing and dance and to honor Durga with the sacrifice of hundreds of buffaloes. On the 10th day of the celebration, Durga images are carried in procession to the Ganga River where they are immersed. Other popular seasonal festivals widely celebrated include Holi (The Festival of Colors) and Divali (The Festival of Lights). The former is a spring festival that celebrates the fertility of the land. During this carnival-like celebration that includes the burning of a great bonfire, peoples of all genders and castes min-

gle freely together to bridge the normal social distinctions between employers and employees or men and women, and young men throw colored powder or colored water on women, just as the youthful Krishna played tricks on the milkmaids of his village. The later Festival of Lights is an autumn harvest celebration that honors, among others, Parvati and Lakshmi, goddesses of wealth and prosperity. In this festival, Hindu fireworks are fired, sweets are exchanged, and males visit and offer gifts to their female relatives. Celebrations such as these fill the religious calendars of Hindus of all sects in every season of the year.

Sacred practices vary greatly among Hindus, in part because of the large number of divisions within the tradition. In addition to the four major sects are thousands of local and regional Hindu cults. Whereas a sect is largely determined by the major god or goddess a family worships, a cult is based on the particular form of the deity that is worshipped in the village in which people live. All family members that worship Shakti, for instance, are known as Shaktas, but there are many different Shakti cults with different sacred practices. Similarly, Hindu sectarians who worship Vishnu or Shiva as their family god also will worship their village god and a personally selected deity whom they rely upon for their individual protection. Hindus acknowledge the existence of 33 million gods, so there are unnumbered combinations of major and minor gods that can be worshipped. One consequence of this complex pantheon of deities is the splintering of Hinduism into a seemingly endless array of cults. For most Hindus, the cult to which he or she belongs has a greater bearing on his or her daily life than the sect to which he or she is associated.

Hindu scholar Lee Siegel uses a television metaphor to describe for Western audiences the subtleties of Hindu religiosity. According to Siegel, *brahman*—that infinite reality that is beyond description—is like a television set without electrical power. Just as few are interested in watching a blank TV screen, few Hindus express an immediate interest in contemplating the unknowable absolute. *Shakti*—the energy of the universe—is like a TV screen connected to a power source but without channel reception. The major Hindu gods—*Brahma, Vishnu,* and *Shiva*—are like the major television networks. *Brahma* can be compared to PBS and CSPAN (everyone knows they exist, but few watch them), *Vishnu* to CBS and NBC, and *Shiva* to FOX and MTV. Hindu sectarians are like American television watchers who are loyal to a given national network. The cults, however, are like the particular television shows (i.e., *I Love Lucy*, *Friends*, *Monday Night Football*). Just as most Westerners turn on the television to watch particular shows rather than to watch whatever is on their favorite network, so are Hindus primarily interested in paying homage to the cult gods and goddesses of their village and on whom they rely for special protection and provisions.

SOURCES

The following anthology includes selections from the vast collections of Hindu writings. About half of the excerpts come from the sacred *Sruti* literature and include selections from the *Rig Veda*, the *Sama Veda*, the *Atharva Veda*, the *Brahmanas*, and the *Upanishads*. The remaining selections are passages from the *Smrti* traditions, including longer segments from the *Law of Manu* and the *Bhagavad Gita* and smaller selections from the *Ramayana*, the *Srimad Bhagavatam*, and the *Vishnu Purana*.

Section 1: Beginnings: God, Time, and the Universe

In many Eastern traditions, the concepts "beginning" and "ending" are less important than the concepts of "being" and "nonbeing." Nonetheless, all Eastern religious traditions include creation stories within their sacred texts, although often the meanings of these narratives differ from the creation accounts of the West. The authors of Eastern texts are more likely to think about the beginning in ontological rather than in historical terms. For these thinkers, the beginning is not reached by tracing linear time backward to the archeological foundations of the universe, but rather by moving from the circumference to the center of a circle that is not made of time.

The opening selections are creation accounts from the *Rig Veda* and the *Upanishads*. Compare these accounts with creation stories within Judaism, Christianity, and Islam. How are the accounts similar and different?

> ## CREATION ACCOUNTS IN THE VEDAS[3]
>
> ### From the Rig Veda X, 129

1. At first was neither Being nor Nonbeing.
   There was not air nor yet sky beyond.
   What was its wrapping? Where? In whose protection?
   Was Water there, unfathomable and deep?

2. There was no death then, nor yet deathlessness;
   of night or day there was not any sign.
   The One breathed without breath, by its own impulse.
   Other than that was nothing else at all.

3. Darkness was there, all wrapped around by darkness,
   and all was Water indiscriminate. Then
   that which was hidden by the Void, that One, emerging,
   stirring, through power of Ardor, came to be.

4. In the beginning Love arose,
   which was the primal germ cell of the mind.
   The Seers, searching in their hearts with wisdom,
   discovered the connection of Being in Nonbeing.

5. A crosswise line cut Being from Nonbeing.
   What was described above it, what below?
   Bearers of seed there were and mighty forces,

6. Who really knows? Who can presume to tell it?
   Whence was it born? Whence issued this creation?
   Even the Gods came after its emergence.
   Then who can tell from whence it came to be?

7. That out of which creation has arisen,
   whether it held it firm or it did not,
   He who surveys it in the highest heaven,
   He surely knows or maybe He does not!

A Creation Account from the Chandogya Upanishad 6, 2[4]

1. "In the beginning there was only that which is (tat svam), one only, without a second. Others say that in the beginning there was only that which is not, one only, without a second; and from that which is not, that which is was born.
2. "But how could that be, my dear son?" the father continued. "How could that which is be born from that which is not? No, dearest son, only that which is and was in the beginning, one only, without a second.

---

[3]*The Vedic Experience: Mantra-manjari*, translated by Raimundo Panikkar (New Delhi: Motilal Banarsidas, 1994), p. 58.

[4]*The Upanishads*. Translated by Max Muller. *Sacred Books of the East*, Vol. 1, 15. (Oxford: Clarendon Press, 1879, 1884).

3. "It thought: 'May I be many things, may I grow forth.' It then sent forth fire. That fire then thought: 'May I be many things, may I grow forth.' It sent forth water. And therefore whenever anybody anywhere is hot and perspires, water is produced on him from fire alone.

4. "Water thought: 'May I be many things, may I grow forth.' It sent forth earth. Therefore, whenever it rains anywhere, most food is then produced. From water alone is edible food produced.

The earliest extant collection of sacred texts from the ancient world is the *Rig Veda*. This collection of 1,028 hymns of praise is addressed to the 33 gods of the ancient Aryans. Each god has control over certain forces of nature. With one notable exception,[5] the gods do not vent their wrath against mortals. Instead, their purpose is to assist humankind by warding off the demons that bring malevolence. When worshippers perform the proper Vedic chants and offer the proper sacrifices, the gods are activated and the universe maintains its order.

The first selection in this section is a hymn addressed to Indra, the favorite national god of the Aryan people. A deity of the thunderbolt, Indra is invoked in more than 250 hymns of the Rig Veda. Exhilarated by Soma, the god of intoxication, Indra unleashes his mighty fury against Vrtra, the serpent demon of drought and darkness, and upon vanquishing the foe, provides humankind with both water and light. A powerful yet amoral god known for his size, strength, drinking, and violence, Indra is the helper of worshippers who seek protection, military victory, and wealth.

ATTRIBUTES OF THE GODS

TO INDRA

From the Rig Veda I, 7[6]

1. Indra the singers, Indra the reciters, Indra the choirs have glorified!

2. Indra the golden, armed with thunder, with his two bay steeds and the Word as his chariot!

3. The Sun is his eye, raised on high. Cloud masses he bursts to release the rain.

4. By your dread power, Indra, most fearsome, help us in battle to win ample spoils.

5. Indra we invoke in all kinds of contests, our Friend who hurls at powers of evil his bolts.

6. Burst open for us yonder cloud in the sky, ever bounteous Indra, irresistible hero!

7. Higher, yet higher, I raise his praises! I find no words worthy of him!

8. He drives on his peoples with strength irresistible, even as the bull drives onward the herds.

9. Sole sovereign is Indra of men and of Gods and of the fivefold race of dwellers on earth.

10. Indra we invoke from all the peoples. May Indra be for us and nobody else.

More Vedic hymns are addressed to Agni than to any other god except Indra. One of the great ritual deities of the *Rig Veda*, Agni is a wise and omniscient deity, the "knower of all created beings." Agni is more closely associated with humans than the other deities. As friend of humankind, he is an immortal who chooses to abide among the mortals. As a "priest" and mediator, he both takes human offerings to the gods and brings the gods to the sacrifices. His flame is the mouth by which the gods eat the sacrifice. The following prayer to Agni is the first hymn in the Rig Veda.

TO AGNI

From the Rig Veda I, 1[7]

1. I magnify the Lord, the divine, the Priest, minister of the sacrifice, the offerer, supreme giver of treasure.

2. Worthy is the Lord to be praised by living as by ancient seers. He makes present for us the Gods.

3. The Lord brings us riches, food in daily abundance, renown, and hero sons to gladden our hearts.

4. Only that worship and sacrifice that you, Lord, guard on every side will reach the heavenly world of the Gods.

5. May the Lord, wise and true offerer, approach, most marvelous in splendor, encircled with his crown of Gods!

6. Whatever gift you may choose to give, O Lord, to your worshiper, that gift, refulgent One, is true.

7. To you, dispeller of the night, we come with daily prayer offering to you our reverence.

8. For you are Lord of sacrifice, enlightener, shepherd of the world, who wax mighty in your own abode.

9. So, like a father to his sons, be to us easy of entreaty. Stay with us, O Lord, for our joy.

---

[5]The god Rudra, later known as Shiva, is the exception.

[6]*The Hymns of the Rigveda*, translated by Ralph T. H. Griffith, (1896), www.sacred-texts.com/hin/rigveda.

[7]*The Vedic Experience*, Panikkar, translator, p. 329.

Surrounded by the 33 gods of the Vedic pantheon, Hindus confront the problem of ultimate power either by affirming all the gods equally or by seeking for a unifying principle behind the multiple expressions of divinity. The following hymns illustrate both approaches to the problem.

From the Rig Veda VIII, 30[8]

Not one of you, ye gods, is small, none of you is a feeble
  child:
All of you, verily, are great.
Thus be ye lauded, ye destroyers of the foe, ye Three and
  Thirty Deities,
The gods of man, the Holy Ones.
As such defend and succor us, with benedictions speak to
  us:
Lead us not from our fathers' and from Manu's path into
  the distance far away.
Ye deities who stay with us, and all ye gods of mankind,
Give us your wide protection, give shelter for cattle and for
  steed.

From the Rig Veda X, 121[9]

1. In the beginning arose the Golden Germ:
  he was, as soon as born, the Lord of Being,
  sustainer of the Earth and of this Heaven.
  What God shall we adore with our oblation?

2. He who bestows life-force and hardy vigor,
  whose ordinances even the Gods obey,
  whose shadow is immortal life—and death—
  What God shall we adore with our oblation?

3. Who by his grandeur has emerged sole sovereign
  of every living thing that breathes and slumbers,
  he who is Lord of man and four-legged creatures
  What God shall we adore with our oblation?

4. To him of right belong, by his own power,
  the snow-clad mountains, the world-stream, and the sea.
  His arms are the four quarters of the sky.
  What God shall we adore with our oblation?

5. Who held secure the mighty Heavens and Earth,
  who established light and sky's vast vault above,
  who measured out the ether in mid-spheres—
  What God shall we adore with our oblation?

6. Toward him, trembling, the embattled forces,
  riveted by his glory, direct their gaze.
  Through him the risen sun sheds forth its light.
  What God shall we adore with our oblation?

7. When came the mighty Waters, bringing with them
  the universal Germ, whence sprang the Fire,
  thence leapt the God's One Spirit into being.
  What God shall we adore with our oblation?

8. This One who in his might surveyed the Waters
  pregnant with vital forces, producing sacrifice,
  he is the God of Gods and none beside him.
  What God shall we adore with our oblation?

9. O Father of the Earth, by fixed laws ruling,
  O Father of the Heavens, pray protect us,
  O Father of the great and shining Waters!
  What God shall we adore with our oblation?

10. O Lord of Creatures, Father of all beings,
  you alone pervade all that has come to birth.
  Grant us our heart's desire for which we pray.
  May we become the lords of many treasures!

The following selections are from the *Upanishads*. Viewed by many as the "culmination of sacred knowledge," the *Upanishads* replaced the Vedic focus on ritualistic religion with an emphasis on the Oneness of all things. As a large collection composed by many authors over a period of three to four centuries, the *Upanishads* do not attempt to present a single coherent view of reality. Rather, the descriptions of the Absolute within the *Upanishads* provide insights that support each of the six philosophical systems that subsequently emerged within Hinduism.

THE ONE OF THE *UPANISHADS*

From the Brhadaranyaka Upanishad III, 9[10]

1. Then Vidagdha Sakalya question him. "How many gods are there, Yajnavalkya?" He answered in accord with the following Nivid (invocationary formula): "As many as are mentioned in the Nivid of the 'Hymn to All the Gods,' namely, three hundred and three, and three thousand and three [=3306]."

[8]*Rig Veda*, Griffith, translator (1896), www.himalayanacademy.com/resources/books/vedic_experience/VEIndex.html.

[9]*The Vedic Experience*, Pannikkar, translator, www.himalayanacademy.com/resources/books/vedic_experience/VEIndex.html.

[10]R. E. Hume, *The Thirteen Principal Upanishads* (London: Oxford University Press, 1931).

"Yes," he said, "but just how many gods are there, Yaj-navalka?"

"Thirty-three."

"Yes," he said, "but just how many gods are there, Yaj-navalka?"

"Six"

"Yes," he said, "but just how many gods are there, Yaj-navalka?"

"Three"

"Yes," he said, "but just how many gods are there, Yaj-navalka?"

"Two"

"Yes," he said, "but just how many gods are there, Yaj-navalka?"

"One and a half"

"Yes," he said, "but just how many gods are there, Yaj-navalka?"

"One . . ."

9. . . . "Which is the one god?" "Breath," said he. "They call him Brahman, the Yon."

From the Kena Upanishad, *Parts 1–2*[11]

1 By whom directed does the mind project to its objects?
By whom commanded does the first life breath move?
By whom impelled are these words spoken?
What god is behind the eye and ear?

That which is the hearing of the ear,
the thought of the mind, the voice of the speech,
the life of the breath, and the sight of the eye.
Passing beyond, the wise leaving this world become
   immortal.

There the eye does not go, nor speech, nor the mind.
We do not know, we do not understand how one can
   teach this.
Different, indeed, is it from the known, and also it is
   above the unknown.
Thus have we heard from the ancients who explained it
   to us.

That which is not expressed by speech,
but that by which speech is expressed:
know that to be God, not what people here adore.

That which is not thought by the mind,
but that by which the mind thinks:
know that to be God, not what people here adore.

That which is not seen by the eye,
but that by which the eye sees:
know that to be God, not what people here adore.

That which is not heard by the ear,
but that by which the ear hears:
know that to be God, not what people here adore.

That which is not breathed by the breath,
but that by which the breath breathes:
know that to be God, not what people here adore.

2 If you think you know it well,
only slightly do you know the form of God.
What refers to you and what refers to the gods
then is to be investigated by you.

I think it is known.
I do not think that I know it well, nor do I think that I
   do not know it.
Those of us who know this know it,
and not those of us who think they do not know it.

The one who has not thought it out has the thought of it.
The one who has thought it out does not know it.
It is not understood by those who understand it;
it is understood by those who do not understand it.

When it is known by an awakening, it is correctly
   known,
for then one finds immortality.
By the soul one finds ability;
by knowledge one finds immortality.

If here one knows it, then there is truth;
if here one does not know it, then there is great loss.
Seeing it in all beings,
the wise on leaving this world become immortal.

From the Shvetashvatara Upanishad
Part 1 (partial)

The soul is infinite, universal, detached.
When one discovers this triad, that is God.
What is perishable is the material.
What is immortal and imperishable is the bearer.
Over both the perishable and the soul the divine one rules.

By meditating on this, by union with this,
and by entering into this being more and more
there finally occurs the cessation of every illusion.
By knowing the divine, every restriction passes away;
with disturbances ended, birth and death cease.

By meditating on this,
there is a third stage at the dissolution of the body, universal
   lordship;
being absolute, one's desire is satisfied.

[11]*Kena Upanishad*, English translation by Sanderson Beck in Sanderson Beck, ed., *Wisdom Bible* (Goleta, CA: World Peace Communications, 2002), pp. 66–67.

That eternal should be known as present in the soul.
Nothing higher than that can be known.

When one recognizes the enjoyer, the object of enjoyment,
and the universal causer, all has been said.
This is the threefold God.

Although not awarded the status of *sruti,* and thus not regulated by the priests, the *Puranas* were the scriptures of the popular masses. Unlike the Vedic scriptures, the *Puranas* could be recited by all groups, including women, outcastes, and men from the lower castes. Initially an oral tradition communicated in local dialects, the *Puranas* often expressed a sense of adoration for personal deities. The following selection is from the *Vishnu Purana,* one of the oldest and best-known *Puranas* that dates from the early fifth century CE.

THE SHAPES OF THE GODS OF THE *PURANAS*

From the Vishnu Purana, 3, 17, 14–34[12]

You are everything, earth, water, fire, air, and space,
the subtle world, the Nature-of-All (pradhana),
and the Person (pums) who stands forever aloof.

O Self of all beings!
From the Creator (Brahma) to the blade of grass
all is your body, visible and invisible,
divided by space and time.

We worship you as Brahma, the Immense Being, the first
shape,
who sprang from the lotus of your navel to create the
worlds.

We, the gods, worship you in our selves,
we, the King of Heaven, the Sun, the Lord of Tears,
the Indweller, the twin gods of agriculture,
the Lord of Wind, the Offering, who all are your shapes
while you are our Selves.

We worship you in your demonic shapes, deceitful and
stupid,
wild in their passions, suspicious of wisdom.

We worship you in the genii, the yakshas,
with their narrow-minds obdurate to knowledge,
their blunt faculties covetous of the objects of words.

O Supreme Man! We bow to your fearful evil shapes
which wander at night, cruel and deceitful

---

[12]*Hindu Polytheism,* translated by Alain Danielou (New York: Bollingen Series LXXIII, 1964), pp. 367–368.

O Giver-of-Rewards (Jundardana)!
We worship you as the Eternal Law
whence virtuous men, who dwell in the heaven,
obtain the blissful fruit of their just deeds.
We bow to the Realized (Siddhas) who are your shapes of joy;
free from contacts, they enter and move within all things.

O Remover-of-Sorrow (Hari)! We bow to you the serpent
shapes,
lustful and cruel, whose forked tongues know no mercy.

O Pervader. We worship you as knowledge
in the peaceful form of the seers,
faultless, free from sin.

O Dweller in the lotus of the Heart! We bow to you
as the self of Time which, at the end of the ages,
infallibly devours all beings.

We worship you as the Lord of Tears,
who dances at the time of destruction,
having devoured gods and men alike.

O Giver of Rewards! We worship your human shape
bound by the twenty-eight incapacities (badha),
ruled by the powers of darkness.

We bow to you as vegetal life (mukhya rupa),
by which the world subsists and which six in kind,
trees, [creepers, bashes, platits, herbs and bamboo]
supports the sacrifcial rites.

O Universal Self! We bow to you under that elemental shape
from which beasts and tnen have sprung,
gods and living beings, ether and the elements,
sound and all the qualities.

O Transcendent Self! We bow to you as the Cause of causes,
the Principal shape beyond compare,
beyond Nature (pradhana) and Intellect.

O All-powerful (Bhagavan)! We bow to your shape
which the seers alone perceive and in which is found
no white nor other colour, no length nor other dimension,
no density nor other quality.

Purer than purity it stands
beyond the sphere of quality.

We bow to you, the birthless, the indestructible,
outside whom there is but nothingness.

You are the ever-present within all things,
as the intrinsic principle of all.

We bow to you, resplendent Indweller (Vasudeva)! the seed
of all that is!
You stand changeless, unsullied.

The Supreme stage is your core, the Universe your shape.
You are the unborn, Eternal.

SECTION 2: Humanity: The Problem of Good and Evil

The scriptures of many world religions describe the human condition as a war between two natures—one good and the other evil. For many, awareness of this human condition is not self-evident but comes to aspirants as they strive to do good. A natural question asked by those who acknowledge this inner contradiction is, What is the source of goodness and evil? Here are two such answers contained within Hindu scripture. The selections are taken from the *Brahmanas* and the *Prasna Upanishad.*

From Brhadaranyaka Upanishad *I, 4, 1–5; 17*[13]

1. In the beginning this was the self alone, in the form of a Man. Looking around he saw nothing what ever except himself. He said in the beginning: "I am" and thence arose the name "I." So, even today, when a Man is addressed, he says in the beginning, "It is I," and then adds any other name he may have. Furthermore, since before the world came to be he had burned up all evils; he is Man. He who knows this also burns up whoever wants to be before him.

2. He was afraid; so, even today, one who is all alone is afraid. He thought to himself: "Since nothing exists except me, of what am I afraid?" Thereupon his fear vanished, for of what should he have been afraid? It is of a second that fear arises.

3. He found no joy; so, even today, one who is all alone finds no joy. He yearned for a second. He became as large as a man and a woman locked in close embrace. This self he split into two; hence arose husband and wife. Therefore, as Yajnavalkya used to observe: "Oneself is like half of a split pea." That is why this void is filled by woman. He was united with her and thence were born human beings.

4. She thought: "How can he unite with me, as he has brought me forth out of himself? Well, I will hide myself." She became a cow, but he became a bull and united with her. Hence cattle arose. She became a mare, he a stallion; she became a she-ass, he a male ass. He united with her and hence singlehoofed animals arose. She became a she-goat, he a he-goat; she became a sheep, he a ram. He united with her and hence goats and sheep arose. In this way he created everything that exists in pairs, down to the ants.

5. He realized: "I indeed am creation, for I produced all this"—for he had become the creation. And he who has this knowledge becomes [a creator] in that same creation. . . .

17. In the beginning there was only the atman, One only. He desired: "May I have a wife in order to have offspring; may I have wealth in order to perform a work!" For desire reaches this far. Even if one wishes, one cannot obtain more than this. Therefore, even nowadays, if a man is alone, he desires: "May I have a wife in order to have offspring; may I have wealth in order to perform a work!" As long as he does not obtain each of these [desires], he thinks himself to be incomplete. His completeness, however, is this: the mind is his Self [atman]; speech is his wife; breath is his offspring; the eye is his human wealth, for he finds it with the eye; the ear is his divine wealth, for he hears it with the ear; the body [atman] is his work, for he works with the body. Fivefold, indeed, is the sacrifice, fivefold is the victim, fivefold is the man. Whatever there is, the whole universe, is fivefold. He attains all this, who knows thus.

From the Prasna Upanishad, *Third Question*[14]

Then Kaushalya Ashvalayana asked him, "Sir, from where
   is this life-breath born?
How does it come into this body?
How does it dividing the soul become established?
By what does it depart?
How does it relate to the external and to the soul inside?"

The seer answered him, "You are asking much,
but because you are very holy, I will tell you.
The life-breath is born from the soul.
As a shadow is cast by a person, so is this life-breath
   extended by the soul,
and for the perfection of the mind it comes into this body.
As a ruler commands the officials, saying, 'Govern these
   villages,'
so this life-breath rules the other breaths.
The out-breath is in the organs of excretion and generation;
the life-breath itself is in the eyes, ears, mouth and nose;
while the equalizing breath is in the middle,
for it equally distributes the offering of food.
From this arise the seven flames.

"The soul lives in the heart.
Here there are one hundred and one channels.
Each of these has one hundred smaller channels.
Each of these has seventy-two thousand branching channels.
Within these moves the diffused breath.
Rising upward through one of these,
the up-breath leads by virtue to the heaven of virtue,
by sin to the hell of sin, and by both back to the human
   world.

---

[13]*The Upanishads,* Muller, translator (1879, 1884), www.sacred-texts.com/hin/rigveda.

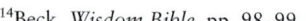

[14]Beck, *Wisdom Bible,* pp. 98–99.

"The sun rises externally as the life-breath,
for it helps the life-breath in the eye.
The goddess of the earth supports a person's out breath.
What is between, namely space, is the equalizing breath.
Air is the diffused breath.
Heat is the up-breath.
Therefore one whose heat has ceased goes to rebirth
with the senses sunk in the mind.

"Whatever is one's consciousness,
with that one enters into the life-breath.
The life-breath joined to the heat together with the soul
lead to whatever world has been imagined.
The wise who know the life-breath thus
do not lose their offspring and become immortal.
As to this there is this verse:
The source, its coming, its staying,
its fivefold division,
and the relation of the soul to the life-breath—
by knowing these one enjoys immortality.
By knowing these one enjoys immortality."

The following selections taken respectively from the *Sama-Vedas,* the *Katha* and *Svetasvatar Upanishads,* and the *Bhagavad Gita* provide insights into Hindu understandings of human nature. According to these passages, are humans essentially divine, demonic, or both? What hope do the texts offer for this human predicament?

Descriptions of Human Nature from the Samaveda Samhita[15]

54 O Lord of Spiritual Knowledge! The devotees have installed Thee in their hearts for the welfare of all—They having elevated their selves and acquired strength and fitness offer salutation to Thee. I am an humble and weak mortal and Thou art the Great, Omnipotent Immortal Principle of Truth. What a gulf of difference! Still I pray that Thou, though so lofty and high, mayest be pleased to condescend to grow in the holiness of my heart by Thy sheer mercy and not by my fitness, to be illumined in my humble heart despite unfitness, and inherent weakness.

From the Katha Upanishad[16]

2   "The good is one thing, and the pleasant quite another.
Both of these with different purposes bind a person.
Of these two, well is it for the one who takes the good;

---

failure of aim is it for the one who chooses the pleasant.
The good and the pleasant come to a person.
The thoughtful mind looking all around them
    discriminates.
The wise chooses the good in preference to the pleasant.
The fool out of getting and having prefers the pleasant.
You, Nachiketas, having examined desires that are
    pleasant
and that seem to be pleasing, have rejected them.
You have not taken that chain of wealth
in which many mortals sink down."

From the Shvetasvatar Upanishad, *Part 5*[17]

5   In the imperishable, infinite, supreme God
two things are hidden: knowledge and ignorance.
Ignorance dies, but knowledge is immortal.

That which is master of both is something else,
the one who rules over every source of creation,
all forms and all sources,
who holds in thought and sees when born
that red seer who was born at the beginning.

That God spreads out every net diversely
and draws it together in this field.
Thus having created the exercisers,
the Lord, the great soul, exercises universal
    sovereignty.

As the radiant sun shines upon all regions above,
    below, and across,
so does this glorious one God of love
rule over whatever creatures are born from a womb.

The source of all who develops its own nature,
who brings to maturity whatever can be ripened,
that one distributes all qualities and rules over this
    whole world.

What is hidden in the secret of the Vedas,
that is, in the Upanishads—
God knows that as the source of the sacred.
The gods and ancient seers who knew that
have become by its nature immortal.

Whoever has qualities performs works that bring
    results;
of such actions one experiences the consequences.
Undergoing all forms, characterized by the three
    qualities,
walking the three paths, the ruler of the vital breaths
wanders around according to one's actions.

---

[15]*Samaveda Samhita,* translated by Bibhor Kumar Lahiri (Calcutta: Firma K. L. Mukhopadhyay, 1963), p. 22.

[16]Beck, *Wisdom Bible,* p. 73.

[17]Beck, *Wisdom Bible,* pp. 111–112.

It is the size of a thumb, bright as the sun,
when coupled with conception and ego.
But with only the qualities of understanding and soul,
it appears the size of the point of an awl.
This life is the hundredth part
of the point of a hair divided a hundred times,
and yet in it is infinity.

Not female nor male nor is it neuter.
Whatever body it takes to itself, with that it is
connected.
By the delusions of imagination, touch, and sight,
and by eating, drinking, and impregnating
there is birth and development of the soul.

According to its actions the embodied one
successively assumes forms in various conditions.
Gross or refined, the embodied one chooses many forms
according to its own qualities.
Subsequently the cause of its union with them can be
seen
because of the quality of its actions and of itself.

The one who is without beginning and without end,
in the middle of confusion, the creator of all,
of diverse form, is the one embracer of the universe.
By knowing the divine, one is released from all
restriction.
The incorporeal is to be apprehended by the heart,
the master of existence and non-existence, the kind one,
the divine maker of all creation and its parts.
Those who know this, leave the body behind.

DIVINE AND DEMONIC QUALITIES FROM THE *BHAGAVAD GITA*[18]

Chapter 16

1. The Supreme Lord said: Fearlessness, purity of heart, perseverance in the yoga of knowledge, charity, sense restraint, sacrifice, study of the scriptures, austerity, honesty;
2. Nonviolence, truthfulness, absence of anger, renunciation, equanimity, abstaining from malicious talk, compassion for all creatures, freedom from greed, gentleness, modesty, absence of fickleness;
3. Splendor, forgiveness, fortitude, cleanliness, absence of malice, and absence of pride; these are the qualities of those endowed with divine virtues, O Arjuna.
4. Hypocrisy, arrogance, pride, anger, harshness, and ignorance; these are the marks of those who are born with demonic qualities, O Arjuna.

---

[18]All the passages in this volume from *Bhagavad Gita,* translated by Ramanand Prasad, (Fremont, CA: American Gita Society, 1988).

5. Divine qualities lead to nirvana, the demonic (qualities) are said to be for bondage. Do not grieve, O Arjuna, you are born with divine qualities.
6. There are two types of human beings in this world: the divine, and the demonic. The divine has been described at length, now hear from Me about the demonic, O Arjuna.
7. Persons of demonic nature do not know what to do and what not to do. They neither have purity nor good conduct nor truthfulness.
8. They say that the world is unreal, without a substratum, without a God, and without an order. The world is caused by lust (or Kaama) alone and nothing else.
9. Adhering to this view these lost souls, with small intellect and cruel deeds, are born as enemies for the destruction of the world.
10. Filled with insatiable desires, hypocrisy, pride, and arrogance; holding wrong views due to delusion; they act with impure motives.
11. Obsessed with great anxiety until death, considering sense gratification as their highest aim, convinced that this (sense pleasure) is everything,
12. Bound by hundreds of ties of desire and enslaved by lust and anger; they strive to obtain wealth by unlawful means for the fulfillment of desires. They think:
13. This has been gained by me today, I shall fulfill this desire, this is mine and this wealth also shall be mine in the future;
14. That enemy has been slain by me, and I shall slay others also. I am the Lord. I am the enjoyer. I am successful, powerful, and happy;
15. I am rich and born in a noble family. I am the greatest. I shall perform sacrifice, I shall give charity, and I shall rejoice. Thus deluded by ignorance;
16. Bewildered by many fancies; entangled in the net of delusion; addicted to the enjoyment of sensual pleasures; they fall into a foul hell.
17. Self-conceited, stubborn, filled with pride and intoxication of wealth; they perform Yajna only in name, for show, and not according to scriptural injunction.
18. Clinging to egoism, power, arrogance, lust, and anger; these malicious people hate Me (who dwells) in their own body and others' bodies.
19. I hurl these haters, cruel, sinful, and mean people of the world, into the wombs of demons again and again.
20. O Arjuna, entering the wombs of demons birth after birth, the deluded ones sink to the lowest hell without ever attaining Me.

SECTION 3: Sacred Stories: Divine Messengers, Prophets, and Priests

Although Hinduism, unlike most of the other great religions, does not have a human founder, its sacred writings include a wealth of stories of heroic and divine figures that came to the earth to provide insights into the nature of ultimate reality. Two of the greatest epics from the ancient world are found within the Hindu sacred canon. The *Ramayana,* the shorter of the epics, is a tragic love story of Prince Rama, an incarnation of the god Vishnu, and his beloved and ever-faithful wife Sita. This virtuous couple along with Hanuman, the monkey friend of Rama who helps retrieve Sita from an evil demon, remains the object of worship for millions of modern day Hindus. The second great epic, the *Mahabharata,* is a 100,000-stanza tale about a family feud between the Pandavas and the Kauravas. Inserted within this story is the single most influential text within Hinduism, the *Bhagavad Gita* (Song of the Lord). This poem is written as a dialogue between a Pandava warrior named Arjuna, and the driver of his chariot, the Blessed Lord Krishna. In the poem, Krishna reveals himself as an avatar or incarnation of the god Vishnu.

The opening selections are taken from the *Bhagavad Gita.* According to these texts, who is Lord Krishna, and what is his essential teaching? Why do you think millions view this poem as the most cherished book in the Hindu canon?

Selections from the *Bhagavad Gita*

Chapter 1

28. Arjuna was overcome with great compassion and sorrowfully said: O Krishna, seeing my kinsmen standing with a desire to fight,

29. My limbs fail and my mouth becomes dry. My body quivers and my hairs stand on end.

30–31. The bow, Gaandeeva, slips from my hand and my skin intensely burns. My head turns, I am unable to stand steady and, O Krishna, I see bad omens. I see no use of killing my kinsmen in battle.

32. I desire neither victory nor pleasure nor kingdom, O Krishna. What is the use of the kingdom, or enjoyment, or even life, O Krishna?

33. Because all those, for whom we desire kingdom, enjoyments, and pleasures, are standing here for the battle, giving up their lives and wealth.

34. Teachers, uncles, sons, grandfathers, maternal uncles, fathers-in-law, grandsons, brothers-in-law, and other relatives.

35. I do not wish to kill them, who are also about to kill, even for the sovereignty of the three worlds, let alone for this earthly kingdom, O Krishna.

36. O Lord Krishna, what pleasure shall we find in killing the sons of Dhritaraashtra? Upon killing these felons we shall incur sin only.

37. Therefore, we should not kill our brothers, the sons of Dhritaraashtra. How can we be happy after killing our kinsmen, O Krishna?

38. Though they, blinded by greed, do not see evil in the destruction of the family, or sin in being treacherous to friends.

39. Why shouldn't we, who clearly see evil in the destruction of the family, think about turning away from this sin, O Krishna?

40. With the destruction of the family, the eternal family traditions are destroyed, and immorality prevails due to the destruction of family traditions.

41. And when immorality prevails, O Krishna, the women of the family become corrupted; when women are corrupted, social problems arise.

42. This brings the family and the slayers of the family to hell, because the spirits of their ancestors are degraded when deprived of ceremonial offerings of rice-ball and water.

43. The everlasting qualities of Varna and family traditions of those who destroy their family are ruined by the sinful act of illegitimacy.

44. We have been told, O Krishna, that people whose family traditions are destroyed necessarily dwell in hell for a long time.

45. Alas! We are ready to commit a great sin by striving to slay our kinsmen because of greed for the pleasures of the kingdom.

46. It would be far better for me if the sons of Dhritaraashtra should kill me with their weapons in battle while I am unarmed and unresisting.

47. Sanjaya said: Having said this in the battle field and casting aside his bow and arrow, Arjuna sat down on the seat of the chariot with his mind overwhelmed with sorrow.

Chapter 2: Transcendental Knowledge

1. Sanjaya said: Lord spoke these words to Arjuna whose eyes were tearful and downcast, and who was overwhelmed with compassion and despair.

2. The Supreme Lord said: How has the dejection come to you at this juncture? This is not fit for an Aryan (or the people of noble mind and deeds). It is disgraceful, and it does not lead one to heaven, O Arjuna.

3. Do not become a coward, O Arjuna, because it does not befit you. Shake off this weakness of your heart and get up (for the battle), O Arjuna.

4. Arjuna said: How shall I strike Bheeshma and Drona, who are worthy of my worship, with arrows in battle, O Krishna?

5. It would be better, indeed, to live on alms in this world than to slay these noble gurus, because by killing them I would enjoy wealth and pleasures stained with (theirs) blood.

6. Neither do we know which alternative (to beg or to kill) is better for us, nor do we know whether we shall conquer them or they will conquer us. We should not even wish to live after killing the sons of Dhritaraashtra who are standing in front of us.

7. My heart is overcome by the weakness of pity, and my mind is confused about Dharma. I request You to tell me, decisively, what is better for me. I am Your disciple. Teach me who has taken refuge in You.

11. The Supreme Lord said: You grieve for those who are not worthy of grief, and yet speak the words of wisdom. The wise grieve neither for the living nor for the dead.

12. There was never a time when I, you, or these kings did not exist; nor shall we ever cease to exist in the future.

13. Just as the Atma acquires a childhood body, a youth body, and an old age body during this life, similarly Atma acquires another body after death. The wise are not deluded by this.

14. (Atma or Atman means consciousness, spirit, soul, self, the source of life and the cosmic power behind the body-mind complex. Just as our body exists in space, similarly our thoughts, intellect, emotions, and psyche exist in Atma, the space of consciousness. Atma cannot be perceived by the senses, because, the senses abide in Atma.) The contacts of the senses with the sense objects give rise to the feelings of heat and cold, and pain and pleasure. They are transitory and impermanent. Therefore, (learn to) endure them, O Arjuna.

15. Because the calm person, who is not afflicted by these feelings and is steady in pain and pleasure, becomes fit for immortality, O Arjuna.

16. There is no nonexistence of the Sat (or Atma) and no existence of the Asat. The reality of these two is indeed certainly seen by the seers of truth. (Sat exists at all times—past, present, and future.) Atma is called Sat. Asat is a notion that does not exist at all (like the horn of a rabbit, or the water in a mirage). The one that has a beginning and an end is neither Sat nor Asat. The body is neither Sat nor Asat, or both Sat and Asat, because, it has a temporary existence. Mithya is the one that appears Sat at first sight, but is really Asat. Body, like the universe or Jagat, is called Mithya.)

17. Know That, by which all this (universe) is pervaded, to be indestructible. No one can destroy the indestructible (Atma).

18. Bodies of the eternal, imperishable, and incomprehensible soul are said to be perishable. Therefore, fight, O Arjuna.

19. The one who thinks that Atma is a slayer, and the one who thinks that Atma is slain, both are ignorant, because Atma neither slays nor is slain.

20. The Atma is neither born nor does it die at any time, nor having been it will cease to exist again. It is unborn, eternal, permanent, and primeval. The Atma is not destroyed when the body is destroyed.

21. O Arjuna, how can a person who knows that the Atma is indestructible, eternal, unborn, and imperishable, kill anyone or cause anyone to be killed?

22. Just as a person puts on new garments after discarding the old ones, similarly Atma acquires new bodies after casting away the old bodies.

23. Weapons do not cut this Atma, fire does not burn it, water does not make it wet, and the wind does not make it dry.

24. This Atma cannot be cut, burned, wetted, or dried up. It is eternal, all pervading, unchanging, immovable, and primeval.

25. The Atma is said to be unmanifest, unthinkable, and unchanging. Knowing this Atma as such you should not grieve.

26. If you think that this (body) takes birth and dies perpetually, even then, O Arjuna, you should not grieve like this.

27. Because, death is certain for the one who is born, and birth is certain for the one who dies. Therefore, you should not lament over the inevitable.

30. O Arjuna, the Atma that dwells in the body of all (beings) is eternally indestructible. Therefore, you should not mourn for any body.

31. Considering also your duty as a warrior you should not waver. Because there is nothing more auspicious for a warrior than a righteous war.

32. Only the fortunate warriors, O Arjuna, get such an opportunity for an unsought war that is like an open door to heaven.

33. If you will not fight this righteous war, then you will fail in your duty, lose your reputation, and incur sin.

34. People will talk about your disgrace forever. To the honored, dishonor is worse than death.

35. The great warriors will think that you have retreated from the battle out of fear. Those who have greatly esteemed you will lose respect for you.

36. Your enemies will speak many unmentionable words and scorn your ability. What could be more painful than this?

37. You will go to heaven if killed, or you will enjoy the earth if victorious. Therefore, get up with a determination to fight, O Arjuna. Treating pleasure and pain, gain and loss, victory and defeat alike, engage yourself in your duty. By doing your duty this way you will not incur sin.

Chapter 7: Self-Knowledge and Self-Realisation

1. The Supreme Lord said: O Arjuna, listen how you shall know Me completely without any doubt, with your mind absorbed in Me, taking refuge in Me, and performing yogic practices.

2. I shall fully explain to you the Self-knowledge together with Self-realization after knowing that nothing more remains to be known in this world.

3. Scarcely one out of thousands of persons strives for perfection of Self-realization. Scarcely any one of the striving, or even the perfected persons, truly understands Me.

4. The mind, intellect, ego, ether, air, fire, water, and earth are the eight fold transformation of My Prakriti. (That which creates diversity, and all that can be seen or known is called Prakriti. Prakriti is also the material cause or the material out of which everything is made. Prakriti is the original source of the material world consisting of three Gunas, and eight basic elements out of which everything in this universe has evolved according to Saamkhya doctrine. Prakriti is also referred to as Asat, perishable, body, matter, nature, material nature, Maya, Mahat Brahma, field, creation, and manifest state.)

5. This Prakriti is My lower energy. My other higher energy is the Purusha by which this entire universe is sustained, O Arjuna. (Purusha is the consciousness that observes, witnesses, watches, and supervises Prakrti. It is the spiritual energy or the efficient cause of the universe. This is also referred to as Sat, imperishable, Atma, consciousness, spirit, self, soul, energy, field knower, creator, and the unmanifest state. Prakriti and Purusha are not two independent identities but the two aspects of Brahman, the Absolute Reality.)

6. Know that all creatures have evolved from this twofold energy, and Brahman is the origin as well as the dissolution of the entire universe.

7. O Arjuna, there is nothing higher than Brahman. Everything in the universe is strung on Brahman like jewels on the thread of a necklace.

8. O Arjuna, I am the sapidity in the water, I am the radiance in the sun and the moon, the sacred syllable OM in all the Vedas, the sound in the ether, and the manhood in men.

9. I am the sweet fragrance in the earth. I am the heat in the fire, the life in all living beings, and the austerity in the ascetics.

10. O Arjuna, know Me to be the eternal seed of all creatures. I am the intelligence of the intelligent, and the brilliance of the brilliant.

11. I am the strength, that is devoid of lust and attachment, of the strong. I am the lust (or Kaama) in human beings that is in accord with Dharma (for procreation), O Arjuna. . . .

25. Veiled by My divine Maya, I am not known by all. Therefore, the ignorant one does not know Me as the unborn and eternal Brahman.

26. I know, O Arjuna, the beings of the past, of the present, and those of the future, but no one really knows Me.

27. All beings in this world are in utter ignorance due to the delusion of dualities born of likes and dislikes, O Arjuna.

28. Persons of virtuous (or unselfish) deeds, whose Karma has come to an end, become free from the delusion of dualities and worship Me with firm resolve.

29. Those who strive for freedom from (the cycles of birth) old age and death by taking refuge in Me know Brahman, the individual self, and Karma in its entirety.

30. The steadfast persons, who know that Brahman is everything, the Adhibhoota, the Adhidaiva, and the Adhiyajna, remember Me even at the time of death (and attain Me).

Chapter 9: Supreme Knowledge and the Big Mystery

1. The Supreme Lord said: I shall reveal to you, who do not disbelieve, the most profound secret of Self-knowledge and Self-realization. Having known this you will be freed from the miseries of worldly existence.

2. This knowledge is the king of all knowledge, is the most secret, is very sacred, it can be perceived by instinct, conforms to Dharma, is very easy to practice, and is imperishable.

3. O Arjuna, those who have no faith in this knowledge follow the cycle of birth and death without attaining Me.

4. This entire universe is pervaded by Me, the unmanifest Brahman. All beings depend on (or remain in) Me (like a chain depends on gold). I do not depend on them. [From a Dvaitic or dualistic view point, waves depend on the ocean, the ocean does not depend on the waves. But, from a Advaitic or non-dualistic point of view, as stated in verse 9.05 below, the question of wave abiding in the ocean or the ocean abiding in the wave does not arise, because there is no wave or ocean. It is water only. Similarly, everything is a manifestation of Brahman only.]

5. And yet beings, in reality, do not remain in Me. Look at the power of My divine mystery. Though the sustainer and creator of all beings, I do not remain in them. (In reality, the chain does not depend on gold; the chain is nothing but gold. Also, matter and energy are different as well as non-different).

6. Consider that all beings remain in Me (without any contact or without producing any effect) as the mighty wind, moving everywhere, eternally remains in space.

7. All beings merge into My Prakriti at the end of a Kalpa (or a cycle of 4.32 billion years), O Arjuna, and I create (or manifest) them again at the beginning of the next Kalpa.

8. Using My Prakriti I create, again and again, the entire multitude of beings that are helpless, being under the control of (the Gunas of) Prakriti.

9. These acts of creation do not bind Me, O Arjuna, because I remain indifferent and unattached to those acts.

10. The Prakriti or nature, under My supervision, creates all animate and inanimate objects; and thus the creation keeps on going, O Arjuna.

11. The ignorant ones, not knowing My supreme natures as the great Lord of all beings, disregard Me when I assume human form.

12. The ignorant persons having false hopes, false actions, and false knowledge, possess the delusive (or Taamasika) qualities of fiends and demons.

13. But great souls, O Arjuna, who possess divine qualities know Me as the (material and efficient) cause of creation and imperishable, and worship Me single-mindedly.

14. Persons of firm resolve worship Me with ever steadfast devotion by always singing My glories, striving to attain Me, and prostrating before Me.

15. Some worship Me by knowledge sacrifice. Others worship the infinite as the one in all (or non-dual), as the master of all (or dual), and in various other ways.

16. I am the ritual, I am the Yajna, I am the offering, I am the herb, I am the mantra, I am the Ghee, I am the fire, and I am the oblation.

17. I am the supporter of the universe, the father, the mother, and the grandfather. I am the object of knowledge, the purifier, the sacred syllable OM, and also the Rig, the Yajur, and the Sama Vedas.

18. I am the goal, the supporter, the Lord, the witness, the abode, the refuge, the friend, the origin, the dissolution, the foundation, the substratum, and the imperishable seed.

19. I give heat, I send as well as withhold the rain, I am immortality as well as death, I am also both the Sat and the Asat, O Arjuna. (Brahman is everything)

20. The knowers of the three Vedas and the drinkers of the juice of Soma (or devotion), whose sins are cleansed, worship Me by Yajna for gaining heaven. As a result of their good Karma they go to heaven and enjoy celestial sense pleasures.

21. Having enjoyed the wide world of heavenly sense pleasures they return to the mortal world upon exhaustion of their good Karma (or Punya). Thus following the injunctions of three Vedas, the fruitive workers take repeated birth and death.

22. To those ever steadfast devotees, who always remember or worship Me with single-minded contemplation, I personally take responsibility for their welfare.

23. O Arjuna, even those devotees who worship demigods with faith, they too worship Me, but in an improper way.

24. Because I alone am the enjoyer of all Yajna, and the Lord. But, people do not know My true transcendental nature. Therefore, they fall (into the repeated cycles of birth and death).

25. Worshippers of the demigods go to the demigods, the worshippers of the ancestors go to the ancestors, and the worshippers of the ghosts go to the ghosts, but My devotees come to Me (and are not born again).

26. Whosoever offers Me a leaf, a flower, a fruit, or water with devotion; I accept and eat the offering of devotion by the pure-hearted.

27. O Arjuna, whatever you do, whatever you eat, whatever you offer as oblation to the sacred fire, whatever charity you give, whatever austerity you perform, do all that as an offering unto Me.

28. By this attitude of complete renunciation (or Samnyasa-yoga) you shall be freed from the bondage, good and bad, of Karma. You shall be liberated, and come to Me.

29. The Self is present equally in all beings. There is no one hateful or dear to Me. But, those who worship Me with devotion, they are with Me and I am also with them.

30. Even if the most sinful person resolves to worship Me with single-minded loving devotion, such a person must be regarded as a saint because of making the right resolution.

31. Such a person soon becomes righteous and attains everlasting peace. Be aware, O Arjuna, that My devotee never falls down.

32. Anybody, including women, merchants, laborers, and the evil-minded can attain the supreme goal by just surrendering unto My will (with loving devotion), O Arjuna.

Chapter 11: The Transfiguration

1. Arjuna said: My illusion is dispelled by Your profound words, that You spoke out of compassion towards me, about the supreme secret of the Self.

2. O Krishna, I have heard from You in detail about the origin and dissolution of beings, and Your imperishable glory.

3. O Lord, You are as You have said, yet I wish to see Your divine cosmic form, O Supreme Being.

4. O Lord, if You think it is possible for me to see this, then O Lord of the yogis, show me Your imperishable Self.

5. The Supreme Lord said: O Arjuna, behold My hundreds and thousands of multifarious divine forms of different colors and shapes.

6. See the Adityas, the Vasus, the Rudras, the Ashvins, and the Maruts. Behold, O Arjuna, many wonders never seen before.

7. O Arjuna, now behold the entire creation; animate, inanimate, and whatever else you like to see; all at one place in My body.

8. But, you are not able to see Me with your physical eye; therefore, I give you the divine eye to see My majestic power and glory.

9. Sanjaya said: O King, having said this; Lord Krishna, the great Lord of (the mystic power of) yoga, revealed His supreme majestic form to Arjuna.

10. (Arjuna saw the Universal Form of the Lord) with many mouths and eyes, and many visions of marvel, with numerous divine ornaments, and holding divine weapons.

11. Wearing divine garlands and apparel, anointed with celestial perfumes and ointments, full of all wonders, the limitless God with faces on all sides.

12. If the splendor of thousands of suns were to blaze forth all at once in the sky, even that would not resemble the splendor of that exalted being.

13. Arjuna saw the entire universe, divided in many ways, but standing as (all in) One (and One in all) in the body of Krishna, the God of gods.

14. Then Arjuna, filled with wonder and his hairs standing on end, bowed his head to the Lord and prayed with folded hands.

15. Arjuna said: O Lord, I see in Your body all the gods and multitude of beings, all sages, celestial serpents, Lord Shiva as well as Lord Brahmaa seated on the lotus.

16. O Lord of the universe, I see You everywhere with infinite form, with many arms, stomachs, faces, and eyes. Neither do I see the beginning nor the middle nor the end of Your Universal Form.

17. I see You with Your crown, club, discus; and a mass of radiance, difficult to behold, shining all around with immeasurable brilliance of the sun and the blazing fire.

18. I believe You are the imperishable, the Supreme to be realized. You are the ultimate resort of the universe. You are the protector of eternal Dharma, and the imperishable primal spirit.

19. I see You with infinite power, without beginning, middle, or end; with many arms, with the sun and the moon as Your eyes, with Your mouth as a blazing fire whose radiance is scorching all the universe.

Chapter 18: The Final Appeal and Conclusion

64. Hear again My supreme word, the most secret of all. You are very dear to Me, therefore, I shall tell this for your benefit.

65. Fix your mind on Me, be devoted to Me, offer service to Me, bow down to Me, and you shall certainly reach Me. I promise you because you are very dear to Me.

66. Setting aside all noble deeds, just surrender completely to the will of God (with firm faith and loving contemplation). I shall liberate you from all sins (or bonds of Karma). Do not grieve.

67. This (knowledge) should never be spoken by you to one who is devoid of austerity, who is without devotion, who does not desire to listen, or who speaks ill of Me.

68. The one who shall propagate this supreme secret philosophy (or the transcendental knowledge of the Gita) amongst My devotees, shall be performing the highest devotional service to Me and shall certainly attain (or come to) Me.

69. No other person shall do a more pleasing service to Me, and no one on the earth shall be more dear to Me.

70. I shall be worshipped with Jnana-Yajna (or knowledge sacrifice) by those who shall study this sacred dialogue of ours. This is My promise.

71. Whoever hears this with faith and without cavil becomes free from sin, and attains heaven (or the higher regions for those whose actions are pure).

72. O Arjuna, did you listen to this with single-minded attention? Has your delusion born of ignorance been destroyed?

73. Arjuna said: By Your grace my delusion is destroyed, I have gained knowledge, my confusion (with regard to body and Atma) is dispelled and I shall obey Your command.

74. Sanjaya said: Thus I heard this wonderful dialogue between Lord and Mahatma Arjuna, causing my hair to stand on end.

75. By the grace of (guru) sage Vyaasa, I heard this most secret and supreme yoga directly from Krishna, the lord of yoga, Himself speaking before my very eyes.

76. O King, by repeated remembrance of this marvelous and sacred dialogue between Lord and Arjuna, I am thrilled at every moment; and

77. Recollecting again and again, O King, that marvelous form of I am greatly amazed and I rejoice over and over again.

78. Wherever is Krishna, the lord of yoga; and wherever is Arjuna, the archer; there will be everlasting prosperity, victory, happiness, and morality. This is my conviction.

The following selections are taken from the great epic, the *Ramayana*, and from the *Srimad Bhagavatam*, one of the best-known *Puranas*. Note the depictions of Rama and Krishna, two avatars of Vishnu. How is each of these avatars portrayed in these stories? In what ways does this portrayal of Krishna differ from the image of Lord Krishna revealed in the *Bhagavad Gita*? What theology is expressed in these accounts?

THE VIRTUES OF RAMA FROM THE *SRIMAD RAMAYANA*[19]

Chapter One, Ayodhya Kanda

Rama, like Brahma among all the living beings, was the most virtuous among those brothers and the mightiest and was a great source of joy for his father. That Rama—was He not the eternal Vishnu who was born on earth after being prayed by celestials to kill the egoistic Ravana? Like Adithi by Indra, best among the celestials, Kausalya shone by her son Rama, the mighty. Rama was beautiful in form, a hero of valour without envy.

By virtues, he was like Dasaratha. In this way, he was an incomparable son on earth. Rama was forever peaceful in mind and spoke softly. He did not react to hard words spoken by others. Rama, because of his good bent of mind, feels glad even by a small good deed done to him. He does not remember any number of bad things done to him. Whenever he finds some time even while practicing archery, Rama conversed with elderly people, elder by way of conduct or wisdom or age or with good natured people. Rama was a wise man. He spoke sweetly. He was the first man to initiate a talk. His speech was compassionate. He was valorous. But he was not arrogant of his mighty valour. He did not speak untruth. He was all-knowing. He used to be receptive and worshipful to elders. People love him and he loved the people. He had compassion. He conquered anger. He was receptive and worshipful to the wise. He had mercy towards the meek. He always knew the task at hand. He was self controlled. He was clean (in conduct). That Rama, having an attitude suitable for his social rank, giving due respect to his kshatriya righteousness, believed that by following the righteousness he would attain great fame and through it the fruit of heaven.

Rama was not interested in actions which were not beneficial. He was a great scholar. He had no taste in tales opposing righteousness. Like Vachaspathi, his eloquent speech contained a series of strategies for action. Rama was a young man without any disease. He was a good speaker. He had a good body. He knew both time and place. He could grasp

[19]*Srimad Ramayana,* translated by Sri Desiraju Hanumanta Rao and Sri M. L. Murthy. Available at www.valmikiramayan.net/ayodhya.

the essence of men. He was the one gentleman born on earth. People loved the virtuous prince Rama and treated him as their spirit moving outside. After completing his education properly, and after knowing the science of archery as prescribed, Rama was better than his father in the use of bow and arrows. Rama, having born in a good clan, was gentle minded. He was not feeble. He spoke truth. He was straightforward. He was properly trained by elderly wise men who knew righteousness. Rama knew the real form of desire, wealth and righteousness. He had a good memory power. He had a spontaneous wisdom. He had skills in arranging customs useful to society prevalent at that time.

Rama was humble. He did not let his feelings appear outwardly. He kept his thoughts to himself. He helped others. His anger and pleasure were not wasteful. He knew when to give and when not to give. Rama had a deep devotion. He had a steadfast mind. He was not stubborn. He did not speak evil words. He shunned idleness and was alert. He could recognise his own errors and those of others. Rama knew the theory and practice of sciences. He understood the differences among men. He could judiciously discriminate whom to protect and whom to punish. Rama was receptive to good people and protected them. He could identify the people to be reprimanded. He knew the ways and means to earn income. He knew the system of spending as enunciated in sciences. Rama could obtain great skill in the groups of sciences along with their subsidiaries. He was interested in enjoying comforts only after understanding the economic realities. He was not an idle man. Rama was acquainted with the fine arts useful for entertainment. He knew how to distribute the wealth. He was efficient in riding and taming of elephants and horses.

Rama was the best of persons knowing the science of archery in the world; and was well appreciated by the champions of archery. He attained skills in marshalling the army. He faced and killed the enemies in battle. Even enraged devas and rakshasas cannot defeat Rama in battle. He had no jealousy. He conquered anger. He had no arrogance and envy. He had not humiliated any living being. He had not surrendered to time. That Prince Rama, with these good virtues, was fair to the people. He was agreeable to the three worlds. By patience and the related virtues, he was equal to Earth, by wisdom to Bruhaspathi and by valour to Devendra.

Rama, by his virtues, was a source of happiness to all people and a spring of joy to his father. As the sun shines with his rays, Rama was shining, thus, with his virtues. The earth wished Rama to be her Lord as he was adorned with self control and norms of behavior, bearing undefeatable valour equal to the universal lords like Indra. Dasaratha, who annihilates enemies, started thinking as follows after observing his son with his many incomparable virtues. The long living and aged Dasaratha thought: "Will Rama become king while I am still alive? Shall I enjoy that happiness?" A great loving thought was ringing in his mind that when he would be able to see his beloved son Rama coronated as king, "Is not Rama, as a raining cloud to the earth, better liked by people than me as he desires the development of the world and has equal compassion towards all living beings. Rama is equal to Yama and Devendra in valour, to Bruhaspati in wisdom and to a mountain in courage. He is more virtuous than me. Shall I attain heaven, after seeing in this age, my son ruling the entire earth?" Rama had many other virtues beyond hitherto stated virtues not to be seen in other kings. His virtues cannot be counted and they are the best in the world.

THE CHILDHOOD OF RAMA AND KRISHNA FROM THE *BHAGAVATA PURANA*[20]

After a little while, Rama and Krishna began to play in the village, crawling on their hands and knees. They slithered about quickly, dragging their feet in the muddy pastures, delighting in the tinkling sound. They would follow someone and then, suddenly bewildered and frightened, they would hasten back to their mothers. Their mothers' breasts would flow with milk out of tenderness for their own sons, whose bodies were beautifully covered with mud, and they would embrace them in their arms and give them their breasts to stick, and as they gazed at the faces with their innocent smiles and tiny teeth they would rejoice. Then the children began to play in the village at those boyish games that women love to see. They would grab hold of the tails of calves and be dragged back and forth in the pastures and the women would look at them and forget their housework and laugh merrily. But the mothers, trying to keep the two very

---

[20]*Hindu Myths*, translated by Wendy Donigar O'Flaherty (New York: Penguin, 1975).

active and playful little boys from horned animals, fire, animals with teeth and tusks, and knives, water, birds, and thorns, were unable to do their housework, and they were rather uneasy.

After a little while, Rama and Krishna stopped crawling, on their hands and knees and began to walk about the pastures quickly on their feet. Then the lord began to play with Rama and with the village boys of their age, giving great pleasure to the village women. When the wives of the cowherds saw the charming boyish pranks of Krishna, they would go in a group to tell his mother, saying, "unties the calves when it is not the proper time, and lie laughs at everyone's angry shouts. He devises ways to steal and eat curds and milk and thinks food sweet only if lie steals it. He distributes the food among the monkeys; if lie doesn't eat the food, he breaks the pot. If he cannot find anything, he becomes angry at the house and makes the children cry before lie runs away. If something is beyond his reach, he fashions some expedient by piling up pillows, mortars, and so on; or if lie knows that the milk and curds have been placed in pots suspended in netting, he makes holes in the pots. When the wives of the cowherds are busy with household duties, he will steal things in a dark room, making his own body with its masses of jewels serve as a lamp. This is the sort of impudent act which he commits; and he pees and so forth in clean houses. These are the thieving tricks that he contrives, but he behaves in the opposite way and is good when you are near." When his mother heard this report from the women who were looking at Krishna's frightened eyes and beautiful face, she laughed and did not wish to scold him.

One day when Rama and the other little sons of the cowherds were playing, they reported to his mother, "has eaten dirt." Yasoda took by the hand and scolded him, for his own good, and she said to him, seeing that his eyes were bewildered with fear, "Naughty boy, why have you secretly eaten dirt? These boys, your friends, and your elder brother say so." He said, "Mother, I have not eaten. They are all lying. If you think they speak the truth, look at my mouth yourself." "If that is the case, then open your mouth," she said to the lord Hari [Vishnu], the god of unchallenged sovereignty who had in sport taken the form of a human child, and he opened his mouth.

She then saw in his mouth the whole eternal universe, and heaven, and the regions of the sky, and the orb of the earth with its mountains, islands, and oceans; she saw the wind, and lightning, and the moon and stars, and the zodiac; and water and fire and air and space itself; she saw the vacillating senses, the mind, the elements, and the three strands of matter. She saw within the body of her son, in his gaping mouth, the whole universe in all its variety, with all the forms of life and time and nature and action and hopes, and her own village, and herself. Then she became afraid and confused, thinking, "Is this a dream or an illusion wrought by a god? Or is it a delusion of my own perception? Or is it some portent of the natural powers of this little boy, my son? I bow down to the feet of the god, whose nature cannot be imagined or grasped by mind, heart, acts, of speech; he in whom all of this universe is inherent, impossible to fathom. The god is my refuge, he through whose power of delusion there arise in me such false beliefs as "I," "This is my husband," "This is my son," "I am the wife of the village chieftain and all his wealth is mine, including these cowherds and their wives and their wealth of cattle."

When the cowherd's wife had come to understand the true essence in this way, the lord spread his magic illusion in the form of maternal affection. Instantly the cowherd's wife lost her memory of what had occurred and took her son on her lap. She was as she had been before, her heart flooded with even greater love. She considered Hari [Vishnu]—whose greatness is extolled by the three Vedas and the *Upanisads* and the philosophies of Sankhya and yoga and all the *Satvata* texts—she considered him to be her son.

SECTION 4: Divine Law: Justice, Reward, and Punishment

Many modern men and women accept the premise that it is possible to do wrong—occasionally or even habitually—and never face the consequences of these improper actions. The idea that there is no connection between act and consequence would have seemed very foreign to the peoples of the ancient world, especially to those who ascribed to the teachings of the Hindu sacred texts. The early Vedas taught a doctrine of order and reciprocity. When humans did their duty, such as chanting hymns and offering sacrifices, the gods performed their tasks and the universal order was upheld. If the goal was not realized, it was because of failed ritual or the work of demons that subsequently could be driven away by the gods when other appropriate rituals were performed. The order and justice of the universe was confirmed in the doctrines of *samsara*

(reincarnation) and *karma*. According to the law of *karma*, every action affects your future destiny, either in this life or in a future existence. Conversely, your present circumstance is a direct result of actions taken in previous lives. No one escapes the consequences of his or her actions.

While the sacred texts of most traditions provide ethical norms and detail rewards and punishments for those who follow or disregard these laws, the rules of conduct within Hinduism often vary according to one's station in life. A proper activity for someone in one caste is not necessarily proper for someone born in a different caste. The following selections from the *Law of Manu* explain the cosmic origins of the four castes and enumerate codes of conduct for men and women of various stations in life. What logic underlies these various prescriptions? How would a devotee of Manu justify these regulations?

CODES OF CONDUCT FROM THE *LAW OF MANU*[21]

Chapter 4

124. The Rig-veda is declared to be sacred to the gods, the Yagur-veda sacred to men, and the Sama-veda sacred to the manes; hence the sound of the latter is impure (as it were).

125. Knowing this, the learned daily repeat first in due order the essence of the three (Vedas) and afterwards the (text of) the Veda.

126. Know that (the Veda-study must be) interrupted for a day and a night, when cattle, a frog, a cat, a dog, a snake, an ichneumon, or a rat pass between (the teacher and his pupil).

127. Let a twice-born man always carefully interrupt the Veda-study on two (occasions, viz.) when the place where he recites is impure, and when he himself is unpurified. . . .

142. A Brahmana who is impure must not touch with his hand a cow, a Brahmana, or fire; nor, being in good health, let him look at the luminaries in the sky, while he is impure.

143. If he has touched these, while impure, let him always sprinkle with his hand water on the organs of sensation, all his limbs, and the navel.

144. Except when sick he must not touch the cavities (of the body) without a reason, and he must avoid (to touch) the hair on the secret (parts).

145. Let him eagerly follow the (customs which are) auspicious and the rule of good conduct, be careful of purity, and control all his organs, let him mutter (prayers) and, untired, daily offer oblations in the fire.

146. No calamity happens to those who eagerly follow auspicious customs and the rule of good conduct, to those who

are always careful of purity, and to those who mutter (sacred texts) and offer burnt-oblations.

147. Let him, without tiring, daily mutter the Veda at the proper time; for they declare that to be one's highest duty; (all) other (observances) are called secondary duties.

148. By daily reciting the Veda, by (the observance of the rules of) purification, by (practicing) austerities, and by doing no injury to created beings, one (obtains the faculty of) remembering former births.

149. He who, recollecting his former existences, again recites the Veda, gains endless bliss by the continual study of the Veda.

Proper Conduct and the Consequences of Misconduct from the Law of Manu

155. Let him, untired, follow the conduct of virtuous men, connected with his occupations, which has been fully declared in the revealed texts and in the sacred tradition (Smriti) and is the root of the sacred law.

156. Through virtuous conduct he obtains long life, through virtuous conduct desirable offspring, through virtuous conduct imperishable wealth; virtuous conduct destroys (the effect of) inauspicious marks.

157. For a man of bad conduct is blamed among people, constantly suffers misfortunes, is afflicted with diseases, and short-lived.

158. A man who follows the conduct of the virtuous, has faith and is free from envy, lives a hundred years, though he be entirely destitute of auspicious marks.

159. Let him carefully avoid all undertakings (the success of) which depends on others; but let him eagerly pursue that (the accomplishment of) which depends on himself.

160. Everything that depends on others (gives) pain, everything that depends on oneself (gives) pleasure; know that this is the short definition of pleasure and pain.

161. When the performance of an act gladdens his heart, let him perform it with diligence; but let him avoid the opposite.

162. Let him never offend the teacher who initiated him, nor him who explained the Veda, nor his father and mother, nor (any other) Guru, nor cows, nor Brahmanas, nor any men performing austerities.

163. Let him avoid atheism, caviling at the Vedas, contempt of the gods, hatred, want of modesty, pride, anger, and harshness.

164. Let him, when angry, not raise a stick against another man, nor strike (anybody) except a son or a pupil; those two he may beat in order to correct them.

INSTRUCTIONS TO KINGS ABOUT CRIMES AND PUNISHMENTS FROM THE *LAW OF MANU*

Chapter 9

270. A just king shall not cause a thief to be put to death, (unless taken) with the stolen goods (in his possession); him who (is taken) with the stolen goods and the implements (of burglary), he may, without hesitation, cause to be slain.

---

[21]All references are to *The Laws of Manu,* translated by George Buhler (Oxford: Clarendon Press, 1886).

warrior

271. All those also who in villages give food to thieves or grant them room for (concealing their implements), he shall cause to be put to death.

274. Those who do not give assistance according to their ability when a village is being plundered, a dike is being destroyed, or a highway robbery committed, shall be banished with their goods and chattels.

275. On those who rob the king's treasury and those who persevere in opposing (his commands), he shall inflict various kinds of capital punishment, likewise on those who conspire with his enemies.

276. But the king shall cut off the hands of those robbers who, breaking into houses, commit thefts at night, and cause them to be impaled on a pointed stake.

277. On the first conviction, let him cause two fingers of a cut-purse to be amputated; on the second, one hand and one foot; on the third, he shall suffer death.

278. Those who give (to thieves) fire, food, arms, or shelter, and receivers of stolen goods, the ruler shall punish like thieves.

279. Him who breaks (the dam of) a tank he shall slay (by drowning him) in water or by (some other) (mode of) capital punishment; or the offender may repair the (damage), but shall be made to pay the highest amercement.

280. Those who break into a (royal) storehouse, an armory, or a temple, and those who steal elephants, horses, or chariots, he shall slay without hesitation. . . .

284. All physicians who treat (their patients) wrongly (shall pay) a fine; in the case of animals, the first (or lowest); in the case of human beings, the middlemost (amercement). . . .

288. Let him [the king?] place all prisons near a high-road, where the suffering and disfigured offenders can be seen.

Castes Duties and Penalties from the Law of Manu

Chapter 10

Priest *duty*

74. Brahmanas who are intent on the means (of gaining union with) Brahman and firm in (discharging) their duties, shall live by duly performing the following six acts, (which are enumerated) in their (proper) order.

75. Teaching, studying, sacrificing for himself, sacrificing for others, making gifts and receiving them are the six acts (prescribed) for a Brahmana.

76. But among the six acts (ordained) for him three are his means of subsistence, (viz.) sacrificing for others, teaching, and accepting gifts from pure men.

77. (Passing) from the Brahmana to the Kshatriya, three acts (incumbent on the former) are forbidden, (viz.) teaching, sacrificing for others, and, thirdly, the acceptance of gifts.

78. The same are likewise forbidden to a Vaisya, that is a settled rule; for Manu, the lord of creatures (Pragapati), has not prescribed them for (men of) those two (castes).

warrior *Merchant Peasants*

79. To carry arms for striking and for throwing (is prescribed) for Kshatriyas as a means of subsistence; to trade, (to rear) cattle, and agriculture for Vaisyas; but their duties are liberality, the study of the Veda, and the performance of sacrifices.

80. Among the several occupations the most commendable are teaching the Veda for a Brahmana, protecting (the people) for a Kshatriya, and trade for a Vaisya. . . .

96. A man of low caste who through covetousness lives by the occupations of a higher one, the king shall deprive of his property and banish.

97. It is better (to discharge) one's own (appointed) duty incompletely than to perform completely that of another; for he who lives according to the law of another (caste) is instantly excluded from his own.

no moving from caste to caste

When sins are committed, penance is necessary to remove the consequences of the wrong actions. Next is a set of prescribed penitential actions for various offenses. What human values support these demands for penance?

Rewards, Punishments, and Penance from the Law of Manu

Chapter 11

48. Some wicked men suffer a change of their (natural) appearance in consequence of crimes committed in this life, and some in consequence of those committed in a former (existence).

49. He who steals the gold (of a Brahmana) has diseased nails; a drinker of (the spirituous liquor called) Sura, black teeth; the slayer of a Brahmana, consumption; the violator of a Guru's bed, a diseased skin;

50. An informer, a foul-smelling nose; a calumniator, a stinking breath; a stealer of grain, deficiency in limbs; he who adulterates (grain), redundant limbs;

51. A stealer of (cooked) food, dyspepsia; a stealer of the words (of the Veda), dumbness; a stealer of clothes, white leprosy; a horse-stealer, lameness.

52. The stealer of a lamp will become blind; he who extinguishes it will become one-eyed; injury (to sentient beings) is punished by general sickliness; an adulterer (will have) swellings (in his limbs).

53. Thus in consequence of a remnant of (the guilt of former) crimes, are born idiots, dumb, blind, deaf, and deformed men, who are (all) despised by the virtuous.

54. Penances, therefore, must always be performed for the sake of purification, because those whose sins have not been expiated, are born (again) with disgraceful marks.

55. Killing a Brahmana, drinking (the spirituous liquor called) Sura, stealing (the gold of a Brahmana), adultery with a Guru's wife, and associating with such (offenders), they declare (to be) mortal sins (mahapataka).

56. Falsely attributing to oneself high birth, giving information to the king (regarding a crime), and falsely accusing one's teacher, (are offenses) equal to slaying a Brahmana.

57. Forgetting the Veda, reviling the Vedas, giving false evidence, slaying a friend, eating forbidden food, or (swallowing substances) unfit for food, are six (offenses) equal to drinking Sura.

58. Stealing a deposit, or men, a horse, and silver, land, diamonds and (other) gems, is declared to be equal to stealing the gold (of a Brahmana).

59. Carnal intercourse with sisters by the same mother, with (unmarried) maidens, with females of the lowest castes, with the wives of a friend, or of a son, they declare to be equal to the violation of a Guru's bed.

60. Slaying kine, sacrificing for those who are unworthy to sacrifice, adultery, selling oneself, casting off one's teacher, mother, father, or son, giving up the (daily) study of the Veda, and neglecting the (sacred domestic) fire,

61. Allowing one's younger brother to marry first, marrying before one's elder brother, giving a daughter to, or sacrificing for, (either brother),

62. Defiling a damsel, usury, breaking a vow, selling a tank, a garden, one's wife, or child,

63. Living as a Vratya, casting off a relative, teaching (the Veda) for wages, learning (the Veda) from a paid teacher, and selling goods which one ought not to sell,

64. Superintending mines (or factories) of any sort, executing great mechanical works, injuring (living) plants, subsisting on (the earnings of) one's wife, sorcery (by means of sacrifices), and working (magic by means of) roots, (and so forth),

65. Cutting down green trees for firewood, doing acts for one's own advantage only, eating prohibited food,

66. Neglecting to kindle the sacred fires, theft, non-payment of (the three) debts, studying bad books, and practicing (the arts of) dancing and singing,

67. Stealing grain, base metals, or cattle, intercourse with women who drink spirituous liquor, slaying women, Sudras, Vaisyas, or Kshatriyas, and atheism, (are all) minor offenses, causing loss of caste (Upapataka).

68. Giving pain to a Brahmana (by a blow), smelling at things which ought not to be smelt at, or at spirituous liquor, cheating, and an unnatural offense with a man, are declared to cause the loss of caste (Gatibhramsa).

69. Killing a donkey, a horse, a camel, a deer, an elephant, a goat, a sheep, a fish, a snake, or a buffalo, must be known to degrade (the offender) to a mixed caste (Samkarikarana).

70. Accepting presents from blamed men, trading, serving Sudras, and speaking a falsehood, make (the offender) unworthy to receive gifts (Apatra).

71. Killing insects, small or large, or birds, eating anything kept close to spirituous liquors, stealing fruit, firewood, or flowers, (are offenses) which make impure (Malavaha).

SECTION 5: Gender: Women and Men in Society

A central idea within Hinduism is nonduality. In a nondualistic world, opposites are mere illusions; true reality is indivisible; ultimately everything (male/female; creature/creator; human/divine) is One. Multiple gods and divas may exist, and these gods may take masculine or feminine forms. Beyond these gods, however, is the One that cannot be described in words. This Absolute Reality is neither male nor female, but rather, a male–female transcendent quality.

Although it is possible to construct a gender-neutral social world from these theological premises, Hindu scriptures generally do not build upon these theological insights. Instead, the Hindu canon, like the sacred texts of many ancient religions, prescribes gender specific roles, and these roles almost always subordinate women to men. The following selections taken from the *Law of Manu* describe the duties of women and men in society, and the various disciplines imposed by men upon women in order to assure coherence to the expected norms. What do these rules and punishments tell us about the status of women in the ancient world? In what ways are they alike and different from the sacred texts of other ancient traditions?

RULES FOR MEN/RULES FOR WOMEN FROM THE *LAW OF MANU*

Chapter 3

1. The vow (of studying) the three Vedas under a teacher must be kept for thirty-six years, or for half that time, or for a quarter, or until the (student) has perfectly learnt them.

2. (A student) who has studied in due order the three Vedas, or two, or even one only, without breaking the (rules of) studentship, shall enter the order of householders.

3. He who is famous for (the strict performance of) his duties and has received his heritage, the Veda, from his father, shall be honored, sitting on a couch and adorned with a garland, with (the present of) a cow (and the honey-mixture).

4. Having bathed, with the permission of his teacher, and performed according to the rule the Samavartana (the rite on returning home), a twice-born man shall marry a wife of equal caste who is endowed with auspicious (bodily) marks.

5. A damsel who is neither a Sapinda on the mother's side, nor belongs to the same family on the father's side, is recommended to twice-born men for wedlock and conjugal union.

6. In connecting himself with a wife, let him carefully avoid the ten following families, be they ever so great, or rich in kine, horses, sheep, grain, or (other) property,

7. (Viz.) one which neglects the sacred rites, one in which no male children (are born), one in which the Veda is not studied, one (the members of) which have thick hair on the body, those which are subject to hemorrhoids, phthisis, weakness of digestion, epilepsy, or white or black leprosy.

8. Let him not marry a maiden (with) reddish (hair), nor one who has a redundant member, nor one who is sickly, nor one either with no hair (on the body) or too much, nor one who is garrulous or has red (eyes),

9. Nor one named after a constellation, a tree, or a river, nor one bearing the name of a low caste, or of a mountain, nor one named after a bird, a snake, or a slave, nor one whose name inspires terror.

10. Let him wed a female free from bodily defects, who has an agreeable name, the (graceful) gait of a Hamsa or of an elephant, a moderate (quantity of) hair on the body and on the head, small teeth, and soft limbs. . . .

15. Twice-born men who, in their folly, wed wives of the low (Sudra) caste, soon degrade their families and their children to the state of Sudras. . . .

17. A Brahmana who takes a Shudra wife to his bed, will (after death) sink into hell; if he begets a child by her, he will lose the rank of a Brahmana.

Chapter 8

352. Men who commit adultery with the wives of others, the king shall cause to be marked by punishments which cause terror, and afterwards banish.

353. For by (adultery) is caused a mixture of the castes (varna) among men; thence (follows) sin, which cuts up even the roots and causes the destruction of everything.

354. A man formerly accused of (such) offenses, who secretly converses with another man's wife, shall pay the first (or lowest) amercement.

355. But a man, not before accused, who (thus) speaks with (a woman) for some (reasonable) cause, shall not incur any guilt, since in him there is no transgression.

356. He who addresses the wife of another man at a Tirtha, outside the village, in a forest, or at the confluence of rivers, suffer (the punishment for) adulterous acts (samgrahana).

357. Offering presents (to a woman), romping (with her), touching her ornaments and dress, sitting with her on a bed, all (these acts) are considered adulterous acts (samgrahana).

358. If one touches a woman in a place (which ought) not (to be touched) or allows (oneself to be touched in such a spot), all (such acts done) with mutual consent are declared (to be) adulterous (samgrahana).

359. A man who is not a Brahmana ought to suffer death for adultery (samgrahana); for the wives of all the four castes even must always be carefully guarded.

360. Mendicants, bards, men who have performed the initiatory ceremony of a Vedic sacrifice, and artisans are not prohibited from speaking to married women.

361. Let no man converse with the wives of others after he has been forbidden (to do so); but he who converses (with them), in spite of a prohibition, shall be fined one suvarna.

362. This rule does not apply to the wives of actors and singers, nor (of) those who live on (the intrigues of) their own (wives); for such men send their wives (to others) or, concealing themselves, allow them to hold criminal intercourse.

363. Yet he who secretly converses with such women, or with female slaves kept by one (master), and with female ascetics, shall be compelled to pay a small fine.

364. He who violates an unwilling maiden shall instantly suffer corporal punishment; but a man who enjoys a willing maiden shall not suffer corporal punishment, if (his caste be) the same (as hers).

THE NATURE AND DUTIES OF WOMEN FROM THE *LAW OF MANU*

Chapter 2

213. It is the nature of women to seduce men in this (world); for that reason the wise are never unguarded in (the company of) females.

214. For women are able to lead astray in (this) world not only a fool, but even a learned man, and (to make) him a slave of desire and anger.

215. One should not sit in a lonely place with one's mother, sister, or daughter; for the senses are powerful, and master even a learned man.

Chapter 5

146. . . . Here now the duties of women.

147. By a girl, by a young woman, or even by an aged one, nothing must be done independently, even in her own house.

148. In childhood a female must be subject to her father, in youth to her husband, when her lord is dead to her sons; a woman must never be independent.

149. She must not seek to separate herself from her father, husband, or sons; by leaving them she would make both (her own and her husband's) families contemptible.

150. She must always be cheerful, clever in (the management of her) household affairs, careful in cleaning her utensils, and economical in expenditure.

151. Him to whom her father may give her, or her brother with the father's permission, she shall obey as long as he lives, and when he is dead, she must not insult (his memory).

152. For the sake of procuring good fortune to (brides), the recitation of benedictory texts (svastyayana), and the sacrifice to the Lord of creatures (Pragapati) are used at weddings; (but) the betrothal (by the father or guardian) is the cause of (the husband's) dominion (over his wife).

153. The husband who wedded her with sacred texts, always gives happiness to his wife, both in season and out of season, in this world and in the next.

154. Though destitute of virtue, or seeking pleasure (elsewhere), or devoid of good qualities, (yet) a husband must be constantly worshipped as a god by a faithful wife.

155. No sacrifice, no vow, no fast must be performed by women apart (from their husbands); if a wife obeys her husband, she will for that (reason alone) be exalted in heaven.

156. A faithful wife, who desires to dwell (after death) with her husband, must never do anything that might displease him who took her hand, whether he be alive or dead.

157. At her pleasure let her emaciate her body by (living on) pure flowers, roots, and fruit; but she must never even mention the name of another man after her husband has died.

158. Until death let her be patient (of hardships), self-controlled, and chaste, and strive (to fulfill) that most excellent duty which (is prescribed) for wives who have one husband only. . . .

163. She who cohabits with a man of higher caste, forsaking her own husband who belongs to a lower one, will become contemptible in this world, and is called a remarried woman (parapurva).

164. By violating her duty towards her husband, a wife is disgraced in this world, (after death) she enters the womb of a jackal, and is tormented by diseases (the punishment of) her sin.

165. She who, controlling her thoughts, words, and deeds, never slights her lord, resides (after death) with her husband (in heaven), and is called a virtuous (wife).

166. In reward of such conduct, a female who controls her thoughts, speech, and actions, gains in this (life) highest renown, and in the next (world) a place near her husband.

Chapter 9

1. I will now propound the eternal laws for a husband and his wife who keep to the path of duty, whether they be united or separated.

2. Day and night woman must be kept in dependence by the males (of) their (families), and, if they attach themselves to sensual enjoyments, they must be kept under one's control.

3. Her father protects (her) in childhood, her husband protects (her) in youth, and her sons protect (her) in old age; a woman is never fit for independence.

4. Reprehensible is the father who gives not (his daughter in marriage) at the proper time; reprehensible is the husband who approaches not (his wife in due season), and reprehensible is the son who does not protect his mother after her husband has died.

5. Women must particularly be guarded against evil inclinations, however trifling (they may appear); for, if they are not guarded, they will bring sorrow on two families.

6. Considering that the highest duty of all castes, even weak husbands (must) strive to guard their wives.

7. He who carefully guards his wife, preserves (the purity of) his offspring, virtuous conduct, his family, himself, and his (means of acquiring) merit.

8. The husband, after conception by his wife, becomes an embryo and is born again of her; for that is the wifehood of a wife (gaya), that he is born (gayate) again by her.

9. As the male is to whom a wife cleaves, even so is the son whom she brings forth; let him therefore carefully guard his wife, in order to keep his offspring pure.

10. No man can completely guard women by force; but they can be guarded by the employment of the (following) expedients:

11. Let the (husband) employ his (wife) in the collection and expenditure of his wealth, in keeping (everything) clean, in (the fulfillment of) religious duties, in the preparation of his food, and in looking after the household utensils.

12. Women, confined in the house under trustworthy and obedient servants, are not (well) guarded; but those who of their own accord keep guard over themselves, are well guarded.

13. Drinking (spirituous liquor), associating with wicked people, separation from the husband, rambling abroad, sleeping (at unseasonable hours), and dwelling in other men's houses, are the six causes of the ruin of women.

14. Women do not care for beauty, nor is their attention fixed on age; (thinking), '(It is enough that) he is a man,' they give themselves to the handsome and to the ugly.

15. Through their passion for men, through their mutable temper, through their natural heartlessness, they become disloyal towards their husbands, however carefully they may be guarded in this (world).

16. Knowing their disposition, which the Lord of creatures laid in them at the creation, to be such, (every) man should most strenuously exert himself to guard them.

17. (When creating them) Manu allotted to women (a love of their) bed, (of their) seat and (of) ornament, impure desires, wrath, dishonesty, malice, and bad conduct.

PROPER TREATMENT OF WOMEN FROM THE *LAW OF MANU*

Chapter 4

55. Women must be honored and adorned by their fathers, brothers, husbands, and brothers-in-law, who desire (their own) welfare.

56. Where women are honored, there the gods are pleased; but where they are not honored, no sacred rite yields rewards.

57. Where the female relations live in grief, the family soon wholly perishes; but that family where they are not unhappy ever prospers.

58. The houses on which female relations, not being duly honored, pronounce a curse, perish completely, as if destroyed by magic.

59. Hence men who seek (their own) welfare, should always honor women on holidays and festivals with (gifts of) ornaments, clothes, and (dainty) food.

60. In that family, where the husband is pleased with his wife and the wife with her husband, happiness will assuredly be lasting.

61. For if the wife is not radiant with beauty, she will not attract her husband; but if she has no attractions for him, no children will be born.

62. If the wife is radiant with beauty, the whole house is bright; but if she is destitute of beauty, all will appear dismal.

SECTION 6: Daily Living: Health, Etiquette, and Holy Days

The ancient Hindu texts place strong emphasis on the proper performance of rituals. Of the more than 300 rituals described in the sacred canons, a large number are related to the concepts of cleanliness and contamination. Only those who are clean—physically, sexually, and spiritually—and who avoid contact with the impure will enjoy health in this life and spiritual advancements in subsequent lives. Other ritual observances are performed to propitiate the gods in order to forestall disaster or ensure security. The following selections from the *Law of Manu* include descriptions of dietary, sexual, and contamination rules and rituals for daily living. Also included are selected hymns and charms from the Vedas. Each of the four selections is directed to a specific purpose: obtaining good health, growing hair, finding a lover, securing protection. What insights about the ancient world can we gain from these passages? In what ways are our modern rules and aspirations alike/unlike those of the authors of these passages?

EATING INSTRUCTIONS FROM THE *LAW OF MANU*

Chapter 2

53. Let a twice-born man always eat his food with concentrated mind, after performing an ablution; and after he has eaten, let him duly cleanse himself with water and sprinkle the cavities (of his head).

54. Let him always worship his food, and eat it without contempt; when he sees it, let him rejoice, show a pleased face, and pray that he may always obtain it.

55. Food, that is always worshipped, gives strength and manly vigor; but eaten irreverently, it destroys them both.

56. Let him not give to any man what he leaves, and beware of eating between (the two meal-times); let him not over-eat himself, nor go anywhere without having purified himself (after his meal).

57. Excessive eating is prejudicial to health, to fame, and to (bliss in) heaven; it prevents (the acquisition of) spiritual merit, and is odious among men; one ought, for these reasons, to avoid it carefully.

Chapter 5

32. He who eats meat, when he honors the gods and manes, commits no sin, whether he has bought it, or himself has killed (the animal), or has received it as a present from others.

33. A twice-born man who knows the law, must not eat meat except in conformity with the law; for if he has eaten it unlawfully, he will, unable to save himself, be eaten after death by his (victims).

34. After death the guilt of one who slays deer for gain is not as (great) as that of him who eats meat for no (sacred) purpose.

35. But a man who, being duly engaged (to officiate or to dine at a sacred rite), refuses to eat meat, becomes after death an animal during twenty-one existences.

36. A Brahmana must never eat (the flesh of animals unhallowed by Mantras; but, obedient to the primeval law, he may eat it, consecrated with Vedic texts.

37. If he has a strong desire (for meat) he may make an animal of clarified butter or one of flour, (and eat that); but let him never seek to destroy an animal without a (lawful) reason.

38. As many hairs as the slain beast has, so often indeed will he who killed it without a (lawful) reason suffer a violent death in future births.

39. Svayambhu (the Self-existent) himself created animals for the sake of sacrifices; sacrifices (have been instituted) for the good of this whole (world); hence the slaughtering (of beasts) for sacrifices is not slaughtering (in the ordinary sense of the word).

40. Herbs, trees, cattle, birds, and (other) animals that have been destroyed for sacrifices, receive (being reborn) higher existences.

RULES REGARDING SEXUAL ACTIVITIES FROM THE *LAW OF MANU*

Chapter 2

93. Through the attachment of his organs (to sensual pleasure) a man doubtlessly will incur guilt; but if he keeps them under complete control, he will obtain success (in gaining all his aims).

94. Desire is never extinguished by the enjoyment of desired objects; it only grows stronger like a fire (fed) with clarified butter.

95. If one man should obtain all those (sensual enjoyments) and another should renounce them all, the renunciation of all pleasure is far better than the attainment of them.

Chapter 3

45. Let (the husband) approach his wife in due season, being constantly satisfied with her (alone); he may also, being intent on pleasing her, approach her with a desire for conjugal union (on any day) excepting the Parvans.

46. Sixteen (days and) nights (in each month), including four days which differ from the rest and are censured by the virtuous, (are called) the natural season of women.

47. But among these the first four, the eleventh and the thirteenth are (declared to be) forbidden; the remaining nights are recommended.

48. On the even nights sons are conceived and daughters on the uneven ones; hence a man who desires to have sons should approach his wife in due season on the even (nights).

49. A male child is produced by a greater quantity of male seed, a female child by the prevalence of the female; if (both are) equal, a hermaphrodite or a boy and a girl; if (both are) weak or deficient in quantity, a failure of conception (results).

50. He who avoids women on the six forbidden nights and on eight others, is (equal in chastity to) a student, in whichever order he may live.

Chapter 4

40. Let him, though mad with desire, not approach his wife when her courses appear; nor let him sleep with her in the same bed.

41. For the wisdom, the energy, the strength, the sight, and the vitality of a man who approaches a woman covered with menstrual excretions, utterly perish.

42. If he avoids her, while she is in that condition, his wisdom, energy, strength, sight, and vitality will increase.

43. Let him not eat in the company of his wife, nor look at her, while she eats, sneezes, yawns, or sits at her ease.

44. A Brahmana who desires energy must not look at (a woman) who applies collyrium to her eyes, has anointed or uncovered herself or brings forth (a child).

RULES GOVERNING RELATIONS WITH THE IMPURE FROM THE *LAW OF MANU*

Chapter 4

60. Let him not dwell in a village where the sacred law is not obeyed, nor (stay) long where diseases are endemic; let him not go alone on a journey, nor reside long on a mountain.

61. Let him not dwell in a country where the rulers are Sudras, nor in one which is surrounded by unrighteous men, nor in one which has become subject to heretics, nor in one swarming with men of the lowest castes. . . .

79. Let him not stay together with outcasts, nor with Kandalas, nor with Pukkasas, nor with fools, nor with overbearing men, nor with low-caste men, nor with Antyavasayins.

80. Let him not give to a Shudra advice, nor the remnants (of his meal), nor food offered to the gods; nor let him explain the sacred law (to such a man), nor impose (upon him) a penance.

81. For he who explains the sacred law (to a Sudra) or dictates to him a penance, will sink together with that (man) into the hell (called) Asamvrita. . . .

244. Let him, who desires to raise his race, ever form connections with the most excellent (men), and shun all low ones.

245. A Brahmana who always connects himself with the most excellent (ones), and shuns all inferior ones, (himself) becomes most distinguished; by an opposite conduct he becomes a Sudra.

246. He who is persevering, gentle, (and) patient, shuns the company of men of cruel conduct, and does no injury (to living creatures), gains, if he constantly lives in that manner, by controlling his organs and by liberality, heavenly bliss.

Chapter 11

181. He who associates with an outcast, himself becomes an outcast after a year, not by sacrificing for him, teaching him, or forming a matrimonial alliance with him, but by using the same carriage or seat, or by eating with him.

182. He who associates with any one of those outcasts, must perform, in order to atone for (such) intercourse, the penance prescribed for that (sinner). . . .

190. Let him not transact any business with unpurified sinners; but let him in no way reproach those who have made atonement.

191. Let him not dwell together with the murderers of children, with those who have returned evil for good, and with the slayers of suppliants for protection or of women, though they may have been purified according to the sacred law.

VEDIC PRAYERS AND CHARMS TO ASSIST IN DAILY LIVING

Healing Prayers from the Rig Veda X, 137[22]

Ye gods, raise up once more the man whom ye have
   humbled and brought low,
O gods, restore to life again the man who hath committed
   sin.
Two several winds are blowing here, from Sindhu, from a
   distant land.

---

[22]Griffith's translation of the *Rig Veda* is found in H. Daniel Smith, ed., *Selections from Vedic Hymns*, pp. 52–53.

May one breathe energy to thee, the other blow disease
   away.
Hither, O Wind, blow healing balm, blow all disease away,
   thou Wind:
For thou who has all medicine comest as envoy of the
   gods.
I am come nigh to thee with balms to give thee rest and
   keep thee safe.
I bring thee blessed strength, I drive thy weakened malady
   away.
Here let the gods deliver him, the Maruts' band deliver him:
All things that be deliver him that he be freed from his
   disease.
The Waters have their healing power, the Waters drive
   disease away.
The Waters have a balm for all: let them make medicine for
   thee.
The tongue that leads the voice precedes. Then with our
   tenfold branching hands, With these two chasers of
   disease we stroke three with a gentle touch.

A Charm to Grow Hair from the
Atharva Veda VI, 136[23]

As goddess upon the Goddess Earth thou wast born, O
   plant!
We dig the up, O Nitatni, that thou mayest strengthen (the
   growth) of hair.
That hair of thine which does drop off, and that which is
   broken root and all,
Upon it do I sprinkle here the all-healing herb.

A Charm to Secure the Love of a Woman
from the Atharva Veda VI, 8

As the creeper embraces the tree on all sides,
Thus do thou embrace me, so that thou, woman,
Shalt love me, so that thou shalt not be averse to me!
As the eagle when he flies forth presses his wings against the
   earth,
Thus do I fasten down thy mind, so that thou, woman,
Shalt love me, so that thou shalt not be averse to me!
As the sun day by day goes about this heaven and earth,
Thus do I about thy mind, so that thou, woman,
Shalt love me, so that thou shalt not be averse to me!

A Charm to Arouse a Man's Passion
from the Atharva Veda VI, 131

From thy head unto thy feet do I implant (love's) longing
   into thee.

Ye gods, send forth the yearning love: may yonder man
   burn after me!
Favor this (plant) Anumati [=a goddess who favors
   consent];
      fit it together, Akuti [=a goddess of schemes]!
Ye gods, send forth the yearning love: may yonder man
   burn after me!
If thou does run three leagues away, (or even) five leagues,
   (or yet) the distance coursed by a horseman,
From there thou shalt return, shalt be the father of our sons!

Prayers for Protection and Green Pastures
from the Rig Veda I, 42[24]

1. Shorten our path, O God, remove
   all stumbling blocks, Deliverer.
   Be at hand to guide.

2. Scare from our road the wicked wolf,
   the ill-intentioned one who lies
   in wait to harm.

3. The robber lurking round our path,
   who cunningly contrives our hurt,
   chase far away.

4. Trample beneath your feet the burning
   brand of the wicked, whoever he be,
   the double-tongued.

5. From you, wise wonder-working God,
   we claim today that selfsame aid
   you gave our Fathers.

6. So, Giver of favors, you who wield
   the golden sword, grant to us riches
   easily won.

7. Help us elude pursuers, O God,
   and make our path both smooth and fair.
   Show us your might.

8. Lead us to pastures green, O God.
   Protect us from untimely heat.
   Show us your might.

9. Be gracious to us, fill us wholly,
   impart to us food and spiritual vigor.
   Show us your might.

10. All that God does shall win our praise.
    We magnify his name with hymns,
    seeking boons from the Mighty.

[23]All *Atharva Veda* selections are in Smith, ed. *Selections from the Vedic Hymns*, p. 68.

[24]*The Vedic Experience*, Panikkar, translator, www.himalayanacademy.com/resources/books/vedic_experience/VEIndex.html.

Section 7: Human Quest: Paths to Salvation and Enlightenment

Within Hinduism, final salvation or enlightenment is less an achievement than a realization. It often begins with the desire to know Who am I?, but it ends when we come to understand the Hindu truth that no individual "I" ultimately exists. To be saved is to recover our true eternal being and to be emancipated from the endless cycle of life, death, and rebirth. Hindus call this state of final emancipation *moksha*.

Sacred Hindu texts suggest that multiple paths lead to *moksha*. There is the path of works, the path of knowledge, the path of devotion, and the path of yoga. Although the sacred canon depicts and values these paths differently, all paths are recognized and respected by orthodox Hindus. The selections included in this anthology are grouped according to their location in scripture. The first set of passages comes from the *Vedas*; the second, from the *Upanishads*, and the third, from the *Gita*. Which path to salvation is predominant in each of the selections? What is the essence of each path? Is each path mutually exclusive, or can the three paths to enlightenment be reconciled?

Paths to Salvations from the *Samaveda*[25]

32. O my Mind! Adore Him—wise, righteous, destroyer of enemies, Ever Resplendent, Embodiment of Knowledge—for visualizing Him in the region of the heart unviolated by the enemies like passion, anger, greed, infatuation, obsession and ego. In other words, it is not proper for you, O my mind, to keep yourself wavering. Concentrate yourself. Engage yourself in non-violent (sacrificial) action (vajna). Follow the virtue of sooth-saying. Keep you inner enemies at a distance. Beware! If you really seek Divine Grace and merger in Supreme Being, do not wander away nor be restless. . . .

36. O Fire, the embodiment of superior knowledge! Mayst Thou protect us first by Thy symbol of Karma (action); secondly by Thy symbol of Jnan (knowledge). O Preserver of Valour! Mayst Thou be propitiated by our hymns and be pleased to maintain us by Thus symbol of Trio—Karma-Jnan-Bhakti (action-knowledge-devotion)! O Lord, the ultimate Abode or Refuge. Mayst Thou save us by Thy four-fold symbol of Karma-Jnan-Bhakti-Moksha (action-knowledge-devotion-emancipation). . . .

82. If, even the insignificant mortals offer oblations devotedly and steadfastly to Agni, and kindle the urge and fire of spiritual knowledge in the regions of their hearts, they can become vastly talented and fit to achieve bliss, notwithstanding their earlier insignificance. . . .

87. O Mankind! If you are really serious in your intentions of approach towards and achievement of the Supreme Being, invoke Him devotedly with your pure and sincere hymns directed to Him who is not only beloved to you but also to all the creatures of the universe and who is assessable like a real friend. May the Fire of Knowledge—the source of all bliss on our fervent solicitation of peace and tranquillity of mind—Ultimate Abode of all beings—be kindled in our hearts by adoration with proper hymns.

Included next are selections from the *Isha* and the *Mundaka Upanishads*. Although not among the oldest, the *Isha Upanishad* holds a special place in the Hindu canon and traditionally is placed at the beginning of the *Upanishads*. In only 18 verses, it discloses the mysteries of the Vedas as it reflects on the transcendence and immanence of the One who is everywhere and nowhere. It declares that the path to true liberty, joy, and wisdom is the path of nonduality, of oneness. The *Mundaka* also is a treasured *Upanishad* that describes the truth that passes understanding.

Paths to Salvation from the *Isha Upanishad*[26]

By the Lord is enveloped
all that moves in the moving world.
By renouncing this, find your enjoyment.
Do not covet the possessions of others.
Working here one may wish to live for a hundred years.
Thus it is up to you—there is no other way than this—
the work does not adhere to you.
Demonic are those worlds named, covered in blinding
    darkness;
there after death go those people who kill the soul.
Unmoving the one is faster than the mind.
The angels do not reach it, as it is always beyond them.
Standing still it passes beyond those who run.
In it the Mother establishes the waters.
It moves, and it does not move.
It is far, and it is near.
It is within all this, and it is also outside all this.

---

[25]Translation by Bibhor Kumar Lahiri, pp. 14–16, 30–32.

[26]Beck, *Wisdom Bible*, pp. 83–84.

Whoever sees all beings in the soul
and the soul in all beings
does not shrink away from this.
In whom all beings have become one with the knowing soul
what delusion or sorrow is there for the one who sees unity?
It has filled all.

It is radiant, incorporeal, invulnerable,
without tendons, pure, untouched by evil.
Wise, intelligent, encompassing, self-existent,
it organizes objects throughout eternity.

Into blind darkness enter those who follow ignorance;
into even greater darkness go those who follow knowledge.
It is distinct, they say, from knowledge.
It is distinct, they say, from ignorance.
So have we heard from the wise who explained it to us.
Knowledge and ignorance, whoever knows the two together
with ignorance passes over death,
with knowledge attains immortality.

Into blind darkness enter those who follow non-becoming;
into greater darkness enter those who follow becoming.
It is distinct, they say, from becoming.
It is distinct, they say, from non-becoming.
So have we heard from the wise who explained it to us.
Becoming and destruction, whoever knows the two together
with destruction passes over death,
with becoming attains immortality.

The face of truth is covered with a golden disc.
Unveil it, nourisher,
for one whose duty is to see the truth.
Nourisher, one seer, controller, sun, child of the creator,
spread your light and gather your brilliance
that I may see your loveliest form.
Whatever is that Spirit, that also am I.
May this life enter into the immortal breath!
This body then ends in ashes. Aum.
Purpose, remember! Action, remember!
Purpose, remember! Action, remember!

Agni, lead us by a good path to success,
you god who knows all ways.
Keep us away from deceitful sins.
We offer ample prayer to you.

FROM THE *MUNDAKA UPANISHAD* PART 2[27]

2

"This is the truth:
as from a blazing fire
thousands of flaming sparks come forth,

———————
[27]Beck, *Wisdom Bible*, pp. 87–92.

so from the imperishable, my friend,
various beings come forth and return there also.
Divine and formless is the Spirit,
which is outside and inside, unborn, not breath, not mind,
pure, higher than the high imperishable.

"From this is produced breath, mind, and all the senses,
space, air, light, water, and earth supporting all.
Fire is its head, its eyes the sun and moon,
the regions of space its ears, the revealed Vedas its speech,
air its breath, its heart the world.
The earth is its footstool.

"It is the inner soul of all beings.
From it comes fire whose fuel is the sun,
from the moon, rain, plants on the earth;
the male pours seed in the female;
thus creatures are produced from the Spirit.

"From it come the hymns, the chants,
the formulas, the rites of initiation,
and all the sacrifices, ceremonies, and offerings,
the year too, and the sacrificer,
and the worlds where the moon shines and the sun.

"From it also are born various gods, the celestials,
people, cattle, birds, the in-breath and the out-breath,
rice and barley, discipline,
faith, truth, chastity, and the law.

"From it come forth the seven life-breaths,
the seven flames, their fuel, the seven oblations,
these seven worlds in which move the life-breaths
set within the secret place, seven and seven.

"From it the seas and mountains all;
from it flow the rivers of all kinds;
from it come all plants and the essence
by which the inner soul lives in the elements.

"The Spirit itself is all this here:
works and discipline and God, beyond death.
Whoever knows that which is set in the secret place,
that one here on earth, my friend,
cuts apart the knot of ignorance.
Manifest, hidden, moving in the secret place, the great home.
In it lives all that moves and breathes and sees.

"Know that as being, as non-being, as most to be desired,
beyond understanding, as what is best of all.
That which is luminous, subtler than the subtle,
in which are set all the worlds and their inhabitants—
that is the imperishable God.
It is life; it is speech and mind.
That is the real; it is immortal.

"It is to be known, my friend; know it.
Taking as a bow the great weapons of the Upanishads,
place on it an arrow sharpened by meditation.

Stretching it with thought directed to that,
know that imperishable as the target, my friend.

"The word AUM is the bow; the soul is the arrow.
God is said to be the target.
By the unfaltering it is to be known.
One becomes united with it as the arrow.

"In whom sky, earth, and atmosphere are interwoven,
and also the mind together with all the life breaths,
this alone know as the one soul.
Other words dismiss. This is the bridge to immortality.

"Where the channels are brought together
like the spokes in the hub of a wheel
there it moves and becomes manifold.

"AUM. Thus meditate on the soul.
May you be successful in crossing over
to the farther shore beyond darkness.

"Whoever is all-knowing, all-wise,
whose is this greatness on the earth,
in the divine city of God
and established in heaven is the soul.

"Using the mind, leading the life-breaths and the body,
established in matter one finds peace in the heart.
By this knowledge the wise perceive
the light of blissful immortality.
The knot of the heart is loosened, all doubts vanish,
and one's works cease when it is seen, the lower and higher.

"In the highest golden sheath is God,
without stain or parts.
Radiant is it, the light of lights,
that which the knowers of the soul know.
The sun does not shine there nor the moon nor the stars;
lightning does not shine; how then could this fire?
The whole world is illuminated by its light.
God truly is this immortal.
God in front, God behind, to the right and the left.
Spread out below and above, God is all this great universe."

3

"Two birds, close companions, cling to the same tree.
Of these two, one eats the sweet fruit,
and the other looks on without eating.
The soul is the one sitting immersed on the same tree,
deluded and sad because helpless.
But seeing the other who is the Lord and beloved,
it realizes its greatness and overcomes the sadness.

"When a seer sees the brilliant creator,
Lord, Spirit, God-source,
then being a knower, shaking off good and evil,
stainless one reaches supreme identity.

Truly it is life that shines forth in all beings.
Understanding this one knows there is nothing else to say.

"Delighting in the soul,
enjoying the soul, doing holy works,
such a one is the best of the knowers of God.
The soul can be attained by truth, by discipline,
by correct knowledge, by studying God.
Within the body, made of light, pure is this
which the ascetics, their faults removed, view.

"Truth alone conquers, not falsehood.
By truth is laid out the path leading to the gods
by which the sages whose desires are satisfied
ascend to where the supreme home of truth is.
Vast, divine, its form unthinkable, subtler than the subtle,
it shines out, farther than the far, yet close-by.
resting in the secret place,
even here it is seen by those with vision.

"It is not grasped by sight nor even by speech
nor by other angels, nor by austerity nor by work.
By the grace of wisdom and mental purity
by meditating one does see the indivisible.
The subtle is to be known by consciousness
in which the five different breaths have centered.
All of human thought is interwoven with the life-breath.
When that is purified, the soul manifests its power.

"Whatever world a person of pure heart
holds clearly in mind,
and whatever desires that one desires,
that world is obtained and those desires.
Therefore whoever desires success
should honor the knower of the self.

"That one knows the supreme home of God,
founded on which the whole world shines radiantly.

"The wise who, free from desires, worship the Spirit,
pass beyond the sperm.
Whoever entertains desires, dwelling on them,
is born here and there on account of these desires;
but one whose desire is satisfied, whose soul is perfected,
all desires here on earth vanish away.

"This soul can not be attained by instruction
nor by intellect nor by much learning.
It can be attained only by the one whom it chooses.
To such a one this soul reveals its own nature.

"This soul can not be attained by one lacking strength
nor by carelessness nor by misdirected discipline;
but the one striving by these means who knows,
this soul enters into the home of God.

"Attaining this, the seers, happy with knowledge,
souls perfected, free from emotion, tranquil,

attaining the one who is universally omnipresent, those wise, united souls enter into the all itself.

"Those who have ascertained
the meaning of the Vedanta knowledge,
ascetics with natures purified by the way of renunciation,
they in the God-worlds at the end of time,
transcending death are all liberated.
The fifteen parts return to their foundations,
and all the angels to their divinities.

"One's actions and the soul composed of wisdom
all become one in the supreme imperishable.
As rivers flowing into the ocean disappear
losing name and form,
so the knower liberated from name and form
reaches the divine Spirit, higher than the highest.

"Whoever knows that supreme God becomes God.
In that family no one is born who does not know God.
This one crosses over sorrow, crosses over sins,
liberated from the knots of the heart, becomes immortal.
This has been declared in the verse:

'Doers of the works, learned in scriptures,
absorbed in God, having faith
make offerings to the one seer,
to those one should declare this knowledge of God,
by whom the rite of the head
has been performed according to rule.' "

This is the truth.
The seer Angiras declared it long ago.
Let no one who has not performed the rite read this.
Salutation to the highest seers!
Salutation to the highest seers!

PATHS TO SALVATION FROM THE *BHAGAVAD GITA*

Chapter 8

In this section of the *Gita,* Arjana asks Krsna several questions about the Absolute and the relation of the Self to the Absolute. Below are Krishna's answers:

5. The One who leaves the body, at the hour of death, remembering Me attains My abode. There is no doubt about this.
6. Remembering whatever object one leaves the body at the end of life, one attains that object, O Arjuna, because of the constant thought of that object (one remembers that object at the end of life and achieves it).
7. Therefore, always remember Me and do your duty. You shall certainly attain Me if your mind and intellect are fixed on Me.
8. By contemplating on Me with an unwavering mind, disciplined by the practice of meditation, one attains the Supreme divine spirit, O Arjuna.

9. The one who meditates on Brahman as the omniscient, the oldest, the controller, smaller than the smallest (and bigger than the biggest), the sustainer of everything, the inconceivable, the self luminous like the sun, and as transcendental or beyond the material reality;
10. At the time of death with steadfast mind and devotion; making the flow of Pranic impulse rise up (to the middle of two eye brows) by the power of yoga and holding there; attains the Supreme divine spirit.
11. I shall briefly explain to you (the process to attain) that goal which the knowers of the Vedas call the imperishable; into which the ascetics, freed from attachment, enter; and desiring which people lead a life of celibacy.
12. Controlling all the (nine) doors of the body, the abode of consciousness; focusing the mind on the heart and Prana in the cerebrum, and engaged in yogic practice;
13. One who leaves the body while meditating on Brahman and uttering OM, the sacred monosyllable sound of Brahman, attains the Supreme goal.
14. I am easily attainable, O Arjuna, by that ever steadfast yogi who always thinks of Me and whose mind does not go elsewhere.
15. After attaining Me the great souls do not incur rebirth, the impermanent home of misery, because they have attained the highest perfection.
16. The dwellers of all the worlds including the world of Brahmaa, the creator, are subject to (the miseries of) repeated birth and death. But, after attaining Me, O Arjuna, one does not take birth again.
17. Those who know that the day of Brahmaa lasts one thousand Yugas (or 4.32 billion years) and that his night also lasts one thousand Yugas, they are the knowers of day and night.
18. All manifestations come out of the unmanifest state or Prakriti at the arrival of Brahmaa's day, and they again merge into the same Prakriti at the coming of Brahmaa's night.
19. The same multitude of beings come into existence again and again at the arrival of the day of Brahmaa, and they are annihilated, inevitably, at the arrival of Brahmaa's night.
20. There is another eternal unmanifest state higher than (both Purusha and) Prakriti that does not perish when all beings perish.
21. This unmanifest state is called the imperishable or Brahman. This is said to be the ultimate goal. Those who reach My Supreme abode do not return (or take rebirth).
22. This Supreme abode, O Arjuna, is attainable by unswerving devotion to Me within which all beings exist, and by which all this universe is pervaded.
23. O Arjuna, now I shall describe different paths departing by which, during death, the yogis do or do not come back.
24. Fire, light, daytime, the bright lunar fortnight, and the six months of the northern solstice of the sun; departing by the path of these gods the yogis, who know Brahman, attain nirvana.

25. Smoke, night, the dark lunar fortnight, and the six months of southern solstice of the sun; departing by these paths, the righteous person attains lunar light (or heaven) and reincarnates.

26. The path of light (of spiritual practice of Kundalini yoga and Self-knowledge) and the path of darkness (of materialism and ignorance) are thought to be the world's two eternal paths. The former leads to nirvana and the latter leads to rebirth.

27. Knowing these two paths, O Arjuna, a yogi is not bewildered at all. Therefore, O Arjuna, be steadfast in yoga (of meditation) at all times.

28. The yogi who knows all this goes beyond getting the benefits of the study of the Vedas, performance of sacrifices, austerities, and charities, and attains the Supreme eternal abode.

SECTION 8. The Religious Life: Worship and Righteousness

How does a person live a religious life? Within Hinduism, the answer to this question, in large part, depends on a person's sex, age, and caste. Although everyone is expected to respect and make daily offerings to the gods, only highly trained Brahmin priests can perform certain religious functions needed to propitiate the gods. The selections in this section include Vedic prayers describing the fire sacrifices to the gods, rules from the *Law of Manu* that detail proper religious behavior in each of the four stages of life through which twice-born Hindu males ideally pass and a description of the true saint contained in a beloved section of the *Gita*.

VEDIC WORSHIP FROM THE *SAMAVEDA SAMHITA*[28]

7. O Fire—O Essence of Revelation! Be pleased to come and accept our hymns well chanted—well enunciated according to the Vedic rules as enjoined in the Vedanga of Siksha. Overlook the short-comings in our pronunciation of the Vedic Mantras. There may be defects in our offerings in the sacrificial fire (Yajna). Pardon the mundane (worldly) aspects in the divine hymns and sacrificial offerings of devotees, conscious or unconscious. Such irregularity in utterance or in sacrificial offerings generally vitiates the hymns and sacerdotal acts rendering them unacceptable, by reason of defects in expression or sacrifice. Still, we beseech THEE TO COME and install THYSELF in our sanctified hearts, where, though great majestic THOU ART THOU SHALT grow and shall be propitiated with the nectar flowing from our devoted hearts in the shape of our extreme inward eagerness, unflinching steadfastness and also sincere and unwavering devotion. We do,

therefore, pray that our sincerity of purpose may attain forgiveness and our faulty expressions and defective sacrificial actions may become acceptable, and faults and defects are overlooked by THEE. O Lord of Wisdom! Unless we are pardoned for our defaults on grounds of our inward eagerness, unflinching steadfastness and sincerity, all our efforts to propitiate THEE shall be ineffective and unproductive. Our hope lies in THY grant of pardons on good and cogent ground. For where THY majesty offsets our humility—THY immortality, our mortality, THY towering strength, and stature, our inherent weakness and short-comings? So, we ever remain to crave THY pardon and to count on THY unlimited patience. For we do not justify our incorrigible short-comings. May we be pardoned and saved from the natural consequence of our faulty words and defective deeds. . . .

15. O God of Fire! Being kindled by the devotional power Thou pervadest the Universe for saving men from sins. Being offered for successful termination of our sacrificial practices, our befitting hymns, or reasonable prayers directed towards Thy Exalted Self may be graciously accepted by Thee. All the prayers may reach Him but all are not granted. Those alone proceeding from the pure hearts of the devotees and based on good and cogent grounds, and made with sincerity of purpose, are granted. Our other prayers are made in vain. . . .

63. O Mortal! Worship the Supreme Being with oblations—propitiate Him with meditation—serve Him installed in your heart, source of your weal and delight the Lord of the Universe—and also the Homes' Lord. Wherever libations are poured, He is worshipped with gifts and homage. Do honor Him worthy of reverence in your house. . . .

85. Agni—the everlasting—much beloved and honorable as a guest of the house of the devotees, where in all mortals offer their oblations—should be adored at dawn. . . .

94. The devotees practicing sacerdotal acts and chanting Vedic hymns, do so all directed to the Supreme Being, who accepts all our spiritual practices. Like the outer circle of the wheel, attached by spokes, He encircles His creation and remains all-pervading.

RELIGIOUS DUTIES IN THE FOUR STAGES OF LIFE FROM THE *LAWS OF MANU*

THE RELIGIOUS LIFE OF A STUDENT

Chapter 2

69. Having performed the (rite of) initiation, the teacher must first instruct the (pupil) in (the rules of) personal purification, of conduct, of the fire-worship, and of the twilight devotions.

70. But (a student) who is about to begin the Study (of the Veda), shall receive instruction, after he has sipped water in

---

[28]Translation by Bibhor Kumar Lahiri, pp. 4, 8–9, 24, 31, 35.

accordance with the Institutes (of the sacred law), has made the Brahmangali, (has put on) a clean dress, and has brought his organs under due control.

71. At the beginning and at the end of (a lesson in the) Veda he must always clasp both the feet of his teacher, (and) he must study, joining his hands; that is called the Brahmangali (joining the palms for the sake of the Veda). . . .

74. Let him always pronounce the syllable Om at the beginning and at the end of (a lesson in) the Veda; (for) unless the syllable Om precede (the lesson) will slip away (from him), and unless it follow it will fade away. . . .

194. In the presence of his teacher let him always eat less, wear a less valuable dress and ornaments (than the former), and let him rise earlier (from his bed), and go to rest later. . . .

199. Let him not pronounce the mere name of his teacher (without adding an honorific title) behind his back even, and let him not mimic his gait, speech, and deportment.

200. Wherever (people) justly censure or falsely defame his teacher, there he must cover his ears or depart thence to another place.

201. By censuring (his teacher), though justly, he will become (in his next birth) an ass, by falsely defaming him, a dog; he who lives on his teacher's substance, will become a worm, and he who is envious (of his merit), a (larger) insect.

THE RELIGIOUS LIFE OF A HOUSEHOLDER

Chapter 3

1. The vow (of studying) the three Vedas under a teacher must be kept for thirty-six years, or for half that time, or for a quarter, or until the (student) has perfectly learnt them.

2. (A student) who has studied in due order the three Vedas, or two, or even one only, without breaking the (rules of) studentship, shall enter the order of householders.

3. He who is famous for (the strict performance of) his duties and has received his heritage, the Veda, from his father, shall be honoured, sitting on a couch and adorned with a garland, with (the present of) a cow (and the honey mixture).

4. Having bathed, with the permission of his teacher, and performed according to the rule the Samavartana (the rite on returning home), a twice-born man shall marry a wife of equal caste who is endowed with auspicious (bodily) marks. . . .

15. Twice-born men who, in their folly, wed wives of the low (Sudra) caste, soon degrade their families and their children to the state of Sudras. . . .

63. By low marriages, by omitting (the performance of) sacred rites, by neglecting the study of the Veda, and by irreverence towards Brahmanas, (great) families sink low.

64. By (practising) handicrafts, by pecuniary transactions, by (begetting) children on Shudra females only, by (trading in) cows, horses, and carriages, by (the pursuit of) agriculture and by taking service under a king,

65. By sacrificing for men unworthy to offer sacrifices and by denying (the future rewards for good) works, families, deficient in the (knowledge of the) Veda, quickly perish.

66. But families that are rich in the knowledge of the Veda, though possessing little wealth, are numbered among the great, and acquire great fame.

THE RELIGIOUS LIFE OF A FOREST DWELLER

Chapter 6

1. A twice-born Snataka, who has thus lived according to the law in the order of householders, may, taking a firm resolution and keeping his organs in subjection, dwell in the forest, duly (observing the rules given below).

2. When a householder sees his (skin) wrinkled, and (his hair) white, and. the sons of his sons, then he may resort to the forest.

3. Abandoning all food raised by cultivation, and all his belongings, he may depart into the forest, either committing his wife to his sons, or accompanied by her.

4. Taking with him the sacred fire and the implements required for domestic (sacrifices), he may go forth from the village into the forest and reside there, duly controlling his senses. . . .

8. Let him be always industrious in privately reciting the Veda; let him be patient of hardships, friendly (towards all), of collected mind, ever liberal and never a receiver of gifts, and compassionate towards all living creatures. . . .

23. In summer let him expose himself to the heat of five fires, during the rainy season live under the open sky, and in winter be dressed in wet clothes, (thus) gradually increasing (the rigor of) his austerities.

24. When he bathes at the three Savanas (sunrise, midday, and sunset), let him offer libations of water to the manes and the gods, and practicing harsher and harsher austerities, let him dry up his bodily frame.

25. Having reposited the three sacred fires in himself, according to the prescribed rule, let him live without a fire, without a house, wholly silent, subsisting on roots and fruit,

26. Making no effort (to procure) things that give pleasure, chaste, sleeping on the bare ground, not caring for any shelter, dwelling at the roots of trees.

27. From Brahmanas (who live as) ascetics, let him receive alms, (barely sufficient) to support life, or from other householders of the twice-born (castes) who reside in the forest.

28. Or (the hermit) who dwells in the forest may bring (food) from a village, receiving it either in a hollow dish (of leaves), in (his naked) hand, or in a broken earthen dish, and may eat eight mouthfuls.

29. These and other observances must a Brahmana who dwells in the forest diligently practice, and in order to attain complete (union with) the (supreme) Soul, (he must study) the various sacred texts contained in the Upanishads,

THE RELIGIOUS LIFE OF AN ASCETIC

Chapter 6

33. But having thus passed the third part of (a man's natural term of) life in the forest, he may live as an ascetic during the fourth part of his existence, after abandoning all attachment to worldly objects.

34. He who after passing from order to order, after offering sacrifices and subduing his senses, becomes, tired with (giving) alms and offerings of food, an ascetic, gains bliss after death.

35. When he has paid the three debts, let him apply his mind to (the attainment of) final liberation; he who seeks it without having paid (his debts) sinks downwards.

36. Having studied the Vedas in accordance with the rule, having begat sons according to the sacred law, and having offered sacrifices according to his ability, he may direct his mind to (the attainment of) final liberation.

37. A twice-born man who seeks final liberation, without having studied the Vedas, without having begotten sons, and without having offered sacrifices, sinks downwards. . . .

41. Departing from his house fully provided with the means of purification (Pavitra), let him wander about absolutely silent, and caring nothing for enjoyments that may be offered (to him).

42. Let him always wander alone, without any companion, in order to attain (final liberation), fully understanding that the solitary (man, who) neither forsakes nor is forsaken, gains his end.

43. He shall neither possess a fire, nor a dwelling, he may go to a village for his food, (he shall be) indifferent to everything, firm of purpose, meditating (and) concentrating his mind on Brahman.

44. A potsherd (instead of an alms-bowl), the roots of trees (for a dwelling), coarse worn-out garments, life in solitude and indifference towards everything, are the marks of one who has attained liberation.

45. Let him not desire to die, let him not desire to live; let him wait for (his appointed) time, as a servant (waits) for the payment of his wages. . . .

49. Delighting in what refers to the Soul, sitting (in the postures prescribed by the Yoga), independent (of external help), entirely abstaining from sensual enjoyments, with himself for his only companion, he shall live in this world, desiring the bliss (of final liberation). . . .

55. Let him go to beg once (a day), let him not be eager to obtain a large quantity (of alms); for an ascetic who eagerly seeks alms, attaches himself also to sensual enjoyments. . . .

57. Let him not be sorry when he obtains nothing, nor rejoice when he obtains (something), let him (accept) so much only as will sustain life, let him not care about the (quality of his) utensils.

58. Let him disdain all (food) obtained in consequence of humble salutations, (for) even an ascetic who has attained final liberation, is bound (with the fetters of the Samsara) by accepting (food given) in consequence of humble salutations.

59. By eating little, and by standing and sitting in solitude, let him restrain his senses, if they are attracted by sensual objects.

60. By the restraint of his senses, by the destruction of love and hatred, and by the abstention from injuring the creatures, he becomes fit for immortality.

61. Let him reflect on the transmigrations of men, caused by their sinful deeds, on their falling into hell, and on the torments in the world of Yama,

62. On the separation from their dear ones, on their union with hated men, on their being overpowered by age and being tormented with diseases,

63. On the departure of the individual soul from this body and its new birth in (another) womb, and on its wanderings through ten thousand millions of existences,

64. On the infliction of pain on embodied (spirits), which is caused by demerit, and the gain of eternal bliss, which is caused by the attainment of their highest aim, (gained through) spiritual merit.

65. By deep meditation let him recognize the subtle nature of the supreme Soul, and its presence in all organisms, both the highest and the lowest. . . .

68. In order to preserve living creatures, let him always by day and by night, even with pain to his body, walk, carefully scanning the ground.

69. In order to expiate (the death) of those creatures which he unintentionally injures by day or by night, an ascetic shall bathe and perform six suppressions of the breath. . . .

73. Let him recognize by the practice of meditation the progress of the individual soul through beings of various kinds, (a progress) hard to understand for unregenerate men.

74. He who possesses the true insight (into the nature of the world), is not fettered by his deeds; but he who is destitute of that insight, is drawn into the circle of births and deaths.

75. By not injuring any creatures, by detaching the senses (from objects of enjoyment), by the rites prescribed in the Veda, and by rigorously practicing austerities, (men) gain that state (even) in this (world). . . .

80. When by the disposition (of his heart) he becomes indifferent to all objects, he obtains eternal happiness both in this world and after death.

81. He who has in this manner gradually given up all attachments and is freed from all the pairs (of opposites), reposes in Brahman alone.

DESCRIPTIONS OF A TRUE DEVOTEE FROM THE *BHAGAVAD GITA*

Chapter 12

1. Arjuna said: Those ever-steadfast devotees (or Bhaktas) who thus worship You (as the manifest or personal God), and those who worship the eternal unmanifest (the formless or impersonal) Brahman (by developing Jnana), which of these has the best knowledge of yoga?

2. The Supreme Lord said: Those ever steadfast devotees who worship with supreme faith by fixing their mind on Me as personal God, I consider them to be the best yogis.

3. But those who worship the imperishable, the undefinable, the unmanifest, the omnipresent, the unthinkable, the unchanging, the immovable, and the eternal Brahman.

4. Restraining all the senses, even minded under all circumstances, engaged in the welfare of all creatures, they also attain Me.

5. Self-realization is more difficult for those who fix their mind on the formless Brahman, because the comprehension of the unmanifest Brahman by the average embodied human being is very difficult.

6. But, to those who worship Me as the personal God, renouncing all actions to Me; setting Me as their supreme goal, and meditating on Me with single minded devotion;

7. I swiftly become their savior, from the world that is the ocean of death and transmigration, whose thoughts are set on Me, O Arjuna.

8. Therefore, focus your mind on Me alone and let your intellect dwell upon Me through meditation and contemplation. Thereafter you shall certainly come to Me.

9. If you are unable to meditate (or focus your mind) steadily on Me, then seek to reach Me, O Arjuna, by practice of (any other) spiritual discipline (or Sadhana of your choice).

10. If you are unable even to do any Sadhana, then be intent on performing your duty for Me. You shall attain perfection just by working for Me (as an instrument, just to serve and please Me, without selfish motives.

11. If you are unable to work for Me then just surrender unto My will with subdued mind, and renounce (the attachment to, and the anxiety for) the fruits of all work (by learning to accept all results, as God-given, with equanimity).

12. Knowledge is better than mere ritualistic practice, meditation is better than mere knowledge, renunciation of the fruit of work is better than meditation, peace immediately follows the renunciation of (the attachment to) the fruit of work.

13. One who does not hate any creature, who is friendly and compassionate, free from (the notion of) "I" and "my," even-minded in pain and pleasure, forgiving; and

14. The yogi who is ever content, who has subdued the mind, whose resolve is firm, whose mind and intellect are engaged in dwelling upon Me; such a devotee is dear to Me.

15. The one by whom others are not agitated, and who is not agitated by others; who is free from joy, envy, fear, and anxiety; is also dear to Me.

16. One who is free from desires; who is pure, wise, impartial, and free from anxiety; who has renounced (the doership in) all undertakings; and who is devoted to Me, is dear to Me.

17. One who neither rejoices nor grieves, neither likes nor dislikes, who has renounced both the good and the evil, and who is full of devotion, such a person is dear to Me.

18. The one who remains the same towards friend or foe, in honor or disgrace, in heat or cold, in pleasure or pain; who is free from attachment; and

19. The one who is indifferent or silent in censure or praise, content with anything, unattached to a place (country, or house), equanimous, and full of devotion; that person is dear to Me.

20. But those devotees who have faith and sincerely try to develop the above mentioned immortal virtues, and set Me as their supreme goal; are very dear to Me.

SECTION 9: Ending: Death, Judgment, and the Afterlife

The final section consists of passages from five major *Upanishads*. How do these beatific visions compare with similar texts in the great religions of the West? In what ways are these visions similar and distinct?

DESCRIPTIONS OF DEATH AND BEYOND FROM THE *PRASNA UPANISHAD* 5TH QUESTION[29]

Then Saibya Satyakama asked: Master, that man who until the end of his life rests on OM his meditation, where does he go after life?

The sage replied: The word OM, O Satyakama, is the transcendent and the immanent Brahman, the Spirit Supreme. With the help of this sacred Word the wise attains the one or the other.

---

[29]*The Upanishads*, with an Introduction by Juan Mascaro (New York: Penguin, 1965), p. 73.

OM, or AUM, has three sounds. He who rests on the first his meditation is illumined thereby and after death returns speedily to this world of men led by the harmonies of the Rig Veda. Remaining here in steadiness, purity, and truth he attains greatness.

And if he rests his mind in meditation on the first two sounds, he is led by the harmonies of the Yajur Veda to the regions of the moon. After enjoying their heavenly joys, he returns to earth again.

But if, with the three sounds of the eternal OM, he places his mind in meditation upon the Supreme Spirit, he comes to the regions of light of the sun. There he becomes free from all evil, even as a snake sheds its old skin, and with the harmonies of the Sama Veda he goes to the heaven of Brahma where from he can behold the Spirit that dwells in the city of the human body and which is above the highest life. There are two verses that say:

"The three sounds not in union lead again to life that dies; but the wise who merge them into a harmony of union in outer, inner and middle actions becomes steady: he trembles no more."

With the harmonies of the *Rig Veda* unto this world of man, and with those of the *Yajur Veda* to the middle heavenly regions; but, with the help of OM, the sage goes to those regions that the seers know in the harmonies of the *Sama Veda*. There he finds the peace of the Supreme Spirit where there is no dissolution or death and where there is no fear.

WHAT REMAINS AT DEATH? FROM THE *KATHA UPANISHAD*, PART 5[30]

5 "By ruling over the city of eleven gates,
  the unborn who is not devious-minded does not grieve,
  but when set free is truly free.
  This truly is that.

"The swan in the sky, the god in the atmosphere,
  the priest at the altar, the guest in the house,
  in people, in gods, in justice, in the sky,
  born in water, born in cattle, born in justice,
  born in rock, is justice, the great one.
  Upwards it leads the out-breath,
  downwards it casts the in-breath.
  The dwarf who sits in the center all the gods reverence.
  When this incorporate one that is in the body
  slips off and is released from the body,
  what is there that remains?
  This truly is that.

---

[30]Beck ed. *Wisdom Bible*, pp. 79–80.

"Not by the out-breath and the in-breath
does any mortal live.
Buy by another do they live
on which these both depend.

"Look, I shall explain to you
the mystery of God, the eternal,
and how the soul fares after reaching death, Gautama.
Some enter a womb for embodiment;
others enter stationary objects
according to their actions and according to their
  thoughts.

"Whoever is awake in those that sleep,
the Spirit who shapes desire after desire,
that they call the bright one.
That is God; that indeed is called the immortal.
On it all the worlds rest, and no one ever goes beyond it.
This truly is that.

"As one fire has entered the world
and becomes varied in shape
according to the form of every object,
so the one inner soul in all beings
becomes varied according to whatever form
and also exists outside.

"As one air has entered the world
and becomes varied in shape
according to the form of every object,
so the one inner soul in all beings
becomes varied according to whatever form
and also exists outside.

"As the sun, the eye of the world,
is not defiled by the external faults of the eyes,
so the inner soul in all beings
is not defiled by the evil in the world, being outside it.

"The inner soul in all beings, the one controller,
who makes this one form manifold,
the wise who perceive this standing in oneself,
they and no others have eternal happiness.

"The one eternal among the transient,
the conscious among the conscious,
the one among the many, who grants desires,
the wise who perceive this standing in oneself
they and no others have eternal happiness.

"This is it.
Thus they recognize the ineffable supreme happiness.
How then may I understand this?
Does it shine or does it reflect?
The sun does not shine there, nor the moon and the
  stars;
lightning does not shine there, much less this fire.
After that shines does everything else shine.
The whole world is illuminated by its light.

The Mystery of the Brahman from the *Taittiriya Upanishad* 3.1–6[31]

Once Bhrigu Varuni went to his father, Varuna and said: "Father, explain to me the mystery of the Brahman."

Then his father spoke to him of the food of the earth, of the bread of life, of the one who sees, of the one who hears, of the mind that knows, and of the one who speaks. And he further said to him: "Seek to know him from whom all beings have come, by whom they all live, and unto whom they all return. He is Brahman."

So Bhrigu went and practiced tapas, spiritual prayer. Then he thought that Brahman was the food of the earth: for from the earth all beings have come, by food of the earth they all live, and unto the earth they all return.

After this he went again to his father Varuna and said: "Father explain further to me the mystery of Brahman." To him his father answered: "Seek to know Brahman by tapas, by prayer, because Brahman is prayer."

So Bhrigu went and practiced tapas, spiritual prayer. Then he thought that Braham was life: for from life all beings have come, by life they all love, and unto life they all return.

After this he went again to his father Varuna and said: "Father explain further to me the mystery of Brahman." To him his father answered: "Seek to know Brahman by tapas, by prayer, because Brahman is prayer."

So Bhrigu went and practiced tapas, spiritual prayer. Then he thought that Brahman was mind: from form mind all beings have come, by mind they all live, and unto mind they all return.

After this he went again to his father Varuna and said: "Father explain further to me the mystery of Brahman." To him his father answered: "Seek to know Brahman by tapas, by prayer, because Brahman is prayer."

So Bhrigu went and practiced tapas, spiritual prayer. Then he thought that Brahman was reason, for from reason all beings have come, by reason they all live, and unto reason they all return.

He went again to his father, asked the same question, and received the same answer.

So Bhrigu went and practiced tapas, spiritual prayer. And then he saw Brahman is joy: for FROM JOY ALL BEINGS HAVE COME, BY JOY THEY ALL LIVE, AND UNTO JOY THEY ALL RETURN.

This was the vision of Bhrigu Varuni which came from the Highest; and he who sees this vision lives in the Highest.

Between Time and Eternity from the *Chandogya Upanishad* 8.4.1[32]

There is a bridge between time and Eternity; and this bridge is Atman, the Spirit of man. Neither day nor night cross that bridge, nor old age, nor death, nor sorrow.

Evil or sin cannot cross that bridge, because the world of the Spirit is pure. This is why when this bridge has been crossed, the eyes of the blind can see, the wounds of the wounded are healed, and the sick man becomes whole from his sickness.

To one who goes over that bridge, the night becomes like unto day; because in the worlds of the Spirit there is a Light which is everlasting.

From the *Brihad-aranyaka Upanishad*[33]

II.4

Maitreyi," said one day Yajnavalkya to his wife, "I am going to leave this present life, and retire to a life of meditation. Let me settle my possessions upon you and Katyayani."

"If all the earth filled with riches belonged to me, O my Lord, " said Maitreyi, "should I thereby attain life eternal?"

"Certainly not," said Yajnavalkya, "your life would only be as in the life of wealthy people. In wealth there is no hope of life eternal!"

"Maitreyi said: "What should I then do with possessions that cannot give me life eternal? Give me instead your knowledge, o my Lord."

On hearing this Yajnavalkya exclaimed: "Dear you are to me, beloved, and dear are the words you say. Come, sit down and I will teach; but hear my works with deep attention."

---

[31]Mascaro, *The Upanishads* (Penguin, 1965), pp. 110–111.

[32]*Mascaro*, The Upanishads, p. 121.

[33]Mascaro, *The Upanishads* (Penguin, 1965), pp 130–132; and S. Radhakrishnan, *The Principal Upanishads* (New York: Harper & Row, 1951), pp. 269–70, 296.

Then spoke Yajnavalkya:

"In truth, it is not for the love of a husband that a husband is dear; but for the love of the Soul in the husband that a husband is dear."

"It is not for the love of a wife that a wife is dear; but for the love of the Soul in the wife that a wife is dear."

"It is not for the love of children that children are dear; but for the love of the Soul in children that children are dear."

"It is not for the love of riches that riches are dear; but for the love of the Soul in riches that riches are dear."

"It is not for the love of religion that religion is dear; but for the love of the Soul in religion that religion is dear."

"It is not for the love of power that power is dear; but for the love of the Soul in power that power is dear."

"It is not for the love of heavens that heavens are dear; but for the love of the Soul in heavens that heavens are dear."

"It is not for the love of the gods that the gods are dear; but for the love of the Soul in the gods that the gods are dear."

"It is not for the love of creatures that creatures are dear; but for the love of the Soul in creatures that creatures are dear."

"It is not for the love of the all that the all is dear; but for the love of the Soul in the all that the all is dear."

"It is the Soul, the Spirit, the Self, that must be seen and be heard and have our thoughts and meditation, O Maitreyi.

When the Soul is seen and heard, is thought upon and is known, then all that is becomes known.

Religion will abandon the man who thinks that religion is apart from the Soul.

Power will abandon the man who thinks that power is apart from the Soul.

The gods will abandon the man who thinks that the gods are apart from the Soul.

Creatures will abandon the man who thinks that creatures are apart from the Soul.

All will abandon the man who thinks that the all is apart from the Soul.

Because religion, power, heavens, beings, gods and all rest on the Soul.

IV, 4, 1–2

When this self gets to weakness, gets to confusedness, as it were, then the breaths gather round him. He takes to himself those particles of light and descends into the heart. When the person in the eye turns away, then he becomes non-knowing of forms.

He is becoming one, he does not see, they say; he is becoming one, he does not smell, they say; he is becoming one, he does not taste, they say, he is becoming one, he does not speak, they say; he is becoming one, he does not hear, they say; he is becoming one, he does not think, they say; he is becoming one, he does not touch, they say; he is becoming one, he does not know, they say. The point of his heart becomes lighted up and by that light the self departs either through the eye or through the head or through other apertures of the body. And when he thus departs, life departs after him. And when life thus departs, all the vital breaths depart after him. He becomes one with intelligence. What has intelligence departs with him. His knowledge and his work take hold of him as also his past experience. . . .

Verily, when a person departs from this world, he goes to the air. It opens out there for him like the hole of a chariot wheel.

Through that he goes upwards. He goes to the sun. It opens out there for him like the hole of a lambara. Through that he goes upwards. He reaches the moon. It opens out there for him like the hole of a drum. Through that he goes upwards. He goes to the world free from grief, free from snow. There he dwells eternal years.

PowerWeb SUPPLEMENTS

1. **Ancient Jewel,** T. R. (Joe) Sundaram, *The World & I,* October 1996.
2. **Seeing the Sacred,** Diana L. Eck, from *Darsan: Seeing the Divine Image in India,* Anima Books, 1985.
3. **The Sacred Is the One True Reality of Brahman,** Swami Nikhilananda, from *Enduring Issues in Religion,* Greenhaven Press, 1995.
4. **The Hindu Ethic of Nonviolence,** *Hinduism Today,* February 1996.

Four *PowerWeb* supplemental readings explore the historic and contemporary relevance of a variety of core South Asian spiritual concepts. In the first selection, T. R. (Joe) Sundaram sketches in large strokes how Indian concepts of divinity have influenced religious thought in several great world traditions. In the ensuing two selections, Diana L. Eck describes the popular Hindu practice of envisioning the divine in sacred objects and places, and Swami Nikhilananda explains for modern readers what is meant by the assertion "Brahman is the One True Reality." Finally, the fourth recommended reading examines the ethic of nonviolence and its influence on the indigenous religions of South Asia. Students interested in understanding the spread of traditional Hindu beliefs into non-Hindu belief systems will particularly enjoy these readings.

These readings from *PowerWeb: Religion* are available at the McGraw-Hill *PowerWeb* website http://www.dushkin.com/powerweb. A personal access code to *PowerWeb: Religion* is provided free with each new copy of this book. Those who purchase a used copy may buy an access code at the website.

SELECTED BIBLIOGRAPHY

Babb, Lawrence A. *Redemptive Encounters: Three Modern Styles in the Hindu Tradition.* Berkeley, CA: University of California Press, 1986.

Basham, A. L. *The Origins and Development of Classical Hinduism.* Kenneth G. Zysk, ed. Boston: Beacon Press, 1989.

Biardeau, Madeleine. *Hinduism: The Anthropology of a Civilization.* New York: Oxford University Press, 1994.

Bowes, Pratima. *The Hindu Religious Tradition.* London: Routledge & Kegan Paul, 1977.

Chapple, Christopher Key, *Nonviolence to Animals, Earth, and Self in Asian Traditions.* Albany: State University of New York Press, 1993.

Copley, Antony, ed. *Hinduism in Public and Private.* New York: Oxford University Press, 2003.

Deutsch, Eliot. *The Bhagavad Gita.* Translated, with Introduction and Critical Essays by Eliot Deutsch. New York: University Press of America, 1968.

Doniger, Wendy, and Brian K. Smith. *The Laws of Manu.* New York: Penguin Books, 1992.

Flood, Gavin. *An Introduction to Hinduism.* Cambridge: Cambridge University Press, 1996.

Ions, Veronica. *Indian Mythology.* New York: Peter Bedrick Books, 1983.

Klostermaier, Klaus K. *A Survey of Hinduism.* Albany: State University of New York Press, 1989.

Lindsey, Harlan, and Paul B. Courtright, eds. *From The Margins of Hindu Marriage: Essays on Gender, Religion, and Culture.* New York: Oxford University Press, 1995.

Perrett, Roy W. *Hindu Ethics: A Philosophical Study.* Honolulu: University of Hawaii Press, 1998.

Pintchman, Tracy. *The Rise of the Goddess in the Hindu Tradition.* Albany: State University of New York Press, 1994.

Potter, Karl. *Advaita Vedanta Up to Samkara and his Pupils.* Princeton, NJ: Princeton University Press, 1988.

Powell, Barbara. *Windows into the Infinite: A Guide to the Hindu Scriptures.* Fremont, CA: Asian Humanities Press, 1996.

Radhakrishnan, Sarvepalli, and Charles A. Moore. *A Source Book in Indian Philosophy.* Princeton, NJ: Princeton University Press, 1957.

The Upanishads. Translations from the Sankrit with an Introduction by Juan Mascaro. London: Penguin Books, 1965.

van Buitenen, J. A. B. *The Bhagavadgita in the Mahabarata.* Chicago: University of Chicago Press, 1981.

Zaehner, R. C. *Hinduism.* New York: Oxford University Press, 1990.

Buddhism 5

About five centuries before the birth of Jesus, an Indian prince left his position of nobility to search for spiritual enlightenment. After six years of searching, the former prince discovered a truth about the human condition and began to share this truth with those around him. His message attracted a large company of followers. One day, those who were amazed at his teachings asked him: "Are you a god? Are you an angel? Are you a saint?" To each question, the wise man answered, "No." At that point, his disciples asked: "Then what are you? To this, the man answered: "I am awake."

Budh is the root of a Sanskrit word that means "to wake up." The word also denotes a state of knowing, or enlightenment. The term *Buddha*, literally the "Awakened One," is the title that loyal disciples gave to this ancient sage who woke up from the coma that entraps humankind.

From the teachings of this man emerged a tradition that today includes more than 350 million followers worldwide. Like most world religions, the tenets and customs of those who embrace Buddhism vary widely. In fact, the distance between Buddhists is so great that scholars often study the three major branches of this tradition separately. Yet, despite their differences, all Buddhists share two affirmations, one negative and one positive. The bad news is that life includes suffering, and that notwithstanding how much money, power, or status a person enjoys, no one is immune to it. The good news, however, is that there is a way to find release from this predicament and that the path to freedom is available to men and women of all classes and clans.

SETTING

Buddhism, much like Christianity, is a religion that was founded by a traveling teacher who renounced the religious establishment of his day. The given name of this rebel saint was Siddhartha, but he was called Gautama, after the name of his family. Gautama was born in the city of Kapilavastu, which is on the slopes of the Himalayas, near the present-day Nepal-Indian border. His father was a feudal lord named Suddhodana; his mother was Queen Maya. The date of his birth is contested. Some believe he was born as early as 624 BCE, while others place his birth as late as 466. It is more common to accept either 567 or 563 BCE as the most likely year of his birth.

To fully appreciate Gautama's teachings and influence, it is important to understand the Hindu world into which he was born. Many scholars believe that early Hinduism was largely shaped by the interactions between two distinct peoples and cultures. It is likely that the original inhabitants of India worshipped human and animal deities, looked with favor upon nonviolence and ascetic virtues, developed yoga meditation techniques, and embraced the idea of reincarnation. To this religious milieu, the Indo-European Aryans added a tradition known as Brahmanism. In contrast to the ascetic religion of the Dravidians, Brahmanism was a this-worldly, life-affirming religion that included a pantheon of powerful, fun-loving, and often amoral gods. The Aryans also brought with them a great reverence for the forces of nature. Impressed with the regularity of natural phenomena, they were convinced that every event had a cause and that good fortune de-

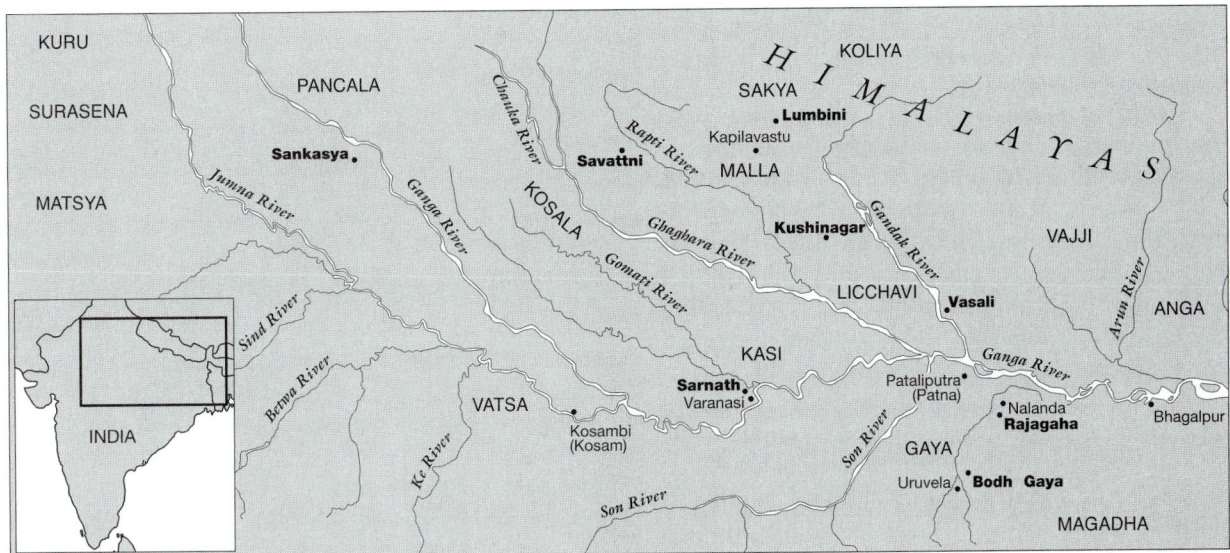

Map of sixth-century BCE India, showing major places of religious interest.

pended on securing the graces of the deities that controlled the natural order. Consequently, to appease the gods and win good favor, the Aryans offered elaborate sacrifices to their gods. These sacred rites were performed by the Brahmins, a special class of priests who served as the intermediators between the humans and the gods.

During the sacred rituals, the priests recite the ancient Vedic hymns that had been passed down orally from generation to generation. The Aryans believed that when these hymns were correctly recited, the gods were pleased and good fortune followed. Because the Brahmins alone knew the magical sounds, and because the survival of the community depended on the proper performance of these sacred duties, the Brahmins enjoyed a privileged social status. Over time, a rigid caste system emerged throughout India that placed the Brahmins and their political-military associates at the top of the social order, and, correspondingly, relegated the conquered native populations into the menial, servant classes.

By the seventh century BCE, many had come to view Brahmanism—with its emphasis on caste, sacrifice, and ritual—to be stale, stagnant, and corrupt. About this time some anonymous ascetic sages began to produce a collection of poems and dialogs known as the *Upanishads*. In time, these texts would become

recognized along with the Vedic hymns as part of the "revealed" Hindu canon. Although some of these verses supported the priestly system of sacrificial offerings, the major thrust of the *Upanishads* was to subordinate the Vedic rituals and even the caste duties to the higher spiritual goal of self-realization. According to the insights of these sages, the many Hindu gods were simply manifestations of an indefinable Absolute that both pervaded and transcended the universe. Moreover, they insisted that the Self within each individual comes from and ultimately will return to the Source of all being. Salvation is achieved when a person comes to understand the spiritual truth that the individual Self (Atman) and the universal Self (Brahman) are one and the same.

Not all Indian thinkers, however, were persuaded by the arguments of the Upanishadic teachers. Among the sixth-century BCE skeptics who rejected both the efficacy of the sacrificial rituals and the metaphysics of the Upanishadic thinkers were the Materialists, also known as the Carvakas. To these Materialists, the only valid source of knowledge was sense perception, and the only true reality was the physical world. Physical laws alone determined human life and behavior. The soul had no existence apart from the body; thus, there was no afterlife, and all discussions about morality and spirituality were meaningless. This form of Naturalism was a bold reaction against the idealistic metaphysics within orthodox Hinduism.

Another nonorthodox sixth-century reformer was the founder of Jainism, Nataputta Vardhamana, a spiritual teacher who is better known by his title Mahavira, which means "Great Hero." Mahavira was born the son of a wealthy Indian ruler. Like other Hindus of his era, Mahavira accepted as a reality the continuous cycle of birth, death, and rebirth. Unlike the orthodox, however, Mahavira challenged the caste system, rejected the authority of the Brahmin priests and the sacredness of the Vedas, and spoke against the efficacy of appealing to the Hindu deities.

Mahavira taught that reality consisted of two separate eternal existences, matter and soul, and that the purpose of life was to liberate the soul from its attachment to matter. As karma (the law of cause and effect by which actions produce good or bad consequences) was believed to unite soul and matter, to be liberated from the birth, death, and rebirth cycle, Mahavira taught that people must learn to avoid actions and to expiate past actions through the practice of severe austerities. After spending 12 years as a wandering ascetic who gave up all his worldly attachments, including even his clothing, Mahavira claimed to have attained release from the bonds of rebirth. He, thus, became a *jina*, which means a conqueror of his or her passions.

A generation after Mahavira, Gautama also would forsake a life of luxury to pursue spiritual enlightenment. Like the Jains and the Caravakas before him, Gautama rejected the superiority of the Brahmin caste, the sacredness of Hindu scripture, and the metaphysics of the Upanishadic thinkers. Like Mahavira, his journey took him down an ascetic path, but unlike Mahavira, in the end the Buddha would not find release through asceticism. The insights he discovered on his journey, however, inspired a movement that more than 25 centuries later has become the world's fourth largest religion.

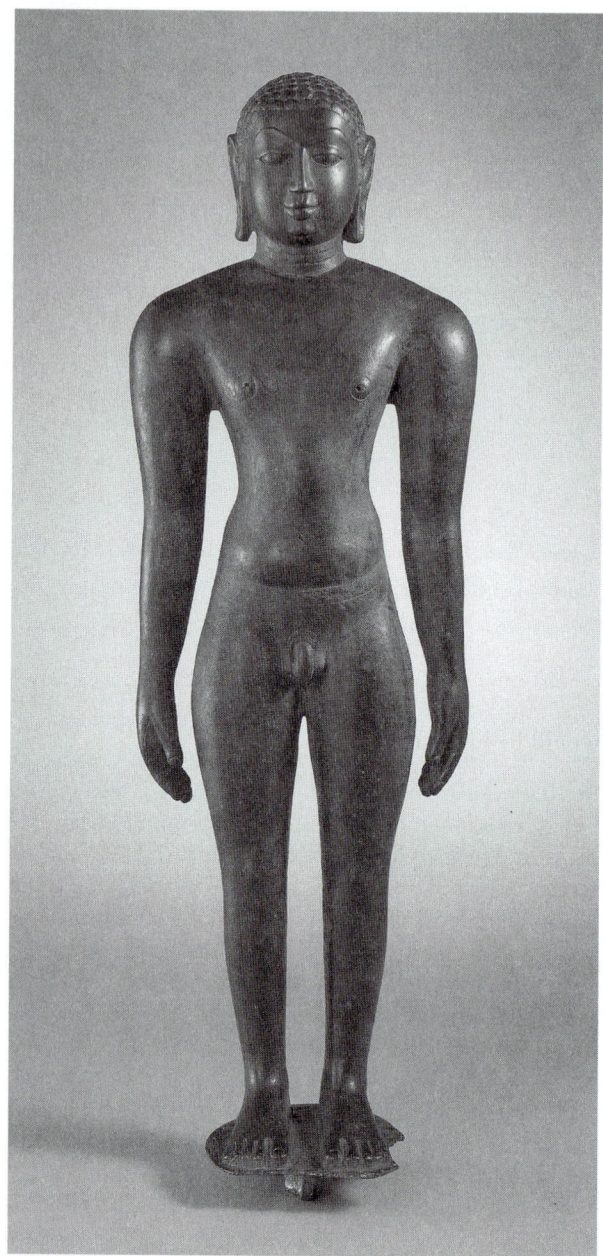

Statue of a naked Mahavira illustrates the priority that Jains place on nonattachment to worldly things.

SACRED STORIES AND BELIEFS

Those who reverently remember the lives of historical figures often embellish the biographies of these men and women, thus making it difficult for future generations to distill the "factual" from the legendary accounts. This is as true for the Buddha as it is for the other great sages of the ancient world. To understand Buddhism, however, it is important to know the sacred stories that have been passed down about the founder of the tradition. From these traditional accounts of Gautama's life, we can gain important insights about both the man himself and about the millions of his followers who have found inspiration from his life and teachings.

Gautama's Birth, Childhood, and Youth

According to tradition, Gautama was not simply a human who founded a religion, but he was a preexistent personage who was born a *Bhodisattva,* a being destined to become a Buddha. Buddhists assert that the Buddha had a supernatural conception that is somewhat analogous to the Virgin Birth of Jesus. During the Midsummer Festival, a white elephant is said to have entered the womb of Queen Maya. Precisely 10 lunar months later, when Maya was traveling to visit her parents, she entered a park called Lumbini. Here she went into labor, and while in a standing position, she gave birth to a son who was received on a golden net held by four angels. The newborn baby then arose and told his mother that this would be his last birth.

There is another story that says at the time of his birth, a Hindu sage noticed that the 32 traditional marks of an "Enlightened One" were apparent in the child's body. This prophesy was corroborated five days later at the child's name-giving ceremony when a soothsayer announced that if the child remained at home, he would become a great king who would rule all of India. If the child left the palace, however, the soothsayer said that he would become a Buddha.

When the baby was only one week old, his mother died, and Gautama was placed under the care of his aunt. His father, the local "king" or chieftain of the city, provided Gautama with all the luxuries that his position allowed. Three palaces were built for him, and servants, including 40,000 dancing girls, responded to all of his requests. One story informs us of Gautama's childhood predispositions. During a public festival, Gautama once was left alone in a tent. When his nurses returned, they found him seated with his legs crossed, absorbed in a meditative trance.

At age 16 (or as some accounts say, age 19), Gautama married a cousin, who was a princess in a neighboring region. Legend has it that she was a perfect wife, always cheerful, charming, and dutiful. Together, they had a child. After the birth of a son, Gautama seemed to have everything: youth, health, wealth, power, marital bliss, and family. Despite all these things, however, Gautama remained dissatisfied with life's limitations.

The Legend of the Four Passing Sights

Desiring his son to become a universal king, Gautama's father went to great lengths to shield his son from all of life's misfortunes. As a result, Gautama grew up in ignorance of the existence of old age, disease, and death. One day, however, a god appeared on the roadside near Gautama in the form of a decrepit old man. Gautama asked his charioteer what this was, and for the first time he learned that the condition of old age awaited all men. On another day, Gautama saw the form of a diseased man, and thus learned that disease and misery were common in life. Later, the prince saw a dead man being carried on a funeral pyre. With this, Gautama learned about the dreadful reality of death. The prince became distraught, until he saw a fourth sight—an ascetic monk walking toward him wearing a yellow robe. From the sight of this man of peace, Gautama gained an insight into how to find freedom from the sufferings of old age, disease, and death. At this point, the prince resolved to leave the palace to search for the way of release. Against the wishes of his father, he shaved his head, exchanged his rich garments for a coarse yellow robe, and left the palace and his family to seek deliverance in the forests.

The Unfulfilled Quest

Although dissatisfied with hedonism, at age 29 Gautama remained unsure as to the true path to enlightenment. According to Buddhist sources, Gautama refused to reject a philosophy until he had fully tested it. Hence, after leaving his palace, he went to Rajagaha, the royal city in a neighboring province, where he became the disciple of two ascetic philosophers schooled in various yogic practices. After testing their teachings, Gautama became convinced that meditation alone could not lead him to enlightenment. Gautama then withdrew further into the forest to test the extreme bodily asceticism that the Jains, among other sects, advocated as the way to liberation.

For five more years, Gautama endured severe austerities in his search for release. He practiced restraint of breath, ate only nauseous foods, stood for long periods in a single posture, slept on thorns and near rotting bodies, let filth accumulate on his body, and finally reduced his daily diet to a single grain of rice. Ultimately, he collapsed from his weakness, and the five ascetics who lived near him thought that he had died. When he awoke, a young woman nursed him to health by offering him some cooked rice and milk. Outraged at this self-indulgence, the ascetics denounced him as a backslider and left him. This experience, however, convinced Gautama that neither of the two widely recognized roads to salvation—meditation or asceticism—brought enlightenment.

Discovering the Truth of the Middle Way

At age 35, Gautama entered a grove now called Bodhgaya and sat down at the foot of a Bodhi-tree. Here he resolved to sit until he attained enlightenment. As he allowed his mind to reflect upon his past experiences, he began to see more clearly. Realizing that he was close to enlightenment, Mara the tempter came to him in an attempt to frustrate his search for truth. Mara first told him that a former enemy had led a revolt, taken his wife, and imprisoned his father and that he must return home immediately to secure the release of his family. Next the tempter appeared in the form of sensuous dancers who tried to seduce him. Finally, Mara appeared in the form of horrific demons that sent deadly missiles at him. Notwithstanding these distractions, Gautama remained unmoved. Thus, having defeated Mara, he spent the night under the tree in meditation. It was here that he passed into the state of "wakefulness."

After having experienced the earthly foretaste of Nirvana, he returned to the world to communicate his saving knowledge to others. The first men he sought were the five ascetics who earlier had deserted him. He found them in the Deer Park at Benares. At first, the ascetics shunned him, but after noticing his radiance and serenity, they received him into their company. Having thus won their attention, the Buddha told them that there were two extremes that ought to be avoided—a life given to pleasures and a life given to mortifications. He then informed them that enlightenment was to be found by pursing the truth of the Middle Way. After sharing his experience with them, he challenged them to embrace the path of the Middle Way. The five ascetics accepted his testimony,

Enlightenment of the Buddha. For several centuries the Buddha was not portrayed in human form since he was believed to have transcended all limitations of space, time, and existence. Instead, he was depicted by symbols standing for the four central events in his life: a lotus for his birth, a tree and a throne for his enlightenment, a wheel for his first teaching (the four Noble Truths), and a stupa for his bodily demise. The carvings on the stupa at *Sanchi* illustrate aniconic portrayals, such as this one where he is portrayed as a tree surrounded by his respectful followers.

and, with their conversion, the first Sangha (the Buddhist monastic order) came into being.

The Four Noble Truths and the Eightfold Path

In this first sermon delivered at Benares, the Buddha outlined "four noble truths" that would become the centerpiece of his future teachings. These truths are as follows:

1. Human suffering (*duhkha*) is universal.
2. Suffering is caused by craving (*trishna*).
3. Release from suffering (*nirvana*) comes by eliminating the craving for material and sensual satisfactions.
4. The way to achieve release is by following an eightfold path, which includes right belief, right aspiration, right speech, right conduct, right means of livelihood, right endeavor, right mindfulness, and right meditation. The eightfold path thus demands wisdom, morality, and concentration, and all are needed to extinguish the cravings that cause human misery.

The Master Teacher and His Disciples

For 45 years following his enlightenment, the Buddha traveled around northeastern India winning disciples, training monks, and overseeing the affairs of the Sangha. He taught lay people about the merits of alms-giving and about the need to keep the five moral precepts—do not destroy life; do not steal; do not commit adultery; do not lie; do not drink intoxicants. He taught them that charity and morality brought harmony and prosperity in this life and a favorable rebirth in the next.

To those ready to seek life's ultimate goal, however, the Buddha taught about the monastic path that leads to *Nirvana*. Advising his monks to abandon the cravings that lead to suffering, he spoke about overcoming the three great poisons (greed, hate, and ignorance) and the five hindrances (sensuous pleasures, ill-will, sloth, restlessness, and doubt). A teacher of practical wisdom, the Buddha avoided speculative metaphysical matters, questions that he insisted brought neither insight nor edification. On several occasions, his disciples asked him, "Is the world eternal or not eternal? Is the world finite or infinite? Is the soul the same as or not the same as the body? Does a Buddha exist or not exist after death?" To each of these questions, tradition informs us that the Buddha remained silent. To him, metaphysical speculations about the unknowable produced sectarian pride and division but did not lead to improved conduct or enlightenment.

During the rainy season of every year, when torrential rains and rising rivers made travel difficult, the Buddha withdrew to a retreat site to spend special times with his monks. Between November and June, however, he was out in the world providing the masses with spiritual counsel and encouragement. Noted for both his great compassion and wisdom, the Buddha attracted a wide range of followers, including men and women from every class and caste. A number of his early disciples were merchants from prominent families who, following their conversions, offered generous gifts to support the Sangha. Others, including Upali the barber, who became one of the Buddha's most trusted disciples, came from the lowly servant classes. Still others came from Hinduism's elite Brahmin caste. Included among the Brahmans were two of his chief disciples: Sariputra, a venerated disciple known for his great wisdom, and Maudgalyayana, the great one renowned for his supernatural powers.

According to tradition, the Buddha returned to his home city of Kapilavastu and there received into the Sangha his son, wife, stepmother, and two of his cousins, Ananda and Devadatta. Among these recruits, Ananda is particularly venerated in Buddhist lore as the Buddha's personal attendant during the last 25 years of his life and as the beloved disciple who recited the entire teachings of the Buddha to the assembly of monks who gathered together at Rajagriha following the master's death. Similarly, his stepmother, Mahaprajapati, also is reverently remembered as the one who pleaded with her son to allow women into the Sangha and then, following the Buddha's acceptance, became the first nun to join the monastic order. His cousin, Devadatta, in contrast, is remembered as the jealous disciple who renounced the Buddha's path of salvation, plotted his murder, and attempted to usurp control of the Sangha. When Devadatta's evil scheme was foiled, however, this "Judas Iscariot" of the Buddhist tradition established his own sect and died in disgrace.

The Buddha's Final Days and Death

At the age of 80, while traveling north from Rajagriha, the Buddha became ill with dysentery. His condition grew worse after he ate a meal of dried boar's flesh in the home of a blacksmith named Cunda. The Buddha retired to a grove near the village of Kushinagari. Here, with his strength departing, he lay down and offered his disciples some final instructions.

Even at his deathbed, the Buddha's thoughts were directed toward others. Concerned that Cunda might feel responsible for his death, he asked his traveling companion Ananda to inform Cunda that his last meal was to him like that hallowed meal he ate while under the Bodi-tree just before his enlightenment. After making this request, the Buddha graciously received a delegation of villagers from Kushinara who had come to give him their respects. According to tradition, as the Buddha breathed his last breaths, flowers dropped from the sky, heavenly music filled the air, and an assembly of gods and powerful spirits surrounded the grove. At this moment, the Buddha is said to have uttered his final words: "All compounded things decay. Work out your own salvation with diligence."

SCRIPTURES

Like Jesus, the Buddha left no writings. His teachings, however, were remembered by his disciples and transmitted orally for several centuries, until they were finally codified into written texts. Because these texts were placed into three collections, the earliest scriptures were known as the *Tripitaka,* meaning the "three baskets" of the Buddha's wisdom.

The Origins and Divisions of *The Three Baskets*

Born a prince in the kingdom of Magadha, Gautama spoke an Indian dialect known as Ardhamagadhi, and hence, his teachings were first delivered and remembered in this form. Following the Buddha's death, the successorless movement splintered into a number of sects, 18 of which are remembered in the tradition. Although each sect attempted to preserve the memory of the Buddha and his words, most of the records of these early sects have been lost, either because the oral tradition was never written down or because the ravages of time have destroyed the written records. No texts from the dialect that Gautama originally spoke are extant. Oral traditions, however, were recorded and preserved in two ancient Indian dialects: Sanskrit, the official language of Brahmanism, and Pali, a simplified form of Sanskrit that was very similar to the dialect spoken by Gautama. In time the Sanskrit version of the *Tripitaka*[1] became the ac-

---

[1] *Tripitika* is the Sanskrit word for "three baskets." In Pali, the term is *Tipitika.*

> ### DIVISION AND SCOPE OF THE TRIPITAKA
>
> The Basket of Discipline (*Vinaya Pitaka*) includes rules for monks and nuns
>
> The Basket of Discourses (*Sutra Pitaka*) includes the Buddha's remembered teachings grouped into five major sections:
> The Long Discourses (*Digha Nikaya*)
> The Middle Length Discourses (*Majjhima Nikaya*)
> The Grouped Discourses (*Samyutta Nikaya*)
> The Numbered Discourses (Anguttara Kikaya)
> The Little Books (*Khuddaka Nikaya*), which includes the *Dhammapada*
>
> The Basket of Elaboration (*Adhidhamma Pitaka*) explores the physics and psychology of existence

cepted text for the Buddhist traditions that originated in northern India, whereas the Pali text became the authorized canon for the Theravadin Buddhist tradition with its origins in southern India.

It is difficult, if not impossible, to determine which portions of the *Tripitaka* date back to the Buddha himself and which are later embellishments of his teachings. One method that scholars use to attempt to date the texts is to compare the extant documents of the various sects. Where the passages in the texts agreed word for word, it is assumed that these texts date to an early period before the emergence of separate schools of Buddhist thought. Similarly, passages that do not agree are taken to be elaborations of the earlier texts. While this scholarship offers us many insights, readers should be aware that this process also is riddled with uncertainties and that modern scholarship cannot always tell whether a particular passage dates close to the time of the Buddha or was produced by an unnamed disciple two or more centuries later.

Where scholarship is silent, however, tradition often speaks loud and clear. According to many of the faithful, shortly after the Buddha's death 500 followers spent the rainy season together at Rajagriha. Although many question the historicity of this so-called

First Council, tradition informs us that the monks at this council recited to each other the remembered spoken words of the Buddha. Because these words were viewed to be words of the Buddha that were remembered and authenticated by his closest disciples, many of the teachings in the *Tripitaka* typically begin with the expression, "Thus have I heard," and then are followed by descriptions of where and to whom the Buddha was speaking at the occasion of the message.

The first of the "pitakas" or baskets of the *Tripitaka* is the *Vinaya Pitaka* (The Basket of Discipline). This collection includes the 227 and 311 rules that monks and nuns, respectively, are instructed to follow while living within their monastic communities. Some of the rules deal with mundane matters such as the feeding, clothing, and housing of the monks and nuns; other rules regulate how the members of the order are to interact among themselves and with those outside the order. The *Vinaya* also offers prescribed punishments for those who violate these rules of discipline. Four offenses—sexual intercourse, theft, murder, and false claim to supernatural powers—are not tolerated and result in immediate expulsion from the order. The lesser offenses demand less harsh punishments and provide opportunities for confession and forgiveness. As the most stable and uncontested words of the *Tripitaka*, the *Vinaya* has been memorized and recited by Buddhist monks and nuns for more than 2 millennia. It is still common for a shorter summary of these rules to be chanted every fortnight by members of the monastic orders.

The second basket of the *Tripitaka* is the *Sutra*[2] *Pitaka* (The Basket of Discourses). This massive collection includes more than 10,000 sermons and sayings delivered by the Buddha during his 45-year teaching ministry, as well as some additional verses recited by members of the Sangha who were contemporaries of the Buddha. This basket of materials is subdivided into five groupings that are arranged according to their length, form, and thematic content:

1. The Division of Long Discourses (*Digha Nikaya*)—34 lengthy sermons that convey the compassion, power, and wisdom of the Buddha. It includes the well-known account of "The Buddha's Last Days."

2. The Division of Medium Length Discourses (*Majjhima Nikaya*)—152 mid-length sermons of the Buddha delivered in a wide variety of contextual settings.

3. The Division of Grouped Discourses (*Samyutta Nikaya*)—7,762 shorter teachings grouped into 56 thematic categories.

4. The Division of Numerically Arranged Discourses (*Anguttara Nikaya*)—9,550 short teachings arranged into 11 divisions according to the number of verses about a single topic.

5. The Division of Little Books (*Khuddaka Nikaya*)—a collection of 15 (17 in the Thai edition and 18 in the Burmese) shorter works that contain some of the earliest and some of the latest material in the canon.

Within this final division of the *Sutra Pitaka* are some of the most beloved passages in the *Tripitaka*. The first book in this division, the *Khuddakapatha* (literally, the "Short Passages"), is essentially a primer for novice monks and nuns that includes prayers and a catechism of basic Buddhist precepts and teachings. Likewise, the *Itivuttaka* (literally, "As It Was Said"), is a popular collection of short sayings of the Buddha. The *Therigatha* ("Songs of the Elder Nuns") and the *Theragatha* ("Songs of the Elder Monks") are inspiring personal accounts of the lives of early monks and nuns. Many of these stories are conversion testimonials that contrast the pre-enlightenment sufferings with the post-enlightenment bliss of these early disciples. Also in this collection are the *Udana*, a rich collection of 80 short sutras, the *Sutra Nipata*, a collection of 71 short teachings, and the *Jataka*, a book of birth stories that relates popular beliefs about 547 previous births of the Buddha. Finally, and most importantly, this division includes the *Dhammapada*—a collection of 423 verses that expresses the basic teachings of Buddhism.

The third basket is the *Abhidhamma Pitaka* (The Basket of Doctrinal Elaboration). This collection contains some of the most difficult material in the *Tripitaka* for it attempts to explore the physics and psychology of existence. According to some sects, the Buddha formulated this collection during the fourth week after his Enlightenment. Most scholars, however, do not consider this to be the work of the Buddha himself but, instead, view it as elaborations of his teachings that were added to the canon several centuries after his death. The contents of the

---

[2]*Sutra* is a Sanskrit word. In Pali, the word is *sutta*. For consistency, in this volume we use the Sanskrit *sutra*.

Abhidhamma vary more widely among the Buddhist sects than the contents of the first two baskets of the *Tripitaka*. Some of the early sects even contested the authenticity of portions of this collection.

The *Abhidhamma* is divided into seven books, each of which is to some extent a technical manual for meditation. The most important books include the *Enumeration of Phenomena* (a text that describes 52 mental factors, 89 possible states of consciousness, 4 primary elements, and 23 physical phenomena), and the *Book of Relations* (a detailed analysis of 24 laws of conditionality that govern the interactions between mind and matter). Some 6,000 pages in the Sinhalese edition, this last book in the *Abhidhamma* has the distinction of being the longest single volume in the *Tripitaka*.

Later Additions to the Sacred Canon

Since ancient times, the early history of Buddhism has traditionally been divided into eras of 500-year durations, with the first period opening with the birth of the Buddha himself. The great literary accomplishment of Buddhism during this formative period was the production of the *Tripitaka*. According to the basic teachings of the *Tripitaka*, the highest goal to which a Buddhist could aspire was to become an *Arhat*—a monk or nun who had experienced enlightenment.

About five centuries after Gautama's birth, however, Buddhism entered into a second era of development. This era, like the first, was a period of great intellectual and literary creativity. According to some scholars, by the first century BCE doctrinal disputes among the sects and growing tensions between the monks and the laity convinced many Buddhists that the central doctrines in the *Tripitaka* had become stale and lifeless, and in response to this growing dissatisfaction, other collections of religious discourses appeared. Although new and innovative, these writings were viewed by their supporters to be the "higher" teachings that were spoken by the Buddha himself, recorded by his disciples, and then hidden for 400 years, only to be rediscovered at a later time when there were humans capable of understanding the deeper implications of the message. In Mahayana parlance, the new sutras were regarded as a "second turning of the Dharma-wheel" that revealed a deeper level of truth than the *Three Baskets*.

> ### DIVISION AND SCOPE OF LATER ADDITIONS TO THE SACRED CANON
>
> **Mahayana Buddhism**
> Goal: Becoming a *Bodhisattva*
> Major Collections:
> The Perfection of Wisdom Sutras
> The Lotus Sutra
> The Three Pure Land Sutras
> The Lankavatara Sutra
> The Garland Sutra
> **Tantric Buddhism**
> Goal: Becoming a *Shiddha*
> Major Collections:
> The Tibetan Book of the Dead
> Songs of Milarepa

A major thrust of these writings was to replace the original goal of becoming an enlightened monk with the still higher goal of becoming a *Bodhisattva*—someone who had obtained perfection, yet who deferred the ultimate bliss of *Nirvana* in order to turn back and show others how to be freed from their sufferings. The appearance and spread of these writings forced the division of monks into two large and opposing traditions: the Mahayana tradition, which embraced the new scriptures, and the Theravada or Hinayana tradition, which rejected them.

The Mahayana Scriptures

The sheer volume of the literary productions of this era is impressive as each of the several Mahayana schools that developed selected particular texts into their sacred canons. These texts were originally written in Sanskrit, although many of them have been preserved via later Chinese and Tibetan translations. Although much of this literature has been translated into English during the last century, some of it remains without an English translation. Owing to the vastness of the Mahayana collections, in this survey we will only discuss five of the most well-known and influential collections in this immense literary tradition.

1. *The Perfection of Wisdom Sutras (Prajnaparamita)*—This massive collection, which includes 40 sutras totaling some

100,000 pages, focuses on the importance of wisdom among the 10 perfections that are found in the *Bodhisattva*. The lengths of these sutras vary from the *Heart Sutra*, a one-page poetic exposition of the faith, to the *Wisdom in Eight Thousand Lines Sutra*, an elaborate teaching that develops the Buddhist doctrine of Emptiness. One of the most influential of the wisdom sutras is the *Diamond Cutter Sutra*, so-called because its teaching is like a sharp diamond that cuts away all unnecessary conceptualizations and brings one to the realization that phenomenal appearances are not ultimate reality but mere illusions. This work, which was written in the first century and printed in Chinese in 868 CE five centuries before the Gutenberg Bible, is believed to be the first book ever printed.

2. *The Lotus Sutra (Saddharma-Pundarika)*—Written in Sanskrit between 100 BCE and 150 CE and translated on several occasions into Chinese in the third to fifth centuries, this collection is recognized by many Mahayana schools as containing the purest expression of the Buddha's teaching about supreme enlightenment. The *Lotus Sutra* places a radical emphasis on devotion and faith as it asserts that the path to Buddhahood is not restricted to those who practiced monastic austerities but is open to all who worship the Buddha (or Buddhas) in a number of ways. The sutra teaches the doctrine of the eternal cosmic Buddha whose universal grace is the source of salvation. This collection is the central text for the T'ien-T'ai sect in China and the several sects inspired by Nichiren in Japan.

3. *The Three Pure Land Sutras*—These sutras—which consist of the *Sutra of Amitabha*, the *Teaching of Infinite Life*, and the *Visualization Sutra*—are the central texts for Mahayana Buddhism's Pure Land schools. These sutras expound the doctrine of Amitabha, the *Bodhisattva* who, upon becoming a Buddha, created a "Pure Land" of infinite positivity where people go after they die in order to realize full enlightenment. The Pure Land is not a final resting place (like the Christian "heaven") but a place for the dead to go to find enlightenment so that they will be able to

return to the earth in a future life in order to help others. The third sutra in this collection teaches 16 methods of visualizing Amitabha Buddha, the *Bodhisattvas*, and the Pure Land paradise. The central message of these sutras— that salvation is not obtained by human efforts but by the total reliance on the grace of Buddha Amitabha—is for Buddhism a doctrine that is comparable to Martin Luther's "justification by faith alone" interpretation of Christian dogma.

4. *The Lankavatara Sutra*—This late-fourth-century Mahayana text asserts that the Buddha went to the island of Lanka to teach this sutra to the Emperor Ravana, a king depicted in the early Hindu epic Ramayana. Although this long, terse, and complex sutra of mixed prose and verse contains almost all of the main ideas of Mahayana Buddhism, it is most famous for its exposition of the Mind-only doctrine that insists that all discriminated entities are empty—nothing but creations of the mind. According to the teachings of this sutra, the key to enlightenment is to be freed from the illusions of dualistic concepts that falsely discriminate between subject and object and cause the cycle of birth and death. The *Lankavatara Sutra* was especially influential in the formulation of a school of Mahayana Buddhism known as Yogacara.

5. *The Garland Sutra* (Avatamsaka)—This text, which was first translated from Sanskrit into Chinese by Buddhabhadra around 420 CE, is one of the most influential texts in East Asian Buddhism and is considered the core scripture of the Chinese Hua-yen school. The vast text encompasses a wide range of subjects, including the teaching that all things are interdependent and interpenetrating (i.e., things are what they are because of their relationship with other things) and that the human mind is the universe itself. One well-known book in this collection, the *Gandhavyuha Sutra*, describes a seeker named Sudhana who travels across India receiving spiritual instruction from 52 teachers before ultimately realizing the highest truth. In the end, Sudhana discovers that a *Bodhisattva* is in fact not separate from the beings that he endeavors to help.

The Tantras and the Third Sacred Canon

About a 1,000 years after the life of Gautama, Buddhism entered a third era of creative development which, like the first two eras, resulted in the production of a new sacred literature. This literature, known as the Tantras (meaning "continuous linage"), departed from earlier forms of Buddhism in several fundamental ways. Whereas the ultimate goals of life as presented in the *Tripitaka* and the Mahayana sutras, respectively, are to become either an enlightened monk (*Arhat*) or a compassionate *Bodhisattva*, in the Tantric texts, the highest aim in life is to become a *Siddha*. Unlike the *Arhat* or the *Bodhisattva*, the *Siddha* is not interested in obtaining Buddhahood at some distant moment. Rather, the *Siddha* is a master teacher with wonder-working, magical powers whose spiritual development is so advanced that he can obtain Buddhahood in a single lifetime.

According to the Tantric literature, this fast-track path to full spiritual realization is a path that appropriates the secret powers that resided within the universe to obtain the goal of enlightenment. To a greater degree than the earlier Buddhist forms, the Tantric canon elevated the role that deities, ghosts, spirits, and demons play in one's spiritual quest. Another unique characteristic of Tantric teaching is its willingness to spurn, and even mock, conventional morality. Just as farmers use impure substances like manure to fertilize the soil, the Tantric teachers insist that it is possible to use the very things that produced suffering (desires and cravings) to transcend all desires and thereby find enlightenment. Hence, in addition to the use of yogic techniques, hand gestures, and magical sounds, Tantric practices incorporate taboos that are shocking to Buddhists outside this tradition, including the use of intoxicating drinks and the performance of sacred sexual rituals.

Like the earlier scriptures, the Tantras were attributed to the Buddha. Unlike the earlier sacred canons, however, the Tantras were not to linked directly to the words of the historic Gautama. Instead, the new teachings were assigned to mythical Buddhas who were alleged to have revealed the esoteric secrets in the Tantras at some remote and distant time.

Perhaps the best-known example of Tantric literature in the West is a book written by Padmasambhava entitled *Bardo Thodol Chenmo*. When this eighth-century piece was translated into English in 1927, it was given its more popular title, *The Tibetan Book of the Dead*. According to tradition, after its production, this work was hidden in caves until revealed in the fourteenth century by Rigzin Karma Linpa, a spiritual master believed to be the reincarnation of Padmasambhava. This work is in essence a self-help guidebook that is intended to help the dying and recently deceased souls to find their way through the difficult stages of the afterlife. The work is reportedly based on accounts of spiritual masters who had total recall of their own between-lives experiences.

Another popular illustration of the Tantric literary tradition is the *Songs of Milarepa*. The hero of this classic is Milarepa, a great Tibetan mediator whose tragic youth and early search for enlightenment were marked by violence and extreme hardship. Milarepa was sent by his master teacher Marpa to meditate in remote caves on the snow-covered Tibetan mountains. Wearing only a cotton-cloak, Milarepa (literally "the cotton-clad one"), kept warm on the frigid mountains only by the inner heat of his yoga mastery. As his spiritual powers grew, disciples traveled great distances to the caves to hear him express his spiritual insights in spontaneous songs, which, according to tradition, are said to number 100,000.

SUBDIVISIONS

By demanding loyalty to no god, leaving no writings, and appointing no successor, the Buddha initiated a great movement that was at once both popular and prone to division. The early appeal of the movement is easy to describe. Unlike the sacred knowledge of Brahmanism, which was transmitted in an elite language known only by the priests, the Buddha's teachings were dispersed in the vernacular languages to peoples of all castes and classes. Moreover, unlike Jainism—another contemporaneous reform movement that rejected the efficacy of the Brahmans and their gods—early Buddhism did not demand either an extreme form of asceticism or a complete rejection of community norms. With religious teachings more accommodating than confrontational, the nonviolent lifestyle fostered by the Sangha appealed to the local rulers and the general population alike.

Without a strong central authority, however, the Sangha also was ripe for frequent schisms. Within a century after the Buddha's death, an assembly of

Padmasambhava, the Buddhist sage with magical powers who exorcised demons and enabled a Buddhist monastery to be built in Tibet.

monks and laity met at Vaisali for the so-called Second Council to discuss matters of doctrine and discipline. Two factions emerged from this council: the Mahasanghika (meaning the "Great Sangha"), and the Theravadins (meaning the "Adherents of the Teaching of the Elders"). This division between the liberals, who wanted to ease the disciplinary restrictions on the Sangha, and the conservatives, who insisted upon a strict adherence to the monastic rules, was only the first of numerous schisms that would splinter the unity of the Sangha. According to tradition, 18 separate groups were established during the several centuries that immediately followed the Buddha's death. Despite their differences over matters of doctrines and discipline, the early Buddhist sects were tolerant of each other. During this early period, it was even common for monks and nuns from the differing sects to live together in the same monastic communities.

Asoka and the Spread of Early Buddhism

About three centuries after the life of Jesus, the Roman Emperor Constantine embraced Christianity, called for a council of bishops to define Christian dogma, and used his influence to spread the religion across the empire. Similarly, about three centuries after the life of the Buddha, King Asoka, a powerful emperor who conquered the whole of India, converted to Buddhism and became interested in promoting its propagation. Publicly professing his sorrow for the wars and sufferings he had caused, he promised his subjects that henceforth he would rule with gentleness and patience. To eliminate unnecessary bloodshed, he abolished the royal hunt and reduced the consumption of meat in the palace. He also issued royal decrees telling the people that they must respect living creatures, speak only the truth, treat slaves and servants properly, honor their teachers, and show liberality to the ascetics.

Although his decrees did not mention doctrines such as the Four Noble Truths or the goal of obtaining *Nirvana,* Asoka worked to spread his understanding of Buddhism across his empire. During his reign, he made pilgrimages to the sacred spots where the Buddha was born, experienced enlightenment, and died. He also opened the original 10 burial mounds (known as *stupas*) where the relics of the Buddha were stored, and he distributed these relics to numerous other locations across India, thus spreading the cult of devotion to the Buddha. Moreover, he issued edicts discouraging schism and, according to tradition, called the Third Council to reorganize and reform the Sangha.

Most importantly, Asoka sent Buddhist missionaries to Syria, Egypt, Cyrene, Greece, Sri Lanka, and Burma. The missions to Africa and the Mediterranean had little effect, but the missionary activity in Sri Lanka bore great fruit. Buddhism became the official state religion of the region. In time the island was declared to belong to the Buddha himself, and only Buddhists were eligible to become its kings. In Sri Lanka, the *Tripitaka* was published and preserved in the Pali dialect. The Pali *Tripitaka* is the only canon of an early school that is preserved completely.

The most successful of the early sects that took root in Sri Lanka was the conservative Theravadin school. This tradition, which accepts only the Pali *Tripitaka* into its sacred canon, holds that a favorable rebirth awaits the morally upright but that normally only those who take monastic vows will obtain *Nirvana.* The term *Thervadin* means "Teachings of the Elders."

The Three Vehicles of Buddhism

In addition to the ancient Thervadin tradition, two other great traditions emerged during the first millennium of Buddhist development. These three great early traditions have been called Hinayana, Mahayana, and Vajrayana. Each of these names contains the Sanskrit root *yana,* a word that literally means "vehicle" but often refers to water vehicles or rafts. Each tradition claims to carry its seekers from the present shores of this world to the distant shore of *Nirvana,* and the names of these traditions are descriptions of the types of rafts that ferry their adherents across the treacherous seas of life to enlightenment.

Hinayana—The Lesser Vehicle

Hinayana means "Lesser Vehicle," whereas *Mahayana* and *Vajrayana,* respectively, mean "Greater Vehicle" and "Diamond Vehicle." Mahayana Buddhists often refer to the Theravadin sect as Hinayana, although it is obvious that the surviving members of this sect reject being called the Lesser Vehicle. However, if the negative connotations are stripped away from the word, the term *Hinayana* is helpful because it conveys a fundamental teaching of the Theravadin tradition, namely that the distant shore of *Nirvana* can normally be reached only by those who board the small raft through the taking of monastic vows. The most conservative of the three traditions, the Hinayana or Theravadin school focuses on the concept of an *Arhat,* a celibate monk or nun who has achieved the goal of liberation or no rebirth. Owing to the location of its flowering in Sri Lanka, Hinayana is sometimes referred to as Southern Buddhism. With about 125 million followers worldwide, this branch remains the dominant expression of Buddhism in Sri Lanka, Burma, Cambodia, Laos, Thailand, and the southern part of Vietnam.

Mahayana—The Greater Vehicle

As discussed earlier, beginning about five centuries after the life of Gautama, tensions within the Sangha led to the production of additional sacred writings that were attributed to the Buddha himself. Those who embraced these sutras and their teachings became known as Mahayanists. The ultimate goal for Mahayana Buddhists is not to strive for individual freedom from suffering and the cycle of birth and death but to become a *Bodhisattva,* striving for awakening for the sake of all sentient beings and vowing to stay in the cycle until all beings are awakened. From the Mahayana perspective, this is the "greater vehicle" because it puts the concern for others above the concern for self.

Just as Protestant Christianity has divided into many denominations, there are many subsets within Mahayana Buddhism. Some of the major groups include the Meditation Schools (Ch'an in China and Zen in Japan), T'ein-t'ai, Hua-yen, and the Pure Land sects of Jodo-shu and Jodo-shin-shu. Mahayana Buddhism is most prominent in China, Korea, Japan, and the northern part of Vietnam; hence, it is often referred to as Eastern Buddhism. With about 185 million adherents worldwide, Mahayana Buddhism is the largest of the three great Buddhist traditions.

Although the doctrines of Mahayana Buddhism vary widely from sect to sect, most Mahayanists view the historical Gautama as an incarnation of an eternal Buddha essence that has existed in all ages. One of the central innovations that separated and continues to separate the Mahayanists from the Hinayanists is the commitment to become a *Bodhisattva* rather than an *Arhat*. *Bodhisattvas* are those who possess complete wisdom yet whose compassion for others compels them to postpone their entrance into *Nirvana* in order to liberate others from their sufferings. According to the Mahayanists, anyone can become a *Bodhisattva* and thereby eventually attain Buddhahood. To become a *Bodhisattva*, it is necessary to win enlightenment for others and begin the journey toward Buddhahood. Mahayanists recognize that the path to Buddhahood will be long and arduous and that *Bodhisattvas* will spend eons and eons practicing the six perfections before obtaining Buddhahood. The six perfections include the perfection of generosity, morality, patience, vigor, meditation, and wisdom.

Mahayanists also speak about 10 stages that *Bodhisattvas* travel on the way to Buddhahood. The first six stages correspond to the eons in which the six perfections are practiced. During the final four stages of the path to Buddhahood, Mahayanists view the *Bodhisattva* to be a supernatural being with miraculous powers. Omnipotent and compassion filled, the "celestial *Bodhisattva*" is considered to be worthy of reverence. Among the celestial *Bodhisattvas* most adorned by Mahayanists include Avalokiteshvara (literally, "the Lord Who Observes") and Maitreya (the "Kindly Friend"). As the all-compassionate *Bodhisattva* who watches over the inhabited world, Avalokiteshvara is said to have come to the earth more than 300 times to save those in peril. He is worshiped in China in female form as Kuan-yin, and in Tibet as Chenrezi, whose reincarnations are said to include the Dalai Lama. Similarly, Maitreya is considered by

Mahayanists to be the fifth and final Buddha (Gautama is considered to be the fourth) who will come to the earth sometime in the future to deliver all those who have not yet reached enlightenment.

In addition to these mythological *Bodhisattvas*, the Mahayanists worship a number of mythological transcendent Buddhas who are said to reside in the 10 directions of the heavens. For example, in the East lives Akshobhya, the "Imperturbable," whose help is sought in overcoming anger; in the West is Amitabha, the "Infinite Light" Buddha to whom the Pure Land denominations look for their salvation. According to Pure Land Buddhists, countless eons ago Amitabha was a monk who became a *Bodhisattva*. Upon attaining Buddhahood, he created the Western Paradise, a "Buddha-Land" known as the Pure Land. As the Lord of this land of bliss, he welcomes into this heaven those who beseech him in faith.

Unlike the Hinayanaists who look upon the historical Buddha as an example for them to follow, many Mahayanists believe that humans are too weak to confront life's sufferings without turning to transcendent Buddhas like Amitabha who are both all-knowing and willing to help those who call on them. Consequently, prayer, worship, and faith in savior-beings are more important among Mahayanists than among Hinayanaists.

Along with the sects there also are two influential Mahayana philosophical systems or schools, Madhyamika and Yogacara. The former dates to the second- or third-century teachings of the philosopher Nagarjuna who argued, among other things, that Ultimate Reality transcends the senses and cannot be conceptualized in thought or speech. From this teaching, he concluded that all statements are equally untenable and that even the current world of everyday experience and *Nirvana* were mere conceptual constructions—empty suggestions that point us toward undifferentiated Reality. In this theory, salvation is gained when all distinctions are dropped and only absolute Emptiness remains. This school never gained wide appeal among the masses, but it has served as the philosophical foundation for Buddhist intellectuals within several sects.

The other major school, Yogacara, emerged in the fourth century with the circulation of the philosophical works of two brothers, Asanga and Vasubandhu. A distinguishing mark of this school is that it denies the reality of the material world and insists that ultimate reality is purely mental. Yogacara also is noteworthy

Timeline of Buddhism.

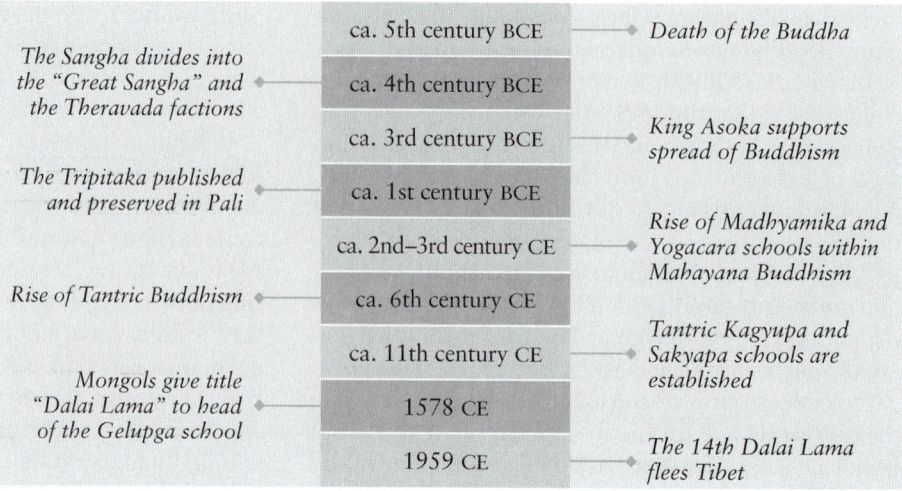

	ca. 5th century BCE	*Death of the Buddha*
The Sangha divides into the "Great Sangha" and the Theravada factions	ca. 4th century BCE	
	ca. 3rd century BCE	*King Asoka supports spread of Buddhism*
The Tripitaka published and preserved in Pali	ca. 1st century BCE	
	ca. 2nd–3rd century CE	*Rise of Madhyamika and Yogacara schools within Mahayana Buddhism*
Rise of Tantric Buddhism	ca. 6th century CE	
	ca. 11th century CE	*Tantric Kagyupa and Sakyapa schools are established*
Mongols give title "Dalai Lama" to head of the Gelupga school	1578 CE	
	1959 CE	*The 14th Dalai Lama flees Tibet*

for developing the doctrine of the three bodies of the Buddha. According to this doctrine, the Buddha exists on three levels. First, the Buddha on occasion comes to earth, as did Gautama, in a "Transformational Body." In some texts this body is viewed as human flesh and blood; in other texts, it is considered to be a phantom body that only appears to be human. Second, the Buddha also has an "Enjoyment Body" that exists for the enjoyment of *Bodhisattvas*. In this glorified form, the Buddha reveals himself to the supernatural beings in the celestial worlds. Enjoyment-body Buddhas preside over their own Buddha-lands, which are mysterious universes that are mentally created by the mind-powers of Enjoyment-body Buddhas for the spiritual benefit of others. Finally, the Buddha exists as the "Dharma body," which is the undifferentiated nature of reality itself. For some Buddhists, the Dharma-body is somewhat analogous to the concept of God in other religions. For others, it is the unknowable, impersonal, eternal void that is the ground of all existence. With Yogacara's emphasis on the use of yogic practices, its premise that reality is "thought only," and its insistence that the world is not different from *Nirvana*, this philosophical school, as well as the Madhyamika school, played an influential role in the development of the third great Buddhist tradition, Vajrayana.

Vajrayana—The Diamond Vehicle

Vajrayana can be translated as either "The Diamond Vehicle" or "the Thunderbolt Vehicle." Because this tradition is an esoteric version of Mahayana Buddhism, it sometimes is called Tantric Buddhism, and

also Mantrayana, "the Vehicle of Mantras." In pre-Buddhist times, the word *Vajra* was the name of the power-packed scepter used by Indra, the ruler of the Vedic gods of India. The word also was used in Mahayana Buddhist texts to refer to a meditative state reached by *Bodhisattvas* in their tenth and final stage on the path to Buddhahood. Vajra, hence, is a symbol of the powerful methods that can be used to bring enlightenment. Like a thunderbolt, it has the power to destroy spiritual obstacles that stand in the way of awakening. As hard as a diamond, it suggests the indestructible nature of the enlightened mind.

The Vajrayana tradition acknowledges that there are two paths to awakening. The common path is the way that is taught in the *Tripitaka* and the Mahayana sutras. This path, which is based on morality, concentration, and wisdom, leads to *Nirvana* but only after eons of time and great human efforts. The uncommon path of the Vajrayana vehicle, however, leads directly to *Nirvana*. This sudden ascent to Buddhahood uses advanced techniques of yoga and tantra adapted from Hinduism, including the use of sacred sounds (mantras) that produce magical effects. These heretofore secret practices produce states of consciousness and out-of-body experiences that conjure visions of celestial Buddhas and *Bodhisattvas*. If the central aim of Tantric Buddhism is to overcome worldly attachments and to recognize that everything is the Dharma-body, then any action that produces these insights could potentially be used to reach enlightenment. Some Tantric rites include unconventional and taboo practices that are sexual in nature. The objective of sexual yoga is to purify the ordinarily forbidden primal urges into wholesome tools for spiritual enlightenment. Because this rapid path to enlightenment is dangerous and requires great skill, it is only to be attempted with the guidance of a spiritual master who understands the secrets of the universe.

This tradition originated in India at the beginning of the sixth century and was considered as orthodoxy in the great monastic centers of Northern India by the eleventh century. Spreading from Northern India, it also took root and flowered in Tibet and is therefore often referred to as Tibetan or Northern Buddhism. Buddhism first entered Tibet when two foreign wives of a Tibetan king converted the king to Buddhism from Bon, the native religion of the region. Bon is a folk religion that is centered on a cult of deceased kings, demonic and spirit possession, magic and exorcism, dragons and vampires, and a belief in rebirth. Tibetan Buddhism did not gain popularity among the masses until the eighth century, when a later king invited a Buddhist sage with magical powers named Padmasambhava to Tibet. According to tradition, the king desired to build a Buddhist monastery but was unable to complete the project because of demonic hindrances. The Tibetan king, hence, summoned Padmasambhava from India to exorcise the demons and oversee the monastery's construction. This Buddhist sage, popularly known as Guru Rinpoche (meaning "Precious Guru"), completed the project and established a community of spiritual teachers known as *lamas*. Padmasambhava converted many Tibetans to Buddhism. He also is said to have converted many of the Bon deities, who, notwithstanding their frightful and ferocious appearances, were embraced by the Tibetan Buddhists as the protectors of the land.

The form of Tantric Buddhism that emerged in Tibet was a mixture of Mahayana Buddhism, tantric mysticism, and Bon folk religion. The first school in this tradition, Nyingmapa, accepts Padmasambhava as its founder. In the eleventh century, an aging scholar-monk Atisa (982–1054) came from India to teach the Tibetans a fuller understanding of the doctrines of Tantric Buddhism. His reforms ultimately led to the establishment of two subsequent Tibetan schools, Kagyupa (meaning the "Whispered Transmission" School) and Sakyapa. The former was founded by a married spiritual guru named Marpa (1012–1096) who taught secret yogic truths that were to be whispered from master to disciple. The other group, which was named after a monastery built on the mountaintops at Saskya, was founded in 1073 by a scholar monk named Nyingpo. For centuries, the Kagyupa was Tibet's most politically powerful sect until it was supplanted by a fourth major school in the sixteenth century.

This fourth and last major school within Tibetan Buddhism, Gelugpa (meaning the "Virtuous School"), was founded by a fourteenth-century reformer who reduced the magical practices, eliminated the sexual yoga for monks, and enforced greater monastic disciplines. The Gelagpa monks were distinguished from other monks by the yellow color of their ceremonial hats, and thus they came to be known as the "Yellow Hats." In the sixteenth century, Sonam Gyatsho, the third spiritual head of the Gelupga sect, converted the Mongol emperor who ruled Tibet to his version of Buddhism. In 1578, the Mongols gave him the title *Dalai Lama*, which means "Ocean Teacher," or the one whose spiritual wisdom is as great as the ocean. Each Dalai Lama was considered to be the reincarnation of the previous spiritual head of the Gelugpas. Because Sonam Gyatsho was the third spiritual head of the Gelugpas, he became known as the third Dalai Lama. In the mid-seventeenth century, the Mongols invaded Tibet and established the fifth Dalai Lama as ruler of Tibet. In 1959, the 14th Dalai Lama along with 80,000 Tibetans fled the country when the Chinese government imposed a military government in the region. Today there are about 20 million Vajrayana Buddhists scattered around the world.

One of the consequences of the great Tibetan exodus has been a growing awareness and distribution of Buddhism worldwide. During the last half-century, a variety of forms of Buddhism have taken root in nations throughout the West. This Buddhist renaissance, particularly in the West, has been so great that many modern Buddhists consider the current age to be the "fourth turning of the wheel" and anticipate the formation of a Buddhist Western tradition that will augment the great Southern, Eastern, and Northern Buddhist traditions.

SACRED OBSERVANCES AND PRACTICES

The practice of mental concentration, or meditation, occupies a central place within Buddhism. The purpose of meditation is to find liberation from suffering, but this expectation is expressed in many ways, including "experiencing the Buddha-nature," "awakening consciousness," "self-realization," "opening the Mind's eye," and "seeing into one's true nature." The methods Buddhists employ to reach these states of joy and mental tranquility vary according to sect, school, and individual preference. Every day devout Buddhists practice silent meditation, yogic exercises with prescribed posture and breathing, various visualization techniques, the chanting of mantras, and/or the continual invocation of the names of various Buddha manifestations. Others meditate on paradoxical statements in order to prepare their mind for self-awareness. These riddles, known as koans, are designed to help individuals transcend dualistic thinking and thereby grasp the unity of all things. When asked to contemplate on the sound of a bell ringing, for instance, a purely rational mind may think the thought: "I am hearing a bell." To the enlightened practitioner who has emptied his or her mind of the artificial constructs of "I," "the bell," and "hearing," these three distinctions dissolve into an understanding of the single reality, which is the sound of a bell ringing. To many Buddhists, particularly to those who live in the West, setting aside time every day in various forms of meditative activities is a distinguishing mark of the tradition.

Buddhist religiosity, however, involves much more than individualistic techniques for self-improvement. Since ancient times Buddhists have enshrined relics, allegedly from the body of the Buddha, in monuments known as *stupas*. When worshippers enter temple grounds in which the relics are preserved, they generally walk around the stupa three times and then kneel or stand before it in reverence, often presenting offerings of food or flowers. Although in earlier ages the Buddha was more likely to be represented by symbols such as a footprint or an eight-spoked wheel than an image, in modern times most Buddhist temples and private homes include images of the Buddha. Many Buddhists set aside a space in their homes as a shrine to the Buddha and surround his image with flowers, decorations, utensils, and candles. Many recite several times each day the well-known Three Refuges invocation: "I go to the Buddha as my Refuge; I go to the Dharma (Doctrine) as my Refuge; I go to the Sangha (Community of Monks) as my Refuge." In Western societies, it has become common for worshippers to gather in congregational meetings and even offer dharma schools for children that are modeled after the Christian Sunday School.

Buddhists also take pilgrimages to holy places, among the most important being the alleged birthplace of the Buddha, the place of his enlightenment, the site where he preached his first sermon, and the sacred grounds on which he died. Like other great religions, Buddhists also observe a number of seasonal festivals that commemorate key events in the sacred history of the tradition. Buddhists worldwide celebrate the Buddha's birthday, although the day for the celebration varies by sect, with Mahayana Buddhists observing his birthday during the Flower Festival (Hanamatsuri) on April 8 and the Theravadas honoring his birthday as well as his enlightenment and entry into nirvana during the Full Moon Day festival (often called Vesak, the name of a month in the Hindu calendar). Mahayana Buddhists celebrate the latter two significant events in the Buddha's sacred story on Bodhi Day (December 8) and Nirvana Day (February 15). Other festivals important to some Buddhist sects include Ohigan and Bon. Ohigan, which literally means the Other Shore, is celebrated during the spring and autumn equinoxes. In Buddhist terminology, the Other Shore refers to the passing to the next life that lies beyond this world of life and death. Because it is believed this shore is reached through the power and perfections of Amida Buddha, worshippers set aside this time to praise Buddha for his great compassion and to recall and commit themselves to his Six Perfections: charity, morality, endurance, endeavor, mediation, and wisdom. This also is an occasion for family members to pay respect to their deceased ancestors by visiting the graves of their parents and grandparents. Similarly, the Bon Festival is another memorial festivity honored by some Buddhists. On this occasion, Buddhists celebrate the lives of their ancestors by dancing a folk dance, offering gifts to the departed spirits, and lighting lanterns to guide these spirits on their yearly visit to the family home. In this as in many Buddhist festivals, ancient traditional customs intermingle with Buddhist ones to create a festive celebration of reflection and merriment that brings family and friends together in religious and social fervor.

SOURCES

One aspect of Buddhism that distinguishes it from many of the other great world religions is the vastness of its sacred literature. With a canon that includes hundreds of volumes and tens of thousands of pages, only a small sampling of the texts in this canon is possible in a single volume. The majority of the selections in this anthology are drawn from the *Tripitaka,* the *Three Baskets* that are considered to be sacred by each of the three great Buddhist traditions. This collection includes selections from the *Vinaya Pitaka* (*The Basket of Discipline*) and from each of the five divisions of the *Sutra Pitaka* (*The Basket of Discourses*). Buddhism's most widely read book of poetry, the *Dhammapada,* has been quoted extensively. Also included are selections from the five major sacred collections within the Mahayana Canon, and a brief selection from the Vajrayana tradition.

SECTION 1: Beginnings: God, Time, and the Universe

One characteristic that separates Buddhism from most of the other world religions is its denial of a creator God. Although its canon includes accounts of the creation of human beings, the theme of these stories is the degeneration of humankind, not the creation of the cosmos by a godhead. The following selections offer insights into Buddhist concepts of Ultimate Truth and into why the Buddha refused to answer questions concerning the beginnings of the cosmos.

The first selection is taken from the *Udana,* which is in the Little Books Division of the *Sutra Pitaka.* This famous parable of the blind men and the elephant describes Gautama's refusal to speculate on nonedifying questions. What types of questions did the Buddha refuse to answer? Why did the Buddha fail to respond to these questions? What insights about Buddhism can you gain from this silence?

THE BUDDHA'S UNANSWERED QUESTIONS

Blind from Birth from the Udana, VI, 4[3]

I have heard that on one occasion the Blessed One was staying in Savatthi at Jeta's Grove, Anathapindika's monastery. Now at that time there were many priests, contemplatives, and wanderers of various sects living around Savatthi with differing views, differing opinions, differing beliefs, dependent

---

[3]*Handful of Leaves,* translated from the Pali by Thanissaro Bhikkhu. (Santa Cruz: Sati Center for Buddhist Studies, 2003). Available at www.accesstoinsight.org.

for support on their differing views. Some of the priests and contemplatives held this view, this doctrine: "The cosmos is eternal. Only this is true; anything otherwise is worthless."

Some of the priests and contemplatives held this view, this doctrine: "The cosmos is not eternal" . . . "The cosmos is finite" . . . "The cosmos is infinite" . . . "The soul and the body are the same" . . . "The soul is one thing and the body another" . . . "After death a Tathagata exists" . . . "After death a Tathagata does not exist" . . . "After death a Tathagata both does and does not exist" . . . "After death a Tathagata neither does nor does not exist. Only this is true; anything otherwise is worthless." And they lived arguing, quarreling, and disputing, wounding one another with weapons of the mouth, saying, "The Dhamma is like this, it's not like that. The Dhamma's not like that, it's like this."

Then in the early morning, a large number of monks, having put on their robes and carrying their bowls and outer robes, went into Savatthi for alms. Having gone for alms in Savatthi, after the meal, returning from their alms round, they went to the Blessed One and, on arrival, having bowed down to him, sat to one side. As they were sitting there, they said to the Blessed One: "Lord, there are many priests, contemplatives, and wanderers of various sects living around Savatthi with differing views, differing opinions, differing beliefs, dependent for support on their differing views . . . and they live arguing, quarreling, and disputing, wounding one another with weapons of the mouth, saying, 'The Dhamma is like this, it's not like that. The Dhamma's not like that, it's like this. . . .' "

The Blessed One replied:

"Once, in this same Savatthi, there was a certain king who said to a certain man, 'Gather together all the people in Savatthi who have been blind from birth.' "

" 'As you say, your majesty,' the man replied and, rounding up all the people in Savatthi who had been blind from birth, he went to the king and on arrival said, 'Your majesty, the people in Savatthi who have been blind from birth have been gathered together.' "

" 'Very well then, show the blind people an elephant.' "

" 'As you say, your majesty,' the man replied and he showed the blind people an elephant. To some of the blind people he showed the head of the elephant, saying, 'This, blind people, is what an elephant is like.' To some of them he showed an ear of the elephant, saying, 'This, blind people, is what an elephant is like.' To some of them he showed a tusk . . . the trunk . . . the body . . . a foot . . . the hindquarters . . . the tail . . . the tuft at the end of the tail, saying, 'This, blind people, is what an elephant is like.'

"Then, having shown the blind people the elephant, the man went to the king and on arrival said, 'Your majesty, the blind people have seen the elephant. May your majesty do what you think it is now time to do.'

"Then the king went to the blind people and on arrival asked them, 'Blind people, have you seen the elephant?'

" 'Yes, your majesty. We have seen the elephant.'

" 'Now tell me, blind people, what the elephant is like.'

"The blind people who had been shown the head of the elephant replied, 'The elephant, your majesty, is just like a water jar.'

"Those who had been shown the ear of the elephant replied, 'The elephant, your majesty, is just like a winnowing basket.'

"Those who had been shown the tusk of the elephant replied, 'The elephant, your majesty, is just like an iron rod.'

"Those who had been shown the trunk of the elephant replied, 'The elephant, your majesty, is just like the pole of a plow.'

"Those who had been shown the body of the elephant replied, 'The elephant, your majesty, is just like a granary.'

"Those who had been shown the foot of the elephant replied, 'The elephant, your majesty, is just like a post.'

"Those who had been shown the hindquarters of the elephant replied, 'The elephant, your majesty, is just like a mortar.'

"Those who had been shown the tail of the elephant replied, 'The elephant, your majesty, is just like a pestle.'

"Those who had been shown the tuft at the end of the tail of the elephant replied, 'The elephant, your majesty, is just like a broom.'

"Saying, 'The elephant is like this, it's not like that. The elephant's not like that, it's like this,' they struck one another with their fists.

"That gratified the king.

"In the same way, monks, the wanderers of other sects are blind and eyeless. They don't know what is

beneficial and what is harmful. They don't know what is the Dhamma and what is non-Dhamma. Not knowing what is beneficial and what is harmful, not knowing what is Dhamma and what is non-Dhamma, they live arguing, quarreling, and disputing, wounding one another with weapons of the mouth, saying, 'The Dhamma is like this, it's not like that. The Dhamma's not like that, it's like this.' "

Then, on realizing the significance of that, the Blessed One on that occasion exclaimed:

"Some of these so-called priests and contemplatives are attached. They quarrel and fight—people seeing one side."

The next selection is one of the rare creation accounts found in the Buddhist canon. It is atypical, and its purpose is to explain the imperfections, not the creation, of humankind. These texts are from *Ekottara Agama* and *Ch'i-shih,* a Chinese version of the *Tripitaka.*

BUDDHIST CREATION STORIES FROM *EKOTTARA AGAMA* 34 AND *CH'I-SHIH CHING*[4]

You must know, monks, that after the floods [that put out the conflagration that ended the last cosmic cycle] receded and the earth came back into being, there was upon the face of the earth a film more sweet-smelling than ambrosia. Do you want to know what was the taste of that film? It was like the taste of grape wine in the mouth. And at this time the gods of the Abhasvara Heaven said to one another, "Let us go and see what it looks like in Jambudvipa now that there is earth again." So the young gods of that heaven came down into the world and saw that over the earth was spread this film. They put their fingers into the earth and sucked them. Some put their fingers into the earth many times and ate a great deal of this film, and these at once lost all their majesty and brightness. Their bodies grew heavy and their substance became flesh and bone. They lost their magic and could no longer fly. But there were others who ate only a little, and these could still fly about in the air. And those that had lost their magic cried out to one another in dismay, "Now we are in a very sad case. We have lost our magic. There is nothing for it but to stay here on earth;

---

[4]Andrew Wilson, ed. *World Scripture: A Comparative Anthology of Sacred Texts* (New York: Paragon House, 1991), p. 305. Also available at www.euro-tongil.org/ws.

for we cannot possibly get back to heaven." They stayed and fed upon the film that covered the earth, and gazed at one another's beauty. Those among them that were most passionate became women, and these gods and goddesses fulfilled their desires and pleasure in one another. And this was how it was, monks, that when the world began love-making first spread throughout the world; it is an old and constant thing. And that woman should appear in the world, this too is an old thing, and not only a matter of today.

And the gods who had returned to heaven looked down and saw the young gods that had fallen, and they came down and reproached them, saying, "Why are you behaving in this unclean way?" Then the gods on earth thought to themselves, "We must find some way to be together without being seen by others." So they made houses that would cover and hide them. Monks, that was how houses first began.

The final passages are from well-known Mahayanan texts, the *Garland Sutra* and the *Lankavatara Sutra*. These sutras suggest that the world is created by the mind, and that when the mind becomes pure, True Reality is realized. Existence, thus, is the essence of Mind.

MAHAYANA DESCRIPTIONS OF TRUE REALITY FROM THE *GARLAND SUTRA* 20[5]

It is like a painter spreading the various colors:
Delusion grasps different forms but the elements have no distinctions.

In the elements there's no form, and no form in the elements;
Yet apart from the elements, no form can be found.

In the mind is no painting, in painting there is no mind;
Yet not apart from mind, is any painting to be found.

That mind never stops, manifesting all forms,
Countless, inconceivably many, unknown to one another.

Just as a painter cannot know his own mind
Yet paints due to the mind, so is the nature of all things.

Mind is like an artist, able to paint the worlds:
The five clusters [aggregates] are born thence;
There is nothing it does not make.

As in the mind, so is the Buddha; as the Buddha, so living beings:
Know that Buddha and mind are in essence inexhaustible.

_____
[5]Wilson, ed. *World Scriptures*, pp. 148–149. See www.euro-tongil. org.

If people know the actions of mind create all the worlds,
They will see the Buddha and understand Buddha's true nature.

Mind does not stay in the body, nor body stay in mind:
Yet it is able to perform Buddha-work, freely, without precedent.

If people want to really know All Buddhas of all times,
They should contemplate the nature of the cosmos:
All is but mental construction.

FROM THE *LANKAVATARA SUTRA* 61, 63, 64[6]

"What is meant by an eternally-abiding reality? The ancient road of reality, Mahamati, has been here all the time, like gold, silver, or pearl preserved in the mine. The Dharmadhatu (Absolute Truth) abides forever, whether the Tathagata[7] appears in the world or not. As the Tathagata eternally abides so does the Reason of all things. Reality forever abides, reality keeps its order, like the roads in an ancient city.

For instance, a man who is walking in a forest and discovering an ancient city with its orderly streets may enter into the city, and having entered into it, he may have a rest, conduct himself like a citizen, and enjoy all the pleasures accruing therefrom. What do you think, Mahamati? Did this man make the road along which he enters into the city, and the various things in the city?"

"No, Blessed One."

"Just so, what has been realized by myself and the other Tathagatas is this Reality, this eternally-abiding reality, the self-regulating reality, the Suchness of things, the Realness of things, the truth itself.

The world of the ignorant is observed as the continuation of birth and death, whereby dualisms are nourished, and because of the perversion [the truth] is not perceived.

There is just one truth, which is *Nirvana*—it has nothing to do with intellection. The world seen as subject to discrimination resembles a plantain tree, a dream, a mirage.

The Mind as norm is the abode of self-nature which has nothing to do with the realm of causation;

_____
[6]Wilson, ed. *World Scriptures*, pp. 102 103. See www.euro-tongil. org.

[7]Tathagata, literally the "Thus-perfected," is the name the Buddha applied to himself in his teachings. The term also can apply to other fully awakened beings, or buddhas.

of this norm, which is perfect existence and the highest Absolute, I speak.

Of neither existence nor non-existence do I speak, but of Mind-only which has nothing to do with existence and non-existence, and which is thus free from intellection.

Suchness, emptiness, Absolute Truth . . . these I call Mind-only.

SECTION 2: Humanity: The Problem of Good and Evil

The sacred texts of most religions address the schizophrenic tendencies of humans. In Judaism, Christianity, and Islam, religions that assert that there is a single creator God who created a moral universe, the appearance of evil in the world demands the development of doctrines that explain the discrepancy between creation's original purity and its subsequent corruption. This problem is less large in traditions such as Hinduism, which is more likely to regard creation as an act of play and without moral purpose. Similarly, in Buddhism, a tradition that lacks a doctrine of creation, there is less need to develop a doctrine of a human fall from grace. Nonetheless, within Buddhism there are texts that seek to understand and explain the discrepancy between an idealized primordial state of purity and the present state of suffering in the world.

The first selection is a Theravada text from the *Sutra Nipata,* a collection of discourses in the Little Books Division of the *Sutra Pitaka.* The passage points to the causes of human downfall.

BUDDHIST DEPICTIONS OF HUMAN NATURE FROM *SUTRA NIPATA,* I, 6[8]

Thus have I heard. Once the Exalted One was dwelling at Anathapindika's monastery, in the Jeta Grove, near Savatthi. Now when the night was far spent a certain deity whose surpassing splendor illuminated the entire Jeta Grove, came to the presence of the Exalted One and, drawing near, respectfully saluted Him and stood at one side. Standing thus, he addressed the Exalted One in verse:

THE DEITY: Having come here with our questions to the Exalted One, we ask thee, O Gotama, about man's decline. Pray, tell us the cause of downfall!

---

[8]*Everyman's Ethics: Four Discourses by the Buddha,* translated by Narada Thera (Kandy: Buddhist Publication Society, 1985). Available at www.accesstoinsght.org.

THE BUDDHA: Easily known is the progressive one, easily known he who declines. He who loves Dhamma progresses; he who is averse to it, declines.

THE DEITY: Thus much do we see: this is the first cause of one's downfall. Pray, tell us the second cause.

THE BUDDHA: The wicked are dear to him, with the virtuous he finds no delight, he prefers the creed of the wicked—this is a cause of one's downfall.

Being fond of sleep, fond of company, indolent, lazy and irritable—this is the cause of one's downfall.

Though being well-to-do, not to support father and mother who are old and past their youth—this is a cause of one's downfall.

To deceive by falsehood a brahmin or ascetic or any other mendicant—this is a cause of one's downfall.

To have much wealth and ample gold and food, but to enjoy one's luxuries alone—this is a cause of one's downfall.

To be proud of birth, of wealth or clan, and to despise one's own kinsmen—this is a cause of one's downfall.

To be a rake, a drunkard, a gambler, and to squander all one earns—this is a cause of one's downfall.

Not to be contented with one's own wife, and to be seen with harlots and the wives of others—this is a cause of one's downfall.

Being past one's youth, to take a young wife and to be unable to sleep for jealousy of her—this is a cause of one's downfall.

To place in authority a woman given to drink and squandering, or a man of a like behavior—this is a cause of one's downfall.

To be of noble birth, with vast ambition and of slender means, and to crave for rulership—this is a cause of one's downfall.

Knowing well these causes of downfall in the world, the noble sage endowed with insight shares a happy realm.

The next parable is from a Mahayana text, the *Mahaparianivana Sutra.* After asserting that every being has the Buddha nature, this passage provides an explanation as to why morally capable humans often fail to make moral progress.

THE PARABLE OF THE HIDDEN TREASURE IN *MAHAPARINIRVANA SUTRA* 214–15[9]

Every being has the Buddha Nature. This is the self. Such a self is, since the very beginning, under cover of innumerable illusions. That is why a man cannot see it. O good man! There was a poor woman who had gold hidden somewhere in her house, but no one knew where it was. But there was a

---

[9]Wilson, ed. *World Scriptures,* p. 147. See www.euro-tongil.org.

stranger who, by expediency, speaks to the poor woman, "I shall employ you to weed the lawn." The woman answered, "I cannot do it now, but if you show my son were the gold is hidden, I will work for you." The man says, "I know the way; I will show it to your son." The woman replies, "No one in my house, big or small, knows where the gold is hidden. How can you know?" The man then digs out the hidden gold and shows it to the woman. She is glad, and begins to respect him. O good man! The same is the case with a man's Buddha Nature. No one can see it. It is like the gold which the poor woman possessed and yet could not locate. I now let people see the Buddha Nature which they possess, but which was hidden by illusions. The Tathagata shows all beings the storehouse of enlightenment, which is the cask of true gold—their Buddha Nature.

The *Dhammapada* is one of the most widely read and cherished books in the Pali Canon. How is human nature depicted in these passages?

DEPICTIONS OF THE SELF FROM THE *DHAMMAPADA* 12[10]

If a person holds oneself dear,
let one watch oneself carefully.
The wise should be watchful
during at least one of the three watches.

Let each person first direct oneself to what is right;
then let one teach others; thus the wise will not suffer.
If a person makes oneself as one teaches others to be,
then being well-controlled, that one might guide others,
since self-control is difficult.

Self is the master of self;
who else could be the master?
With self well-controlled
a person finds a master such as few can find.

The wrong done by oneself, born of oneself,
produced by oneself, crushes the fool,
just as a diamond breaks even a precious stone.

The one whose vice is great brings oneself down
to that condition where one's enemy wishes one to be,
just as a creeper overpowers the entangled sala tree.
Bad actions and actions harmful to ourselves are easy to do;
what is beneficial and good, that is very difficult to do.

The fool who scorns the teaching of the saintly,
the noble, and the virtuous, and follows wrong ideas,
bears fruit to one's own destruction,
like the fruits of the katthaka reed.

By oneself is wrong done; by oneself one suffers;
by oneself is wrong left undone; by oneself is one purified.
Purity and impurity come from oneself;
no one can purify another.

Let no one neglect one's own duty
for the sake of another's, however great;
let a person after one has discerned one's own duty,
be always attentive to this duty.

The final selection in this section addresses the question, Why do bad things happen to some, and good things to others? Gautama provides an answer to this perplexing question in a discourse that is contained in his Middle Length Discourses of the Pali Canon's *Sutra Pitaka*. According to the Buddha, each person reaps his or her own fruits, but the future does not need to be like the present. Knowing what karma to make is the mark of the wise.

THE BUDDHA ON THE CONSEQUENCES OF ACTIONS IN THE *MAJJHIMA NIKAYA* 135[11]

1. Thus have I heard. On one occasion the Blessed One was living at Savatthi in Jeta's Grove, Anathapindika's Park.

Then Subha the student (brahmin), Todeyya's son, went to the Blessed One and exchanged greetings with him, and when the courteous and amiable talk was finished, he sat down at one side. When he had done so, Subha the student said to the Blessed One:

2. "Master Gotama, what is the reason, what is the condition, why inferiority and superiority are met with among human beings, among mankind? For one meets with short-lived and long-lived people, sick and healthy people, ugly and handsome people, insignificant and influential people, poor and rich people, low-born and high-born people, stupid and wise people. What is the reason, what is the condition, why superiority and inferiority are met with among human beings, among mankind?"

3. "Student, beings are owners of kammas, heirs of kammas, they have kammas as their progenitor, kammas as their kin, kammas as their homing-place. It is kammas that differentiate beings according to inferiority and superiority."

4. "I do not understand the detailed meaning of Master Gotama's utterance spoken in brief without expounding the detailed meaning. It would be good if Master Gotama taught me the Dhamma so that I might understand the detailed meaning of Master Gotama's utterance spoken in brief without expounding the detailed meaning."

"Then listen, student, and heed well what I shall say."

---

[10]All of the passages from the *Dhamapada* in this volume are from the English translation of Sanderson Beck found in the *Wisdom Bible*.

[11]Khantipalo Bhikkhu, ed., *The Buddha's Words on Kama: Four Discourses from the Middle Length Collection.* (Kandy: Buddhist Publishing Society, 1993). See www. accesstoinsight.org.

"Even so, Master Gotama," Subha the student replied. The Blessed One said this:

5. "Here, student, some woman or man is a killer of living beings, murderous, bloody-handed, given to blows and violence, merciless to all living beings. Due to having performed and completed such kammas, on the dissolution of the body, after death, he reappears in a state of deprivation, in an unhappy destination, in perdition, in hell. If, on the dissolution of the body, after death, instead of his reappearing in a state of deprivation, in an unhappy destination, in perdition, in hell, he comes to the human state, he is short-lived wherever he is reborn. This is the way that leads to short life, that is to say, to be a killer of living beings, murderous, bloody-handed, given to blows and violence, merciless to all living beings.

6. "But here some woman or man, having abandoned the killing of living beings, abstains from killing living beings, lays aside the rod and lays aside the knife, is considerate and merciful and dwells compassionate for the welfare of all living beings. Due to having performed and completed such kammas, on the dissolution of the body, after death, he reappears in a happy destination, in the heavenly world. If, on the dissolution of the body, after death, instead of his reappearing in a happy destination, in the heavenly world, he comes to the human state, he is long-lived wherever he is reborn. This is the way that leads to long life, that is to say, to have abandoned the killing of living beings, to abstain from killing living beings, to lay aside the rod and lay aside the knife, to be considerate and merciful, and to dwell compassionate for the welfare of all living beings.

7. "Here, student, some woman or man is one who harms beings with his hands or with clods or with sticks or with knives. Due to having performed and completed such kammas, on the dissolution of the body, after death, he reappears in a state of deprivation. . . . If instead he comes to the human state, he is sickly wherever he is born. This is the way that leads to sickness, that is to say, to be one who harms beings with one's hands or with clods or with sticks or with knives.

8. "But here some woman or man is not one who harms beings with his hands, or with clods, or with sticks, or with knives. Due to having performed and completed such kammas, on the dissolution of the body, after death, he reappears in a happy destination. . . . If instead he comes to the human state, he is healthy wherever he is reborn. This is the way that leads to health, that is to say, not to be one who harms beings with his hands or with clods or with sticks or with knives. . . .

13. "Here, student, some woman or man is not a giver of food, drink, cloth, sandals, garlands, perfumes, unguents, bed, roof and lighting to monks or brahmins. Due to having performed and completed such kamma,[1] on the dissolution of the body, after death he reappears in a state of deprivation. . . . If instead he comes to the human state, he is poor wherever he is reborn. This is the way that leads to poverty, that is to say, not to be a giver of food, drink, cloth, sandals,

garlands, perfumes, unguents, bed, roof and lighting to monks and brahmins.

14. "But here some woman or man is a giver of food, drink, cloth, sandals, perfumes, unguents, bed, roof and lighting to monks and brahmins. Due to having performed and completed such kamma, on the dissolution of the body, after death, he reappears in a happy destination. . . . If instead he comes to the human state, he is rich wherever he is reborn. This is the way that leads to riches, that is to say, to be a giver of food, drink, cloth, sandals, garlands, perfumes, unguents, bed, roof and lighting to monks and brahmins. . . .

19. "So, student, the way that leads to short life makes people short-lived, the way that leads to long life makes people long-lived; the way that leads to sickness makes people sick, the way that leads to health makes people healthy; the way that leads to ugliness makes people ugly, the way that leads to beauty makes people beautiful; the way that leads to insignificance makes people insignificant, the way that leads to influence makes people influential; the way that leads to poverty makes people poor, the way that leads to riches makes people rich; the way that leads to low birth makes people low-born, the way that leads to high birth makes people high-born; the way that leads to stupidity makes people stupid, the way that leads to wisdom makes people wise.

20. "Beings are owners of kammas, student, heirs of kammas, they have kammas as their progenitor, kammas as their kin, kammas as their homing-place. It is kammas that differentiate beings according to inferiority and superiority."

21. When this was said, Subha the student, Todeyya's son, said to the Blessed One: "Magnificent, Master Gotama! Magnificent, Master Gotama! The Dhamma has been made clear in many ways by Master Gotama, as though he were turning upright what had been overthrown, revealing the hidden, showing the way to one who is lost, holding up a lamp in the darkness for those with eyes to see forms.

22. "I go to Master Gotama for refuge, and to the Dhamma and to the Sangha of bhikkhus. From today let Master Gotama accept me as a lay follower who has gone to him for refuge for life."

SECTION 3: Sacred Stories: Divine Messengers, Prophets, and Priests

The primary source of our knowledge of Gautama comes from the *Tripitaka*. The oldest portions of this three-part collection, the *Sutra Pitaka* (*The Basket of Discourses*) and the *Vinaya Pitaka* (*The Basket of Disciplines*), were derived from memories of the Buddha and his teachings that were preserved in the monastic communities. These remembered words, like those of most sacred texts, were transmitted orally for centuries before taking their written form. The following selections from the *Sutra Pitaka* depict several important moments in the life story of the Buddha. These passages recount well-known stories of his birth, his life as an ascetic, his temptation by Mara, his teaching ministry, and his death. The first passage tells the story of the annunciation and birth of Gautama.

JATAKA TALES: THE BIRTH OF THE BUDDHA[12]

At that time, it is said, the Midsummer festival was proclaimed in the City of Kapilavastu, and the people were enjoying the feast. During the seven days before the full moon the Lady Maha Maya had taken part in the festivity, as free from intoxication as it was brilliant with garlands and perfumes. On the seventh day she rose early and bathed in perfumed water: and she distributed four hundred thousand pieces in giving great largesse. Decked in her richest attire she partook of the purest food: and vowing to observe the Eight Commandments, she entered her beautiful chamber, and lying on her royal couch she fell asleep and dreamt this dream.

The four archangels, the Guardians of the world, lifting her up in her couch, carried her to the Himalayan mountains, and placing her under the Great Salatree, seven leagues high, on the Crimson Plain, sixty yojanas broad, they stood respectfully aside. Their queens then came toward her, and taking her to the lake of Anotatta, bathed her to free her from human stains; and dressed her in heavenly garments; and anointed her with perfumes; and decked her with heavenly flowers. Not far from there is the Silver Hill, within which is a golden mansion; in it they spread a heavenly couch, with its head towards the East, and on it they laid her down. Then the future Buddha, who had become a superb white elephant, and was wandering on the Golden Hill, not far from there, descended thence, and ascending the Silver Hill, approached her from the North. Holding in his silvery truck a white lotus flower, and uttering a far-reaching cry, he entered the golden mansion, and thrice doing obeisance to his mother's couch, he gently struck her right side, and seemed to enter her womb.

Thus was he conceived at the end of the Midsummer festival. And the next day, having awoke from her sleep, she related her dream to the raja. The raja had sixty-four eminent Brahamans summoned. . . . And when he had thus satisfied their every desire, he had the dream told to them, and then he asked them, "What will come of it?"

The Brahmans said, "Be now anxious, O King! your queen has conceived: and the fruit of her womb will be a man-child; it will not be a woman-child. You will have a son. And he, if he adopts a householder's life, will become a king, a Universal Monarch; but if, leaving his home, he adopt the religious life, he will become a Buddha, who will remove from the world the veils of ignorance and sin.". . .

From the moment of the incarnation, thus brought about, of the future Buddha, four angels, with swords in their hands, stood guard over the Bodisat and his mother, to shield them from all harm. Pure in thought, having reached the highest aim and the highest honor, the mother was happy and unwearied; and she saw the child within her as plainly as one could see a thread passed through a transparent gem. But as a womb in which a future Buddha has dwelt, like a sacred relic shrine, can never be occupied by another; the mother of the Bodisat, seven days after his birth, died, and was reborn in the City of Delight.

Now other women give birth, some before, some after, the completion of the tenth month, some sitting, and some lying down. Not so the mother of the Bodisat. She gives birth to the Bodisat, standing, after she has cherished him in her womb for exactly ten months. This is a distinctive quality of the mother of a Buddha elect. . . .

That very moment the four pure-minded Haha Brahma angels came there bringing a golden net; and receiving the future Buddha on that net, they placed him before his mother, saying, "Be joyful, O Lady! a mighty son is born to thee!"

Now other living things, when they leave their mother's womb, leave it smeared with offensive and impure matter. Not so a Bodisat. The future Buddha left his mother's womb like a preacher descending from a pulpit or a man from a ladder, erect, stretching out his hands and feet, unspoiled by any impurities from contact with his mother's womb, pure and fair, and shining like a gem placed on fine muslin of Benares. But thought this was so, two showers of water came down from heaven in honor of them and refreshed the Bodisat and his mother.

The next selection from the Middle Length Discourses of the Pali Canon describes the time when

---

[12]V. Fausboll, *Buddhist Birth Stories or Jataka Tales,* translated by T. W. Rhys Davids (London: Truber & Company, 1880), pp. 62–67.

Gautama attempted to find life's true meaning through austerities. It was only after these attempts failed that he realized the truth of the middle way. This famous sermon is so powerful that it often is refereed to as the "Hair-Raising" discourse.

THE BODHISATTA'S AUSTERITIES FROM THE GREAT DISCOURSE ON THE LION'S ROAR[13]

44. "Sariputta, I recall having lived a holy life possessing four factors. I have practiced asceticism—the extreme of asceticism; I have practiced coarseness—the extreme of coarseness; I have practiced scrupulousness—the extreme of scrupulousness; I have practiced seclusion—the extreme of seclusion.

45. "Such was my asceticism, Sariputta, that I went naked, rejecting conventions, licking my hands, not coming when asked, not stopping when asked; I did not accept food brought or food specially made or an invitation to a meal; I received nothing from a pot, from a bowl, across a threshold, across a stick, across a pestle, from two eating together, from a pregnant woman, from a woman giving suck, from a woman lying with a man, from where food was advertised to be distributed, from where a dog was waiting, from where flies were buzzing; I accepted no fish or meat, I drank no liquor, wine or fermented brew. I kept to one house, to one morsel; I kept to two houses, to two morsels; . . . I kept to seven houses, to seven morsels. I lived on one saucerful a day, on two saucerfuls a day . . . on seven saucerfuls a day; I took food once a day, once every two days . . . once every seven days, and so on up to once every fortnight; I dwelt pursuing the practice of taking food at stated intervals. I was an eater of greens or millet or wild rice or hide-parings or moss or rice bran or rice-scum or sesamum flour or grass or cowdung. I lived on forest roots and fruits, I fed on fallen fruits. I clothed myself in hemp, in hemp-mixed cloth, in shrouds, in refuse rags, in tree bark, in antelope hide, in strips of antelope hide, in kusa-grass fabric, in bark fabric, in wood-shavings fabric, in head-hair wool, in animal wool, in owls' wings. I was one who pulled out hair and beard, pursuing the practice of pulling out hair and beard. I was one who stood continuously, rejecting seats. I was one who squatted continuously, devoted to maintaining the squatting position. I was one who used a mattress of spikes; I made a mattress of spikes my bed. I dwelt pursuing the practice of bathing in water three times daily including the evening. Thus in such a variety of ways I dwelt pursuing the practice of tormenting and mortifying the body. Such was my asceticism.

46. "Such was my coarseness, Sariputta, that just as the bole of a tinduka tree, accumulating over the years, cakes and flakes off, so too, dust and dirt, accumulating over the years, caked off my body and flaked off. It never occurred to me: 'Oh, let me rub this dust and dirt off with my hand, or let another rub this dust and dirt off with his hand'—it never occurred to me thus. Such was my coarseness.

47. "Such was my scrupulousness, Sariputta, that I was always mindful in stepping forwards and stepping backwards. I was full of pity even for (the beings in) a drop of water thus: 'Let me not hurt the tiny creatures in the crevices of the ground.' Such was my scrupulousness.

48. "Such was my seclusion, Sariputta, that I would plunge into some forest and dwell there. And when I saw a cowherd or a shepherd or someone gathering grass or sticks, or a woodsman, I would flee from grove to grove, from thicket to thicket, from hollow to hollow, from hillock to hillock. Why was that? So that they should not see me or I see them. . . . Such was my seclusion.

49. "I would go on all fours to the cow-pens when the cattle had gone out and the cowherd had left them, and I would feed on the dung of the young suckling calves. As long as my own excrement and urine lasted, I fed on my own excrement and urine. Such was my great distortion in feeding. . . .

53–55. "Sariputta, there are certain recluses and brahmins whose doctrine and view is this: 'Purification comes about through food.' They say: 'Let us live on beans' . . . 'Let us live on sesamum' . . . 'Let us live on rice,' and they eat rice, they eat rice powder, they drink rice water, and they make various kinds of rice concoctions. Now I recall having eaten a single rice grain a day. Sariputta, you may think that the rice grain was bigger at that time, yet you should not regard it so: the rice grain was then at most the same size as now. Through feeding on a single rice grain a day, my body reached a state of extreme emaciation. Because of eating so little . . . the hair, rotted at its roots, fell from my body as I rubbed.

56. "Yet, Sariputta, by such conduct, by such practice, by such performance of austerities, I did not attain any superhuman states, any distinction in knowledge and vision worthy of the noble ones. Why was that? Because I did not attain that noble wisdom which when attained is noble and emancipating and leads the one who practices in accordance with it to the complete destruction of suffering.

57. "Sariputta, there are certain recluses and brahmins whose doctrine and view is this: 'Purification comes about through the round of rebirths.' But it is impossible to find a realm in the round that I have not already passed through in this long journey, except for the gods of the Pure Abodes; and had I passed through the round as a god in the Pure Abodes, I would never have returned to this world. . . .

60. "There are certain recluses and brahmins whose doctrine and view is this: 'Purification comes about through sacrifice.'

[13] *The Middle Length Discourses of the Buddha: A New Translation of the Majjhima Nikaya*, translated from the Pali by Bhikkhu Nanamoli and Bhikkhu Bodhi (Boston: Wisdom Publications, 1995), pp. 173–178.

But it is impossible to find a kind of sacrifice that has not already been offered up by me in this long journey, when I was either a head-anointed noble king or a well-to-do-brahmin.

61. "There are certain recluses and brahmins whose doctrine and view is this: 'Purification comes about through fire-worship.' But it is impossible to find a kind of fire that has not already been worshipped by me in this long journey, when I was either a head-anointed noble king or a well-to-do brahmin.

62. "Sariputta, there are certain recluses and brahmins whose doctrine and view is this: 'As long as this good man is still young, a black-haired young man endowed with the blessing of youth, in the prime of life, so long is he perfect in his lucid wisdom. But when this good man is old, aged, burdened with years, advanced in life, and come to the last stage, being eighty, ninety or a hundred years old, then the lucidity of his wisdom is lost.' But it should not be regarded so. I am now old, aged, burdened with years, advanced in life, and come to the last stage: my years have turned eighty. Now suppose that I had four disciples with a hundred years' lifespan, perfect in mindfulness, retentiveness, memory and lucidity of wisdom. Just as a skilled archer, trained, practiced and tested, could easily shoot a light arrow across the shadow of a palm tree, suppose that they were even to that extent perfect in mindfulness, retentiveness, memory and lucidity of wisdom. Suppose that they continuously asked me about the four foundations of mindfulness and that I answered them when asked and that they remembered each answer of mine and never asked a subsidiary question or paused except to eat, drink, consume food, taste, urinate, defecate and rest in order to remove sleepiness and tiredness. Still the Tathagata's exposition of the Dhamma, his explanations of factors of the Dhamma, and his replies to questions would not yet come to an end, but meanwhile those four disciples of mine with their hundred years' lifespan would have died at the end of those hundred years. Sariputta, even if you have to carry me about on a bed, still there will be no change in the lucidity of the Tathagata's wisdom.

63. "Rightly speaking, were it to be said of anyone: 'A being not subject to delusion has appeared in the world for the welfare and happiness of many, out of compassion for the world, for the good, welfare and happiness of gods and humans,' it is of me indeed that rightly speaking this should be said."

64. Now on that occasion the Venerable Nagasamala was standing behind the Blessed One fanning him. Then he said to the Blessed One: "It is wonderful, venerable sir, it is marvelous! As I listened to this discourse on the Dhamma, the hairs of my body stood up. Venerable sir, what is the name of this discourse on the Dhamma?"

"As to that, Nagasamala, you may remember this discourse on the Dhamma as 'The Hair-raising Discourse.'"

That is what the Blessed One said. The Venerable Nagasamala was satisfied and delighted in the Blessed One's words.

The next selection from the Little Books Division of the *Sutra Pitaka* describes Gautama's temptation by Mara. Compare this temptation with the New Testament's account of Satan's temptation of Jesus. What are the similarities and the differences?

MARA'S TEMPTATION OF THE BUDDHA FROM THE *SUTRA NIPATA*, III, 2[14]

"When, near the river Neranjara, I exerted myself in meditation for attaining to security from bondage, there came Namuci speaking words of compassion:

" 'You are emaciated and ill-looking, you are near to death! A thousand parts of you belong to death and only a fraction of you is alive. Live, good Sir! It is better to live. Living you may perform meritorious deeds. From practicing celibacy and tending the sacrificial fire much merit is made, but what is obtained from striving? It is difficult to enter the path of exertion, it is difficult to do, difficult to maintain.' "

Mara spoke these words whilst standing in the presence of the Awakened One. To Mara speaking thus, the Lord replied:

"You who are the friend of the negligent, O Evil One, for what reason have you come here? Those who still have use for merit Mara may consider worthwhile addressing. I have faith and energy and wisdom. Being thus bent on striving why do you ask me to live? This wind will wither the currents of the rivers, why should not my exertion dry up even the blood? When the blood dries up, the bile and phlegm wither. On the wasting away of the flesh the mind becomes more and more serene and my mindfulness, wisdom and concentration are established more firmly. In me, who abides enduring such an extreme experience, the mind does not long for sensual pleasures. See the purity of a being!

"Sensual desire is your first army, the second is called discontent, the third is hunger and thirst, the fourth craving, the fifth sluggishness and laziness, the sixth fear, the seventh indecision, and the eighth disparagement of others and stubbornness: gain, fame, honor, prestige wrongly acquired and whoever praises himself and despises others—these, Namuci, are your armies, the Dark One's striking forces. A

[14]*The Discourse Collection: Selected Texts from the Sutta Nipata,* translated by John D. Ireland (Kandy: Buddhist Publication Society, 1983). See www.accesstoinsight.org.

lazy, cowardly person cannot overcome them, but by conquering them one gains bliss.

"I wear munja-grass! Shame on life here in this world! It is better for me to die in battle than to live defeated. Some recluses and brahmanas are not seen (exerting themselves) here, so immerse dare they (in worldliness). They are not aware of that path by which those of perfect conduct walk.

"Seeing the surrounding army ready and Mara mounted (on his elephant), I am going out to fight so that he may not shift me from my position. This army of yours which the world together with the devas is unable to subdue, that I will destroy with wisdom, like an unbaked clay-bowl with a stone. Having mastered the mind and firmly established mindfulness I shall wander from country to country guiding many disciples. And they will be diligent and energetic in practicing my teaching, the teaching of one without sensual desire, and they will go where, having gone, one does not grieve."

Mara: "For seven years I followed the Lord step by step but did not find an opportunity to defeat that mindful Awakened One. A crow flew around a stone having the colour of fat: 'Can we find even here something tender? May it be something to eat?'

"Not finding anything edible the crow left that place. As with the crow and the stone, we leave Gotama, having approached and become disheartened." Overcome by sorrow his lute fell from his arm and thereupon the unhappy spirit disappeared from that place.

The following excerpt is one among the thousands of dialogues contained in the *Tripitaka*. In this passage from the Numerically Arranged Division of the *Sutra Pitaka*, a Brahmin seeker asks the Buddha, "Who are you?" What insights about Buddhism and its relationship with Hinduism are expressed in this exchange?

A Brahmin Asks the Buddha, "Who are you?" from the *Anguttara Nikaya* II, 37–39[15]

At one time the Lord was journeying along the high-road between Ukkattha and Setabbya; so also was

the brahmin Dona. He saw on the Lord's footprints the wheels with their thousand spokes, their rims and hubs and all their attributes complete, and he thought, "Indeed, how wonderful and marvelous—it cannot be that these are the footprints of a human being."

Then Dona, following the Lord's footprints, saw that he was sitting under a tree, comely, faith-inspiring, his sense-faculties and his mind peaceful. . . . Dona approached the Lord and said, "Is your reverence a god?"

"No indeed, brahmin, I am not a god."

"Then an angel?"

"No indeed, brahmin."

"A fairy, then?"

"No indeed, brahmin, I am not a fairy."

"Then is your reverence a human being?"

"No indeed, brahmin, I am not a human being."

"You answer No to all my questions. Who then is your reverence?"

"Brahmin, those outflows whereby, if they had not been extinguished, I might have been a god, angel, fairy, or a human being—those outflows are extinguished in me, cut off at the root, made like a palm-tree stump that can come to no further existence in the future. Just as a blue, red, or white lotus, although born in the water, grown up in the water, when it reaches the surface stands there unsoiled by the water—just so, brahmin, although born in the world, grown up in the world, having overcome the world, I abide unsoiled by the world. Take it that I am Buddha."

Between about 100 BCE and 200 CE, a number of new scriptures appeared alongside the *Tripitaka*. According to the Mahayanas who embrace these scriptures, the new sutras taught the "higher" wisdom of the Buddha, teachings that had been hidden for centuries to allow time for the monks to purify and prepare the people for the Buddha's messianic message. Among these texts is the *Lotus Sutra*, one of the most important works in world history. Millions use it as a religious textbook, reading primer, moral guide, and means of salvation. The following selection from the *Lotus Sutra* details Buddha explanation as to why he is to enter extinction. According to this text, what is the Buddha's nature? What was his ultimate goal, and what should be the goal of these who follow his teachings?

---

[15]Wilson, *World Scripture*, p. 468. See www.euro-tongil.org.

The Buddha's Nature from the *Lotus Sutra*[16]

"Since I attained Buddhahood, an extremely long period of time has passed. My life span is an immeasurable number of asamkhya kalpas, and during that time I have constantly abided here without ever entering extinction. Good men, originally I practiced the bodhisattva way, and the life span that I acquired then has yet to come to an end but will last twice the number of years that have already passed. Now, however, although in fact I do not actually enter extinction, I announce that I am going to adopt the course of extinction. This is an expedient means which the Thus Come One uses to teach and convert living beings.

"Why do I do this? Because if the Buddha remains in the world for a long time, those persons with shallow virtue will fail to plant good roots but, living in poverty and lowliness, will become attached to the five desires and be caught in the net of deluded thoughts and imaginings. If they see that the Thus Come One is constantly in the world and never enters extinction, they will grow arrogant and selfish, or become discouraged and neglectful. They will fail to realize how difficult it is to encounter the Buddha and will not approach him with a respectful and reverent mind.

"Therefore as an expedient means the Thus Come One says: 'Monks, you should know that it is a rare thing to live at a time when one of the Buddhas appears in the world.' Why does he do this? Because persons of shallow virtue may pass immeasurable hundreds, thousands, ten thousands, millions of kalpas with some of them chancing to see a Buddha and others never seeing one at all. For this reason I say to them: 'Monks, the Thus Come One is hard to get to see.' When living beings hear these words, they are certain to realize how difficult it is to encounter the Buddha. In their minds they will harbor a longing and will thirst to gaze upon the Buddha, and then they will work to plant good roots. Therefore the Thus Come One, though in truth he does not enter extinction, speaks of passing into extinction.

"Good men, the Buddhas and Thus Come Ones all preach a Law such as this. They act in order to save living beings, so what they do is true and not false.

"Suppose, for example, that there is a skilled physician who is wise and understanding and knows how to compound medicines to effectively cure all kinds of diseases. He has many sons, perhaps ten, twenty, or even a hundred. He goes off to some other land far away to see about a certain affair. After he has gone, the children drink some kind of poison that makes them distraught with pain and they fall writhing to the ground.

"At that time the father returns to his home and finds that his children have drunk poison. Some are completely out of their minds, while others are not. Seeing their father from far off, all are overjoyed and kneel down and entreat him, saying: 'How fine that you have returned safely. We were stupid and by mistake drank some poison. We beg you to cure us and let us live out our lives!'

"The father, seeing his children suffering like this, follows various prescriptions. Gathering fine medicinal herbs that meet all the requirements of color, fragrance and flavor, he grinds, sifts and mixes them together. Giving a dose of these to his children, he tells them: 'This is a highly effective medicine, meeting all the requirements of color, fragrance and flavor. Take it and you will quickly be relieved of your sufferings and will be free of all illness.'

"Those children who have not lost their senses can see that this is good medicine, outstanding in both color and fragrance, so they take it immediately and are completely cured of their sickness. Those who are out of their minds are equally delighted to see their father return and beg him to cure their sickness, but when they are given the medicine, they refuse to take it. Why? Because the poison has penetrated deeply and their minds no longer function as before. So although the medicine is of excellent color and fragrance, they do not perceive it as good.

"The father thinks to himself: My poor children! Because of the poison in them, their minds are completely befuddled. Although they are happy to see me and ask me to cure them, they refuse to take this excellent medicine. I must now resort to some expedient means to induce them to take the medicine. So he says to them: 'You should know that I am now old and worn out, and the time of my death has come. I will leave this good medicine here. You should take it and not worry that it will not cure you.' Having given these instructions, he then goes off to another land, where he sends a messenger home to announce, 'Your father is dead.'

---

[16]*Lotus Sutra*, translated by Burton Watson (New York: Columbia University Press), pp. 224–232.

"At that time the children, hearing that their father has deserted them and died, are filled with great grief and consternation and think to themselves: If our father were alive he would have pity on us and see that we are protected. But now he has abandoned us and died in some other country far away. We are shelterless orphans with no one to rely on!

"Constantly harboring such feelings of grief, they at last come to their senses and realize that the medicine is in fact excellent in color and fragrance and flavor, and so they take it and are healed of all the effects of the poison. The father, hearing that his children are all cured, immediately returns home and appears to them all once more.

"Good men, what is your opinion? Can anyone say that this skilled physician is guilty of lying?"

"No, World-Honored One."

The Buddha said: "It is the same with me. It has been immeasurable, boundless hundreds, thousands, ten thousands, millions of nayuta and asamkhya kalpas since I attained Buddhahood. But for the sake of living beings I employ the power of expedient means and say that I am about to pass into extinction. In view of the circumstances, however, no one can say that I have been guilty of lies or falsehoods." At that time the World-Honored One, wishing to state his meaning once more, spoke in verse form, saying:

[Part "C"] Since I attained Buddhahood the number of kalpas that have passed is an immeasurable hundreds, thousands, ten thousands, millions, trillions, asamkhyas. Constantly I have preached the Law, teaching, converting countless millions of living beings, causing them to enter the Buddha way, all this for immeasurable kalpas. In order to save living beings, as an expedient means I appear to enter nirvana but in truth I do not pass into extinction. I am always here, preaching the Law. I am always here, but through my transcendental powers I make it so that living beings in their befuddlement do not see me even when close by. When the multitude see that I have passed into extinction, far and wide they offer alms to my relics. All harbor thoughts of yearning and in their minds thirst to gaze at me. When living beings have become truly faithful, honest and upright, gentle in intent, single-mindedly desiring to see the Buddha, not hesitating even if it costs them their lives, then I and the assembly of monks appear together on Holy Eagle Peak. At that time I tell the living beings that I am always here, never entering extinction, but that because of the power of an expedient means at times

I appear to be extinct, at other times not, and that if there are living beings in other lands who are reverent and sincere in their wish to believe, then among them too I will preach the unsurpassed Law.

The final selection in this section is an account of the death of the Buddha. According to this passage from the Long Discourses Division of the *Sutra Pitaka*, what were the final concerns and instructions of the Buddha? How did his disciples interpret his passing?

THE DEATH OF THE BUDDHA FROM *THE GREAT PASSING* IN *DIGHNA NIKAYA*, 16[17]

Now the Exalted one addressed the venerable Ananda, and said: "It may be, Ananda, that in some of you the thought may arise, 'The word of the master is ended, we have no teacher more!' But it is not thus, Ananda, that you should regard it. It is Dhamma, and the rules of the Order, which I have set forth and laid down for you all; let them, after I am gone, be the teacher to you.

"Ananda! when I am gone address not one another in the way in which the brethren have heretofore addressed each other—with the epithet, that is, of 'Avuso' (Friend). A younger brother may be addressed by an elder with his name, or his family name, or the title 'Friend.' But an elder should be addressed by a younger brother as 'Sir' or as 'Venerable Sir.'

"When I am gone, Ananda, let the Order, if it should wish, abolish all the lesser and minor precepts."

"Then the Exalted One addressed the brethren, and said: "It may be brethren, that there may be doubt or misgiving in the mind of some brother as to the Buddha, or the doctrine, or the path, or the method. Inquire, brethren, freely. Do not have to reproach yourselves afterwards with the thought: 'Our teacher was face to face with us, and we could not bring ourselves to inquire of the Exalted One when we were face to face with him.' "

And when he had thus spoken the brethren were silent. And again the second and third time the Exalted One addressed the brethren. And even the third time the brethren were silent.

Then the Exalted One addressed the brethren and said: "It may be, brethren, that you put no questions

[17]This translation of the *Dighna Nikaya* is found in Paul Carus, *Buddha, The Gospel* (Chicago: Open Court Publishing Company, 1894). See also www.sacred-texts.com/bud/btg/btg98.htm.

out of reverence for the teacher. Let comrade communicate to comrade."

And when he had thus spoken the brethren were silent.

And the venerable Ananda said to the Exalted One: "How wonderful a thing it is, lord, and how marvelous! Verily, I believe that in this whole assembly of the brethren there is not one brother who has any doubt or misgiving as to the Buddha, or the doctrine, or the path, or the method!"

Dedication to Buddha

"It is out of the fullness of faith that thou hast spoken, Ananda! But, Ananda, the Tathagata knows for certain that in this whole assembly of the brethren there is not one brother who has any doubt or misgiving as to the Buddha, or the doctrine, or the path, or the method! For even the most backward, Ananda, of all these five hundred brethren has become converted, is no longer liable to be born in a state of suffering, and is assured of hereafter attaining to the enlightenment of Arahantship." *The Theravada Arhat*

Then the Exalted One addressed the brethren and said: "Behold now, brethren, I exhort you, saying: 'Decay is inherent in all component things! Work out your salvation with diligence!'"

This was the last word of the Tathagata.

Then the Exalted One entered into the first stage of rapture. And rising out of the first stage he passed into the second. And rising out of the second he passed into the third. And rising out of the third stage he passed into the fourth. And rising out of the fourth stage of rapture, he entered into the state of mind to which the infinity of space is alone present. And passing out of the mere consciousness of the infinity of space he entered into the state of mind to which the infinity of thought is alone present. And passing out of the mere consciousness of the infinity of thought he entered into a state of mind to which nothing at all was specially present. And passing out of the consciousness of no special object he fell into a state between consciousness and unconsciousness. And passing out of the state between consciousness and unconsciousness he fell into a state in which the consciousness both of sensations and of ideas had wholly passed away. Then the venerable Ananda said to the venerable Anuruddha: "O my lord, O Anuruddha, the Exalted One is dead!"

"Nay, brother Ananda, the Exalted One is not dead. He has entered into that state in which both sensations and ideas have ceased to be!"

Nirvana

SECTION 4: Divine Law: Justice, Reward, and Punishment

Like Moses, Jesus, and Mohammed, Gautama was an outspoken critic of the religious orthodoxy of his culture. Rejecting the authority of the Hindu scriptures, gods, and Brahmin priests, Gautama instructed his followers to find refuge in the Dharma, the way of truth. Unlike the founders of the three great Western religions, however, when offering rules for living, Gautama did not make reference to "divine law." His ethical insights did not come from above as revelations from the gods but were discovered after extensive personal striving, study, and meditation.

Gautama's refusal to speak in terms of divine law did not limit the impact of his words. To the contrary, his ethical teachings and suggested societal rewards and punishments were considered authoritative by his disciples. The words of the Buddha, like the sacred words in the canons of other traditions, teach basic principles of conduct that humans violate at their own peril. The opening selections from the Little Book and Middle Length Divisions of the *Sutra-nipata* provide Gautama's answers to questions posed by a layman named Dhammika and by a group of brahmin householders. In the first, Gautama distinguishes between the modes of conduct expected of monks and laity. In the second, he analyzes what kind of karma it will take to be reborn in low states.

A DIALOG WITH DHAMMIKA FROM THE *SUTRA-NIPATA*, II, 14[18]

Thus have I heard. At one time the Lord was staying near Savatthi in the Jeta Grove at Anathapindaka's monastery. Now the lay-follower Dhammika with five hundred other lay-followers approached the Lord. Having drawn near and having saluted the Lord respectfully he sat down at one side. Sitting there the lay-follower Dhammika addressed the Lord.... "You are an illustrious Awakened One (Buddha). Having investigated all knowledge and being compassionate towards beings you have announced the Dhamma, a revealer of what is hidden, of comprehensive vision, stainless, you illuminate all the worlds. This Dhamma, subtle and pleasing and taught so clearly by you, Lord, it is this we all wish to

---

[18]*The Discourse Collection*, translated by Ireland.

hear. Having been questioned, foremost Awakened One, tell us (the answer). All these bhikkhus and also the lay followers who have come to hear the truth, let them listen to the Dhamma awakened to (anubuddham) by the Stainless One as the devas listen to the well-spoken words of Vasava."

(The Lord:) "Listen to me, bhikkhus, I will teach you the ascetic practice (dhamma dhutam), the mode of living suitable for those who have gone forth. Do you all bear it in mind. One who is intent upon what is good and who is thoughtful should practice it.

"A bhikkhu should not wander about at the wrong time but should walk the village for food at the right time, as one who goes about at the wrong time is (liable to be) obsessed by attachment, therefore Awakened Ones do not walk (for alms) at the wrong time. Sights, sounds, tastes, scents and bodily contacts overwhelm (the minds of) beings. Being rid of desire for these sense objects, at the right time, one may enter (the village) for the morning meal. Having duly obtained food, going back alone and sitting down in a secluded place, being inwardly thoughtful and not letting the mind go out to external objects, a bhikkhu should develop self-control.

"If he should speak with a lay-disciple, with someone else or with another bhikkhu, he should speak on the subtle Dhamma, not slandering others nor gossiping. Some set themselves up as disputants in opposition to others; those of little wisdom we do not praise; attachments bind them and they are carried away by their emotions.

"Having heard the Dhamma taught by the Sugata and considered it, a disciple of Him of excellent wisdom should wisely make use of food, a dwelling, a bed, a seat and water for washing the robe. But a bhikkhu should not be soiled by (clinging to) these things, as a lotus is not wetted by a drop of water.

"Now I will tell you the layman's duty. Following it a lay-disciple would be virtuous; for it is not possible for one occupied with the household life to realize the complete bhikkhu practice (dhamma).

"He should not kill a living being, nor cause it to be killed, nor should he incite another to kill. Do not injure any being, either strong or weak, in the world.

"A disciple should avoid taking anything from anywhere knowing it (to belong to another). He should not steal nor incite another to steal. He should completely avoid theft.

"A wise man should avoid unchastity as (he would avoid falling into) a pit of glowing charcoal.

If unable to lead a celibate life, he should not go to another's wife.

"Having entered a royal court or a company of people he should not speak lies. He should not speak lies (himself) nor incite others to do so. He should completely avoid falsehood.

"A layman who has chosen to practice this Dhamma should not indulge in the drinking of intoxicants. He should not drink them nor encourage others to do so; realizing that it leads to madness. Through intoxication foolish people perform evil deeds and cause other heedless people to do likewise. He should avoid intoxication, this occasion for demerit, which stupefies the mind, and is the pleasure of foolish people.

"Do not kill a living being;
do not take what is not given;
do not speak a lie;
do not drink intoxicants;
abstain from sexual intercourse;
do not eat food at night, at the wrong time;
do not wear flower-garlands nor use perfumes;
use the ground as a bed or sleep on a mat.

"This is called the eight-factored observance made known by the Awakened One who has reached the end of suffering.

With a gladdened mind observe the observance day (uposatha), complete with its eight factors, on the fourteenth, fifteenth and eighth days of the (lunar) fortnight and also the special holiday of the half month. In the morning, with a pure heart and a joyful mind, a wise man, after observing the uposatha, should distribute suitable food and drink to the community of bhikkhus. He should support his mother and father as his duty and engage in lawful trading. A layman who carries this out diligently goes to the devas called "Self-radiant."

A DIALOG WITH THE BRAHMINS FROM THE MIDDLE LENGTH DISCOURSES, *MAJJHIMA NIKAYA* 41[19]

3. The brahmin householders of Sala went to the Blessed One; and some paid homage to the Blessed One and sat down at one side . . .

4. When they were seated, they said to the Blessed One: "Master Gotama, what is the reason, what is the condition,

_____
[19]Bhikkhu, *The Buddha's Words on Kama.*

why some beings here, on the dissolution of the body, after death, reappear in states of deprivation, in an unhappy destination, in perdition, even in hell; and what is the reason, what is the condition, why some beings here, on the dissolution of the body, after death, reappear in a happy destination, even in the heavenly world?"

5. "Householders, it is by reason of conduct not in accordance with the Dhamma, by reason of unrighteous conduct, that beings here on the dissolution of the body, after death, reappear in states of deprivation, in an unhappy destination, in perdition, even in hell. It is by reason of conduct in accordance with the Dhamma, by reason of righteous conduct, that some beings here on the dissolution of the body, after death, reappear in a happy destination, even in the heavenly world."

6. "We do not understand the detailed meaning of this utterance of Master Gotama's spoken in brief without expounding the detailed meaning. It would be good if Master Gotama taught us the Dhamma so that we might understand the detailed meaning of Master Gotama's utterance spoken in brief without expounding the detailed meaning."

Then, householders, listen and heed well what I shall say."

"Yes, venerable sir," they replied. The Blessed One said this:

7. "Householders, there are three kinds of bodily conduct not in accordance with the Dhamma, unrighteous conduct. There are four kinds of verbal conduct not in accordance with the Dhamma, unrighteous conduct. There are three kinds of mental conduct not in accordance with the Dhamma, unrighteous conduct.

8. "And how are there three kinds of bodily conduct not in accordance with the Dhamma, unrighteous conduct? Here someone is a killer of living beings: he is murderous, bloody-handed, given to blows and violence, and merciless to all living beings. He is a taker of what is not given: he takes as a thief another's chattels and property in the village or in the forest. He is given over to misconduct in sexual desires: he has intercourse with such (women) as are protected by the mother, father, (mother and father), brother, sister, relatives, as have a husband, as entail a penalty, and also with those that are garlanded in token of betrothal. That is how there are three kinds of bodily conduct not in accordance with the Dhamma, unrighteous conduct.

9. "And how are there four kinds of verbal conduct not in accordance with the Dhamma, unrighteous conduct? Here someone speaks falsehood: when summoned to a court or to a meeting, or to his relatives' presence, or to his guild, or to the royal family's presence, and questioned as a witness thus, 'So, good man, tell what you know,' then, not knowing, he says 'I know,' or knowing, he says 'I do not know,' not seeing, he says 'I see,' or seeing, he says 'I do not see'; in full awareness he speaks falsehood for his own ends or for another's ends or for some trifling worldly end. He speaks maliciously: he is a repeater elsewhere of what is heard here for the purpose of causing division from these, or is a repeater

to these of what is heard elsewhere for the purpose of causing division from those, and he is thus a divider of the united, a creator of divisions, who enjoys discord, rejoices in discord, delights in discord, he is a speaker of words that create discord. He speaks harshly: he utters such words as are rough, hard, hurtful to others, censorious of others, bordering on anger and unconducive to concentration. He is a gossip: as one who tells that which is unseasonable, that which is not fact, that which is not good, that which is not the Dhamma, that which is not the Discipline, and he speaks out of season speech not worth recording, which is unreasoned, indefinite, and unconnected with good. That is how there are four kinds of verbal conduct not in accordance with the Dhamma, unrighteous conduct.

10. "And how are there three kinds of mental conduct not in accordance with the Dhamma, unrighteous conduct? Here someone is covetous: he is a coveter of another's chattels and property thus: 'Oh, that what is another's were mine!' Or he has a mind of ill-will, with the intention of a mind affected by hate thus: 'May these beings be slain and slaughtered, may they be cut off, perish, or be annihilated!' Or he has wrong view, distorted vision, thus: 'There is nothing given, nothing offered, nothing sacrificed, no fruit and ripening of good and bad kammas, no this world, no other world, no mother, no father, no spontaneously (born) beings,[1] no good and virtuous monks and brahmins that have themselves realized by direct knowledge and declare this world and the other world.' That is how there are three kinds of mental conduct not in accordance with the Dhamma, unrighteous conduct.

"So, householders, it is by reason of conduct not in accordance with the Dhamma, by reason of unrighteous conduct, that some beings here, on the dissolution of the body, after death, reappear in states of deprivation, in an unhappy destination, in perdition, even in hell."

At the heart of Buddhism is the Noble Eightfold Path. A brief yet complete statement of the Eightfold Path is printed below.

TEACHINGS ON THE EIGHTFOLD PATH FROM THE *MAJJHIMA NIKAYA*, 141[20]

The Noble Truth of the Path leading to the cessation of suffering is this Noble Eightfold Path, namely: right view, right aspiration, right speech, right action, right livelihood, right effort, right mindfulness, right concentration.

What is right view? Knowledge of suffering, knowledge of the arising of suffering, knowledge of

---

[20]Wilson, *World Scripture,* p. 113. See www.euro-tongil.org.

the cessation of suffering, knowledge of the path leading to the cessation of suffering—this is called right view.

What is right aspiration? Aspiration for renunciation, aspiration for non-malevolence, aspiration for harmlessness—this is called right aspiration.

What is right speech? Refraining from lying speech, refraining from slanderous speech, refraining from harsh speech, refraining from gossip—this is called right speech.

What is right action? Refraining from violence against creatures, refraining from taking what has not been given, refraining from going wrongly among the sense-pleasures, this is called right action.

What is right livelihood? A disciple of the Noble Ones, getting rid of a wrong mode of livelihood, makes his living by a right mode of livelihood. This is called right livelihood.

What is right effort? A monk generates desire, effort, stirs up energy, exerts his mind and strives for the non-arising of evil unskilled states that have not arisen . . . for the getting rid of evil unskilled states that have arisen . . . for the arising of skilled states that have not arisen . . . for the maintenance and completion of skilled states that have arisen. This is called right effort.

What is right mindfulness? A monk fares along contemplating the body in the body . . . the feelings in the feelings . . . the mind in the mind . . . the mental states in the mental states . . . ardent, clearly conscious of them, mindful of them so as to control the covetousness and dejection in the world. This is called right mindfulness.

And what is right concentration? A monk, aloof from the pleasures of the senses, aloof from unskilled states of mind, enters on and abides in the first meditation which is accompanied by initial thought and discursive thought, is born of aloofness, is rapturous and joyful. By allaying initial thought and discursive thought, with the mind subjectively tranquilized and fixed on one point, he enters on and abides in the second meditation which is devoid of initial thought and discursive thought, is born of concentration, and is rapturous and joyful. By the fading out of rapture . . . he enters on and abides in the third meditation . . . the fourth meditation. This is called right concentration.

The following passages are from the widely read collection in the Little Books Division, the *Dhammapada*. These passages describe the characteristics, consequences and causes of wrong action.

THE CAUSES AND CONSEQUENCES OF WRONG ACTIONS FROM THE *DHAMMAPADA*

The Punishment, 129–144

Everyone trembles at punishment; everyone fears death.
Likening others to oneself,
one should neither kill nor cause killing.

Everyone trembles at punishment; everyone loves life.
Likening others to oneself,
one should neither kill nor cause killing.

Whoever seeking one's own happiness
inflicts pain on others who also want happiness
will not find happiness after death.

Whoever seeking one's own happiness
does not inflict pain on others who also want happiness
will find happiness after death.

Do not speak anything harsh.
Those who are spoken to will answer you.
Angry talk is painful, and retaliation will touch you.
If you make yourself as still as a broken gong,
you have attained nirvana, for anger is not known to you.

Just as a cowherd with a staff
drives the cows into the pasture,
so old age and death drive the life of living beings.

A fool committing wrong actions does not know
that the stupid person burns through one's own deeds,
like one burned by fire.

Whoever inflicts punishment
on those who do not deserve it
and offends against those who are without offense
soon comes to one of these ten states:
cruel suffering, infirmity, injury of the body, fearful pain,
or mental loss, or persecution from the ruler,
or a fearful accusation, loss of relations,
or destruction of possessions,
or lightning fire burning one's houses,
and when one's body is destroyed the fool goes to hell.

Neither nakedness nor matted hair nor mud
nor fasting nor lying on the ground
nor rubbing with dust nor sitting motionless
purify a mortal who is not free from doubt and desire.

Whoever though dressed in fine clothes, lives peacefully,
is calm, controlled, restrained, pure,
and does not hurt any other beings,
that one is holy, an ascetic, a mendicant.

Is there in the world anyone
who is so restrained by modesty
that they avoid blame like a trained horse avoids the
    whip?

Like a trained horse when touched by a whip,
be strenuous and eager, and by faith, by virtue, by energy,
by meditation, by discernment of the truth
you will overcome this great sorrow,
perfected in knowledge, behavior, and mindfulness.

Engineers of canals guide the water;
fletchers make the arrow straight;
carpenters shape the wood;
good people mold themselves.

The final selections contain rules of discipline (Patimokkha) for ordained monks (*bhikkhus*) and nuns (*bhikkhunis*) who live together in a Buddhist community known as the Sangha. These sutras detail how those within the Sangha are to interact with each other and with others living outside the community. Altogether there are 227 Patimokkha rules for the monks and 311 for the nuns. The rules are arranged into categories according to the severity of the punishment for violating the rules. Listed are the most important laws to be followed by those within the Sangha.

RULES OF DISCIPLINE IN THE *VINAYA PITAKA*[21]

PRECEPTS WHOSE VIOLATION REQUIRES EXPULSION

These are the Four Rules that require expulsion from the Order.

1. If One of this Sangha, having been properly ordained and having accepted the Full Precepts, engages in adultery or impure conduct, defiling himself or others, such a one is expelled and cut off.
2. If One of this Sangha, having left the boundaries of the temple or monastery, takes from others, either by force or by guile, what is not freely given, and such theft is discovered so that such a one is brought before a worldly tribunal and this tribunal finds such a one to be guilty, . . . such a one is expelled and cut off.
3. If One of this Sangha, by intent or in anger, causes the death of a human being or one with the form of a human being, or employs some agent for this purpose, or by his actions or words encourages another to disregard his own life, to place his life in danger, or even to take his own life, or in any way recommends that dying is preferable to living, thus causing another's death, such a one is expelled and cut off.

---

[21]All the passages from the *Vinaya Pitaka* included in this volume are available on the Internet at www.dragonflower.org/pratimoksa.html#main.

4. If One of this Sangha, having no true understanding or knowledge, boasts of having attained the "Law above Men" or says: "I have the complete perfect enlightenment, the Treasury of the True Dharma Eye," and if such a one at another time, whether asked or unasked, desiring absolution says: "Indeed, I neither know nor do I understand; when I claimed thus to know I was speaking falsely," unless this first was spoken because of pride, such a one is expelled and cut off.

PRECEPTS WHOSE VIOLATION REQUIRES SUSPENSION

Venerable Ones, I now recite the thirteen laws verging on expulsion which require open confession before the Assembly and absolution by the Assembly.

1. If One of this Sangha by pampering lustful thoughts is conquered by them, wantonly dissipating his energy, except in a dream, let such a one be suspended.
2. If One of this Sangha comes into contact with another person and touches them in a way that encourages lustful desires and a perverted mind in himself or this other, let such a one be suspended. . . .

4. If One of this Sangha, having a corrupt mind and lustful desires, advocates sexual favors saying: "Honored One, this is the highest act, that you minister to me who is pure in the Dharma and follows the Path of Virtue," let such a one be suspended.
5. If One of this Sangha acts as an intermediary, bringing a man and a woman together, whether for the purpose of marriage or for a single act of intercourse, let such a one be suspended.
6. If One of this Sangha builds a house for personal use, care must be taken that it is no more than twelve of the Buddha's spans in length and seven of the Buddha's spans in width. . . . If such a one does not observe these regulations, let such a one be suspended. . . .

8. If One of this Sangha, due to anger or hostility, falsely accuses another of breaking the Precepts which call for expulsion, and at later time, either asked or unasked, confesses that the charge was made in malice, let such a one be suspended.
9. If One of this Sangha, being angry or resentful, takes one matter and calls it another so as to be able to falsely accuse another of breaking Precepts which call for expulsion, and at a later time, whether asked or unasked, confesses that the charge was made in malice. let such a one be suspended.
10. If One of this Sangha attempts to divide a Sangha which is harmonious or takes up a legal question so as to cause the taking of sides and persists in such a course, this one should be spoken to thus: "Venerable One, do not continue in this way, causing a division in this harmonious Sangha. Let us come to terms so as to be united and without dispute, dwelling peacefully, learning from one Master, being like milk and water, illuminating the Buddha's Dharma." If this one then abandons that course, that is good. But if this one does

not give up that course, let him be questioned and admonished by others—once, twice, even three times; if even at the third time such a one abandons that course, that is good. Should such a one, having been spoken to in this way three times, not abandon that course, let such a one be suspended.

11. If there are comrades of one such as was spoken of in the previous rule and these comrades side with and follow the schism-minded one, saying to others: "Venerable Ones, do not speak of this one, neither good nor bad, for this one speaks according to the Dharma and *Vinaya*; this one speaks knowledgeably and what pleases this one pleases us also," then these comrades should be spoken to thus: "Venerable Ones, do not speak this way. The maker of schisms does not speak according to the Dharma or Vinaya. Do not say such a one speaks knowingly; likewise do not take delight in this division of the Sangha. Instead, among us should be harmony and the desire to see harmony, peace without disorder, learning from one Master, being like milk and water, illuminating the Buddha's Dharma." If they then abandon that course, that is good. But if they do not give up that course, let them be questioned and admonished by others—once, twice, even three times; if even at the third time such ones abandon that course, that is good. Should they, having been spoken to in this way three times, not abandon that course, let such ones be suspended.

12. If One of this Sangha lives in a fixed place, dependent on a household or community, and pollutes this living place by impure conduct so that all may see or hear of it, such a one should be told: "Venerable One, your conduct is disorderly and you bring disgrace upon yourself and the Order by your impure living. All men see and speak of it. Now you must leave this place; depart and go elsewhere so that this disgrace is ended." If such a one replies to this admonition: "Venerable Ones, this Sangha is one-sided and foolish. Others have faults more serious than my own, yet no one speaks of them. I shall go my own way and you should do likewise," then such a one should be spoken to thus: "Venerable One, do not defame the Order in this way; do not say that this Sangha contains such persons. It is your conduct which is seen and spoken to the discredit of all." Should such a one who is thus admonished thereupon leave this place and return to Pure Living, that is good; but should there be need for further admonition beyond the second and third time, let such a one be suspended.

13. If One of this Sangha, being of bad disposition, refuses to be spoken to according to the Dharma and the Vinaya, and if such a one when admonished on this account says, "Venerable Ones, do not speak to me of these matters, not of the good nor of the bad, and I will also not speak of these things to you," let such a one be spoken to thus: "Venerable One, do not refuse to be spoken to. One who cannot be spoken to is not in accord with the Dharma and Vinaya; therefore do not be one like this. It is better that you be spoken to in accord with the Dharma and Vinaya, for it is by admonishing and helping one another that faults are discovered and eliminated. How else can this Sangha be in harmony with the

Dharma of the Tathagata, the Blessed One; how else can we be bound together? Venerable One, do not thus separate yourself from this principle." If such a one, having been spoken to thus, abandons this course, that is good. If not, let such a one be admonished for a second and third time, and if the course is abandoned, that is good. But should such a one after even a third admonition not abandon this course, let such a one be suspended.

SECTION 5: Gender: Women and Men in Society

Buddhist scriptures, like most ancient sacred texts, contain contradictory statements about the nature of women and the proper place of women in society. Often these ancient texts portray women primarily as seductresses who, because of their carnal sensual nature, are a threat to the spiritual welfare of men. In these texts, women generally are viewed not only as social inferiors but also as members of a biologically, mentally, and spiritually weaker sex. In other texts, women are presented as domestic paragons created for motherhood. In still other discourses, Buddhist scripture rejects any inherent differences between men and women.

The opening selections are from a collection in the Little Books Division of the *Sutra Pitaka* known as the *Therigatha* (*Psalms of the Sisters*). The presence of this collection of female witnesses in the sacred Buddhist canon suggests a higher status level for women within the Buddhist community than in the larger society. Yet, even in these writings, women often are associated with unflattering stereotypical images. What do these accounts tell us about ancient attitudes toward women? How do you explain the popularity of these attitudes?

THE STORY OF VIMALA FROM THE *THERIGATHA* 5.2[22]

Intoxicated with my complexion figure, beauty, and fame;
   haughty with youth,
I despised other women.
Adorning this body embellished to delude foolish men,

I stood at the door to the brothel: a hunter with his snare
   laid out.
I showed off my ornaments, and revealed many a private part.
I worked my manifold magic, laughing out loud at the crowd.

---

[22]All of the passages from the *Therigatha* are taken from *Therigatha: Verses of the Elders Nuns*, translated by Thanissaro Bhikkhuy. See www.accesstoinsight.org.

Today, having gone for alms, my head shaven, wrapped in a
   double cloak,
I sit at the foot of a tree and attain the state of no-thought.
All ties have been cut, divine and human.
Having cast off all effluents, cooled am I, unbound.

THE STORY OF SONA, MOTHER
OF TEN FROM *THERIGATHA* 5.8

Ten children I bore from this physical heap.
Then weak from that, aged, I went to a nun.
She taught me the Dharma: aggregates, sense spheres, and
   elements.
Hearing the Dharma, I cut off my hair and ordained.
Having purified the divine eye while still a probationer,
I know my previous lives, where I lived in the past.
I develop the theme-less meditation, well-focused
   singleness.
I gain the liberation of immediacy—from lack of clinging,
   unbound.
The five aggregates, comprehended, stand like a tree with its
   root cut through.
I spit on old age.
There is now no further becoming.

THE STORY OF CANDA, THE BEGGAR
FROM *THERIGATHA* 5.12

Before, I had fallen on evil times:
   no husband, no children,
   no relatives, no friends,
   no way to obtain clothing and food.
So, taking a staff and bowl in hand, begging for alms from
   house to house,
feverish from the cold and heat, I wandered for seven full
   years.
Then seeing a nun obtaining food and drink,
I approached her and said:
   "Let me go forth into homelessness."
She, Patacara, out of compassion, let me go forth.
Then, exhorting me, she urged me on to the highest goal.
Hearing her words, I followed her message.
Her exhortation was not in vain.
   Endowed with the three knowledges,
   I'm effluent-free.

THE STORY OF ANOPAMA, THE MILLIONAIRE'S
DAUGHTER FROM *THERIGATHA* 6.5

Born in a high-ranking family with much property, great
   wealth,
consummate in complexion and figure, I was the daughter
   of the treasurer, Majjha.

The sons of kings sought for me, the sons of rich merchants
   longed for me.
One of them sent my father a messenger, saying, "Give me
   Anopama.
I will give in return eight times her weight in jewels and
   gold."
But I, having seen the One Self-awakened, unsurpassed,
   excelling the world,
paying homage to his feet, sat down to one side.
He, Gautama, out of compassion, taught me the Dharma.
And as I was sitting in that very seat, I attained the third
   fruit [of nonreturn.]
Then I cut off my hair, and went forth into homelessness.
Today is the seventh day since I made craving wither away.

THE STORY OF SUBHA AND THE LIBERTINE
FROM *THERIGATHA* 14

As Subha the nun was going through Jivaka's delightful
   mango grove,
a libertine (a goldsmith's son) blocked her path, so she said
   to him:
'What wrong have I done you that you stand in my way?
It's not proper, my friend, that a man should touch a
   woman gone forth.
I respect the Master's message, the training pointed out by
   the one well-gone.
I am pure, without blemish:
Why do you stand in my way?
You—your mind agitated, impassioned;
I—unagitated, unimpassioned, with a mind entirely freed:
Why do you stand in my way?'
'You are young and not bad-looking, what need do you
   have for going forth?
Throw off your ochre robe—
Come, let's delight in the flowering grove.
A sweetness they exude everywhere, the towering trees with
   their pollen.
The beginning of spring is a pleasant season—
Come, let's delight in the flowering grove.
The trees with their blossoming tips moan, as it were, in the
   breeze:
What delight will you have if you plunge into the grove
   alone?
Frequented by herds of wild beasts, disturbed by elephants
   rutting and aroused:
you want to go unaccompanied into the great, lonely,
   frightening grove?
Like a doll made of gold, you will go about, like a goddess
   in the gardens of heaven.
With delicate, smooth Kasi fabrics, you will shine, O beauty
   without compare.
I would gladly do your every bidding if we were to dwell in
   the glade.

For there is no creature dearer to me than you, O nymph
    with the languid regard.
If you do as I ask, happy, come live in my house.
Dwelling in the calm of a palace, have women wait on you,
wear delicate Kasi fabrics, adorn yourself with garlands and
    creams.
I will make you many and varied ornaments of gold, jewels,
    and pearls.
Climb onto a costly bed, scented with sandalwood carvings,
with a well-washed coverlet, beautiful, spread with a
    woolen quilt, brand new.
Like a blue lotus rising from the water where no human
    beings dwell,
you will go to old age with your limbs unseen, if you stay as
    you are in the holy life.'
'What do you assume of any essence, here in this cemetery
    grower, filled with corpses,
this body destined to break up?
What do you see when you look at me, you who are out of
    your mind?'
'Your eyes are like those of a fawn, like those of a sprite in
    the mountains.
Seeing your eyes, my sensual delight grows all the more.
Like tips they are, of blue lotuses, in your golden face—
    spotless:
Seeing your eyes, my sensual delight grows all the more.
Even if you should go far away, I will think only of your
    pure, long-lashed gaze,
for there is nothing dearer to me than your eyes, O nymph
    with the languid regard.'
'You want to stray from the road, you want the moon as a
    plaything,
you want to jump over Mount Sineru, you who have
    designs on one born of the Buddha.
For there is nothing anywhere at all in the cosmos with its
    gods, that would be an object of passion for me.
I don't even know what that passion would be, for it's been
    killed, root and all, by the path.
Like embers from a pit—scattered, like a bowl of poison—
    evaporated,
I don't even see what that passion would be, for it's been
    killed, root and all, by the path.
Try to seduce one who hasn't reflected on this,
or who has not followed the Master's teaching.
But try it with this one who knows and you suffer.
For in the midst of praise and blame, pleasure and pain, my
    mindfulness stands firm.
Knowing the unattractiveness of things compounded,
my mind cleaves to nothing at all.
I am a follower of the one well-gone, riding the vehicle of
    the eightfold way:
My arrow removed, effluent-free, I delight, having gone to
    an empty dwelling.
For I have seen well-painted puppets, hitched up with sticks
    and strings, made to dance in various ways.

When the sticks and strings are removed, thrown away,
    scattered, shredded,
smashed into pieces, not to be found, in what will the mind
    there make its home?
This body of mine, which is just like that, when devoid of
    dhammas doesn't function.
When, devoid of dhammas, it doesn't function, in what will
    the mind there make its home?
Like a mural you've seen, painted on a wall, smeared with
    yellow orpiment,
there your vision has been distorted, meaningless your
    human perception.
Like an evaporated mirage, like a tree of gold in a dream,
    like a magic show in the midst of a crowd – you run blind
    after what is unreal.
Resembling a ball of sealing wax, set in a hollow,
with a bubble in the middle and bathed with tears, eye
    secretions are born there too:
The parts of the eye are rolled all together in various ways.'
Plucking out her lovely eye, with mind unattached she felt
    no regret.
'Here, take this eye. It's yours.'
Straightway she gave it to him.
Straightway his passion faded right there, and he begged her
    forgiveness.
'Be well, follower of the holy life.
This sort of thing won't happen again.
Harming a person like you is like embracing a blazing fire,
It is as if I have seized a poisonous snake.
So may you be well. Forgive me.'
And released from there, the nun went to the excellent
    Buddha's presence.
When she saw the mark of his excellent merit, her eye
    became as it was before.

The next excerpt contains the Buddha's teaching to monks about renunciation. The passage is in the *Itivuttaka*, a collection in the Little Books Division of the *Sutra Pitaka*. What images of women appear in this passage?

IMAGES OF WOMEN FROM THE *ITIVUTTAKA* 114–15[23]

Suppose, monks, a man is carried along a river by a current which looks delightful and charming. Then a sharp-sighted man standing on the bank sees him and calls out, "My friend! Though you are being carried along in the river by a current which seems delightful and charming, yet further down here is a pool with waves and whirlpools, with monsters and demons.

---

[23]Wilson, *World Scriptures*, p. 385. See www.euro-tongil.org.

My friend, when you get there you will come by your death or mortal pain!" Hearing the other's call, that man struggles against the stream with hands and feet.

This parable, monks, I use to explain my meaning. The river current is craving; 'looking delightful and charming' refers to one's own sphere of perception. The pool lower down is the five fetters belonging to this lower world; its waves are the five pleasures of sense; monsters and demons refer to women. His going against the stream refers to renunciation; struggle with hands and feet means to put forth energy. The sharp-sighted man standing on the bank is the Wayfarer, Arahant, a Rightly-awakened One.

The following passages from the Long Discourses Division of the *Sutra Pitaka* contain the Buddha's advice to lay people about parent/child and husband/wife relations. What do these texts inform us about familial relationships within early Buddhism?

TEACHINGS TO LAY PEOPLE ON FAMILIAL RELATIONS FROM THE *DIGHA NIKAYA*, 31[24]

There are five ways in which a son should minister to his mother and father . . . [He should think:] "Having been supported by them, I will support them. I will perform their duties for them. I will keep up the family tradition. I will be worthy of my heritage. After my parents' deaths I will distribute gifts on their behalf." And there are five ways in which the parents, so ministered to by their son . . . will reciprocate: they will restrain him from evil, support him in doing good, teach him some skill, find him a suitable wife and in due time, hand over his inheritance to him. . . .

There are five ways in which a husband should minister to his wife, By honoring her, by not disparaging her, by not being unfaithful to her, by giving authority to her, by providing her with adornments. And there are five ways in which a wife, thus ministered to by her husband . . . will reciprocate: by properly organizing her work, by being kind to the servants, by not being unfaithful, by protecting stores, and by being skillful and diligent in all she has to do.

The section of the *Tripitaka* that provides rules for monastic living includes a number of gender specific regulations. Below are some of the rules relating to relations between monks and nuns. What do these

rules tell us about common assumptions about the nature of men and women?

RULES FOR MONKS AND NUNS IN THE *VINAYA PITAKA*

PRECEPTS REQUIRING CONFESSION AND ABSOLUTION

Venerable Ones! I now recite the ninety rules that require confession and absolution.

5. If One of this Sangha, not the supervisor of a temple, teaches the Dharma to one outside the Order and of the opposite sex in excess of five or six sentences, except in the presence of a discreet person, this requires confession and absolution. . . .
21. If a Bhiksu, not having a commission to do so, instructs or admonishes Bhiksunis, this requires confession and absolution.
22. If a Bhiksu, even having a commission to do so, instructs or admonishes Bhiksunis at an unseemly hour, this requires confession and absolution.
23. If One of this Sangha says to others, "The Bhiksunis are being admonished for some worldly purpose," this requires confession and absolution. . . .

26. If a Bhiksu and Bhiksuni travel together, except on allowed occasions, this requires confession and absolution. The allowed occasions are when traveling in the company of others or when there is the possibility of danger. This is the rule.
27. If a Bhiksu and a Bhiksuni who are not related board a single boat together, to go either upstream or downstream, except to cross to the opposite shore, this requires confession and absolution.
28. If One of this Sangha sits with an unrelated person of the opposite sex in secret or in a concealed spot, this requires confession and absolution.
29. If One of this Sangha stands or sits in secret with another of this Assembly of the opposite sex, this requires confession and absolution.

Some have suggested that Mahayana Buddhism looks upon women more favorably than Theravada Buddhism. Like many generalizations, this statement is misleading since one can find within the vast Mahayana canon both unfavorable and favorable portraits of women. It is more accurate to say that the universe of expression about the status of women is larger in Mahayana texts. The final selection in this section is from a Mahayanan text, *The Vimalakirti Sutra*. This passage challenges the notion that there are inherent differences between the sexes, insisting that commonly accepted differences between women and

[24]*Digha Nikaya: The Long Discourses of the Buddha*, translated from the Pali by Maurice Walshe (Boston: Wisdom Publication, 1995), p. 467.

men are the result of misguided conceptualization. The setting for this passage is a dialogue in the house of Vimalakirti between a goddess and Shariputra, one of the key Brahmin converts of the Buddha and symbol of the intellectual who does not understand the notion of emptiness.

ON THE DIFFERENCES BETWEEN THE SEXES FROM THE *TEACHING OF VIMALAKIRTI SUTRA* 6.6–16[25]

A goddess who lived in the house of Vimalakirti, having heard the doctrinal teaching of the bodhisattvas, the great beings, was very pleased, delighted, and moved. She took on a gross material form and scattered heavenly flowers over the great bodhisattvas and great hearers. When she had thrown them, the flowers that landed on the bodies of the bodhisattvas fell to the ground, while those that fell on the bodies of the great hearers remained stuck to them and did not fall to the ground. Then the great hearers tried to use their supernatural powers to shake off the flowers, but the flowers did not fall off. Then the goddess asked the venerable Shariputra: "Honorable Shariputra, why do you try to shake off the flowers?"

"Goddess, flowers are not fitting for monks; that is why we reject them."

"Honorable Shariputra, do not speak thus. Why? These flowers are perfectly fitting. Why? The flowers are flowers and are free from conceptuality; it is only yourselves, the elders, who conceptualize them and create conceptuality toward them. Honorable Shariputra, among those who have renounced the world to take up monastic discipline, such conceptualizations and conceptuality are not fitting; it is those  who do not conceive either conceptualizations nor conceptuality who are fit.

"Honorable Shariputra, take a good look at these bodhisattvas, great beings: the flowers do not stick to them because they have abandoned conceptuality. . . . Flowers stick to those who have not yet abandoned the defilements; they do not stick to those who have abandoned them. . . ."

"Well done! Well done, Goddess! What have you attained, what have you gained that enables you to have such eloquence?"

"It is because I have not attained anything nor gained anything that I have such eloquence. Those who think that they have attained or gained something are deluded with respect to the well-taught disciplinary doctrine. . . ."

"Goddess, why do you not change your womanhood?"

"During the twelve years [that I have lived in this house], I have looked for womanhood, but have never found it. Honorable Shariputra, if a skillful magician created an illusory woman through transformation, could you ask her why she does not change her womanhood?"

"Every illusory creation is unreal."

"In the same way, honorable Shariputra, all phenomena are unreal and have an illusory nature; why would you think of asking them to change their womanhood?"

Then the goddess performed a supernatural feat that caused the elder Shariputra to appear in every way like the goddess and she herself to appear in every way like the elder Shariputra. Then the goddess who had changed into Shariputra asked Shariputra who had been changed into a goddess: "Why do you not change your womanhood, honorable sir?"

[SHARIPUTRA:] "I do not know either how I lost my male form nor how I acquired a female body."

[GODDESS:] "Elder, if you were able to change your female form, then all women could change their womanhood. Elder, just as you appear to be a woman, so also all women appear in the form of women, but they appear in the form of women without being women. It was with this hidden thought that the Exalted One said: 'Phenomena are neither male nor female.' "

Then the goddess cut off her supernatural power and the venerable Shariputra regained his previous form. Then the goddess said to Shariputra: 'Honorable Shariputra, where is your female form now?'

[SHARIPUTRA:] "My female form is neither made nor changed."

[GODDESS:] "Well done! Well done, honorable sir! In the same way, all phenomena, just as they are, are neither made nor changed. Saying that they are neither made nor changed is the word of the Buddha. . . ."

[SHARIPUTRA:] "Goddess, how long will it be before you reach enlightenment?"

[GODDESS:] "Elder, when you yourself return to being a worldly person, with all the qualities of a worldly person, then I myself will reach unsurpassed, perfect enlightenment."

---

[25]Teaching of *Vimalakirti Sutra* 6. 6–16. See www.anu.edu. asianstudies/buddhism.maha.html.

[SHARIPUTRA:] "Goddess, it is impossible that I could return to being a worldly person, with all the qualities of a worldly person; it cannot occur."

[GODDESS:] "Honorable Shariputra, in the same way, it is impossible that I will ever attain unsurpassed, perfect enlightenment; it cannot occur. Why? Because unsurpassed, perfect enlightenment is founded on a non-foundation. Thus, since there is no foundation, who could reach unsurpassed, perfect enlightenment?"

[SHARIPUTRA:] "But the Tathagata has said: 'Tathagatas as innumerable as the sands of the Ganges river attain, have attained, and will attain unsurpassed, perfect enlightenment.'"

[GODDESS:] "Honorable Shariputra, the words, 'buddhas past, future, and present' are conventional expressions made up of syllables and numbers. Buddhas are neither past, nor future, nor present, and their enlightenment transcends the three divisions of time. Tell me, elder, have you already attained the level of arhat?"

[SHARIPUTRA:] "I have attained it because there is nothing to attain."

[GODDESS:] "It is the same with enlightenment: it is attained because there is nothing to attain."

SECTION 6: Daily Living: Health, Etiquette, and Holy Days

As practitioners of "the middle way," Buddhists are called to live a life of discipline, self-control, and simplicity. The following excerpts from the Grouped Discourses, the Numerically Arranged Discourses, and the Long Discourses Divisions of the *Sutra Pitaka* illustrate some of the basic principles that should order the daily lives of those who choose to follow the teachings of the Buddha.

ON THE NEED FOR DISCIPLINE FROM THE *SAMYUTTA-NIKAYA*, II, 123[26]

The Exalted One said: "Once upon a time, brethren, a cat was standing in a dust-bin, on a dust-heap, watching for a mouse (and said) 'As soon as a mouse comes out in search of food, I will catch and swallow it.'

"Well, brethren, that mouse came out in search of food, the cat pounced suddenly upon it, caught and swallowed it. But the mouse gnawed away at his inside and gnawed his bowels, as a result of which the cat came by his death and mortal pain.

"Even so, brethren, such and such a brother rises up at an early hour, roves himself, and taking bowl and robe, enters a village or suburb to beg for alms, with bodily senses unguarded, with mindfulness unsteadied, and senses unrestrained.

"There he catches sight of some womenfolk, lightly clad or incompletely clad, and on seeing womenfolk thus clad passion torments his mind. With his mind thus tormented by the stings of passion, he comes by his death or else by mortal pain.

"Now, herein, brethren, 'death' means to desert the training of the Ariyan discipline and to return to the lower life (of the world): 'mortal pain,' brethren, means to fall into some grievous offense, (but) an offense of such a sort that recovery from it can be made.

"Therefore, brethren, thus must ye train yourselves: 'Guarded in body-senses, in speech and in mind, with mindfulness established and senses restrained will we enter a village or suburb to beg for alms.'

"Even so, brethren, must ye train yourselves."

ON MUSIC, DANCING AND LAUGHING FROM THE *ANGUTTARA-NIKAYA*, I, 261[27]

"In the Ariyan discipline, brethren, music is lamentation. In the Ariyan discipline, dancing is sheer madness. In the Ariyan discipline, laughing that displays the teeth is childishness.

"Wherefore, brethren, do ye break down the bridge that causes music, dancing, laughter? Enough for you just to smile if you have any cause to show your pleasure."

ON CLOTHING, FOOD AND LODGING FROM THE *DIGHA-NIKAYA*, III, 130[28]

The Exalted One said: "A new teaching, Cunda, do I show you for the control of the asavas which belong to this life. Nay, I do not show you a teaching for the prevention of the asavas of some future life, but for the control of them here and now, as well as for the prevention of them in the future.

"Wherefore, Cunda, as to the robe I have permitted you,—let that be enough for you to keep off cold,

---

[26]*Some Sayings of the Buddha*, translated by F. L. Woodward (London: Oxford University Press, 1973), p. 74.

[27]*Sayings of the Buddha*, p. 72.
[28]*Sayings of the Buddha*, pp. 74–75.

to keep off heat, to prevent the touch of gnats and stinging flies, of wind and sun and snakes, and for modesty.

"As to the food you beg, permitted by me,—let that be enough for the setting up, for the keeping up, for the safeguarding of the body, and for the adoption of the holy life, bearing this in mind: 'Thus do I destroy my old feeling and produce no new feeling, so that I shall be blameless and may live at ease.'

"And as to the lodging that I have permitted, let that be enough to keep off cold, to keep off heat, to keep off the touch of gnats and stinging flies, and wind and sun and bite of snakes,—just enough to provide shelter from the stress of seasons and for solitude.

"And as to the supply of drugs and requisites in case of sickness, which I have permitted,—let those be enough to keep off the pains of sickness that have arisen and as a bare sufficiency of relief."

ON INDULGENCES THAT DESTROY WEALTH FROM THE *DIGHA-NIKAYA*, III, 181[29]

(a) Now, young master, there are these six disadvantages of indulging in intoxicants: loss of wealth, increase of quarreling, liability to sickness, loss of good name, immodest acts, weakening of brain power. These six.

(b) Now, young master, there are these six disadvantages of roaming the streets at unseasonable hours: One is off one's guard and unprotected, one's wife and children are unprotected, one's property likewise: one is suspected of evil doings: false rumors about one have weight: one is exposed to many states of ill. These are the six.

(c) Now, young master, these are these six disadvantages of frequenting festivals. (One keeps thinking) "Where is the dancing? Where is the singing? Where is the music? Where is the recital? Where is the tambour-playing? Where are the tam-tams?" These are the six.

(d) Now, young master, there are these six disadvantages of being given to gambling: If one wins, he wins a foe. If he lose, he has to lament his loss. Gone is his visible means of subsistence. He goes to the Mote-Hall, but his word has no weight there. Friends and ministers of state treat him with contempt. He is not sought after by those who give and take in marriage: for they say, "A gambler is not competent to support a wife." Such are the six disadvantages of being given to gambling.

(e) Now, young master, there are these six disadvantages of bad companions. All the rogues, drunkards, topers, cheats,

frauds, and rowdies are his friends and boon companions. These are the six.

(f) Now, young master, there are these six disadvantages of idling. (The idlers says) "It's too cold," and does no work: or "It's too hot," and does no work: or "It's too early," and does no work: or "It's too late, " and does no work: or "I'm too hungry," and does no work: or "I'm too full," and does not work. So as he lives with all these excuses about work, the wealth that has not yet come to him does not arise, and the wealth that has come goes to destruction.

Thus spake the Exalted One.

In the Buddha's instruction to the monks in the *Vinaya Pitaka*, he informs them of their obligations to care for each other. The following excerpt expresses this expectation.

ON TENDING THE SICK FROM THE *VINAYA*. *MAHAVAGGA*, VIII, 26[30]

Now at that time a certain brother was suffering from dysentery and lay where he had fallen down in his own excrements. And the Exalted One was going his rounds of the lodgings, with the venerable Ananda in attendance, and came to the lodging of that brother. Now the Exalted One saw that brother lying where he had fallen in his own excrements, and seeing him he went towards him, came to him, and said: "Brother, what ails you?"

"I have dysentery, Lord,"

"But is there anyone taking care of you, brother?"

"No, Lord."

"Why is it, brother, that the brethren do not take care of you?"

"I am useless to the brethren, Lord: therefore the brethren do not care for me."

"Then the Exalted One said to the venerable Ananda: 'Go you, Ananda, and fetch water. We will wash this brother.' "

"Yes, Lord," replied the venerable Ananda to the Exalted One. When he had fetched the water, the Exalted One poured it out, while the venerable Ananda washed that brother all over. then the Exalted One taking him by the head and the venerable Ananda taking him by the feet, together they laid him on the bed.

Then the Exalted One, in this connection and on this occasion, gathered the Order of Brethren together, and

---

[29]*Sayings of the Buddha*, pp. 102–103.

[30]*Sayings of the Buddha*, pp. 84–85.

questioned the brethren, saying: "Brethren, is there in such and such a lodging a brother who is sick?"

"There is, Lord."

"And what ails that brother?"

"Lord, that brother has dysentery."

"But, brethren, is there anyone taking care of him?"

"No, Lord."

"Why not? Why do not the brethren take care of him?"

"That brother is useless to the brethren, Lord. That is why the brethren do not take care of him."

"Brethren, ye have no mother and no father to take care of you. If ye will not take care of each other, who else, I ask, will do so? Brethren, he who would wait on me, let him wait on the sick."

Like sacred works in other traditions, Buddhist scriptures encourage believers to journey in reverence to selected holy sites. The following passage taken from the well-known *The Great Passing Discourse* in the *Sutra Pitaka* identifies four holy places within the Buddhist tradition. What events in the life of the Buddha took place at these locations? How are pilgrims expected to approach these sites? How do you explain the importance of pilgrimages in the various world religious?

ON THE ESTABLISHMENT OF PILGRIMAGE PLACES FROM *THE MAHA PARINIBBANA SUTRANA*[31]

Ananda said: "In times past, lord, the brethren, when they had spent the rainy season in different districts, used to come to see the Tathagata, and we used to receive those very reverend brethren to audience, and to wait upon the Exalted One. But, lord, after the end of the Exalted One, we shall not be able to receive those very reverend brethren to audience, and to wait upon the Exalted One."

"There are four places, Ananda, which the believing clansman should visit with feelings of reverence. Which are the four?"

"The place, Ananda, at which the believing man can say: 'Here the Tathagata was born!' is a spot to be visited with feelings of reverence.

"The place, Ananda, at which the believing man can say: 'Here the Tathagata attained to the supreme and perfect insight!' is a spot to be visited with feelings of reverence."

"The place, Ananda, at which the believing man can say: 'Here was the kingdom of righteousness set on foot by the Tathagata!' is a spot to be visited with feelings of reverence."

"The place, Ananda, at which the believing man can say: 'Here the Tathagata passed finally behind!' is a spot to be visited with feelings of reverence. These are the four places, Ananda, which the believing clansman should visit with feelings of reverence."

"And they, Ananda, who shall die while they, with believing heart, are journeying on such pilgrimage, shall be reborn after death, when the body shall dissolve, in the happy realms of heaven."

SECTION 7: The Human Quest: Paths to Enlightenment

From what can humans be delivered? How is this enlightenment obtained? The following two selections from the *Tripitaka* provide basic Buddhist answers to these haunting questions. The first passage, "The Sorrow of Visakha," is from the *Udana* in the Little Books Division; the second, "The Discourse on Right View," is contained in the Middle Length Discourses of the *Sutra Pitaka*.

THE SORROW OF VISAKHA FROM THE *UDANA*[32]

Thus have I heard: On a certain occasion the Exalted One was staying near Savatthi in East Park, at the storied house of Migara's mother.

Now at that time the dear and lovely granddaughter of Visakha, Migara's mother, had died. So Visakha, Migara's mother, with clothes and hair still wet from washing, came at an unseasoned hour to see the Exalted One, and on coming to him, saluted him and sat down at one side. As she sat thus the Exalted One said this to Visakha, Migara's mother:

"Why, Visakha! How is it that you come here with clothes and hair still wet at an unseasonable hour?"

"O, sir, my dear and lovely grand-daughter is dead! That is why I come here, with hair and clothes still wet at an unseasonable hour."

[31]*Maha Parinibbana Suttanta*, translated by T. W. Rhys Davis (Oxford: Clarendon Press, 1881). See www.buddhistinformation.com.

[32]*Udana*, translated from the Pali by Thanissaro Bhikkhu. See www.accesstoinsight.org.

"Visakha, would you like to have as many sons and grandsons as there are men in Savatthi?"

"Yes, sir, I would indeed!"

"But how many men do you suppose die daily in Savatthi?"

"Ten, sir, or maybe nine or eight. Maybe seven, six, five, or four, three, two; maybe one a day dies in Savatthi, sir. Savatthi is never free from men dying, sir."

"What think you, Visakha? In such case would you ever be without wet hair and clothes?"

"Surely not, sir! Enough for me, sir, of so many sons and grandsons."

"Visakha, whose have a hundred things beloved, they have a hundred sorrows. Whoso have ninety, eighty, . . . thirty, twenty things beloved . . . whoso have ten . . . whoso have but one thing beloved, have but one sorrow. Whoso have no one thing beloved, they have no sorrow. Sorrowless are they and passionless. Serene are they, I declare."

All griefs or lamentations whatsoever
And diverse forms of sorrow in the world—
Because of what is dear to these become.
Thing dear not being, these do not become.
Happy are they therefore and free from grief
To whom is naught at all dear in the world.
Wherefore aspiring for the griefless, sorrowless,
Make thou in all the world naught dear to thee.

THE DISCOURSE ON RIGHT VIEW FROM THE *MAJJHIMA NIKAYA*, 9[33]

1. Thus have I heard. On one occasion the Blessed One was living at Savatthi in Jeta's Grove, Anathapindika's Park. There the Venerable Sariputta addressed the bhikkhus thus: "Friends, bhikkhus."—"Friend," they replied. The Venerable Sariputta said this:

2. "'One of right view, one of right view' is said, friends. In what way is a noble disciple one of right view, whose view is straight, who has perfect confidence in the Dhamma, and has arrived at this true Dhamma?"

"Indeed, friend, we would come from far away to learn from the Venerable Sariputta the meaning of this statement. It would be good if the Venerable Sariputta would explain the meaning of this statement. Having heard it from him, the bhikkhus will remember it."

---

[33]*The Discourse on Right View: The Sammaditthi Sutta and Its Commentary*, edited and translated by Phikkhu Bodhi (Kandy: Buddhist Publication Society, 1991).

"Then, friends, listen and attend closely to what I shall say."

"Yes, friend," the bhikkhus replied. The Venerable Sariputta said this:

THE WHOLESOME AND THE UNWHOLESOME

3. "When, friends, a noble disciple understands the unwholesome, the root of the unwholesome, the wholesome, and the root of the wholesome, in that way he is one of right view, whose view is straight, who has perfect confidence in the Dhamma, and has arrived at this true Dhamma.

4. "And what, friends, is the unwholesome, what is the root of the unwholesome, what is the wholesome, what is the root of the wholesome? Killing living beings is unwholesome; taking what is not given is unwholesome; misconduct in sensual pleasures is unwholesome; false speech is unwholesome; malicious speech is unwholesome; harsh speech is unwholesome; gossip is unwholesome; covetousness is unwholesome; ill will is unwholesome; wrong view is unwholesome. This is called the unwholesome.

5. "And what is the root of the unwholesome? Greed is a root of the unwholesome; hate is a root of the unwholesome; delusion is a root of the unwholesome. This is called the root of the unwholesome.

6. "And what is the wholesome? Abstention from killing living beings is wholesome; abstention from taking what is not given is wholesome; abstention from misconduct in sensual pleasures is wholesome; abstention from false speech is wholesome; abstention from malicious speech is wholesome; abstention from harsh speech is wholesome; abstention from gossip is wholesome; non-covetousness is wholesome; non-ill will is wholesome; right view is wholesome. This is called the wholesome.

7. "And what is the root of the wholesome? Non-greed is a root of the wholesome; non-hate is a root of the wholesome; non-delusion is a root of the wholesome. This is called the root of the wholesome.

8. "When a noble disciple has thus understood the unwholesome, the root of the unwholesome, the wholesome, and the root of the wholesome, he entirely abandons the underlying tendency to lust, he abolishes the underlying tendency to aversion, he extirpates the underlying tendency to the view and conceit 'I am,' and by abandoning ignorance and arousing true knowledge he here and now makes an end of suffering. In that way too a noble disciple is one of right view, whose view is straight, who has perfect confidence in the Dhamma and has arrived at this true Dhamma."

NUTRIMENT

9. Saying, "Good, friend," the bhikkhus delighted and rejoiced in the Venerable Sariputta's words. Then they asked him a further question: "But, friend, might there be another

way in which a noble disciple is one of right view . . . and has arrived at this true Dhamma?"—"There might be, friends.

10. "When, friends, a noble disciple understands nutriment, the origin of nutriment, the cessation of nutriment, and the way leading to the cessation of nutriment, in that way he is one of right view . . . and has arrived at this true Dhamma.

11. "And what is nutriment, what is the origin of nutriment, what is the cessation of nutriment, what is the way leading to the cessation of nutriment? There are these four kinds of nutriment for the maintenance of beings that already have come to be and for the support of those seeking a new existence. What four? They are physical food as nutriment, gross or subtle; contact as the second; mental volition as the third; and consciousness as the fourth. With the arising of craving there is the arising of nutriment. With the cessation of craving there is the cessation of nutriment. The way leading to the cessation of nutriment is just this Noble Eightfold Path; that is, right view, right intention, right speech, right action, right livelihood, right effort, right mindfulness and right concentration.

12. "When a noble disciple has thus understood nutriment, the origin of nutriment, the cessation of nutriment, and the way leading to the cessation of nutriment, he entirely abandons the underlying tendency to greed, he abolishes the underlying tendency to aversion, he extirpates the underlying tendency to the view and conceit 'I am,' and by abandoning ignorance and arousing true knowledge he here and now makes an end of suffering. In that way too a noble disciple is one of right view, whose view is straight, who has perfect confidence in the Dhamma and has arrived at this true Dhamma."

THE FOUR NOBLE TRUTHS

13. Saying, "Good, friend," the bhikkhus delighted and rejoiced in the Venerable Sariputta's words. Then they asked him a further question: "But, friend, might there be another way in which a noble disciple is one of right view . . . and has arrived at this true Dhamma?"—"There might be, friends.

14. "When, friends, a noble disciple understands suffering, the origin of suffering, the cessation of suffering, and the way leading to the cessation of suffering, in that way he is one of right view . . . and has arrived at this true Dhamma.

15. "And what is suffering, what is the origin of suffering, what is the cessation of suffering, what is the way leading to the cessation of suffering? Birth is suffering; aging is suffering; sickness is suffering; death is suffering; sorrow, lamentation, pain, grief and despair are suffering; not to obtain what one wants is suffering; in short, the five aggregates affected by clinging are suffering. This is called suffering.

16. "And what is the origin of suffering? It is craving, which brings renewal of being, is accompanied by delight and lust, and delights in this and that; that is, craving for sensual pleasures, craving for being and craving for non-being. This is called the origin of suffering.

17. "And what is the cessation of suffering? It is the remainderless fading away and ceasing, the giving up, relinquishing, letting go and rejecting of that same craving. This is called the cessation of suffering.

18. "And what is the way leading to the cessation of suffering? It is just this Noble Eightfold Path; that is, right view . . . right concentration. This is called the way leading to the cessation of suffering.

19. "When a noble disciple has thus understood suffering, the origin of suffering, the cessation of suffering, and the way leading to the cessation of suffering . . . he here and now makes an end of suffering. In that way too a noble disciple is one of right view . . . and has arrived at this true Dhamma."

AGING AND DEATH

20. Saying, "Good, friend," the bhikkhus delighted and rejoiced in the Venerable Sariputta's words. Then they asked him a further question: "But, friend, might there be another way in which a noble disciple is one of right view . . . and has arrived at this true Dhamma?"—"There might be, friends.

21. "When, friends, a noble disciple understands aging and death, the origin of aging and death, the cessation of aging and death, and the way leading to the cessation of aging and death, in that way he is one of right view . . . and has arrived at this true Dhamma.

22. "And what is aging and death, what is the origin of aging and death, what is the cessation of aging and death, what is the way leading to the cessation of aging and death? The aging of beings in the various orders of beings, their old age, brokenness of teeth, grayness of hair, wrinkling of skin, decline of life, weakness of faculties—this is called aging. The passing of beings out of the various orders of beings, their passing away, dissolution, disappearance, dying, completion of time, dissolution of the aggregates, laying down of the body—this is called death. So this aging and this death are what is called aging and death. With the arising of birth there is the arising of aging and death. With the cessation of birth there is the cessation of aging and death. The way leading to the cessation of aging and death is just this Noble Eightfold Path; that is, right view . . . right concentration.

23. "When a noble disciple has thus understood aging and death, the origin of aging and death, the cessation of aging and death, and the way leading to the cessation of aging and death . . . he here and now makes an end of suffering. In that way too a noble disciple is one of right view . . . and has arrived at this true Dhamma."

BIRTH

24. Saying, "Good, friend," the bhikkhus delighted and rejoiced in the Venerable Sariputta's words. Then they asked him a further question: "But, friend, might there be another

way in which a noble disciple is one of right view . . . and has arrived at this true Dhamma?"—"There might be, friends.

25. "When, friends, a noble disciple understands birth, the origin of birth, the cessation of birth, and the way leading to the cessation of birth, in that way he is one of right view . . . and has arrived at this true Dhamma.

26. "And what is birth, what is the origin of birth, what is the cessation of birth, what is the way leading to the cessation of birth? The birth of beings into the various orders of beings, their coming to birth, precipitation (in a womb), generation, manifestation of the aggregates, obtaining the bases for contact—this is called birth. With the arising of being there is the arising of birth. With the cessation of being there is the cessation of birth. The way leading to the cessation of birth is just this Noble Eightfold Path; that is, right view . . . right concentration.

27. "When a noble disciple has thus understood birth, the origin of birth, the cessation of birth, and the way leading to the cessation of birth . . . he here and now makes an end of suffering. In that way too a noble disciple is one of right view . . . and has arrived at this true Dhamma."

BEING

28. Saying, "Good, friend," the bhikkhus delighted and rejoiced in the Venerable Sariputta's words. Then they asked him a further question: "But, friend, might there be another way in which a noble disciple is one of right view . . . and has arrived at this true Dhamma?"—"There might be, friends.

29. "When, friends, a noble disciple understands being, the origin of being, the cessation of being, and the way leading to the cessation of being, in that way he is one of right view . . . and has arrived at this true Dhamma.

30. "And what is being, what is the origin of being, what is the cessation of being, what is the way leading to the cessation of being? There are these three kinds of being: sense-sphere being, fine-material being and immaterial being. With the arising of clinging there is the arising of being. With the cessation of clinging there is the cessation of being. The way leading to the cessation of being is just this Noble Eightfold Path; that is, right view . . . right concentration.

31. "When a noble disciple has thus understood being, the origin of being, the cessation of being, and the way leading to the cessation of being . . . he here and now makes an end of suffering. In that way too a noble disciple is one of right view . . . and has arrived at this true Dhamma."

In Mahayana texts, the goal of living often is described in other terms. In the following passage from the 8,000-line *Perfection of Wisdom Sutra,* the Buddha instructs Subhuti about the differences between the attitudes of Hinayanists and Mahayanists. According to this text, what are these basic differences?

What, according to this Mahayanist point of view, is the ideal to which humans should strive?

HINAYANA AND MAHAYANA DIFFERENCES FROM THE *PERFECTION OF WISDOM IN 8000 LINES*[34]

[Buddha answered:] "Subhuti, bodhisattvas, great beings, should not train in the way that persons of the hearer vehicle and solitary realizer vehicle train. Subhuti, in what way do persons of the hearer vehicle and the solitary realizer vehicle train? Subhuti, they think thus, '[I] should discipline only myself; [I] should pacify only myself; [I] should attain nirvana by myself.' In order to discipline only themselves and pacify themselves and attain nirvana, they begin to apply themselves to establishing all the virtuous roots. Also, Subhuti, bodhisattvas, great beings, should not train in this way. On the contrary, Subhuti, bodhisattvas, great beings, should train thus, 'In order to benefit all the world, I will dwell in suchness; and, establishing all sentient beings in suchness, I will lead the immeasurable realms of sentient beings to nirvana.' Bodhisattvas, great beings, should begin applying themselves in that way to establishing all virtuous roots, but should not be conceited because of this. . . .

"Those who say, 'In this very life, having thoroughly freed the mind from contamination, without attachment, [I] will pass beyond sorrow' are 'at the level of hearers and solitary realizers.' With respect to this, bodhisattvas, great beings, should not give rise to such thoughts. Why is this? Subhuti, bodhisattvas, great beings, abide in the great vehicle and put on the great armor; they should not give rise to thoughts of even a little elaboration. Why is this? These supreme beings thoroughly lead the world and are a great benefit to the world. Therefore, they should always and uninterruptedly train well in the six perfections."

In Hinayana Buddhism, the road to enlightenment in this life is a narrow path open only to the ordained. Moreover, while this tradition assumes that all people have had many past lives as males and females, it also teaches that it is impossible for a female, while being a female, to obtain Buddhahood. Select Mahayana sutras, however, view women in more favorable light. The following selection from the *Lotus Sutra* illus-

---

[34]*Perfection of Wisdom in 8000 Lines* (Dharamsala, India: Tibetan Cultural Printing Press, 1985). See www.anu.edu/asianstudies.

trates one of these passages. This chapter provides some words of encouragement that the Buddha gave to the two most important women in his life—Gautami, his aunt and stepmother, and Yasodhara, his wife before his renunciation.

The setting of this encounter is near the end of the Buddha's life. In the preceding chapters, the Buddha has exhorted his disciples to uphold and propagate his teachings after his passing. In response to the exhortation, his followers appear before him making vows to preach in other worlds the message of salvation. At this point, the Buddha notices the sad expression of Gautami. What does the following interview between the Buddha and Gautami and Yasodhara tell us about a Mahayana understanding of enlightenment among women?

ENLIGHTENMENT AMONG WOMEN WITHIN MAHAYANA BUDDHISM: *THE LOTUS SUTRA*[35]

Then the noble matron Gautami, the sister of the Lord's mother, along with six hundred nuns, some of them being under training, some being not, rose from her seat, raised the joined hands towards the Lord and remained gazing up to him. Then the Lord addressed the noble matron Gautami: Why dost thou stand so dejected, gazing up to the Tathagata? (She replied): I have not been mentioned by the Tathagata, nor have I received from him a prediction of my destiny to supreme, perfect enlightenment. (He said): But, Gautami, thou hast received a prediction with the prediction regarding the whole assembly. Indeed, Gautami, thou shalt from henceforward, before the face of thirty-eight hundred thousand myriads of kotis of Buddhas, be a Bodhisattva and preacher of the law. These six thousand nuns also, partly perfected in discipline, partly not, shall along with others become Bodhisattvas and preachers of the law before the face of the Tathagatas. Afterwards, when thou shalt have completed the course of a Bodhisattva, thou shalt become, under the name of Sarvasattvapriyadarsana (i.e., lovely to see for all beings), a Tathagata, an Arhat, endowed with science and conduct. And that Tathagata Sarvasattvapriyadarsana, O Gautami, shall

give a prediction by regular succession to those six thousand Bodhisattvas concerning their destiny to supreme, perfect enlightenment.

Then the nun Yasodhara, the mother of Rahula, thought thus: The Lord has not mentioned my name. And the Lord comprehending in his own mind what was going on in the mind of the nun Yasodhara said to her: I announce to thee, Yasodhara, I declare to thee: Thou also shalt before the face of ten thousand kotis of Buddhas become a Bodhisattva and preacher of the law, and after regularly completing the course of Bodhisattva thou shalt become a Tathagata, named Rasmisatasahasrapari-purnadhvaga, an Arhat, endowed with science and conduct, in the world Bhadra; and the lifetime of that Lord Rasmisatasahasraparip-tirnadhvaga shall be unlimited.

When the noble matron Gautami, the nun, with her suite of six thousand nuns, and Yasodhara, the nun, with her suite of four thousand nuns, heard from the Lord their future destiny to supreme, perfect enlightenment, they uttered, in wonder and amazement, this stanza: "O Lord, thou art the trainer, thou art the leader; thou art the master of the world, including the gods; thou art the giver of comfort, thou who art worshipped by men and gods. Now, indeed, we feel satisfied."

The final selection in this section is the *Heart Sutra,* one of the shortest and the most popular sutras in Mahayana Buddhism. This sutra, regarded by many as the summation of the wisdom of Buddha, is recited on a daily basis in Buddhist monasteries and households around the world. Central to this sutra is the concept of nonattachment, the doctrine of emptiness.

THE DOCTRINE OF EMPTINESS FROM THE *HEART SUTRA*[36]

When Avalokitesvara Bodhisattva is practicing the profound Prajna-paramita, He sees and illuminates to the emptiness of the five skandhas, and Thus attains deliverance from all suffering.

Sariputra, matter is not different from emptiness, and Emptiness is not different from matter. Matter is

---

[35]*Holy Saddharma Pundarika, or The Lotus of the True Law,* English translation by H. Kern. *Sacred Books of the East,* Vol. 21 (1884). See www.sacred-texts.com/bud/lotus.

[36]*Heart Sutra,* translated from the Chinese by Hsuan Tsang Dharma Master. See www.buddhistdoor.com/archive/sutra_comm/heart.

emptiness and emptiness is matter. So too are sensation, recognition, volition and consciousness.

Sariputra, the emptiness character of all dharmas, neither arises nor ceases, is neither pure nor impure, and neither increases nor decreases. Therefore, in emptiness: there is no matter, no sensation, recognition, volition or consciousness, no eye, ear, nose, tongue, body, or mind, no sight, sound, scent, taste, tangibles, or dharma, no field of the eye up to no field of mental consciousness, no suffering, no cause of suffering, no ending of suffering, and no path, no wisdom and also no attainment. Because there is nothing obtainable, Bodhisattvas through the reliance on Prajna-paramita have no attachment and hindrance in their minds. Because there is no more attachment and hindrance, there is no more fear, and Far away from erroneous views and wishful-thinking, Ultimately: The Final Nirvana.

Buddhas of the past, present, and future all rely on Prajna-paramita to attain Annutara-samyak-sambodhi. Therefore, realize that Prajna-paramita is the great wondrous mantra, the great radiant mantra, the unsurpassed mantra, and the unequaled mantra. It can eradicate all suffering, and It is genuine and not false. Therefore, utter the Prajna-paramita mantra— Chant: Gate Gate Paragate Parasmagate Bodhisvaha!

Section 8: The Religious Life: Worship and Righteousness

Gautama often spoke about the religious life. Many of his words, however, challenged hearers to question the benefits of sectarian religious practices. The following selections sample some of the Buddha's thoughts about the ideal religious life. As you read these passages, try to identify the distinguishing marks of the enlightened. Compare this ideal with Gautama's portrait of Brahmin priests. What do Buddhist monks and Hindu Brahmins have in common? In what ways are they different?

The first selection is from the *Dhammapadda*. These beautiful verses describe standards of piety expected of those on the road to enlightenment.

MARKS OF THE AWAKENED ONE
FROM THE *DHAMMAPADDA* 14

The one whose conquest cannot be conquered again,
into whose conquest no one in this world enters,
by what track can you lead that one,
the awakened, the omniscient, the trackless?

The one whom no desire
with its snares and poisons can lead astray,
by what track can you lead that one,
the awakened, the omniscient, the trackless?

Even the gods emulate those who are awakened and aware,
who are given to meditation, who are wise,
and who find joy in the peace of renunciation.

It is difficult to be born as a human being;
difficult is the life of mortals;
difficult is the hearing of the true path;
difficult is the awakening of enlightenment.

Not to do wrong, to do good, and to purify one's mind,
that is the teaching of the awakened ones.
The awakened call patience the highest sacrifice;
the awakened declare nirvana the highest good.

The one who strikes others is not a hermit;
one is not an ascetic who insults others.
Not to blame, not to strike,
to live restrained under the law,
to be moderate in eating, to live alone,
and to practice the highest consciousness—
this is the teaching of the awakened ones.

There is no satisfying lusts,
even by a shower of gold pieces.
Whoever knows that lusts have a short taste
and cause pain is wise.
Even in heavenly pleasures one finds no satisfaction;
the disciple who is fully awakened
finds joy only in the destruction of all desires.

People driven by fear go for refuge
to mountains and forests, to sacred groves and shrines.
That is not a safe refuge; that is not the best refuge.
After having got to that refuge,
a person is not delivered from all pains.

Whoever takes refuge with the awakened one,
the truth, and the community,
who with clear understanding perceives the four noble
    truths:
namely suffering, the origin of suffering,
the cessation of suffering, and the eightfold holy way
that leads to the cessation of suffering,
that is the safe refuge; that is the best refuge;
having gone to that refuge,
a person is delivered from all pains.

A person of true vision is not easy to find;
they are not born everywhere.
Wherever such a sage is born, the people there prosper.
Blessed is the arising of the awakened;
blessed is the teaching of the truth;
blessed is the harmony of the community;
blessed is the devotion of those who live in peace.

Whoever gives reverence to those worthy of reverence,
whether the awakened or their disciples,
those who have overcome the army
and crossed the river of sorrow,
whoever gives reverence to such as have found deliverance
and are free of fear,
their merit cannot be measured by anyone.

On one occasion the Venerable Punnaka asked Gautama about the reasons for making sacrificial offerings to the gods. The following piece from the Little Books Division in the *Sutra Pitaka* contains the Buddha's answer. What hope does the Buddha place in finding Enlightenment through the performance of rituals?

ON MAKING SACRIFICES TO THE GODS FROM PUNNAKA'S QUESTIONS IN THE *SUTRA NIPATA*[37]

THE VENERABLE PUNNAKA: "To him who is free from craving, who has seen the root (of things) I have come with a question: for what reason did sages, warriors, brahmanas and other men prepare, here in this world, various sacrificial gifts for the gods (devata)? I ask the Lord this, let him tell me the answer."

THE LORD: "Whatever sages, warriors, brahmanas and other men, Punnaka, prepared various sacrificial gifts for the gods, they did so in the hope of this or that (future) existence, being induced by (the fact of) old age and decay."

PUNNAKA: "By preparing various sacrificial gifts for the gods, being zealous in sacrificing, do they cross beyond birth and decay, Lord?"

THE LORD: "They hope and extol, pray and sacrifice for things of the senses, Punnaka. For the sake of such reward they pray. These devotees of sacrifice, infatuated by their passion for existence, do not cross beyond birth and decay, I say."

PUNNAKA: "If these devotees of sacrifice do not cross beyond birth and decay through sacrifice, Sir, then by what practice does one cross beyond birth and decay in this world of gods and men?"

THE LORD: "He who has comprehended in the world the here and the beyond, in whom there is no perturbation by anything in the world, who is calm, free from the smoldering fires, untroubled and desireless,—he has crossed beyond birth and decay, I say."

The next selection is from the *Tevigga Sutra* in the Long Discourses Division of the *Sutra Pitaka*.

This collection, often called the "Knowledge of the Three Vedas," includes a dialogue between the Buddha and two young Brahmans who are seeking to understand the true path that leads to union with Brahma.

THE PATH TO UNION WITH BRAHMA FROM THE *DIGNA NIKAYA*, 13[38]

Then the young Brahmana Vasettha and the young Brahmana Bharadvaga went on to the place where the Exalted One was. . . . The young Brhamana Vasettha said to the Exalted One: "As we, Gotama, were taking exercise and walking up and down, there sprang up a conversation between us on which was the true path, and which the false. I thus said: 'This is the straight path, this the direct way which makes for salvation, and leads him, who acts according to it, into a state of union with Brahma. I mean that which has been announced by the Brahmana Pokkharasadi.' "

Bharadvaga said thus: " 'This is the straight path, this the direct way which makes for salvation, and leads him, who acts according to it, into a state of union with Brahma. I mean that which has been announced by the Brahman Tarukkha.' Regarding this matter, Gotama, there is a strife, a dispute, a difference of opinion between us."

"Wherein, then, O Vasettha, is there a strife, a dispute, a difference of opinion between you?"

"Concerning the true path and the false, Gotama. Various Brahmanas, Gotama, teach various paths. The Addhariya Brahmanas, the Tittiriya Brahmanas, the Khandoka Brahmanas, the Bsavhariga Brahmanas. Are all those saving paths? Are they all paths which lead him, who acts according to them, into a state of union with Brahma?"

"Just, Gotama, as near a village or a town there are many and various paths, yet they all meet together in the village—just in that way are all the various paths taught by various Brahmanas. Are all these saving paths? Are they all paths which lead him, who acts according to them, into a state of union with Brahma?"

"Do you say that they all lead aright, Vasettha?"

"I say so, Gotama."

---

[37]*Sutra Nipata*, translated by John D. Ireland. See www.accesstoinsight.org.

[38]*Dialogues of the Buddha: The Digha-Nikaya*, translated from the Pali by T. W. Rhys Davids (London: Oxford University Press, 1899). See www.sacred-texts.com/bud.

"Do you really say that they all lead aright, Vasettha?"

"So I say, Gotama."

"But yet, Vasettha, is there a single one of the Brahmanas versed in the three Vedas who has ever seen Brahma face to face?"

"No, indeed, Gotama."

"Or is there then, Vasettha, a single one of the pupils of the teachers of the Brahmanas versed in the three Vedas who has seen Brahma face to face?"

"No, indeed, Gotama."

"Or is there then, Vasettha, a single one of the Brahmanas up to the seventh generation who has seen Brahma face to face?"

"No, indeed, Gotama."

"Well, then, Vasettha, those ancient Rishis of the Brahmanas versed in the three Vedas, the authors of the verses, the utterers of the verses, whose ancient form of words so chanted, uttered, or composed, the Brahmanas of today chant over again or repeat; intoning or reciting exactly as has been intoned or recited; did even they speak thus, saying: 'We know it, we have seen it, where Brahma is, whence Brahma is, whither Brahma is'?"

"Not so, Gotama."

"Then you say, Vasettha, that none of the Brahmanas, or of their teachers, or of their pupils, even up to the seventh generation, has ever seen Brahma face to face. And that even the Rishis of old, the authors and utterers of the verses, of the ancient form of words which the Brahmanas of today so carefully intone and recite precisely as they have been handed down—even they did not pretend to know or to have seen where or whence or whither Brahma is. So that the Brahmanas versed in the three Vedas have forsooth said thus: 'What we know not, what we have not seen, to a state of union with that we can show the way, and can say: "This is the straight path, this is the direct way which makes for salvation, and leads him, who acts according to it, into a state of union with Brahma!"'"

"Now what think you, Vasettha? Does it not follow, this being so, that the talk of the Brahmanas, versed though they be in the three Vedas, turns out to be foolish talk?"

"In sooth, Gotama, that being so, it follows that the talk of the Brahmanas versed in the three Vedas is foolish talk!"

The following is the Buddha's response to an ascetic named Nigrodha who asked the Exalted One

about the views and practices of other sects. This excerpt also is taken from the Long Discourses Division of the *Sutra Pitaka*.

ON THE PRACTICES OF OTHER SECTS FROM THE *DIGHA-NIKAYA*[39]

Now this is what I say to you, Nigrodha: "Let any intelligent man come to me, any man who is also without guile, not a deceiver, but an upright man. I will teach him. I will show him the Norm. And if he practices according to my instructions, to know and realize for himself even in this very life that unsurpassed holy life for the sake of which clansmen go forth from home to the homeless in its perfection, he too shall know and realize in seven years. Do I say seven years? Why, Nigrodha, even if he do so, as I have said, for six, five, four, three, two years, even one year, half a year; five, four, three, two months, even one month . . . nay, if he so practice for seven days, Nigrodha . . . such a man coming to me shall so realize. . . .

Now this I say, Nigrodha, not desiring to win pupils, not wishing to make others fall from their religious vows, not wishing to make others give up their ways of life, not wishing to establish you in wrong ways or to make you give up ways that are good. Not so!

But, Nigrodha, there are bad things not put away, things that have to do with corruption, things that draw one down again to rebirth, things causing suffering, having Ill for their fruit, things concerned with rebirth, decay, and death in time to come. It is for the rejection of these things that I teach to you the Norm, walking according to which these things that are concerned with corruption shall be put away by you, and wholesome things shall be brought to increase; by which even in this present life by his won abnormal powers a man shall realize and abide in the full knowledge and realization of perfect wisdom."

The final passage in this section contains one of the more than five hundred birth stories in the *Jatakas* that detail a previous life of the Buddha. Although presented in childlike simplicity, the stories of the *Jatakas* contain deep truths that attempt to teach profound moral lessons. This tale is often called "The Goat That Laughed and Wept."

---

[39]*Sayings of the Buddha*, p. 58.

PREVIOUS LIVES OF THE BUDDHA FROM
MATAKABHATTA JATAKA: JATAKA NO. 18[40]

One day, while the Buddha was staying in Jetavana, some bhikkhus asked him if there was any benefit in sacrificing goats, sheep, and other animals as offerings for departed relatives.

"No, bhikkhus," replied the Buddha. "No good ever comes from taking life, not even when it is for the purpose of providing a Feast for the Dead." Then he told this story of the past.

Long, long ago, when Brahmadatta was reigning in Baranasi, a brahmin decided to offer a Feast for the Dead and bought a goat to sacrifice. "My boys," he said to his students, "take this goat down to the river, bathe it, brush it, hang a garland around its neck, give it some grain to eat, and bring it back."

"Yes, sir," they replied and led the goat to the river.

While they were grooming it, the goat started to laugh with a sound like a pot smashing. Then, just as strangely, it started to weep loudly.

The young students were amazed at this behavior. "Why did you suddenly laugh," they asked the goat, "and why do you now cry so loudly?"

"Repeat your question when we get back to your teacher," the goat answered.

The students hurriedly took the goat back to their master and told him what had happened at the river. Hearing the story, the master himself asked the goat why it had laughed and why it had wept.

"In times past, brahmin," the goat began, "I was a brahmin who taught the Vedas like you. I, too, sacrificed a goat as an offering for a Feast for the Dead. Because of killing that single goat, I have had my head cut off 499 times. I laughed aloud when I realized that this is my last birth as an animal to be sacrificed. Today I will be freed from my misery. On the other hand, I cried when I realized that, because of killing me, you, too, may be doomed to lose your head five hundred times. It was out of pity for you that I cried."

"Well, goat," said the brahmin, "in that case, I am not going to kill you."

"Brahmin!" exclaimed the goat. "Whether or not you kill me, I cannot escape death today."

"Don't worry," the brahmin assured the goat. "I will guard you."

"You don't understand," the goat told him. "Your protection is weak. The force of my evil deed is very strong."

The brahmin untied the goat and said to his students, "Don't allow anyone to harm this goat." They obediently followed the animal to protect it.

After the goat was freed, it began to graze. It stretched out its neck to reach the leaves on a bush growing near the top of a large rock. At that very instant a lightning bolt hit the rock, breaking off a sharp piece of stone which flew through the air and neatly cut off the goat's head. A crowd of people gathered around the dead goat and began to talk excitedly about the amazing accident.

A tree deva [Devas are celestial beings, ranging from the highest gods to simple tree spirits.] had observed everything from the goat's purchase to its dramatic death, and drawing a lesson from the incident, admonished the crowd: "If people only knew that the penalty would be rebirth into sorrow, they would cease from taking life. A horrible doom awaits one who slays." With this explanation of the law of kamma the deva instilled in his listeners the fear of hell. The people were so frightened that they completely gave up the practice of animal sacrifices. The deva further instructed the people in the Precepts and urged them to do good.

Eventually, that deva passed away to fare according to his deserts. For several generations after that, people remained faithful to the Precepts and spent their lives in charity and meritorious works, so that many were reborn in the heavens.

The Buddha ended his lesson and identified the Birth by saying, "In those days I was that deva."

SECTION 9: Endings: Death, Judgment, and the Afterlife

Without promising a heaven paved with streets of gold, numerous Buddhist texts offer followers ways to cope with the pain of death. One popular story included in the Psalms of the Sisters[41] concerns a woman who was so completely overwhelmed by grief owing to the loss of her son that she went from door to door with his corpse asking for medicine that could revive him. Upon seeing the woman, the Buddha told her: "Go, enter the town, and bring from any house

[40]*Jataka Tales of the Buddha*, retold by Ken and Visakha Kawaski (Kandy: Buddhist Publication Society, 1995). See www.buddhistinformation.com/jataka_tales_of_the_buddha_part1.htm.

[41]*Therigatha*, Canto X, LXIII.

where yet no man has died a little mustard seed." After obeying this instruction, the woman found consolation in realizing that no family had escaped the pain that comes from the death of loved ones. This message of consolation through the realization of the impermanence of all things is also the central teaching in the following passage taken from "The Arrow," one of 71 sutras in the *Sutra Nipata* of the Little Book Division of the *Sutra Pitaka*.

THE STORY OF THE GRIEVING WOMAN FROM THE *SUTRA NIPATA*[42]

"Unindicated and unknown is the length of life of those subject to death. Life is difficult and brief and bound up with suffering. There is no means by which those who are born will not die. Having reached old age, there is death. This is the natural course for a living being. With ripe fruits there is the constant danger that they will fall. In the same way, for those born and subject to death, there is always the fear of dying. Just as the pots made by a potter all end by being broken, so death is (the breaking up) of life.

"The young and old, the foolish and the wise, all are stopped short by the power of death, all finally end in death. Of those overcome by death and passing to another world, a father cannot hold back his son, nor relatives a relation. See! While the relatives are looking on and weeping, one by one each mortal is led away like an ox to slaughter.

"In this manner the world is afflicted by death and decay. But the wise do not grieve, having realized the nature of the world. You do not know the path by which they came or departed. Not seeing either end you lament in vain. If any benefit is gained by lamenting, the wise would do it. Only a fool would harm himself. Yet through weeping and sorrowing the mind does not become calm, but still more suffering is produced, the body is harmed and one becomes lean and pale, one merely hurts oneself. One cannot protect a departed one (peta) by that means. To grieve is in vain.

"By not abandoning sorrow a being simply undergoes more suffering. Bewailing the dead he comes under the sway of sorrow. See other men faring according to their deeds! Hence beings tremble here with fear when they come into the power of death. Whatever they imagine, it (turns out) quite different from that. This is the sort of disappointment that exists. Look at the nature of the world! If a man lives for a hundred years, or even more, finally, he is separated from his circle of relatives and gives up his life in the end. Therefore, having listened to the Arahant, one should give up lamenting. Seeing a dead body, one should know, 'He will not be met by me again.' As the fire in a burning house is extinguished with water, so a wise, discriminating, learned and sensible man should quickly drive away the sorrow that arises, as the wind (blows off) a piece of cotton. He who seeks happiness should withdraw the arrow: his own lamentations, longings and grief.

"With the arrow withdrawn, unattached, he would attain to peace of mind; and when all sorrow has been transcended he is sorrow-free and has realized Nibbana."

Although a characteristic of Buddhism is its emphasis on the here-and-now rather than on the hereafter, Buddhist texts when discussing death often invoke images of heaven and hell. The following selections from the *Guide to the Bodhisattva's Way of Life* and from the *Dhammapada* illustrate these tendencies. What are the central messages of these passages? In what ways do the promises of a future life give purpose and meaning to this life?

HEAVEN AND HELL IN THE *GUIDE TO THE BODHISATTVA'S WAY OF LIFE* 2.33–41[43]

The untrustworthy lord of death waits not for things to be
    done or undone;
Whether I am sick or healthy, This fleeting life span is
    unstable.

Leaving all I must depart alone.
But through not having understood this
I committed various kinds of evil
For the sake of my friends and foes.

Yet my foes will become nothing.
My friends will become nothing.
I too will become nothing.
Likewise all will become nothing.

---

[42]*The Discourse Collection*, translated by Ireland.

[43]Wilson, *World Scriptures*, pp. 239–240. See www.euro-tongil.org.

Just like a dream experience, whatever things I enjoy will
  become a memory.
Whatever has passed will not be seen again.

Even within this brief life many friends and foes have passed,
But whatever unbearable evil I committed for them
Remains ahead of me. . . .

While I am lying in bed,
Although surrounded by my friends and relatives,
The feeling of life being severed will be experienced by me
  alone.

When seized by the messengers of death,
What benefit will friends and relatives afford?
My merit alone shall protect me then,
But upon that I have never relied.

DESCRIPTIONS OF HELL FROM THE *DHAMMAPADA* 22

Whoever says what is not goes to hell,
also whoever having done something says, "I did not do it."
After death both are equal,
being people with wrong actions in the next existence.

Many who wear the yellow robe
are ill-behaved and unrestrained.
Such wrong-doers by their wrong actions go to hell.
It would be better for a bad, unrestrained person
to swallow a ball of red-hot iron
than to live off the charity of the land.

A reckless person who wants another's wife
gains four things:
fault, bad sleep, thirdly blame, and finally hell.
There is fault and the wrong path;
there is brief pleasure
of the frightened in the arms of the frightened,
and heavy penalty from the ruler.
Therefore do not run after another's wife.

As a blade of grass wrongly handled cuts the hand,
so also asceticism wrongly practiced leads to hell.
An act carelessly performed, a broken vow,
unwilling obedience to discipline—
all these bring no great reward.
If anything is to be done, let one do it vigorously.
A careless recluse only bespatters oneself
with the dust of desires.

A wrong action is better left undone,
for a wrong action causes suffering later.
A good action is better done,
for it does not cause suffering.

Like a frontier fort
that is well guarded inside and outside,
so guard yourself.
Not a moment should escape,
for those who allow the right moment to pass
suffer pain when they are in hell.

Those who are ashamed of
what they should not be ashamed of
and are not ashamed of
what they should be ashamed of,
such people, following false doctrines, enter the wrong path.

Those who fear what they should not fear
and do not fear what they should fear,
such people, following false doctrines, enter the wrong path.

Those who discern wrong where there is no wrong
and see nothing wrong in what is wrong,
such people, following false doctrines, enter the wrong path.

Those who discern wrong as wrong
and what is not wrong as not wrong,
such people, following true doctrines, enter the good path.

One of the core texts within the Pure Land School of Mahayana Buddhism is the *Visualization Sutra*. In this text, the historical Buddha teaches 16 visualizations that, when perfected, allow a person to obtain in this lifetime a vision of the Amitabha Buddha, the Amitabha's Bohdisattvic attendants, and the Pure Land itself. This selection is taken from the 14th visualization in this sutra.

VISIONS OF REBIRTH IN PURE LAND BUDDHISM FROM THE *VISUALIZATION SUTRA*[44]

The Buddha said to Ananda and Vaidehi, "In all, there are nine levels of sentient beings who are reborn in the Western Quarter. The sentient beings in the highest level of the highest grade of rebirth are those who vow to be reborn there. By awakening the three kinds of mind they are reborn there. What are the three? The first is the most sincere mind, the second is the mind of deep faith, and the third is the mind which aspires for rebirth by transferring merit. Those who possess those three minds will be reborn in that land without fail.

---

[44] *Visualization Sutra*, available at www.buddhistinformation.com/pureland.

"There are three other kinds of beings who will be reborn there. What are the three? First are the compassionate ones who refrain from killing and observe the precepts; second are those who read and recite the Mahayana Vaipulya Sutras; and third are those who cultivate the six kinds of mindfulness. Transferring the merit for rebirth, they vow to be reborn in that land. By accomplishing these virtuous acts for a period of from one to seven days, they immediately attain rebirth.

"When an aspirant is about to be reborn in that land, a result of unconquerable resolve, the Tathagata Amitayus appears along with Avalokitesvara, Mahasthamaprapta, countless transformation Buddhas, a great assembly of a hundred thousand bhiksus and sravakas, and countless heavenly beings in their seven-jeweled palaces.

"Holding a diamond pedestal, Bodhisattva Avalokitesvara approaches the aspirant along with Bodhisattva Mahasthamaprapta. The Buddha Amitayus sends forth a great light that illuminates the aspirant's body, and along with the Bodhisattvas, offers welcoming hands. Avalokitesvara and Mahasthamaprapta, along with countless other Bodhisattvas, then encourage the aspirant's mind by offering praise. Upon seeing this, the aspirant dances with joy, is self-seen seated atop the diamond pedestal, and, following after the Buddha, is reborn into that land as quickly as the snap of a finger.

"Once reborn in that land, the aspirants see the Buddha's body and the perfection of the Buddha's myriad characteristics. The perfection of the Bodhisattvas' physical characteristics is also seen. The light of the jeweled forests widely proclaim the wondrous Dharma, and having heard it, the aspirants will instantly awaken the insight into the non-origination of all existence.

"Then, in an instant, the aspirants will visit and venerate all the Buddhas of the Ten Quarters, and in the presence of each Buddha receive a prediction of their future Buddhahood. Upon returning to the land from whence they came, they attain countless hundreds of thousands of Dharma-gates of dharanis. These are called the sentient beings in the highest level of the highest grade of rebirth."

The ultimate goal within Buddhism, however, is not rebirth in paradise, but the attainment of *Nirvana*. Literally, this word means "extinction" or "to blow out." The following passages from the *Sutra Pitaka* contain a selection of the Buddha's teachings on *Nirvana*. According to the hints included in these passages, what is the Buddha's understanding of *Nirvana*? Is *Nirvana* a condition, a state of being, both, or neither? Explain your answers.

Discussions of *Nirvana* from *Udana* 80, VIII[45]

Thus have I heard. On a certain occasion the Exalted One was staying near Savatthi in Anathapindika's Part at Jeta Grove. Now on that occasion the Exalted One was instructing, stirring, firing, and gladdening the brethren with a pious talk about Nibbana, and those brethren understood its meaning, paid attention to it, grasped with their minds the whole teaching, listened to the teaching with ready ears.

Then on that occasion the Exalted One, seeing the application of it, uttered these solemn words:

"There is, brethren, a condition wherein there is neither earth, nor water, nor fire, nor air, nor the sphere of infinite space, nor the sphere of infinite consciousness, nor the sphere of the void, nor the sphere of neither perception nor non-perception: where there is no 'this world' and no 'world beyond': where there is no moon and no sun. That condition, brethren, do I call neither a coming nor a going nor a standing still nor a falling away nor a rising up: but it is without fixity, without mobility, without bias. THAT IS THE END OF WOE:

Hard to behold the Selfless, so 'tis called.
Not easy is it to perceive the Truth.
But craving is pierced through by one who knows:
He who sees all clings not to anything.

And again, on that occasion, the Exalted One uttered these solemn words:

"There is, brethren, an unborn, a not-become, a not-made, a not-compounded. If there were not, brethren, this that is unborn, not-become, not-made, not compounded, there could not be made any escape from what is born, become, made, compounded."

And again, on that occasion, the Exalted One uttered these solemn words:

"In him who depends (on others), there is wavering. In him who is independent, there is no wavering. Where there is no wavering, there is tranquillity. Where there is tranquillity, there is no passionate delight. Where there is no passionate delight, there is no coming and going (in rebirth). Where there is no

---

[45] *Udana*, translated by Ireland.

coming and going (in rebirth), there is no falling from one state to another. Where there is no falling from one state to another there is no 'here', no 'beyond,' no 'here-and-yonder.' THAT IS THE END OF WOE."

THE FIVE DESTINATIONS FROM THE *GREAT DISCOURSE ON THE LION'S ROAR*[46]

35. "Sariputta, there are these five destinations. What are the five? Hell, the animal realm, the realm of ghosts, human beings and gods.

36. (1) "I understand hell, and the path and way leading to hell. And I also understand how one who has entered this path will, on the dissolution of the body, after death, reappear in a state of deprivation, in an unhappy destination, in perdition, in hell.

(2) "I understand the animal realm, and the path and way leading to the animal realm. And I also understand how one who has entered this path will, on the dissolution of the body, after death, reappear in the animal realm.

(3) "I understand the realm of ghosts, and the path and way leading to the realm of ghosts. And I also understand how one who has entered this path will, on the dissolution of the body, after death, reappear in the realm of ghosts.

(4) "I understand human beings, and the path and way leading to the human world. And I also understand how one who has entered this path will, on the dissolution of the body, after death, reappear among human beings.

(5) "I understand the gods, and the path and way leading to the world of the gods. And I also understand how one who has entered this path will, on the dissolution of the body, after death, reappear in a happy destination, in the heavenly world.

(6) "I understand Nibbana, and the path and way leading to Nibbana. And I also understand how one who has entered this path will, by realizing it for himself with direct knowledge, here and now enter upon and abide in the deliverance of mind and deliverance by wisdom that are taintless with the destruction of the taints."

PowerWeb SUPPLEMENTS

1. **The Beginnings of Buddhism,** Ian Mabbett, *History Today,* January 2002.
2. **The Sacred Is Complete Emptiness,** Daisetz T. Suzuki, from *Enduring Issues in Religion,* San Diego: Greenhaven Press, 1995.

3. **"Shinran and Jodoshinshu,"** Hisao Inagaki, *Inaugural Lecture for the Numata Chair at Leiden University,* April 7, 1992.
4. **An Essential Commitment,** J. L. Walker, *Parabola,* Fall 2000.

Students who wish to better understand what unites and what divides those who look to the Buddha for spiritual guidance will enjoy the *PowerWeb* readings for this chapter. The first selection, which is written by historian Ian Mabbett, surveys central teachings of the Buddha that have inspired his followers for 2,500 years. The following selections, in contrast, illuminate some of the colorful variations that exist within this world religion. Daisetz T. Suzuki, for example, explores the concept of nonattachment within Zen Buddhism, Hisao Inagaki examines the core teachings of the large but lesser known Japanese Buddhist denomination, the Jodoshin School, and J. L. Walker discusses the importance of the role of teacher in Tibetan Buddhism. These supplemental texts will better enable students to speak with confidence about the core beliefs that unite Buddhists of diverse cultures as well as several distinctive regional and doctrinal variations within this global tradition.

Readings from *PowerWeb: Religion* are available at the McGraw-Hill *PowerWeb* website http://www.dushkin.com/powerweb. A personal access code to *PowerWeb: Religion* is provided free with each new copy of this book. Those who purchase a used copy may buy an access code at the website.

SELECTED BIBLIOGRAPHY

Boucher, Sandy. *Opening the Lotus: A Woman's Guide to Buddhism.* Boston: Beacon Press, 1997.

Buddhist Birth Stories. Translated by Thomas William Rhys Davids. New York: Arno Press, 1977.

Conze, Edward. *Buddhism: Its Essence and Development.* Oxford: Cassirer, 1960.

Conze, Edward. *A Short History of Buddhism.* London: George Allen and Unwin, 1980.

Conze, Edward, I. B. Horner, David Snellgrove, and Arthur Waley, trans. and ed. *Buddhist Tests Through the Ages.* Oxford: One World Press, 1995.

Cuevas, Bryan J. *The Hidden History of the Tibetan Book of the Dead.* New York: Oxford University Press, 2003.

Fields, Rick. *How the Swans Came to the Lake.* Boston: Shambala, 1986.

Harvey, Peter. *An Introduction to Buddhism: Teachings, History and Practices.* Cambridge: Cambridge University Press, 1998.

Kitagawa, Joseph, and Mark Cummings, eds. *Buddhism in Asian History.* New York: MacMillan, 1988.

La Fleur, William. *Buddhism: A Cultural Approach.* Englewood Cliffs, NJ: Prentice Hall, 1988.

Lester, Robert C. *Buddhism.* San Francisco: Harper & Row, 1987.

---

[46]*Majjhima Nikaya: The Great Discourse on the Lion's Roar.* translated from the Pali by Nanamoli Thera, edited and revised by Bhikkhu Bodhi (Kandy: Buddhist Publication Society).

Lopez, Donald S., Jr., ed. *Buddhism in Practice*. Princeton, NJ: Princeton University Press, 1995.

Mullin, Glenn H. *Death and Dying: The Tibetan Perspective*. London: Arkana, 1986.

Murcott, Susan. *The First Buddhist Women: Translations and Commentaries on the Therigata*. Berkeley, CA: Parallax Press, 1991.

Nanamoli, Bhikkhu, and Bhikkhu Bodhi, trans. *The Middle Discourses of the Buddha: A New Translation of the Majjhima Nikaya*. Boston: Wisdom Publications, 1995.

Schober, Juliane, ed. *Sacred Biography in the Buddhist Traditions of South and Southeast Asia*. Honolulu: University of Hawaii Press, 1997.

Snelling, John. *The Buddhist Handbook: A Complete Guide to Buddhist Schools, Teaching, Practice, and History*. New York: Barnes and Noble Books, 1991.

Walshe, Maurice. *The Long Discourses of the Buddha. A Translation of the Digha Nikaya*. Boston: Wisdom Publications, 1995.

Williams, Paul. *Mahayana Buddhism*. London: Routledge and Kegan Paul, 1989.

Chinese Religions   6

The story is often told about the emperor who approached a Chinese scholar and asked, "Are you a Buddhist?" Without speaking, the scholar pointed to his Daoist robe. "So you are a Daoist," stated the emperor. The scholar then lifted his robe to show the emperor his Buddhist sandals. The confused emperor then asked, "Are you then a Buddhist?" The scholar replied only by pointing to the Confucian hat that he was wearing.

This story illustrates a tendency that has prevailed in China at least since the sixth century of the Common Era when philosopher Li Shiquian[1] wrote: "Buddhism is the sun, Daoism is the moon, and Confucianism the five planets." Li's poetic words suggest a degree of integration between Buddhism, Daoism, and Confucianism that is sometimes puzzling to the more compartmentalized Western mind. Like the celestial lights that shine from above, each of the three great religions exists as a separate identity, yet together they illuminate the order of the natural world as it relates to humankind. They are, as is commonly stated, "three roads to the same destination." From a Chinese perspective, the three traditions are not mutually exclusive, and it is not uncommon for the religious to embrace all three of these traditions concurrently.

Buddhism, as discussed in Chapter 5, was introduced into China from India in the early centuries of the Common Era and is currently the world's fourth largest religion. In this chapter, we will describe the origins and sacred histories of the two native Chinese traditional religions, Confucianism and Daoism. Notwithstanding the late-twentieth-century attempts by the People's Republic of China to curtail the influence of these religions, Confucianism and Daoism continue to attract the loyalty of more than 0.25 billion partisans and together represent the fifth largest religious tradition in the world.

SETTING

Establishing specific times for the origins of Confucianism and Daoism can be more complicated than first meets the eye. For instance, although we know that Confucius lived in the sixth century BCE during the Zhou dynasty, most scholars would agree that the religious/philosophical system known as Confucianism emerged several centuries later during the Han dynasty. Similarly, while Daoism traditionally is said to have sprung from the teachings of Lao-zi (the "old-master" allegedly 50 years older than Confucius), most scholars doubt the historical existence of Lao-zi and suggest that Daoism as a religion did not develop before the second century of the Common Era. Consequently, when discussing the origins of these traditions, we will be wise to remember that our date-setting efforts depend as much on semantic arguments about how the traditions are defined as on the known facts regarding the circumstances of their founders.

We can be assured, however, of two indisputable statements about the origins of these traditional Chinese religions:

1. Both traditions are indigenous to China.
2. Both religions are based on a matrix of distinctively Chinese beliefs and practices that existed hundreds of years before the evolution of these systems.

---

[1]Chinese names and titles have generally been transliterated using pinyin, with the exception of some Taiwanese terms and personal names. The term "Confucian" has been used because of its familiarity.

The Land and Peoples of China

With more than 1 billion people living on nearly 10 million square kilometers of land, China is first among the countries of the modern world in population and third in land mass. Bordered to its east by the Pacific Ocean, this immense modern nation-state shares its northern, western, and southern boundaries with more than a dozen nations, the largest being Mongolia, Russia, India, and Burma. Although the land area controlled by Chinese rulers was not as great in ancient times as it is today, the vast population of China has always been a distinctive characteristic of the region. Even 2,000 years ago China was one of the world's most populated areas, housing 60 million people—as many as then lived in all the regions under the domain of the Roman Empire.

The geography of China is extremely diverse. Its mostly mountainous terrain includes high plateaus; great deserts in the west; and plains, deltas, and hills in the east. The Yangtze River divides China into its northern and southern regions. To the north of the Yangtze, wheat is produced in the drier and colder climate. In the hot and humid region south of the Yangtze, more rain, rivers, and lakes allow for the production of rice. Despite the great variations in China's geography, the peoples of this region share a common culture that is as remarkable for its resiliency as it is for its beauty and brilliance.

Early Chinese History and Religion

Preliterate tribes have existed in China for thousands of years. Our understanding of these ancient peoples is derived from fragmented physical evidence (such as tools, pottery, and jade ornaments found in the tombs of the dead) and from traditional lore that was passed

down and later codified into the Chinese classic known as the *Book of History*. In many ways these ancient tales are distinctively Chinese. Whereas many Western traditions attributed the beginnings of culture to divine activities, the Chinese tended to give less credit to the deities and more to the revered legendary sages who, according to tradition, studied the operations of the heavens and then applied the harmony of the natural world to human circumstances.

Among the first of these cultural heroes was Fu Xi, the serpent-bodied emperor who allegedly ruled during an age when the people survived by hunting wild game. He is credited with teaching his people how to domesticate animals, use iron in hunting, play musical instruments, write with pictograms, and understand celestial secrets by the use of trigrams. The hero of the ensuing agricultural era was Shen-nung, the ox-headed farmer who is said to have invented the ox-cart and to have given his people knowledge of agriculture and medicine. Another cultural hero was Huang-di, the alleged inventor of bricks who founded the first cities. His descendants were considered to be the founders of the Xia Dynasty, a dynasty that lasted for 500 years and is renowned for its production of black-lacquered pottery. According to the *Book of History*, the last Xia emperor lost what is called the "mandate of heaven" for his misconduct and was overthrown by a ruler who founded the ensuing Shang dynasty.

China's recorded history begins only with the Shang Dynasty (ca. 1750–1100 BCE). It was during the Shang period that the Chinese peoples developed a method of casting bronze, a precious metal that was used to make swords, spearheads, bowls, and other useful objects. The hereditary kings of the Shang period built large-walled cities, although most of the ordinary folk continued to live as they had for thousands of years as farmers in small villages. The

Timeline of ancient China.

2200–1750 BCE	*Traditional dates of the legendary Xia Dynasty*
1750–1100 BCE	*Shang Dynasty*
1100–771 BCE	*Western Zhou*
771–256 BCE	*Eastern Zhou*
221–206 BCE	*Qin Dynasty*
206 BCE–220 CE	*Han Dynasty*

Shang elite also developed a written script, the ancestor of modern Chinese, and used this script to record their petitions to their ancestors. This tradition of communicating with one's ancestral spirits has been a hallmark of Chinese religious practices for more than 3,000 years. When writing was first invented in Mesopotamia, it was originally used for accounting and commercial purposes (i.e., to keep track of the possessions of the king). In China, however, the most ancient written records were religious in nature. These early scripts, which we label as "oracle texts," indicate that the Shang kings established a ritual center along the banks of the Huan River near the end of the second millennium BCE. At this site near their royal palaces and tombs, diviners employed by the king used specialized techniques to communicate with the spirit world. These diviners were experts in a form of *pyromancy,* the art of foretelling the future by the use of fire. After first performing a preparatory ritual that summoned the spirits to the sacred site, the diviners drilled holes in turtle shells or in ox shoulder bones and then applied heat to the holes, causing the shells and bones to expand and crack. As the diviners applied the heat, they asked questions of the spirits, who allegedly answered the questions through the cracking of the shells. The diviners then interpreted the meanings of the cracks and thus disclosed the advice of the spirits to the royal questions. After the divination, the name of the diviner and the words of the question were sketched near the cracks, and the shells with inscriptions were meticulously stored. Although the cosmological worldview of the ancient Chinese emphasized the efficacy of human over divine efforts, the oracle texts inform us that the ancient Chinese not only acknowledged the existence of spiritual beings, but they also expected their Shang kings to consult these spirits prior to undertaking important royal activities.

During the Shang period, the highest of all the deities addressed in the oracle texts was Shang Di, a title that can be translated as the "Lord on High" or the "Supreme Ruler." Scholars disagree over whether Di was considered to be a particular ancestor of a king, the collective ancestral spirits of the ruling household, or an abstract personification of Nature itself. It is clear, however, that Di's status in heaven was analogous to that of the supreme ruler on earth and that no other deity rivaled Di's range and power.

In later dynasties, the earlier notion of Shang Di merged with a new concept known as Tian. Some scholars speculate that Tian was originally a non-Shang high deity who, in time, was equated with the Shang deity Di. The word *Tian,* which often is translated simply as "Heaven, " is a less personal and more vaguely defined term that refers to the universal power that regulates human affairs. Rulers of later dynasties proclaimed that Tian (Heaven) had given them the authority to rule. However, if Heaven could award this mandate, it also could transfer the divine right to rule to others if the leaders became corrupted. This "mandate of heaven" concept served as an ethical and religious check against the otherwise absolute powers of the earthly rulers. Chinese history is filled with rebellions initiated by individuals who have claimed the "mandate of heaven" for themselves.

According to the *Book of History,* the last Shang emperor lost the "mandate of heaven" because of his drunkenness and corruption and was replaced by Wen Wang and his son Wu, rulers of the nearby kingdom of Zhou. In founding the Zhou dynasty (ca. 1100–256 BCE), Wu was assisted by his brother, the Duke of Zhou. When Wu died, the Duke acted as regent of the kingdom until Wu's son, Ch'eng, came of age. During this time, the Duke repressed a revolt against Ch'eng. Later, after Ch'eng reached maturity, the Duke voluntarily retired and

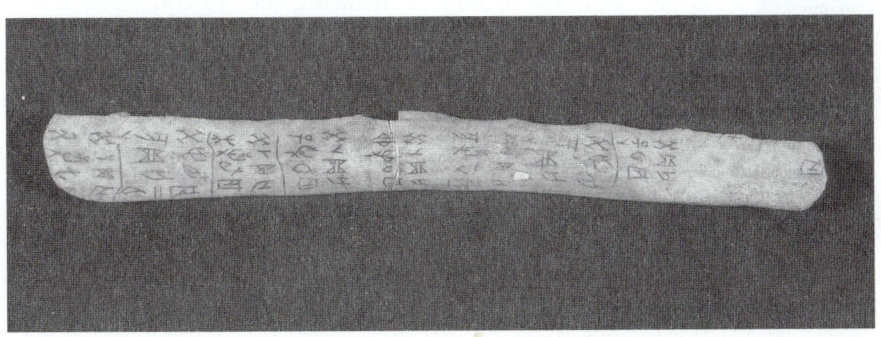

Inscriptions on oracle bones from the Shang Period.

gave the kingdom back to his nephew. For these actions, the Duke of Zhou is warmly remembered in Chinese historiography as the personification of the virtuous ruler whose sole duty was to provide for the welfare of his subjects.

Yin-Yang and the Ten Thousand Things

An important concept that has helped to shape and unify Chinese culture through the ages is a distinctively Chinese belief about the world and the place of humans within it. In the great religions of the West, a Creator deity alone is considered worthy to be worshipped, although humans are uniquely honored as the prime object of his creation. Within the Hindu tradition, on the other hand, creation itself is often considered to be either an illusion or a transitory phenomenon. Chinese cosmology, however, rejects all of these assertions. Rather than doubting the reality of the natural world, or relegating it to a status that is inferior to a Creator deity, the Chinese consider the world to be a holy place that is worthy of veneration. Furthermore, the Chinese insist that no boundaries separate humankind, the domain of nature, and the supernatural world.

Since ancient times, Chinese thinkers have assumed that the world is a complex organism, a living system in which everything that exists is interconnected by shared rhythms. Because humanity and the environment are inseparable, human actions produce cosmic consequences. If humans misbehave, the heavens become upset and the earth

A visual representation of yin-yang.

does not prosper. Rather than viewing the universe as being created from nothing by an all-powerful God, the Chinese assume that the cosmos has evolved into its present complex condition from an earlier state of undifferentiated simplicity. The universe continues to change, but according to the Chinese, there is a consistent pattern to these changes that is discernable to the wise. For at least 3,000 years, the Chinese have attributed the ongoing changes in the cosmos to the interaction of two cosmic forces, *yin* and *yang*.

Unlike Western philosophers who view reality as being composed of invisible particles or atoms, many Chinese call the stuff out of which all things are made *qi* (pronounced chee). For these thinkers, everything that exists and that has ever existed—rocks, rivers, animals, humans, the sky, emotions, demons, ghosts—is composed of *qi*, the basic element of the universe. Although this "energy" source is a single entity, it moves between two cosmic forces known as *yin* and *yang*. *Yin* represents that which is passive, cold, earthly, wet, dark, soft, changeable, and female. *Yang* is associated with that which is active, hot, heavenly, dry, bright, hard, steadfast, and male.

A basic difference between the Chinese conception of *yin* and *yang* and other classical philosophical dualisms (i.e., good and evil) is that whereas most dualisms are forever in conflict, *yin* and *yang* always act in harmony, and both are considered to be necessary to maintain the order of the universe. According to the Chinese, every object at times shows *yin* characteristics and at other times, *yang* characteristics. Moreover, it is desirous to allow the natural ebb and flow between *yin* and *yang*, and dangerous to impede it. For instance, to be healthy, sleep, which is *yin*, should be balanced with periods of activity, *yang*. When the natural flow of *qi* is obstructed, however, then the imbalance between *yin-yang* causes destruction and illness. At death, the *yin* components of a person move downward into the corpse, where it, if not propitiated by sacrifices performed by surviving relatives, may return as a ghost to haunt the living. In contrast, the *yang* parts of the person ascend into the heavens, where they may influence the surviving descendants for the good.

Hence, from a Chinese perspective, the gods are essentially *yang* spirits, and the demons or malignant beings, *yin* spirits. Both are composed of the same stuff, *qi*, and there is no ontological distinction between the gods and the demons, or for that matter, between the gods, humans, and the mountains and rivers. Everything alive is *qi*, and all of the "Ten Thousand Things" that comprise the universe come from the interactions of the *yin-yang* union.

SACRED STORIES AND BELIEFS

During the early Zhou period, China was divided into hundreds of vassal states ruled by relatives of the hereditary king. The semi-independent states were subdivided into districts that were ruled by governors. Hence, the population was stratified into a feudal bureaucratic system in which authority flowed downward from the king, to the nobles, to the governors and their petty officers, to the common people. Social harmony was maintained when the subjects gave their loyalty and gifts to their lords and the nobility vowed their loyalty and provided their gifts to the king. Every male subject also was responsible for performing certain sacred rites that only he could perform.[2] For instance, the common people offered sacrifices at their family shrine to their ancestral spirits, and the princes paid homage to the spirits at the ancestral temples dedicated to the deities of the nearby mountains and rivers. Correspondingly, the king, as heaven's representative on earth, approached on behalf of the people the higher gods and the spirits of the great rivers. As *Tian-zi* (which means the Son of Heaven), the king performed rituals to the great deities, who, in turn, were supposed to protect the state. Misfortune at any level was attributed to angry spirits who had been neglected or had not received sufficient sacrificial offerings to satisfy their needs.

In the eighth century BCE, an invasion of non-Chinese tribes from the west weakened the feudal system. The ensuing war forced the Zhou king to move his capital further to the east. Consequently, historians divide the Zhou dynasty into the

Confucius.

Western Zhou (1100–771 BCE) and Eastern Zhou (771–256 BCE) periods.

Confucius and the legendary Lao-zi were born several centuries into the Eastern Zhou period. During this era the Zhou kings still held the title Son of Heaven, but their hold over the kingdom had dissipated, even as the feudal lords became more ruthless and engaged in ambitious and destructive civil wars. As often happens during periods of social dissolution, growing numbers began to question the traditional values that had been accepted for more than 1,000 years. New schools of thought emerged that addressed these concerns, some attacking the old feudal system and others seeking to restore it. Among the reformers of the period was Chiu from the family of Kung. The English name, Confucius, is derived from the Latinized form of K'ung Fu Tzu, which means "Master Kung."

---

[2]Because sons alone were eligible to perform these rites, it followed that every married man considered the birth of a son to be of cosmic importance. The Chinese tradition of embracing secondary wives and concubines stems from this concern.

PART A

CONFUCIAN STORIES AND BELIEFS

The Life and Legend of Confucius

Confucius was born in 551 BCE in the state of Lu, which is located in northeastern China in the modern province of Shantung. Since the earliest biographies of Confucius appeared five centuries after his death (after he had attained a semidivine status), separating the factual from the legendary can be as difficult for Confucius as it is for most of the other founders of religious systems. According to traditional accounts, however, Confucius's father was a distinguished soldier who died, along with Confucius's mother, when he was a young boy. Although poor, Confucius was a talented and ambitious child with a heart for learning. He married at age 19 and had a son and a daughter. His son became one of his disciples, but nothing is known about Confucius's wife or daughter.

As a young man, Confucius worked as a clerk in the Memorial Temple of the Duke Zhou. Here he performed the sacred ceremonies and gained a reputation as an expert in the ancient rituals. Confucius tried on several occasions to pass the qualifying exams for a government post, but he was unsuccessful. Disappointed but not embittered, he withdrew from the competition and gave himself to teaching. As a tutor he broke tradition by accepting the children of the rich and poor alike, but he refused students who did not possess high mental capabilities and a strong desire to learn.

According to tradition, at age 50 Confucius finally passed the civil service exam and became the chief magistrate of a remote town west of the Lu capital. Although his intellect was noted, his advice was rarely heeded. Frustrated at his superiors' lack of interest in his policies, he resigned his position and never again held an official post. For the next 15 years, he traveled across the states of Zhou with those who would accompany him. Going first to the north and then to the south, he visited the rulers of multiple vassal states. Officials listened to him but never granted him an opportunity to demonstrate the effectiveness of his reforms. At age 68, the disheartened Confucius returned to his hometown in the state of Lu. Here he spent his final years teaching and editing the ancient writings later known as the *Five Classics*.

Shortly before his death, Confucius succinctly encapsulated his career and life-quest with the statement: "At fifteen I set my heart on learning; at thirty I took my stand; at forty I came to be free from doubts; at fifty I understood the Decree of Heaven; at sixty my ear was attuned; at seventy I followed my heart's desire without overstepping the line."[3] He died in 479 BCE believing that he had failed to achieve his major goal—which was to save the edifice of civilization by restoring the moral foundations of antiquity.

Basic Confucian Teachings

Confucius lived in an era not unlike that of Palestine during the period of Confederation when, according to the Book of Judges, "there was no king . . . and every man did what was right in his own eyes." Alarmed by the unraveling of the social fabric, Confucius perceived it his divine mission to instruct rulers on how to restore the peace that had existed during the golden age of the ancient sage kings. He believed that China was corrupt, but not beyond redemption, and he offered unsolicited advice in the hopes of restoring the ancient harmony. Although Confucius denied that he was an innovator, he was a creative thinker who interpreted the ancient tradition in ways that carried novel if not revolutionary overtones. For these reasons it is not surprising that the feudal lords were reluctant to embrace his reforms.

Confucius's central ideas can be expressed through a discussion of four key Chinese terms—*de* (moral virtue), *jun-zi* (superior person), *ren* (benevolence), and *li* (propriety):[4]

---

[3] Analects 2.4.

[4] Before entering into a discussion of these concepts, we first should acknowledge the difficulty in translating from the Chinese language. Precision is lost in all translations, but the problem is compounded in translating from Chinese because there were no universal grammatical rules in classical Chinese and because its written script consisted primarily of picture symbols (pictograms) and combinations of picture symbols (ideograms). Some Confucians even insist that Confucianism cannot be communicated in non-Chinese, a caution almost never considered in other traditions. Few, for example, would argue that Plato could not be understood without knowing Greek, that the Bible could not be interpreted without knowing Hebrew, or that the sayings of the Buddha could not be communicated without knowing Pali. This textbook, of course, presumes that communication through translations is viable, but readers should be aware that not all Confucianists would agree with this premise.

- *De (Moral Virtue):* The word *de* signifies the moral force that is given to rulers from Heaven. Without this power, states cannot long survive. According to Confucius, rulers who relied on physical force to control the people were doomed to failure; however, one who ruled by *de* was "like the pole-star, which remains in its place while all the lesser stars do homage to it."[5] Confucius contrasted the sage kings of antiquity who ruled by moral example with the warlords of his day who used brutal force to subjugate the people. He insisted that if a ruler exemplified *de*, then he truly would be Tian-zi, the Son of Heaven who demonstrated to his subjects the way of Heaven. To Confucius, virtuous living among the people could not be obtained through legislation or force; it could only be established through example. Moral reform, however, had to begin at the top, and it was the responsibility of the ruler to set the moral example for his people.

- *Jun-Zi (Superior Person):* As a teacher, Confucius's quest was to make his disciples into *jun-zis*. Originally, the singular form of this term meant the "son-of-a-ruler" and it signified noble birth. Victorian English would translate the original meaning of this word as "gentleman." Confucius, however, adjusted the definition of *jun-zi* to mean not nobility by birth but nobility by virtue. To Confucius, the truly noble were not those merely born into the aristocratic ranks, but rather, those who cultivated their character to become the best that they could be. Anyone could become a *jun-zi*. It would not be easy. It would require great commitment and perseverance; however, all humans possess the nature to become a superior person. Confucius contrasted the noble or superior person with the petty person, saying "the superior person is concerned with virtue, the inferior person with land; the superior person understands what is right, the inferior person what is profitable."[6] According to Confucius, peace and harmony will dominate the land only when the people are transformed into *jun-zis*, that is, into superior persons who cultivate the cardinal virtues that will make them into mature, nonpetty human beings.

- *Ren (Benevolence):* Among the greatest of the cardinal virtues is *ren*. Although this word does not even appear in the oracle texts, Confucius elevated this concept to the center of his teaching, speaking more about *ren* in his recorded conversations than any other topic. As a general virtue, *ren* means humanity; as a particular virtue, it means benevolence or love. Etymologically, the word is a combination of the character "human being" and the number 2; hence, it carries with it the idea of being fully human toward others. The person of *ren* is one who obeys Confucius's golden rule, "Do not impose on others what you yourself do not desire" and its corollary, "You yourself desire rank and standing; then help others attain rank and standing."[7] According to Confucius, failing to seek the good of others breeds strife, but living according to *ren* restores the harmony of the ancient sages. Similarly, the wise ruler governs by *ren* and makes the welfare of the people his primary end.

- *Li (Propriety):* Although difficult to translate, the word *li* expresses better than any other term Confucius's formula for reform. In one sense, *li* means propriety—doing things the way they should be done in any given social situation; in another sense, *li* means ritual—performing your sacred duties. Thus, *li* refers both to doing right and performing rites. What is right conduct and what rites should be conducted are not the same for all people at all times, but rather, *li* varies depending on age, gender, social status, and context. According to Confucius, the ancients lived harmoniously in a just social order in which superiors and inferiors knew their places and behaved accordingly. To him, reform required returning to the hierarchical social structure of a past golden age. Confucius was most interested in *The Five Relationships* that he considered to be the most vital to the health of society. These relations were the relationship between Ruler and Subject, Parent and Child,

---

[5]Analects 2.1.

[6]Analects 4.11.

[7]Analects 15.24; 7:28.

Husband and Wife, Elder Sibling and Younger Sibling, and Elder Friend and Younger Friend. Practicing *li* meant behaving in ways appropriate to a person's role. In practice, it required benevolent rulers and loyal subjects, protective husbands and obedient wives, loving parents and reverential children, gentle elder siblings and respectful younger siblings, and mentoring elder friends and deferential younger friends.

Confucius minced no words promoting the importance of propriety and ritual. The following passage from the *Book of Rites* expresses his understanding that harmony in the empire, in the village and in the home depends on the practice of *li*.

> What I have learned is this, that of all the things that people live by, *li* is the greatest. Without *li*, we do not know how to conduct a proper worship of the spirits; or how to establish the proper status of the king and the ministers, the ruler and the ruled, and the elders and the juniors; or how to establish the moral relationships between the sexes, between parents and children, and between brothers; or how to distinguish the different degrees of relationships in the family. That is why a gentleman holds *li* in such high regard.

The Religious Dimensions of Confucian Thought

Much ink has been spilled debating the question, Is Confucianism a philosophy or a religion? The answer to the question, of course, depends on how religion is defined. It certainly is true that Confucius was more concerned with ethics than theology, was reticent to speculate about the nature of the spirit world, and held a rationalistic and humanistic worldview. However, to conclude from this that Confucius advanced a form of humanism that was devoid of religious character is to stretch the evidence and, according to Rodney Taylor,[8] to fail to understand the central religious dimension within Confucian thought.

Confucius, after all, was intensely loyal to Heaven, which he felt had given him a mandate to reform the world. On one occasion when an enemy, Huan Tui,

threatened his life, he responded: "Heaven begat the power that is in me. What have I to fear from such a one as Huan Tui?" When he felt neglected and misunderstood, he took comfort in the thought, "There is Heaven that knows me." His primary teachings focused on the need to return to the virtuous ways of the sage-kings of antiquity who followed the way of Heaven. He insisted that the ancient kings were fortunate because after their deaths, their descendants continued to offer them sacrifices for many generations. He praised King Wu and the Duke of Zhou for repairing the ancestral temple and for continuing the family sacrifices. He never denied that the spirits of the dead existed, and he performed the sacred ceremonies treating them as if they were present.

Moreover, he never repudiated the traditional Chinese views about the continuum of Heaven and Earth or about the need for the Earth to communicate with Heaven through ritual sacrifices. He avoided discussions of supernatural phenomena, not because he disbelieved in the spirit world but because he felt that it was more productive to speak about the purpose of life on this earth than to speculate about the unknowable. His mission was to bring about political reform, but the aim of the reform was to restore the world of the sage kings, a world that was impregnated with religious meaning.

From Confucius to Confucianism

Confucius did not consider himself to be the founder of a new school of thought, and his reputation for achieving this distinction did not arise until several centuries after his death. Two scholars who helped to create this image of Confucius were Meng-zi (ca. 371–289 BCE) and Xun-zi (ca. 298–238 BCE). Following in the Confucian tradition, both men aspired to advise rulers to bring about reform using the Confucian model. Meng-zi taught a program for perfecting individuals by cultivating their innate tendencies for the good. Xun-zi embraced the same goal but taught that more needed to be done to achieve the goal. According to Xun-zi, humans must restrain their base instincts and have their behavior modified through law and following rules of propriety. Although the former viewed human nature as fundamentally good, and the latter as originally evil, both believed in human perfectibility, in kingly government, and in the importance of education in achieving moral reform.

[8]Rodney L. Taylor, *The Religious Dimensions of Confucianism* (Albany, NY: State University of New York Press, 1990).

In the middle of the third century BCE, the western state of Qin (Ch'in) gained control over lands previously controlled by the Zhou, thus ending a dynastic line that had lasted for some 800 years. By 221 BCE, the Qin solidified its control over the remaining states and established an empire that embraces most of the land we now call China. The name China comes from Qin or Ch'in, the name of this state. During this short-lived dynasty (221–207 BCE), Chinese writing was standardized, the Great Wall of China was begun, and totalitarian principles that emphasized state sovereignty over human freedoms were enforced. The Confucian school opposed these principles, and Confucian scholars were executed and Confucian writings burned. Fortunately, the reactionary Qin dynasty did not last long, and the first emperor of the succeeding Han Dynasty ended the period of brutality and persecution, although he also maintained some of the Qin innovations, including the replacing of the feudal principalities with provinces run by state-appointed officials.

It was during the Han Dynasty (202 BCE–220 CE) that the ideas promoted by Confucius and his disciples received official state support and thus were dispersed among the intellectuals throughout the empire. In 136 BCE, the state adopted the writings advanced by Confucian scholars to be the foundation of the official system of education. At about this same time the state also erected temples in Confucius's honor and provided support for making his ancestral home into a national shrine. With these developments, the teachings of Confucius and his followers became systematized into the tradition that is known to us today as Confucianism.

Traditional sketch of Lao-zi riding on a water buffalo towards the western frontiers.

support any system that demanded rigid structure and social conformity. Whereas Confucius wanted to cultivate human virtue through learning and ritual, some of his critics rejected all efforts to organize society with references to eternal rules. To these mystics, some who later would be known as Daoists, human needs were best met when individuals rejected all artificial restraints and lived spontaneously in harmony with nature.

Although Daoism has played a central role in the development of Chinese culture, it is not a tradition that is easily defined in terms of its founders, beliefs, deities, practices, or scriptures. Most scholars would agree, however, that any definition of Daoism must include a discussion of three key ingredients: the ancient philosophy expressed in the *Dao-de-jing* and the *Zhang-zi*; the goals and practices developed by the magico-technicians of the Han Dynasty; and the organizations of the messianic movements of mass salvation that arose in the second century of the Common Era.

PART B

DAOIST STORIES AND BELIEFS

The Other Way: The Rise of Daoism

Confucius was not the only philosopher of the Eastern Zhou period to offer a vision for a better world. To Confucius, restoring the ancient feudal order through political reform was a worthy and accomplishable goal. Other thinkers, however, refused to

The Legend and Philosophy of Lao-Zi

All forms of Daoism express reverence for a mysterious figure known affectionately by his title *Lao-zi*, which means "the Grand Old Master." Little is known about Lao-zi, and many scholars consider him to be a fictitious character invented by later Daoists to establish a pre-Confucian historical priority. According to tradition, Lao-zi is said to have been born about a half-century before Confucius, around the year 604 BCE. Fantastic stories of his birth abound. For instance, he is said to have been conceived by a shooting star, carried in his mother's womb for 82 years, and born with white hair as a wise old man. His given name was Erh; his surname, Li; and his public name, Tan. With a surname Li, later emperors of the Tang Dynasty (616–907 CE) would claim him as their ancestor. His other two names, Erh and Tan, mean "ears" and "long ears," descriptive terms associated with the great sages known for their wisdom and long life.

Lao-zi lived in the Yangtze River region. This region, unlike the Yellow River area where Confucius matured, housed a population that was generally opposed to the feudal stronghold of the Zhou Dynasty. Lao-zi allegedly worked as an archivist in the Zhou court, although he left this position after becoming disenchanted with the corruption of the dynasty. According to tradition, he was a man of great understanding who came to realize that even the search for knowledge was vain, for it perverted the simplicity that can be known intuitively by living in harmony with nature. In one account, Lao-zi met Confucius, and after the meeting, Confucius was reported to have said, "The dragon is beyond my knowledge; it ascends into heaven on the clouds and the wind. Today I have seen Lao-zi, and he is like the dragon." In still other accounts, Lao-zi is said to have tutored Confucius in the knowledge of the ancient rites.

The Grand Old Man also was considered to be a person of ambitionless virtue. After realizing the unwillingness of the people to cultivate their natural goodness, he allegedly climbed upon a water buffalo and headed west beyond the world of deluded, corrupted men. At the Hanku Pass on the western border, a gatekeeper tried to persuade him to turn back. Failing at this, the gatekeeper then asked him to at least leave a record of his wisdom. Lao-zi agreed, and in three days he wrote a tiny volume of 5,000 characters that is known to us as the *Dao-de-jing*, or the *Sacred Book of the Dao and De*. Lao-zi then rode off into the western sunset and was never heard from again.

Although the *Dao-de-jing* is credited to Lao-zi, most scholars agree that it was the product of authors who lived in the late-Zhou period during an era of advanced feudal order disintegration. Historians label this era the Warring States Period (ca. 481–221 BCE), but it could just as well be called the Period of the Philosophers because it was a time of great intellectual creativity. The themes in the *Dao-de-jing* were transmitted and amplified in another fourth-century BCE text that is named after its author *Zhuang-zi* (ca. 370–301 BCE). These two texts form the bases of an early form of Daoism that has come to be known as Philosophical Daoism.

Philosophical Daoism advances the idea that when things are allowed to follow their natural course, they will move in harmony with *Dao*, the way of the universe. Defining the *Dao* is impossible, because reason cannot comprehend it. However, although the *Dao* is indescribable, living in harmony with it is the chief aim of life. Those who do not follow the *Dao* may find temporary success, but their success will not last, for all conditions—the seasons of the year, *yin* or *yang*, love or hate, adversity or prosperity—will ultimately be transformed according to the law of reciprocal causality. The wise, therefore, do not fret about their condition or about what is right and wrong; instead, they simply learn to enjoy the ride, letting happen what will according to the transformations of the *Dao*. Because the *Dao* is not personal, it is not formally worshipped. Nonetheless, the wise will meditate on it and will become one with the "Ten Thousand Things" when they live in harmony with it.

Whereas the followers of Confucius applauded the wisdom of the legendary sage-kings, the early Daoists looked for inspiration to an even more distant past. The golden age for the Daoists was an epoch before civilization was born—before society developed distinctions based on gender and class. In this golden era, lines between states, between occupational groups, and even between humans and animals were not clearly distinguishable. In this embryonic state the world existed as chaotic wholeness, a state that is often imagined as an "uncarved block." Within the uncarved block, everything existed and everything was possible. From a Daoist perspective, prior to birth there was no distinction between life and death. With the carving of the block, however, the world descended into a state of imperfection.

Unlike the Western religions that tend to identify human sin as the act that separated humanity from God, the Daoist version of the Fall identifies the dividing of the whole into nameable parts as the cause of imperfection. This idea is expressed in the *Dao-de-jing* verse: "The *Dao* gave birth to the One, the One gave birth to the Two, the Two gave birth to the Three, and the Three gave birth to the Ten Thousand Things" (*Dao-de-jing* 42). But just as division, birth, and aging lead to imperfection, reversing this process leads back to the purity of the original uncarved block. Daoist thinkers believe that by understanding the path that the *Dao* followed in its descent, a person can return to the embryonic state and thereby regain perfection and immortality.

The Pursuit of Immortality

During the Early Han Dynasty,[9] growing numbers of wandering ascetics and healers committed themselves to the pursuit of advanced longevity and immortality. For Daoists, the quest for immortality always meant physical immortality since it was believed that one's personality or soul consisted of several interrelated souls that were dispersed at death. In an attempt to reach physical immortality, these magico-technicians experimented with forms of divination, including astrology, numerology, and dream interpretation; developed advanced medical techniques, including forms of acupuncture, sexual yoga, and dietetics; and performed purification rituals, including exorcisms and visualization exercises. Some Daoist adepts also practiced the art of alchemy, which involved the assembling of secret ingredients to concoct an elixir, that when digested, either physically or spiritually, promised to bring immortality. These magicians (known as *fangshi*) gained access to the kings, who on occasion, not only digested their elixirs but also funded expositions to distant regions in search of the legendary islands of the immortals that were believed to exist in the ocean between China and Japan. Daoists believed that on these Isles of the Blessed grew plants that could restore life and renew youth. On one oc-

casion during the reign of Wu Ti (140–87 BCE), a *fangshi* persuaded the emperor to attempt to transmute cinnabar into gold by making sacrifices to the God of the Stove. This was a significant event in the development of Religious Daoism because the sacrifice to the traditional Chinese God of the Stove anticipated the incorporation of other deities into Daoism and thus, the subsequent enlargement of the Daoist pantheon. By the first century of the Common Era, *fangshi* magicians who sought immortality through the use of drugs and the avoidance of grain were renowned across China for their austerities and unworldly tendencies.

The Later Han Dynasty (25–220 CE) was a critical period in the development of Religious Daoism. During times of political instability when the emperors were weakened by uprisings in the provinces, gifted visionaries received from the high gods numerous revelations of sacred texts. These revelations often inspired further rebellions against the existing social order, rebellions that either had to be crushed or ameliorated by the ruling authorities. As communities embraced the new revelations, alliances were forged between the rulers and the priests of the emerging sects. Another important development of the Later Han Period was the elevation of Lao-zi to deity status. Although previously venerated as the author of the *Dao-de-jing*, by the beginning of the Common Era Lao-zi was worshipped as *Taishang Laojun*, "the Most High Lord Lao." As the personification of the eternal *Dao*, Lao-zi was seen as a savior figure who often appeared to advise rulers about the way of the universe.

The Establishment of Daoism as an Organized Religion

One appearance of Lao-zi was said to have taken place in 142 CE. On this occasion, the Most High Lord Lao allegedly visited Zhang Daoling and instructed him to replace the corrupted religious practices of the people with the pure doctrines of Lao-zi. These teachings emphasized correct actions and good works, which if appropriated, promised to bring community health and prosperity. Owing largely to his faith healing abilities, Zhang emerged as cultural hero, was given the title of "Celestial Master" (a title that also would be bestowed upon his earthly successors), and according to tradition, triumphantly ascended to heaven.

The movement founded by Zhang and his followers was the most successful, yet not the only messianic

---

[9]Han emperors ruled China from 206 BCE to 220 CE, except for a brief interruption in the early first century when a commoner secured the throne after a power struggle in the Han household. Historians distinguish the eras before and after the Interregnum with the labels Early Han and Later Han Periods.

Zhang Daoling, the Celestial Master, riding a tiger.

movement of the second century. As it grew, it was able to divide the regions it occupied into parishes. The focal point of each parish was the chamber of quietness or the temple, which was a sacred center of communication between the powers on high and the priestly representatives of the people. Moreover, the sect was able to require every household to contribute five pecks of rice annually to support the church and to administer the parish. Owing to its leadership and its tax, the emerging sect was known by two names, "The Way of the Celestial Masters" and "the Way of the Five Pecks of Rice." After the grandson of Zhang pledged his loyalty to the Wei Dynasty (220–265 CE) of northern China, the Wei emperors granted official recognition to the Celestial Masters. This alliance gave the Celestial Masters an advantage over the other Daoist sects of the period. Within a century, the Celestial Masters emerged as the dominant religious body in China, complete with an elaborate set of rituals performed in communal temples by an authorized professional priesthood.

Although Western scholars once drew sharp distinctions between Philosophical Daoism (an unorganized, reflective movement for intellectuals) and Religious Daoism (the liturgical church of immortality seekers), recent scholars are more prone to emphasize the continuities between these two traditions.

Daoism, like many of the great world religions, is a complex tradition that has emerged from the waters of several streams. Its formation and early development can be best understood as a succession of revelations, with each revelation accepting the insights of the former ages but also claiming to surpass them in wisdom and purity.

SCRIPTURES

The Chinese word used to describe the authoritative Confucian and Daoist texts is *jing*. Literally the word denotes the lengthwise threads on a weaver's loom onto which the cross threads are woven. When *jing* is applied to written texts, it refers to those authoritative documents that shape the fabric of society. After Buddhism came to China, this same word was used to translate the Sankrit word *sutra*, which referred to the collection of writings attributed to the Buddha. Consequently, the same word *jing* describes the literary canon for each of China's religions, although the connotations regarding the meaning of this word differ among the three traditions.

For most Daoists, the authoritative texts are literally viewed as translations from a "celestial script" that was frozen in time from a distant and less corrupted past. During the formative period of Religious Daoism, these revelations of the eternal *Dao* were considered sacred books, which could be surpassed in authority only by the reception of additional revelations from even more authoritative deities from an even more distant past. The Confucian canon, however, was not considered to be revelations from the gods, and many scholars, although not all, insist that the proper translation of the term *jing* regarding these texts is "classic" rather than "sacred book."

PART A
CONFUCIAN CLASSICS

The Confucian Canon

The term *jing* has been applied to various collections of works at different points in the history of the Confucian tradition. In the early Han period, the Confu-

---

CONFUCIAN CLASSICS

The Five Classics
- The Book of Changes
- The Book of History
- The Book of Odes
- Spring and Autumn Annals
- The Book of Rites

The Four Books
- The Analects
- The Book of Mencius
- The Doctrine of the Mean
- The Great Learning

---

cian canon included nine books, but in later dynasties some of the early material was reorganized and additional works were added, thus making a total of Thirteen Classics in the canon. Among these, the more important include the *Five Classics*, which pre-date or are continuous with Confucius, and the *Four Books*, which post-date Confucius's lifespan.

The earliest authoritative texts within the Confucian tradition expressed the presumed teachings of the venerable sage-kings of antiquity. Originally, there were six works in this grouping, but one work, the *Book of Music*, is no longer extant. According to tradition, Confucius was the author or editor of these classics, although scholars question his contribution to all of these works. The *Five Classics* that are extant include the following:

The Book of Changes

Perhaps the earliest text of Chinese antiquity, the *Book of Changes* (*I Jing*), is a divinatory handbook that rests on the assumption that the universe is continually regenerating itself according to rhythmic patterns. The work contains a directory of 64 symbols (called hexagrams) that are made up of combinations of solid and broken lines. Each hexagram is associated with a concept, such as Retreat or Progress, which is described in the book with cryptic commentaries. To seek advice as to how to act in harmony with the patterns of nature, a diviner asks a question and then throws to the ground some longer and shorter "yarrow stalks." The patterns of the fallen stalks are observed and then associated with 1 of the

64 hexagrams. Diviners then reflect on the textual commentary about the hexagram before deciding on an appropriate plan of action. For example, if a military general is concerned with a question of war strategy and he throws a combination of short and long lines that conform to the hexagram "Retreat," then he would reflect on that commentary in the *I Jing* and plan his military operations accordingly. Scholars believe that the hexagrams in the *Book of Changes* date to the Shang Dynasty, but the commentaries were written centuries later during the Zhou Dynasty.

The Book of History

This work purports to be a history of ancient China from the third millennium to the seventh century BCE. It opens with a description of the acts of the legendary ruler Shun, who performed ritual offerings to the spiritual beings and established a new cosmic order. Throughout the work, the cultural heroes of antiquity are portrayed as wise sages, not because they received divine directives from the gods but because they were able to observe the cyclical patterns of nature and apply these insights to human relations. The cosmological worldview of the *Book of History* acknowledges the existence of the spirits and *Shang Di*, the Most High God, even as it celebrates the efficacy of human effort. The work suggests that humans who possess *de* (virtue) can communicate with spirits that can provide assistance in worldly matters. The task of the ruler is to provide for the welfare of the people by maintaining the harmony of the universe. Failure to perform these responsibilities, however, will result in the loss of the "mandate of heaven" that is bestowed by Heaven upon morally upright sovereigns. The central teaching, thus, is that true authority is not automatic; it must be earned.

The Books of Odes

Also known as the *Book of Poetry* and the *Book of Songs*, this classic is a collection of 305 sacrificial hymns, praise songs to the cultural heroes, and love poems. According to tradition, Confucius selected these from a larger number of ancient poems and taught that their study would free the mind from depraved thoughts. A few of the pieces date to the Shang Dynasty, but most are Zhou Period pieces from about 1000 to 600 BCE. From the *Book of Odes* we learn how the Zhou nobles honored their ancestors with great feasts, a practice that suggests the idea that

Heaven would respond favorably to the supplications of pious petitioners.

Spring and Autumn Annals

This work outlines a record of historic events in Lu, the birth-state of Confucius, from 711 to 481 BCE. The work includes a concise, year-by-year listing of events, allegedly written by Confucius, and three commentaries about the events ascribed to later disciples. Scholars believe that the first part probably pre-dates Confucius, but it may have been revised and edited by him. The latter parts appear to have been written no earlier than the fourth century BCE.

The Book of Rites

A ritual text of the late Zhou and early Han eras, the *Book of Rites* describes and discusses the philosophical meanings of the rituals performed by the ancient sage-kings. The rites encompass a wide variety of ritualized public and private behavior, from simple table manners to the ways of governing human relations through sacrificial offerings. Portions of this work were considered of such importance to later neo-Confucianists that two chapters of this work were removed and elevated into independent texts that became two of the authoritative *Four Books* that formed the basis of Confucian education from the fourteenth through the twentieth centuries of the Common Era.

The New Scriptural Tradition of Neo-Confucianism

For more than 1,000 years after the *Five Classics* were codified (during the early Han dynasty), Confucianists accepted the classics as authoritative teachings from antiquity that were written or edited by Confucius. By the Tang Dynastic Period (618–907 CE), an orthodox interpretation of the *Five Classics* was well established in an official commentary entitled *The Correct Meanings of the Five Classics*. Not all scholars, however, accepted this version of orthodoxy, and over time, new commentaries appeared that challenged the authenticity and authority of the *Five Classics* themselves.

Among the greatest of the philosophers of this Neo-Confucian movement was Zhu Xi (1130–1200 CE). According to Zhu Xi, the purpose of the Classics was to help thinkers understand correct principles, but once the principles were understood, the Classics themselves were no longer needed. Zhu Xi was able to shift attention away from a concern for the historical facts of the sages of antiquity to philosophical principles that revealed the metaphysical structure in all things. As a consequence of this teaching, the authority of the Classics was diminished, even as a new canon of authoritative texts was accepted. The authoritative works, known as the *Four Books,* were not actually new writings, but their combination, and the authority given to them were both innovative and revolutionary. The *Four Books* of the neo-Confucian canon include the following:

The Analects

Generally recognized as the most reliable source of Confucian doctrine, the *Analects* is a collection of Confucian sayings that were compiled by his disciples after his death. Most of the work consists of the remembered words of Confucius himself, although some passages also contain the words of his disciples. The Chinese name for the book is *Lun Yu*, which means "selected sayings." The verses are arranged into 20 chapters or books. At least three versions of the *Lun Yu* circulated during the Early Han Period. In the early third century CE, Ho Yen compiled an eclectic edition drawn from these earlier versions. The current version of the *Lun Yu* is from the edition edited by Ho Yen.

The Book of Mencius

The longest of the *Four Books*, this work is a collection of essays that contains a series of conversations between Meng-zi and his disciples, friends, rulers, and rival philosophers. The central theme expressed throughout this work is Meng-zi's conviction about the essential goodness of human nature. The work, which is divided into seven books—each subdivided into two parts — was most likely compiled by the disciples of Meng-zi shortly after his death in the third century BCE.

The Doctrine of the Mean

Originally Chapter 28 of the *Book of Rites*, this work is an excellent philosophical exposition of Confucian thought. Its teachings emphasize the trinity of humanity, Heaven, and Earth and its corollary, the unity of humankind and Heaven. Although the work is tra-

Ming dynasty depiction of Confucius.

ditionally attributed to Confucius's grandson Zi Si, scholars speculate that portions of it were written after the time of Meng-zi in the second century BCE.

The Great Learning

Originally Chapter 39 of the *Book of Rites*, this introduction to Confucian thought is a treatise designed to educate gentlemen, and it has served as the first classical Chinese text studied by schoolboys for many centuries. The work teaches that before ordering the states, the ancient sages regulated their families; before regulating their families, they cultivated themselves; before cultivating themselves, they perfected their minds; before perfecting their minds, they established sincere thoughts and extended their knowledge. Hence, a central message of the work is that a harmonious society is the result of the extension of personal virtues.

PART B
DAOIST SCRIPTURES

The Canon of Philosophical Daoism

The two great literary classics in philosophical Daoism are the *Dao-de-jing* and *Zhuang-zi*. The books differ greatly in size, language, and style. Originally, the *Dao-de-jing* was known as the *Lao-zi*, after its alleged author. During the Han Period, it was given its new name, a title that identified it as a book of *jing*, thus placing it on equal footing with the Confucian classics. The *Dao-de-jing* is a book of poetry that contains slightly more than 5,000 characters. It traditionally is divided into 81 chapters, the opening 37 of which deal with the *Dao* (the way of the cosmos), and the remaining 44 with the *De* (the power of virtue). Although the concepts within it are recognized as ancient, the text itself most likely dates only from the third century BCE and includes remembered sayings from several wise masters. Owing to its cryptic style, it can be interpreted in many ways, but it is generally read as a utopian tract that advocates a return to the primitive. With more than 100 English translations, this alluring and mysterious work has been read by Westerners more than any other classical Chinese text.

After the *Dao-de-jing*, the second most respected ancient Daoist classic is the *Zhuang-zi*. Almost 20 times the size of the *Dao-de-jing*, the *Zhuang-zi* in its present form consists of 33 discrete chapters that are largely arranged according to topic and are written mostly in prose. Although the work no doubt includes selections from several philosophers of the Warring States Period (481–221 BCE), scholars attribute the first seven chapters to Zhuang-zi, the brilliant fourth-century BCE writer who popularized and extended the teachings of Lao-zi much like Meng-zi did for Confucius and the apostle Paul did for Jesus. The text is known for its high literary quality, humor, and insight. Rich in imagery and metaphor, it presents deep philosophical insights in simple and profane ways, often poking fun at serious philosophers who would constrict individual freedom and spontaneity. The range of the work is wide, including, for example, fanciful accounts of holy men who mount dragons and soar through the clouds on celestial journeys, and collections of witty aphorisms of the boundless Master Zhuang-zi. The worldview presented throughout the *Zhuang-zi* is distinctively anti-Confucian in that it associates order and symmetry with death, and chaos and disarray with life.

The Sacred Books of Religious Daoism

Just a generation ago, we knew little about the nearly 1,500 sacred texts that comprise the present canon of Religious Daoism. In recent decades, an explosion in Daoist scholarship has resulted in the publications of the first English translations of many of these sacred books. This scholarship has greatly enhanced our knowledge of the Daoist canon, but much remains to be done before the West will be able to fully appreciate this diverse religious tradition.

It is not simply the size of the canon that impedes our understanding of Daoist scriptures. Most of the

sacred texts were not even written for the broader audience of its time,[10] much less for a modern readership with vastly different cultural expectations. Moreover, the texts attempted to reveal cosmic secrets to specialized priests, so much that we would like to know about terminology and context was silently passed over without explanation. Consequently, the already difficult task of translating Chinese script into Western languages is made even more complex by the esoteric nature of these sacred works themselves.

Like the recognized holy books of many traditions, the Daoist canon has evolved over time. The current canon, excepting several supplements that were added in the seventeenth and twentieth centuries of the Common Era, was compiled and printed during the Ming Dynasty (1368–1644 CE) in the middle of the fifteenth century. During the preceding millennium, the Daoist canon was edited, rearranged, and enlarged seven or eight times. On most of these occasions, the new edition was produced on the order of the Emperor.[11]

The earliest known catalog was ordered by Emperor Song Mingdi and compiled by Lu Xiujing in the year 471 CE. Influenced by the Buddhist tradition that divided its scripture into the Three Baskets (*Tripitaka*), the Lu Xujing canon organized the Daoist sacred writings into the Three Caverns. The material in each cavern was subdivided into 12 thematic categories: Fundamental Texts, Talismans, Commentaries, Charts and Illustrations, Histories and Genealogies, Precepts, Ceremonies, Rituals, Various Arts, Biographies, Hymns, and Memorials. All subsequent editors of the Daoist canon have used the Lu Xujing method of organizing the sacred books into three caverns with 36 subdivisions. The Lu Xujing canon included 1,200 juan or chapters, but the size of the canon has increased in subsequent editions. The Ming Dynasty canon, for instance, includes more then 5,300 juan.

The Three Caverns and the Four Supplements

According to Religious Daoist cosmology, during three cosmic eras, the three august gods, each living in separate heavens, sent out three teachings or cav-

---

[10]In fact, it was considered to be a sacrilegious act for a lay person to read these cosmic secrets.

[11]For a note on the various editions of the Daoist canon, see Kenneth Dean, *Daoist Ritual and Popular Cults of South-East China* (Princeton, NJ: Princeton University Press, 1993), pp. 221–222.

erns. Each cavern corresponded to one of the three major Daoist sects that emerged in southern China during the Early Six Dynasties Era. The three teachings included the *Dongzhen* (the Authentic Cavern), the *Dongxuan* (the Mysterious Cavern), and the *Dongshen* (the Spirit Cavern). The Authentic Cavern incorporated the writings of the *Shangquing* tradition, the Mysterious Cavern included the texts of the *Lingbao* tradition, and the Spirit Cavern contained the writings of the *Sanhuang* tradition. Each sect added a supplemental text that described the origins of the sacred revelations. A fourth collection, the *Zhengyi fu,* also was acknowledged to be sacred. This Fourth Supplement included the revelations of the Celestial Masters School, an earlier, second-century movement that is generally recognized as the sect that launched Religious Daoism. Hence, the "Bible" of Religious Daoism includes a rich and diverse assortment of writings that are contained in a catalog of works known to us as the Three Caverns and the Four Supplements.

Space does not permit a thorough discussion of the history of each component within this immense canon. The following comments, however, provide a concise introduction to three important collections of Daoist writings that have been translated into the English language and studied by Western scholars. The three collections include the *Zhengyi, Shangqing,* and *Lingbao* scriptures.

DAOIST CLASSICS

Philosophical Daoism
  Dao-de-jing
  Zhuang-zi

Religious Daoism
  The Xiujing Canon

The Three Caverns
  Authentic Cavern (Shangquing tradition)
  Mysterious Cavern (Lingbao tradition)
  Spirit Cavern (Sanhuang tradition)

The Four Supplements (one supplement from each tradition, plus the *Zhengyi fu* from the Celestial Masters School)

The Zhengyi *Scriptures*

Although this collection of writings from the Celestial Masters School is not included among the works contained in the Three Caverns, it is included in the Daoist canon as the fourth supplement. According to the Celestial Masters, in 142 CE the deified Lao-zi appeared to Zhang Daoling, a small landowner who lived in western China in the mountains of Sichuan. Lao-zi presented Zhang Daoling with the *Zhengyi* revelations and proclaimed him to be the first Celestial Master. In addition to establishing a pact between Lao-zi, the incarnation of the eternal Dao, and the descendants of the first Celestial Master, the revelations instituted new moral guidelines, established communal rituals, and promised protection and immortality to those who embraced the new revelations.

The Shangqing *Scriptures*

These scriptures allegedly were revealed between 364 and 370 CE by celestial beings to Yang Xi (330–386 CE), a visionary medium who was employed as a spiritual advisor to a southern gentry family in the county of Jiankang, near modern Nanjing. The texts were called *Shangqing* (meaning Highest Clarity), after the name of the heaven from which the divine beings came. Yang Xi gave the scriptures to members of the Xu family, which included Xu Hui, a court official who had converted, perhaps for political reasons, to the Celestial Masters School. After receiving the new scriptures, Xu Hui left the Celestial Masters School and his governmental post and retired to Mt. Mao, where he devoted his time to studying and practicing the new methods of immortality proclaimed in the *Shangqing* scriptures.

The *Shangqing* scriptures were written in an exalted and poetic language, and suggest a familiarity with the Confucian classics as well as the *Dao-de-jing* and the *Zhuang-zi.* Although they did not deny the Celestial Masters revelations, they insisted that these scriptures were received from lower emissaries of the celestial order and thus advanced inferior immortality techniques. In comparison with the communal rites of the Celestial Masters, the *Shangqing* practices were aimed at taking adepts individually to the realms of the immortals, first by visualization exercises, then by ecstatic spirit journeys, and finally by swallowing elixirs concocted from secret recipes. The *Shangqing* texts were the first scriptures to closely integrate a religious sect with the ancient Chinese art of alchemy.

Later *Shangqing* texts appeared during the ensuring centuries, and in the sixth century, Dao Hongjing (456–536 CE) gathered the various manuscripts and produced a work that contained the revelations given to Yang Xi, plus some correspondences between Yang Xi and the Xu family. Dao Hongjing also established a formal *Shangqing* School on Mt. Mao. Owing in part to its favorable relations with the emperors, the *Shangquing* School flourished throughout the remainder of the Six Dynasties and Tang Periods as one of the foremost schools of Daoism.

The Lingbao *Scriptures*

In the same region of China, but three decades after Yang Xi's revelations, another set of sacred writings appeared. These scriptures were compiled about the year 400 CE by Ge Chaofu, a relative of the famous fourth-century alchemist Ge Hong (283–343). Ge Chaofu did not claim to have received these texts from the celestial deities himself. Rather, he asserted that about two centuries earlier, the Great Lord of the Highest Heaven sent three perfected sages to visit his distant relative, Ge Xuan, a virtuous Daoist magician. According to tradition, the perfected worthies gave Ge Xuan these sacred texts, which he then passed down through the Ge clan to Chaofu. This alleged line of transmission enabled the *Lingbao* School to claim that its scriptures predated the *Shangqing* scriptures that were revealed to Yang Xi.

The *Lingbao* texts, unlike the *Shangqing* scriptures, are not named after the heaven of their origin. Instead, the word *Lingbao* means "Numinous Treasure." This term denotes the claim that these scriptures were fragments from heaven that were formed from mysterious graphs that flickered from within the *Dao* at the time when the heaven and earth were divided. More communal and less elitist than the Highest Clarity School, the *Lingbao* scriptures promised salvation for all, rich and poor alike. It also advanced simpler immortality techniques than the *Shangqing* texts, requiring merely the recitation of its scriptures to ensure a place among the perfected. The *Lingboa* texts also were the first Daoist scriptures to accept aspects of Buddhist cosmology and doctrine. For instance, the *Lingbao* embraced the Buddhist notion of rebirth. It taught that by reciting scriptures and participating in the communal rites of salvation, a person might rescue his or her ancestors from low rebirth, and even move them directly into the heavens, where they could assist in the salvation of others. The *Lingbao* emphasis on rescuing humanity from the terrors of bondage also reflects the Buddhist bodhisattva ideal that elevates the salvation of others to the chief aim of life. With this universalist vision of salvation, the *Lingbao* School, much like Mahayana Buddhism, claimed to be Daoism's Greater Vehicle, even as it relegated the *Shangqing* to the status of the Lesser Vehicle.

SUBDIVISIONS

PART A

CONFUCIAN SUBDIVISIONS

Confucianism through the Ages

Although Confucian thought has circulated in China for about 2.5 millennia, its history includes as many ups and downs and twists and turns as a modern roller-coaster ride. Following its formation and infancy during the Eastern Zhou and Warring States periods (pre-221 BCE), it became a persecuted doctrine during the short-lived Qin Dynasty (221–206 BCE) but then emerged as the orthodox ideology of the state during the ensuing Han Dynasty (206 BCE–220 CE). Under the Hans, the non-Confucian philosophers were shunned as the imperial academies made the Confucian classics and commentaries the foundation of the state educational system.

After the fall of the Han Emperors, China entered into an era of political instability (often called the Six Dynasties Period, 221–589 CE). During this period of disunity, the growth of Daoist sects and the arrival of Buddhism from India broke apart the Confucian monopoly and even succeeded in shifting Confucian ideology from the center to the margins of Chinese culture. For several centuries, the most distinguished philosophers in China were Buddhists, not Confucians. When this period of unrest ended with the rise of the Sui Dynasty (589–618 CE) and its successor the Tang Dynasty (618–907 CE), Confucianism regained some of its former influence, although it never fully recouped the privileged status that it once enjoyed during the Han period.

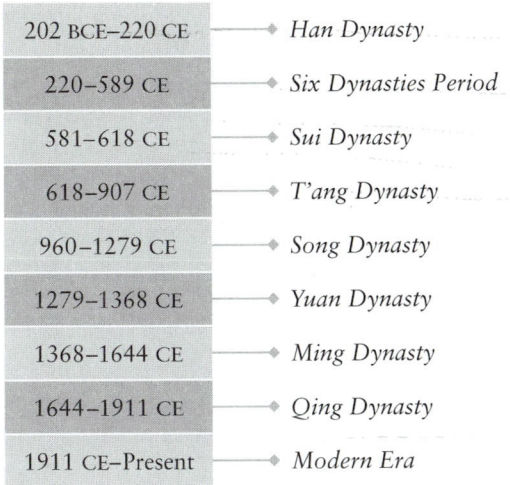

202 BCE–220 CE	→	*Han Dynasty*
220–589 CE	→	*Six Dynasties Period*
581–618 CE	→	*Sui Dynasty*
618–907 CE	→	*T'ang Dynasty*
960–1279 CE	→	*Song Dynasty*
1279–1368 CE	→	*Yuan Dynasty*
1368–1644 CE	→	*Ming Dynasty*
1644–1911 CE	→	*Qing Dynasty*
1911 CE–Present	→	*Modern Era*

Timeline of Chinese History.

After invaders from the north toppled the Tang Dynasty in the early seventh century, a series of struggles erupted among competing warlords. Five decades and five dynastic changes later, the turmoil ended when general Chao K'uang-yin reunited China and established the Song Dynasty (960–1279 CE). Memories of this era of anarchy and rebellion provoked scholars to think about ways to strengthen the social fabric. This interest, along with a growing concern with the spread of Buddhist devotional societies across China, triggered a scholarly reaction against all ideologies deemed to be alien and non-Chinese. In this atmosphere, a new form of Confucianism emerged that blamed China's problems on the "heterodox" teachings of Buddhism and Daoism. Scholars use the label "Neo-Confucianism" to distinguish this expression of Confucian thought from its earlier pre-Song era forms.

The Rise of Neo-Confucian Schools

The foremost school of Neo-Confucianism that emerged during the Song Period has been called both Ch'eng-Chu, after the names of its early masters,[12] and the School of Principle, after its central philosophical

focus. The greatest proponent of this school was Zhu Xi (1130–1200 CE), an astute synthesizer who was to Neo-Confucianism what Thomas Aquinas was to Catholic Christianity. According to the philosophy of Zhu Xi, the world consists of two inseparable elements: Principle (*li*)[13] and Material Force (*qi*). The former is immaterial, one, unchanging, and eternal; the latter is material, many, changing, and transitory. The ultimate origin of Principle is called the Great Ultimate, which emanates from Heaven. The School of Principle teaches that there is an immutable Principle that gives form to all things and that the task of the philosopher is to investigate things in order to understand the Principle in each object. When able to comprehend the universal Principle that is inherent in all things, a person becomes a sage.

Although this philosophic system incorporated selected Daoist and Buddhist ideas, its primary intent was to subordinate these elements into a thoroughly Confucian worldview. For instance, Zhu accepted ancestor worship and the veneration of the spirits of the Chinese sages but denied that the souls of ancestors existed and opposed the popular gods of Daoism. Again, following Buddhist practices, Zhu advocated spending a portion of every day in "silent-sitting," but he denied Buddhist notions of rebirth and salvation and insisted that the purpose of meditation was to achieve moral development, not metaphysical insight. Like the ideas of most great thinkers, the central meanings and merits of Zhu's philosophy have been interpreted differently by modern academics. Some scholars, noting his refusal to use anthropomorphic language to describe the spirit world and his abstract references to Heaven, suggest that Zhu was an atheist and that his school encouraged the agnostic tendencies that were latent in the earlier forms of Confucianism.[14] Other scholars assert, however, that Zhu's insistence that Principle existed before Heaven and Earth and that Principle is the cause of the existence of opposites (*yin-yang*) but has no opposite itself, signifies a theistic form of Neo-Confucianism that has similarities with Lao-zi's

---

[12]The early philosophers who influenced Zhu Xi and the development of Song Neo-Confucianism are Zhou Dun-yi (1017–1073), Zhang Zai (1020–1077), Ming-dao (1032–1085), and Yi-chuan (1033–1107). For a selected anthology of their writings, see *A Source Book in Chinese Philosophy,* translated and compiled by Wing-Tsit Chan (Princeton, NJ: Princeton University Press, 1963), pp. 460–571.

[13]The Latinized word *li,* which here means Principle, is derived from a different Chinese character or ideogram than a second Latinized word *li,* which is translated as "propriety" or "ritual." Although when read in English the words look the same, they are different words in the Chinese script and convey different meanings.

[14]For example, see the chapter on "Chu His, Leibniz and the Philosophy of Organism" in Volume II of Joseph Needham, *Science and Civilization in China* (London: Cambridge University Press, 1954).

Undifferentiated Eternal *Dao* and with Aquinas's First Cause/Creator God of the universe.[15]

Notwithstanding its metaphysical implications, it was the pragmatic value of Zhu's doctrines that made them historically significant. The Song emperors liked Zhu's system because it affirmed the existing political order and emphasized the importance of obedience to superiors. In time, Zhu's interpretations of the Confucian classics became the basis of the civil service examination questions that all Chinese scholars had to master before they could assume a government post. This rigid form of Neo-Confucianism also spread to Korea and Japan, where it rooted and emerged as a serious challenger to Buddhism.

In the late thirteenth century, China was torn and then unified by Genghis Khan, a Mongol empire builder who cared little for the philosophical intricacies of the Chinese literati. During the rule of the Mongols (Yuan Dynasty, 1279–1368 CE), the Confucian civil service exams were initially discontinued, but later, in 1313, reinstated, not so much for their merit but as an effective means for recruiting administrative officials. With few exceptions, throughout the Yuan Dynasty the great scholars were proponents of Zhu's School of Principle.

After a century of foreign rule, rebel Chinese armies drove out the Mongols and established the Ming Dynasty (1368–1644 CE). This highly centralized and despotic dynasty would be able to maintain order in China for three centuries. Throughout this period, the Chinese government maintained a large bureaucracy (ranging in size from 10,000 to 15,000 officials) that was staffed by scholars who completed the elaborate civil service examination process. The Ming examination system was based on knowledge of the *Four Books*, edited by Zhu, and on Zhu's orthodox interpretations of these Confucian classics.

During the later Ming era, however, a new school of Neo-Confucianism emerged that challenged the merits of an educational system that placed such an emphasis on book learning and memorization. This sect, often called the School of Mind, embraced the teachings of the statesman-scholar Wang Yang-Ming (1472–1529 CE).

The School of Mind differed from the School of Principle in that it insisted that true knowledge comes intuitively from within rather than empirically from without. Like Meng-zi and Zhu Xi, Wang believed in the innate goodness of human nature, but he went beyond his predecessors in arguing that it was only through the self-discovery of this truth that humans could achieve sagehood. For Wang, since the mind contained every Principle of the universe, it was unnecessary to go beyond examining a person's own mind. The Way was attainable without investigation and study. Good works were unnecessary. "My nature is . . . sufficient for me to attain sagehood," wrote Wang. "I have been mistaken in searching for Principle in external things and affairs."[16] If Zhu was the Thomas Aquinas of Neo-Confucianism, Wang was its Martin Luther.

Although Wang's views did not receive official acceptance during his lifetime, they did exert a strong influence on later Chinese philosophers. Wang's influence also extended into Japan, where his School of Mind (Yomeigaku) rivaled the School of Principle (Shushigaku) from the seventeenth through the nineteenth centuries.

Without accepting the exaggerated theories of the critics of Wang who associated the growth of his school with the eventual fall of the Ming Empire, Wang's distrust of using external criteria to locate truth did foster a sense of moral relativism that inspired some radical sects of the late-Ming era to denounce all conventional moral precepts. However, the degenerate followers of Wang did not single-handedly cause the collapse of the Ming. Equal blame must be placed on the rigidity of Zhu Xi's system, which, according to historian John Fairbank, became a "strait-jacket on the Chinese mind." Denouncing the intellectual sterility of the period, Fairbank chastised the Ming rulers for their rigid demands on orthodoxy, concluding: "The Four Books and Five Classics became the intellectual fare of all ambitious men, as though Chinese society could find refuge by turning back into its own cultural heritage and could protect itself by staying within an established framework of ideas."[17]

---

[15]Michael O. Billington, "Toward the Ecumenical Unity of East and West: The Renaissances of Confucian China and Christian Europe," *Fidelio*, Vol. II, no. 2 (Summer 1993).

[16]Tu Wei-ming, *Neo-Confucian Thought in Action: Wang Yang-ming's Youth*, 1472–1509 (Berkeley: University of California Press, 1976).

[17]John King Fairbank, *The United States and China* (Cambridge, MA, 1958): pp. 63–64. For a more favorable interpretation of the impact of Neo-Confucianism on China, see William Theodore De Bary, *The Unfolding of Neo-Confucianism* (New York: Columbia University Press, 1975).

מעל הבית נגע בינינו שאומרים הההודה

During the Middle Ages, Jewish schools dedicated to the study of the Talmud (known as Yeshivot) flourished throughout the diaspora. The custom of reading the Talmud at Yeshivot continues to this day within Jewish communities around the world.

Michelangelo's *The Conversion of St. Paul* from the ceiling of the Sistine Chapel depicts Jesus stretching his hand from the sky toward the fallen Paul.

The Black Stone, called "Hajratul-Aswad."

Rama and Sita, the Hindu prototype of the perfect couple.

The "Eight Immortals" that Daoists believe descended into heaven after having reached perfection in eight different ways.

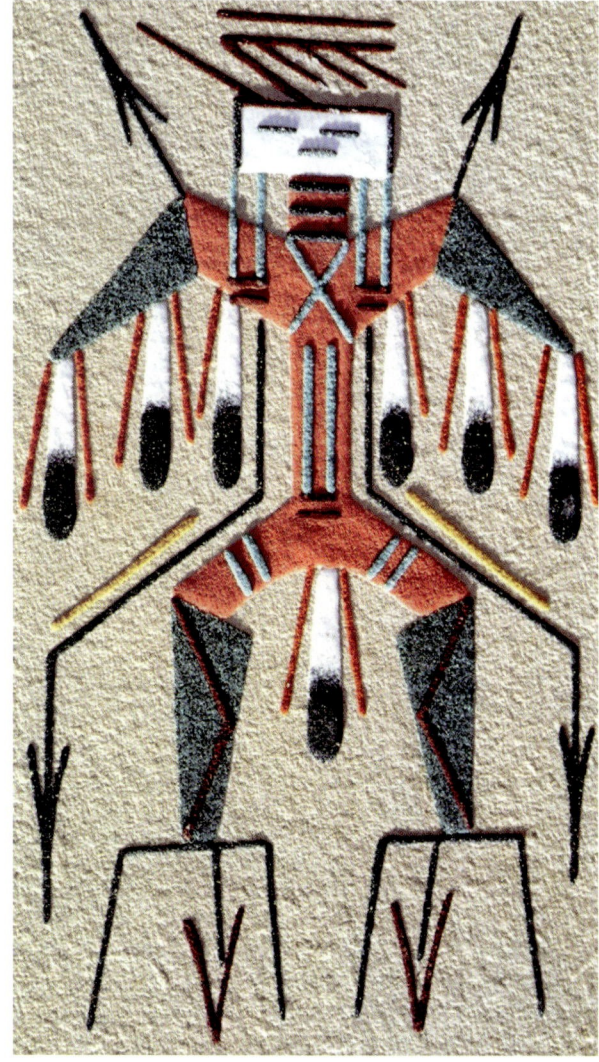

Sandpainting is a central element in Diné (Navajo) healing ceremonies.

Ritual initiation ceremony of the Krobo tribe with the ritual mother.

The Rapa Nui peoples on the remote Polynesian island known by Westerners as "Easter Island" carved more than 800 massive statues, most of which weigh 14 tons and stand 13 feet. Much controversy surrounds the religious and secular meanings of these impressive works of art.

In 1644, with an army of bandits surrounding the capital, the last Ming Emperor committed suicide. The Manchus from the northeast took advantage of this opportunity and sent troops into China, allegedly on the pretext of helping the Ming suppress the bandits. Instead of assisting, however, they took the capital city and announced the establishment of a new Qing dynasty. Qing emperors would rule China until Sun Yat-sen's revolution of 1911 established the Republic of China. This revolution brought China's extensive imperial history to an end. Ironically, China's last emperor would not be Chinese, but Manchu.

Although foreign invaders, the early Qing emperors expressed a keen interest in Chinese culture and philosophy and defended with vigor the orthodoxy of the Song Neo-Confucians. For about a century under the Qing, the rationalistic School of Principle dominated Confucian scholarship. In the eighteenth century, however, the influence of Zhu Xi's school subsided as growing numbers of scholars expressed a preference for practical learning over abstract thinking. Refusing to accept anything without evidence, Qing era scholars such as Tai Chen (1723–1777) argued that the proper way to investigate Principle was not by intellectual speculation (as advocated by Zhu Xi) or by introspection (as advocated by Wang Yangming), but by a critical, analytical, objective study of concrete objects. This Investigations-Based-on-Evidence School never attained the stature of the two earlier Neo-Confucianist schools, but its inductive and comparative methodology did produce significant advances in the textual criticism of the Confucian classics.

PART B

DAOIST SUBDIVISIONS

The Daoist Sects of Medieval and Early Modern China

Although Daoism never monopolized the Chinese educational system like Confucianism, state events did affect its organization and propagation. Official recognition was at least implicitly given to Religious Daoism as early as the Han Dynasty when the emperors ordered that offerings be made to the deified Lao-zi and that temples be built in his honor. It, however, was not until the fifth century CE, after the *Shangqing* and *Lingboa* revelations, that an emperor of the Northern Wei Dynasty (386–535 CE) proclaimed Daoism to be the official religion of the Empire. According to tradition, in 415 CE the deified Lao-zi appeared to a Daoist visionary named Kou Qianzhi (365–448 CE), proclaimed him to be the Celestial Master and instructed him to cleanse Daoism from its sexual irregularities[18] and mercenary tendencies and to place greater emphasis upon the importance of good works and hygiene. Kou took his new revelations to the imperial court, where, in 440 CE, he persuaded Emperor Tai Wu Ti to accept Daoist initiation and promote the reforms that promised to bring harmony to the northern empire.

While Kou's theocratic state only survived briefly, imperial support for Daoism continued. In the following centuries, Sui (589–618 CE) and Tang (618–907 CE) emperors established Daoist monasteries and passed decrees exempting Daoist monks from military service and from most forms of taxes. In time, the monasteries began issuing ordination certificates that attested that the holders of the certificates were monks who had reached a stated level of proficiency in Daoist doctrines. To limit the potential for abuse, in the eighth century the imperial government assumed control of the Daoist ordination process and accepted only certificates at officially sanctioned ordination ceremonies. Daoism reached its greatest splendor during the Tang Dynasty, when the Tang rulers claimed to be descendants of Lao-zi himself. During this era, the most respected and influential leaders within Daoism were members of the Highest Clarity School who were trained in the *Shangqing* revelations.

During the Song Dynasty (960–1279 CE), a number of new Daoist schools appeared. These sects are often grouped according to the regions of their origins into the Southern and the Northern Daoist traditions.

---

[18]Kou specifically was rejecting the practice performed in some early Daoist sects known as the Union of Breaths. This immortality ritual involved a collective sexual orgy in which men and women had intercourse with successive partners without regard to family ties. The practice was based on the theory that semen is the essence of *yang*, which is necessary for long life. According to this theory, because *yang* is considered to be nourished by female orgasm (*yin*), males can prolong life by a ritual that involves intercourse with a succession of female partners, inducing an orgasm in each, while postponing male ejaculation and preserving the vital essence of life.

Southern School Daoism

Among the major Daoist sects that emerged in southern China during the Song Period were the *Tianxin* (Heart of Heaven Sect), the *Shenxiao* (Divine Empyrean Sect), and the *Zhengyi* (Orthodox Unity Sect). Although remnants of each tradition can be found today, the only Southern Daoist tradition that survives as a sect is the Zhengyi.

The Tianxin (Heart of Heaven Sect) was a tradition of healing rituals that were based upon some tenth-century scriptures codified at the Song court by Yuan Mian-tsung. These scriptures taught priests how to heal mental illnesses by drawing spiritual power from the sun, moon, and stars. Its doctrines are still practiced among the Yao in Thailand. The Shenxiao (Divine Empyran Sect) was an early-twelfth-century liturgical tradition that was established by Li Lingsu (1076–1120 CE) during the reign of Song emperor and Daoist patron, Huizong (1100–1125 CE). According to Li, Huizong was a deity (the older brother of the Jade Emperor) who came to the Earth to bring salvation to his subjects. The sect was named after the new liturgy instituted by Li, the Shenxiao ritual, which itself was named after a Heaven that allegedly is above all other heavens. This liturgy, a revision of the earlier *Lingbao* rituals, is still practiced in Taiwan, but it is considered by most modern Daoists to be of inferior quality.

The Zhengyi (Orthodox Unity Sect) is a renovated form of the second-century CE Celestial Masters School. During the Tang Period, the Celestial Masters School was overshadowed by the *Shangqing* and *Lingbao* traditions. At the end of the Northern Song period, however, the Celestial Masters School was renewed by the influence of the 30th Celestial Master, Chang Chi-hsiem, who started the Orthodox Unity movement. Like the Celestial Masters School, this sect is based on the revelations from the Lord Lao to Zhang Daoling. The masters of this school are "hearth dwellers"; that is, they work out of their own homes rather than live in monasteries. Their priests marry, and the priesthood is hereditary, with one son per generation selected to act as the chief priest and carry forward the tradition. People purchase talismans (which allegedly protect them from demons, disease and misfortune) from Zhengyi priests and hire them to perform rites that summon the souls of the dying back into the body, or after death, help them to get through hell. On special occasions, the priests also perform village rituals in temples dedicated to local gods and conduct exorcisms and healing rituals. The ritual tradition is centered on the practice of public confession of sins and on the administration of talismans and amulets to cure disease. The sect is strongest today in Taiwan.

Northern School Daoism

After invasions from the north forced the Song government to retreat to the south of the Yangtze River (1126 CE), a number of new Daoist sects were founded in the occupied North. Attracting followers from all levels of society, the northern sects tended to discard the earlier liturgical traditions, including the use of elixirs of immortality, and attempted to integrate elements of Confucianism and Buddhism into Daoism. Among the major northern sects that emerged during the twelfth century were the *Tai-I* (Supreme Unity Sect), the *Chen-Ta-Dao* (Perfect and Great Way Sect), and the *Chuan-chen* (Complete Perfection Sect).

The Supreme Unity Sect was founded in 1140 CE by the spiritual healer Hsiao Pao-chen. This sect embraced ascetic virtues, prohibited the use of intoxicants, and insisted that its priests remain celibate. It briefly received state patronage after Emperor Hsitung learned of Hsiao's healing powers and invited him to the imperial court. At about this same time, the Perfect and Great Way Sect was founded (1142 CE) by Liu te-jen. Basing its teachings on the *Dao-de-jing* and not on new revelations, this school also discouraged magical practices such as the use of talismans and elixirs and placed a strong emphasis on matters of practical morality and healing through prayer rather than rituals. Both of these sects flourished briefly but died out during the fourteenth century.

The only Northern School tradition to survive into the twenty-first century was the Complete Perfection Sect. This sect was founded in 1163 CE by the soldier-turned-scholar-turned-priest, Wang Zhe (1112–1170 CE). According to tradition, Wang was a disciple of Lu Tung-pin, one of the Eight Immortals[19] of the

---

[19]The belief in the Eight Immortals (Chang Kuo Lao, Chung Li-ch'uan, Ts'ao Kuo-chiu, Lu Tung-pin, Ho Hsien-ku, Li Hsuan, Han Hsiang-tzu, and Lan Ts'ai-ho) developed during the Tang Dynasty. These immortals, who symbolize good fortune, are said to inhabit Mount K'un-lun and are ruled by the Queen Mother of the West who grows the Peaches of Immortality that bestow perpetual life.

Tangs who had ascended into Heaven three centuries earlier. Wang taught that immortality can be achieved by withdrawing from the affairs of the world, cultivating internal spiritual gifts, and harmonizing them with external life. To nurture the *yang* (heaven) and suppress the *yin* (earth), Wang advocated what some would call fanatical asceticism, which included not only moral discipline, meditation, celibate living, and abstinence from meat and wine, but also sleep deprivation. Some members of the sect were said to have lived for a decade without lying down. Supported by the Yuan (Mongol) rulers, the Complete Perfection Sect attained a position of high influence that it has never fully lost. The monastic Complete Perfection Sect along with the communal Orthodox Unity Sect are the two major forms of Daoism today.

Chinese Religions in the Twentieth Century

The Revolution of 1911 ended the imperial system, and with it, institutional Confucianism. Over the ensuing decades there were sporadic attacks on Confucian, Daoist, and Buddhist temples by radicals who argued that the old religions must be removed to make room for the emergence of a new China. After the Communist takeover of China in 1949, government pressures on religion became more systematic. Land owned by monasteries and temples were given to peasants to farm; priests were put to work in the fields like everyone else; and Marxist ideology taught the people that the ancient religions were feudal superstitions that obstructed progress. Before 1966, however, religious activities remained somewhat protected by a Chinese constitution that promised both freedom for and protection from religion.

In 1966, Mao-Ze-dong (1893–1976 CE) led China into a new era. During this phase known as the Great Proletarian Cultural Revolution, Mao stirred the young to revolt against their teachers and to attack all remnants of the evil past that existed before the revolution of 1949. At Mao's urging, Red Guards ransacked temples, destroyed sacred images, and burned the old books. For more than a decade, almost all outward expressions of religion on the mainland disappeared as popular sects were shut down and their leaders humiliated, imprisoned, or executed.

Despite the destruction in mainland China of religious artifacts, after the death of Mao and the removal from power of his wife and top associates (the Gang of Four), many ancient traditions began to resurface. Since the 1980s, China has liberalized its policies toward religion. Temples and a few theological seminaries have been built, and priests and scholars once again are afforded the opportunity to study and write about religion. There also is some evidence to support the revival of popular forms of Chinese religious expressions, including a renewal of interest in Confucian ancestor worship and Daoist funeral rituals. Spirit mediums and sectarian groups, however, are still prohibited, and the willingness of the Marxist regime to continue its liberalization policies and tolerate the spread of organized religion remains in doubt.

SACRED OBSERVANCES AND PRACTICES

Even as the traditional Chinese religions have been waning on the mainland, the ancient religious ideals of the Chinese people have been growing in popularity in overseas communities. From Taiwan to San Francisco, from Tokyo to London, practitioners are adopting Buddhist meditation techniques, using the Confucian divination text *Yi-jing* to assist them in decision making, and turning to Daoist medical practices to maintain their health. China's Three Teachings continue to attract their advocates, although to a lesser degree on the mainland than during China's glorious past.

The willingness of the Chinese to intermingle elements such as Confucian ancestor worship, Daoist funeral rituals, and Buddhist devotional rites has produced a rich and colorful constellation of sacred practices and festivals. On public occasions, worshippers visit the temples to make offerings and ask supplications before the deities they deem to be the most able to meet their circumstantial needs. Popular deities include Kuan Kung, a god of war, healing, and wealth, and Matsu, the Queen of Heaven, who is particularly revered in Taiwan, although multiple other deities also are worshipped throughout the Chinese world at various times and places.

Meanwhile, sacred rites also are performed privately in the homes of the Chinese people across the globe. Some continue to turn to talismans, amulets, or elixirs to protect them from demons and disease, while others seek protection from harm by focusing on moral living, meditation, abstinence from meat and wine, and/or prayers to their household deities. Many also set aside a space in their homes as a shrine to their ancestral spirits and hang above the stove an image of Zao Jun, the guardian kitchen god. In a popular celebration held as the lunar New Year approaches, many Chinese ritually dispatch Zao Jun to heaven to report to the Jade Emperor Yu Huang how each family member has behaved during the year. The New Year Festival continues with the worship of the tutelary deities of the home, of Heaven and Earth, and of the ancestors; it concludes with a feast that honors the eldest couple in the family followed by several days of familial visitation.

Other major seasonal observances include the early spring Clear and Brightness Day, the early summer Dragon Boat Festival, and the mid-autumn Harvest Moon Festival. Clear and Brightness Day is a day set aside for mourning the dead, for cleaning and repairing grave sites, and for enjoying amusements such as kite-flying and dog races. This festival falls during the third lunar month at the onset of warmer weather and the budding of new life. On the fifth day of the fifth month, the Dragon Boat Festival commemorates the death of the despondent poet Qu Yuan who drowned himself in the third century BCE after losing the trust of his lord. To celebrate this occasion, people row boats into a local river and throw bamboo filled with rice as an offering to the great ancient poet. Later in the year, at the appearance of the full moon around the time of the autumn equinox, the Harvest Moon Festival commemorates the ancient custom of the emperor asking Heaven for a prosperous year. On this occasion families reunite, exchange gifts, and eat circular moon cakes traditionally presented as offerings to the moon goddess. Like the seasonal festivals of many great religions, these once-sacred observances have evolved in modern times into more secular celebrations of playful amusement and familial visitations.

SOURCES

The most important works in the Confucian canon are the *Five Classics* and the *Four Books*. In the following collection, all nine of these Confucian classics are represented, including extensive selections from the *Analects*, the recorded words of Confucius. This anthology also includes numerous passages from the most influential works within Philosophical Daoism, the *Dao-de-jing* and the *Zhuang-zi*, as well as selected excerpts from the *Zhengyi, Shangqing,* and *Lingbao* scriptures—the sacred writings of the major traditions within Religious Daoism.

SECTION 1: Beginnings: God, Time, and the Universe

PART A

CONFUCIAN TEXTS

Within the traditional Confucian canon of the *Five Classics* and the *Four Books*, a beautiful poem about the birth of the father of the Chinese people is found in the *Book of Odes*. This book, which contains 305 ancient poems, is one of the *Five Classics* traditionally ascribed to Confucius. As you read this song, reflect on its meaning. What is special about the birth of How-tsieh? What ancient sacred traditions does the song affirm?

CREATION STORIES FROM THE *BOOK OF ODES*

The Song of How-tsieh[20]

The first birth of our people
Was from Keang Yuen.
How did she give birth to our people?
She had presented a pure offering and sacrifice,
that her childlessness might be taken away.
She then trod on a toe-print made by God, and was moved,
In the large place where she rested.
She became pregnant; she dwelt retired;
She gave birth to, and nourished a son,
Who was How-tsieh.

When she had fulfilled her months,
Her first-born son came forth like a lamb,
There was no bursting, nor rending,
No injury, no hurt;—
Showing how wonderful he would be.
Did not God give her the comfort?
Had he not accepted her pure offering and sacrifice,
So that thus easily she brought forth her son?

---

[20]*The Chinese Classics*, Vol. IV, translated by James Legge, *The Shih King*, Parts I and II (London: Trubner and Company, 1871).

He was placed in a narrow lane,
But the sheep and oxen protected him with loving care.
He was placed in a wide forest,
Where he was met with by the woodcutters.
He was placed on the cold ice,
And a bird screened and supported him with its wings.

When the bird went wasy,
How-tsieh began to wail;
His cry was long and loud,
So that his voice filled the whole way.

When he was able to crawl,
He looked majestic and intelligent.
When he was able to feed himself,
He fell to planting large beans.
The beans grew luxuriantly;
His rows of paddy shot up beautifully;
His hemp and wheat grew strong and close;
His gourds yielded abundantly.

We load the stands with the offerings,
The stands both of wood and of earthenware.
As soon as the fragrance ascends,
God, well pleased, smells the sweet savour.
Fragrant is it, and in its due season!
How-tsieh founded the sacrifice,
And no one, we presume, has given occasion for blame or
    regret
In regard to it, down to the present day.

Another collection in the *Five Classics* is the *Book of Rites*. The following selection from this classic discusses the origins of the universe. According to this passage, what is the relationship between creation itself and human nature?

CREATION STORIES FROM THE *BOOK OF RITES*[21]

The Nature of the Universe and Man

Man is a product of the attributes of heaven and earth, by the interaction of the dual forces of nature, the union of the animal and intelligent souls, and the finest subtle matter of the five elements.

Heaven exercises the control of the strong and light force and hangs out the sun and stars. Earth exercises the control of the dark and weaker force and gives vent to it in the hills and steams. The five ele-

---

[21]Robert Ballou, ed. *The Bible of the World* (New York: The Viking Press, 1939), pp. 379–380, taken from the translation by James Legge in *Sacred Books of China* (Oxford: The Clarendon Press, 1885).

ments are distributed through the four seasons, and it is by their harmonious action that the moon is produced, which therefore keeps waxing for fifteen days and waning for fifteen.

The five elements in their movements alternately displace and exhaust one another. Each one of them, in the revolving course of the twelve months of the four seasons, comes to be in its turn the fundamental one for the time.

The five notes of harmony, with their six upper musical accords, and the twelve pitch tubes, come each, in their revolutions among themselves, to be the first note of the scale.

The five flavors, with the six condiments, and the twelve articles of diet, come each one, their revolutions in the course of a year, to give its character to the food.

The five colors, with the six elegant figures, which they form on the two robes, come each one, in their revolutions among themselves, to give the character of the dress that is worn.

Therefore man is the heart and mind of heaven and earth, and the visible embodiment of the five elements. He lives in the enjoyment of all flavors, the discriminating of all notes of harmony, and the enrobing of all colors.

Thus it was that when the sages would make rules for men, they felt it necessary to find the origin of all things in heaven and earth; to make the two forces of nature the commencement of all; to use the four seasons as the handle of their arrangements; to adopt the sun and stars as the recorders of time, the moon as the measure of work to be done, the spirits breathing in nature as associates, the five elements as giving substance to things, rules of propriety and righteousness as their instruments, the feelings of men as the field to be cultivated, and the four intelligent creatures as domestic animals to be reared.

The origin of all things being found in heaven and earth, they could be taken in hand, one after the other.

The idea that the cosmos operates through forces of its own, without anthropomorphic deities, also is expressed in the famous Confucian classic the *Book of Changes*. Originally a book of divination, the *Book of Changes* later became the subject of numerous philosophical commentaries by eminent Chinese thinkers. The first 2 of the 64 symbols presented in the *Book of Changes* are Ch'ien (The Creative,

Heaven) and K'un (The Receptive, Earth). Presented here is the Commentary section for each of these hexagrams. What philosophical principles regarding the creation process are suggested in these commentaries?

COMMENTARIES ON HEAVEN AND EARTH FROM THE *BOOK OF CHANGES*[22]

Ch'ien (The Creative, Heaven)

Commentary: Great indeed is ch'ien the ultimate source. The ten thousand things receive their beginnings from it. It governs Heaven. The clouds drift by and the rain falls. All things flow into their forms. The ends and the beginnings are greatly illuminated. The six lines of the hexagram take shape at their own times.

In timely fashion they ride the six dragons and so rule over the heavens. The way of ch'ien is change and transformation. Each thing thereby achieves its true nature and destiny and assures that it is in accord with great harmony. There is great benefit and constancy. It stands out from all the things of the world, and the nations of the earth enjoy peace.

K'un (The Receptive, Earth)

Commentary: Great indeed is that originating in k'un. The ten thousand things all receive life from it when it is in harmonious union with Heaven. K'un contains everything in abundance. Its virtue is in harmony with the infinite. It encompasses all things and illuminates the universe. Each individual thing achieves perfect success. The mare is an animal of the land. It wanders freely over the land. It is gentle and obedient and symbolizes great benefit through perseverance. The gentleman should conduct himself in like manner. At first he may lose his way, but later by being humbly obedient he will achieve it forever. In the west and south there are friends. One may associate with people of a sympathetic nature. In the east and north there are no friends, but in the end one may gain benefit from this. The good fortune of peaceful perseverance will result from being in harmony with the forces of the Earth.

---

[22]Quoted from Deborah Sommer, ed. *Chinese Religion: An Anthology of Sources* (New York: Oxford University Press, 1995), p. 5.

PART B
DAOIST TEXTS

The sacred texts of the great Western traditions offer answers to questions pertaining to the origins of humanity and to the beginnings of the cosmos itself. The authors of these texts were generally content to assert that creation was an act of a God who was before the beginning. Eastern sages, however, pushed the boundaries of time back even further, pondering the still earlier questions, Who created God, and what was before there was being? For the ancient Chinese, the answers to these perplexing questions were contained in the concept *Dao*. This single word, sometimes translated into English as "The Way," cannot be defined in a short phrase. In fact, according to the Chinese texts, *Dao* cannot be defined at all. Yet, for many ancients, to become one with *Dao* was the ultimate purpose of creation.

The opening selections in this section are taken from the two most important collections within Philosophical Daoism, the *Dao-de-jing* and the *Zhuang-zi*. How do the authors of these passages attempt to describe the indescribable *Dao*? In what ways are their concepts of *Dao* similar to and different from Judaism's Yahweh, Christianity's Holy Trinity, Islam's Allah, and Hinduism's Brahma?

DESCRIPTIONS OF THE *DAO* FROM THE *DAO-DE-JING*[23]

1. The Dao that can be told is not the eternal Dao
   The name that can be named is not the eternal Name.
   The unnameable is the eternally real.
   Naming is the origin of all particular things.
   Free from desire, you realize the mystery.
   Caught in desire, you see only the manifestations.
   Yet mystery and manifestations arise from the same source.
   This source is called darkness.
   Darkness within darkness.
   The gateway to all understanding.

2. When people see some things as beautiful, other things become ugly.
   When people see some things as good, other things become bad.

---

[23]Translation by S. Mitchell.

Being and non-being create each other.
Difficult and easy support each other.
Long and short define each other.
High and low depend on each other.
Before and after follow each other.
Therefore the Master acts without doing anything
and teaches without saying anything.
Things arise and she lets them come;
things disappear and she lets them go.
She has but doesn't possess, acts but doesn't expect.
When her work is done, she forgets it.
That is why it lasts forever. . . .

4. The Dao is like a well: used but never used up.
It is like the eternal void: filled with infinite
   possibilities.
It is hidden but always present.
I don't know who gave birth to it.
It is older than God. . . .

7. The Dao is infinite, eternal.
Why is it eternal?
It was never born; thus it can never die.
Why is it infinite?
It has no desires for itself; thus it is present for all
   beings.
The Master stays behind; that is why she is ahead.
She is detached from all things; that is why she is one
   with them.
Because she has let go of herself, she is perfectly
   fulfilled. . . .

14. Look, and it can't be seen.
Listen, and it can't be heard.
Reach, and it can't be grasped.
Above, it isn't bright.
Below, it isn't dark.
Seamless, unnameable, it returns to the realm of
   nothing.
Form that includes all forms, image without an image,
subtle, beyond all conception.
Approach it and there is no beginning; follow it and
   there is no end.
You can't know it, but you can be it, at ease in your
   own life.
Just realize where you come from: this is the essence of
   wisdom. . . .

25. There was something formless and perfect before the
   universe was born.
It is serene. Empty. Solitary. Unchanging. Infinite.
   Eternally present.
It is the mother of the universe.
For lack of a better name, I call it the Dao.
It flows through all things, inside and outside, and
   returns

to the origin of all things.
The Dao is great. The universe is great. Earth is great.
   Man is great.
These are the four great powers.
Man follows the earth.
Earth follows the universe.
The universe follows the Tao.
The Dao follows only itself. . . .

52. In the beginning was the Dao.
All things issue from it; all things return to it.
To find the origin, trace back the manifestations.
When you recognize the children and find the mother,
you will be free of sorrow.
If you close your mind in judgments and traffic with
   desires,
your heart will be troubled.
If you keep your mind from judging and aren't led by
   the senses,
your heart will find peace.
Seeing into darkness is clarity.
Knowing how to yield is strength.
Use your own light and return to the source of light.
This is called practicing eternity.

DESCRIPTIONS OF THE *DAO* FROM THE *ZHUANG-ZI*, 6

The Dao has its reality and its signs but is without action or form. You can hand it down but you cannot receive it; you can get it but you cannot see it. It is its own source, its own root. Before heaven and earth existed it was there, firm from ancient times. It gave spirituality to the spirits and to God; it gave birth to heaven and to earth. It exists beyond the highest point, and yet you cannot call it lofty; it exists beneath the limit of the six directions, and yet you cannot call it deep. It was born before heaven and earth, and yet you cannot say it has been there for long; it is earlier than the earliest time, and yet you cannot call it old.

Creation texts also abound in the canons of Religious Daoism. Two such creation stories are presented here. The first is a Tang Dynasty (618–906 CE) text from the *Shangqing* tradition that is included in *The Scripture of How the Highest Venerable Lord Opens the Cosmos.* This piece attempts to integrate the early philosophical views on the origins of the cosmos first expressed in the Confucian classic, the *Book of Changes,* with the later Daoist beliefs regarding the transformations and reappearance of the Lord Lao-zi. Its opening, "Thus I have heard," also suggests the influence of Buddhism. The second selection is taken from *The Scripture of Purity and Tranquility.* This scripture became prominent in the Song Dynasty (960–1260 CE) and remains a popular devotional text that is often recited by monks in the Complete Perfection Sect. What do these texts tell us about Religious Daoist beliefs concerning creation?

CREATION STORIES WITHIN RELIGIOUS DAOISM
From the Scripture of How the Highest Venerable Lord Opens the Cosmos[24]

[1a] Thus I have heard. Before heaven and earth opened, all was endless beyond Great Clarity; all was limitless in Barren Nonbeing. Desolate and vast it was, and without bounds.

> No heaven nor earth: no yin nor yang,
> no sun nor moon: no brightness nor radiance,
> no east nor west: no green nor yellow,
> no south nor north: no soft nor hard,
> no cover nor support: no embrace nor closeness,
> no wisdom nor sageliness: no loyalty nor goodness,
> no going nor coming: no arising nor passing,
> no front nor back: no round nor square.

It transformed hundreds of millions of times, all grand and vast, vast and grand! No shape nor sign. Pure so-being and emptiness! Oh, how unfathomable!

> No measure nor end: no high nor low,
> no even nor odd: no left nor right,
> Above and below, in pure so-being alone.

The Venerable Lord, the Dao, was at rest in open mystery, beyond silent desolation, in mysterious emptiness. Look and do not see, [1b] listen and do not hear. Say it/he is thee and do not see a shape; say it/he is not there, yet all beings follow him for life. Beyond the eight bonds—slowly, slowly—first it divides. Sinks to form the subtle and the wondrous, to make the world.

Then there was Vast Prime [Hongyuan]. In the time of Vast Prime, there still was no heaven and no earth, the empty void had not yet separated, clear and turbid were not yet divided. In mysterious barrenness and silent desolation, Vast Prime continued for a myriad kalpas.

Then Vast Prime divided, and there was Coagulated Prime [Hunyan]. Coagulated Prime continued for a myriad kalpas until it reached its perfection. Its perfection lasted for eighty-one times ten thousand years.

Then there was Grand Antecedence [Taichu]. In the time of Grand Antecedence, the Venerable Lord descended from barren emptiness to be the teacher of grand Antecedence. His mouth brought forth the Scripture of Opening the Cosmos in one section and forty-eight times ten thousand characters. Each character was one hundred square miles in size. Thus he taught Grand Antecedence.

In Grand Antecedence, for the first time he separated heaven and earth, the clear and the turbid. [2a] He divided boundless galaxies and vast nebulae. He set up shapes and signs. He secured north and south. He ordered east and west. He opened the darkness and made light. He positioned the four universal mainstays.

Above and below, inside and out, within and without, long and short, gross and subtle, female and male, white and black, big and small, noble and humble—all were constantly moving along in darkness.

But when Coagulated Prime attained the Scripture of Opening of the Cosmos of The Venerable Lord, clear and turbid were separated. Clear energy rose up and formed heaven. Turbid energy sank down and formed earth. The three spheres were established. Then, for the first time, there were heaven and earth.

From the Scripture of Purity and Tranquility[25]

The Great Dao has no form;
It brings forth and raises heaven and earth.
The Great Dao has no feelings;
It regulates the course of the sun and the moon.
The Great Dao has no name;
It raises and nourishes the myriad beings.
I do not know its name—
So I call it Dao.
The Dao can be pure or turbid, moving or tranquil.
Heaven is pure, earth is turbid;
Heaven is moving, earth is tranquil.
The male is moving, the female is tranquil.
Descending from the origin,
Flowing toward the end,
The myriad begins are being born.

---

[24]Livia Kohn, *The Taoist Experience: An Anthology* (Albany, NY: State University of New York Press, 1993), pp. 35–37.

[25]Kohn, *The Taoist Experience*, p. 25.

Purity—the source of turbidity,
Movement—the root of tranquility.
Always be pure and tranquil;
Heaven and earth
Return to the primordial.

SECTION 2: Humanity: The Problem of Good and Evil

PART A

CONFUCIAN TEXTS

Most sacred canons do not present a monolithic and consistent philosophy of human nature, but rather include an assortment of statements about the human condition that subsequent commentators use to construct systematic belief systems. In this respect, the Confucian canon is no exception. Although a distinguishing mark of traditional Confucianism is the belief in the natural goodness of humanity, ancient poems in the *Book of Odes* and the words ascribed to Confucius in the *Analects* are more ambiguous about human nature than are subsequent statements contained in the sacred canon. Included in this section are selections from the ancient *Book of Odes* and the *Analects* followed by selections from later Confucian scholars, Mencius (Men-zi) and Hsun Tzu (Xun-zi). In what ways do the arguments of the later Confucians agree with the thoughts of Confucius and the poets of antiquity? On what do these thinkers agree and disagree?

CONFUCIAN DESCRIPTIONS OF HUMAN NATURE FROM THE BOOK OF ODES

How vast is God,
The ruler of men below!
How arrayed in terrors is God,
With many things irregular in his ordinations.
Heaven gave birth to the multitudes of the people,
But the nature it confers is not to be depended on.
All are good at first,
But few prove themselves to be so at the last.

King Wan said, "Alas!
Alas, you sovereign of Shang,
People have a saying,
'When a tree falls utterly,
While its branches and leaves are yet uninjured,

It must first have been uprooted,'
The beacon of iu is not far distant;—
It is in the age of the last sovereign of Hsia."

FROM THE ANALECTS

4:6 Confucius said: "I have never seen one who really loves ren or really hates non-jen. If you really loved ren you would not place anything above it. If you really hated the non-jen, you would not let it near you. Is there anyone who has devoted their strength to ren for a single day? I have not seen anyone who has lacked the strength to do so. Perhaps there has been such a case, but I have never seen it."

5:10 Confucius said: "I have not yet met a really solid man." Someone said, "What about Shan Ch'ang?" Confucius said, "Ch'ang is ruled by lust. How could he be solid?"

5:26 Confucius said: "It's all over! I have not yet met someone who can see his own faults and correct them within himself."

6:17 Confucius said: "People are straightforward at birth. Once they lose this, they rely on luck to avoid trouble."

6:19 Confucius said: "You can teach high-level topics to those of above-average ability, but you can't teach high-level topics to those of less than average ability."

6:27 Confucius said: "Even over a long period of time, there have been few people who have actualized the Mean into Manifest Virtue."

8:12 Confucius said: "It is quite rare to see someone who applies himself to the study of something for three years without having a noticeable result."

9:17 Confucius said: "I have never seen one who loves virtue as much as he loves sex."

9:21 Confucius said: "There are some who sprout but do not blossom, some who blossom but do not bear fruit."

15:3 Confucius said: "Yu, those who understand virtue are few and far between."

17:2 Confucius said: "People are similar by nature, but through habituation become quite different from each other."

17:3 Confucius said: "Only the most wise and the most foolish do not change."

FROM THE BOOK OF MENCIUS[26]

6A:2 Kao Tzu said: "Human nature is like whirling water. If you let it out on the east side, it will go east. If you let it out on the west side, it will go west. Similarly, human nature has no predisposition for good or evil, just as water has no predisposition for east or west."

Mencius said: "It is true that water has no predisposition for east or west. But doesn't it have a predisposition for up

---

[26]The source of the material is an Internet translation by Charles Muller.

and down? The goodness of the human nature is just like the downward tendency of water. Just as all water has a down-going tendency, all people have a tendency toward goodness." "Now you can splash water and make it fly over your head, or you can dam it and force it uphill, but these are after all, forcing it. You can push people into doing evil, but that is not their basic nature."

6A:6 Kung Tu-tzu said: "Kao Tzu says that human nature is neither good nor evil. Others say that human nature can be made good or evil. That is why when Kings Wen and Wu were in power, the people loved goodness, and when Yu and Li were in power, they enjoyed inflicting pain.

"Still others say that some people are inherently good and some are inherently evil. Therefore, under a good ruler like Yao, there was such an evil man as Hsiang; and to such a bad father as Ku-sou, a good son Shun was born; and with a nephew of the senior branch as evil as Chou on the throne, such good uncles as Ch'i, Viscount of Wei, and Prince Pi Kan lived.

"Now you say that human beings are inherently good. Then are all the others wrong?"

Mencius said: "When I say human beings are inherently good, I am talking about their most fundamental emotional qualities. If someone does evil, it is not the fault of their natural endowment. Everyone has the feeling of concern for the well-being of others; everyone has the sense of shame and disgust at their own evil; everyone has the sense to treat others courteously and respectfully; everyone has the sense of right and wrong.

"The feeling of concern for the well-being of others is ren. The sense of shame and disgust is Righteousness; the sense to treat others with courtesy and respect is Propriety. The sense of right and wrong is Wisdom.

"Ren, Righteousness, Propriety and Wisdom are not forced onto us from the outside. They are our original endowments—you have really not thought it through, have you?

"Thus it is said: 'If you strive for it, you will gain it; if you ignore it, you will lose it.' Men differ in terms of actualization: some are double, some fivefold and some manifest it to an incalculable degree. This difference is because some are not able to fully develop their natural endowments. . . ."

6A:7 Mencius said: "In years of good harvest the children are wholesome; in years of bad harvest, they are incorrigible. This is not because Heaven sends down different endowments of ability, but because their minds being sunk in depression.

"Now if you plant wheat and barley and cover them, and the soil is the same and the cultivation times are the same, they will all grow strongly. When it comes to their ripening time and there are differences, it is because of differences in soil fertility, the nourishment from rain or the amount of care-taking done by the farmers.

"So whenever things are of the same species, they will resemble each other. This being so, how could we doubt that it is the same with men? I and the sage are of the same species. Therefore, Lung-tzu said: 'Even if I don't know the foot-size

when making sandals, I know enough that I won't make bushel baskets.' The similarity in sandals is because of the similarity in feet.

"We also have similarities in taste. That's how Yi Ya [*A legendary famous cook in ancient China.*] knows what I like beforehand. Imagine if his taste was inherently different than that of others like that of another species such as dog or horse. How could everybody love the taste of Yi Ya's cooking? The fact that everybody agrees that Yi Ya's cooking is the best shows the sameness in people's taste.

"It is the same with the ear. The fact that everyone takes the music of Conductor K'uang as the best, shows the sameness in the ears of everyone.

"It is the same with the eyes. Everyone knows that there is no one in the world as attractive as Tzu Tu. And if you don't think she is beautiful, you are blind.

"Therefore I say, there is a standard for taste, there is a standard for music, and there is a standard for beauty. Shouldn't it also be so with the things of the mind? What is it that is the same with people's minds? It is that they know the same principle and the same Righteousness. The sage knows the sameness of our minds beforehand. Therefore his principles and Righteousness fit to our minds, in the same way that the meat of grain-eating animals fits our taste."

FROM HSUN TZE'S "HUMAN NATURE IS EVIL"[27]

Human nature is evil; its goodness is conscious effort. The nature of people today is such that from birth they covet profit. To accommodate their covetousness they struggle and fight for their lives, and courtesy and civility vanish. From birth they bear violent hatreds, and to accommodate those hatreds they resort to violence and banditry, and loyalty and good faith disappear. From birth they have the desires of the ear and eye and fondness for sound and color; to accommodate those desires they resort to wanton behavior, and refined principles of ritual and righteousness evaporate. If people follow their natures and accommodate their emotions, struggling and fighting will invariable ensue, and they will transgress their stations in life, upset principles, and turn to violence. Only with the transformations of standards and teachers and the ways of ritual and righteousness can courtesy and civility appear, and under those circumstances, people can develop refined culture and principles and turn to good governance. If one looks at it

People must change to stop evil

[27]Deborah Sommer, ed. *Chinese Religion: An Anthology of Sources* (New York: Oxford University Press, 1995), p. 69.

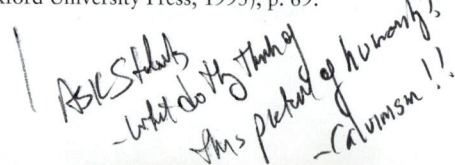

Ask Students – what do they think of this picture of humanity? –Calvinism!!

How do people change? How is evil quelled?

6 / Chinese Religions   289

this way, then it is clear that human nature is evil, and that goodness is conscious effort.

A bent piece of wood can only be straightened by steaming, and a dull piece of metal can only be sharpened by grinding it against a whetstone. Now considering that human nature is evil, it can only be rectified with standards and teachers, and it can only be well governed with the application of ritual and righteousness. If people have no standards or teachers, they will waver perilously and lack rectitude; without rites or righteousness they will be intractable, disorderly, and badly governed. In antiquity the sage kings perceived all this. They initiated rituals and righteousness and formulated standards and various measures to straighten and enhance human nature and emotions; they did this to rectify them, to train and transform them, and to guide them. Thus everything was well governed and everything accorded with the Way. People today who are transformed by teachers and standards, who develop refined culture and learning, who follow the ways of ritual and righteousness, become honorable persons. Those who just go along with their natures and emotions, are satisfied with wantonness, and go contrary to ritual, are small-minded people. If one looks at it this way, it is clear that human nature is evil.

Importance of Teachers

PART B

DAOIST TEXTS

The scriptures of Philosophical Daoism also confront questions regarding the human condition. The following selections from the *Zhuang-zi* detail a Daoist understanding of the original condition of humanity. According to *Zhuang-zi,* how has the human condition changed since ancient times? How can humans reclaim their original mind?

DAOIST DESCRIPTIONS OF HUMAN NATURE FROM THE *ZHUANG-ZI*

He [the sage] wears the human form without human passions. Because he wears the human form he associates with men. Because he has not human passions the questions of right and wrong do not touch him. Infinitesimal indeed is that which belongs to the hu-

man; infinitely great is that which is completed in God.

Hueitse said to Zhuangzi, "Do men indeed originally have no passions?"

"Certainly," replied Zhuangzi.

"But if a man has no passions," argued Hueitse, "what is it that makes him a man?"

"Dao," replied Zhuangzi, "gives him his expressions, and God gives him his form. How should he not be a man?"

"If then he is a man," said Hueitse, "how can he be without passions?"

"Right and wrong (approval and disapproval)," answered Zhuangzi, "are what I mean by passions. By a man without passions I mean one who does not permit likes and dislikes to disturb his internal economy, but rather falls in line with nature and does not try to improve upon (the materials of) living."

"But how is a man to live this bodily life," asked Hueitse.

"He does not try to improve upon (the materials of) his living?"

"Dao gives him his expression," said Zhuangzi, "and God gives him his form. He should not permit likes and dislikes to disturb his internal economy. But now you are devoting your intelligence to externals, and wearing out your vital spirit. Lean against a tree and sing; or sit against a table and sleep! God has made you a shapely sight, yet your only thought is the hard and white."

ON TOLERANCE

Ts'ui Chu: asked Lao Tan {57}, saying, "If the empire is not to be governed, how are men's hearts to be kept good?"

"Be careful," replied Lao Tan, "not to interfere with the natural goodness of the heart of man. Man's heart may be forced down or stirred up. In each case the issue is fatal. By gentleness, the hardest heart may be softened. But try to cut and polish it, and it will glow like fire or freeze like ice. In the twinkling of an eye it will pass beyond the limits of the Four Seas. In repose, it is profoundly still; in motion, it flies up to the sky. Like an unruly horse, it cannot be held in check. Such is the human heart."

Of old, the Yellow Emperor first interfered with the natural goodness of the heart of man, by means of charity and duty. In consequence, Yao and Shun wore the hair off their legs and the flesh off their arms in endeavoring to feed their people's bodies. They tortured the people's internal economy in order to conform to charity and duty. They exhausted the people's energies to live in accordance with the laws and statutes. Even then they did not succeed. Thereupon, Yao (had to) confine Huantou on Mount Ts'ung, exile the chiefs of the Three Miaos and their people into the Three Weis, and banish the Minister of Works to Yutu, which shows he had not succeeded. When it came to the times of the Three Kings, {58} the empire was in a state of foment. Among the bad men were Chieh and Cheh; among the good were Tseng and Shih. By and by, the Confucianists and the Motseanists arose; and then came confusion between joy and anger, fraud between the simple and the cunning, recrimination between the virtuous and the evil-minded, slander between the honest and the liars, and the world order collapsed. Then the great virtue lost its unity, men's lives were frustrated. When there was a general rush for knowledge, the people's desires ever went beyond their possessions. The next thing was then to invent axes and saws, to kill by laws and statutes, to disfigure by chisels and awls. The empire seethed with discontent, the blame for which rests upon those who would interfere with the natural goodness of the heart of man.

In consequence, virtuous men sought refuge in mountain caves, while rulers of great states sat trembling in their ancestral halls. Then, when dead men lay about pillowed on each other's corpses, when cangued prisoners jostled each other in crowds and condemned criminals were seen everywhere, then the Confucianists and the Motseanists bustled about and rolled up their sleeves in the midst of gyves and fetters! Alas, they know not shame, nor what it is to blush!

SECTION 3: Sacred Stories: Divine Messengers, Prophets, and Priests

Among the founders of the two great religious traditions indigenous to China, Confucius and Lao-zi, much is known about one, and little is known of the other. Of Confucius, we know a great deal. For centuries, Confucius was credited with editing or writing the *Five Classics* of Chinese history and culture. Although modern scholars no longer attribute all the classics to him, there is little doubt that Confucius

both drew his teachings from these writings and left his imprint upon them. In addition to the *Five Classics*, the disciples of Confucius converted a collection of his teachings to memory, and following his death, produced a collection of Confucian sayings and dialogues known as the *Analects*. Although not written as a narrative, this text provides us with a wealth of knowledge about both the humanity and the teachings of Confucius.

Unfortunately, few details about the life of Lao-zi are extant. Scholars still are debating the question as to whether Lao-zi was a legendary figure or a historic individual. The name *Lao-zi* means simply "Old Master." More is known about Daoism's other founder, Zhuang-zi, a thinker who was to Lao-zi what Plato was to Socrates and St. Paul was to Jesus. By popularizing and expounding the Old Master's obscure teachings, Zhuang-zi was largely responsible for creating the Daoist philosophical tradition.

PART A

CONFUCIAN TEXTS

The opening selections are taken from the *Analects*. From these historical nuggets, attempt to construct a life portrait of Confucius. What type of individual was he? In what ways was he like and unlike the founders of the other traditions you have studied in this volume?

THE LIFE OF CONFUCIUS FROM THE *ANALECTS*

2:4 Confucius said: "At fifteen my heart was set on learning; at thirty I stood firm; at forty I had no more doubts; at fifty I knew the mandate of heaven; at sixty my ear was obedient; at seventy I could follow my heart's desire without transgressing the norm."

3:15 When Confucius entered the Grand Temple, he asked about everything. Someone said, "Who said Confucius is a master of ritual? He enters the Grand Temple and asks about everything!" Confucius, hearing this, said, "This is the ritual."

4:14 Confucius said: "I don't worry about not having a good position; I worry about the means I use to gain position. I don't worry about being unknown; I seek to be known in the right way."

4:31 Tzu Kung was correcting people. Confucius said, "Ssu (Tzu Kung) must be a superman. I have no spare time to do this."

5:1 Confucius said of Kung Ye Chang that he was fit for marriage. Even though he was arrested once, he had been innocent; therefore Confucius gave him his daughter in marriage. Confucius said of Nan Yung that if the Dao prevailed in the state he would never lack an official post. If the Dao was lacking in the state, he would avoid getting into trouble. He gave him the daughter of his own elder brother in marriage.

5:25 Yen Yüan and Tzu Lu were by the Master's side. He said to them: "Why don't each of you tell me of your aspirations?" Tzu Lu said, "I would like to have wagons, horses and light fur coats to give to my friends, and if they damaged them, not to get angry." Yen Yüan said, "I would like not to be proud of my good points and not to show off my works." Tzu Lu said, "What are your wishes, Teacher?" Confucius said, "I would like to give comfort to the aged, trust to my friends and nurturance to the young."

5:27 Confucius said: "In a hamlet of ten families there must be someone as loyal and trustworthy as I. But I doubt there will be someone as fond of study."

7:1 Confucius said: "I am a transmitter, rather than an original thinker. I trust and enjoy the teachings of the ancients. In my heart I compare myself to old P'eng."

7:2 Confucius said: "Keeping silent and thinking; studying without satiety, teaching others without weariness: these things come natural to me."

7:3 Confucius said: "Having virtue and not cultivating it; studying and not sifting; hearing what is just and not following; not being able to change wrongdoing: these are the things that make me uncomfortable."

7:4 During the Master's leisure time he was relaxed and enjoyed himself.

7:7 Confucius said: "From the one who brought a bundle of dried meat (the poorest person) upwards, I have never denied a person my instruction."

7:8 Confucius said: "If a student is not eager, I won't teach him; if he is not struggling with the truth, I won't reveal it to him. If I lift up one corner and he can't come back with the other three, I won't do it again."

7:9 If the Master sat beside a person in mourning, he would not eat to the full. If he had wept on a certain day, he would not sing.

7:12 The things with which the Master was cautious, were fasting, war and sickness.

7:15 Confucius said: "I can live with coarse rice to eat, water for drink and my arm as a pillow and still be happy. Wealth and honors that one possesses in the midst of injustice are like floating clouds."

7:17 Topics which the Teacher regularly discussed were the Book of Odes, the Book of History, and the maintenance of propriety. These were the topics which he regularly discussed.

7:18 The Duke of Sheh asked Tzu Lu about Confucius. Tzu Lu didn't answer him. The Teacher said, "Why didn't you just tell him that I am a man who in eagerness for study forgets to eat, in his enjoyment of it, forgets his problems and who is unaware of old age setting in?"

7:19 Confucius said: "I was not born with wisdom. I love the ancient teachings and have worked hard to attain to their level."

7:20 The master never discussed strange phenomena, physical exploits, disorder or ghost stories.

7:24 The Master taught four things: Culture, correct action, loyalty and trust.

7:26 When the Master went fishing, he did not use a net; when he hunted, he would not shoot at a perched bird.

7:31 When the Teacher was singing with someone, and he found out that they sang well, he would make them start over again, and he would sing the harmony.

7:32 Confucius said: "In literature, perhaps I am equal to others. But I cannot manifest the behavior of the Superior Man."

7:33 Confucius said: "I dare not claim to be a sage or a man of ren. But I strive for these without being disappointed, and I teach without becoming weary. This is what can be said of me." Kung Hsi Hua said, "It is exactly these qualities that cannot be learned by the disciples."

7:37 The Master was mild yet strict, authoritative yet not mean, courteous, yet relaxed.

9:4 There were four things the master had eliminated from himself: imposing his will, arbitrariness, stubbornness and egotism.

9:15 Confucius said: "When out in the world, I served my ruler and ministers. At home I served my father and elder brothers. I never dared to take funerals lightly and I didn't get into trouble with alcohol. What problems could I possibly have?"

10:12 There was a fire in the stables. When the Master returned from court, he asked: "Was anybody hurt?" He didn't ask about the horses.

11:8 When Yen Yüan died, the master cried: "How cruel! Heaven is killing me! Heaven is killing me!"

11:9 When Yen Hui died, the Master wept uncontrollably. The disciples said, "Master, you are going overboard with this!" Confucius said, "Going overboard?! If I can't cry now, when should I cry?"

16:13 Ch'an K'ang asked Po Yu (Confucius' son): "Have you heard anything from your father different than we disciples have?" Po Yu replied, "Not yet. Once, when my father was standing by himself, I passed by the hall quickly, and he said, 'Have you learned the Book of Odes yet?' I said, 'Not yet.' So I went and studied the Book of Odes. On another day, the same scene occurred, and he asked me, 'Have you learned the Record of Propriety yet?' I said, 'Not yet.' He said, 'If you don't learn propriety you will have no structure.' So I went and studied the Propriety. I have only heard these two things." Ch'an K'ang left, elated, saying, "I questioned on

one thing and got three! I learned about the Poems, I learned about the Propriety and I learned that the Superior Man is not partial to his son."

PART B

DAOIST TEXTS

Despite the lack of historical evidence about the life of Lao-zi, the canon of Religious Daoism is filled with stories of his deified status. The following excerpt about the life of Lao-zi is taken from an early fourth-century CE text *Introduction to the Scripture of Lao-zi's Ascension to the West and Conversion of the Barbarians.*

THE LIFE OF LAO-ZI FROM THE INTRODUCTION TO THE SCRIPTURE OF LAO-ZI'S ASCENSION[28]

In the year *gengchen,* on the fifteen day of the second month, [Lao-zi] was born in Bo. Nine dragons sprinkled water over him to rinse and wash his body; then they transformed into nine springs.

At that time, the Venerable Lord had white hair. He was able to walk upon birth. A lotus flower spouted under each step he took. After nine steps, he pointed to heaven with his left hand, to the end with his right hand and announced to the people: "In heaven above, on the earth below, I alone am venerable. I shall reveal the highest law of the Dao. I shall save all things moving and growing, the entire host of living beings. I shall wander across the ten directions and reach to the dark prisons of the underworld. I shall lead all those not yet saved and all those lost in error to certain salvation."

Hidden and apparent among humanity, he served as the teacher of dynasties. Reaching in position to the Great Ultimate itself, he is highest among gods and immortals.

At the time of his birth he possessed a naturally beautiful body. He was clad in heavenly garments, a divine fragrance pervaded his rooms, and brilliant sunlight radiated from him. In nine days, his body

grew nine feet. Everybody, startled and amazed, recognized him for a sage.

Since he was born with the appearance of old age, he was called Lao-zi, "Old Child." The gods of heaven in the void, however, praise him with ten different titles. They are:

Highest Venerable Lord
Highest Venerable of Perfect Spirit and the Wisdom of Nonbeing
Teacher of Emperors and Kings
Great Officer
Great Venerable among Immortals
Father of Heavenly Beings
Highest One of Non-Action
Benevolent Master of Great Compassion
Heavenly Venerable of Primordial Beginning
Old Child

. . . Crossing the Hangu Pass, he transmitted the Scripture of the Dao and the Virtue in 5,000 words, the Wondrous True Scripture of Western Ascension, and other sacred texts to Yin Xi [the guardian of the Pass]. In addition, he taught him the highest methods of Great Clarity, the true writ of the Three Caverns, the talismans and charts of Numinous Treasure, the application of Great Mystery, and other secret ways. He ordered Yin Xi to teach these to people of utmost purity and humanity, so that they could undergo the transformation of wings and become spirit immortals. He commanded him to never let the transmission be interrupted.

With this he crossed over to the west. Passing through the floating sands, he reached the town of Bimo in the land of Khotan. At that time, he raised his Tathagata staff and summoned all his followers. They appeared in an instant: There were Master Redpine, the Elder of the Yellow Center, the Heavenly King of Primordial Beginning, the Goddess of the Great One, the Jade Maiden of the Six Heavenly Branches, the Divine Lord of the Eight Trigrams, the dragon and tiger lords, as well as large numbers of meritorious celestial officials.

In addition, there were the lads of the Golden Carriage, and those of the Benevolent Radiance, the officials of heaven and earth, as well as all the rulers of water and air, the sun and moon, of mountains and the sea. There were the governors of yin and yang, of wood, fire, metal and earth, as well as the gods of the five sacred mountains and the four majestic streams—and many more. . . .

Using his divine powers, he then summoned all the barbarian kings. Without question they appeared

---

[28]Kohn, *The Taoist Experience,* pp. 72–76.

from far and near. There were numerous kings and nobles . . . [1267a] They all came with their wives and concubines, families and other dependents. They crowded around the Venerable Lord, coming ever closer in order to hear the law.

At this time the Venerable Lord addressed the assembled barbarian kings:

"Your hearts are full of evil! You engage in killing and harm other beings! Since you feed only on blood and meat, you cut short manifold lives!

"Today I will give you *the Scripture of Yaksa Demons*. It will prohibit meat-eating among you and leave you with a diet of wheat and gruel. This will take care of all that slaughter and killing! Those among you who cannot desist shall themselves become dead meat!

"You barbarians are greedy and cruel! You make no difference between kin and stranger. You are intent only to satisfy your greed and debauchery! Not a trace of mercy or sense of social duty within you!

"Look at you! Your hair and beards are unkempt and too long! How can you comb and wash it? Even from a distance you are full of rank smell! Bah! How awfully dirty your bodies must be!

"Now that you are made to cultivate the Dao all these things will be great annoyances to your practice. I therefore order all of you to shave off your beards and hair. According to your native customs, all your garments are made of felt and fur. By teaching you the Lesser Way, I will, by and by, lead you to more cultivated manners. In addition, I will give you a number of precepts and prohibitions, so that you gradually get to exercise mercy and compassion. Each month on the fifteenth day, you shall repent your sins."

The following selection is a *Zhengyi* text from the *Scripture of the Inner Explanations of the Three Heavens*. This work tells the sacred story of Lao-zi's visitation to Zhang Daoling, the founder of the Celestial Masters sect that launched Religious Daoism.

LAO-ZI'S VISITATION TO ZHANG DAOLING FROM THE *SCRIPTURE OF THE INNER EXPLANATIONS OF THE THREE HEAVENS*[29]

On the first day of the fifth month in the renwu year, the first year of the Han peace reign period [11 June 142 CE], Lord Lao met with the Daoist Zhang Daol-ing in a stone chamber on Mount Quting in the Commandery of Shu. Lord Lao, in his role as the Newly Emerged Most High, brought Zhang to visit him at the Great Parish on Mount Kunlun.[30]

The Most High announced to him: "The people of this generation do not hold in awe the True and Correct, but fear [only] the deviant and demonic. Thus I have proclaimed myself the Newly Emerged Lord Lao. He forthwith honored Zhang as the "Master of Three Heavens of the Correct and Unified Pneumas of the Grand Mystic Metropolis" and entrusted to him the Way of the Covenanted Authority of Correct Unity, to govern in the name of the Newly Emerged Lord Lao. In doing so, Lord Lao abrogated all authority of the age of the Six Heavens with its Three Ways.

Zhang was to stabilize and correct the Three Heavens, eradicating the frivolous and returning the people to simplicity and truth. [For this purpose,] he received the true scriptures of the Most High and established regulations and ordinances.

After sixteen years had elapsed, in the dingyou year, the third year of the Eternal Longevity reign period [157 CE], Zhang went to the court of the Han thearch as subject and made a covenant with the thearch sealed with the blood of a white horse and with an iron tally inscribed in cinnabar as verification. This covenant was made by the two together before the Three Offices of Heaven, Earth, and Water and before the General of the Year Star [Jupiter]. Both vowed that they would eternally employ the correct law of the Three Heavens and not proscribe the people of heaven. The people were not to wantonly carry out improper sacrifice to the demons or spirits belonging to other groups. This was to deprive demons of sacrificial sustenance. . . .

Zhang Daoling established twenty-four parishes, placing male and female officers called Libationers to head them and to take charge of the converted populace of the true law of the Three Heavens. They were to receive families into the faith by means of a pledge of five pecks of rice. The converted numbered ten thousand families in a hundred days. The people came in masses, like clouds.

Zhang made statutory articles and petitions in ten thousand copies. He entrusted these to his son and grandson, who succeeded him as masters to the

---

[29]Stephen R. Bokenkamp, *Early Daoist Scripture* (Berkeley, CA: University of California Press, 1997), pp. 215–217.

[30]Mount Kunlun was the mythical residence of the goddess Queen Mother of the West, which was believed to be located in far western reaches of the world.

kingdom. Once the affairs of the law were settled and the divisions between humans and demons safely delineated, Zhang rose up in broad daylight to take up the position of Celestial Master in the heavens. The Celestial Master's son, Zhang Heng, as well as his grandson, Zhang Lu, together with their wives, achieved liberation from the corpse and ascended into heaven. Thus there are three Masters and three Ladies.

SECTION 4: Divine Law: Justice, Reward, and Punishment

Many have argued that the two great Chinese traditions differ dramatically in their attitudes toward governance. According to some scholars, Confucius advocated an "authoritative government" led by superior men who aspired to a life of virtue. Lao-zi and Zhuang-zi, in contrast, supported a "laissez-faire" approach to government and frowned upon ambitious reformers with lofty aspirations of benevolence.

The opening selections include passages on governance from the Confucian and the Philosophical Daoist canons. The Confucian texts are from the *Analects* and the *Doctrine of the Mean*; the Daoist selections are from the *Dao-de-jing* and the *Zhuang-zi*. Note that *Zhuang-zi* often places words in the mouth of Confucius, but followers of Confucius do not accept as authentic these words from the Daoist canon. As you read these selections, consider how each tradition would answer three basic questions: How should society be governed? What guidelines should direct the actions of would-be reformers? In what ways are the two traditions in agreement and disagreement?

PART A

CONFUCIAN TEXTS

GUIDELINES FOR GOVERNING FROM THE *ANALECTS*

2:1 Confucius said: "If you govern with the power of your virtue, you will be like the North Star. It just stays in its place while all the other stars position themselves around it."

2:3 Confucius said: "If you govern the people legalistically and control them by punishment, they will avoid crime, but have no personal sense of shame. If you govern them by means of virtue and control them with propriety, they will gain their own sense of shame, and thus correct themselves."

2:19 The Duke of Ai asked: "How can I make the people follow me?" Confucius replied: "Advance the upright and set aside the crooked, and the people will follow you. Advance the crooked and set aside the upright, and the people will not follow you."

2:20 Chi K'ang Tzu asked: "How can I make the people reverent and loyal, so they will work positively for me?" Confucius said, "Approach them with dignity, and they will be reverent. Be filial and compassionate and they will be loyal. Promote the able and teach the incompetent, and they will work positively for you."

4:12 Confucius said: "If you do everything with a concern for your own advantage, you will be resented by many people."

12:7 Tzu Kung asked about government. The Master said, "Enough food, enough weapons and the confidence of the people." Tzu Kung said, "Suppose you had no alternative but to give up one of these three, which one would be let go of first? The Master said, 'Weapons.' Tzu Kung said "What if you had to give up one of the remaining two which one would it be?" The Master said, "Food. From ancient times, death has come to all men, but a people without confidence in its rulers will not stand."

12:9 Duke Ai asked Yu Zo: "It has been a year of famine and there are not enough revenues to run the state. What should I do?" Zo said, "Why can't you use a 10% tax?" The Duke answered: "I can't even get by on a 20% tax, how am I going to do it on 10%?" Zo said, "If the people have enough, what prince can be in want? If the people are in want, how can the prince be satisfied?"

12:19 Chi K'ang Tzu asked Confucius about government saying: "Suppose I were to kill the unjust, in order to advance the just. Would that be all right?" Confucius replied: "In doing government, what is the need of killing? If you desire good, the people will be good. The nature of the Superior Man is like the wind, the nature of the inferior man is like the grass. When the wind blows over the grass, it always bends."

13:1 Tzu Lu asked about how to govern. Confucius said, "Lead the people and work hard for them." "Is there anything else?" "Don't get discouraged."

13:6 Confucius said: "When you have gotten your own life straightened out, things will go well without your giving orders. But if your own life isn't straightened out, even if you give orders, no one will follow them."

15:27 Confucius said: "If everybody hates something, you'd better check into it. If everybody loves something, you'd better check into it."

GUIDELINES FOR GOVERNING FROM *THE DOCTRINE OF THE MEAN*[31]

20. The Duke of Ai asked about government. Confucius said: "The records of the governments of Wen and Wu are

---

[31]Translated by Charles Muller.

on the ancient tablets. When they had the right people, the government functioned, and when they didn't have the right people, government failed. When people are right, the government flourishes; when the ground is right, plants flourish; the governments of Wen and Wu flourished like fast-growing weeds."

Therefore, the skillful handling of government is contingent upon having the right people. You attract the right people by your own character. You cultivate your character through the Dao and you manifest the Dao by means of ren. Ren is "humanity" and its most obvious function is in love for relatives. "Justice" means "setting things right" and its most obvious function is in venerating the Good. The differing levels in loving relatives and venerating the good are expressed through propriety.

Thus, if your rank is low, and you do not have the support of those in power, you cannot hope to have an influence on government. Therefore the Superior man cannot but cultivate his character.

Wanting to cultivate his character, he cannot do it without serving his parents. Wanting to serve his parents, he cannot do it without understanding others. Wanting to understand others, he cannot do it without understanding Heaven.

There are five pervasive (ta) relationships in this world, which are carried out in three ways. The relationships are those between ruler and minister, father and son, husband and wife, older brother and younger brother, and between friends. The three ways of practice are wisdom, ren and courage, but they are practiced in unison.

Some are born knowing it; some know it by learning and some have to struggle to know it. Nonetheless, the knowledge is the same.

Some practice it by being comfortable within it; some practice it by benefiting from it; and some have to struggle to practice it. But when the practice is perfected, it is the same."

Confucius said: "Loving study, you approach wisdom; loving energetic practice, you approach ren. Understanding shame, you approach courage. If you understand these three, you know how to polish your character; knowing how to polish your character, you know how to handle others; knowing how to handle others, you know how to govern a state or clan."

In general, in the handling of the realm, a state or a clan, there are nine basic patterns of treatment. These are: polishing your own character; venerating the Good; caring for your relatives; respecting the high ministers; making the lower ministers feel like they have a significant role; treating the common people as your children; making the artisans feel welcome; treating foreign guests gently and embracing the nobles. . . .

Fasting in ceremonial dress, not acting against the norms of propriety; this is how you polish your character. Letting go of slander, freeing yourself from lust, disregarding wealth and

prizing virtue: This is how you promote goodness. Respecting their rank, paying them well, going along with their likes and dislikes: this is the way to take care of your relatives. Giving them enough officers to dole out their responsibilities: this is the way to encourage the high ministers. To reward well trustworthiness and loyalty: this is the way to encourage the lower officers. Employing the people around their own farming schedules and taxing them lightly: this is the way to encourage the people. Daily and monthly examining their works and giving merit where due: this is the way to encourage the artisans. Sending out envoys to meet foreign visitors and bestowing kindness and pity on the handicapped: this is the way to be gentle to visitors from afar. To renew their broken lineages, restore their vanquished states, quell their rebellions and protect them from danger; giving them rich presents and expecting little in return: this is how you embrace the nobles.

While altogether there are these nine patterns of treatment, there is a single way to carry out all of them. In all affairs, if you plan ahead you can be successful, and if you don't plan ahead, you will fail. If you are prepared before you speak, you won't be tongue-tied. If you are prepared before you begin a job, you won't have complications. If you are prepared before you act, you won't have to be sorry. If you are prepared before teaching, you won't run out of material.

PART B
DAOIST TEXTS

GUIDELINES FOR GOVERNING
FROM THE *DAO-DE-JING*

29. Do you want to improve the world?
    I don't think it can be done.
    The world is sacred. It can't be improved.
    If you tamper with it, you'll ruin it.
    If you treat it like an object, you'll lose it.
    There is a time for being ahead,
    a time for being behind;
    a time for being in motion,
    a time for being at rest;
    a time for being vigorous,
    a time for being exhausted;
    a time for being safe,
    a time for being in danger.
    The Master sees things as they are,
    without trying to control them.
    She lets them go their own way,
    and resides at the center of the circle.

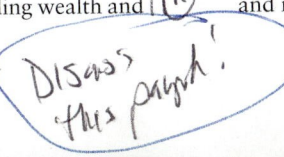

57. If you want to be a great leader,
    you must learn to follow the Dao.
    Stop trying to control.
    Let go of fixed plans and concepts,
    and the world will govern itself.
    The more prohibitions you have,
    the less virtuous people will be.
    The more weapons you have,
    the less secure people will be.
    The more subsidies you have,
    the less self-reliant people will be.
    Therefore the Master says:
    I let go of the law, and people become honest.
    I let go of economics, and people become prosperous.
    I let go of religion, and people become serene.
    I let go of all desire for the common good,
    and the good becomes common as grass.

58. If a country is governed with tolerance,
    the people are comfortable and honest.
    If a country is governed with repression,
    the people are depressed and crafty.
    When the will to power is in charge,
    the higher the ideals, the lower the results.
    Try to make people happy,
    and you lay the groundwork for misery.
    Try to make people moral,
    and you lay the groundwork for vice.
    Thus the Master is content to serve as an example
    and not to impose her will.
    She is pointed, but doesn't pierce.
    Straightforward, but supple.
    Radiant, but easy on the eyes.

GUIDELINES FOR GOVERNING FROM THE *ZHUANGZI*

This Human World

[Confucian said:] "The Sages of old first strengthened their own character before they tried to strengthen that of others. Before you have strengthened your own character, what leisure have you to attend to the doings of wicked men? Besides, do you know into what virtue evaporates by motion and where knowledge ends? Virtue evaporates by motion into desire for fame and knowledge ends in contentions. In the struggle for fame men crush each other, while their wisdom but provokes rivalry. Both are instruments of evil, and are not proper principles of living.

"Besides, if before one's own solid character and integrity become an influence among men and before one's own disregard for fame reaches the hearts of men, one should go and force the preaching of char-

ity and duty and the rules of conduct on wicked men, he would only make these men hate him for his very goodness. Such a person may be called a messenger of evil. A messenger of evil will be the victim of evil from others. That, alas! will be your end.

"On the other hand, if the Prince loves the good and hates evil, what object will you have in inviting him to change his ways? Before you have opened your mouth, the Prince himself will have seized the opportunity to wrest the victory from you. Your eyes will be dazzled, your expression fade, your words will hedge about, your face will show confusion, and your heart will yield within you. It will be as though you took fire to quell fire, water to quell water, which is known as aggravation. And if you begin with concessions, there will be no end to them. If you neglect this sound advice and talk too much, you will die at the hands of that violent man. . . ."

The disdain for societal norms expressed in the *Dao-de-jing* and the *Zhuang-zi* did not prevent Religious Daoists from proscribing rules of proper conduct. Most early Religious Daoists supported the five Buddhist prohibitions against killing, stealing, lying, misbehaving sexually, and getting intoxicated. In addition to these prohibitions, Daoist sects created other standards of conduct that were expected to be observed by Daoist adepts. The following selection of 10 divine precepts is taken from the *Red Writings and Jade Instructions,* a *Lingbao* scripture that dates to the early fifth century CE. What similarities do you find between these precepts and the Ten Commandments of the Western Religions?

RULES OF CONDUCT IN RELIGIOUS DAOISM FROM THE *HIGHEST AND WONDROUS SCRIPTURE OF NUMINOUS TREASURE IN THE MYSTERY CAVERN CONTAINING RED WRITINGS AND JADE INSTRUCTIONS*[32]

The Ten Precepts

1. [2b] Don't harbor hatred or jealousy in your heart! Don't give rise to dark thieving thoughts! Be reserved in speech and wary of transgressions! Keep your thoughts on the Divine Law!
2. Maintain a kind heart and do not kill! Have pity for and support all living beings! Be compassionate and loving! Broadly reach out to bring universal redemption to all!
3. Maintain purity and be withdrawing in your social interactions! Be neither lascivious nor thieving, but constantly harbor good thoughts! Always take from yourself to aid others!

---

[32]Kohn, *The Taoist Experience,* pp. 98–100.

4. Don't set your mind on sex or give rise to passions! Be not licentious in your heart but remain pure and behave prudently! Make sure your actions are without blemish or stain!

5. Don't utter bad words! Don't use flowery and ornate language! Be straightforward within and without! Don't commit excesses of speech!

6. Don't take liquor! Moderate your behavior! Regulate and harmonize your energy and inner nature! Don't let your spirit be diminished! Don't commit any of the myriad evils!

7. Don't be envious if others are better than yourself! Don't contend for achievement and fame! [3a] Be retiring and modest in all things! Put yourself behind to serve the salvation of others!

8. Don't criticize or debate the scriptures and teachings! Don't revile or slander the saintly texts! Venerate the Divine Law with all of your heart! Always act as if you were face to face with the gods!

9. Don't create disturbance through verbal argumentation! Don't criticize any believers, be they monks, nuns, male or female laity, or even heavenly beings! Remember, all censure and hate diminishes your spirit and energy!

10. Be equanimous and of whole heart in all of your actions! Make sure that all exchanges between humankind and the gods are proper and respectful!

SECTION 5: Gender: Women and Men in Society

Although neither Confucius nor Lao-zi and Zhuang-zi provided many detailed instructions about how women and men were to interact in society, the words attributed to the founders of the two great traditions have played a major role in shaping the status of women in Chinese culture. Printed in this section are excerpts from the teachings of these founders that have influenced gender expectations in China for more than two millennia.

PART A

CONFUCIAN TEXTS

A basic Confucian teaching was that all social relations must be harmonious and reciprocal. To Confucius, however, harmony and reciprocity did not mean equality. To the contrary, Confucius assumed that there was a hierarchical relationship between husband and wife, just as there were hierarchical relationships between ruler and subject, elder brother and

younger brother, and parent and child. As a result, the words of Confucius often have been used to support the absolute rights of husbands over wives, parents over children, and rulers over subjects.

Examine the following passages from the *Analects*. How important is the family to Confucius? What are the specific responsibilities of the various members of the family? What gender assumptions are contained in his teachings? Which of the ideas in the *Analects* about the family and gender appear in the sacred canons of the other traditions you have studied? What ideas seem to be unique to this tradition?

FAMILY RELATIONSHIPS WITHIN CONFUCIANISM FROM THE *ANALECTS*

1:11 Confucius said: "When your father is alive, observe his will. When your father is dead observe his former actions. If, for three years you do not change from the ways of your father, you can be called a 'real son.'"

2:5 Meng I Tzu asked about the meaning of filial piety. Confucius said, "It means 'not diverging (from your parents).'" Later, when Fan Chih was driving him, Confucius told Fan Chih, "Meng Sun asked me about the meaning of filial piety, and I told him 'not diverging.'" Fan Chih said, "What did you mean by that?" Confucius said, "When your parents are alive, serve them with propriety; when they die, bury them with propriety, and then worship them with propriety."

2:7 Tzu Lu asked about the meaning of filial piety. Confucius said, "Nowadays filial piety means being able to feed your parents. But everyone does this for even horses and dogs. Without respect, what's the difference?"

2:8 Tzu Hsia asked about filial piety. Confucius said, "What is important is the expression you show in your face. You should not understand 'filial' to mean merely the young doing physical tasks for their parents, or giving them food and wine when it is available."

4:18 Confucius said: "When you serve your mother and father it is okay to try to correct them once in a while. But if you see that they are not going to listen to you, keep your respect for them and don't distance yourself from them. Work without complaining."

4:19 Confucius said: "While your parents are alive, it is better not to travel far away. If you do travel, you should have a precise destination."

4:20 Confucius said: "If, for three years (after your father's death) you don't alter his ways of doing things, you can certainly be called 'filial.'"

11:21 Tzu Lu asked if it was a good idea to immediately put a teaching into practice when he first heard it. Confucius said, "You have a father and an older brother to consult. Why do you need to be so quick to practice it?" Zan Yu asked the same question. Confucius said, "You should practice it immediately."

Kung Hsi Hua said, "When Yu asked you, you told him he should consult his father and elder brother first. When Ch'iu (Zan Yu) asked you, you told him to practice it immediately. May I ask why?" Confucius said, "Ch'iu has a tendency to give up easily, so I push him. Yu (Tzu Lu) has a tendency to jump the gun, so I restrain him."

13:18 The Duke of Sheh told Confucius: "In my land, there are Righteous men. If a father steals a sheep, the son will testify against him." Confucius said, "The Righteous men in my land are different from this. The father conceals the wrongs of his son, and the son conceals the wrongs of his father. This is Righteousness!"

17:25 Confucius said: "Girls and inferior men are hard to raise. If you get familiar with them, they lose their humility; if you are distant, they resent it."

17:26 Confucius said: "One who has reached the age of forty and is disliked, will be disliked to the end."

18:4 The people of Ch'i sent Lu a present of girl musicians. Chi Huan (ruler of Lu) received them, and for three days did not hold court. Confucius left.

PART B

DAOIST TEXTS

The following selections illustrate the wide range of gender images used to describe the *Dao* in the *Dao-de-jing*. According to these texts, is the *Dao* predominately a masculine or feminine principle? Do these texts affirm the superiority of women, the superiority of men, or the equality of the sexes? Defend your answer.

GENDER IMAGES FROM THE *DAO-DE-JING*[33]

6. The Dao is called the Great Mother:
   empty yet inexhaustible,
   it gives birth to infinite worlds.
   It is always present within you.
   You can use it any way you want.

10. Can you coax your mind from its wandering
    and keep to the original oneness?
    Can you let your body become
    supple as a newborn child's?
    Can you cleanse your inner vision
    until you see nothing but the light?

Can you love people and lead them
without imposing your will?
Can you deal with the most vital matters
by letting events take their course?
Can you step back from you own mind
and thus understand all things?
Giving birth and nourishing,
having without possessing,
acting with no expectations,
leading and not trying to control:
this is the supreme virtue.

28. Know the male, yet keep to the female:
    receive the world in your arms.
    If you receive the world,
    the Dao will never leave you and you will be like a
       little child.
    Know the white, yet keep to the black:
    be a pattern for the world.
    If you are a pattern for the world,
    the Dao will be strong inside you and there will be
       nothing you can't do.
    Know the personal, yet keep to the impersonal:
    accept the world as it is.
    If you accept the world,
    the Dao will be luminous inside you and you will
       return to your primal self.
    The world is formed from the void, like utensils from a
       block of wood.
    The Master knows the utensils, yet keeps to the block:
    thus she can use all things.

52. In the beginning was the Dao.
    All things issue from it; all things return to it.
    To find the origin, trace back the manifestations.
    When you recognize the children and find the mother,
    you will be free of sorrow.
    If you close your mind in judgements and traffic with
       desires,
    your heart will be troubled.
    If you keep your mind from judging and aren't led by
       the senses,
    your heart will find peace.
    Seeing into darkness is clarity.
    Knowing how to yield is strength.
    Use your own light and return to the source of light.
    This is called practicing eternity.

55. He who is in harmony with the Dao is like a newborn
       child.
    Its bones are soft, its muscles are weak, but its grip is
       powerful.
    It doesn't know about the union of male and female,
    yet its penis can stand erect, so intense is its vital
       power.
    It can scream its head off all day,

[33]Translated by Stephen Mitchell (New York: Harper and Row, 1988).

yet it never becomes hoarse, so complete is its harmony.
The Master's power is like this.
He lets all things come and go effortlessly, without
   desire.
He never expects results; thus he is never disappointed.
He is never disappointed; thus his spirit never grows old.

SECTION 6: Daily Living: Health, Etiquette, and Holy Days

The word *li* often appears in the ancient Chinese texts. Translated into English as "propriety" or "ritual," this word refers to the wide variety of rites that permeated early East Asian society. Confucius was considered an expert on the proper handling of all sorts of rituals—from the simple rules of etiquette in day-to-day human interactions to the elaborate ceremonies performed at funerals and other special and holy occasions. For Confucius, maintaining proper manners and observing the rituals produced both a harmonious society and a reformed human heart.

Daoists, however, view Confucius's preoccupation with outward piety with contempt. Throwing social conventions to the wind, the followers of Lao-zi and Zhuang-zi encourage spontaneity and independence in thought and conduct. Going with the flow of the natural order is the primary Daoist imperative.

According to the following passages from the two canons, in what ways are the attitudes of the Daoists and the Confucianists toward social decorum and the pleasures of this world alike and different? What does it mean to embrace a Confucian lifestyle? What does it mean for a disciple of Lao-zi to follow the Way? Is it accurate to describe Confucianism as puritanical, and Daoism, as amoral? Why or why not?

PART A

CONFUCIAN TEXTS

ADVICE FOR DAILY LIVING FROM THE *ANALECTS*

3:4 Lin Fang asked about the fundamentals of ritual. Confucius said, "What an excellent question! In ritual, it is better to be frugal than extravagant; in funerals deep sorrow is better than ease."

3:10 Confucius said: "At the Great Sacrifice, after the pouring of the libation, I have no further desire to watch."

3:11 Someone asked for an explanation of the Great Sacrifice. Confucius said, "I don't know. If there were someone who knew this, he could see the whole world as if it were this": He pointed to the palm of his hand.

3:12 "Sacrificing as if present" means sacrificing to the spirits as if they were present. Confucius said, "If I do not personally offer the sacrifice, it is the same as not having sacrificed at all."

3:13 Wang Sun Chia asked: "What do you think about the saying 'It is better to sacrifice to the god of the stove than to the god of the family shrine.'?" Confucius said, "Not so. If you offend Heaven, there is no one you can pray to."

8:8 Confucius said: "Be aroused by poetry; structure yourself with propriety, refine yourself with music."

11:1 Confucius said: "Common people develop their understanding of music and ritual earlier. The nobility develop these later. In terms of practicality, earlier development is better."

16:5 Confucius said: "There are three kinds of enjoyment which are beneficial and three kinds of enjoyment which are harmful. The enjoyment of cultivation in music and ritual, the enjoyment of speaking of the goodness of others and the enjoyment of being surrounded by friends of good character are all beneficial. The enjoyment of arrogance, the enjoyment of dissipation and the enjoyment of comfort are all harmful."

PART B

DAOIST TEXTS

ADVICE FOR DAILY LIVING FROM THE *ZHUANG-ZI*

Joined Toes

Joined toes and extra fingers seem to come from nature, yet, functionally speaking they are superfluous. Goiters and tumors seem to come from the body, yet in their nature, they are superfluous. And (similarly), to have many extraneous doctrines of charity and duty and regard them in practice as parts of a man's natural sentiments is not the true way of Dao. For just as joined toes are but useless lumps of flesh, and extra fingers but useless growths, so are the many artificial developments of the natural sentiments of men and the extravagances of charitable and dutiful conduct but so many superfluous uses of intelligence. . . . All these are superfluous and devious growths of knowledge and are not the correct guide for the world. He who would be the ultimate guide never loses sight of the inner nature of life. Therefore with him, the united is not like joined toes, the separated is not like extra fingers, what is long is not considered as excess, and what is short is not regarded as wanting. For duck's legs, though short, cannot be lengthened without dismay to the duck, and a crane's legs, though long, cannot be shortened without misery to the crane. That which is long in nature must not be cut off, and that which is short in nature must not be lengthened. Thus will all sorrow be avoided.

I suppose charity and duty are surely not included in human nature. You see how many worries and dismays the charitable man has! Besides, divide your joined toes and you will howl: bite off your extra finger and you will scream. In the one case, there is too much, and in the other too little; but the worries and dismays are the same. Now the charitable men of the present age go about with a look of concern sorrowing over the ills of the age, while the non-charitable let loose the desire of their nature in their greed after position and wealth. Therefore I Suppose charity and duty are not included in human nature. Yet from the time of the Three Dynasties downwards what a commotion has been raised about them! . . .

Why then should the doctrines of charity and duty continue to remain like so much glue or cords, in the domain of Dao and virtue, to give rise to confusion and doubt among mankind? Now the lesser doubts change man's purpose, and the greater doubts change man's nature. How do we know this? Ever since the time when Shun made a bid for charity and duty and threw the world into confusion, men have run about and exhausted themselves in the pursuit thereof. Is it not then charity and duty which have changed the nature of man? Therefore I have tried to show {42} that from the time of the Three Dynasties onwards, there is not one who has not changed his nature through certain external things. If a common man, he will die for gain. If a scholar, he will die for fame. If a ruler of a township, he will die for his ancestral honors. If a Sage, he will die for the world. The pursuits and ambitions of these men differ, but the injury to their nature resulting in the sacrifice of their lives is the same. . . .

What I call good is not what is meant by charity and duty, but taking good care of virtue. And what I call good is not the so-called charity and duty, but following the nature of life. What I call good at hearing is not hearing others but hearing oneself. What I call good at vision is not seeing others but seeing oneself. For a man who sees not himself but others, or takes

possession not of himself but of others, possessing only what others possess and possessing not his own self, does what pleases others instead of pleasing his own nature. Now one who pleases others, instead of pleasing one's own nature, whether he be Robber Cheh or Po Yi, is just another one gone astray. Conscious of my own deficiencies in regard to Dao, I do not venture to practice the principles of charity and duty on the one hand, nor to lead the life of extravagance on the other. . . .

If each man keeps his own sense of sight, the world will escape being burned up. If each man keeps his own sense of hearing, the world will escape entanglements. If each man keeps his intelligence, the world will escape confusion. If each man keeps his own virtue, the world will avoid deviation from the true path.

ADVICE ON DAILY LIVING FROM THE *DAO-DE-JING*

19. Throw away holiness and wisdom,
    and people will be a hundred times happier.
    Throw away morality and justice, and people will do
        the right thing.
    Throw away industry and profit, and there won't be
        any thieves.
    If these three aren't enough,
    just stay at the center of the circle and let all things
        take their course.

53. The great Way is easy, yet people prefer the side paths.
    Be aware when things are out of balance.
    Stay centered within the Dao.
    When rich speculators prosper while farmers lose their
        land;
    when government officials spend money on weapons
        instead of cures;
    when the upper class is extravagant and irresponsible
    while the poor have nowhere to turn—all this is
        robbery and chaos.
    It is not in keeping with the Dao.

54. Whoever is planted in the Dao will not be rooted up.
    Whoever embraces the Dao will not slip away.
    Her name will be held in honor from generation to
        generation.
    Let the Dao be present in your life and you will
        become genuine.
    Let it be present in your family and your family will
        flourish.
    Let it be present in your country and your country will
        be an example

to all countries in the world.
Let it be present in the universe and the universe will
sing.
How do I know this is true? By looking inside myself.

The ritual of sending documents to the gods in order to gain their assistance in healing illness was an essential component of the Celestial Masters tradition within Religious Daoism. The following selection is an excerpt from *The Great Petition for Sepulchral Plaints,* a scripture from this early tradition. This text was a model text that was personalized and dispatched by Daoist priests to celestial officials on behalf of human clients who were suffering from ills believed caused by aggrieved spirits of the dead. The model petition included three elements: a description of the client's problem, a statement of repentance, and a request for celestial aid to alleviate the suffering. According to this text, what is the cause and remedy of misfortune?

HEALTH AND HEALING IN RELIGIOUS DAOISM FROM *THE GREAT PETITION FOR SEPULCHRAL PLAINTS*[34]

Complete religious title [of the priest]

We address our superiors:

Now (so-and-so), of (such-and-such) region . . . has provided a full statement in which he has said that the auspices of his house are in disastrous decline, and the members of his household have been burdened with successive illnesses. Their activities are unprofitable; their dwelling is unquiet. Thus he has pleaded for a petition for the dispersal and elimination of a sepulchral plaint.

Now, judging by the appearance of the situation, one might seek out the [plaint's] roots in a rough fashion. One must suspect that among his ancestors . . . [there was someone who,] since when alive his or her trespasses were excessive, after death became subject to all manner of inquisitions and punishments. His descendants having yet to redeem him, in the darkness he is crying out bitterly.

Perhaps it is a plaint over burial on a spring, or over a funeral's having encroached on a god's temple. Perhaps it is a plaint over a grave having been dug into a cavern, or over a coffin having been damaged. . . .

---

[34]Peter Nickerson, in Stephen R. Bokenkamp, *Early Daoist Scriptures* (Berkeley, CA: University of California Press, 1997), pp. 261–271.

Your servant, relying completely on the Protocols of the Twelve Hundred Officials and the rituals for curing illness and extinguishing evil . . . respectfully invites his superiors:

The Lord of Celestial Glory and his hundred thousand troops dressed in yellow to apprehend these demons in (so-and-so's) household—the hundred and twenty harmful anomalies, the violent harmers within and without, and the twelve punishing killers—and annihilate them all.

Also we invite the Supreme Lord of the High Storehouse and his ten thousand troops. On behalf of (so-and-so's) household they are to apprehend and place under their control those demons of the five tombs that come and go, wounding and killing, attaching themselves to the descendants and causing harmful anomalies and calamitous injuries, making (so-and-so) ill to the point that his deadly wounds are unceasing. Annihilate them all. . . .

If in the family of (so-and-so) . . . someone in his or her burial has offended . . . [the celestial powers], thus violating the prohibitions and taboos. . . . as for all these things that cause punishment and calamity and bring disquiet, causing illness among the descendants, let them be entirely dissolved and let harmony be restored. Trace [the case] to its origins and repair the situation; change the inauspicious into the auspicious. Turn calamities into blessings, so that life and death, dark and light, do not interfere with one another. . . .

From now on, as for (so-and-so) and his family, let divine pneumas radiate all about them and celestial numina aid and protect them. Let their five organs be attuned and their six viscera be open and clear, replete with perfected essence, with the hundred illnesses put to rest. Let their enterprises be successful and their merit be renewed daily. Let all auspicious things descend and wickedness be dissipated. Let both their public and private affairs flourish, with the living and the departed [beneficially] relying on one another.

As for the Celestial Officials, Lords, Generals, Clerks, and Soldiers—both civil and military officials— who have been invited, if they diligently achieve results and drive off demonic injury, and in apprehending and executing [the malefactors] establish merit, then we beg directly to state their merit and reward them with promotion, adding to their offices and advancing their rank, in order of high and low in accordance with the constant codes of the Celestial Bureaux, so that they shall be without resentment.

As for the pledges offered by (so-and-so)—forty feet of figured purple cloth, one bushel and two pecks of Destiny Rice, twelve hundred cash, one set of pure clothes for wearing, one hundred and twenty sheets of deposition paper, two sticks of ink, two brushes, one ounce of cinnabar, one scholar's knife, a pure mat, and one pure turban—they are for requiting the Officials, Lords, Generals, and Clerks for their efficacious diligence.

We pray to the Most High, etc. . . . Because (so-and-so) is ill, and in order to disperse the inquisitory pneumas and seizing infusions of those departed earlier or dead later, your servant respectfully offers up the Great Petition for Sepulchral Plaints and presents himself on high, etc. etc.

While Religious Daoists used exorcisms and healing rituals to combat disease, they also advocated special breathing exercises, physical gymnastics, and the use of diet and drugs as means for maintaining good health. Many of the theories that support modern Chinese Medicine were articulated centuries ago in the voluminous works within the Daoist canons that were devoted to health and longevity. Two selections from this vast literature are provided below. The first is from *The Numinous Treasure Way of Eating the Essence of the Five Wonderplants*, a fourth century CE text from the *Lingbao* tradition. The second is an eleventh-century CE teaching from the Complete Perfection School entitled *Chongyang's Fifteen Articles on Establishing the Teaching*.

FROM *THE NUMINOUS TREASURE WAY OF EATING THE ESSENCE OF THE FIVE WONDERPLANTS*[35]

Pine Resin

[2.1a] The Venerable Lord said: When a pine tree has grown for a thousands years, its resin is so concentrated that, by eating it, you can pervade all in your spirit. You can enter into the depth of the earth, hide your true identity, and change your name at will.

The needles and stem of a pine tree are rather large, following the plant's roots in their shape. Its resin is also called "magnificent joy" [black amber] or again "truffle fungus."

With its help you can become immune to weapons. You can pass freely over land and through water, leave the obscure and enter the serene. You will be free from hunger and thirst and live as long as the sun and the moon.

If you can find the resin of a thousand-year-old pine, you can truly live long.

Sesame

The Venerable Lord said: Nourish your body with the "little louse" and you will recover a healthy complexion and return to youthfulness.

Another name of this plant is "barbarian hemp." The reason for this is that it originally comes from Ferghana in the lands of the barbarians. After it had grown there wild for ten thousand years, it crossed the border and came east.

If kept deep in the earth, it is a powerful drug against all danger and fierceness. If soaked in boiled water, it can ward off wind and expel cold.

It has the most appropriate name of "giant victor." This is due to the fact that it repels all kings of evil and demonic powers and pursues them to their end.

Pepper

[1b] The Venerable Lord said: Pepper grows in both the regions of Shu and of Han [southwest and central China].

Since it contains the energy of great yin, it will allow you to live as long as heaven and earth, to transform and change your body at will, and to pass freely over land and through water. With pepper you can ward off dampness.

None of the many pathogenic influences will dare to come near you. As long as you eat pepper, there is not a single demon, magical evil, or poison that you cannot stop in its tracks.

If you nourish on it permanently, you can fulfill all the wishes of your heart's desire. However, you must keep the method hidden from the world, since the practice is very profound. Keep it in strict confidence and never give it away. Then you won't need a lot of gold to realize your goals.

FROM *CHONGYANG'S FIFTEEN ARTICLES ON ESTABLISHING THE TEACHING*[36]

Article 4. The Preparation of Medicines

Herbs are the finest energy of mountains and streams, the essential florescence of grasses and trees. They

---

[35]Kohn, *Taoist Experience*, pp. 150–151.

[36]Kohn, *Taoist Experience*, p. 88.

may be warm, or they may be cool; one uses them to supplement or drain energy. They may be thick, or they may be thin; one uses them externally or from within.

Studying herbs in their essence allows you to support your inner nature and destiny. On the other hand, if you apply herbs blindly, you will waste your body and physical constitution.

All those who study the Dao must penetrate herbal lore. If you do not do so, you have no means to support the Dao. Yet in doing so, you must not develop attachments, for they will diminish the hidden merits of past lives. You will then hanker after material goods on the outside and waste your efforts at cultivation within.

Not only does this lead to grave transgressions and errors in this life, but it will also cause retribution in the lives to come. Oh, noble disciples of my teaching! Heed this and be very careful.

SECTION 7: The Human Quest: Paths to Salvation and Enlightenment

What do humans desire to achieve? What paths are they willing to take to reach these goals? The founders of the two great Chinese traditions provided answers to these eternal questions, but their answers were not always similar. Confucius accepted the deities and spirits acknowledged by his culture and insisted on the proper performance of the ancient sacred rituals. Yet, despite these traditional leanings, Confucius was a practical humanist who had little interest in metaphysical speculation. His goals were social and this worldly, and his instructions centered principally on issues of relational ethics. Lao-zi, in contrast, was a social rebel who ridiculed popular forms of outward religious expression. An ascetic with little regard for established conventions, Lao-zi, nonetheless, was profoundly interested in learning how to develop the inward spiritual life. He called his disciples to become one with the natural order by intuitively following the directions that came from within.

The following selections illustrate a variety of Confucianist and Philosophical Daoist answers to questions about life's purpose and direction. The Confucian teachings are taken from *The Great Learning* and *The Doctrine of the Mean*, two pieces originally in the ancient *Book of Rites* that were edited and made into independent works by the twelfth-century CE scholar Zhu Xi. The Daoist answers come from the two most sacred works within Philosophical Daoism, the *Dao-de-jing* and *Zhuang-zi*. Based on these readings, what insights do these traditions offer about the meaning of life? How does each tradition define enlightenment, and how is this goal realized? What thoughts do these ancient Chinese thinkers share with the authors of the *Bhagavad Gita* and the *Tripitaka*?

PART A

CONFUCIAN TEXTS

PATHS TO ENLIGHTENMENT FROM *THE GREAT LEARNING*

The way of great learning
    consists in manifesting one's bright virtue,
    consists in loving the people,
    consists in stopping in perfect goodness.
When you know where to stop, you have stability.
When you have stability, you can be tranquil.
When you are tranquil, you can be at ease.
When you are at ease, you can deliberate.
When you can deliberate you can attain your aims.
Things have their roots and branches, affairs have their end
    and beginning.
When you know what comes first and what comes last, then
    you are near the Dao.

The ancients who wanted to manifest their bright virtue to
    all in the world
    first governed well their own states.
Wanting to govern well their states, they first harmonized
    their own clans.
Wanting to harmonize their own clan, they first cultivated
    themselves.
Wanting to cultivate themselves, they first corrected their
    minds.
Wanting to correct their minds, they first made their wills
    sincere.
Wanting to make their wills sincere, they first extended their
    knowledge.

Extension of knowledge consists of the investigation of
    things.
When things are investigated, knowledge is extended.
When knowledge is extended, the will becomes sincere.
When the will is sincere, the mind is correct.
When the mind is correct, the self is cultivated.

Superior person

When the self is cultivated, the clan is harmonized.
When the clan is harmonized, the country is well governed.
When the country is well governed, there will be peace
   throughout the land.

From the king down to the common people, all must regard the cultivation of the self as the most essential thing. It is impossible to have a situation wherein the essentials are in disorder, and the externals are well-managed. You simply cannot take the essential things as superficial, and the superficial things as essential.

PATHS TO ENLIGHTENMENT FROM *THE DOCTRINE OF THE MEAN*

Chapters 21–27[37]

21. The enlightenment that comes from sincerity is our own nature. The sincerity that comes from enlightenment is called "education." If you are sincere you will be enlightened. If you are enlightened, you will be sincere.

22. Only the perfectly sincere person can actualize his own essence. Actualizing his own essence, he can fully actualize the essence of others. Fully actualizing the essence of others, he can fully actualize the essence of all things. Being able to fully actualize the essence of all things, he can assist Heaven and Earth in their transformation and sustenance. Able to assist in Heaven and Earth's transformation and sustenance, he forms a trinity with Heaven and Earth. . . .

24. Once you are in the Path of fully actualized sincerity, you have foreknowledge of things. When a nation or clan is about to rise up, there are always omens of their fortune. When a nation or clan is about to fall, there are always omens of their misfortune. It can be seen in the milfoil stalks, tortoise shells and in the movements of the body. When good or evil fortune is imminent, the perfectly sincere person will know without obstruction. With fully actualized sincerity, you are like a god.

25. Sincerity is just 'perfecting' and the Dao is just 'following.' Sincerity is the beginning and end of all things. Without sincerity there is nothing. Thus the Superior Man values the process of "becoming-sincere." But sincerity is not "just-perfecting"; it also means "perfecting all things." To perfect yourself, you need ren. To perfect others, you need wisdom. The virtue of our nature is that it is none other than the Dao by which inner and outer are merged. Thus we can always use it to set things right. . . .

27. How great is the Dao of the sage! Superabundant, it develops all things, extending up to Heaven. How excellent it is! It embraces the three hundred rules of ceremony, and the three thousand rules of conduct; it waits for the right per-

son and then functions. Hence it is said: "If you do not perfect your virtue, the perfect Dao cannot be actualized." Therefore the Superior Man esteems his virtuous nature and follows the path of inquiry, extending himself in breadth and greatness, penetrating all subtleties, penetrating its height and brilliance, following the course of the actualization of the Mean. He reviews the old and learns the new, thickening his character through the valorization of propriety.

Therefore he abides in a position of power without arrogance, and abides in a low position without being rebellious. When the government is just, he can speak and be praised. When the government is wicked, he can conceal himself by silence. The Book of Odes says: "His intelligence and wit were his protection."

Does this not reflect the same meaning?

This world

PART B

DAOIST TEXTS

TEACHINGS ON ENLIGHTENMENT FROM THE *DAO-DE-JING*

16. Empty your mind of all thoughts.
   Let your heart be at peace.
   Watch the turmoil of beings, but contemplate their
      return.
   Each separate being in the universe returns to the
      common source.
   Returning to the source is serenity.
   If you don't realize the source, you stumble in
      confusion and sorrow.
   When you realize where you come from,
   you naturally become tolerant, disinterested, amused,
      kindhearted as a grandmother, dignified as a king.
   Immersed in the wonder of the Dao,
   you can deal with whatever life brings you and when
      death comes, you are ready.

22. If you want to become whole, let yourself be partial.
   If you want to become straight, let yourself be crooked.
   If you want to become full, let yourself be empty.
   If you want to be reborn, let yourself die.
   If you want to be given everything, give everything up.
   The Master, by residing in the Tao, sets an example for
      all beings.
   Because he doesn't display himself, people can see his
      light.
   Because he has nothing to prove, people can trust his
      words.

---

[37]Translated by Charles Muller.

Because he doesn't know who he is, people recognize
    themselves in him.
Because he has no goal in mind, everything he does
    succeeds.
When the ancient Masters said,
"If you want to be given everything, give everything up,"
they weren't using empty phrases.
Only in being lived by the Dao can you be truly yourself.

33. Knowing others is intelligence; knowing yourself is
    true wisdom.
Mastering others is strength; mastering yourself is true
    power.
If you realize that you have enough, you are truly rich.
If you stay in the center and embrace death with your
    whole heart,
you will endure forever.

41. When a superior man hears of the Dao, he immediately
    begins to embody it.
When an average man hears of the Dao, he half
    believes it, half doubts it.
When a foolish man hears of the Dao, he laughs out loud.
If he didn't laugh, it wouldn't be the Dao.
Thus it is said:
The path into the light seems dark,
the path forward seems to go back,
the direct path seems long,
true power seems weak,
true purity seems tarnished,
true steadfastness seems changeable,
true clarity seems obscure,
the greatest art seems unsophisticated,
the greatest love seems indifferent,
the greatest wisdom seems childish.
The Dao is nowhere to be found.
Yet it nourishes and completes all things.

47. Without opening your door, you can open your heart
    to the world.
Without looking out your window, you can see the
    essence of the Tao.
The more you know, the less you understand.
The Master arrives without leaving,
sees the light without looking,
achieves without doing a thing.

48. In pursuit of knowledge, every day something is added.
In the practice of the Dao, every day something is
    dropped.
Less and less do you need to force things,
until finally you arrive at non-action.
When nothing is done, nothing is left undone.
True mastery can be gained by letting things go their
    own way.
It can't be gained by interfering.

56. Those who know don't talk. Those who talk don't know.
Close your mouth, block off your senses,
blunt your sharpness, untie your knots,
soften your glare, settle your dust.
This is the primal identity.
Be like the Dao.
It can't be approached or withdrawn from,
benefited or harmed, honored or brought into disgrace.
It gives itself up continually. That is why it endures.

70. My teachings are easy to understand and easy to put
    into practice.
Yet your intellect will never grasp them,
and if you try to practice them, you'll fail.
My teachings are older than the world. How can you
    grasp their meaning?
If you want to know me, look inside your heart.

81. True words aren't eloquent; eloquent words aren't true.
Wise men don't need to prove their point;
men who need to prove their point aren't wise.
The Master has no possessions.
The more he does for others, the happier he is.
The more he gives to others, the wealthier he is.
The Dao nourishes by not forcing.
By not dominating, the Master leads.

The following dialogues are from the *Zhuang-zi*.
What are the central messages within these teachings?
In what ways do these messages differ from those
within the *Analects*?

FROM THE *ZHUANG-ZI*

Yen Huei spoke to Chungni (Confucius), "I am getting on."

"How so?" asked the latter.

"I have got rid of charity and duty," replied the
former.

"Very good," replied Chungni, "but not quite
perfect."

Another day, Yen Huei met Chungni and said, "I
am getting on."

"How so?"

"I have got rid of ceremonies and music," answered Yen Huei.

"Very good," said Chungni, "but not quite perfect."

Another day, Yen Huei again met Chungni and
said, "I am getting on."

"How so?"

"I can forget myself while sitting," replied Yen Huei.

"What do you mean by that?" said Chungni,
changing his countenance.

"I have freed myself from my body," answered Yen Huei. "I have discarded my reasoning powers. And by thus getting rid of my body and mind, I have become One with the Infinite. This is what I mean by forgetting myself while sitting."

"If you have become One," said Chungni, "there can be no room for bias. If you have lost yourself, there can be no more hindrance. Perhaps you are really a wise one. I trust to be allowed to follow in your steps."

The Yellow Emperor withdrew. He resigned the Throne. He built himself a solitary hut, and sat upon white straw. For three months he remained in seclusion, and then went again to see Kuangch'engtse.

The latter was lying with his head towards the south. The Yellow Emperor approached from below upon his knees. Kowtowing twice upon the ground, he said, "I am told that you are in possession of perfect Tao. May I ask how to order one's life so that one may have long life?"

Kuangch'engtse jumped up with a start. "A good question indeed!" cried he. "Come, and I will speak to you of perfect Tao. The essence of perfect Dao is profoundly mysterious; its extent is lost in obscurity. "See nothing; hear nothing; guard your spirit in quietude and your body will go right of its own accord.

"Be quiet, be pure; toil not your body, perturb not your vital essence, and you will live for ever.

"For if the eye sees nothing, and the ear hears nothing, and the mind thinks nothing, your spirit will stay in your body, and the body will thereby live for ever.

"Cherish that which is within you, and shut off that which is without for much knowledge is a curse.

"Then I will take you to that abode of Great Light to reach the Plateau of Absolute Yang. I will lead you through the Door of the Dark Unknown to the Plateau of the Absolute Yin.

"The Heaven and Earth have their separate functions. The yin and yang have their hidden root. Guard carefully your body, and material things will prosper by themselves.

"I guard the original One, and rest in harmony with externals. Therefore I have been able to live for twelve hundred years and my body has not grown old."

The Yellow Emperor kowtowed twice and said, "Kuangch'engtse is surely God.

"Come," said Kuangch'engtse, "I will tell you. That thing is eternal; yet all men think it mortal. That thing is infinite; yet all men think it finite. Those who possess my Dao are princes in this life and rulers in the hereafter. Those who do not possess my Dao behold the light of day in this life and become clods of earth in the hereafter.

"Nowadays, all living things spring from the dust and to the dust return. But I will lead you through the portals of Eternity to wander in the great wilds of Infinity. My light is the light of sun and moon. My life is the life of Heaven and Earth. Before me all is nebulous; behind me all is dark, unknown. Men may all die, but I endure for ever."

Salvation is arguably the central goal of Religious Daoism, although the path to realizing this goal varies among the differing sects. Among the most influential texts within the Religious Daoist canon is the *Lingbao* text entitled *The Wondrous Scriptures of the Upper Chapters on Limitless Salvation*. Early in the Tang Dynasty this scripture was declared to be one of the three texts to be studied by Daoists for the examination that led to Daoist investiture. This scripture is still recited in liturgy wherever Daoist adepts practice. Included here is the Preface to this scripture. According to this *Lingbao* text, what are the manifestations of salvation and how is it manifested?

PATHS TO SALVATION WITHIN RELIGIOUS DAOISM FROM *THE WONDROUS SCRIPTURES OF THE UPPER CHAPTERS ON LIMITLESS SALVATION*[38]

PREFACE

The [Most High Lord of] the Dao said:

Of old, in the Bilu kongge dafuli land in the midst of the Inaugural Azure Heavens, I received the Boundless Upper Chapters of the Scripture of Salvation of Primordial Commencement. When the Celestial Worthy of Primordial Commencement pronounced this scripture, he made ten complete recitations to summon in the ten directions the Great Spirits of Heavenly Perfection, the Most Honored of the Exalted Sages, and the Perfected of Wondrous Deeds in all their countless multitudes who might attend his throne. These beings came, mounted on air. They arrived in flying clouds and cinnabar-red cirrus wisps, in green chariots with rose-gem wheels. Their feathered canopies shrouded the land, while their streaming essences glittered with gemmy light, so that the five

---

[38]Bokenkamp, *Early Daoist Scriptures*, pp. 405–407.

colors billowed forth, flashing penetratingly throughout the Grand Void.

For the space of seven days and seven nights, the suns and moons, stars and lodgings, even to the Cogs, Armils, and Jade Transverses of all the Dippers of all the heavens, stopped at once in their rotations. The spirit-driven winds were still and silent. The mountains and seas hid away their cloudy emanations. The heavens lacked even floating haze; the air was perfectly clear in all directions. Throughout the whole kingdom, the earth—all mountains and rivers, forests and groves—became uniform and flat, so that there were no longer high and low places. All became as cyan jade; there were no other colors. As the multitude of Perfected attended his throne, the Celestial Worthy of Primordial Commencement sat suspended in the air, floating above a pentachromatic lion. When he spoke the scripture through for the first time, all of the assembled great Sages voiced their approval. At once all those in the kingdom afflicted with deafness, both male and female, were able to hear again. When he expounded the scripture a second time, the eyes of the blind were opened to the light. When he expounded the scripture for the third time, the mute were able to speak. When he expounded the scripture for the fourth time, those long lame or paralytic were able to arise and walk. When he expounded the scripture for the fifth time, those with chronic illnesses or diseases were immediately made whole. When he expounded the scripture for the sixth time, white hair turned black again and lost teeth were regrown. When he expounded the scripture for the eighth time, wives became pregnant, while birds and beasts' wombs were quickened. Not only were those already born made whole, but the unborn as well came whole into life. When he expounded the scripture for the ninth time, the stores of earth were leaked forth; gold and jade lay revealed. When he expounded the scripture for the tenth time, desiccated bones were revivified; all rose up to become human beings again. At once the whole kingdom, both male and female, inclined their hearts to the Dao. All received protection and salvation. All achieved long life.

Section 8: The Religious Life: Worship and Righteousness

The sacred texts of most traditions describe the character and virtues of special exemplars of the faith that rise above the norms of others within the tradi-

tion. Judaism and Islam has its prophets; Christianity, its saints; Hinduism, its gurus and sages; and Buddhism, its arahants and bodhisattvas. The ancient Chinese used several words to describe that idealized human who was worthy to be imitated. The word *jun-zi*, often translated as the "superior man," technically meant "the son of a prince." This person of nobility was one who had made significant progress in the Way (*Dao*) of self-cultivation. A second Chinese term, *ren*, is often translated into English as "benevolence," "perfect goodness," or "humanity." This term is difficult to translate in a single word because it does not refer so much to a particular type of virtue as to the inner capacity within all humans to do good. To be called *ren* in the sacred Chinese texts was a high compliment. To be a person of *ren* was to be fully human.

The following selections from the Confucian *Analects* and the Daoist *Zhuang-zi* offer descriptions of sages and saints who were worthy to be venerated. How did each tradition characterize these role models of virtue? Compare these descriptions with the exemplars of the faith of the other great religious traditions. What similarities and differences are there in the various manifestations of sainthood?

PART A

CONFUCIAN TEXTS

Characteristics of the Superior Man in the *Analects*

4:10 Confucius said: "When the Superior Man deals with the world he is not prejudiced for or against anything. He does what is Right."

4:11 Confucius said: "The Superior Man cares about virtue; the inferior man cares about material things. The Superior Man seeks discipline; the inferior man seeks favors."

4:24 Confucius said: "The Superior Man desires to be hesitant in speech, but sharp in action."

5:15 Confucius said that Tzu Chan had four characteristics of the Superior Man: In his private conduct he was courteous; in serving superiors he was respectful, in providing for the people he was kind; in dealing with the people he was just.

6:25 Confucius said: "The Superior Man who studies culture extensively, and disciplines himself with propriety can keep from error."

14:24 Confucius said: "The Superior Man penetrates (ta) that which is above. The inferior man penetrates that which is below."

14:25 Confucius said: "The ancient scholars studied for their own improvement. Modern scholars study to impress others."

14:28 Tseng Tzu said: "The Superior Man doesn't worry about those things which are outside of his control."

14:29 Confucius said: "The Superior Man is humble in his speech but superb in his actions."

15:18 Confucius said: "The Superior Man suffers from his own lack of ability, not from lack of recognition."

15:19 Confucius said: "The Superior Man is concerned about the kind of reputation he will have after he passes away."

15:20 Confucius said: "The Superior Man seeks within himself. The inferior man seeks within others."

15:21 Confucius said: "The Superior Man strives but does not wrangle. He has friends, but doesn't belong to a clique."

15:22 Confucius said: "The Superior Man does not promote a man because of his words, and does not disregard the words because of the man."

17:24 Tzu Kung asked, "Does the Superior Man also have things that he hates?" Confucius said, "He does. He hates those who advertise the faults of others. He hates those who abide in lowliness and slander the great. He hates those who are bold without propriety. He hates those who are convinced of their own perfection, and closed off to anything else. How about you, what do you hate?" Tzu Kung said, "I hate those who take a little bit of clarity as wisdom; I hate those who take disobedience as courage; I hate those who take disclosing people's weak points to be straightforwardness."

CHARACTERISTICS OF THE PERSON OF *REN* IN THE *ANALECTS*

4:1 Confucius said: "As for a neighborhood, it is its ren that makes it beautiful. If you choose to live in a place that lacks jen, how can you grow in wisdom?"

4:2 Confucius said: "If you lack ren you can't handle long periods of difficulty or long periods of comfortability. Ren men are comfortable in ren. The wise take advantage of ren."

4:3 Confucius said: "Only the ren person is able to really like others or to really dislike them."

4:4 Confucius said: "If you are really committed to jen, you will have no evil in you."

4:5 Confucius said, "Riches and honors are what all men desire. But if they cannot be attained in accordance with the Dao they should not be kept. Poverty and low status are what all men hate. But if they cannot be avoided while staying in accordance with the Tao, you should not avoid them. If a Superior Man departs from ren, how can he be worthy of that name? A Superior Man never leaves ren for even the

time of a single meal. In moments of haste he acts according to it. In times of difficulty or confusion he acts according to it."

6:20 Fan Ch'ih asked about the marks of wisdom. Confucius said, "Working to give the people justice and paying respect to the spirits, but keeping away from them, you can call wisdom." He asked about the marks of jen. Confucius said, "Ah yes, jen. If you suffer first and then attain it, it can be called ren."

6:21 Confucius said: "The wise enjoy the sea, the ren enjoy the mountains. The wise are busy, the ren are tranquil. The wise are happy, the ren are eternal."

7:29 Confucius said: "Is ren far away? If I aspire for ren it is right here!"

14:7 Confucius said: "There are some cases where a Superior Man may not be a man of ren, but there are no cases where an inferior man is a man of ren."

14:11 Confucius said: "To be poor without resentment is difficult. To be rich without arrogance is easy."

14:13 Tzu Lu asked what constitutes a 'perfected man.' Confucius said: "If you have the wisdom of Tsang Wu Chung, the desirelessness of Kung Ch'o, the courage of Pien Chuang Tzu and the abilities of Zan Ch'iu, and are also refined through propriety and music, you might indeed be called a 'perfected man.' But if you want to perfect yourself right now, why would you need all of that? When you see an opportunity for advantage, think of Righteousness. When you meet danger, leave it up to destiny. When someone reminds you of an old promise and it doesn't rattle you at all, you can be regarded as a 'perfected man.'"

17:6 Tzu Chang asked Confucius about ren. Confucius said, "If you can practice these five things with all the people, you can be called ren." Tzu Chang asked what they were. Confucius said, "Courtesy, generosity, honesty, persistence, and kindness. If you are courteous, you will not be disrespected; if you are generous, you will gain everything. If you are honest, people will rely on you. If you are persistent you will get results. If you are kind, you can employ people."

PART B

DAOIST TEXTS

DESCRIPTIONS OF THE TRUE SAGE IN THE *ZHUANG-ZI*

Deformities, or Evidence of a Full Character

In the state of Lu there was a man, named Wang T'ai, who had had one of his legs cut off. His disciples were as numerous as those of Confucius. Ch'ang Chi asked

Confucius, saying, "This Wang T'ai has been mutilated, yet he has as many followers in the Lu State as you. He neither stands up to preach nor sits down to give discourse; yet those who go to him empty, depart full. Is he the kind of person who can teach without words and influence people's minds without material means? What manner of man is this?"

"He is a sage," replied Confucius, "I wanted to go to him, but am merely behind the others. Even I will go and make him my teacher,—why not those who are lesser than I? And I will lead, not only the State of Lu, but the whole world to follow him."

"The man has been mutilated," said Ch'ang Chi, "and yet people call him 'Master.' He must be very different from the ordinary men. If so, how does he train his mind?"

"Life and Death are indeed changes of great moment," answered Confucius, "but they cannot affect his mind. Heaven and earth may collapse, but his mind will remain. Being indeed without flaw, it will not share the fate of all things. It can control the transformation of things, while preserving its source intact."

"How so?" asked Ch'ang Chi. "From the point of view of differentiation of things," replied Confucius, "we distinguish between the liver and the gall, between the Ch'u State and the Yueh State. From the point of view of their sameness, all things are One. He who regards things in this light does not even trouble about what reaches him through the senses of hearing and sight, but lets his mind wander in the moral harmony of things. He beholds the unity in things, and does not notice the loss of particular objects. And thus the loss of his leg is to him as would be the loss of so much dirt."

Autumn Floods

"Therefore, the truly great man does not injure others and does not credit himself with charity and mercy. He seeks not gain, but does not despise the servants who do. He struggles not for wealth, but does not lay great value on his modesty. He asks for help from no man, but is not proud of his self-reliance, neither does he despise the greedy. He acts differently from the vulgar crowd, but does not place high value on being different or eccentric; nor because he acts with the majority does he despise those that flatter a few. The ranks and emoluments of the world are to him no cause for joy; its punishments and shame no cause for disgrace. He knows

that right and wrong cannot be distinguished, that great and small cannot be defined.

The Perfected of Old[39]

What, then, is a perfected?

The perfected of old did not fight it if he had little, did not grow proud if he had much. He never planned his affairs. Someone like this would make a mistake and not feel bad about it; he would attain success and not claim credit for it. Someone like this would climb into high places and not get nervous. He would enter water and not get wet; he would enter fire and not get burned. All this is because his knowledge could reach to the Dao itself. . . .

The perfected of old did not know how to delight in life, nor did he know how to loathe death. He came to be without pleasure and went back to nonbeing without refusal. He came in an instant, he went in an instant, and that was all. He never forgot where he began; he never pursued where he would end. He received life and enjoyed it. But then he forgot about it and returned it when the time came. This is what we mean by not using the mind to repel the Dao, nor using humanity to assist heaven. Such indeed is the perfected. . . .

The perfected of old bore himself with dignity and did not bulge. He appeared to lack, yet he would receive nothing. He was upright in his correctness but never insistent. He was strong in his position, yet never showed off.

Mild and cheerful—he seemed joyous.
Reluctant—he would not help himself.
Annoyed—he let it show in his face.
Giving—he found rest in his virtue.
Tolerant—he seemed like the common world.
Imposing—he would never be controlled.
Withdrawn—he seemed to prefer solitude.
Bemused—he forgot what he was going to say.

Within Religious Daoism, it was not uncommon to find meditation manuals that included depictions of goddesses descending from the heavens in order to offer physical and spiritual comfort to male adepts in search of immortality. One such encounter is contained in the *Shangqing* text from the Tang Period entitled *Scripture of the Mysterious Perfected*. What insights about Daoist spirituality during the Tang Period can be gleaned from this passage?

---

[39]Kohn, *Taoist Experience*, pp. 282–283.

VISUALIZATION TECHNIQUES IN RELIGIOUS DAOISM FROM *SCRIPTURE OF THE MYSTERIOUS PERFECTED*[40]

[2a] Make the sun or the moon stand right in front of your mouth, about nine feet away. The rays of their light should be directed toward your mouth so they can easily enter.

Now visualize a young lady in the sun or the moon. On her head she is wearing a purple cap; her cloak and skirt are of vermilion brocade. She calls herself Jade Maiden of Cinnabar Morning Light of Greatest and Highest Mystery. Her taboo name is Binding Coil, and she is also known as the Secret Perfected.

From her mouth she now emits a red energy, which fills the space between the light rays of the sun or the moon. See how the light rays merge and combine with the morning light of the Jade Maiden. When they have amalgamated completely, let them enter your mouth.

[2b] Hold on to the light and swallow it; then visualize the Jade Maiden emit another stream of light. Practice this nine times ten, then stop.

Now visualize the Jade Maiden and order the luminants of either the sun or the moon to press intimately on your face. Make the Jade Maiden press her mouth tightly upon your own, and allow her energy fluids to enter deeply into you.

Softly utter the following incantation:

[3a] Oh, Purple Perfected of Great Empyrean,
Hidden Goddess of the Hall of Light!
Oh, Living Essence of the Sun and the Moon,
Binding Coil, Jade Maiden!
Oh, goddess born prior even to emptiness,
Known as the Secret Perfected!
Your head is crowned by purple radiance,
A numinous cap of lotus leaves.
Your body is wrapped in a brocade cloak,
A flying skirt of vermilion cinnabar.
Oh, come out of the sun and enter the moon,
You celestial light of enchanting fragrance!
May your mouth emit red energy—
Oh, let it drip into my Three Primes!
May my face gave upon the Well of Heaven,
Softer become my spirit soul, strong my material parts.
May the mysterious fluid come floating to me
And the embryo essence within grow to completion!
May my five orbs within develop florescence!
May my pupils be open to look back inside!
May I suspect and control the myriad spirits!
May I be a flying immortal near the Ruler of Fates!

Following this incantation, visualize the mouth of the Jade Maiden spouting forth salival fluid. Let it flow into your own mouth. Then rinse with this fluid and swallow it. Perform this ninety times, then stop.

Once this is accomplished, just calm your mind and open your thoughts. At this point you can perform the practice frequently, no longer the subject to various limitations. . . .

[4a] Practice this for five years, and the Jade Maiden of Greatest Mystery will descend to you and lie down to share your mat. The Jade Maiden might even divide her shape for you into a host of like jade maidens who will serve your every whim.

This is due to the proper accordance of impulses, to the right combination of essences. It is the pure transformation of life, the essential vision of the true inner forms of all.

With this you have reached the perfect state of superior essence, the wondrous response to the divine impulse.

The perfected officers on high have developed this method of the sun's morning light and the practice involving the two luminants in order to allow human beings to pervade the universal numen and reach utter perfection. People with this practice can embody pure life and develop jade-like glow.

[4b] With this you can command the myriad spirits and ascend to the halls of the emperor-on-high.

SECTION 9: Ending: Death, Judgment, and the Afterlife

What happens to the human personality at death? One answer to this question is suggested in the following excerpt from the ancient Confucian classic *Tso Chuan* (*Master Tso's Commentary on the Spring and Autumn Annals*). This text is a compilation of historical tales and legends about northern China between 722 and 481 BCE. Tradition credits Confucius as its editor. This excerpt assumes that the human personality consists of two souls. According to this selection, what happens to these souls at death?

PART A

CONFUCIAN TEXTS

WHAT HAPPENS AT DEATH FROM *MASTER TSO'S COMMENTARY ON THE SPRING AND AUTUMN ANNALS*

The Wraith of Po-yu[41]

The people of Cheng were all frightened of Po-yu, and if someone said, "Po-yu is here!" they would all run away heedless of where they went. In the second

---

[40]Kohn, *Taoist Experience*, pp. 269–271.

[41]Translation from Sommer, *Chinese Religions*, pp. 25–26.

month, when the punishments were being decided, someone dreamed that Po-yu appeared in armor and walked around, saying, "On the day *jen-tze* I will kill Ti, and next year, on the day *jen-yin*, I will kill Tuan." When the *jen-tze* arrived and Ti did actually die, the people became even more frightened; when Kung-sun Tuan died on the day *jen-yin* in the month when the states Ch'i and Yen made peace, they became absolutely terrified. In the next month, Tzu-ch'an gave appointments to Kung-sun Hsieh and to Liang Chih, the son of Po-yu, to placate the wraith. The incidents stopped. When Tzu-t'ai Shu asked Tzu-ch'an why he did this, he replied, "When ghosts have a place to return to, they do not become wraiths, and now I have given them a place to return to. . . ."

When Tzu-ch'an went to Chin, Chao Ching-tzu asked him whether it was possible that Po-yu really had become a ghost. Tzu-ch'an replied, "It is possible. When humans are born, they first develop what is called the corporeal soul. When the yang force develops, then there is the anima soul. By interacting with things their subtle energies increase, and the corporeal and anima souls strengthen. Eventually their energies intensity until they become numinous and bright. If average men or women should die violently, they are able to linger near people as malevolent wraiths. . . . Po-yu was from a family that held political power for three generations. He had access to many things, and his subtle energies were strong. He came from a great and distinguished clan. Doesn't it stand to reason that it was possible for him to become a wraith when he suffered a violent death?"

Like the Buddha, Confucius refrained from metaphysical speculation and therefore made few comments about that which lies beyond death. Lao-zi and Zhuang-zi, in contrast, spoke often about the return of humankind to its source—the eternal *Dao*. The final selections include some rare Confucian statements in the *Analects* about death and the great beyond. These words are followed by selections from the *Dao-de-jing* and the *Zhuang-zi* that offer Daoist insights into that which is unknowable and that which can be known.

WHAT LIES BEYOND DEATH?
FROM THE *ANALECTS*

4:8 Confucius said: "If I can hear the Dao in the morning, in the evening I can die content."

7:34 The Master was very sick, and Tzu Lu said that he would pray for him. Confucius said, "Is there such a thing?" Tzu Lu said, "There is. The Eulogies say: 'I pray for you to the spirits of the upper and lower realm.'" Confucius said, "Then I have been praying for a long time already."

8:3 Tseng Tzu was ill. He summoned his disciples and said, "Uncover my feet and hands. The Book of Odes says: 'He was cautious, Apprehensive. As if at the edge of a deep chasm; As if treading on thin ice.' From now, I know that I have gotten past this (sickness)."

8:4 While Tseng Tzu was ill, Meng Cheng Tzu went to see him. Tseng Tzu said, "When a bird is about to die, its song is melancholy. When a man is about to die, his words are excellent. The Way prized by the Superior Man has three aspects: In his behavior and deportment he avoids brashness and arrogance. When paying attention to his facial expressions he is guided by honesty. When speaking, he avoids vulgarity and slander. As far as attending to the sacrificial tables—there are specialists hired for these jobs."

11:11 Chi Lu asked about serving the spirits. Confucius said, "If you can't yet serve men, how can you serve the spirits?" Lu said, "May I ask about death?" Confucius said, "If you don't understand what life is, how will you understand death?"

14:37 Confucius said: "Aah! No one understands me!" Tzu Kung said, "What do you mean, 'No one understands you'?" Confucius said, "I have no resentment against Heaven, no quarrel with men. I study from the bottom and penetrate to the top. Who understands me? Heaven does!"

17:18 Confucius said: "I wish I could avoid talking." Tzu Kung said, "Master, if you didn't speak, what would we disciples have to pass on?" Confucius said, "Does Heaven speak? Yet the four seasons continue to change, and all things are born. Does Heaven speak?"

PART B
DAOIST TEXTS

FROM THE *DAO-DE-JING*

50. The Master gives himself up to whatever the moment brings.
He knows that he is going to die, and he has nothing left to hold on to:
no illusions in his mind, no resistances in his body.
He doesn't think about his actions; they flow from the core of his being.
He holds nothing back from life; therefore he is ready for death,
as a man is ready for sleep after a good day's work.

74. If you realize that all things change,
there is nothing you will try to hold on to.
If you aren't afraid of dying, there is nothing you can't achieve.
Trying to control the future is
like trying to take the master carpenter's place.
When you handle the master carpenter's tools,
chances are that you'll cut your hand.

76. Men are born soft and supple; dead, they are stiff and hard.
Plants are born tender and pliant; dead, they are brittle and dry.
Thus whoever is stiff and inflexible is a disciple of death.
Whoever is soft and yielding is a disciple of life.
The hard and stiff will be broken. The soft and supple will prevail.

FROM THE *ZHUANG-ZI*

The Preservation of Life

Human life is limited, but knowledge is limitless. To drive the limited in pursuit of the limitless is fatal; and to presume that one really knows is fatal indeed!

In doing good, avoid fame. In doing bad, avoid disgrace. Pursue a middle course as your principle. Thus you will guard your body from harm, preserve your life, fulfill your duties by your parents, and live your allotted span of life. . . .

When Laotse died, Ch'in Yi went to the funeral. He uttered three yells and departed. A disciple asked him saying, "Were you not our Master's friend?"

"I was," replied Ch'in Yi.

"And if so, do you consider that a sufficient expression of grief at his death?" added the disciple.

"I do," said Ch'in Yi. "I had thought he was a (mortal) man, but now I know that he was not. When I went in to mourn, I found old persons weeping as if for their children, young ones wailing as if for their mothers. When these people meet, they must have said words on the occasion and shed tears without any intention. (To cry thus at one's death) is to evade the natural principles (of life and death) and increase human attachments, forgetting the source from which we receive this life. The ancients called this 'evading the retribution of Heaven.'

"The Master came, because it was his time to be born; He went, because it was his time to go away. Those who accept the natural course and sequence of things and live in obedience to it are beyond joy and sorrow. The ancients spoke of this as the emancipation from bondage. The fingers may not be able to

supply all the fuel, but the fire is transmitted, and we know not when it will come to an end."

Like the scriptures of most world religions, the sacred canons of Religious Daoism contain apocalyptic writings that suggest a coming cataclysm of great proportions. Such an event was prophesied in one of the early scriptures of the Celestial Masters School entitled the *Commands and Admonitions for the Families of the Great Dao*. This mid-third-century CE text, which allegedly was the work of the Celestial Master Zhuang Lu, offers a brief history of the five occasions when the Lord Dao intervened among humans: (1) during the Zhou Dynasty, when the *Scripture of Great Peace* was revealed to Gan Ji; (2) in the fifth century BCE, when the historical Lao-zi produced the *Dao-de-jing*; (3) during the lifetime of the "Perfected Person" (meant to be the historical Buddha), when a simplified revelation of the *Dao* was given for the barbarians; (4) at the beginning of the Han Dynasty, when the Master Yellow Stone gave a revelation to Zhang Liang; and finally, (5) on June 11, 142 CE, when the Lord Lao-zi bestowed on Zhang Daoling the title of Celestial Master, thus launching the sects of the Celestial Masters. Interestingly, the text does not promise a further epiphany of the *Dao* to inaugurate the coming age of Great Peace. Instead, its purpose is to warn the people of the dangers of forsaking the *Dao* and to urge them to return to the teachings of their founders. According to this text, how have the people become corrupted during the century since the origins of the Celestial Masters, and what judgments and rewards are in store for this fallen generation? Compare the teachings of this scripture with the apocalyptic prophecies in the sacred canons of the other world religions. How do you explain the similarities and differences?

APOCALYPTIC WRITINGS WITHIN RELIGIOUS DAOISM FROM *COMMANDS AND ADMONITIONS FOR THE FAMILIES OF THE GREAT DAO*[42]

On the first day of the fifth month in the first year of the Han Peace reign period [11 June 142 CE] the Dao created the Way of the Covenantal Authority of Correct Unity at Red-Stone Wall at Quting of Lin'ang County, the Commandery of Shu. Binding tallies were formed with heaven and earth, and the twenty-four

---

[42]Bokenkamp, *Early Daoist Scriptures*, pp. 165–185.

parishes were established to promulgate the primal, original, and inaugural pneumas to rule the people.

You do not know even the basics of the Dao, nor can you distinguish its true revelations from the false. You only strive with one another for high status in the world and worry about assigning one another a social standing. In so doing, you turn your backs on the Dao and revel against its powers. You wish to follow human understanding, but the human understanding delights in chaos! . . .

The prohibitions of the Dao, the origins of the True and Correct, the explanations of the divine Transcendents—all were promulgated to you by the Dao. This is the extent to which the Dao thinks of you! How regrettable, how injurious it is to consider the [Scriptures] to be not True and not Correct, and on this basis to proclaim that the Dao deceives its people.

Coming to the time when the kingdom of the righteous toppled, those who fled into exile and those killed were numbered by the tens of thousands.[43] Since the exile, we have been scattered over the entire kingdom. The Dao has often saved your lives. Sometimes it has broken through the pneumas to speak to you; sometimes a minister or magistrate of the earlier days [in Hanzhong] has tried to reform you, but still you do not keep faith. This is extremely regrettable.

If you wish morning, you must first have evening. If you desire Great Peace, you must first experience chaos. Since the evil of humanity could not be rooted out, you must first pass through war, illness, flood, drought, and even death. Your life spans have been depleted, and so it is appropriate that you must come up against these things. Though this is so, the favored will be without injury, since such persons have practiced the Dao in the past in order to prepare against such things as have come upon us today. Even if you die without reaching the age of Great Peace, your children and grandchildren will be blessed with Heaven's favor.

Those of these final generations are frivolous and lacking in substance. They are not resolute of heart. Both the prior and the new families [of Daoists], observing the people of this generation and perceiving the coming change, should be able to reform their

hearts. If you performed good deeds, practicing humanity and duty, then all will be well with you. You will see Great Peace. You will pass thought the catastrophes unscathed and become the seed people of the later age. Although there will be disasters of war, illness, and flood, you will confront them without injury. Thus you are named after the Dao. If you keep your mind fixed on the Dao, the Dao will keep you in mind. If you do not, the Dao will not be mindful of you. . . .

Henceforth, all people under Heaven will be harassed and in panic like sheep. War and pestilence presses on all sides; evil pneumas circulate. You should keep in mind the good of the day, revering Heaven and honoring the spirits. If you cherish life and practice the Dao with your thoughts on the True and Correct, the Dao will cherish you. If you do not remain mindful of the Dao, the Dao will distance itself from you. When you are suddenly confronted with disaster or injury, you should be careful not to regret [your service to the Dao], since this will cause suffering later. . . .

By now the Three Heavens are infuriated, and killing pnemas criss and cross throughout the world. The five planets have lost their measured movement, and the Grand White shines forth. There are perverse winds, thunders in winter, and aphelial and parhelian comets that dip and rise. In these ways, Heaven suspends images in the sky to inform people that if they do not keep faith with the Dao, the Dao will become enraged. Those who die will find their pneumas resting in the dark valley. . . .

In recent years, there have been plagues in the four quarters that have swept away all of the inauspicious. This was merely the slaughter of evil persons. Those who clung to the Dao and delighted in goodness were personally protected by Heaven as babes would be guarded from harm. Confronted by danger, they pass through it as easily as the tongue avoids the teeth. Do you all know now what I mean?

From this time on, it is impermissible for you to recklessly establish anyone in any official parish position. If you disobey me again, you will incur injury. Do not blame me [when this happens].

When Libationers cure the ill, they should do so at the onset of the illness. But, once the illness is cured, if it returns again, that person is evil. Do not again treat or cure them.

All of our households should transform one another through loyalty and filiality, so that fathers are

---

[43]This reference refers to the events that followed the year 215 CE after Zhuang Lu submitted to the founder of the Wei Dynasty and the members of the Celestial Masters sect were dispersed from Hanzhong, the region of their origins.

magnanimous and sons filial, husbands faithful and wives chaste, elder brothers respectful and the younger obedient. Mornings and evenings you should practice "clarity and stillness." Root out all covetousness, abandon the pursuit of personal profit, and rid yourself of desire. Reform your evil cravings. Pity the poor and cherish the old. Be liberal in supplying others and in giving way to them. Drive from you heart excesses of jealousy, joy, and anger so that your emotions are constantly harmonious and your eyes and belly in accord. Aid the kingdom in strengthening its mandate. Abandon all of your past evil pursuits. Those who from today on, practice good actions will find that disaster and disease melt away form them, and will become the seed people of the later age.

The people should not complain of their poverty and suffering, or covert riches, happiness, and high position. You have seen with your own eyes and heard with your own ears: From ancient times, have the rich and honored ever endured? Their possessions are abandoned on the ground and their bodies perish in the marketplace. Looked at in this way, the old proverb is correct: "A dead prince is not worth a live rat." What you achieve will be life, and the Dao is where you should seek it.

You should remember that the Dao conceals itself and is nameless. Name is an axe that hacks at the body. "Good actions leave no trace." If they wish to make it so that others do not see their "traces," those who practice the Dao should regulate their bodies and nurture their lives to seek blessing. Instead of which you teach others to give free rein to the self. If the self is given free rein, people will see its traces and the axe will be keen. If the axe that hews down the body is keen, good fortune departs and bad arrives. Should you not be cautious? Should you not be fearful? The reason heaven and earth endure is because they lack willfulness. And that which "does not act falsely, leaves nothing left undone." Only when one does not allow others to see one's traces can one truly accomplish wonders.

You vulgar people are truly comical: When you do some small good deed, you always want others to know of it, and when you differ by so much as a grain of rice from others, you expect to be considered worthy. These are the sorts of benefit derived from what is not the Dao. In all cases, such behavior is a violation of the proscriptions of the Dao.

Now I transmit my teachings so that you people [of the Dao], both those who joined previously and new members, shall know my heart. Do not forsake it.

PowerWeb SUPPLEMENTS

1. **Confucius**, Jonathan D. Spence, *The Wilson Quarterly*, Autumn 1993.
2. **Supernatural Retribution and Human Destiny**, Cynthia Brokaw, *from Religions of China in Practice*, Princeton University Press, 1996.
3. **Stories from an Illustrated Explanation of the** *"Tract of the Most Exalted on Action and Response,"* Catherine Bell, *from Religions of China in Practice*, Princeton University Press, 1996.
4. **Daoist Sitting Meditation**, Zhu Hui, *The Empty Vessel*, Summer 2002.

In an elegant piece from the *Wilson Quarterly*, historian Jonathan Spence illustrates the influence of Confucian ideas on Chinese culture and then comments on the recent revival of scholarly interest in Confucian studies. After surveying this brief introduction into the Chinese mind, readers will enjoy examining several additional supplemental sources that describe the ethical and spiritual sides of Chinese religiosity. Two *PowerWeb* selections taken from *Religions of China in Practice* highlight the traditional Chinese preoccupation with matters of morality. In these pieces, Catherine Bell discusses the importance of morality books in China's religious culture, and Cynthia Brokaw interprets the thoughts of a seventeenth century Confucian who elaborated a method of calculating one's accumulation of merit and demerit throughout life. Finally, the spiritual side of Chinese religious practice is presented in a piece by Zhu Hui that introduces readers to "Static Gong," a Daoist meditation that practitioners claim brings physical, mental and spiritual well-being. After reading these selections, students will be better able to express an opinion on the proposition that traditional Chinese religions focus more on practical and ethical concerns than on speculative and theological ones.

Readings from *PowerWeb: Religion* are available at the McGraw-Hill *PowerWeb* website http://www.dushkin.com/powerweb. A personal access code to *PowerWeb: Religion* is provided free with each new copy of this book. Those who purchase a used copy may buy an access code at the website.

SELECTED BIBLIOGRAPHY

Birrell, Anne. *Chinese Mythology: An Introduction.* Baltimore: Johns Hopkins University Press, 1993.
Bokenkamp, Stephen R. *Early Daoist Scriptures.* Berkeley, CA: University of California Press, 1997.

Chan, Wing-Tsit, translated and compiled. *A Source Book in Chinese Philosophy*. Princeton, NJ: Princeton University Press, 1973.

Clart, Philip, and Charles B. Jines, ed. *Religion in Modern Taiwan*. Honolulu: University of Hawaii Press, 2003.

Confucius: The Analects. Translated with an Introduction by D. C. Lau. New York: Penguin Books, 1979.

Dean, Kenneth. *Taoist Ritual and Popular Cults of South-east China*. Princeton, NJ: Princeton University Press, 1993.

Eskildsen, Stephen. *Asceticism in Early Taoist Religion*. Albany, NY: State University of New York Press, 1998.

Kaltenmark, Max. *Lao Tzu and Taoism*. Stanford, CA: Stanford University Press, 1969.

Kohn, Livia. *Monastic Life in Medieval Daoism: A Cross Cultural Perspective*. Honolulu: University of Hawaii Press, 2003.

Kohn, Livia, ed. *The Taoist Experience: An Anthology*. Albany, NY: State University of New York Press, 1993.

Kwang-Ching, Liu, and Richard Shek. *Heterodoxy in Late Imperial China*. Honolulu: University of Hawaii Press, 2004.

Legge, James, trans. *The Sacred Books of China*. Oxford: The Clarendon Press, 1885.

Lopez, Donald S., Jr., ed. *Religions of China in Practice*. Princeton, NJ: Princeton University Press, 1996.

Mair, Victor. *Wandering on the Way*. Honolulu: University of Hawaii Press, 1998.

Mitchell, Stephen, trans. *Dao-de-jing*. New York: Harper & Row, 1988.

Ng, Wai-ming. *The I-Ching in Tokugawa Thought and Culture*. Honolulu: University of Hawaii Press, 2000.

Overmyer, Daniel L. *Religions of China*. San Francisco: Harper, 1986.

Pines, Yuri. *Foundations of Confucian Thought*. Honolulu: University of Hawaii Press, 2002.

Robinet, Isabelle. *Taoism: Growth of a Religion*. Stanford, CA: Stanford University Press, 1997.

Sommer, Deborah, ed. *Chinese Religion: An Anthology of Sources*. New York: Oxford University Press, 1995.

Spence, Jonathan D. *The Search for Modern China*. New York: W. W. Norton, 1999.

Taylor, Rodney L. *The Religious Dimensions of Confucianism*. Albany, NY: State University of New York Press, 1990.

Tu, Wei-ming. *Neo-Confucian Thought in Action*. Berkeley, CA: University of California Press, 1976.

Welch, Holmes, *The Parting of the Way: Lao Tzu and the Taoist Movement*. London: Methuen, 1957.

Native American Religions

7

What's in a name? To make any statement about the religions of the descendants of the original inhabitants of the Western Hemisphere is a dangerous task. First, among the thousands of languages of these peoples, it is difficult to find a language with a word that corresponds to the English word "religion." These inhabitants were deeply spiritual, but few viewed themselves as religious. Second, this diversely populated group encompasses cultures spread across more than 16 million square miles of land in a multitude of climate and geological regions. Nonetheless, amidst the many differences are some common features. Our task in this chapter will be to point toward those commonalities, while always remembering that great diversity exists within these peoples.

Even selecting a noun to identify these peoples is controversial. The word *Indian* is the legacy of the European sailors of 1492 who mistook what we now know as the Western Hemisphere for another continent further to the west, the continent that included India. Technically, that term was not incorrect, since the sixteenth-century Spanish word for Indians referred at that time to all peoples living east of the Indus River, which is where the inhabitants of the Western Hemisphere live. Many dislike the use of this term, however, not only because it erroneously associates these peoples with those living in India but also because this is the official term that made its way into the laws and treaties of the United States and Canada. Likewise, the phrase *Native American* is troublesome to some because it also owes its origins to the European Amerigo Vespucci, an explorer who had few positive words to say about the inhabitants of this part of the world. Similarly, the expression *Native Peoples* also is prob-

lematic; anyone born in this hemisphere, no matter what the heritage of his or her descendants, may claim to be native to this land.

Generally, the preferred way to identify the peoples of the Western Hemisphere is through a reference to their specific tribal names. With more than 600 officially recognized tribal peoples in this population, however, few nonspecialists have the knowledge and the vocabularies to make these distinctions. Moreover, even these tribal names are often clouded in controversy. For instance, the people widely known as Navajo prefer to be called Dineh, which means in their language "First People." Likewise, the Lakota and Dakota peoples prefer these labels over the more widely used term Sioux, which itself was derived from a French variation of a Chippewa word for "enemy."

So how should one identify these peoples? When addressing persons of a particular tribal group, it would be courteous to be more concerned with what is respectful than what academic authorities claim to be the correct label. Thus, simply to call them as they wish to be called would be the preferred way. This courtesy is not possible in a generalized textbook, so in this chapter we shall use all of the terms interchangeably, and in advance, apologize to those who may find our terminology to be offensive.

SETTING

The origins of Native American spiritualities must be traced to the ancestors of the indigenous peoples of the Americas. Who were these distant people, and when did they arrive in the New World? From the perspective of modern scholars, the first people to

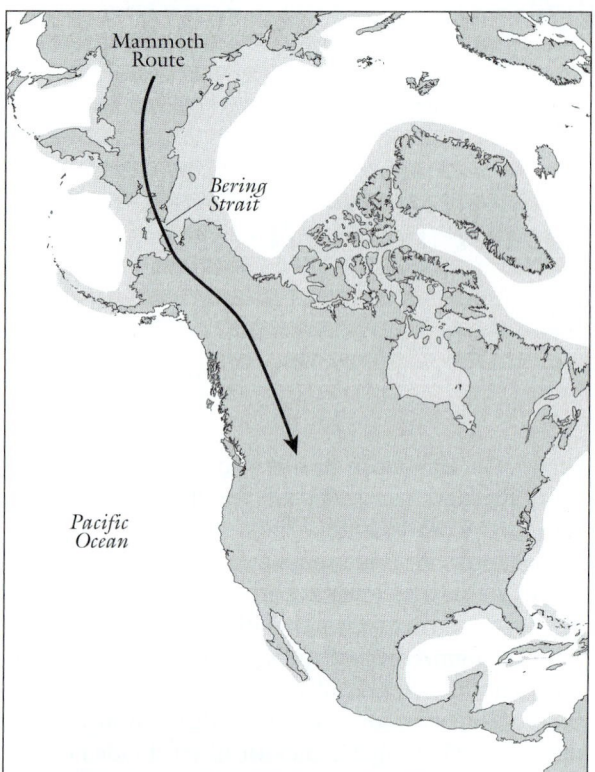

The mammoth route across the Bering Strait.

most likely arrived during one of these intervals. Some controversial data, including human artifacts from a site in Brazil allegedly 33,000 years old, provides support for the earlier period of migration. However, because the preponderance of the uncontested archeological evidence dates to only about 15,000 years ago, most regard the later era to be the most likely time of arrival. Thus, while both arguments are plausible, the majority opinion holds that some time about 15,000 years ago, near the end of the last Ice Age, the first peoples unknowingly migrated to North America over a 1,000-mile-wide land bridge that connected Asia and Alaska.

Over the centuries these nomadic peoples probably followed herds of large animals southward, including the mammoth (a gigantic, hairy, elephantlike creature that became extinct about 8,000 years ago), along an ice-free corridor in the western High Plains that lay between the impassable glaciers in eastern Canada and the mountain glaciers of the Rockies and Coast ranges. These nomads, often called "Paleo-Indians," were anatomically identical to modern humans and held skills comparable to other Old World peoples at the time. They, for instance, knew how to make and use fire and how to survive in cold environments with no domesticated animal save the dog. Without agricultural knowledge, they survived by hunting the game that they tracked. By about 10,000 years ago, these peoples had developed great skills in manufacturing spears and other weapons capable of killing large game. Spear points dating to the tenth millennium BCE were discovered about 100 years ago in New Mexico, and since then, similar "Clovis" blades have been found throughout the United States. The presence of these points at numerous locations demonstrates the mobility of the Paleo-Indians and confirms that pockets of these hunters lived in small, armed family units in every corner of the continent.

About 10,000 years ago, the planet began to enter what geologists call the Holocene Period, a label that refers to postglacial times. During the next 5 millennia the earth warmed, glaciers receded toward the poles, and sea levels rose. The warming temperatures produced changes in vegetation patterns, which resulted in the extinction of the mammoths and a number of other large animals, including the American horse and camel. Other animals, such as the bison, survived by evolving through natural selection into a smaller species about half the size of

inhabit the Western Hemisphere arrived during what geologists call the Pleistocene Ice Age. Because physical and genetic data link contemporary Native Americans to Asian populations, most scholars believe that humans entered North America from Asia. The most likely route of this journey was through the region that connects Siberia and Alaska. Today this area is known as the Bering Sea, although in previous geological ages, when earth temperatures were cooler, a land bridge connected these regions, thus making land transit possible. On this arid and steeped tundra was an open landscape with sparse grass and brush that supported game animals and nomadic humans who hunted them. It is likely that nomadic hunters entered North America even without knowing it while tracking game.

The 1,000-mile-wide land bridge, commonly referred to as Beringia, was created by low sea levels in two recent geological periods, about 50,000 years ago, and then again between about 25,000 to 13,000 years ago. Consequently, if the first peoples came to America from Asia on foot via Beringia, then they

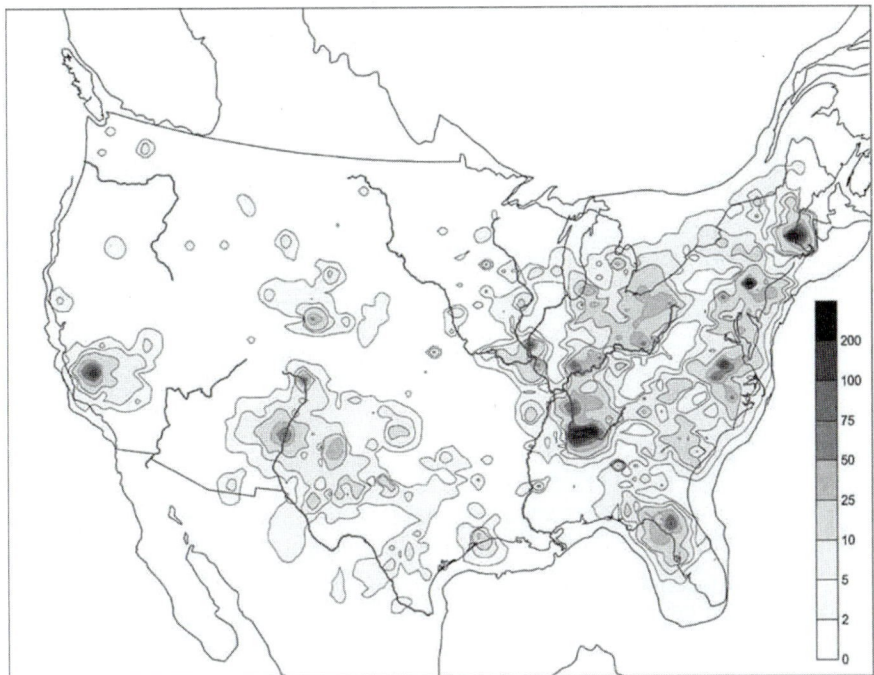

Fluted points dating back some 10,000 years have been discovered across large regions of the North American continent.

their Pleistocene predecessors. The nomadic peoples who lived off these animals were forced to either adapt to the new environment or die.

From Hunter-Gatherers to Cultivators

One adjustment of the hunter-gatherer societies was to broaden their food base. Circumstances forced them to hunt a wider variety of animals, including rodents and other small species. They also invented the bow and arrow as they strove to find more efficient ways to hunt. In addition, early in the Holocene Period those living in temperate latitudes began to focus more on plant resources than did their ancestors. They learned to burn forest edges to weed out shrubs that inhibited the spread of grasslands. Through these human efforts they expanded the acreage of grassland on which the game they hunted could live.

Archaeologists call the era from about 7000 to 1800 BCE the Archaic (meaning "old") Age. During this era regional variations became more distinct. In the Central Plains, bison, antelope, and elk were major food sources. In the Southwest, Archaic peoples hunted smaller animals such as deer, rabbits, and squirrels and supplemented their diets by eating seeds,

nuts, berries, and a variety of insects. The Northwest Coast peoples developed an effective drying and storage technology to preserve salmon taken in spring and fall harvestings. Meanwhile, in the forested coastal Eastern Woodlands, the women and older men collected shellfish, while the younger men hunted for deer.

Often limitation of resources is an engine for cultural change. Late in the Archaic Period, growing population densities in some areas placed a strain on food supplies, thus creating circumstances that demanded new food-getting strategies. Around this time a major cultural breakthrough—the advent of agriculture—took place in some regions. The shift from gathering food to relying upon the cultivation of seeds for food was gradual, but its effects were radical. Some form of New World soil cultivation dates back nearly 10,000 years. At this time the food gatherers in Mexico's Oaxaca Valley (pronounced Wha-ha-ka) survived by traveling from one wild food source to another. Occasionally, they would clear small patches of land near their favorite rock shelters, place seeds in the ground, and later return to the rock shelters to harvest the wild foods seasonally. Over time they noticed that the seeds from the patches they prepared often grew a little larger than

Chronology of the major eras in North and Meso-American civilizations.

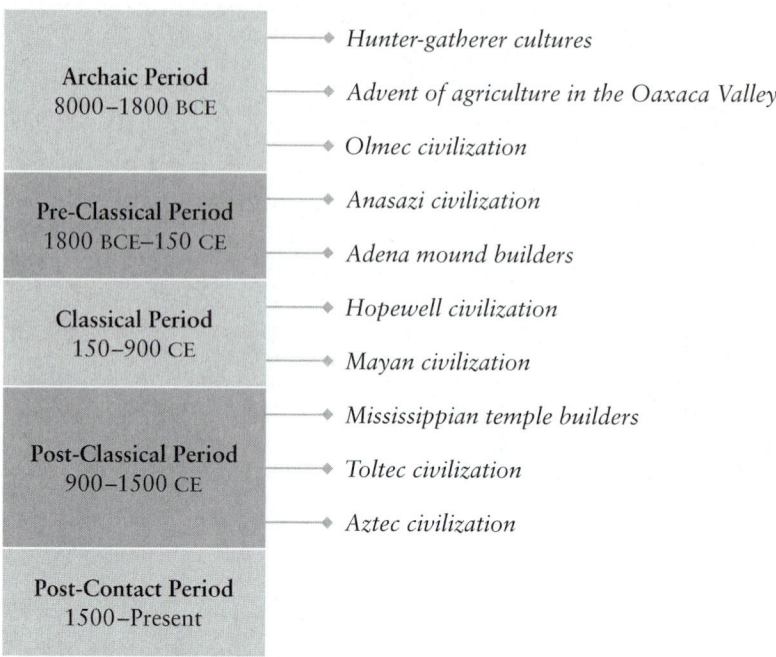

Archaic Period 8000–1800 BCE	➤ *Hunter-gatherer cultures*
	➤ *Advent of agriculture in the Oaxaca Valley*
	➤ *Olmec civilization*
Pre-Classical Period 1800 BCE–150 CE	➤ *Anasazi civilization*
	➤ *Adena mound builders*
Classical Period 150–900 CE	➤ *Hopewell civilization*
	➤ *Mayan civilization*
	➤ *Mississippian temple builders*
Post-Classical Period 900–1500 CE	➤ *Toltec civilization*
	➤ *Aztec civilization*
Post-Contact Period 1500–Present	

those collected from the wild. Around 3500 BCE, these Oaxacans noticed that a mutant of the wild grass teosinte produced large kernels on a cob. Wisely, they cultivated this mutant plant known as maize, or Indian corn. Scholars estimate that as early as 5000 BCE about 10 percent of their diet came from the resources of their garden patches. Following the cultivation of maize, however, upward of 30 percent of their diets came from their agricultural labors. In time, some former food gatherers made the decision to risk their survival on full-time gardening. The risk paid off. After learning how to cultivate beans, an important source of protein, these early sedentary farmers survived on a moderately healthy diet that consisted of what they called the "three sisters": squash, maize, and beans. When interplanted, these crops serendipitously replenished the soil with nitrogen and phosphorus through bacteria and fungi in their roots, thus resulting in a fertilization process that made each crop stronger.

The advent of agriculture triggered other cultural advances as it released growing numbers from the burdens of subsistence activities and provided them with the time/luxury to specialize in other things—artisanship, government, religion, art, engineering, and philosophy. Full-scale agriculture encouraged both the exchange of goods produced by specialized labor

and a rise in urban villages. By Late Archaic times, the Meso-Americans were building densely packed cities with defensive walls. Each city had its public plazas with temples and palaces constructed on impressive platform mounds. Stone altars, giant sculptured heads (perhaps intended as portraits of the mighty rulers), and towering earthen pyramids filled the landscape, while aqueduct systems were constructed to carry water inside the city walls. This Olmec Culture, the first highly advanced civilization created by New World peoples, may have been the "mother culture" that influenced many subsequent developments in this hemisphere. In time other Meso-American states would flourish, only later to weaken and be succeeded by others. Following the Olmecs, various groups of Mayans dominated the Valley of Mexico (ca. 150–900 CE). Later, the Toltecs (ca. 900–1200 CE), and finally the Aztecs (1200–1500 CE), the last peoples to control Meso-America in precontact times, dominated the region.

Cultural Developments North of Mexico

Although few North Americans made any attempt to copy the architectural styles of these Meso-Americans, the cultivation of corn did spread across

This eighth-century Mayan temple to a serpent god has 365 outer steps (one for each day of the year) and a ball court where carvings suggest a custom of sacrificing players following the match.

the southern and southwestern portions of what is presently the United States. Domesticated corn appeared among the peoples of New Mexico by about 3300 BCE and, shortly thereafter, also among the peoples of the Southeast. Unlike wild seeds, corn had to be planted and then given almost daily attention. Watering the crops, weeding the soil, and protecting the gardens from rodents and rabbits took time. As a consequence, the peoples choosing to adopt plant cultivation had to modify their nomadic ways. Overtime, settlements became more permanent and population densities increased. The creation of village life also resulted in more competition for resources and social prestige, changes that eventually would be expressed in greater degrees of social differentiations between the peoples.

Another characteristic of the Archaic Period was the invention of pottery. The invention of pottery not only gave preliterate peoples an avenue for artistic expression, but it also brought benefits to their diet and health through its water carrying and cooking functions. Because pottery-making tools have been found in the graves of women, we assume that women were the potters. The invention of pottery, like the advent of all significant cultural breakthroughs, had an impact on the gender roles of the sexes.

Archaeologists label the next stages of cultural development the Pre-Classical or Formative Stage, the Classical Stage, and Post-Classical Stage. Owing to space limitations, we will only outline developments in two significant American cultures that flourished

during these periods: the Anasazi of the Southwest and the Mound Builders of the East.

The Anasazi of the Southwest

The Anasazi were the ancestors of the Pueblo Indians who live in the Four Corners Region of Arizona, Utah, Colorado, and New Mexico. The term *Anasazi* comes from a Navajo word meaning "enemy." In ancient times theses peoples lived on the cool and relatively wet Colorado Plateau, which enabled them to cultivate corn, beans, and squash without having to dig large irrigation systems. With plenty of wood for fuel and lodges, early Anasazi peoples built ground-level "pit" structures with stone or adobe walls and ceilings supported by timbers overlaid with grass and dirt. Later they built more elaborate cliff dwellings that could be reached through ladders made from timber and chipped niches in cliff walls. Such high and dry cliff lodging not only provided protection from intruders and from climatic conditions, but they also were ideal places to store perishable foods.

One of the largest excavated ancient cliff dwelling sites, Pueblo Bonito in Chaco Culture National Historical Park, has more than 650 rooms and once stood five stories high. Another amazing engineering feat of the Anasazi was the construction of 400 miles of straight, 30-foot-wide roads that radiated outward from the Chaco Canyon in northwestern New Mexico to southwestern Colorado and southeastern Utah. Much effort was taken to build the roads in a straight-line pattern that did not bend to the natural terrain. Mystery remains as to the purpose of this labor-intensive project built by people who did not have the wheel or beasts of burden to use these roads. Some scholars speculate the roads were used for military purposes; others argue they were used for the movement of timber; still others assert the roads were constructed for religious pilgrims traveling to and from sacred sites in Chaco.

A common feature found in many Anasazi lodges was a circular room that was cut into the ground. This room, known as a *kiva,* had a fireplace in the middle of the floor with a hatch in the ceiling. People entered the *kiva* by a ladder that extended through the hatch. Some *kivas* had benches around the interior walls to seat guests and to hold ritual objects such as a tiny pot or a piece of jewelry. The *kivas* were used both as community gathering places and as places for religious ceremonies. Many modern Pueblo peoples believe that long ago their ancestors came to this world from a world below. The modern Hopis and Zunis, for instance, believe that the Grand Canyon was the spot of emergence. Small holes found in the floor of excavated ancient Anasazi *kiva* sites may have symbolized the emergence of earth people from the world below. Modern Hopis call this hole that provides symbolic access to the lower worlds a *sipapu,* which means "the navel of the earth." Just as the emergence spot is the center of the earth, the *sipapu* in every lodge centers that household within the cosmos.

In comparison with many Native Peoples of the era, the Anasazi were culturally advanced, producing elaborate fineries such as woven baskets, turquoise beaded necklaces, embroidered cotton cloth, and beautiful pottery. Their cultural legacy also includes thousands of pictures of animals, birds, snakes, people, and mythological creatures engraved into the rock formations across the Southwest. Among the more common figures inscribed in their rock art are *Avanyu,* the horned water-snake associated with water, and the famous Southwestern fertility figure *Kokopelli,* the humpback creature carrying a flute. After surviving for more than 2 millennia, the Anasazi culture peaked in the early decades of the thirteenth century CE and then entered into rapid decline. The reasons for its demise remain contested. One popular theory is that droughts in the thirteenth century caused severe food shortages that resulted in starvation and disease. Whatever the cause, by the beginning of the fourteenth century the Anasazi no longer occupied the mesas that had been occupied since ancient times.

The Mound Builders of the East

While the Anasazi Culture was flourishing in the Southwest, the Mound Builders of Adena (ca. 1000 BCE–200 CE) and Hopewell (ca. 300 BCE–700 CE) and later the Mississippian Temple Mound Builders

Ceremonial kiva at Chaco Canyon Indian ruins.

(ca. 750 CE–1450 CE) established great centers of cultural activity in the eastern half of the continent. To a greater degree than the Indians of the West, these peoples took great interest in producing burial monuments for their deceased. The first builders, named the Adena people, lived in the forested lands of Pennsylvania, West Virginia, Kentucky, and Indiana. The earth monuments they constructed were often circular-shaped mounds that resembled living creatures. The Hopewell culture flourished over large areas of the Midwest, with its most flamboyant features located in the Ohio Valley near Chillicothe. The earth monuments built in this region are the largest geometric earth constructions known on the planet. At Mound City, Ohio, for instance, a vast complex of circular, square, and octagonal mounds within a 4-square-mile enclosure are linked by causeways up to 30 miles in length. Similarly, the design at the Great Serpent Mound in Ohio is equally impressive. This site consists of a twisting serpent-shaped earthwork that ends in one direction with encampments that look like a tightly curved serpent tail, and in the other direction with what appears to be a serpent mouth with opened jaws enclosing an oral burial mound. There is much disagreement over the meaning of the structures, but certainly such gigantic efforts would have not been attempted if they did not carry symbolic significance. Inside the enclosures were log tombs that contained human bones and a large quantity of goods, including

flint and obsidian chips, spear-throwers, stone knives, and polished axes. Many of the artifacts came from distances far away, signifying a culture with extensive exchange zones. Interestingly, no one lived permanently within the gigantic geometric embankments. Hopewell, thus, has appropriately been called "unique" because it was a "civilization without cities." The culture endured throughout the Midwest until the beginning of the fifth century, at which time, for not well-understood reasons, the mound building discontinued.

The third group of earth architects in the East, the Mississippian Tradition, represents the highest stage of cultural evolution among the indigenous inhabitants in what currently constitutes the United States. With remarkable earth monuments built in sites that extend from Oklahoma to the eastern coast, the Mississippian peoples constructed flat-topped mounds that served as platforms for elaborate timber temples. Included with the human remains interned at these burial sites were expensive valuables, including copper and mica ornaments, pearls, stone axes, and pottery in the form of trophy heads. Their pottery often was decorated with pictures of weeping eyes, winged/flying human figures, and sun images. Near the mounds were urban centers and rural zones of permanent villages that were supported by maize cultivation. One of the urban sites, Cahokia (located in Illinois just across the Mississippi River from

Great Serpent Mound in Ohio.

St. Louis) once housed a population of some 30,000 inhabitants. Within a five-square-mile land area, the Cahokia people constructed more than 100 earthen mounds of various shapes and sizes, including the fabulous Monk's Mound that towered 100 feet in the air and occupied a base that covered 16 acres. The labor required to build such an edifice signifies the presence of a centralized political organization that was much larger than the small-scale chiefdoms found elsewhere in North America.

Amazingly, this marvelous city survived only 200 years before it entered into rapid decline about 1250 CE. With Meso-American motifs abounding at its site, some speculate that the great wealth and re-markable rise of the Cahokia was tied to a trading al-liance between its rulers and the emperors of the powerful Toltec Empire of Mexico. Consequently, ac-cording to these scholars, Cahokia was fated to fall as rapidly as it rose, following the demise of the Toltec culture in the thirteenth century. Other scholars, how-ever, downplay the Toltec connection and speculate that a depletion of natural resources following cli-matic changes likely caused Cahokia's abandonment. Like many topics of study in the prehistory of North America, much remains to be known about this ar-chitectural marvel, the grandest built in prehistorical times north of Mexico.

The Range of Cultural Diversity

The prehistorical peoples of the Americas varied widely in language, livelihood, and culture. While all in the far distant past were hunter-gatherers, over time some became settled farmers (Southwest and Southeast peoples) while others remained primarily hunters (Plains Indians) or gatherers (California and the Desert Region peoples). Some were primarily fish-ers (Northwest Coast peoples), others hunter-fishers (The Sub-Arctic peoples), and still others fisher-gatherers (Plateau Indians). Still others were hunter-farmers (Northeast and Central Plains peoples). They also varied widely in the styles of their crafts and ar-chitecture. Some built great urban centers (Meso-Americans and Mississippian Temple Builders), while others remained roaming nomads. Some lived pri-marily in small family units, while others had elabo-rate kin and political organizations.

Despite their great differences, for more than 10,000 years the inhabitants of the Americas shared a few things in common—similar DNA, relative iso-lation from Old World technologies and intellectual influences, and, for the overwhelming majority, an absence of a written script. Even these statements, however, cannot be stated absolutely. Some pre-Columbian, trans-Atlantic and trans-Pacific contact probably occurred. From these commonalities—a dis-tant heritage, the New World environment, and the primacy of oral tradition—shared expressions of spir-itualities appeared. These distinctive values include the three common features described in the next sec-tion: a deep respect for sacred place and cyclical time, a metaphysics of nature, and an appreciation of the transformative power of ritual.

SACRED STORIES AND BELIEFS

"A Tewa is not interested in the world of archaeolo-gists," wrote Alfonso Ortiz for the *National Geo-graphic* in 1991. "A Tewa is interested in our own story of our origin, for it holds all that we need to know about our people, and how one should live as a human. The story defines our society. It tells me who I am, where I came from."

These words by this modern Tewa express an opin-ion shared by many Native Americans. For Western-ers who share a time-centered, chronologically arranged worldview, questions such as when and where people originated are questions of interest. For many Native Peoples, however, academic accounts of origins, like the one presented in the previous section, carry less meaning and significance than the sacred tales of origins that have been passed down around campfires from the beginning. Through the sharing of these sacred stories, the world of the gods and the cos-mic order of all things become known.

Native American Cosmologies: Sacred Places in Sacred Time

Especially important for all peoples are the sacred stories that explain the emergence of cosmos from chaos. In Western religious traditions, these stories generally assume the presence of an all-powerful Cre-ator who decides how things should be and brings them into being. This motif is not present in most Native American creation accounts. More common to the Native American peoples are "earth-diver" stories and "emergence" stories that trace a migration of humans from lower worlds.

The *earth-diver* stories explain how the world was formed in the midst of a great body of water. Often in these stories the Earth-Maker sends a variety of animals down into the water to bring up a piece of earth, and from this mud, land is formed. Unlike the classic Genesis account of the West, in this story the earth is not formed out of nothingness because the stuff of which the earth was fashioned already preexisted. Also unlike the Genesis account, in these stories the animals are not simply creatures of an omnipotent Creator but, rather, co-exist with Him and assist Him in the creation process.

According to those who embrace *emergence* creation stories, the universe consists of many layers, some above and some below the human world. In the beautiful but complex Zuni creation story, the cosmos consists of seven spheres. The highest of the spheres is the realm of the life-giving, supreme, bisexual power. Lower spheres are identified with Sun Father, who gives light during the day, and Moon Mother, who gives light at night while demonstrating the natural cycles of all life forms. Humans inhabit the middle world, the fourth sphere, which is associated with Earth Mother, the source of all vegetation. Before the Zuni came to this terrestrial world, however, they lived in an underworld, where Father Sun did not shine until Sun decided it was time to bring them into His presence. To do this He created two sons with supernatural powers to lead the people out of the lower world. In their escape, they climbed through other worlds, learning as they traveled to respect the plants and animals that helped them proceed, until they finally emerged at the surface where Father Sun shined on them. In an emergence story of the Tewa, humans are seen originating in a lower world, but in this account, the underworld was a world in which humans once lived with the supernaturals and did not know death. Thus, emergence for the Tewa is a story of the ascension of humanity away from the sacred into the profane.

Variations on these accounts of a multiworld universe are contained in the cosmologies of many other Native American peoples. In many traditions the cosmos is viewed as three tiered. The Upper World is the world beyond the sky that is inhabited by spiritual powers and departed souls. This world is associated with order, permanence, and clarity. The Lower World, in contrast, is the world below the sky, earth, and waters. This world also is inhabited by spiritual beings, but these beings express qualities opposite to those of the Upper World: chaos, fertility, and madness. The Middle World, where humans live, exists in a precarious balance between the Upper and Lower Worlds. In these stories, the cosmos exists in two complementary parts that cannot be separated, and out of this duality comes forth life. It should be noted that while the Upper and Lower Worlds in these accounts represent different and opposing forces, they do not symbolize the good versus evil, or God versus Satan, duality that is common in Western worldviews.

The cosmologies in these accounts suggest an attitude about time and space that is a distinctive feature of Native American spirituality. In most Western traditions, time is viewed linearly, moving from the past to the present in straight-line progressions. Every event has a consequence, which then is a cause of a subsequent event. The dominant status given to linear time is conveyed within the idioms of Western languages. In English, when we wish to stress clear thought, we say, "Let's get it straight," whereas when we are confused, we state that someone is "talking in circles." Similarly, before proceeding ahead we encourage people to "line up," but when frustrated at our lack of accomplishment we say that we are "moving in circles." To Native Americans, this conception of linear time appears foreign and unnatural. To these peoples, the true nature of time is like the rhythms of the natural world. Each day the sun rises in the east and sets in the west. Each month the moon completes its cycle. Each year the seasons come and go, even as the birds migrate and return. Likewise, every life is born and decays. This, however, does not mean that death is the "end of the line," since within cyclical time there is no beginning or end, only transitions.

The different time concepts of American Indians and non-Indians have produced cultural misunderstandings. An old Arapaho noted this truth when he observed:

> White people . . . [who do not understand our concept of time] thought we were all lazy. That was because we took a different attitude toward time from theirs. We enjoyed time; they measured it. . . . We had no set time for coming back [from the hunt] for that depended on the buffalo and on the

weather. When we had meat enough and the skins were dry enough to pack, we started back to the home camp.[1]

Coexisting on the same land with Western peoples, who monitor time by the ticks of a clock, has not been easy for Native American peoples, who are more comfortable moving to the rhythms of moon cycles and animal migrations. Nonetheless, a cyclical view of time carries with it at least two distinct spiritual advantages.[2]

1. Seamless, cyclical time encourages people to focus on the present rather than to consume their lives with guilt over the past or worry about the future. Among the thousands of Native American languages and dialects, it is hard to find one that uses past and future verb tenses. Such references are not necessary because, to these people, time is repeatable. All things important that happened once can project themselves into the present at any moment. Even the sacred stories that explain the creation of the cosmos are not understood as stories of a single, one-time event from a distant past. Rather, to Native peoples the time described in these accounts—a time when the gods were active in the creative process—is contemporaneous time that can be reclaimed through the reenactments of the sacred rituals that have existed from the beginning.

2. Cyclical time also is advantageous because it locates humanity in sacred space. Unlike linear time, which is fragmented and lacks a center, cyclical time orients people with reference to all other times in the cosmos. In some world religions, strong emphasis is placed on living in obedience to divine commands. This concept of "sin" is not primary among indigenous peoples, but the expectation that one should be centered within a sacred place is among the fundamental concepts that define Native American spirituality. To be centered is to be in proper relationship with all things. Living

outside one's sacred place is not only dangerous, but it also threatens the balance of the cosmos.

Virtually every creation story underscores the importance of sacred place. In the seven-world cosmos of the Zuni creation story, for example, humans are found at work and play in the Middle World, which is equivalent to the center point $(0,0,0)$ on a three-dimensional x,y,z axis. This fourth, middle world, thus, is more than just one of seven worlds. It also represents the sum of all opposites in the three-dimensional time-space continuum. As the one point in the universe that is common to all other domains, it is the symbol of totality. Consequently, Zunis believe that humans were intended to live in a sacred space in the center of the cosmos.

This preoccupation with sacred space is expressed in all aspects of the daily lives of Native American peoples. People return to the holy sites where happenings described in their sacred stories took place long ago. Here on these sacred grounds they pray, fast, gather herbs, and conduct ceremonies that they believe literally result in a reenactment of the mysterious event associated with the site. These sacred places nurture the people by giving them songs for ceremonies, medicines for healing, and visions for strength, even as the people honor the land by treating it with respect and singing to it songs of thanksgiving. Respect for sacred geography also is manifested in the architecture, art, and religious ceremonies of Native Americans. In the Navajo creation story, First Man and First Woman created the four sacred mountains that define the boundaries of Navajoland.[3] Consequently, when the Navajo build a *hogan* (a ceremonial lodge where all tribal planning takes place), they place four ceremonial poles in the four directions to recreate the mythic time when First Man and First Woman placed the four mountains as their *hogan* posts. Similarly, the *kivas* of the Pueblo peoples are centered around the *sipapus* (a sacred hole in the floor) that represent the place the first peoples emerged from the underworld. For these people the fixing of a center establishes the circumference that delineates the sacred space provided for human activities.

---

[1]Carl Sweezy, "We Counted Time by Sleeps," in *Native Heritage*, Arlene Hirschfelder, ed. (New York: Macmillan, 1995), p. 174.

[2]For a discussion of Native American views of time, see Joseph Epes Brown, *Teaching Spirits: Understanding Native American Religious Traditions* (New York: Oxford University Press, 2001), pp. 9–21.

---

[3]The four sacred mountains are Mt. Blanca and Mt. Hesperus in Colorado, Mt. Taylor in New Mexico, and the San Francisco Peaks in Arizona.

Coyote is pictured in rock art throughout the Southwest.

Just as the creation stories orient humans to a particular place in the cosmos, the trickster stories that are common to almost every Native American tradition also serve to establish appropriate human boundaries. The form of the hero/culprit trickster varies from region to region. In many cultures, particularly in the Southwest, the trickster is presented as Coyote; in the Northwest he often is Raven; among the Lakota Sioux he generally is presented as Iktomi the Spider. Notwithstanding his original form (which is irrelevant because Trickster has the power to change forms at will), in each case the trickster represents the desire for unfettered freedom, the wish to live in a world free from rules. In many of his adventures Trickster is driven by his hunger for food; in others he is obsessed with sexual urges. In every case the powerful but foolish Trickster exceeds the boundaries of acceptable behavior and in the end is punished for allowing his appetites to get the best of him. The messages of the stories are clear. Only the foolish ignore the boundaries placed on them.

The Metaphysics of Nature: Sacred Beliefs

Another insight that defines Native American spirituality is the belief that the universe is inhabited by spirits. The idea that the cosmos is alive is not unique to Native Americans, but it is a concept that permeates most indigenous American traditions. Native Americans contend that all things—supernaturals, humans, animals, plants, stones, rivers, mountains, the heav-

THE FOUR SOULS OF THE LAKOTA

Niya: the life breath that departs at death
Nagi: the ancestral spirit that carries one's personality
Sicum: the power inherit in all beings that makes medicines effective
Nagali: the immortal cosmic energy that is the essence of all life

enly bodies—have spirits that are alive and communicate with each other. Each spirit contains specific powers, so the wise do not offend the spirits by violating the sacred taboos that have established the boundaries of conduct since the beginning. Instead, the wise appeal to the spirits through prayer and sacrifices in the hopes that they may win their approval and receive the gifts of their special abilities. This insight does not exclude a belief in a unitary Supreme Being that is understood to be the composite of all things. The Oglala call this Supreme Being *Waken-Tanka*, often translated the "Great Mysterious." *Waken-Tanka* is the invisible energy of the cosmos that the Oglala believe is manifested in 16 gods. Although not a singular, personal deity, *Waken-Tanka* is the divine conglomerate of all the immortal beings that never were born and never will die.

When the cosmos is viewed as alive with spirits that can bring blessings or harm, there is incentive to treat with reverence all aspects of the environment.

This reverence also flows from the belief that all things share a spiritual reality that transcends physical differences. According to the Lakota, all things are related because each thing has four souls. The first soul, *niya*, is the life-breath that infuses all forms. When the life-breath is absent, the form may seem lifeless, but when it reenters the physical form, the body is strengthened. The second soul, the *nagi*, is the ghost or mirror image of the physical form that carries the personality of its possessor. The *nagi* understands a spirit language and thus can communicate with the *nagi* of other beings. When going on a vision quest to seek the guidance of spirit guardians, it is a person's *nagi* that speaks with the *nagi* of the animals or forces that come to the seeker's aid. After death, however, the *nagi* lingers for awhile and then departs on a journey to a spirit world via the Milky Way. The third soul, *sicum*, is the power within all beings. A person can acquire the *sicum* of others and become powerful, or loan his or her own *sicum* to those in need. The *sicum* is what makes the sacred medicines effective. Paradoxically, the *sicum* in the cosmos is finite. The more an individual shares, the more *sicum* he or she gives away and the less power he or she maintains. The fourth soul, the *nagali*, is the cosmic energy that causes all things to move. It is the original source of all things, the essence of life. It is like the smoke that rises from the flames of all things consumed in fire. According to this worldview, the four souls are the bases for the interrelatedness of all things.

Within the unity of things, there also is a hierarchy of power. While all beings have *sicum*, some have more than others. The bison, the eagle, and the bear are the most powerful among animals, but each animal, even the lowly chipmunk, has *sicum* that can provide strength to those in need. Humans have a unique position in the cosmic order. While each animal reflects an aspect of *Waken-Tanka* (the Great Mysterious), humans include within themselves all of its aspects. Humans, thus, are a universe in miniature—beings full of potential that nonetheless must rely upon the animals and forces of nature to recognize their full potential. Native American peoples believe benevolent spirits are pleased to assist humans in this regard. When the animals see that a person is seeking a vision experience, these creatures hold a council to decide which animal possesses the powers that can meet the seeker's particular needs. Consequently, for humans to become fully human, they must learn from the wisdom of the animals and natural forces that serve as their guardian spirits.

If humans expect to receive powers from the spirits, they also must reciprocate by following sacred protocols. To illustrate, when a hunter kills an animal, he must thank the animal by blowing breath into the animal's nostrils. This act ensures the animal's safe return to the spirit world and thereby increases the likelihood that the hunter will be successful on the next hunt. Similarly, if a human acts selfishly and dishonors the plant and animal spirits by exploitation or wasteful consumption, then the spirits will cease to offer their healing and sustaining powers. A sacred pact must exist between humans and the beings of the cosmos in order for the cycle of life to be sustained. Black Elk described this pact and the spiritual interconnectedness of all things with these words:

> Peace . . . comes within the souls of men when they realize their relationship, their oneness, with the universe and all its powers, and when they realize that at the center of the Universe dwells *Waken-Tanka*, and that this center is really everywhere, it is within each of us.[4]

Repairing Broken Cycles: Sacred Actions, Numbers, and Objects

Despite the quest for harmony, humans sometimes allow the natural world to fall out of balance. The sacred pact can be broken by many careless acts: abusing the environment, wasting food, forgetting the protocols that honor the spirits, and violating the sacred taboos. A consequence of such disrespectful acts may bring sickness, famine, bad weather, or other misfortune. In these times, people must turn to the sacred rituals to restore the delicate balance that is necessary for the cycle of life to continue. In these rituals it is believed that sacred power is released that recreates and sustains the cosmos, and humanity again is recentered within sacred time and place.

The primary purpose of the ceremonies is to renew the partnership between humans and the spirit world. According to Joseph Epes Brown, to restore this sacred pact three things must occur: purification, expansion, and identification.[5] First, cleansing is nec-

---

[4]Joseph Epes Brown, *The Sacred Pipe* (Norman, OK: University of Oklahoma Press, 1953), p. 115.

[5]Brown, *Teaching Spirits*, pp. 110–113.

essary because the impure may not be united with sacred power. The sweat lodge in many traditions is a place for the purification of the body and mind. Second, the imperfect human fragment must be expanded so that the whole universe lies within the self. Only then will a human proceed to the final stage of the ritual, which is to become one in identity with all things. Brown uses the Pipe Ceremony of the Plains Indians to illustrate the elements of these restorative actions. The pipe with its stem, bowl (or heart), and foot represents humanity, which is first cleansed with sweet grass before the ritual proceeds. Upon purification, the ceremonial leader fills the bowl with seven pieces of tobacco, points the pipe in the six directions (north, south, east, west, up, down), and then gives thanks to birds, animals, waters, and all the other spirit beings. When the tobacco fills the bowl, the totality of the universe is then present within it. The fire used to light the pipe comes from the Great Mysterious that is the essence of all things. As the fires consume the tobacco, it rises to the heavens as smoke, and a sacrificial community of identity is reenacted. Through this action the smoker understands that he or she is one with all things.

Often the sacred ceremonies involve fasting, dancing, creating artwork, cleansing, and, occasionally, ritualistically violating certain taboos. Through dance, usually accompanied by song, the beating of drums, and the shaking of rattles, the participants prepare themselves for contact with the spirit world. In the Sun Dance performed by some Plains traditions, the dancers even place thongs through the flesh of the pectoral muscles and hang from the center pole of lodge, thus attaching themselves to the divine. In other rituals such as in Navajo healing ceremonies, artists create sand paintings, the sand of which is used to press against the body of the ill person to emphasize the unity between the person and the powers contained in the sacred art. After the ceremony, the sand painting is destroyed so that the power within it will not be released outside the ritual content. On other occasions, sacred objects such as prayer sticks and medicine bundles are used to release healing powers. Often the chants and actions of the ceremonial leaders involve the use of sacred numbers, most commonly the numbers 4 and 7, which represent, among other things, the four two-dimensional directions, the four seasons, and the seven points (north, south, east, west, up, down, and center). In still other sacred rituals, such as the Pueblo *kachina* dances, clowns inter-

rupt the rites with demonstrations of sexual gestures that outside the ceremony would be considered taboo, but within the confines of the ritual serve to awaken the people to spiritual realities through humor. In sum, Native American communities in a wide variety of ways make use of sacred time, place, dance, numbers, objects, art, and buffoonery to communicate with the spirit world and to repair the sacred pact that connects all things in the cosmos.

SCRIPTURES (SACRED ORAL TRADITIONS)

The term *Scriptures* when applied to Native American religions can be misleading. The scriptures of the great Western religions and, to a lesser degree, the scriptures and sacred classics from the East, all underwent an evolutionary process that included the following stages: words spoken, words committed to memory, words codified into script, and finally, scripted words formally approved (canonized) by some authoritative body that rendered them as especially worthy of reverence for those within the tradition. At each stage there was a pruning process at work. Not all of the spoken words of spiritual insight were considered worthy of remembrance; not all of the oral traditions were placed into script; not all of the collections of religious writings were accepted into the sacred canon. Moreover, inevitably there were disagreements over the selections, and not everyone ultimately would embrace what became the officially sanctioned canon. Nonetheless, as a result of this process, large numbers within each tradition came to acknowledge that a given collection of religious writings had authority over their lives.

The sacred insights of the indigenous peoples of America, however, do not share this same history. With few exceptions, Native American peoples had no written script before European contact. In addition, the thousands of nations and tribes that collectively we refer to in the singular as Native American have never been culturally, politically, or religiously united. As a result, there has never been a pan-Indian authoritative council that has given its sanction to any collection of spiritual insights. This, of course, does not mean that Native Americans are lacking in oral traditions that convey sacred knowledge. It only means that the sacred stories and words of Native

Americans have not been culled into collections of written texts officially sanctioned by some authoritative council of religious elders. Consequently, *Sacred Oral Traditions* rather than *Scriptures* is a more accurate descriptor of the words that express common features of Native American spirituality.

The Sanctity of Spoken Words

Notwithstanding these caveats, in many ways Native American oral traditions have much in common with the scriptures of other world religions. A fact too little appreciated is that all of the Holy Writings of the great religions fundamentally were texts meant to be heard, not read. The Hindus tell us that the very sounds of the Vedas are sacred, and, when verbalized, these sounds release spiritual forces that alter the cosmos. Jews, Christians, and Muslims also recognize the powers of spoken words as their scriptures teach that creation itself was the result of the spoken words of the Creator. In addition, although both Jesus and the Buddha were literate, neither left any writings. Nonetheless, the remembered words they spoke—ultimately codified in Christian and Buddhist scriptures—exert tremendous influence on their followers. Even the Apostle Paul's letters, which comprise much of the Christian New Testament, were written to be orally presented to the congregations to which they were addressed. Just as it is the sound of music, not the written score, that moves our emotions, so it is the oral presentation of the written scriptures that have transformed the lives of the religious throughout time and place. Until recently, Native Americans have been without written texts, but they have never been without sacred oral traditions that evoke life-changing powers.

According to the Native American scholar Sam D. Gill,[6] the nonliteracy of the indigenous peoples has largely shaped the content and expression of Native American spirituality. The cultural impact of nonliteracy can be understood by contrasting the consequences of the various modes of communication. In written cultures, sight tends to be the dominant sense. To see is to become persuaded, and failure to see can lead to disbelief. Communication through an alphabetic script also promotes a bias in favor of that which is linear and progressive. Circular and reciprocal perspectives often embraced by nonliterate cultures are neglected. Written words also are less fragile, more permanent, and more easily dissected by the human mind. Writing permits and encourages extensive criticism of words and concepts and thereby contributes to great precision in knowledge. When words are placed in script, however, the original author loses control of them; they become available to be scrutinized and interpreted in other contexts and to be commented on by others about their original meaning. Such an intellectual interplay promotes speculation and philosophical abstraction. Finally, writing reduces the importance of time and place because written scripts can be readily stored and retrieved, any time, any place. This allows for a separation between author and audience, both in time and distance. In modern times, reading and writing have become private, silent acts, performed in solitude. Written expression, thus, can be characterized as convenient, precise, abstract, permanent, and impersonal.

These advantages, however, come at a price. Even the Western philosopher Plato referred to this cost when he commented: "If men learn [writing], it will implant forgetfulness in their souls. They will cease to exercise memory because they rely on that which is written, calling things to remembrance no longer from within themselves, but by means of external marks."[7] Oral communication by necessity demands personal, face-to-face communication, an intimacy that can be lost through written forms. Spoken words are transmitted by breath, which in many Native American languages is the word for life, soul, and poetry. When sounds through breath or wind are released, they are free to be received by the total environment. All of creation—humans, animals, birds, rocks—is surrounded by the sound. Once released, the sound of the spoken words is immediate, but it survives only a brief moment. Speaking is a sacred act that carries within it many responsibilities. To name or to speak of a person is to call forth the spiritual essence of that which is named. To Native Americans, names and words are not simply metaphors of concepts, but rather they are conveyors of spiritual realities. Owing to the sacred nature of acts of speech, tribal languages generally do not contain profanities; thus, to express profanities Native Americans must borrow words from nontribal languages. To sum, spoken words to a greater degree

---

[6]Sam Gill, *Native American Traditions: Sources and Interpretations* (Belmont, CA: Wadsworth Publishing, 1983), pp. 43–59.

[7]Plato, *Phaedrus*, translated by R. Hackforth (Cambridge, MA: Harvard University Press, 1952), pp. 274–275.

than written discourse are spontaneous, temporary, concrete, personal, and sacred.

The sacred importance of speech is expressed in a variety of ways in the customs and sacred stories of Native American traditions. In numerous Pueblo and California Indian creation stories, the first figure to exist was Thought-Woman who, through her thought, formed the world. Those who followed her in creation then assisted her in the creative process by naming the things that she, by thought, had formed. Naming thus gives distinction and identifies that which exists. Native Americans hold that "a life proceeds from a name like a river flows from its source," so it is not surprising that they give utmost care to the names they select for each other. Often names are announced in sacred naming ceremonies. Most Native Americans acquire several names throughout their lives. After a young warrior excels in battle, for example, in a ceremony following the return of the war party the tribal leader will give him a new name that is reflective of his accomplishments. When a stranger would ask an Indian his name, often the Indian would remain silent and allow another to respond to the question, since modesty would not permit him to boast about himself by announcing the honorific title included in his name. Names are important in Native American cultures because it is assumed that one's name is who one is and who one will become.

Rules of Speech and the Art of Storytelling

In comparison with written cultures, oral traditions tend to give primacy to sound rather than sight. Within many Native American traditions, what is seen often is considered untrustworthy because the shifting world of appearances is not always as it seems. Each tradition has its sacred stories that depict the foolishness of those who mistake the apparent for the real. The trickster Coyote is always changing his form to lure women into his embraces or to steal food from unsuspecting victims. Other stories warn men not to approach beautiful maidens outside of camp because they could be an evil power in disguise. Even while distrusting the visual, Native American traditions attest to the powers of sound, viewing songs, prayers, stories, and other oral events as spiritual forces that shape the cosmos. To Native Americans, spoken or sung words are more than a means of conveying information or entertaining. In the Beaver language, the word for *song* is also the word for *prayer,*

and the word for *medicine,* is "his song," or the song that was given to a person by the spirits. When pronounced in ritual contexts, words spoken or sung have the power to create or destroy, cure or cause disease, produce beauty and orderliness or release chaos and disorder.

In nonliterate societies, the whole culture must be held in memory. Only that which is transmitted through a chain of face-to-face conversations will be preserved for future generations. This reality places a heavy responsibility on the community to find forms of communication that will ensure this transference of knowledge. Two ideal forms of transmitting culture are through song and stories. The elders who sing the songs and tell the stories must not only be experts in tribal knowledge, but they also must be performers who have mastered the artforms of singing and storytelling, actors with the rhetorical skills that enable them to engage the listeners and to convey to them the relevance of the message. To accomplish these sacred duties, skilled oral transmitters make use of props, hand gestures, intensity of voice, puns, metaphors, and even silence to communicate and preserve the wisdom of their culture.

Because spoken words contain powers that can be used for good or evil, it is important that these artists fully understand the protocols of speech making so as not to violate any of the sacred taboos. To illustrate, singers and storytellers must be cognizant of the proper time and place to relate their stories. To name and thus to call forth a dangerous power at an inauspicious time invites disaster. Trickster tales, in particular, must be told with care. Among the Kiowa, for instance, it was feared that if a trickster story was told during the day hours, the trickster would bite off the noses of the peoples at night. Similarly, the Santee Sioux refused to tell a snake story during the summer months for fear that the snake would cause harm to the storyteller. Other traditions refused to recite Coyote tales between the first thunder in the spring and the last thunder in the fall when the Thunder-Beings were most active. Even as the timing of singing and storytelling must be monitored, so must consideration be given to the place or setting of the speech-act. For instance, for a prayer to be effective, it should be performed in a ceremonial context according to a sacred protocol. Silent prayer recited by an individual outside a ritual context is not common among many Native American traditions. However, participating in the oral performance of a prayer in a ceremonial setting can be a life-renewing experience that engages all the senses. The extensive rules and restrictions associated with public acts of speech add an aura to oral discourse and preserve the sanctity of the oral traditions that express the spiritual wisdom of the people.

THE EVOLUTION OF NATIVE AMERICAN SPIRITUALITIES

Most of the world religions with ancient scriptures have undergone significant changes since the canonization of these sacred writings. A common feature within the evolution of these traditions has been the tendency to splinter, under historical pressures, into a variety of groups or sects. Each sect of the tradition shares and rejects portions of the religious expressions of the other sects within the tradition. To illustrate, Christianity has divided into Catholics, Orthodox, and Protestants; Islam into Sunnis and Shiites; Buddhism into the Theravada and Mahayana; and so forth. The history of Native American religion differs from these other major world traditions in this area just as it differs from them in its absence of canonized sacred writings. This does not mean that historic pressures and contact with foreign religions have not altered Native American religious expressions. Indeed, the spirituality of Native American peoples has been undergoing change for millennia, and the rate of change has been particularly rapid in recent centuries. However, the directional movement from unity to schism that characterizes many other major world religions is not a part of the history of Native American religious expressions. In fact, the reverse is true. In recent years the pressures exerted upon Native Americans have brought about a greater degree of religious cohesion among these peoples than existed before European contact.

The relative isolation of Native American peoples from Old World influences was shattered in 1492 when Columbus made his famous voyage across the Atlantic. Great controversy exists over the number of people in the Western hemisphere before European contact, but the numbers were exceedingly high. A midrange estimate is that about 7 million indigenous peoples lived in the North American continent alone. Although great in population, these peoples were geographically, politically, linguistically, and culturally divided into some 600 autonomous societies, 200 to 300 spoken languages, and, depending on definition, a dozen or so separate "culture areas." Many of these tribal peoples shared some religious insights, but no

Timeline of Native American history.

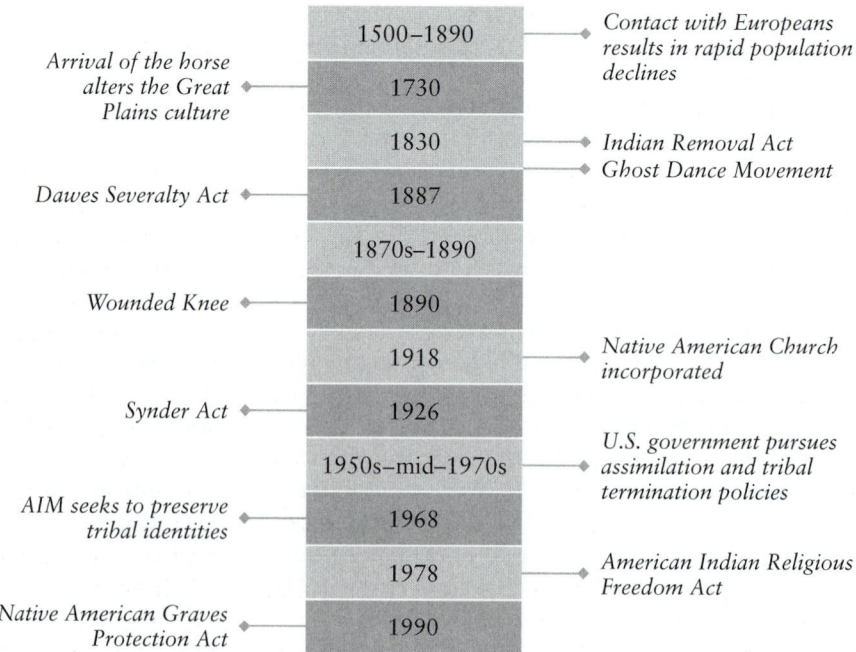

	1500–1890	Contact with Europeans results in rapid population declines
Arrival of the horse alters the Great Plains culture	1730	
	1830	Indian Removal Act / Ghost Dance Movement
Dawes Severalty Act	1887	
	1870s–1890	
Wounded Knee	1890	
	1918	Native American Church incorporated
Synder Act	1926	
	1950s–mid–1970s	U.S. government pursues assimilation and tribal termination policies
AIM seeks to preserve tribal identities	1968	
	1978	American Indian Religious Freedom Act
Native American Graves Protection Act	1990	

singular Native American religious tradition existed. Just 400 years after contact, however, the number of indigenous people in North America had been reduced to about 250,000. Simultaneous with this devastating population decline was a coast-to-coast Indian religious revitalization movement that brought with it a greater degree of spiritual unity among the diversity of tribes than had ever been achieved. What factors contributed to these indelible changes in the size, culture, and spirituality of these Native American peoples?

Effect of Contact: 1500–1700 CE

In 1493 Roman Catholic Pope Alexander VI divided the non-European world between Spain and Portugal. As the map of the "unexplored" regions of the world became better known, it became obvious that Spain got the better end of the bargain, receiving papal entitlement to all of the Western hemisphere except Brazil. By Spanish royal decree, all of the native peoples in these lands were to be converted to Catholicism. Early in the sixteenth century, the Spanish Crown established the *encomienda* system, a system that granted Spanish landholders paper titles to the land and to the labor of the native populations living on it. In return, the landholder paid a tax to the Crown, promised to provide proper care for the natives and to convert them to Christianity and Spanish culture. This system wreaked havoc upon many indigenous cultures in the Caribbean, Mexico, South America, and Florida. The system was later reformed and replaced by the *reduccion* system that entrusted the native populations to church authorities. Under this system the indigenous peoples generally were treated more humanely, although the priority to convert the "savage heathens" into Catholic Christians remained.

For several centuries, Spain dominated vast regions of the New World. In the North American West, Spanish explorers searched for the Seven Cities of Cibola, the cities of gold. While no gold was found, conquistadors accompanied by Catholic priests successfully subdued the Pueblo peoples of the Rio Grande. After the establishment of Franciscan missions, the Pueblo peoples were forced to work for the colonial governors and settlers. Because it was Franciscan policy to rotate the priests, the missionaries as a rule did not learn the native languages. As a result, the missions did little to persuade the natives to embrace Christian doctrine, although by punishing offenders with whippings, they did enforce the laws that required all na-

tives to be baptized and attend mass. The Spanish also were highly successful in using forced labor to construct Christian chapels. By 1630, some 90 chapels dotted the landscape of the Southwest.

These accomplishments also produced antagonism and distrust that had the effect of driving Pueblo religion underground. In 1660, the Pueblos revolted, killing 400 of the 2,500 Spanish colonists in the Rio Grande, including 21 of the 33 missionaries to the region. Like most Native American military victories against Europeans, the gains were short-lived. Soon the Spanish returned, and many Pueblo peoples scattered to the West to join other Pueblo communities or to settle among non-Pueblos like the Navajo and Apache. During these centuries of Spanish domination, many cultural benefits went to the Native peoples. Wheat, melons, apricots, tomatoes, apples, peaches, and pears were added to their diets; for the first time they acquired goats, sheep, and chickens as domesticated animals. In addition, from the Spanish they learned how to utilize horses, mules, and donkeys for transportation and for assistance with their labor. In many ways, Spanish influences brought about beneficial and dramatic cultural changes. These changes, however, did not extend to religion. Other than driving native religious practices underground, two centuries of Catholic missions had little effect on the religious beliefs of the peoples of the Southwest.

Meanwhile, in the East from Florida to Canada, other Native Americans confronted and suffered the consequences of European contact. Beginning with the Spanish settlement of St. Augustine, Florida, in 1585, sixteenth-century interactions between Eastern Native Americans and Europeans often resulted in the forced labor of native peoples and in a rapid population decline that nearly exterminated the indigenous peoples in Florida. Later, during the seventeenth-century European colonists from England, France, and the Netherlands joined the Spanish in establishing permanent settlements in North America. English colonists—initially at Jamestown (1607), Plymouth (1620), and Massachusetts Bay (1630) and later at other coastal regions—settled on lands inhabited by Eastern Woodlands peoples. At each settlement, early years of peaceful coexistence were followed by periods of violence. Even more devastating to the Native populations than warfare was the exchange of germs for which the isolated peoples of the New World had no natural immunities. Through disease and bloodshed, population levels of the indigenous peoples dropped in the East as they did in the West. In just 200 years the indigenous population of North America fell by 95 percent. Restated, for every 100 North Americans in 1492, there were only 5 natives occupying the same land area two centuries later. The efforts of the English Protestants to Christianize the native peoples in the East met with no more success than the efforts of the Spanish Catholics in the West. The history of this era seems to affirm the adage that when cultures are threatened by oppressive forces, they respond with actions that strengthen tradition and intensify solidarity. Native American religious understandings shifted following contact, largely because the encounters forced the suffering indigenous peoples to make sense of their great losses and to find new sacred medicines that would assist them in their struggles.

Eighteenth- and Nineteenth-Century Adaptations

Living on the same continent with growing numbers of Old World colonizers brought about lifestyle changes, but in many ways the changes of the eighteenth century were not as threatening to some Native peoples as were those that occurred in the previous centuries. In the Southwest, Spanish efforts to Christianize the Pueblos were relaxed, and with the reduced external pressures, the acculturative processes were accelerated. On the Central Plains, there was little contact between the Native tribes and Europeans, although tribal acquisition of European guns did alter the way of life and the balance of power among the tribes of the region. Moreover, in the mid-eighteenth century with the arrival of the horse, the tribes of this region made cultural adaptations that enabled them to achieve a commanding control over the Great Plains. Moreover, owing to the arrival of the horse, new tribes formed and other tribes—such as the Comanche, Kiowa, and Pawnee of the South Plains and the Crow, Cheyenne, Lakota, and Sioux of the North Plains— were greatly empowered. Meanwhile, in the East, most English colonists still lived only near the Atlantic coastlines, so violence between the Anglos and Native peoples was constrained for much of the century.

Native American tribes, however, often were caught up in the chronic European wars of the era. Warfare was commonplace for the empire building Old World peoples who, for more than a century, were in states of declared war as often as they were at peace. In each of the six European wars of the pe-

riod,[8] Indian nations often were forced to choose sides among the European powers, which sometimes resulted in wars against each other. Occasionally the eastern tribes formed military confederations to protect themselves from European invasions. Two such confederations included the six-nation Iroquois Confederacy of the Northeast and the Creek or Muskogee Confederacy of the Southeast. By the end of the eighteenth century, the newly created United States of America had replaced the Old World Empires as the primary threat to Native American ways.

The nineteenth century was a critical century for Native American peoples. As U.S. citizens moved westward from the original 13 seaboard states, tensions with Native Americans intensified. In 1830, the U.S. Congress enacted an Indian Removal Act that forced the displacement of southeastern peoples onto reservation lands in Oklahoma territory. By midcentury, 70,000 Indians had forcibly been relocated from their ancestral homes east of the Mississippi River. Meanwhile, after the United States annexed the Louisiana Territory (1803) and Texas (1845) and acquired the Great American West from Mexico in the Treaty of Guadalupe Hidalgo (1848), gold was discovered in California. These events opened the floodgates of American migration onto Indian lands. Death by disease and violence followed. During the second half of the century, the population of the California Indians alone plummeted from about 100,000 to 15,000. Elsewhere in the Northwest and in the Central Plains, military clashes took place between U.S. armies and Native American peoples who sometimes fought as individual tribes and sometimes as confederations of pan-Indian alliances. By late century, the so-called Indian Wars had largely come to an end with the forced surrender of the Native American nations. Placed on reservation lands that prohibited war, hunting, or raiding parties, the defeated nations lost their traditional means of securing wealth, prestige, and social rank. With their tribal economies collapsed, they had no option but to accept U.S. government rations in exchange for the promise to become settled farmers on the lands allotted to them by governmental authorities. After the reservations were established, the U.S. government

---

[8]These wars included King William's War (1689–1697), Queen Anne's War (1702–1713), King George's War (1740–1748), the French and Indian War (1754–1763), the War for Independence (1775–1783), and the wars of the Napoleonic Era (1793–1802, 1803–1815).

This 1900 photo of students at the Phoenix Indian School demonstrates the late nineteenth and early twentieth century attempts to assimilate native Americans into mainstream culture. The white dresses, hair ribbons, and kneeling in prayer are not artifacts of traditional native American culture.

contracted with Christian denominations to manage the reservations. Christian missionaries were given responsibility for educating and "civilizing" the Natives, and the denominations received Indian lands for the building of churches and boarding schools.

The decade of the 1880s saw a rapid collapse of traditional Indian ways. The Carlisle Indian School in Pennsylvania was established as the first of many boarding schools designed to assimilate Indian youth into Anglo culture. In an attempt to live up to its motto, "From Savagery into Civilization," the school moved Indian youth away from their home environments to Carlisle; taught them a Western educational curriculum; and forbade them from speaking their native languages, wearing their traditional dresses, or performing any of their traditional ceremonies. During the next half-century, some 50,000 Indian youth were educated in off-reservation schools like Carlisle. Traditional Native American religious practices were further attacked when, in 1883, the U.S. Bureau of Indian Affairs prohibited a religious practice known as the Sun Dance and other tribal dances and banned medicine men from performing some of their sacred rituals. The impact of this policy was that Native Religions and practitioners were systematically persecuted and, in some cases, imprisoned. That same year Buffalo Bill's Wild West Show opened to entertain au-

diences by portraying Native American customs as primitive curiosities.

In 1887 the U.S. Congress enacted the Dawes Severalty Act that empowered the president to convert Indian tribal lands into parcels of 160 acres (the same acreage that had been given to non-Indians in the Homestead Acts) and to allow each Indian head-of-household to receive title to this land. After this allotment, the remaining reservation lands were sold to non-Indians. Designed to achieve the assimilation of Indians into American culture, this act was popular both among the greedy leaders of corporate America who desired the lands protected in former treaties, and among the so-called reformers, who believed Native Americans would benefit by assimilation into Western ways.

As other means of arresting America's cultural takeover failed, Native American millenarian movements appeared and spread among the various tribes. Early in the century the Shawnee prophet Tenskwataya, the brother of the famous chief and warrior Tecumseh, predicted that the land the Europeans had taken from them would be restored by divine intervention if the First peoples would return to their traditional ways. This prophecy resonated among the Native Peoples and aided in the formation of a pan-Indian alliance against Anglo western expansion. The movement dispersed, however, following the death of Tecumseh and Tenskywataya during the War of 1812. A generation later another movement coalesced around the teachings of the Washington state Wanapum medicine man Smohallo, who bemoaned that Mother Earth was being raped by American agricultural technologies. He prophesied that if the Native peoples would maintain their traditional hunting-based lifestyle and conduct the sacred Prophet Dance ceremonies that the spirits had given to him, then the white people would be destroyed and dead Indians would rise to enjoy a new earth replenished with abundant game. These teachings contributed to the popularity of the Ghost Dance movement that appeared later in the century when Wovoka, a Paiute from Nevada, received similar visions about a coming millennial age. Wovoka, known by Anglos as John Wilson, promised Native peoples that the end of the world was near and that if they would stop drinking, fighting, and quarrelling and would perform the sacred Ghost Dance, then in the new coming age all would be reborn into a world filled with abundance. To some Native tribes, the Ghost Dance also carried military overtones. According to the once-powerful Sioux, for example, dancers who wore special "ghost shirts" would be protected from the bullets of white people. Such talk made U.S. civilians and soldiers nervous. This Ghost Dance hysteria set the stage for the senseless and tragic U.S. massacre of Sioux women and children at Wounded Knee in December 1890.

The Ghost Dance movement, which sought a return to traditional Native American ways, failed in its goals, but, in its failure, it played a key role in unifying tribes that previously had little association. Ironically, the rapid loss of tribal functions in the late nineteenth century gave birth among Native peoples to the concept of the "American Indian." Before the devastation of their cultures, Native Americans viewed themselves as tribal peoples with tribal identities. By the turn of the twentieth century, however, more and more also came to see themselves as Indians, individuals united by their common sufferings at the hands of non-Indian peoples.

Twentieth-Century Religious Developments

U.S. policies toward Native Americans in the twentieth century shifted with the political winds of the nation. For the first quarter of the century the assimilationist

This 1926 photo is of Wovoka, the Paiute prophet, and a motion picture actor, T.J. McCoy.

goals of the Dawes Act remained largely intact. Several years before the United States celebrated its 150th birthday, Congress passed the Snyder Act, which finally extended citizenship rights to all Native Americans. Shortly thereafter, during the so-called Indian New Deal, the Bureau of Indian Affairs, under the leadership of John Collier, adopted a more liberal policy that advocated preservation of traditional Native American culture as its central goal. In the politically more conservative post–World War II era, however, official U.S. policy again was reversed as governmental authorities adopted "assimilation, compensation, and termination" as its central objectives. Desiring again to mainstream Native Americans into the larger culture, the government at mid-century established protocols that would provide for a one-time compensation to tribal peoples for any illegalities the government may have committed against these peoples. Following this payoff, the government would terminate their tribal identity, thus eliminating any special treatment (no tax-ation, hunting and fishing privileges, etc.) that previous treaties had granted the Indian nation. Following the lobbying successes of AIM (American Indian Movement) during the late 1960s and 1970s, official U.S. policies again shifted in an attempt to protect and preserve Native American tribal identities and custom. For example, the American Indian Religious Freedom Act of 1978 was passed to guarantee the continued free expression of religion for Native Americans. Since its passage, the limits of this act have been legally tested on numerous occasions as federal and state courts have been asked to settle such questions as to whether the act entitles Native Americans the legal right to kill endangered species like the bald eagle in order to use them in their religious ceremonies. Federal actions such as the Religious Freedom Act and the Native American Graves Protection Act (1990), however, also have contributed significantly to the renaissance in Tribal Religion that is sweeping across Native America.

SACRED OBSERVANCES AND PRACTICES

During the twentieth and twenty-first centuries, religiously minded Native Americans have responded in a variety of ways to the government's periodic efforts to force assimilation. Some simply have attempted to resist these pressures by reviving the sacred customs of their past (e.g., the forbidden Sun Dance ceremony). Others have struggled to encourage the formation of a pan-Indian identity that blends together and mixes old tribal ways even while adopting new trans-tribal ceremonies (e.g., the annual powwows). Still others have embraced the idea of assimilation, dispelled their traditional religious ceremonies, and joined Christian churches.

One religious innovation of the past 150 years that has appealed to a number of Indians within each of these groups is peyote religion. Peyote (*Lophophora williamsii*) is a cactus plant that, when ingested, produces psychophysiological effects including sharpened acuity, exhilaration, relaxation, and euphoria. The cactus, which is native to regions of southern Texas and Mexico, may have been used in religious ceremonies by the peoples of Mexico since ancient times. In the late nineteenth century, its use was introduced to the Kiowa and Comanche tribes in the southern plains. With the formation of the pan-Indian alliances

that accompanied the Ghost Dance movement, knowledge of peyote spread more widely. By the early twentieth century, it was used in religious ceremonies of Native peoples in all regions of the country. When governmental authorities attempted to prohibit its use, the supporters of peyote religion incorporated the "Native American Church" (1918) in an attempt to find legal protection for the ceremony under the freedom of religion clauses in the U.S. Constitution. Numerous legal battles have been waged in the federal courts over the religious use of peyote since the creation of this denomination that combines elements of Christianity and peyote religion.

The popularity of peyote religion can, in part, be ascribed to its capacity for meeting the complex needs of Native Americans during a difficult time in their history. As a healing and vision-seeking ritual, it carries forward aspects of traditional Native American spiritualities. As a successful means of combating the problem of alcoholism that is rampant among Native American communities, it has won the support of those seeking to preserve tribal loyalties. Meanwhile, it fosters the growth of a pan-Indian identity, and, by embracing aspects of Christianity, it also has support among some of those who seek Native American assimilation into the broader American culture. The ascension of peyote religion is yet another example of the flexibility of Native Americans to adapt to the exigencies of their history.

SOURCES

Because there are no canonized writings for the indigenous American spiritual traditions, the selections presented in this section are not authoritative in the same sense as the Hebrew Bible is to Jews or the Qu'ran is to Muslims. Moreover, the true meaning or even the authenticity of some of the texts may be problematic, not only because of the difficulty in translating an oral language with non-Western ideas into the English written language but also because of the motives and collection methods of those who translated these stories. Students should be aware that these texts were collected by various types of people for different purposes and with a variety of technologies. Some were produced by missionaries writing for Christian church publications; others were produced by anthropologists writing for academic

The tribes of North America and where they lived.

publications. The mindset of the collector of the oral traditions may have influenced what was recorded and how it was translated.

Notwithstanding these cautions, these selections, drawn from more than 40 different tribes, are pre-sented with the hope of capturing a representative sampling of the great diversity of religious expres-sions found among Native American peoples. The corresponding map identifies the location of the tribes represented in this anthology.

SECTION 1: Beginnings: God, Time, and the Universe

Looking at the vastness and beauty of the earth and sky, humans across all cultures have reflected on the origins of the universe and on the powers that brought it into being. Most creation stories offer explanations of how chaos or disorder was transformed into cosmos or order. In the Hebrew creation story that has shaped the development of the religions of the West, an omnipotent God speaks and the heavens and the earth are formed. In an orderly, sequentially linear six-day process, the cosmos is created, the earth is populated with living things, and humans are created and given reign over the material world. The stories of creation told by the native inhabitants of America share some similarities with this account, but there also are many differences. In typical Native American accounts, for instance, the present earth populated by humans appears to be formed as the offspring of world parents, as a product of an earth-diving process of concerned animals, or as a world that emerged from other worlds below the surface.

Here are accounts of cosmic origins from four geographically and culturally diverse Native American peoples: the Zuni of the Southwest, the Lakota of the Central Plains, the Lenape (Delaware) of the Eastern Woodlands, and the Yuchi of the Southeast. Compare these accounts with each other and with the creation accounts of other major religious traditions. From these sacred stories, what insights can we discover about Native American understandings of the divine, time, and the cosmos?

A ZUNI GENESIS STORY[9]

Before the beginning only the All-Father, Awonawilona, the Maker and Container of All, had being. Throughout the great space of ages there was nothing else but black darkness and everywhere a desolate and endless void.

Pondering this emptiness and desiring a better condition, the All-Father conceived within himself and projected his thoughts outward in space where the mists of increase, potent steams of growth, were evolved and coalesced. Through his omniscience, the All-Container shaped himself into the person and form of the Sun whom we hold to be our father and who thus came to exist and appear. With his appearance as the Sun came the brightening of the spaces with light and in this luminescence the great mist clouds.

From his surface the Sun Father, Yatoka, drew substance to form the seed for two differing worlds and therewith impregnated the great waters. Under the heat of his light, the water grew warm and green. Upon the sea a scum arose, waxing ever greater and dividing until it became AwitelinTsita, the four-fold enclosing Earth Mother and Apoyan Ta'chu, the all-covering Sky Father lying close together upon the Great Waters.

From this lying together the two conceived all of the beings of earth, men and creatures, in the four-fold womb of the world. Growing large with her children, the Earth Mother sank into the embrace of the waters below leaving the Sky Father clasped by the waters above.

Now like all Supernal Begins, the Earth Mother and the Sky Father were amorphous, changeable, even as smoke in the wind, transmutable as thought, capable of manifesting themselves in any form at will, as dances may with mask making. Thus as man and woman they spoke to one another.

TWO LAKOTA SIOUX STATEMENTS ABOUT THE GREAT MYSTERY AND CREATION

Waken Tanka: The Great Mystery[10]

There was, and is, and will be Wakan Tanka, the Great Mystery. He is one yet many. He is the Chief God, the Great Spirit, the Creator, and the Executive. He is the Gods-Kindred, both the Subordinates and the Gods-like. He is the good and evil gods, the visible and invisible, the physical and immaterial, for He is all in one.

The Gods had no beginning and they will have no end. Some are before others; some are related as parent and child. Yet the Gods have no mother or father, for anything that has birth will have death. Since the Gods were created, not born, they will not die. Mankind cannot fully understand these things, for they are the Great Mystery. . . .

Everything significant or important, whether it is understood or not, is part of Wanka Tanka. Wanka

[9]Frank Hamilton Cushing, *The Mythic World of the Zuni*, edited and illustrated by Barton Wright (Albuquerque, NM: University of New Mexico Press), pp. 1–2.

[10]Vivian One Feather, *Oglala History and Culture—Teachers' Resource Book* (Pine Ridge, SD: Red Cloud Indian School, Research Project 1972, 1974), pp. 17–18.

Tanka is the highest God force. Wanka Tanka is really sixteen Gods; anything whether it be visible or invisible, material or without material, human or animal, can be represented as a God. For example, Inyan is a rock, and Maka is earth. The Gods control everything, but people are not entirely separated from the Gods, for they are closely related to the Great Mystery. People are related to the Gods because Gods have human qualities, even faults.

A Lakota Sioux Creation Story[11]

Long, long ago before there was any other thing or any time, Inyan was. His spirit was Wakan Tanka. Hanhepi was then, but she was not a thing. She was only the black of darkness. Inyan was soft and shapeless, but he had all powers. The powers were in his blood, and his blood was blue. He desired that there might be another thing so that he might exercise his power over it. But there could be no other, unless he created it from himself. If he created it, he would have to give it part of his spirit and a portion of his blood. How much power the new creature would have depended on how much blood was taken from him.

Inyan finally decided to create another, but as part of himself so that he could still have control of the powers. So he took part of himself and spread it over and around himself in the shape of a great disk. He named this disk Maka. To create Maka he took so much from himself that he opened all his veins, and all his blood flowed from him, and he shrank and became hard and powerless. As his blood flowed, it became water. But powers cannot live in water, so they separated themselves and became a being in the shape of a great blue dome, whose edge is near the edge of Maka. The powers are a spirit, and the blue dome is the sky and is the great spirit Mahpiyato. Inyan, Maka, and the waters are the world, and Mahpiyato is the sky above.

Maka was quarrelsome and scolded Inyan because he did not create her as a separate being and demanded that he banish Hanhepi. Inyan said that he was not powerless, and then she insulted him for his lack of power and nagged him until he agreed to appeal to Mahpiyato. Mahpiyato heard the complaint

of Maka and the plea of Inyan that she be satisfied. So Mahipyato was created a judge, the final supreme judge of all things.

Mahpiyato decreed that Maka must remain forever attached to Inyan, just as she was created. But to satisfy her, he created Anpetu, who is not a thing, for he is only the red of light. Then Mahpiyato banished Hanhepi to the regions under the world, and placed Anpetu on the world. Then there was light everywhere in the world, but there was no heat nor any shadow.

Maka looked at herself and saw that she was naked and cold, and then she complained to Mahpiyato about this. Mahpiyato took something from Inyan, from Maka, from the waters, and from himself, and with it he made a shinning disk. He called the disk Wi and he gave a spirit to it. He then placed Wi above the blue dome, and commanded him to shine on all the world, giving heat to everything and to make a shadow of each thing. Wi did as he was commanded and all on the world was hot. Maka had no comfort except in the shadow, and she implored Mahpiyato to return Hanhepi to the world. Then Mahpiyato commanded Anpetu and Hanhepi to follow each other and remain for a space in the world. He commanded Wi to go before to the regions under the world and to follow him above the world. They did all that they were commanded.

The Lenni Lenape (meaning "Original People") are an Algonquian-speaking people with ancestral homelands along the East Coast of North American. The English referred to them as the Delaware. They are unique among Native American peoples in that they claim a national epic that was committed to writing. This account, the *Wallam Olum* (or the "Red Record") is composed of 183 symbols combined with words that tell the story of the Lenape before the coming of the Europeans. Scholars disagree as to its authenticity. The epic opens with the following creation story.

THE CREATION OF THE COSMOS ACCORDING TO THE LENAPE RED RECORD[12]

At the beginning, the sea everywhere covered the earth. Above extended a swirling cloud, and within it, the Great Spirit moved.

[11]Amelia Lamont and Reva High Horse, compilers, *Oglala Sioux Elementary Unit, Grades K–6: Native American Teacher Training Institute* (Lincoln, NE: University of Nebraska, ca. 1970), pp. 15–16.

[12]*The Red Record: The Wallam Olum*, translated by David McCutchen, (Garden City Park, NY: Avery Publishing, 1993), pp. 52–56.

Primordial, Everlasting, Invisible, Omnipresent—the Great
  Spirit moved.
Bringing forth the sky, the earth, the clouds, the heavens.
Bringing forth the day, the night, the stars.
Bringing forth all of these to move in harmony.
Stirred to action strong winds blew, cleansing the sky in
  rapid streams.
Pure as snow arose the lands to be inhabited.
Again, the Great Spirit created: the creator spirits,
Living beings, immortals, the Souls of Everything.
Then the Spirit, Ancestor, Grandfather of Men,
Gave the First Mother, Mother of Life.
[Who] gave the fish, gave the turtles, gave the beasts, gave
  the birds.
But the bad spirit brought forth bad creatures: the snakes
  and sea monsters.
It brought forth flies; it brought forth Mosquitoes.
Friends were all living things with each other.
The Benefactor and the helpful spirits were busy.
Those ancestors, the first men, were alone; the first women
  were brought them.
Hungry for the first food, those ancestors gathered it.
All were delighted, all were carefree, all were happy.
But then, very secretly at the end, an evil snake, a sorcerer
  came to the earth.
Wickedness, wrongfulness, criminal acts—these came there.
Black weather came, sickness came, death came.
All of this was long ago in the land beyond the great flood,
  the first world there was.

A Yuchi Account of the Origin of Dry Land[13]

When the Creator resolved to make a home for the
living beings he had no solid matter to start with, and
hence called a council of various animals to deliberate upon the matter. Among those that he gathered
were the wolf, the raccoon, the bear, the turkey buz-
zard, the crawfish, the loon, and the ring-necked
duck. They decided that earth should be taken from
the bottom of the waters, and selected the loon for the
purpose, as he was known to be the best diver. The
loon put white beads around his neck and plunged
into the water, but the water was deep and its pressure
forced the beads into the skin of his neck, so that they
could not be removed, and they are sticking there
even now. As he returned to the surface without obtaining any earth or mud, the beaver was ordered to

accomplish the task. He dived, but the water suffo-
cated him and his dead body reappeared on the surface largely swelled up. This is the reason why all
beavers now show a thick, swollen exterior. Another
beast had to plunge down on the same errand. The
crawfish took a dive and soon yellow dirt appeared
on the water's surface. He came near being drowned,
but on reappearing he stretched up his claws, which
were examined by the animals assembled. They found
some mud sticking on the inside of them, between the
extremities, and handed it over to the Creator, who
rolled it out to a flat mass, spread it on the surface of
the waters, and it became land. The fish, whose domain was the bottom of the water, noticed the coming down of the crawfish and pursued him for the
theft, but the crawfish managed to elude him and escape to the surface.

Peoples from all cultures express their sentiments
toward the deities in their pantheon not only via creation myths, but also through prayers and hymns. The
selections here include a variety of songs of praise addressed to the high deities of the most technologically
advanced Native American civilizations in pre-
Columbian times: the Incas of Peru and the Aztecs of
Meso-America. Compare these hymns with the words
of praise contained in the Hebrew Book of Psalms and
in the Hindu Rig Veda. What commonalities and differences do you find when comparing these accounts?

Prayers to Viracocha, Creator God of the Incas[14]

O conquering Viracocha!
Everpresent Viracocha!
Thou who art without equal upon the earth!
Thou who art from the beginnings of the world until its end!
Thou gavest life and valour to men, saying,
"Let this be a man."
And to woman saying,
"Let this be a woman."
Thou madest them and gavest them being.
Watch over them, that they may live in health and in peace.
Thou who art in the highest heavens,
And among the clouds of the tempest,
Grant them long life,
And accept this sacrifice,
O Creator.

---

[13]Bill Grantham, *Creation Myths and Legends of the Creek Indians*
(Gainesville, FL: University of Florida Press, 2002), pp. 50–51.

[14]Philip Ainsworth Means, ed., *Ancient Civilizations of the Andes*
(New York: Charles Scribner's Sons, 1931), pp. 438–439.

O Pachacamac!
Thou who hast existed from the beginning,
Thou who shalt exist until the end,
Powerful but merciful,
Who didst create man by saying,
"Let man be."
Who defendest us from evil,
And preservest our life and our health,
Art thou in the sky or upon the earth?
In the clouds or in the deeps?
Hear the voice of him who implores thee.
And grant him his petitions.
Give us life everlasting,
Preserve us, and accept this our sacrifice.

HYMNS TO THE HIGH GODS OF THE AZTECS[15]

The Hymn of Huitzilopochtli

Huitzilopochtli is first in rank, no one, no one is like unto him: not vainly do I sing (his praises) coming forth in the garb of our ancestors; I shine, I glitter.

He is a terror to the Mixteca; he alone destroyed the Picha-Huasteca, he conquered them.

The Dart-Hurler is an example to the city, as he sets to work. He who commands in battle is called the representatives of my God.

When he shouts aloud he inspires great terror; the divine hurler, the god turning himself in the combat, the divine hurler, the god turning himself into combat.

Amanteca, gather yourselves together with me in the house of war against your enemies, gather yourselves together with me.

Pipiteca, gather yourselves together with me in the house of war against your enemies; gather yourselves together with me.

HYMN TO TELEOINAM, THE MOTHER OF THE GODS

This Aztec genius of fertility was the patroness of women in childbirth. Her temple at Tepeyacac was one of the most renowned in ancient Mexico. Later the Christian "Our Lady of Guadalupe" made her appearance on this celebrated holy site.

Hail to our mother, who caused the yellow flowers to blossom, she who scattered the seeds of the maguey, as she came forth from Paradise.

Hail to our mother, who poured forth white flowers in abundance, she who scattered the seeds of the maguey, as she came forth from Paradise.

Hail to the goddess who shines in the thorn bush like a bright butterfly,

Ho! She is our mother, goddess of the earth, she supplies food in the desert to the wild beasts, and causes them to live.

Thus, thus, you see her to be an ever-fresh model of liberality toward all flesh,

And as you see the goddess of the earth do to the wild beasts, so also does she toward the green herbs and fishes.

SECTION 2: Humanity: The Problem of Good and Evil

According to a Mohawk Traditional proverb, "Every person has both a bad heart and a good heart. No matter how good a man seems, he has some evil. No matter how bad a man seems, there is some good about him. No man is perfect."[16] But what constitutes a good and bad heart? Although Native American oral traditions generally are less likely than many Old World traditions to define "sin" or misconduct as human violations of specific divine injunctions, the New World peoples often did wonder about questions of good and evil. Their thoughts about the nature of humankind and about the origins of good and evil are reflected in the creation stories of the various peoples. This section contains selections from stories of origins from the traditions of three Native American peoples: the Oneidas from the Northeast, the Navajos from the Southwest, and the Caddos from the South. As you read these accounts, think about how each group viewed the moral condition of humans. In what ways do these points of view complement and conflict with the ideas about good and evil expressed in other Old World scared traditions?

---

[15]*Rig Veda Americanus: Sacred Songs of the Ancient Mexicans with a Gloss in Nahuatl*, edited with a paraphrase, notes, and vocabulary by Daniel G. Brinton (1890). Scanned at sacred-texts.com, March 2001.

[16]*World Scripture: A Comparative Anthology of Sacred Texts* (New York: Paragon House, 1991), p. 277.

THE ONEIDA CREATION STORY[17]

When I was a child, I used to hear the old people tell stories about how it came to pass that people began to live on the Earth.

Once there lived people in a certain place, among whom there was a very rich man. They had everything that they needed there; nothing was lacking; they were so happy that there was no sickness, and no one ever died. It is said that this rich man had a lot of servants who always kept him entertained; they were playing lacrosse. The man and his wife were sitting and watching them play ball. He sent her off, saying, "Would you go and get some water, I want a drink." So she went to the spring. She went to get water, and one of the ball players came along. He was very sweaty, that ball player; and he said, "Couldn't I have a drink?" So then she gave him something to drink, enough that he drank his fill; then she refilled the water and took it back to where her husband was sitting. He said, "Why did you put another before me? I sent you to get water."

It is said that she replied, "He was so sweaty, I took pity on him, that is why I gave the water to him, because he was playing ball." He said, "I told you before that you should never let another man come between us. But now, you have broken your promise to me. Now we will have to fulfill what we agreed upon. For if ever our minds become separated, then we will truly go our different ways."

Then, it is said, he called to some strong men, saying, "that tree over there, the one with the long root (the white pine), uproot it. Throw her down there because now we are divided." At that, they uprooted the tree; he sat her down on the hole and pushed her; then she reached out to her right side; there she grabbed onto a strawberry plant, and carried it along with her; and with the other hand, it is said, a tobacco plant; and so these are the things she brought with her when she fell into the hole.

Down and down she falls, and as she is enveloped by darkness, she keeps falling down and down. Then, at last, a light suddenly appears in the direction towards which she is falling. There were already creatures living in the water. There was no earth, just

muddy water. Then one of these, a muskrat, they say, was looking up; he said, 'What's that way up there, flying this way?' So then they were all looking up; and finally they saw something flying down; and they kept looking and looking up there.

There were also birds living there, and they went flying up; the one in front said, "It's a human coming down; it's a human coming down!"

[The animals then discuss how to help the woman. Ultimately it was decided that the birds would soften her fall and that Turtle would support the woman when she landed.]

Thus they came, with the woman standing on them as they flew. Very slowly, they left her on the back of the turtle that was floating there. There she stood: the back of the turtle was only big enough for her to stand there with her feet together. So it was, for some time there was daylight, and then darkness fell upon her.

[At this point in some versions, the water animals dive down to get mud from the bottom and bring it to the surface. From this mud the Earth grows.]

Then, some time later, she became pregnant, this one who stood upon the Earth. And then, when her term had come, one male child was born the right way; he was born the way a person should be born. But the other one was in such a hurry to come out that he came right through her body; he killed their mother. So then they were all alone, these two twin brothers.

The name of one of them was Thaluhyawaku, and the other, Tawiskalu. The way they were, they had different kinds of minds. And now, whatever this Thaluhyawaku would think of doing, Tawiskalu would change it to the opposite way. . . .

[The story continues with Thaluhyawaku making figurines of animals that would wander on the Earth for meat. Tawiskalu, however, locked up the animals that Thaluhyawaku had made for meat and created other dangerous animals that would kill people.]

Then after some time, Thaluhyawaku made another figurine, a human. He made both man and woman. He made them out of clay. And when he had completed it, then he said, 'arise, you two' and so the two of them stood up and came to life. And then, when they came alive, then he gave them permission to start raising a family. And these dangerous animals that were wandering around would fear them; and also there were those wandering around that humans would be able to eat; those are the edible ones of his

[17]Demus Elm and Harvey Antone, *The Oneida Creation Story*, translated and edited by Floyd G. Lounsbury and Bryan Gick (Lincoln, NE: University of Nebraska Press, 2000), pp. 30–53.

creation. Then it was that he gave them dominion over whatever was on the Earth. They themselves would control everything; they would be responsible for whatever he created on the Earth; and he gave them nothing that would make them have to work for a living. All the animals that he left for them would be what the two of them would live on.

Then his brother [Tawiskalu] wanted to copy what had happened, the figures that he [Thaluhyawaku] had created that had come to life. So now he too made a figurine; he wanted a human, as his brother had made. But it was a monkey, with a long tail; that is what this one was that he made. And when it came to life, he was not satisfied then with the way it looked. And he said, "You will have your home in the forest; that is where you will dwell." Then he formed yet another figure; but again it was only another of the same sort. Again it was a monkey that he formed, only this time it did not have a tail sticking out. Now it was one of the great apes. He brought it to life also, this one that he had formed. But he was not satisfied with how this one looked either. That one also he sent into the forest that is where you will dwell."

Now then he formed another figurine. This time he picked some foam from the water, and that is what he made it out of, the figure that he now formed. It was much finer looking. But he was not able to bring it to life, this figure that he had made.

So then he asked his brother to bring it to life, this figure that he had made. If there should be offspring, his brother would have half control of it and he himself half. And indeed he [Thaluhyawaku] did bring this one to life. He said, "To the East is where I will send him." It was to the place of the 'Little Garden,' as they call it, that is where he placed him. He would live very well there. There were lots of fruit-bearing plants there, and that is what he would live on. And that indeed is how he helped him.

Then, when the offspring survived, then he [Thaluhyawaku] went back and took possession of everything for himself; he took control again. And then he said, "The children will be without sin. It is I who will be in control." He [Tawiskalu] said, "So be it, but later on, they will start to talk; and later on, someone will also grow stronger. I will say [to some human], "You say something to that person," and so shall it be in his thoughts. I will say, "You go and hit somebody with something," and so shall it be in his thoughts. And then I will take control of them again." And that is what Tawiskalu said.

And then it will come to pass that someone will say something—when one is also stronger than the other—then one person can speak ill of another person; and then one person will hit another with something; and then he [Tawiskalu] will once again take control of everything for himself. And indeed it seems that this is the way it was fixed for that man he had placed in the Little Garden.

SELECTIONS FROM THE NAVAJO CREATION STORY[18]

The Navajo creation story is a lengthy, complex story that details the origins of five worlds. It opens with the emergence of insectlike people from deep within the earth describing how they made their way to the surface, where in time they evolved into "earth surface people" and formed human clans. As the people became more complex, they learned how to mitigate evil with good by developing relationships with the supernatural powers and among themselves. A major theme is the tension between male and female that results in disharmony and destruction. In Navajo thought, the quest for sexual harmony epitomizes the universal pattern for attaining harmony in all relationships: earth and sky, night and day, mortals and immortals, summer and winter.

Previous to the selection printed here, the story details how First Man learns of First Woman's infidelity and strikes her, thus causing her to flee to her mother Woman Chief. In anger, Woman Chief berates First Man, telling him that he is a braggart who claims cosmic importance, although in reality, she says, all things ripen through her. Following this insult, the men remove themselves to the other side of the stream. For four years the men and women are separated. During this time hardships take place for both groups, but especially for the women who deteriorate when left alone to themselves. After a council, First Man sends a raft to bring the starving women across the stream. The sexes are reunited, but a flood threatens their survival. To escape the water, the people climb through an opening in a fast growing reed plant that takes them to the surface of the fifth world. The story continues as follows:

[18]Paul G. Zolbrod, *Dine bahane: The Navajo Creation Story* (Albuquerque, NM: University of New Mexico Press, 1984), pp. 94–97.

It is also said that with more room in the fifth world the people began to travel. First they journeyed east. And after one day's walk they reached "White Spot on the Earth." There they camped. And during that night a young woman gave birth.

She was a beautiful maiden who, during the separation of the men and the women in the world below, had reached the age where she longed for the company of a man.

So early one morning she had torn off an antelope horn, which was fuzzy at the time as growing antelope horns usually are. And after warming it all day long in the light, she had inserted it into herself as darkness fell. With it she spent the whole night trying to make *bijoozh* her vagina shout.

Now she was bringing forth the fruit of that self-abuse: an offspring that looked nothing like an ordinary child. Instead, this infant was a round, misshapen creature with no head.

When the people saw, they were frightened and ashamed. So they held a council and decided that this baby should be abandoned. They threw it into a gully and left it there to die.

Nonetheless it lived, as they were to learn. It would grow up and become a terrible creature *Deelgeed* the Horned Monster. And eventually he would destroy many of the people.

[The next day after traveling further to the east a second woman goes into labor. She had abused herself during the separation of the sexes with an eagle wing and gave birth to Monster Eagle, who later would carry away many people. Again, on the next day after traveling further to the east, a third woman who had abused herself with a stone gave birth to Monster Who Kicks People Down the Cliff, a creature that would cause many people to be crushed in the canyon. Finally, after traveling another day to the east, a fourth woman who had abused herself with a cactus gave birth to twin mutants knows as Monsters That Kill with Their Eyes. These mutants would flee to the brush and later paralyze many with their deadly stare. Then the story continues.]

[This] explains how monsters came to exist in this world, bringing disorder wherever they went. Such creatures were the fruit of transgressions that took place in the fourth world, where the men and the women were separated.

Like the men, the women could not endure living apart. And for as long as they lived separately on opposite banks of the same stream, both groups made a mockery of marriage by masturbating.

As the march to the east continued, other monsters were likewise born. They too were the result of the foolish quarrel that had taken place between the First Man and the First Woman.

Still other monsters sprang from the blood that was shed during the birth of the first four. And all of them would likewise grow up, as the people were soon to learn.

They would all become enemies and destroyers. Soon they would begin to lurk under rocks and along cliff-paths. They would spring upon passersby and kill them. Then they would devour them. And because of those monsters the people would live in daily fear, it is said.

The final excerpt is from the oral traditions of the Caddo Indians who, in distant times, lived in Louisiana and since 1859 have settled in what is currently western Oklahoma. Like their close kin the Wichitas, the Caddos survived by agricultural and buffalo hunting. How might the economy of this Plains Indian culture influence the contents of this story? According to this story, what is a source of civil strife?

A CADDO TALE: THE EFFEMINATE MAN WHO INTRODUCED CIVIL STRIFE[19]

One time there lived among the people a man who always did the women's work and dressed like the women and went with them, and never went with the men. The men made fun of him, but he did not care, and continued to work and play only with the women. A war broke out with some other tribe, and all of the men went to fight but this man, who stayed behind with the women. After the war party had gone, an old man, who was too old to go with them, came to him and told him that if he would not go to fight he was going to kill him, for it was a disgrace to have such a man in the tribe. The man refused to go, saying that the Great Father did not send him to earth to fight and did not want him to. The old man paid no attention to his excuse, and told him if he did not go to fight he would have the warriors kill him when they returned from battle with the enemy. The man said that they could not kill him, that he would always come to life,

---

[19]George A. Dorsey, *Traditions of the Caddo* (Washington, D.C.: Carnegie Institution of Washington, 1905), p. 19.

and would bewitch people and cause them to fight and kill one another. The old man did not believe him, and when the war party came home he told the men that they would have to kill the man because he was a coward, and they could not let a coward live in the tribe. They beat him until they thought he was dead, and were just ready to bury him when he jumped up alive. Again they beat him until he fell; then they cut off his head. He jumped up headless and ran about, frightening all of the people. They were just about to give up killing him when some one noticed a small purple spot on the little finger of his left hand. They cut that out; then he lay down and died. Soon after many people began to fight and quarrel, and some even killed their own brothers and sisters and fathers and mothers. The other people tried to stop the fighting, but could not, because the people were bewitched and could not help themselves. Then the old man remembered what the coward had said, and he told the people, and they were all sorry that they had killed him.

SECTION 3: Sacred Stories: Divine Messengers, Prophets, and Priests

Within the oral traditions of the Native American peoples are thousands of cultural hero tales. In these tales a superhuman hero uses his cunning and power to bring great benefits to humanity by giving the world its present form, by ridding the land of monsters and giants, and by giving to humankind those things that make life worth living.

One common tale told among numerous Native American peoples is a story that explains how light or fire was brought to the earth. In this story the world originally was in darkness until the hero departed from the human world to the home of the keeper of light and, through trickery or battle, secured light for humankind. A second widely told story is the tale of how a hero comes to the earth to subdue the wild beasts that threaten humankind. A third common type of tale explains how humans received the sacred medicines that provide them with protection and healing powers. The following selections from the Tsimshian peoples of the Northwest, and the Arikara and Ogalala of the Great Plains are representative tales from these genres. Note how metamorphosis or transformation in form is a major motif in these tales. What does the content and structure of these tales tell us about the theology and worldview of these Native American peoples?

THE THEFT OF LIGHT—A TSIMSHIAN TALE[20]

Giant flew inland (toward the east). He went on for a long time, and finally he was very tired, so he dropped down on the sea the little round stone which his father had given to him. It became a large rock way out at sea. Giant rested on it and refreshed himself, and took off the raven skin.

At that point there was always darkness. There was no daylight then. Again Giant put on the raven skin and flew toward the east. Now, Giant reached mainland and arrived at the mouth of Sheena River. There he stopped and scattered the salmon roe and trout roe. He said while he was scattering them, "Let every river and creek have all kinds of fish!" Then he took the dried sea lion bladder and scattered the fruits all over the land, saying, "Let every mountain, him, valley, plain, the whole land, be full of fruits!"

The whole world was still covered with darkness. When the sky was clear, the people would have a little light from the stars; and when clouds were in the sky, it was very dark all over the land. The people were distressed by this. Then Giant thought that it would be hard for him to obtain food if it were always dark. He remembered that there was light in heaven, whence he had come. Then he made up his mind to bring down the light to our world. On the following day Giant put on his raven skin, which his father the chief had given to him, and flew upward. Finally he found the hole in the sky and he flew through it. Giant reached the inside of the sky. He took off the raven skin and put it down near the hole of the sky. He went on, and came to a spring near the house of the chief of heaven. There he sat down and waited.

Then the chief's daughter came out, carrying a small bucket in which she was about to fetch water. She went down to the big spring in front of her father's house. When Giant saw her coming along, he transformed himself into the leaf of a cedar and floated on the water. The chief's daughter dipped it up in her bucket and drank it. Then she returned to her father's house and entered.

After a short time she was with child, and not long after she gave birth to a boy. Then the chief and the chieftianess were very glad. They washed the boy regularly. He began to grow up. Now he was beginning

---

[20]Gill, *Native American Traditions: Sources and Interpretations* (Belmont, CA: Wadsworth Publishing, 1983), pp. 30–31.

to creep about. They washed him often, and the chief smoothed and cleaned the floor of the house. Now the child was strong and crept about every day. He began to cry, "Hama, hama!" He was crying all the time, and the great chief was troubled, and called in some of his slaves to carry about the boy. The slaves did so, but he would not sleep for several nights. He kept on crying, "Hama, hama!" Therefore the chief invited all his wise men, and said to them that he did not know what the boy wanted and why he was crying. He wanted the box that was hanging in the chief's house.

This box, in which the daylight was kept, was hanging in one corner of the house. Its name was ma. Giant had known it before he descended to our world. The child cried for it. The chief was annoyed, and the wise men listened to what the chief told them. When the wise men heard the child crying aloud, they did not know what he was saying. He was crying all the time, "Hama, hama, hama!"

One of the wise men, who understood him, said to the chief, "He is crying for the ma." Therefore the chief ordered it to be taken down. The man put it down. They put it down near the fire, and the boy sat down near it and ceased crying. He stopped crying, for he was glad. Then he rolled the ma about inside the house. He did so for four days. Sometimes he would carry it to the door. Now the great chief did not think of it. He had quite forgotten it. Then the boy really took up the ma, put it on his shoulders, and ran out with it. While he was running, some one said, "Giant is running away with the ma!" He ran away the hosts of heaven pursued him. They shouted that Giant was running away with the ma. He came to the hole of the sky, put on the skin of the raven, and flew down, carrying the ma. Then the hosts of heaven return to their houses, and he flew down with it to our world.

THE HOLY BOY WHO STOPPED ANIMALS FROM KILLING HUMANS—AN ARIKARA TALE[21]

Now, I am going to tell a story. It isn't a long story.

Long, long ago when mysterious things occurred during the holy period, the different kinds of animals

---

[21]Douglas R. Parks, *Traditional Narratives of the Arikara Indians: Stories of Alfred Morsette*, English Translations, Vol. 3 (Lincoln, NE: University of Nebraska Press, 1991), pp. 131–134.

that roam around today used to hate us human beings. When they would see a human, the stags, buffalo, or whatever they were, would burn him. And these birds that fly around—geese and cranes—would fly in a circle over a human whenever they saw him. Then while he was looking for food for himself, the poor thing—whether man or a youth—he would become dizzy as he watched them and be knocked to the ground, as he went about wherever he was going, seeking to find food for himself. Things were not good for human beings during the holy period. I don't know when that time was.

Well, then a boy cam down from up there in the sky. Before he came down here, he said, "I don't like what these animals are doing down there, molesting human beings, the poor things. Now I am coming. I'm going to hurt them." Well, then he came down to earth.

Then as he traveled around, he would knick an arrow in his bow and shoot it into the brush. In this way he felled stags, elks, bears, and other ferocious animals when he shot at them. He would also fell a buffalo whenever he released an arrow and let it fly somewhere. Likewise, whenever he shot an arrow up into the air, it would land and then there would be a flock of dead geese or cranes lying there.

Then the living powers became angry. "Eh, he has killed a multitude of us, this holy boy who goes around shooting us. Now let him die of thirst."

Then all the water disappeared. There was no more water. Wherever the creek and river valleys were, the water disappeared entirely. And the boy would go to different places looking for water while he just wandered all around. When he came to a bank there would be only mud there.

One day while he was looking at things along a dry bank, he saw what is called a spring peeper, the one that makes sounds in the evening at the edge of a creek or spring.

Then this boy sang:

"Tell me where the water is, and I shan't jab you.
Tell me where the water is, and I shan't jab you.
    Tell me where the water is!
Tell me where the water is, and I shan't jab you.
    Tell me where the water is!"

Now the spring peeper, poor thing, became very frightened since the boy was kicking it around, molesting it. Then it stood up and thought, "I might save myself."

And so the spring peeper went to a mud flat where the ground was damp. The spring peeper put its two forelegs into the mud and then backed off. Oh my, then water emerged. And as the water came out, it grew in volume. Why, now this boy began to drink his fill!

Then the boy said, "Now, you creatures who did this to me, my vengeance will fall upon you."

And after he nocked an arrow, he felled an elk or whatever kind of animal it might be, as he was killing different ones. "Now do not do it again!" he warned. "If I return, the consequences will be even worse." When he shot an arrow into the air, he brought down geese and cranes, killing them too. "Let that also be all of your killing of these human beings of mine, the poor things! If I must come again, it will be even worse."

Then the boy returned to the sky.

Now that is why animals no longer molest us poor human beings like they used to do long, long ago. When the different kinds of wild animals used to oppose us in those times, they must have been ferocious. When the stags bellowed, they burned a person up. The stags and elk and other such animals were fierce and attacked human beings. [Then this boy came and] here they were the ones that became frightened! The boy said, "It's no longer the way it used to be. It's not going to be that way again."

And then this boy went back up into the sky to wherever he had come from.

The White Buffalo Woman and the Gift of the Sacred Pipe—An Oglala Tale[22]

Once two men were out hunting with bows and arrows when they saw in the distance something wondrous approaching them. As the object came closer, they saw that it was a beautiful woman dressed in white buckskin and carrying a bundle on her back. The woman was so beautiful that one of the men had bad intentions toward her. She told this man to come forward, and as he neared her they were both enveloped by a mist. When the mist lifted, the man was nothing but bones and terrible snakes were eating him.

She told the other man to return to his camp and tell his chief to prepare a great lodge and tell all the people to gather. She had something of great importance to tell them. The man returned and told what

had happened. The chief ordered that several tipis be taken down and made into a large lodge. The people dressed in their finest clothes and awaited the appearance of the mysterious woman. The woman arrived and entered the lodge in a sunwise direction. She bore the bundle in her hands and offered it to the chief, saying that it was a sacred pipe and with it the people would send their voices to *Wakantanka*. From her bundle she took the sacred pipe and a round stone, placing the latter on the ground. She took the pipe and offered the stem to the heavens, saying "With this sacred pipe you will walk upon the Earth; for the Earth is your Grandmother and Mother and She is sacred."

She told the people that the pipe bowl was made of red stone and represented the earth. Carved in the stone was a buffalo calf which represented all four-legged creatures. The stem of the pipe was made of wood and represented all growing things. And the twelve feathers which decorated the pipe represented the Spotted Eagle and all the winged creatures of the air. All the peoples and the things of the universe would be joined with whoever smoked the sacred pipe. The woman then touched the pipe to the round stone, saying, "With this pipe you would be bound to all your relatives: your Grandfather and Father, your Grandmother and Mother."

She told the people to behold the seven circles inscribed on the round stone and that these represented the seven rites in which the pipe would be used. The first large circle represented the rite she would teach them on this day, and others represented rites that would later be revealed to them. She told the chief that through the pipe the people would increase. Then she instructed them in the first rite, which was the ghost-keeping ceremony. In this ceremony the people could send their voices to Wakantanka through the soul of a deceased person. The day on which the soul is released to return to Wakantanka would be sacred, and on this day four women would be made sacred and in time bear children.

As the sacred woman was about to leave, she addressed the chief, saying that he must always treat the pipe in a sacred manner. "Remember," she said, "in me there are four ages. I am leaving now but I shall look back upon your people in every age, and at the end I shall return."

Moving around the lodge in a sunwise manner, the woman left, but after walking a short distance she sat down. When she arose the people were amazed to see that she had turned into a red and brown buffalo calf.

[22]William K. Powers, *Oglala Religion* (Lincoln, NE: University of Nebraska Press, 1977), pp. 81–83.

The calf walked on, lay down, rolled and when it got up it was a white buffalo calf. Again the white buffalo walked farther, and turned back into a black buffalo. The black buffalo walked farther away, stopped, and after bowing to each quarter of the universe, disappeared over a hill.

Another genre of tales within most traditions is the trickster tale. Many trickster figures portray chaos and disorder. Others represent all of the polarities of this world: creator/destroyer, intelligence/stupidity, goodness/evil. Both powerful and foolish, they are characters that often follow the base desire for freedom, including sexual freedom. The consequences they suffer as a result of the violations of social taboos teach us the necessity for establishing boundaries for human conduct. In the American West, the trickster most often presented is Coyote. The following selections include several well-known Coyote tales that appear in various forms in numerous Native American oral traditions. The versions offered in this section are from Utes of Utah and the Wasco-Warm Springs Indians of the Northwest.

Trickster Tales from the Utes[23]

Coyote and the Originals of Pain, Death, and Winter

Wolf wanted women to be pregnant in their arms and suffer no pain, but Coyote said: "Let them bear children in their abdomens and suffer lots of pain."

Wolf wanted the dead buried in anthills and wanted them to come to life again the next day, but Coyote said, "No, let them be put in the ground and let families all cut their hair and be sad and cry."

Wolf wanted no winter, wanted it always to be nice weather, but Coyote said, "No, let it be cold part of the time."

Coyote Seeks a Name

Coyote wanted a name for his little son, so he went over to see Woodchucks to see if they had a good one. Coyote asked the names of all the Woodchuck children. One little fellow, just about the size of Coyote's son, had a real cute name. Coyote liked it and asked if he could have the name for his son. Woodchuck said yes and Coyote started home with the name.

He had not gone very far when he stumbled and fell and when he got up he had lost the name. So back he went to the Woodchucks to get the name again. They told him again and Coyote started home. He got a little farther this time before he stumbled and fell and lost the name again. So back he went once more, poor old fellow. He started home again, and again he fell and lost the name and had to go back. This happened several times till Coyote was ashamed to go back again and went home without any name for his son.

Coyote's Carelessness: A Trickster Tale of the Wasco-Warm Springs[24]

Coyote was going along, and he came to a river where five pretty sisters were bathing and washing clothes some distance from each other. "What pretty girls," said Coyote to himself, "I wonder how I can enjoy them all." He thought a little, and then turned himself into a baby laced up in a papoose-board, and set himself adrift on the river.

Pretty soon he drifted down to the oldest sister. "Oh, what a beautiful baby!" she said and pulled it ashore and picked it up. Well, that Coyote turned back into himself before she knew what was happening, and he had his way with her; then he became a baby again and drifted to the second oldest sister. "Oh, my, what a cute baby!" she said, "I must save it!"—but when she picked it up it was that Coyote! And so he fooled two more sisters in the same way, until he got down to the last one, the youngest.

When she saw the baby drifting down she said, "There's something funny about this; let me see"—and she held the baby in the water with one hand and quickly unlaced it with the other. Sure enough, it was that Coyote! When he turned himself into a baby, he just forgot to change his penis too, and when the youngest sister saw he was no baby, she threw him far out into the river. He was careless, but she was careful.

Section 4: Divine Law: Justice, Reward, and Punishment

With no written tradition dating to distant times, there is no singular Native American code of ethics that is equivalent to the divine laws that are contained in sacred writings such as the Hebrew *Torah* or in the

---

[23]Anne M. Smith and Alden Hayes, ed. *Ute Tales* (Salt Lake City: University of Utah Press, 1992), pp. 53, 67.

[24]Gill, *Traditions*, pp. 32–33.

Hindu *Law of Manu.* Strong ethical injunctions, however, permeated the oral traditions of all Native American peoples. Many of these teachings emphasize the necessity of remembering that the entire universe is sacred and interconnected. Consequently, it is not surprising that Native American spirituality often places a high priority on matters related to ecological ethics. The first selections are taken from contemporary Native American voices. Some of these words are directed as much to non-Indians as to Indians. What are the major themes contained in these passages? What do these selections teach us about Native American ecological ethics?

"Scraps from a Diary—Chief Seattle"[25]

This text allegedly is a translation of the Duwamish Chief Seal'th's speech that was delivered to his people when they were making preparations to move across Puget Sound, away from the city that was named in Chief Seattle's honor.

Every part of this earth is sacred to my people. Every shining pine needle, every sandy shore, every mist in the dark woods, every meadow, every humming insect. All are holy in the memory and experience of my people.

We know the sap which courses through the trees as we know the blood that courses through our veins. We are part of the earth and it is part of us. The perfumed flowers are our sisters. The bear, the deer, the great eagle, these are our brothers. The rocky crests, the juices in the meadow, the body heat of the pony, and man, all belong to the same family. . . .

Will you teach your children what we have taught our children? That the earth is our mother? What befalls the earth befalls all the sons of the earth.

This we know: the earth does not belong to man, man belongs to the earth. All things are connected like the blood that unites us all. Man did not weave the web of life, he is merely a strand of it. Whatever he does to the web, he does to himself.

The following brief excerpt was taken in 1885 from Smohalla, a prophet and chief of the Wanapun Indians of the Columbia River valley.[26]

After awhile, when God is ready, he will drive away all the people except the people who have obeyed his laws.

Those who cut up the lands or sign papers for lands will be defrauded of their rights, and will be punished by God's anger.

Moses was bad. God did not love him. He sold his people's houses and the graves of their dead. It is a bad word that comes from Washington. It is not a good law that would take my people away from me to make them sin against the laws of God. You ask me to plow the ground! Shall I take a knife and tear my mother's bosom? Then when I die she will not take me to her bosom to rest.

You ask me to dig for stone! Shall I dig under her skin for her bones? Then when I die I cannot enter her body to be born again. You ask me to cut grass and make hay and sell it, and be rich like white men, but how dare I cut off my mother's hair?

Finally, the following words were expressed in 1925 by Katie Luckie, an elder from the Californian Wintu tribe.[27]

The White people never cared for land or deer or bear. When we Indians kill meat, we eat it all up. When we dig roots, we make little holes. When we built houses, we make little holes. When we burn grass for grasshoppers, we don't ruin things. We shake down acorns and pinenuts. We don't chop down trees. We only use dead wood. But the White people blow up the ground, pull down trees, kill everything. The tree says, "Don't, I am sore. Don't hurt me." But they chop it down and cut it up. The spirit of the land hates them. . . . Everything the White man has touched, it is sore.

These modern comments reflect themes that have been expressed in the rites and oral traditions from the more distant past. The following selections are accounts and stories about the deer hunt. The first comes from the agricultural Acoma Pueblo culture of New Mexico. The second is a story of the largely hunting Loucheux peoples of the sub-Arctic. Although selections from diverse cultures, both suggest that hunting is not just an economic activity but also a religious activity that assumes a spiritual relationship between humans and animals. Native

---

[25]William Young, *Quest for Harmony: Native American Spiritual Traditions* (New York: Seven Bridges Press, 2002), p. 335.

[26]Gill, *Traditions*, pp. 156–157.

---

[27]Young, *Quest for Harmony*, pp. 348–349.

peoples often view animals as under the control of a spiritual master who releases them to be hunted. Consequently, the hunt, the kill, and even the disposal of the animal must follow a sacred protocol. Failure to follow this protocol can carry with it severe punishments.

DESCRIBING THE DEER HUNT (ACOMA), BY JAMES PAYTIAMO[28]

When an Indian has hit a deer, he runs to the fallen animal. First he takes a small branch of a tree and brushes him off, as he has a religious belief that the deer is made of sheets of clouds, and he has to brush off the clouds to get at him. Then, he reaches down in his pocket for the yellow pollen he has collected from flowers, takes it between his thumb and forefinger, drops a little on the deer's mouth, then carries it to his own breath, and makes a sign with the pollen towards the hunter's camp, which is supposed to lead the spirit of the deer to the camp.

Then he pulls the deer around by the forelegs, until he lies with his head towards the camp. The next thing is to take the little flint animals in the shapes of lions, wolves and bears, as many as he carries, and place them on the deer to feed and get back the power they gave him. They always come first. While these animals are on the deer, the hunter rolls a cigarette of cornhusks, and while he smokes he talks to the dead creature just as if he were telling a human where to go. When he finishes he gathers his flint animals, carefully places them in his bag, and talks to them while he puts them in the bag with these animals round his neck under his shirt. . . .

After skinning the deer and placing the meat on these juniper twigs, the hunter starts to cut the animal into part like a beef. He is always sure that he takes the entrails out first. He digs in the ground a shallow hole, and washes his hands. If there is not water nearby, he wipes his hands on a cloth. He reaches down with his hands into the blood and dips it up four times, and places it in the shallow hole on the earth. This is to feed the mother earth. Then he takes out the spleen, and places it nearby on a twig of a tree to feed the crow. Then he cuts him up.

A LOUCHEUX MORALITY TALE[29]

Once, a long time ago, a child asked his parents to let him make some "medicine" for deer-hunting, so that his father might kill a great many fat deer whenever he wanted to; but he was so young that he could barely walk as yet, and his father did not want him to do so, thinking that the medicine would not be strong enough. The boy implored him, and being again refused permission, he began to cry. Day and night he cried, until the Indians in the neighborhood were concerned, and inquired from the hunter about the cause of all these tears. But when they were told the reason why, they were satisfied that the boy was too small to prepare a "medicine." So disturbed were they by the cries, however, that in the end they persuaded the hunter to humor his son. So the boy made some medicine, and said to the people, "You shall now kill as many deer as you wish, but you must always give the fattest animals to my father."

Now, then, they went out hunting, and killed a great number of deer, many of which were very fat. Instead of complying with their promise, however, some Indians kept the fattest game for themselves, and gave only the next choice to the child's father; and from this time on the hunters failed to kill any deer. Soon the people began to starve. The boy again made a "medicine" for he and his father, like the others, had no longer anything to eat. "You must take a fine and clean deer-skin," said he to his father, "and make it into a bag. When it is done, lay it on your sledge, outside the lodge. Then take a deer's shoulder, cut all the meat off it, and when only the clean bone is left, put it along with a bit of blood into the bag on the sledge." So it was done; and the next morning, as the hunter looked at the bones in the pouch, he found them covered with flesh. Day after day the same thing happened, the bones being found with new flesh every day, in the morning. So the boy and his father had enough to eat, while, as long as the famine lasted, the other Indians were starving.

Moral standards also are communicated from the elders to the young through instructions given to those about to enter into adulthood. The following selections include advice given to a Winnebago young

---

[28]Gill, *Traditions,* pp. 122–123.

[29]Penny Petrone, *First Peoples, First Voices* (Toronto: University of Toronto Press, 1983), p. 129.

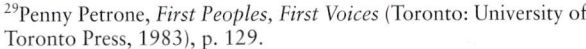

man by his father. This passage sheds light on what it meant to be a responsible man in Winnebago culture. What do these instructions tell us about gender expectations among these Eastern Woodlands peoples?

A WINNEBAGO FATHER'S TEACHINGS TO HIS SON[30]

You ought to be of some help to your fellowmen and for that reason I counsel you to fast. Our grandfather who stands in our midst [the fire] sends forth all kinds of blessings. Try them and obtain one of these. Try to have one of our grandfathers, one of the war chiefs [the spirits in control of the powers for victory on the warpath] pity you. Then some day as you travel along the road of life you will know what to do and encounter no obstacles. Without any trouble you will then be able to seek the prize you desire. . . .

If . . . you do what we call throwing away a human life [taking a life needlessly], you will have committed the greatest of all shameful acts. Why, a mourner might hurt you and burn you with embers, and then all your relatives would feel sad on your account. . . .

If you cast off your dress for many people [give to the needy], they will be benefited by your deeds. You will likewise have helped your people. It is good to be honored by all the people and they will then certainly like you if you obtain a limb [war honors]. . . . However, when you are recounting your war deeds in behalf of departed souls, do not try to add to your honor by claiming more than you actually accomplished. You will thereby merely make the souls of the departed stumble on their journey to spirit-land. If you tell a falsehood there and exaggerate your account, you, in consequence, will die soon after. Those spirits who are in control of war blessings will hear you. Tell less than you did. The old men claim that it is wiser.

It is good to die on the warpath. If you die in war, your soul will not become unconscious. You will then be able to do what you please with your soul. Your soul will always remain in a happy condition. If you choose to go back to earth as a human being and live again you can do so. You can live a second life on earth, or live in the form of those who walk on the light [birds], or in the form of an animal, if

you choose. All of these benefits will you obtain if you die in battle. . . .

Do not abuse your wife. If you make your wife suffer, you will die in a short time. Our grandmother, the earth, is a woman, and in mistreating your wife, you are abusing her. Most certainly will you be abusing our grandmother if you act thus. Since it is she who takes care of us, by your action you will be practically killing yourself. . . .

Never do anything wrong to your children. Whatever your children ask you to do, do it for them. If you act in this manner people will say that you are good-natured.

If anyone in the village loses a friend through death, if you are worth anything [wealthy], cover the expenses of the funeral of the deceased if you can. Help the mourners likewise, if you can, in defraying the expenses of feeding the departed [food brought to the grave for the first four nights after burial when the spirit of the deceased is still hovering around]. If thus you act, you will do well. All the people you have helped will then know you; everyone will know you. For the good you do, all will love you.

It is not good to be a winner in gambling. You might become rich thereby, but that is no life for anyone to lead. If you are blessed with the luck of a gambler, you might indeed win and have plenty of wealth, but none of the children you have will live. . . .

When you get married, do not make an idol of the woman you marry; do not worship her. If you worship a woman, she will insist upon greater and greater worship as time goes on. . . . It may also be that if you are married, you will listen to the voice of your wife, and you will refuse to go on the warpath. You will appear as if you had been brought up like a girl. All who are men perform the deeds of men; you, on the other hand, will never perform a real man's deed. When you are invited to a war bundle feast, they will only give you a lean piece of meat. That is what they will place before you. Why should you run the risk of thus subjecting yourself to the risk of being made fun of? . . . It is for these reasons that it is not good to listen to women. Guard yourself against it. Do not listen to women. You will be regarded as different from other people. It is not good. . . .

On the warpath is the place where you will have fun! However, do not go on the warpath unless you have fasted. You must fast for that particular warpath, for if you do not and you nevertheless try to join such a war party, then when you are present at a

[30]Elisabeth Tooker, ed. *Native North American Spirituality of the Eastern Woodlands: Sacred Myths, Dreams, Visions, Speeches, Healing Formulas, Rituals and Ceremonies* (New York: Paulist Press, 1979), pp. 70–83.

fight, when you are in the very midst of it, a bullet will come your way and kill you. That will be due to the fact that you did not fast. People know this and if, therefore, you depend upon yourself, you will certainly do a man's deed.

The final selections include rare lists of laws or regulations produced by Native American peoples. The first piece is a recollection of the principles advanced by the Shawnee leader Tecumseh and his brother, Tenskwatawa the Prophet. The prophetic religion described here spread briefly during the early nineteenth century but rapidly declined following Tecumseh's death at the Battle of Thames in 1813. The second reading is an excerpt from the "Laws of the Creek Nation" as recorded on March 15, 1824. Note the moral precepts that guided these peoples during the early decades of the nineteenth century. How wise and just were these social and religious rules?

RULES OF TENSKWATAWA THE PROPHET[31]

The Prophet with all his brothers are pure Indians of the Shawnee nation, and when a boy, was a perfect vagabond and as he grew up would not hunt and become a great drunkard. . . . [He] refrained from drinking any kind of spirituous liquor, and recommended it strongly to all the Indians far and near to follow his example. I shall here give you as many of those laws or regulations as I can now remember, but I know I have forgot many.

1st Spirituous liquor was not to be tasted by any Indians on any account whatever.

2nd No Indian was to take more than one wife in future, but those who now had two or three or more wives might keep them, but it would please the Great Spirit if they had only one wife.

3rd No Indian was to be running after the women; if a man was single let him take a wife.

4th If any married woman was to behave ill by not paying proper attention to her work, etc., the husband had a right to punish her with a rod, and as soon as the punishment was over, both husband and wife were to look each other in the face and laugh, and to bear no ill will to each other for what had passed.

5th All Indian women who were living with whitemen were to be brought home to their friends and relations, and their children to be left with their fathers, so that the nations might become genuine Indians.

6th All medicine bags, and all kinds of medicine dances and songs were to exist no more; the medicine bags were to be destroyed in *presens* of the whole of the people collected for that purpose, and at the destroying of such medicine, etc., every one was to make open confession to the Great Spirit in a loud voice of all the bad deeds that he or she had committed during their lifetime, and beg for forgiveness as the Great Spirit was too good to refuse.

7th No Indian was to sell any of their provision to any white people, they might give a little as a present, as they were sure of getting in return the full value in something else.

8th No Indian was to eat any victuals that were cooked by a White person, or to eat any provision raised by White people, as bread, beef, pork, fowls, etc.

9th No Indian must offer skins or furs or any thing else for sale, but ask to exchange them for such articles that they may want.

10th Every Indian was to consider the French, English, and Spaniards, as their fathers or friends, and to give them their hand, but they were not to know the Americans on any account, but to keep them at a distance.

11th All kind of white people's dress, such as hats, coats, etc., were to be given to the first whiteman they met as also all dogs not of their own breed, and all cats were to be given back to white people.

12th The Indians were to endeavor to do without buying any merchandise as much as possible, by which means the game would become plenty, and then by means of bows and arrows, they could hunt and kill game as in former days, and live independent of all white people.

13th All Indians who refused to follow these regulations were to be considered as bad people and not worthy to live, and must be put to death. . . .

14th The Indians in their prayers prayed to the earth, to be fruitful, also to the fish to be plenty, to the fire and sun, etc., and a certain dance was introduced simply for amusement, those prayers were repeated morning and evening, and they were taught that a divination form these duties would offend the Great Spirit.

LAWS OF THE CREEK NATION, 1824[32]

Law 1st Murder shall be punished with death. The person who commits the act shall be the only one punished and only upon good proof

Law 2nd If a man Kill another person and it can be provened to have done by accident he shall not be punished

Law 3rd If a negro Kill an Indian the negro shall suffer death and if an Indian Kill a negro he shall pay the owner the value . . .

[31]Gill, *Traditions*, pp. 152–153.

[32]Antonil J. Waring, *Laws of the Creek Nation* (Athens, GA: University of Georgia Press, 1960), pp. 17–27.

Law 8th Stealing shall be punished as follows for the first offense the thief shall be whipped for the second offence shall be cropped. for the third offence he shall be put to death. . . .

Law 14th Friendly Indians must pay all debt due to each other . . .

Law 32nd No person belonging to the Creek Nation shall go into any of the United States Territories or Cherokee Nation and procure goods or any thing else upon a Credit. . . .

SECTION 5: Gender: Women and Men in Society

Creation stories often express the attitudes of people regarding the "proper" duties of men and women in society. The opening selections are excerpts from the creation stories of the Mandan Indians of Central Canada and of the Navajo of the Southwest. The first account is given by a Mandan woman named Scattercorn. The second is another excerpt from the Navajo Creation story. To review the storyline of this tale, review the readings provided in Section 2. Like other parts of the Navajo myth, this story is rich in sexual images. What insights about gender roles and relationships are imbedded in these stories?

A MANDAN EMERGENCE STORY BY SCATTERCORN[33]

The Corn people were living under the ground by a lake. One day some of the people saw an opening reaching to the land above, and there was a vine growing in this hole. They asked the Fox to climb up and see this land. He climbed up, but, when he stuck his nose out, he got only a brief look at the beautiful land above because Sun burned his nose.

Then they asked Elk to go up and dig the hole larger with his horns. He made the hole large so the people could get through. The people started up, following the vine. They came up continuously for four days, but on the last day a woman heavy with child broke the vine and ended the migration forever. All these people had been raising the corn on this land beneath the earth.

There were four leaders in the group that reached the earth. They were the three brothers and a sister. Their names were Good Furred Robe, Cornhusk Earrings, Uses His Head for Rattle, and a sister named Waving Corn Stalk. Good Furred Robe began to lay

———
[33]Gill, *Traditions*, pp. 69–70.

out the villages and fields. He laid out the lodges in rows like the rows of corn, and he assigned the garden plots to each family. Then he distributed corn, beans, squash, and sunflower seeds to each family.

In those days the sister would be out in the fields all day overseeing the work. One day a stranger came to the gardens and wanted to talk to her, but she would not see him. He came four times to see her, but each time she refused. That man was Sun. On his fourth visit he said, "What you plant you will not harvest."

The next day when the sun came up, the air was so hot that the corn wilted. After the sun had set, she went through the gardens with her robe singing the holy songs, and the corn plants revived. Sun scorched the gardens four times, and each time she revived them with her robe and songs. . . .

Good Furred Robe also told the people that, when working in the gardens, they should burn sage and rub themselves with it to remove the bad spirits of the fields. In those days when he instructed them in that manner, worms and bugs fell from their robes, so the Mandan women set the rules of always burning sage at the close of the day's work in the fields.

Then he organized two societies, one for the men and the other for the women. He called the society for the men "Brave Warrior Society" or "Black Mouths." He brought in the men to dance. Two were given cornstalks, for only the bravest were to carry them, and he told them that these plants represented the bravest men. In war these two men could get a stick and attach raven feathers to represent the corn. If this staff was stuck into the ground, they could hold the enemy back, and, if the Mandan wanted to retreat, they could pull up the staffs and retreat without being killed. The men were between thirty and forty years old.

He organized a women's society and called it the Goose Society. The older ones would be around thirty years of age and would keep the society for five years. He selected two little girls about eight years old and stood them in the middle of the group. One girl's mouth was painted blue, the other's was black, and both represented geese. Each member wore a gooseskin and head for a headdress. Whenever anyone made an offering to the waterbirds when they came north in the spring or in the fall when they returned to the south, this society met and danced. All others with rights in the Corn ceremonies came out at those times also. The leader of the Goose Society and the last woman in the line both carried small clay pots. People could come to these dances and make offerings of horses, guns, or robes which entitled them to dance in the line, going around the Corn Priest four times, which was a sign that the giver would live to be old.

THE NAVAHO CREATION STORY[34]

Altse hastiin the First Man became a great hunter in the fourth world. So he was able to provide his wife *Altse asdzaa* the First Woman with plenty to eat. As a result, she grew very fat.

Now one day he brought home a fine, fleshy deer. His wife boiled some of it, and together they had themselves a hearty meal. When she had finished eating, *Altse asdzaa* the First Woman wiped her greasy hands on her sheath.

She belched deeply. And she had this to say: "Thank you *shijoozh* my vagina," she said.

To which *Altse hastiin* the First Man replied this way: "Why do you say that?" he replied. "Why not thank me? Was it not I who killed the deer whose flesh you have just tasted on?" Was it not I who carried it here for you to eat? Was it not I who skinned it? Who made it ready for you to boil? Is *nijoozh* your vagina the great hunter, that you should thank it and not me?"

To which *Altse asdzaa* offered this answer: "As a matter of fact, she is," offered she. In a manner of speaking, it is *joosh* the vagina who hunts. Were it not for *joosh* you would not have killed that deer. Were it not for her you would not have carried it here. You would have not skinned it. You lazy men would do nothing around here were it not for *joosh*. In truth, *joosh* the vagina does all the work around here."

To which *Altse hastiin* the First Man had this to say: "Then perhaps you women think you can live without us men," he said. "Maybe you need only *nihijoozh* your vaginas. *Nihijoozh* your great huntress. *Nihijoozh* your tireless workers."

Quickly came this reply from *Altse asdzaa* the First Woman: "All things do not exist thanks alone to you," she replied quickly. "We could live alone if we wanted to. We are the ones who till the fields, after all. We are the ones who gather the food, after all. We can live on the crops that we grow. We can live on the seeds that we gather. We can live on the berries that

we find and on the fruits that we bring. Things exist thanks as much to us as to you. We have no need of you men."

On and on they argued that way, *Altse hastiin* the First Man permitting himself to grow angrier and angrier with each reply his wife made; *Altse asdzaa* the First Woman permitting herself to grow more and more vexing with each reply she offered. Until at length he stalked out of the shelter where they had lived together as man and wife. Out he stalked and jumped across the fire in front of their home, where he remained all that night with only his anger to keep him company.

Because the survival of horticultural societies depends on the fertility of both the people and the soil, it is not surprising that Native American peoples appealed to the life-renewing forces in their sacred ceremonies. In these religious rites, women often received instructions on how to perform their sacred duties, which included birthing and raising children and planting and tilling the fields. The following selections are taken from the initiation ceremonies of the Osages, a Plains Indian people akin to the Omahas, Kaws, Poncas, and Quapaws. Like many Indians of the Central Plains, the Osages depended on both the hunt and the soil for their survival.

INSTRUCTIONS TO THE WOMAN AS TO HER DUTIES AS MOTHER[35]

You have a child. Other children are yet to be born to you. There is in you the same desire that there is in all good mothers to bring your children successfully to maturity. In this you need the aid of a power that is greater than that of the human being. There is a rite by which an appeal can be made to this power. It is this: Let the father of your child secure the skin on an old male buffalo. You will dress and soften the skin with your own hands. When you have made it soft and pliable, take some red paint and with it draw a straight, narrow line from the head, through the length of the body of the skin, to the tip of the tail. This straight line represents the path of the power of day that liveth forever. You will paint all four legs of the robe red, to represent the dawn, the coming of the

---

[34]Zolbrod, *Dine bahane*, pp. 58–59.

[35]Garrick A. Bailey, ed., *The Osage and the Invisible World from the Works of Francis Las Flesche* (Norman, OK: University of Oklahoma Press, 1995), pp. 177–179.

force of day and of life. Let each child to whom you have given birth sleep in the consecrated robe and you will have aid in bringing to maturity your children.

INSTRUCTIONS TO THE WOMAN AS TO THE CEREMONIAL PLANTING OF THE CORN

The planting of the field is also a responsibility that has been bestowed upon you and has to do with the feeding of your children. In this duty also you need aid such as no human effort can give you. There is a way by which you can appeal for aid in performing this duty and reach the power that controls all things. When the time for planting has come, aim to rise with the sun so that your task will begin at the same time the sun begins to take its course. The parting of your hair must be painted red for this work. The red line will represent the path of the force of day and will make the paths of all the animals converge toward you, for upon them you and your children must depend for food. When you reach your field you must, first of all, prepare seven hills which you shall regard as the "Mysterious Hill." Open the first hill with your planting stick and put into it one grain of corn, after which you will cover up the opening and tap it with your foot; in the second hill you will put two grains in the same manner; three in the third hill; four in the fourth; five in the fifth; six in the sixth; and seven in the seventh. This ceremony is a supplication for three things: first, the growing of the corn to maturity; second, the success of the hunter; third, the success of the warrior who protects the home and field. When you have finished planting the seven sacred hills you may proceed to plant the rest of your field without further ceremony. . . .

Young girls also received instruction on proper female etiquette through the folktales that were passed down from generation to generation. Two examples of these stories are included here. The first is a selection from the Algonkian-speaking Chippewa oral tradition. The Chippewas of the Great Lakes region are a combination agricultural and hunting people with a marked division of labor between the sexes. Within their oral tradition are many tales about two sisters, Matchikwesis and Oshkikwe. These sister stories generally follow a common pattern: The older sister seeks something she should not have and suffers disappointment, while the other sister abstains from the taboo and is rewarded. These tales were mostly cautionary tales told by women to young girls to illus-

trate proper female behavior. The second selection is a tale with a similar moral that is taken from the Micmac peoples of northern New England. In these selections, what were the misdeeds of the young women? According to these tales, what traits do the Chippewas and Micmac expect from young girls?

THE SISTERS AT LEECH LAKE[36]

At Leech Lake there were two young women in a canoe, crossing the lake. One of them began to wonder why the lake was called Leech Lake. While they were paddling, they began to notice that the current was going just like a rapid. The canoe began to stand straight up, and the women sitting in front took off all her ornaments. Indian girls used to wear a lot of beads. She took them all off and put them into the lake. The other one didn't know that she should do this. That was the one that had wondering why it was called Leech Lake. She fell out of the canoe. But before she fell off, she saw a great big leech—three or four feet wide. The other girl saw it too. He was coming through the water in big up-and-down motions, like a worm crawling fast. The girl drowned and died. The leech probably took her to the bottom of the lake. But that showed her why it was called Leech Lake. She should have taken off her ornaments and put them in the lake. That story shows why Indians respect everything. If that girl hadn't asked herself, "Why is this called Leech Lake?" nothing would have happened to her.

THE WOMAN WHO MARRIED HORNED SERPENT[37]

In the old times, there was a family with a daughter who was very proud. She would not sit down where anyone else sat, and when she combed her hair and oiled it, when she bathed and painted her face, she would not do it with the others of the People, but by herself. When young men came to the wigwam, she would not talk with them. She refused to marry.

An old man says to the father, "You better be careful. Something is feeling wrong. Unless you make her

[36]Victor Barnouw, *Wisconsin Chippewa Myths & Tales* (Madison, WI: The University of Wisconsin Press, 1977), pp. 111–112.

[37]Ruth Holmes Whitehead, *Stories from the Six Worlds: Micmac Legends* (Halifax: Nimbus Publishing Limited, 1988), p. 47.

marry the next boy who comes, some bad thing will happen."

Now this girl is going to the spring to get water. She takes the bark bucket with her, to carry home the water in. She kneels before the spring, and begins to dip out water. And there, deep in the water, she sees a man. He is very beautiful. And he sits under the water, cross-legged as any hunter sits who has killed his first moose, and with his arms folded across his chest.

The heart of this girl goes to him.

The man from under the water rises out of the spring. He smiles at her, and he carried home her bucket of water. When he comes into the wigwam, her mother greets him as "daughter's husband," and so the thing is done. This girl is wed.

And when the time comes that this girl has had a son, her husband says to her, "Come. Let us go to my home. My parents would like to see the baby."

All the people went with them to the lake. There this man from the world under the water tells his wife to remove the clothes from the baby. And there, before all the people, the three of them begin to change. Their bodies thicken and lengthen, lying upon the ground. They become Horned Serpent Persons, jip-ijka'maq: the man, the woman, and the child.

"Goodbye, you of the People," calls the man as he changes. "Do not look to see us any more." Then he and his wife and child slide into the lake, into the world under the water. The People never found that girl again.

This is what pride will do.

SECTION 6: Daily Living: Health, Etiquette, and Holy Days

Modern societies view sexuality in terms of X and Y chromosomes and define health as the absence of a pathological condition or disease. To many peoples, this medical terminology is not as insightful as explanations of physical conditions that are detailed in their sacred traditions. Like other predominantly oral cultures, Native Americans understand that an individual's health, and even his or her sex, is often affected by such things as living in harmony with nature, avoiding sacred taboos, and using the secret medicines that have been provided by the mysterious guardian spirits.

The opening selections come from a genre that can be called prenatal memories. The first is an account of a Hopi, who recalls the actions of his parents before his birth. Note in this account how the parents were expected to behave during the pregnancy to ensure the health of the baby. The second account is an intrauterine memory of an Inuit from the Arctic. Note in this account the predominance of the idea of reincarnation. What other cultural values are suggested in these readings?

TWINS TWISTED INTO ONE[38]

When we were within our mother's womb, we happened to hurt her. She has told me how she went to a medicine man in her pain. He worked on her, felt her breasts and belly, and told her that we were twins. She was surprised and afraid. She said, "But I want only one baby." "Then I will put them together," replied the doctor. He took some corn meal outside the door and sprinkled it to the sun, and tied it around my mother's left wrist. It is a powerful way to unite babies. We twins began, likewise, to twist ourselves into one child. My mother also helped to bring us together by her strong wish for only one baby.

My mother has described how carefully she carried me. She slept with my father right along, so that he could have intercourse with her and make me grow. It is like irrigating a crop: if a man starts to make a baby and then stops, his wife has a hard time. She had intercourse with my father so that I could have an easy birth and resemble him.

She refused to hold another woman's child on her lap and took care not to breathe into the face of small children and cause them to waste away. She had nothing to do with the tanning of skins or the dyeing of anything lest she spoil the goods and also injure me. When she grew big, she was careful to sit in such a way that other people would not walk in front of her and thus make my birth difficult. She would not look at the serpent images displayed in the ceremonies, lest I turn myself into a water snake while still in her womb and raised up my head at the time of birth, instead of lying with head down seeking a way out.

My father has related how he took care to injure no animal and thus damage my body. If he had cut off the foot of any living creature, I might have been born without a hand or with a clubfoot. Any cruel treatment

[38] Don C. Talayesva, *Sun Chief: The Autobiography of a Hopi Indian*, ed. Leo W Simmons (New Haven, CT: Yale University Press, 1942), pp. 25–26.

of a dumb beast would have endangered my life. If he had drawn a rope too tightly around the neck of a sheep or burro, it might have caused my navel cord to loop itself around my neck and strangle me in birth. Even if I had been able to free myself from the cord, I might have remained half choked and short of breath for a long time.

Iqallijuq's Description of Intra-uterine Memories[39]

[This scene takes place in the uterus, which is in the shape of the mother's igloo:]

As I was looking out the door, I started to think that I would like to pass through it. . . . However, I did not reach the entrance way. Situated to the left of the entrance were male instruments. . . . I extended my hand towards them and grabbed them, but the idea that I would be very cold when I used them made me put them back, and grabbing instead the female equipment, a little oil lamp and a little knife (crescent-shaped), I emerged with great effort. . . . Savviuqtalik, my eponym, had expressed the wish to be reborn as a female. . . . Indeed, I took my time at birth as I had first grabbed the knife of the male, a harpoon and the tip of a harpoon; this is the reason why I took so long [to be born]. . . . In fact I had become cross-gendered because Savviuqtalik had not wanted to return as a man, but as a woman. He did not want to hunt because it was too demanding and there was the great risk of being cold. Thus I became a girl after my sex was changed at birth. First I had a penis, but then I had a vulva; this is the way of the "cross-gendered."

Among many Native American peoples, names are generally more than labels that distinguish persons from each other. Names also are ways to describe the character of the persons. It is common for individuals to receive multiple names during their lives. The following excerpt from Chief Buffalo Child Long Lance describes the naming practices followed by the Blackfoot of the Northwest.

What's in an Indian Name? by Long Lance[40]

When I was a youngster every Indian had at least three names during his lifetime. His first name, which he received at birth and retained until he was old enough to go on the war-path, was descriptive of some circumstances surrounding his birth. As an instance, we have a man among the Blackfeet whose name is Howling-in-the-Middle-of-the-Night. When he was born along the banks of the Belly River in southern Alberta, the Indian woman who was assisting his mother went out to the river to get some water with which to wash him. When she returned to the teepee she remarked, "I heard a wolf howling across the river." "Then," said the baby's mother, "I shall call my son 'Howling-in-the-Middle-of-the-Night.' "

The birth name of the youngster was supposed to be retained by him until he was old enough to earn one for himself; but always when he grew old enough to play with other children his playmates would give him a name on their own by which he would be known among them, no matter what his parents called him. And this name often was not flattering; for we Indian boys were likely to choose some characteristic defect on which to base our names for our playmates-such as Bow Legs, Crazy Dog, Crooked Nose, Bad Bay, or Wolf Tail. . . .

But the real name of the Indian was earned in the latter instance: when he was old enough to go out for his first fight against the enemy. His life name depended on whatever showing he should make in his first battle. When he returned from the war-path the whole tribe would gather to witness the ceremony in which he would be given his tribal name by the chief of the tribe. If he made a good showing, he would be given a good name, such as Uses-Both-Arms, Charging Buffalo, Six Killer, Good Striker, Heavy Lance, or Many Chiefs. But if should make a poor showing his name might be: Crazy Wolf, Man-Afraid-of-a-Horse, or Smoking-Old-Woman. Thus, an Indian's name tells his record or what kind of man he is. . . .

The foregoing is the reason why no old Indian will ever tell you his own name. If you ask him he will turn to some third person and nod for him to tell you. The reason for this is that he is too modest to brag of his exploits on the war-path.

[39]Bernard Saladin D'Anglure, "From Foetus to Shaman: The Construction of an Inuit Third Sex," in Antonia Mills and Richard Slobodin, eds. *Amerindian Rebirth: Reincarnation Belief among North American Indians and Inuit* (Toronto: University of Toronto Press, 1994), pp. 86–87.

[40]Gill, *Traditions*, p. 89.

The following selections offer insights into Native American healing practices. According to most native traditions, human beings, unlike the bear and eagle, are frail creatures who depend on the blessings or medicines received from guardian spirits for the maintenance of their health. The spirits communicate with humans through visions and dreams and through sacred songs that have healing (or killing) powers. The spirits also have taught certain privileged humans about the curing powers of the plants, roots, and flowers. The first selection is a beautiful creation account that comes from the Salish (Flathead) tradition of the Rocky Mountain West. The next piece is a description of the life and rituals of a Sioux medicine man. From these texts, how would you describe these peoples' understandings of the relationship between spirituality and health?

A Salish Story of Origins[41]

For thousands of years the Salish people lived a happy and contented life. They had a special relationship with the earth and all that was around them. The people knew how to take care of themselves and how to help each other.

But long ago, in one village, people were dying and they had no cure. One night the oldest of four brothers had a vision in which he was told to go into the mountains to the east and after three days' travel he would come upon an old man who would help them. So in the morning, the oldest brother told his other brothers of his dream, and they all started on the journey into the mountains. On the evening of the third day, they came upon a place with many lakes, and there they found the lodge of the old man. The old man asked them to enter and instructed his daughter to give them drink. Then the old man told them, "In the morning we will talk."

In the morning the old man asked the brothers why they had come to see him. The middle brother said, "Our people are sick and dying. We have no medicine to help them. I want to be tall and strong so I can help my brothers and my people." So the old

man told him to go out of the lodge, and to turn back and face him. When the brother turned around, he was transformed into a tall tree, a tree that can see all around. "In this way," said the old man, "you can help your people."

The next brother told the old man, "I want to be strong and tough so I can help my people too." And the old man told him to leave the lodge and then turn back and face him. When he did, the old man turned him into a rock that would be strong and endure all kinds of hardship.

And then the old man told the oldest brother to go back to his people and make a little lodge facing east. He should build a fire using his brother the tree, and he should heat his brother the rock in the fire. After bringing the rock into the lodge, he should pray with sincerity. "Always take care of this lodge and pray to me," the old man said. "If you are sincere, then I will help you."

And the old man gave the oldest brother his daughter, who would teach him the proper way to gather and use plants, roots, flowers, and grasses, telling him what is good for this or that sickness. The brothers thanked the old man and left. Each step of the journey home, the young woman instructed them about plants and roots and how to use them to cure illnesses.

Descriptions of the Life and Rituals of a Sioux Medicine Man[42]

People and this world and all that is in it are only a part of Wakan Tanka, the lesser part when you consider the limitlessness of eternity and the universe, and the limits and relative insignificance of matter as we know ourselves and this world to be.

Yet from the holy goodness of Waken Tanka a way was given to us—for he loves his children and this creation—that we may pray and have a glimpse, a little knowledge of the Great Mystery that is this life. . . .

You must know that a medicine man among our people is in possession of a special office. He is a servant of the people and of the gods. He enters upon a

[41]Jacqueline Peterson and Laura Peers, *Sacred Encounters: Father De Smet and the Indians of the Rocky Mountain West* (Norman, OK: The University of Oklahoma Press, 1993), p. xi.

[42]Arthur Amiotte, "Eagles Fly Over," in Gill, *Traditions*, pp. 91–92.

way that is sometimes not of his choosing, sometimes because he chose. I have known people who have bought their office. Some are good and some use it to their own advantage.

I did not ask for my office. My work was made for me and given to me by the other world, by the Thunder Beings. I am compelled to live this way that is not of my own choosing, because they chose me. I am a poor man; see how I dress and the house I live in. My whole life is to do the bidding of the Thunder Beings and of my people and to pay heed to what the Grandfathers tell me. . . .

To enter into any ceremony is a most sacred act. It begins in the mind of a person either by himself or because other beings chose him for their purposes. When it is clear that a man has an intention, he must prepare himself by being honest with himself about what it is he desires and intends to do. If after he has examined himself well he feels confident that he wants and needs the help of a counselor, an intercessor, he must fill a good pipe with red willow bark tobacco and seek out the medicine man he wishes to see and whose help he wants. When he approaches the home of the medicine man he should rid himself of all undesirable thoughts so that his mind might be clear to utter his request as a petition prayer.

As a man with a filled pipe approaches a medicine man, he should realize that this man, depending on his predilections and his ability to read the intent of his visitor, has the right to refuse the offered pipe. A petitioner should be prepared to offer the filled pipe four times, each time stepping back and extending the pipe at arm's length. . . . If the medicine man accepts the pipe on the first or any other offering, it means he is willing to listen to your request, but it does not mean he will grant it. He will either light the pipe himself or ask you to light it. While he smokes the pipe, you must make your request. Since the pipe is being smoked in a sacred manner, you must make your petition as simply and as honestly as you can, for depending on what you say and how you say it, the medicine man will deliberate and make his decision. When the smoking is finished and after the bowl has been emptied of its ashes, a less formal conversation will follow.

For Native Americans, there were medicines for all needs, including the need to attract a lover, to become beautiful, and to cause a separation between the one you love and a competitor. The following selections are Cherokee "sacred formulas," which perhaps are better described as magical charms, since the intended purpose of some of these chants is far from sacred. Many chants follow a typical pattern, opening with a device to command attention (i.e., "Now! Listen!"), followed by the name, ritualistic color, and place of residence of the spirit being petitioned; an assurance that the spirit has the power to carry out the request; and a statement that asserts the deed has already been accomplished. The arrangements of the chants also make use of the magic numbers, four and seven. According to the tradition, these songs produced the desired affect only when chanted in the Cherokee tongue. To more fully interpret these selections, consult the following data that connects the seven colors of Cherokee magical symbolism with their qualities:

> Red: *East, Victory, Power*
> Blue: *North, Failure, Weakness, Spiritual Depression*
> Black: *West, Death, Oblivion*
> White: *South, Happiness, Peace*
> Brown: *Normality, the Earth*
> Purple: *Witchcraft, Evil*
> Yellow: *A Sinister Influence, Power*

LOVE INCANTATIONS AMONG THE CHEROKEES[43]

This chant is to be used before a young man attends a gathering where girls would be present:

Now! Ha, then! You women of the Seven Clans!

Ha! Now it has surely become time!

All of you have just come to put White Eyes on me.

Ha, then! All of you will not be able to glance elsewhere. It will be my body alone upon which all of you will be gazing!

---

[43]Jack Frederick Kilpatrick and Anna Gritts Kilpatrick, *Walk in Your Soul: Love Incantations of the Oklahoma Cherokees* (Dallas: Southern Methodist University Press, 1965), pp. 18–19, 86–87, 91–92, 129–130.

This chant is to be repeated four times. After each recitation, the male blows his breath towards the girl of his choice.

Now! I am as beautiful as the very blossoms themselves!

I am a man, you lovely ones, you women of the Seven Clans! (Now these are my people, ____, and this is my name, ____)

Now! You women who reside among the Seven Peoples, I have just come to intrude myself among you.

All of you have just come to gaze upon me alone, the most beautiful.

Now! You lovely women, already I just took your souls!

I am a man! You women will live in the very middle of my soul.

Forever I will be as beautiful as the bright red blossoms.

The following is introduced with the words: "Before going where girls are like to be present, one can make himself attractive to them by saying [this chant] four times, and by blowing one's breath upon one's hands and chest after each recitation of the spell."

Now! Ha! I alone am as beautiful as the Meadowlark! (I am their only friend.)

I am alone in the Seven Clan Districts! (I am their only friend.)

The Seven Eyes will be seeking me alone! (I am their only friend.)

My name is ____; my people are ____.

SECTION 7: The Human Quest: Paths to Salvation and Enlightenment

At the core of many Native American spiritual traditions is the vision quest. The vision quest refers to any sacred time of retreat in which an individual seeks to experience the presence and powers of the guardian spirits. Generally this experience is first sought in adolescence as the individual prepares to enter adulthood, but it also can be repeated on other special occasions later in life. The first selection is a description of the vision quest and its importance. The description is told by Yellowtail, a Crow Medicine Man and Sun Dance Chief. Note the spiritual preparation that Yellowtail insists must be undertaken before going on a vision quest.

THE VISION QUEST[44]

One of the main rites of the Sun Dance religion is the vision quest. It is a period set aside for solitary prayer at a remote place.

A person will usually spend three or four days of fasting on the vision quest, saying his prayers during all that time. He goes away up in the hills, gets away from people, and goes off by himself, and there he fasts and prays for either the three- or four-day period he selected before he began his quest.

There are many intentions that a person may have when he prepares to make a vision quest. He may want medicine, some kind of power to help him in battle or in all of his life. Strong medicine powers would protect the man so that he would not be wounded and could not be hit by an enemy's arrow. That kind of medicine would make a man successful in battle with the enemy. A lot of men seek those kinds of powers, and that is what they have in mind when they start out on the vision quest.

Some men might seek different kinds of medicine power or understanding. They may want to be able to heal or doctor people. They may seek the answer to a question or a problem that is bothering them or their family or tribe. And above all, a man may want to pray in this way because this is a way to come closer to Acbadadea. In this rite each man may awaken in his heart the knowledge of the Maker of All Things Above. A man may pray for any of these things because they would be helpful to him, his family, and his tribe, but a man also must pray for virtue and the correct understanding with which to face life. ....

When a person is on a vision quest, he must have certain attitudes and intentions for his prayers to be sincere, and then he must carry these over into his daily life. It is easy to forget what you learned during this trial; unless you remember to carry on your prayer continually during every day of your life, you will not have learned one of the most important purposes of the vision quest. Each time we talk about one of our sacred rites, you will hear me talk about the spiritual attitudes which a person must possess as that person

[44]*Yellowtail Crow Medicine Man and Sun Dance Chief: An Autobiography as told to Michael Oren Fitzgerald.* Introduction by Fred Voget. (Norman, OK: University of Oklahoma Press, 1991), pp. 69–76, 115–119.

participates in any rite. It is possible to learn the outer steps that must be accomplished in a rite without learning the inner meanings that are the keys to the sacred traditions. Each seeker must therefore open his heart to the Great Mystery as he tries to follow the sacred way, because the perfect accomplishment of the outer steps of a rite will be worth nothing without the knowledge of the inner meanings. If the intention of a person is to achieve outward glory and superiority over other people, then that person will never be given great medicine, because that person's intention and attitudes are not in harmony with the correct spiritual purpose. If the reason you participate in a rite is wrong, then you will receive no reward. If you participate because you know the purpose of the rites and you want to express your gratitude and love of the sacred ways, then you may eventually receive a great reward.

Yellowtail also describes the "sweat lodge" ceremony, another sacred rite designed to purify the body and to awaken the mind to the secrets of the spiritual world. Seekers are encouraged to participate in this ceremony on numerous occasions throughout the year. Like in the Vision Quest, preparation is necessary before a person can expect to receive the inner cleansing that is promised through this ceremony. As you read Yellowtail's description of this sacred occasion, reflect upon the symbolism of the rite. Why would this ceremony have special meaning to peoples who embrace an emergence view of creation?

First, a small lodge must be built. You cut twelve small poles from tree saplings and bend them over and tie them together. You should say a prayer before cutting each tree, because the tree has allowed us to use it for our prayer ceremony. You put each sapling into the ground in a circle, with the doorway to the east. When the twelve poles are put in the ground in an upright position, they are like the twelve upright poles of the Sun Dance lodge. The sweat lodge can be made any size, but it generally holds five or six men, who will be seated about the pit where the hot rocks will be placed. . . .

Now we are ready to bring the rocks into the lodge. Everyone is quiet and prayers are being said by one and all. A man is selected to bring the rocks from the fire into the lodge. This man makes a vow or request in his heart and does not speak. No one talks during this time, but everyone is making his own vow in his heart. . . .

Anyone can take a pipe into the sweat lodge. It is one of the best ways to pray, and this is good. We should always offer a smoke and prayer before and after each sweat lodge ceremony. . . . It is always necessary to smudge the lodge with some type of incense before we start, but it is up to the participants to choose the type to be used.

When we are in the sweat lodge and all the covers are closed, there is no light in the lodge except the red glow of the hot rocks. The smell of the sacred incense fills the air. We have entered into another world which is beyond our physical world. When the water is thrown onto the rocks, the heat does not merely cleanse us on the outside; it also goes all the way into our hearts. We know that we must suffer the ordeal of the heat in order to purify ourselves. In that way, we can re-emerge from the sweat lodge at the end of the ceremony as new men who have been shown the light of the wisdom of our spiritual heritage for the first time. This allows us to participate in all of our daily tasks with the fresh remembrance of our position on earth and our continuous obligation to walk on this earth in accordance with the sacred ways.

Adult vision seekers from several tribal traditions also participate in the sacred Sun Dance. This dance was held when someone had a dream about the dance. While failure to respond to the dream could result in death, obedience to the call would bring good fortune and spiritual blessings. The following is a Shoshoni story of the origins of the Sun Dance, a dance they called "Dagoo Winode," or the Thirst Stand Dance.

THE SHOSHONI SUN DANCE[45]

One night when [a] man was asleep, he saw a vision of himself sitting on a hill. Looking toward the place of the rising sun, he thought he saw a little, black, moving speck, and he wondered what it was that was moving toward him so rapidly. When the object came near, he saw that it was a buffalo. The man got scared and was about to leave, but the buffalo spoke to him. "Do not be scared of me," it said. "Do not be afraid. I will not harm you. I only bring you a message."

The man was mystified. He was so astonished that he sat very still. The buffalo came up to him and said, "I am set to tell you about a dance. You will call it *Dagoo Winode*. It is a dance in which you will not eat or

---

[45]Ella E. Clark, *Indian Legends from the Northern Rockies* (Norman, OK: University of Oklahoma Press, 1966), pp. 187–189.

drink for three days and three nights. You will do nothing but worship during those three days and nights. If you will pray for your people, the sick ones in this dance and the others who are brought to you will get well."

Then he told the man that from time to time the Sun Dance would change. The buffalo showed him, in a vision, a brush structure like a windbreak. Near it four men were dancing. As they danced up to the center pole of the brush structure, they passed two old women on each side of the entrance. They sat there holding willows tied in bunches. With these willow branches the old women brushed out the footprints the dancers made in the dirt. The reason for rubbing out the tracks is not know.

Later, another Shoshoni saw the same vision. He saw a large structure made of brush, and noticed that it had a forked center pole. He saw many people dancing, all of them men. In the man's vision, the buffalo called his attention to the twelve long poles and said, "Those twelve poles mean something good. Everything in the Sun Dance Lodge is a prayer. Each part of it is a symbol, a symbol of something good."

Then the buffalo told this man, in his vision, the first step he should take before he put up the Sun Dance Lodge. "You must go out and kill a buffalo," it said. "You will take only the hide and the head. They will remind you that the Great Mystery came to the Shoshonis in the form of a buffalo and that the buffalo brought them this message that is called the Sun Dance. Tell your people that this dance was given to you and to them by the Father, the Great Mystery."

Then the buffalo taught the man four prayer songs to be used in the Sun Dance, saying "All four songs are to be sung sixteen times."

During the preparation of the Sun Dance Lodge, seven prayers are made. After the poles have been selected, but before they had been cut, before the twelve forked poles are cut, before the tree for the center pole is felled, before it is placed in the center hole of the lodge area, and before the buffalo head is fastened over the bunch of willows tied to the center pole—at each of these times, an old man or the Sun Dance leader prays. Then there are prayers with songs as men and women fasten strips of blue and green cloth to the center pole and raise it. There is a prayer after the people have been bathed in the river and are assembled in the Sun Dance place. The green cloth stands for the green things of the spring and summer months; the blue stands for the clean, fresh air we breathe and for the blue skies, where the Great Mystery, our Father, lives.

When the dancers are in place, the leader stands under the center pole and makes this prayer: "Our Father, bless me now that my people and I have built this place, a gift from you, our Father, a gift which you have given to our forefathers, which through them you gave to us. Bless us, that all of these men who came in to dance with me may be well, that the sick ones may be made well through this Sun Dance. Bless us, even though we may become dry and weak from thirst and hunger. Protect us through these days and nights, so that at the end of three days, when we get out, with your blessing, we may take of your precious gifts, water and food, and receive our strength back. Grant that we may become healthy, the sick and weak become strong, both old and young be protected from diseases. Bless us, I pray to you, our Father, that my people who are sick may be made well through you, our Father. Amen."

Native American children, like children of all cultures, are taught the stories of their sacred traditions from birth. As they reach puberty, however, they are encouraged to experience for themselves the powers of the spiritual forces. To prepare for their first vision quest, Native American youth entering puberty construct a small lodge in a secluded place, place charcoal on their faces to make them look "pitiful," and depart to their sacred places away from camp. Their hope during this three- or four-day retreat to an isolated place is to receive a vision that will transform their lives. Owing to the sacredness of the occasion, few puberty visions have been recorded. The following selections, however, are detailed summaries of the visions of two Ojibwa youth. The dates for these experiences were 1848 and 1936, respectively.

PUBERTY FASTING AND VISIONS AMONG THE OJIBWAS[46]

Account 1: Schoolcraft 1848

At the age of twelve or thirteen, when I had my first menstruation, my mother sent me to the forest and encouraged me to fast for a vision, "asking pity of the

[46]Christopher Vecsey, *Traditional Ojibwa Religion and Its Historical Changes* (Philadelphia: American Philosophical Society, 1983), pp. 130–131.

Master of Life, to help my poor family." It was the middle of winter. On the sixth night I heard a voice saying, "Poor child! I pity your condition." I followed the voice as it summoned me, on a shining path going upward. After a short distance I saw on the right a new moon with a bright flame coming from it, giving great light. On the left was the setting sun. The Everlasting Woman told me her name. She gave me her name and said that I could give it to another. She gave me long life on earth and skill in saving life in others. I went on and saw a man with a large, circular body and rays from his head like horns. He said not to fear; he was the Little Man Spirit. This name was for my first son. He told me to continue. The path led to an opening in the sky. There was a man with a halo, whose breast was covered with squares. His name was The Bright Blue Sky, the veil that covers the opening to the sky. He said not to be afraid. He gave me the gifts of life and the power to endure and withstand. I saw myself encircled with bright points which rested against me like needles; there was no pain; they fell at my feet. This happened several times. Each time he reassured me. Then awls and nails stuck into my flesh but still no pain. He said it was good and told me to continue; I would live long. I got to the beginning of the opening to the sky. I had arrived; I could go no further, he said. He told me to return to my lodge on a kind of fish swimming in the air. He told me to eat when I got back. I rode the fish back, with my hair floating behind me. After this, animal food disgusted me.

Account 2: Radin, 1936

When I was twelve I blackened my face and fasted. On the third night a man came and told me he was coming for me, that I would be blessed if I believed him. I refused to go with him having been warned by my father against taking the first visitor. Then another man came, telling me that they had seen my pitiable condition, that I would never be killed if I went with him. I would live to be an old man, blind before dead, and my body would be as solid as his back. He was the leader of a number of men. I was to return home, and he told me to turn around toward him as I left. I turned and saw he was Turtle. Turtle had blessed me.

The following excerpt from an Iglulik Eskimo Shaman Initiation describes the enlightenment a shaman experiences upon making contact with the spirit world.

AN IGLULIK ESKIMO SHAMAN EXPERIENCES ENLIGHTENMENT[47]

The enlightenment consists of a mysterious light which the shaman suddenly feels in his body, inside his head, within the brain, an inexplicable searchlight, a luminous fire . . . for he can now, even with closed eyes, see through darkness and perceive things and coming events which are hidden from others: thus they look into the future and into the secrets of others.

The candidate obtains this mystical light after long hours of waiting, sitting on a bench in his hut and invoking the spirits. When he experiences it for the first time, it is as if the house in which he is suddenly rises, he sees far ahead of him, though mountains, exactly as if the earth were one great plain, and his eyes could reach to the end of the earth. Nothing is hidden from him any longer; not only can he see things far, far away, but he can also discover souls, stolen souls, which are either kept concealed in far, strange lands or have been taken up or down to the land of the Dead.

Although personal descriptions of the vision quest are rare, the oral literature of Native Americans is filled with tales of these encounters. The following is a story told among the Cree Indians of Sandy Lake about Mis-qua-day-sih, the Turtle and guardian spirit for those blessed to be chosen by him. Such tales reinforce the teachings that guardian spirits hear and respond to the sincere prayers of fasting vision seekers.

MIS-QUA-DAY-SIH, THE GUARDIAN SPIRIT—A CREE TALE[48]

Once one of our men went out to fast and he remained in the forest for many days. When he came back he told the people that he had dreamed of the turtle, mis-qua-day-sih. This caused a great commotion in the village because very few people had the fortune to have the turtle for a protector throughout life.

Mis-qua-day-sih had told this man that when he was on water he would be as safe as if he were on land. The water would be as solid as the ground and would not be an obstacle like it was to other people. If an or-

---

[47] *World Scriptures*, p. 382.

[48] James R. Stevens, *Sacred Legends of the Sandy Lake Cree* (Toronto: McClelland and Steward Limited, 1971), p. 83.

dinary person went on water he would sink to the bottom and drown, but this man would have the power to walk on water. After the man had survived some terrible storms on the lakes, the people realized that mis-qua-day-sih must have been his guardian spirit.

Once this man was hunting in the Fort Severn area with two of his friends. The two friends had taken the canoe up the river to get some geese. When they were coming back they missed a portage because they were not familiar with the river and their canoe was carried into the roaring rapids. The canoe was turned over in the white water and the men fell into the stream. It appeared that they would be victims for certain, but the man with mis-qua-day-sih as guardian spirit walked out on the water and pulled his friends to the shore, saving their lives.

This is a true story, held in the minds of many of the old people at Sandy Lake.

SECTION 8: The Religious Life: Worship and Righteousness

Unlike Judaism, Christianity, and Islam, Native American religions generally do not designate a single day of the week to honor their deities. Most, however, have specific times for sacred events scattered throughout the seasons of the year. Few groups, in fact, would undertake anything of importance without first enacting sacred ceremonies. Many of these rituals celebrate changes in the life cycle, or what many Native Americans call "the road of life." Others are performed on special occasions when circumstances call for the guidance and protection of the sacred powers. Often these times of worship involve the use of sacred objects, fire, songs, and dances. Holy words appropriately chanted and sung, even if not understood by the participant, were known to effectively resolve crises that confront the human condition.

Among the sacred rituals observed by many was the celebration of a young woman's first menstruation. After this event, women were treated differently during their menstruation cycles. In some traditions it was believed that women had great powers during these times, so special rules applied to their conduct during their menstruations. For example, in some traditions menstruating women were not allowed to cross behind where a man sleeps (where his medicine bundle was kept) for fear of tampering with a man's secret medicines. The Navajo word for a girl's puberty ritual is *kinaalda*. This rite is modeled after the

story of when the cultural hero Changing Woman came of age. The following selection entitled "Kinaalda of Changing Woman" tells this story. The second selection, entitled "Why Women Menstruate," is taken from the oral tradition of the Havasupai Indians. As in many stories of the Southwest, the Coyote is the culprit who is blamed for this unpleasantry. Why do you think rituals of first menstruation were important to these Native American peoples?

KINAALDA OF CHANGING WOMAN[49]

It was a long time ago that Changing Woman had her Kinaalda. She made herself become kinaalda. This happened after the creation of the Earth People. The ceremony was started so women would be able to have children and the human race would be able to multiply. . . .

Nine days after [her second menstruation] Changing Woman gave birth to Monster Slayer and Born for Water, twin boys. These two were put on earth so that all the monsters which were eating human beings would be killed. They rid the earth of all these monsters; that is why they were called Holy People. As soon as they had done this, their mother, Changing Woman, who was then living at Gobernador Knob, left and went to her home in the west, where she lives today.

After she moved to her home in the west, she created the Navaho people. When she had done this, she told these human beings to go to their original home, which was the Navaho country. Before they left, she said: "After this, all the girls born to you will have periods at certain times when they become women. When the time comes, you must set a day and fix the girl up to be kinaalda; you must have these songs sung and do whatever else needs to be done at that time. After this period, a girl is a woman and will start having children."

WHY WOMEN MENSTRUATE— A HAVASUPAI TALE[50]

Long ago, when the world was still wet, before the human race was here and when the animals were like human beings, Squirrel lived in the San Francisco

[49]Gill, *Traditions*, pp. 104–105.

[50]Carolyn Niethammer, *Daughters of the Earth: The Lives and Legions of American Indian Women* (New York: Macmillan Publisher, 1977), pp. 37–38.

Mountains. One day he took the tibia of a deer and painted on it a design. After sundown he threw the bone to the east with a prayer that a young girl would come to him with the next rising sun. The girl came just as Squirrel had prayed she would. She lived happily for a time there at the camp with her guardian Squirrel and her brothers, Coyote and White Dog.

One day Coyote called to his sister saying, "Sister, you must stay here while I go out to hunt." After the girl waited a while, Coyote returned carrying a fawn he had killed. The girl was glad to see the fawn and sat nearby thinking how good the meat would taste. While Coyote was butchering she felt the fawn's smooth hair and touched its ears and face. Presently Coyote asked the girl to hand something to him and when turned away to reach it, Coyote put his hand in the fawn's flesh blood and flipped it on the girl's thighs close to her vagina. Then Coyote cried out: "Oh, Sister, you are menstruating. Now you cannot eat meat until you are clean, after four days have passed." The girl was angry because she couldn't eat the meat. Coyote said to her, "From now on it will happen like this to you once every month. After four days you must bathe."

The girl went to bed unhappy and the next morning when she awoke she was still angry with Coyote so she left camp saying nothing to her relatives. She ran away to a land in the west where she lived from then on.

Special ceremonies also celebrated changes in the "road of life" of males. In addition to the puberty rites of young men (see Section 7), initiation rites also were required before men received the powers of the medicine bundles of their respective clans. Because these medicines could be used for good or evil, the initiates took vows not to misuse their powers. Failure to live according to these vows could evoke severe penalties. The following selection is part of an Osage initiation ceremony that bestows rain-making powers to those joining a particular clan. Note the consequences for breaking the vows of clan membership.

THE GREAT RAIN SONGS[51]

It has been said, in this house,
That an avenger of the little one,

---

[51]Bailey, *The Osage and the Invisible World from the Works of Francis Las Flesche*, pp. 209–210.

Amid the winds of the west,
My grandfather, the avenger travels.
Even amidst the winds that rush before the storms,
He travels and moves.
With a power of discernment from which no evil act can be
    concealed.
It is he who is chosen to guard with watchful care the
    penalties.
It is he shadow,
My grandfather, who travels amidst the winds; verily with a
    power from which no evil act can be concealed.
He stands ever at the back of the man who takes the vow,
Or ever hovers about his head.
Even as the man violates his vow and goes upon his life
    journey, unmindful of his broken vow,
The skin of his face shall become shallow and of sickly hue;
Blood shall gush from his nostrils with twirling motion,
Even as the man goes upon his journey, unmindful of his
    broken vow,
His spirit shall be suddenly taken from him, when
    demanded.
The avenger of the little one
Shall forever stand. . . .

In addition to rites that celebrate changes in an individual's life cycle, seasonal and special occasion ceremonies also were performed to ensure success in community activities such as agricultural, hunting, and war. In most traditions, nothing of importance would be undertaken without first seeking the blessings of the mysterious powers. In Pawnee culture, for example, before beginning a hunt, planting corn, or starting a war, prayers and sacrifices would be offered to *Ti-ra'-wa*, the high god of the Plains. Likewise, after success has been achieved, the Pawnees gathered again to give thanks to *Ti-ra'-wa* for his provisions. If the hunt was successful, the first animal killed was burned as an offering while the warriors marched around the fire, rubbing the smoke over their bodies and singing: "Now, you, *Ti-ra'-wa*, the Ruler, look at your children and bless them; keep them and have mercy upon them."

The intermediary between *Ti-ra'-wa* and the Pawnees was the tribal priest who understood the mysteries of the sacred bundles that every male adult hung on the west side of his lodge (the farthest side from the door). These bundles physically contained such things as eagle feathers, a pipe, and tobacco—revered objects that, when activated in appropriate rituals, released secret medicines for the use of the community. Among the sacred ceremonies performed each year by the Pawnees was the Corn Dance. This ceremony is described in the following selection that was given to George Bird Brinnell by Curly Chief in the late nineteenth century.

SACRED BUNDLES, SONGS AND DANCES AMONG THE PAWNEE[52]

The windy month [March] was the one in which Ti-ra'-wa gave us the seed to cultivate. The first moon in April is the one during which they had a special worship about the corn. Until these ceremonies had been performed no one would clear out the patch where they intended to plant the crop. Everybody waited for this time. . . .

The preparations for this dance are always made by a woman. . . . The high priest stands at the back, of the lodge with the sacred bundles of the three bands before him. Then this leading woman comes forward, and presents to the high priest the dried meat and the sack of corn, and two ancient, sacred hoes, made from the shoulder-blade of a buffalo, bound to a handle by the neck ligament. She places them on the ground before the sacred bundles, the corn in the middle, and the tow hoes on either side. With these things she also presents a sacred pipe, filled and ready for lighting, taken from a sacred bundle. Then she steps back.

The old high priest must well know the ceremonies to be performed. He prays to Ti-ra'-wa and light the sacred pipe, blowing smoke to heaven, to the earth, and to the four points of the compass. . . .

After these ceremonies the women come forward, holding their hoes in their hands, and dance about the lodge one after another in single file, following the leading women. Four times they dance about the lodge. She cannot pass the priest the fifth time. These ceremonies and the songs and prayers were to ask for a blessing on the hunt and on the corn, and to learn whether they would be blessed in both. . . .

The next day after these ceremonies every one would begin to clear up their patches and get ready to plant corn. The leading woman who prepared the dance is respected and highly thought of. After that she is like a chief.

This ceremony is the next principal thing we have after the burnt offering of the animal and of the scalp. We did not invent this. It came to us from the Ruler, and we worship him through it. By it we are made strong. We are like seed and we worship though the corn.

For centuries Native American peoples have used tobacco in their worship ceremonies. In more recent times, many New World peoples also have incorporated the use of peyote in their worship experiences. Its use in southern Texas and Mexico where it grows dates back centuries, but the spread of the use of peyote outside this region is a more recent phenomenon. It was introduced to the Kiowa and Comanche tribes around 1870; spread slowly throughout Plains in the final decades of the nineteenth century; and then, notwithstanding periodic attempts of United States authorities to prohibit it, continued to expand into all regions of North America during the last century.

The final section includes several pieces that deal with peyote religion. The first is a Kiowa tale about the origins of peyote. The next reading is a modern account of the practices of the Huichol of Northern Mexico as they go on their annual pilgrimage to their ancestral lands to collect the peyote. The last selection is a late-nineteenth-century account of an Arapaho peyote ceremony. How do you explain the growing popularity of the use of peyote among Native Americans during the last 150 years?

A KIOWA TALE ABOUT PEYOTE WOMAN[53]

Two young men had gone upon a war expedition to the far south. They did not return at the expected time, and after long waiting their sister, according to Indian custom, retired to the hills to bewail their death. Worn out with grief and weeping, as night came on she was unable to get back to camp and lay down where she was. In her dreams the peyote spirit came to her and said: "You wail for your brothers, but they are still alive. In the morning look, and where your head now rests, you will find that which will restore them to you." The spirit then gave her instructions and was gone. With the daylight she arose, and on looking where she had slept, she found peyote, which she dug up and took back with her to camp. Here she summoned the priests of the tribe, to whom she told her vision and delivered the instructions which she had received from the spirit. Under her direction the sacred tipi was set up with its crescent

[52]George Bird Brinnell, *Pawnee Nero Stories and Folk-Tales*, introduction by Maurice Frink (Lincoln, NE: University of Nebraska Press, 1961), pp. 369–373.

[53]Young, *Quest for Harmony*, p. 314.

mound, and the old men entered and said prayers and sang the songs and ate the peyote—which seems to have been miraculously multiplied—until daylight, when they saw in their visions a picture of the two young warriors, wandering on foot and hungry in the far off passes of the Sierra Madre. A strong party was organized to penetrate the enemy's country and after many days the young men were found and restored to their people. Since then, the peyote is eaten by Indians with a song and prayer that they may see visions and know inspirations, and the young girl who first gave it is venerated as the "Peyote Woman."

ACTS OF REVERSAL ON THE PILGRIMAGE FOR PEYOTE[54]

On the trails in which we travel to the peyote country, as we see different things we make this change. That is because peyote is very sacred, very sacred. That is why it is revered. Therefore, when we see a dog, it is a cat, or it is a coyote. Ordinarily, when we see a dog, it is just a dog, but when we walk for the peyote it is a cat or a coyote or even something else. . . .

When we say come, it means go away. When we say "shh, quiet," it means to shout and when we whistle or call to the front we are really calling a person behind us. We speak in this direction here. That one over there turns because he already knows how it is, how everything is reversed. To say, "Let us stay here," means to go. . . .

Women, you call flowers. For the woman's skirts, you say, "bush," and for her blouse you say "palm roots." And a man's clothing, that too is changed. His clothing you call fur. His hat, that is a mushroom. Or it is his sandal. Begging your pardon, but what we carry down here, the testicles, they are called avocados. And the penis, that is his nose. That is how it is.

When we come back with the peyote, the peyote which has been hunted, they make a ceremony and everything is changed back again. And those who are at home, when one returns they grab one and ask, "What is it you call things" How is it that now you call the hands hands but when you left you called them feet?" Well, it is because they have changed the

names back again. And they all want to know what they called things. One tells them, and there is laughter. That is how it is. Because it must be as it was said in the beginning, in ancient times.

ARAPAHO PEYOTE CEREMONY DESCRIBED BY ALFRED L. KROEBER[55]

The participants in the ceremony gather outdoors; and the leader of the ceremony, the one in whose tent it is held, selects a fire-tender, . . . silently pointing to him with an eagle wing-feather. This feather the fire-tender uses as a fan for the fire during the ceremony. The place of the fire-tender is just inside the door, to its left or north. The fire chief goes first, and starts the fire inside the tent. When this begins to be illuminated, the other worshippers gather their blankets about them, and in single file walk to the tent. The fire chief kneels or stands on the prairie, outside the door, with his bead bowed, facing the tent. . . . The conductor of the ceremony, who has led the row of men, stands, and prays in a low voice, and then enters. He is followed by others singly. The fire chief goes last, and closes the door of the tent. The worshippers then sit down. . . .

Usually corn-husk cigarettes are first smoked, and are lighted with a stick taken from the fire by the fire-tender. The leader of the ceremony then produces from a small beaded purse or pouch a mescal-plant, which he keeps permanently often carrying it on his person. The plant selected is usually large, round, and even. He carefully smoothes a little space at the middle point of the crescent of reddish earth before him. Breaking eight short stems of sage, he lays them on this spot in the form of two superimposed crosses, the ends of the stems pointing in the cardinal directions and between. On this sage his mescal-plant is then laid (usually a head feather plume, which may have been worn in the hair on entering the tent, is stuck in the ground so that its tip nods over the plant); then, starting from the plant, the leader makes a crease along the top of the crescent of earth, first to the right, then to the left. This is continued at its two ends by the worshippers sitting on each side of the leader, and their neighbors carry it farther until the end of the crescent is reached. This crease or line is made by pressing the thumb into the loose earth. It represents

---

[54]Ramon Medina Silva, "How the Names Are Changed on the Peyote Journey," in Gill, *Traditions*, pp. 82–83.

[55]Gill, *Traditions*, pp 163–166.

the path by which the thoughts of the worshippers travel to the mescal-plant.

After this altar, as it might be called, has been completed, the peyote is eaten. The director gives to each of the participants four of the plants. . . . After the first four plants have been disposed of by all, the leader takes up his rattle and begins to sing. . . . During the night, the songs usually refer to the peyote itself, to the birds regarded as its messengers, and to the long duration of the night. In the morning as the tent begins to become diffused with light, the songs refer to the morning star and the end which it brings to the ceremony. At sunrise the woman [usually the wife of the leader] leaves the tent, and after a short time re-appears with four dishes of food and drink, which she places in a row on the ground, between the fire and the door. On one occasion, the woman on this re-appearance wore a symbolically painted buckskin dress. Soon after her entrance, the last round of singing is completed, the rattle is laid aside, and the fire is allowed to burn out. . . .

It is perhaps eight in the morning when the tent is left. For the rest of the day the worshippers lie on blankets in a pleasant spot under trees, under a shade, or in the house. From time to time one of them sings, shaking the rattle softly. The drum is no longer used. Occasionally more than one man will sing different songs at the same time. The effect of the drug is still very strong. The physiological discomforts have usually worn off, and the pleasurable effects are at their height. It appears that new songs, inspired perhaps by the visions of the night, are often composed during this day. At noon a meal is again served, most of the food at which is sweet. At this meal only one spoon is allowed in the company, and food requiring the use of this is therefore passed around from one participant to the other. At dark the worshippers saddle their horse and ride home, or go to bed if they live at the leader's house.

SECTION 9: Endings: Death, Judgment, and the Afterlife

Stories of the origin of death are common among Native American oral traditions. Here are several examples of how Native peoples explain the universality of death. Note that among the peoples living in the Northwest coastal region, the Raven is treated as the trickster culprit, much like the Coyote is in other areas of the continent.

THE ORIGIN OF BIRTH AND DEATH (TAHLTAN VERSION)[56]

Once the tree and the Rock were pregnant and were about to give birth. The Tree woman held on to a stick or bar, as Indian woman do, while the Rock woman used nothing to hold on to. Her child, when half born, turned into a rock, and died. Raven came along afterwards, and found the women. He said, "I am very sorry. I have come too late. Had I been here, this would not have happened. Now people must die, because Tree gave birth, and Rock did not. If Rock had given birth, and Tree had not, people would never die. People would then have been like rocks, and lasted forever. As it is now, people are like trees. Some will live to be very old, and decay and die, as some trees do; while others, when only partly grown, will die like young trees that die without decay and fall down. Thus death comes to people of all ages, just as among trees, and none lives very long."

THE ORIGIN OF HUMANS; THE ORIGINS OF DEATH (TLINGIT VERSION)[57]

After all the human beings had been destroyed Raven made new ones out of leaves. Because he made this new generation, people know that he must have changed all of the first people who had survived the flood, into stones. Since human beings were made from leaves people always die off rapidly in the fall of the year when flowers and leaves are falling off.

THE ORIGIN OF DEATH (SAHAPTIN VERSION)[58]

Coyote's married daughter was accidentally burned to death. Her husband moved away, and left Coyote alone. One night, as Coyote was sleeping, his daughter came and talked to him. "I have just come to see you," she said. "I am going on to where the dead people live. You cannot go with us, because you are alive, and we are dead." Coyote said that he would follow her. "You can come along if you throw yourself into the fire," the girl told him. Coyote threw himself into

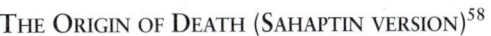

[56]Gill, *Traditions*, p. 114.

[57]Peter Goodchild, ed. *Raven Tales* (Chicago: Chicago Review Press, 1991), p. 17.

[58]Gill, *Traditions*, pp. 115–116.

the flames, but as soon as he felt the pain, he jumped out again. He was so badly blistered, however, that his daughter allowed him to go along. "You will never see us again," she told him, "but you will hear us later. There is nothing to eat on the trail. You must stick your hand in your mouth. That will satisfy you."

The girl led the way, and Coyote followed her voice. It often led him into rocks and trees. There was noise of laughter ahead of him, and Coyote followed the sound. Though it was daylight, Coyote could see nothing. They talked only when evening came, and then Coyote would follow the sound. They traveled for five days. At the end of that time Coyote could almost see them. In five days more they would be like people to him.

When they finally arrived at the land of the dead, they feared they would have to bar him from it, because he was alive. They made him sleep at some distance from the others. The land of the dead was very close to the sea. All about him Coyote saw all kinds of eggs. They gave him a bag full of holes in which to gather eggs. He filled the bag, and saw that all the eggs fell through the holes. Therefore, he did not even tie it up. "Next time fill up the bag; and even if it falls together, as if there were nothing in it, be sure to tie it up. Then it will be full." "That is what I thought," replied Coyote. He went back to gather more eggs. He filled the bag and tied it up. He threw it on his back, but it seemed as though there were nothing in it. Soon, however, it grew heavy; and when he reached the house, it was quite full. Henceforth it became his duty to gather eggs.

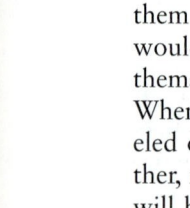

Though he heard people talk, he could not see them. He would laugh over their jokes, and they would talk about him. They said that they would put themselves into a bag, which he was to carry home. When they were ready, they told him to start. He traveled over five mountains. The girl said to him, "Father, now we are going home. Four of the mountains will be easy to climb, but do not under any circumstances open your pack. When you have reached the side of the last mountain, untie the bundle, and there will be people in it. When later others die, they too will come back in a little while." Coyote promised not to untie the bags. "I may be able to cross the mountains in two days," he said. He threw the pack on his back and started on the journey. This time he had a little food with him. He crossed three mountains, and the load began to get heavy. He heard the people laugh and talk, and he was very glad. He crossed the

fourth mountain, and now there was only one more to climb. He started to climb it, and managed to get within a few feet of the top. He was very tired, still he forced himself to go about four feet more, that that was as far as he could go. Though he had only about six feet to travel, he opened his pack. Those in the pack then said to him, "Father, now we must go back, and you will have to go home. Henceforth when people die, they will be dead forever." Then Coyote cried, and said, "I shall not be the only one to mourn a child. All people shall do the same as I. When a person dies, they shall never see him again." Thus he said, and went home. That is the end.

The attempt to visit the land of the dead to retrieve the spirit of a loved one was a common motif within the stories of many Native American peoples. The following selection from the Alabama peoples of the South is one of these stories. According to this reading, what is the Alabama understanding of the afterlife?

An Alabama Tale: The Men Who Went to the Sky[59]

There were two men and a woman living in a certain place. The woman had a little child. By and by the child's mother died. Then the two men determined to try and get her back, and about March they started off to heaven. They traveled on and on until at last they came to where an old woman lived and stayed at her house all night. She gave each of them a boiled pumpkin to eat, and they thought that these would not be enough, but the minute one of them was consumed another appeared in its place, and they ate on until they were filled. Going on farther, they came to some little people who were going to war on ducks and geese. Passing on, they came to where another old woman lived, and they spent the night with her. She said to them, "You are not to cross rivers on the way." She gave each a gourd with which they were to dip away the water of the streams they came to so that they could pass through them. Then they came to a third old woman and spent the night with her also. She said, "On the way are many great snakes," so she gave them bark of the bass tree to tie about their legs. Having fastened this on, they continued their journey and came to masses of snakes piled together. They

---

[59]Grantham, *Creation Myths and Legends of the Creek Indians,* pp. 175–176.

walked through these and the snakes bit them but did them no harm. By the time they had gotten through, however, their barks were worn out with the biting. Again they came to an old woman with whom they passed the night. She said, "There is a battle on the way. If you have tobacco, cut it up ready for smoking." They cut their tobacco up and she made cigarettes for them. She said, "When you see the battle, smoke cigarettes." They went on and by and by found the battle. Then they smoked cigarettes and the smoke covered everyone as with clouds, so they passed safely through. Finally they came to the end of the land and found the sky, which was moving up and down. One of them said, "I am the panther," and jumped up upon it. The other said, "I am a wildcat," and did the same thing. Then they were carried far up and found some people living there. One day, as they traveled on, they came to a man and some dens. The man told them not to stop at the dens but to go by, which they did. Next night they came to another man and spent the night with him. He said, "The woman's town is next. They will try to stop you, but do not stop." They found this town as he had said, and the women tried to stop them, but they passed right on.

Finally, they came to where God (aba ski djo kole, "high living") dwelt. He said, "Why did you come here?" and they told him that they had come for the mother of the child. Then he told them to stay there to the dance and he gave them a watermelon to eat. The men thought that the watermelon seed would be a good thing to save and plant at home, but he told them not to keep a single seed. He had it divided for them, and when they were through eating they put the seeds back, and God put the rind together and made it into a whole watermelon once more. He said, "You have come a long way," and they agreed that this must have been the case, for they had traveled an entire year. Then God took the cover off from something and let them look inside. They saw the house from which they had come just beneath. At the dance they saw the woman they were in search of but could not catch her. Then God gave them pieces of corncob and said, "When you see that woman again throw these at her." When they again saw her at the dance they threw the pieces of corncob at her. The last piece struck her, she fell down, and they seized her. Then God brought a big jug, put the woman into it, and screwed on the top. He said, "When you want to go back tell me." They said, "We will go tomorrow." Then they went to sleep, but when they woke up they

found they were sleeping in their own house. The woman inside of the jar was groaning, saying "You have bought me here and killed me." They were so sorry for her that they put the jar in the shade and unscrewed the top a little, whereupon she stopped groaning. Then they thought they would go to sleep, but when they woke up and opened the jar she was gone. She went back to heaven. If they had left the cover screwed on until she died she would have come back again. God gave the woman to them but they lost her again. If they had left this cover screwed down, people would still come back to earth; but since they did not, people do not come back anymore.

Within the oral traditions of a large number of tribes are prophecies about the coming of white men and the consequences that will follow. Some of the stories are cautionary warnings; others are eschatological projections about the end of time. Here are several such stories. What do these prophecies tell us about the thoughts and concerns of Native Americans during the last several centuries?

PROPHECIES OF THE END

A Nez Perce Warning About the Coming of White Men[60]

An old man in Lapwai—I forget his name—used to see the future in his dreams. He would see white-faced animals a little bigger than deer coming over the hill. They would come down Thunder Hill, between Lapwai and the Clearwater River. Behind the white-faced deer was a white-faced man.

"Another kind of human being is going to be here soon," the old man would tell his people.

Other men laughed at him.

"We are going to have some writing given us," he told them. "We must have our ears open so that we can understand it. A white-faced man will explain it. We will have seven sleeps, and the seventh day will be a holy day.

The earth will be plowed up. There will be many ways of going fast to other places. People will go fast on the land and fast in the air, like big birds."

People laughed at the old man's dreams, laughed at what he said would happen. But everything he prophesied came true.

This is a true story, not a myth or legend.

---

[60]Clark, *Indian Legends from the Northern Rockies*, p. 55.

The Prophesy of Sweet Medicine— A Cheyenne Cultural Hero[61]

Many centuries ago the prophet and savior Sweet Medicine came to the prairie people. Before his birth the people were bad, living without law and killing one another. But with his life those things changed. Indians are often called savages, and it was true of the Cheyennes at first, but not after Sweet Medicine's time. . . .

Sweet Medicine's Death: The tribe was camped in a big village near Devil's Tower in Wyoming when Sweet Medicine knew his time had come. He called the military societies together and ordered them to build him a hut of cedar poles, covered with rye grass and cottonwood bark and bedded inside with rye grass. Then, since he was helpless with old age, he had them carry him to this place and lay him on the bedding inside. When this was done he ordered the camp moved farther down, several miles away from him, so that in the end he would be alone. After the camp was set up there he sent word for the people to come back to hear the last things he had to tell them. When they had surrounded the place and stood there waiting, he began to speak:

"There is a time coming, though, when many things will change. Strangers called Earth Men will appear among you. There skins are light-colored, and their ways are powerful. They clip their hair short and speak no Indian tongue. Follow nothing that these Earth Men do, but keep your own ways that I have taught you as long as you can.

The buffalo will disappear, at last, and another animal will take its place, a slick animal with a long tail and split hoofs, whose flesh you will learn to eat. But first there will be another animal you must learn to use. It has a shaggy neck and a tail almost touching the ground. Its hoofs are round. This animal will carry you on his back and help you in many ways. These far hills that seem only a blue vision in the distance take many days to reach now; but with this animal you can get there in a short time, so fear him not. Remember what I have said.

But at last you will not remember. Your ways will change. You will leave your religion for something new. You will lose respect for your leaders and start quarreling with one another. You will lose track of your relations and marry women from your own families. . . . I am sorry to say these things, but I have seen them, and you will find that they come true."

Then people were all quiet, thinking of what Sweet Medicine had said. But they did not believe him. At last they left him there alone and he was not seen again.

The final reading is a free rendering of a message by Wovoka, a Paiute Indian who was known by the English as John Wilson. During the winter of 1888–1889, Wovoka fell asleep and was taken to another world where he received a message from the Supreme God that he was told to deliver to the Native peoples of all tribes. As word spread of his visions, thousands came to Wovoka to receive instructions about the Ghost Dance ceremonies and about the soon coming of a new age. The following message that was received in August 1891 has become known as the "Messiah Letter."

THE MESSIAH LETTER[62]

When you get home you must make a dance to continue five days. Dance four successive nights, and the last night keep up the dance until the morning of the fifth day, when all must bathe in the river and then disperse to their homes. You must all do in the same way.

I, Jack Wilson, love you all, and my heart is full of gladness for the gifts you have brought me. When you get home I shall give you a good cloud [rain?] which will make you feel good. I give you a good spirit and give you all good paint. I want you to come in three months, some from each tribe there [the Indian territory]. There will be a good deal of snow this year and some rain. In the fall there will be such a rain as I have never given you before.

Grandfather says, when your friends die you must not cry. You must not hurt anybody or do harm to anyone. You must not fight. Do right always. It will give you satisfaction in life. . . .

Do not tell the white people about this. Jesus is now upon the earth. He appears like a cloud. The dead are alive all again. I do not know when they will be here; maybe this fall or in the spring. When the time comes there will be no more sickness and everyone will be young again.

---

[61]John Stands in Timber and Margot Liberty, with the Assistance of Robert M. Utley, *Cheyenne Memories* (New Haven, CT: Yale University Press, 1998), pp. 27, 39–41.

[62]Young, *Quest for Harmony*, p. 277.

Do not refuse to work for the whites and do not make any trouble with them until you leave them. When the earth shakes [at the coming of the new age] do not be afraid. It will not hurt you.

I want you to dance every six weeks. Make a feast at the dance and have food that everybody may eat. Then bathe in the water. That is all. You will receive good words again from me some time. Do not tell lies.

The words of the final piece expresses the spiritual attitudes of a contemporary Cherokee.

Walk On—A Contemporary Cherokee Poem[63]

Good morning, Grandfather.
I entered this life a ways back
and put skin on to walk two-legged on this Creation—
and what a glorious time it was.

It taught me about breath
and about sensing and feeling and caring through my heart.
And I walked on around that Red Road,
Looking and trying to understand more
about the mystery and the secrets She holds.

And You spoke to me through the wind,
and You sang to me through the birds.
And You brought challenges forth so that
I might listen to the message You bring me more sincerely.
And I kept walking down this road.

And I came 'round the bend
at the middle of that curve in the road
and I began to find a secret in the Spirit of my Self. . . .

And still I walked on, sometimes blind and deaf,
and sometimes with pain.
But I fought with my fears and I embraced my
    unknowingness—
and still I walked on.
And my children and my family stood with me
and we came to know each other in those later years more
    than we
had before—for some of our falseness had fallen away—
and still I walked on.

And I kept walking on this road towards You,
towards that other world that grew closer to me with each
    step.
And as the door of the Great Spirit world came closer
my fear loomed up inside sometimes. . . .

But something called me forth—
the Morning Star rose with each day—
and my prayer became a centering—and still I walked on,
until I began to hear the Song of the Mother,
and Her arms embraced me so,
that instead of walking She carried me right to the door.
And as the door opened, I heard Her Song,
And Her Song lifted me up, so I could soar.

PowerWeb SUPPLEMENT

1. **Becoming Part of It,** Joseph Epes Brown, *Parabola,* August 1982.

Contemporary Native American spiritual practices often focus on the experience of connecting individuals with the world around them. In this recommended selection, Joseph Epes Brown explains how rituals such as pipe smoking or sand painting are designed to create and maintain this connection with nature. Readings from *PowerWeb: Religion* are available at the McGraw-Hill *PowerWeb* website http://www.dushkin.com/powerweb. A personal access code to *PowerWeb: Religion* is provided free with each new copy of this book. Those who purchase a used copy may buy an access code at the website.

SELECTED BIBLIOGRAPHY

Andrien, Kenneth J. *Andean Worlds: Indigenous History, Culture and Consciousness Under Spanish Rule, 1532–1825.* Albuquerque, NM: University of New Mexico Press, 2001.

Bailey, Garrick A., ed. *The Osage and the Invisible World from the Works of Francis Las Flesche.* Norman, OK: University of Oklahoma Press, 1995.

Barnouw, Victor. *Wisconsin Chippewa Myths & Tales.* Madison, WI: University of Wisconsin Press, 1977.

Bross, Kristina. *Dry Bones and Indian Sermons: Praying Indians in Colonial America.* Ithaca, NY: Cornell University Press, 2004.

Brown, Jennifer S. H., and Elizabeth Vibert. *Reading Beyond Words: Contexts for Native History.* Orchard Park, NY: Broadview Press, 2003.

Brown, Joseph Epes. *Teaching Spirits: Understanding Native American Religious Traditions.* New York: Oxford University Press, 2001.

Calloway, Colin G., ed. *First Peoples: A Documentary Survey of American Indian History.* New York: Bedford/St. Martin's, 2004.

Cebula, Larry. *Plateau Indians and the Quest for Spiritual Power, 1700–1850.* Lincoln, NE: University of Nebraska Press, 2003.

Collins, John James. *Native American Religions: A Geographical Survey.* Lewiston, NY: The Edwin Mellen Press, 1990.

[63]Michael Stillwater and Gary Malkin, eds. *Graceful Passages: A Companion for Living and Dying* (Novato, CA: New World Library, 2003), pp. 32–33.

Dill, Sam D. *Native American Traditions: Sources and Interpretations.* Belmont, CA: Wadsworth Publishing, 1983.

Eastman, Charles A. *The Soul of the Indian.* Lincoln, NE: University of Nebraska Press, 1980.

Elm, Demus, and Harvey Antone. *The Oneida Creation Story.* Translated and edited by Floyd G. Lounsbury and Bryan Gick. Lincoln, NE: University of Nebraska Press, 2000.

Grantham, Bill. *Creation Myths and Legends of the Creek Indians.* Gainesville, FL: University of Florida Press, 2002.

Grounds, Richard A., George E. Tinker, and David E. Wilkins. *Native Voices: American Indian Identity and Resistance.* Lawrence, KS: University of Kansas Press, 2003.

Grumet, Robert S., ed. *Northeastern Indian Lives, 1632–1816.* Amherst, MA: University of Massachusetts Press, 1996.

Hittman, Michael. Edited by Don Lynch. *Wovoka and the Ghost Dance.* Lincoln, NE: University of Nebraska Press, 1997.

Irwin, Lee. *Native American Spirituality: A Critical Reader.* Lincoln, NE: University of Nebraska Press, 2000.

Judson, Katharine Berry, ed. *Myths and Legends of the Pacific Northwest.* Lincoln, NE: University of Nebraska Press, 1997.

Linderman, Frank B. *Pretty-shield: Medicine Woman of the Crows.* Lincoln, NE: University of Nebraska Press, 2003.

Linderman, Frank B. *Old Man Coyote.* Lincoln, NE: University of Nebraska Press, 1996.

Luckert, Karl W., ed. *Navajo Coyote Tales: The Curlo to Aheedliinii Version. By Father Berard Haile.* Lincoln, NE: University of Nebraska Press, 1984.

Malokti, Ekkehart, ed. *Hopi Stories and Tales.* Lincoln, NE: University of Nebraska Press, 2001.

Malotki, Ekkehart and Ken Gary. *Hopi Stories of Witchcraft, Shamanism, and Magic.* Lincoln, NE: University of Nebraska Press, 2001.

McCutchen, David, trans. *The Red Record: The Wallam Olum.* Garden City Park, NY: Avery Publishing, 1993.

Mills, Antonia, and Richard Slobodin, ed. *Amerindian Rebirth: Reincarnation Belief among North American Indians and Inuit.* Toronto: University of Toronto Press, 1994.

Peterson, Jacqueline, and Laura Peers. *Sacred Encounters: Father De Smet and the Indians of the Rocky Mountain West.* Norman, OK: University of Oklahoma Press, 1993.

Petrone, Penny. *First Peoples, First Voices.* Toronto: University of Toronto Press, 1983.

Powers, William K. *Oglala Religion.* Lincoln, NE: University of Nebraska Press, 1977.

Robinson, Sherry. *Apache Voices: Their Stories of Survival as Told to Eve Ball.* Albuquerque, NM: University of New Mexico Press, 2000.

Smith, Anne M. and Alden Hayes, ed. *Ute Tales.* Salt Lake City: University of Utah Press, 1992.

Swanton, John R. *Creek Religion and Medicine.* Lincoln, NE: University of Nebraska Press, 2000.

Terraciano, Kevin. *The Mixtecs of Colonial Oaxaca.* Palo Alto, CA: Stanford University Press, 2001.

Tooker, Elisabeth, ed. *Native North American Spirituality of the Eastern Woodlands.* New York: Paulist Press, 1979.

Vecsey, Christopher. *Traditional Ojibwa Religion and Its Historical Changes.* Philadelphia: American Philosophical Society, 1983.

Wissler, Clark, and D. C. Duvall, comp. *Mythology of the Blackfoot Indians.* Lincoln, NE: University of Nebraska Press, 1995.

Young, William A. *Quest for Harmony: Native American Spiritual Traditions.* New York: Seven Brides Press, 2002.

Zolbrod, Paul G. *Dine bahane: The Navajo Creation Story.* Albuquerque, NM: University of New Mexico Press, 1984.

Traditional African Religions 8

Although Africa played a significant role in the early histories of each of the three major religions of the West,[1] only a century ago the majority of African peoples embraced one of the numerous non-Western religious traditions indigenous to the continent. In recent decades, the rapid expansion of Christianity and Islam throughout Africa has reduced the percentage of peoples who remain practitioners of traditional African religions. Large numbers of African Christians and Muslims, however, remain influenced by traditional African religious worldviews. Moreover, traditional African religions no longer are limited to the African continent but are visible in numerous regions of the world, particularly in Brazil, Cuba, and the United States. According to one recent estimate, as many as 800 million people worldwide celebrate life through practices that resemble the religious rites observed by indigenous African cultures of previous centuries.[2]

SETTING

While fossil evidence suggests that humanlike creatures have been walking upright for more than 2 million years, most scientists agree that *Homo sapiens* or "Wise Man" emerged on this planet about 500,000 years ago. Whenever the origins of human life actually transpired, it is likely that this took place in the heartlands of Africa. Thus, over the past half-million years, migrations out of Africa have produced a world population of more than 6 billion people, all of whom are in some sense descendants of the early Africans. Currently about 800 million live in the 12 million square miles that comprise Africa, making the continent slightly larger in population than Europe and slightly less than the combined populations of the two Americas. About 600 million of the contemporary Africans live below the Sahara Desert in those regions of the continent that historically have been more isolated from foreign influences than northern Africa. This chapter focuses primarily on the indigenous peoples of the sub-Sahara, since the major religions of North Africans already have been treated in the chapters that cover the great religions of the West.

The Peoples of Africa

Modern Africans are diverse peoples who speak, depending on language definitions, more than 1,000 different tongues. In a continent with so many nonintercomprehensible languages, multilingualism is the norm within virtually every nation-state. To illustrate, in Nigeria alone nearly 400 languages are spoken. Linguists often group these languages into four major phylums. Geographically, the largest division is the Niger-Kordofan phylum. This broad division comprises hundreds of languages, including the Bantu languages, and covers territory that stretches from Gambia throughout western and central Africa, down to the southern regions of the continent. In contrast, the Khoisan or "Click" linguistic family is a small language group that includes primarily only the Bushmen and Hottentots in southwest Africa. The Afro-Asian phylum, which includes among others, linguistic families the Egyptian, Semitic, and Berber

---

[1]See Chapters 1, 2, and 3.

[2]Toyin Falola, ed. *Africa: Vol. 5: Contemporary Africa* (Durham, NC: Carolina Academic Press, 2003), p. 553.

languages, is found in the populous northern portions of the continent, while the Nilo-Saharan phylum is sandwiched between the Afro-Asian and the Niger-Kordofanian divisions.[3]

Although most contemporary Africans speak multiple languages, historically communication across the regions of the continent has been difficult. Moreover, sharing language similarities that modern linguists use to differentiate language phylum does not unite diverse peoples into a common ethnic heritage. Ethic diversity in Africa, like linguistic diversity, is significant. In the sub-Sahara, only three ethnic groups have populations that approach 10 million, while hundreds of ethnic traditions include less than 1 million people each. In comparison with peoples of other continents, the average size of an ethnic unit in Africa is small. As a result of these linguistic and ethnic divisions, cultural diversity (and often ethnic tension) is correspondingly great.

Influences of Land and Climate

Environmental factors along with linguistic incompatibilities and relative (not absolute) isolation from the outside world have contributed to the cultural diversity of the African peoples. Much of the continent lies within the tropics, the regions of the earth within 23.5 degrees of the equator where the sun is located directly above the surface at noon on at least one day of the year. The climate of tropical regions is generally hot and wet. Often seasons in the tropics are characterized more by changes in rainfall than in temperatures. Some rain forest areas of Africa receive upward of 200 inches of rain per year. The abundant moisture makes possible in some regions the growth of densely packed gigantic trees reaching 200 feet in the air. The high tree lines provide a canopy of shade to the semidark forest floor that is covered with fungi and other lifeforms that require little light. In less dense wooded areas, an abundance of species of plants and animals inhabit the junglelike forest floor. Beyond the areas of deciduous forests are the drier savanna grasslands that serve as home for beautiful, wild, and, to Westerners, exotic large animals. Africa also has towering mountains such as Mount Kenya and Mount Kilimanjaro with their year-round snowcapped peaks that stand more than three miles above their wet and hot tropical bases. North and south of the tropics are drier regions that include some of the largest, hottest, and most barren deserts on earth. Together, the impenetrable forests, towering mountains, and insufferable deserts have encouraged the continuation of relatively isolated, self-sufficient, and small-scale nomadic and rural cultures. In recent centuries, cosmopolitan, urban, and multiethnic centers have grown, but most of these high-density population regions are located in coastal areas of northern and southern Africa.

Owing in part to the plethora of microorganisms that inhabit tropical regions, life expectancy in the heart of Africa has always been relatively low. While until recent historic times the unhealthy human environment insulated portions of the sub-Sahara from foreign invasions, the awe-inspiring terrains, high death rates, and relative isolation of the inner continent contributed to the rise of indigenous religious traditions that seek to make sense of a world characterized by natural beauty, wilderness, disease, and hardship. In contrast to the religions of many cultures, indigenous African oral traditions are lacking in expressions of heaven-bound sentimentality but are articulate in portraying a stark realism that anchors humanity on an earth inhabited with both kind and dangerous spirits.

Although writing was developed in Egypt 5,000 years ago, literacy did not spread to the sub-Saharan regions until recent times. Consequently, like the indigenous traditions of the Americas, the native cultures of the sub-Sahara are largely nonliterate. Without written records, the indigenous religious traditions of these diverse peoples must be constructed solely from the extant artifacts, which decay rapidly in the hot and humid climate, and from the living oral traditions, which may have been influenced by non-Africans who have penetrated into the inner continent in recent centuries. Reconstructing the history of traditional African religions from these limited and uncertain sources can be a difficult and challenging task.

SACRED STORIES AND BELIEFS

Two words that aptly describe traditional African religions are *variety* and *ubiquity*. We speak of African religions in the plural because the continent houses a

---

[3]Falola, *Africa: Vol. 5*, pp. 735–757.

thousand ethnic traditions, each of which has its own religious system. Great diversity exists within these systems. Some peoples, such as the Dinka and Nuer, spend the majority of their lives in acts of worship, while other peoples participate in religious ritual on only infrequent occasions. Some peoples give reverence to only one or two divinities below the high God or Supreme Being (who is nearly universally recognized), while others, such as the Yoruba, have some 1,700 divinities (known as *orisa*) that serve as intermediaries between the high God and humanity. Amidst the great variety of religious expressions, however, most traditional African religions share a belief in a Supreme Being and a belief in the notion that the spiritual and the physical are two dimensions of the same universe. For African indigenous societies, the spiritual and physical are so intertwined that it is difficult to isolate the sacred from the profane. Like many religious peoples, traditional Africans live in a profoundly religious world where names of people carry religious meanings, where the sounds of African instruments are expressions of a sacred language, and where solar and lunar eclipses are perceived not simply as acts of nature but as divine warnings that all is not well. Relations with the sacred in traditional African cultures are more communal than personal. No atheists or nonreligious persons exist among these peoples: to eliminate religion from your life is to excommunicate yourself from society. The starting point to understanding traditional African religions is to appreciate the centrality of the idea that the universe and all activity within it are fundamentally religious in nature.

Traditional African Ontology

Traditional African ontology is anthropocentric in that it places humanity in the center of the cosmos. Below humankind in the chain of being are the animals, plants, and other living organisms. Lower still are the natural objects that do not have biological life. Above humanity, yet below the high God, are the various types of Spirits. Some Spirits were created as divinities by God; some were superhuman heroes who achieved divinity status; still others are the spiritual remains of humans who died long ago.

Africans view the high God as the creator and sustainer of humanity. The various Spirits, in turn, are recognized as the intermediaries that communicate between the high God and humankind. The lower orders

comprise the environment in which humans live, thus providing humankind with the sustenance needed to survive without immediate contact with God. Most indigenous cultures view the high God more in concrete than abstract terms. According to a number of creation stories, the high God once lived near the earth, but, owing to the bothersome annoyances sometimes ascribed to a woman, He withdrew far away into the sky where He now dwells. Generally, people refer to Him as "The Wise One," "He who knows all and see all," "He who is everywhere," "The All-Powerful," "The One who fills everything," "The Fathomless Spirit," "The Unknown," and in numerous other ways that suggest an omnipotent, omnipresent, mysterious, and masculine or androgynous deity. Although no idols bear His image and, with few exceptions, no lavish temples provide Him sanctuary, the high God of traditional African religions is known and respected throughout the continent.

African Concepts of Time

According to the renowned African scholar John S. Mbiti, the key to understanding the indigenous religions of Africa is to comprehend traditional African concepts of time.[4] Unlike most modern cultures that view time as threefold (past, present, and future), in traditional African societies time exists only in two dimensions—a long past and a present that includes an immediate but not a distant future. Not only do most African languages lack a future verb tense, but there are few concrete words that convey the idea of a distant future. To indigenous Africans, only experienced time is meaningful. Because the distant future has not been experienced, little attention is given to it. Only the near future that can be understood as part of the inevitable rhythms of nature has meaning to traditional societies.

Also unlike other modern and Western concepts of time, Africans do not view time as a commodity that can be quantified with precision. Dated calendars and clocks are rare in traditional African cultures. Africans instead live by *phenomenon* calendars that reckon time in relation to the rhythms of nature. Pregnant women, for instance, know the number of lunar months that will transpire during their pregnancy,

---

[4]John S. Mbiti, *African Religions and Philosophy* (Garden City, NY: Anchor Books, 1970), pp. 19–36.

and travelers state how many days it takes to go from one place to another. These timed events, however, are not based on precise abstractions such as seconds and minutes but are understood in reference to natural phenomena that reoccur but are not easily quantified with exactness. Every day begins with the rising of the sun, but it does not matter to traditional African cultures if this takes place at 5 or 7 in the morning. People retire at night to sleep, and African words express this experience, but whether this takes place at 9 or midnight is not a meaningful concept. Similarly, in equatorial regions, the year consists of two rainy and two dry seasons and is deemed completed when each season is experienced, regardless of whether this occurs in 340 or 390 days.

In the Swahili language, two words are associated with concepts of time: *Sama* and *Zamani*. *Sama* refers to experienced and remembered time, whereas *Zamani* refers to the distant past that is beyond human memory. *Sama* time moves toward *Zamani* as the present and recent past moves into the unremembered past. *Zamani* is the final destination of all human existence; it is the graveyard of history since in traditional African cultures time seemingly moves backward into the *Zamani* period, not forward toward some expectant future golden age. Unlike many religions of the world, indigenous African religions are lacking in sacred myths about the end of the world. Rather, traditional Africans expect the flow of time to continue to move from *Sama* to *Zamani* as it always has.

Life and Death in African Cultures

This two-dimensional understanding of time influences traditional African attitudes toward life, death, and the afterlife. According to traditional African worldviews, the death of a soul or personality is not a single datable event but a long process that moves individuals gradually from the *Sama* into the *Zamani* periods. After physical death, it is believed that the soul of the deceased remains in the *Sama* period as long as he or she is remembered by family members. In this "living-dead" state, the individuals keep their names and personalities. If the deceased has no family, however, then the spirit of a man or woman cannot remain in *Sama* time, and his or her personality is lost. Many widespread traditional African customs such as polygamy, the inheritance of wives from deceased brothers, and abhorrence to homosexuality

are anchored in this belief. In virtually every indigenous African culture, marriage and procreation are viewed not as optional but as sacred duties. Anyone who rejects the responsibility of procreation is a curse to the community because to die without offspring is to cease to live.

In life, most indigenous societies affirm the legitimate pursuit of physical enjoyments such as food and drink, dance, and sexual pleasures. Correspondingly, it is assumed that the living-dead also have such desires, and it is the responsibility of their families to provide for these needs. In most cultures, the living-dead are believed to maintain in the spirit world the same sex and social status they experienced in life. Traditional African funeral feasts are both mournful and celebratory events because they are rituals that bring the spirits of the departed back to the families that will respect and care for them through offerings and animal sacrifices. Many indigenous peoples note that they have heard or seen the living-dead. Sometimes their reappearance is in human form, but more often it is in the form of totem (sacred) animals that vary among ethnic groups. In many societies, tribal leaders are associated with great snakes such as mambas, while commoners reappear as grass snakes. In some cultures, the living-dead on rare occasions are believed to be reincarnated into a newborn child who will carry the name and the personal traits of the deceased member of the family.

The living-dead naturally have an interest in the affairs of their family and, consequently, serve like a police force that punishes misdeeds such as the abuse of a husband, the unfaithfulness of a wife, the overambitiousness of a younger brother, or the disobedience of a son. When misfortune comes to a family member, it is sometimes assumed that it was caused by the ghost of a living-dead who died with a grudge against the victim. In former ages, the ghosts of war captives or domestic slaves were particularly feared. Although the ancestral ghosts have greater power and wisdom than the living, they are not worshiped as deities because, within four or five generations, they will be forgotten and become nameless spirits without identities. While among the living-dead, however, the physically departed speak the languages of both the spirit and physical worlds and thus can serve as intermediaries who can take human concerns to the high God or lesser deities of the cosmos.

The living-dead can both cause harm and good will, so attitudes toward them are ambiguous. They must be respected, but it is dangerous for humans to associate too closely with them. People call upon them mostly in times of trouble when there is a need to understand the cause of some misfortune. After several generations pass, if no living member of the family remembers the name of the departed, the living-dead move from a state of personal immortality into a state of collective immortality that is associated with *Zamani* time. In this final state, their spirits exist as empty names without personalities. This is the final destination for all, except for the cultural heroes to whom God awards deity status. With only rare exceptions, the collective spirit world is the ultimate destiny of all humankind.

The Spirits and the Lower Deities

Above the living and the living-dead in the cosmos are the collective spirits and the lower deities. The collective spirits were once living and living-dead personalities who passed from *Sama* to *Zamani*. There are several possible origins of the deities. A few were superhuman cultural heroes whom God raised to divinity status. Other Spirits were created by God as lower deities. One category of these deities can be understood as the personifications of the high God. Called by different names among different cultures, many of these deities are associated with natural phenomena such as the sun, moon, thunder, lightning, rain, mountains, lakes, and rivers. Although timeless, these phenomena are directly experienced by humans; thus, they are closer to humanity than the mysterious high God and can be asked in religious rituals to serve as intermediaries between humans and the divine. The names, numbers, forms, genealogies, and colors associated with these lower deities vary among the peoples. Deities can be benevolent or malevolent, but most, like humans, are mixtures of good and evil. Some are known as tricksters who enjoy causing mischief. Among some peoples, trickster deities serve as divine enforcers who punish those who fail to make proper sacrifices. Owing to their great powers, people pray to them and honor their taboos, hoping that such actions will halt the tricksters from causing them harm.

Communicating with the Spirit World

When misfortune comes, it is assumed that some higher power is upset. Almost all native cultures believe that offended ancestral ghosts cause human suffering and disease, although generally not death. The appropriate timing of death, it is widely believed, is determined before birth when the individual soul receives its destiny from the high God or in some traditions, from one of his intermediaries. Early death, which is common, is not feared, because it implies that some beings prefer to live in the spirit world that is closer to God. However, premature death (dying before your allotted time), which can be caused by suicide or witchcraft, is considered a tragedy that can carry cosmic consequences, including the annihilation of the soul before it evolves back into *Zamani* time.

While it is believed that the living-dead cause diseases among family members, massive epidemics and natural catastrophes are ascribed to the angered deities in the spirit world. When calamity strikes, the besieged family or community must first discover the spirit who is causing the torment and then perform rituals that will satisfy the offended power and thereby restore the necessary cosmic balance. To determine the cause of the misfortune, the indigenous people use the art of divination. In some cultures, particularly those in western Africa, religious specialists or priests approach the spirits on behalf of those in their community. Other peoples, particularly traditions in eastern and central Africa, have no ordained priests but rely on lay diviners who are known for their skills in communicating with the spirit world. Often these diviners are females who when not divining, hold no advanced status in the community.

There are numerous ways that traditional Africans communicate with the spirit world. Using techniques similar to the Chinese diviners who employ *I Jing* to assist in decision making, some African diviners throw palm nuts or seashells on the ground and then count the sides of the fallen objects to answer the questions asked to the diviner. Others toss chains of snake bones to find their answers. Still others examine the entrails of animals, especially fowls. Among the most universal forms of divination on the African continent is divination through spirit possession. Generally speaking, a person cannot be possessed by a living-dead until he or she has been initiated into the spirit possession cult. The initiation process can be long, arduous, and dangerous. After the neophytes are trained in the sacred languages and receive a new name and new personality, they become able to invite the offended spirits into their body. During spirit possession, the diviner-mediums lose their own personalities and take on the personalities of the spirits, allowing the ancestral ghosts to speak through them to inform the people of the offense that has been committed.

Once the cause of misfortune has been determined, two steps remain: restitution by ritual and medical treatment. As in many traditions, traditional African religions use prayer and sacrifice in their sacred healing rituals. In some circumstances, an ox, cow, or goat is sacrificed, although more typically the most common sacrifice to the spirits is a chicken. Human sacrifice is not unknown but is exceedingly rare and generally used only as an act of desperation. The blood of the sacrificed animal often is smeared on the body of the victim to symbolically unite the divine and the human. After the offended spirit has been appeased, the subject may need to receive medical treatment from another religious specialist, the tribal healer. This "traditional doctor" (inappropriately labeled a "witch doctor" by uninformed Westerners) treats the victim by dispensing roots, bark, and leaves as herbal medicines. At times, doctors also seek cures through body massages, incantations, and the appropriate use of medicinal objects such as needles and feathers. Although many women are diviners, fewer women are herbalists, in part because this work involves trips into the bush to collect herbs, an activity that demands public contact with strangers. This type of behavior is considered taboo for women in many traditional African societies.

Witchcraft and Evil Magic

Alongside the herbalists and diviners are those who use their spiritual knowledge for evil purposes. Although this group can include men, often these "witches" are women who, it is believed, operate in secret at night, flying from their sleeping bodies to feed on their victims. Witches also are believed to be able to manipulate flies, bats, reptiles, and other beasts into assisting them in doing their nefarious work. Their powers to torment and kill are so great that no village can feel entirely safe from their presence. When misfortune comes, often husbands and wives accuse the co-wives in the household of causing the troubles by evil magic. Traditional societies once had harsh measures of dealing with accused witches. As modern courts have curtailed some of these ancient practices, many traditional Africans believe that sorcery is more common today than it was in the past.

As fear of witchcraft escalates, so escalates the prestige of traditional healers who are looked upon to protect the community from the evils of sorcery by removing curses and controlling the spirits of the living-dead. Notwithstanding the modernization that is currently transforming many African nation-states, traditional religious sentiments remain strong as Africans throughout the continent hold to the view that the physical and spiritual worlds are intimately intertwined and that a mysterious power is ever-present that can be used for good or for evil purposes. Many contemporary scholars are examining intersections between these indigenous views and "Africanized" Christian and Islamic practices.

SCRIPTURES (AFRICAN ORAL TRADITIONS)

Like the indigenous cultures of the Americas and Oceania, traditional African peoples do not condense their religious beliefs and practices into a systematic set of dogmas. No creeds are recited other than the individual expressions of heartfelt convictions. No sacred scriptures have been codified into textual units and canonized by religious authorities to serve as standards of religious beliefs and practices. African religions have no founders, although some have incorporated legendary heroes into the oral traditions that are passed forward from generation to generation. Traditional African understandings of the sacred, however, are believed to have come from the ancestors. Each generation receives this sacred tradition and makes use of it by interpreting and modifying it in ways that meet the needs and circumstances of the community. Unlike the great religions of the East or the West, traditional African religions make no claims to universality. Instead, they are tribal or national religions that are deemed appropriate to those among whom the particular tradition evolved. This is not to say that religious ideas do not spread among the peoples by migrations, intermarriages, and conquest, but there are no missionaries who seek to convert members of other tribes, and conversion from one tradition to another is rare.

Although there are no written sacred texts, creeds, or formulated systematic theologies, the sacred traditions and philosophical underpinnings of African indigenous religions are preserved in many wood carvings and sculptures expressing religious content and in the recited proverbs, prayers, songs, rituals, and stories that are taught to the young by the elders within each tribe. Insights into traditional African understandings of God, human nature, morality, and the afterlife can be found in the abundant creation stories and origins of disease and death stories that permeate throughout the continent. Selections from each of these oral styles are included in the Sacred Texts section of this chapter.

THE ONGOING HISTORY OF RELIGIONS IN AFRICA

All history, including African religious history, is largely composed of long periods marked by gradual change, interrupted occasionally by trigger-point events that evoke more violent changes. One critical development that influenced the future of African religions was the seventh-century CE migrations of Bantu-speaking peoples into central and southern Africa. The independent chiefdoms established by these traditional peoples in southeastern Africa would flourish with little foreign interference for nearly 1,000 years. Even as the Bantu were migrating toward the south, the Islamic tradition was gaining strongholds in North Africa. For more than a millennium, the northern regions above the 10th parallel have been predominantly Muslim. Moreover, medieval trans-Saharan trade between the Islamic world and the peoples of West Africa fostered the rise of a secession of powerful African empires that governed hundreds of thousands of subjects. Between the eleventh and fifteenth centuries, these powerful West African empires exported gold, ivory, and other local commodities into Arabia, Europe, India, and China. Later, in late-fifteenth- and sixteenth-century Portugal, other Christian European nations also attempted to establish strong commercial and religious ties with these kingdoms.

When African chiefs, either for political or religious reasons, converted to Islam or Christianity, these nonindigenous religious traditions began to make headway into the sub-Sahara. The drift of traditional peoples toward these ancient Western religions was easy for some since the God of Abraham, Isaac, and Jacob seemed, at first glance, to be compatible with the high God of Africa. The famous autobiography of

When twins are born in Nigeria, parents often commission the carving of a pair of figurines known as "Ibeji," which means "twice born." Since it is believed that the souls of twins are linked, if one twin dies, the figurine of the departed will be cared for as if it were living. Failure to feed and wash the Ibeji may result in harm for the parent or the surviving twin.

Olaudah Equiano, an eighteenth-century African who was brought to America as a slave, comments on the similarities that this Christian convert found between his new faith and his childhood religious upbringing. After reading the Bible, Equiano remarked: "I was wonderfully surprised to see the laws and rules of my own country written almost exactly here."*

Of course, there are limits to the similarities between traditional African religious worldviews and

---

*Olaudah Equiano: The Interesting Narrative of the Life of Olandah Equiano, or Gustavus Vassa, the African (London, 1789, Vol. 1), p. 172. Available at http://history.hanover.edu/texts/Equiano.

Timeline of African history.

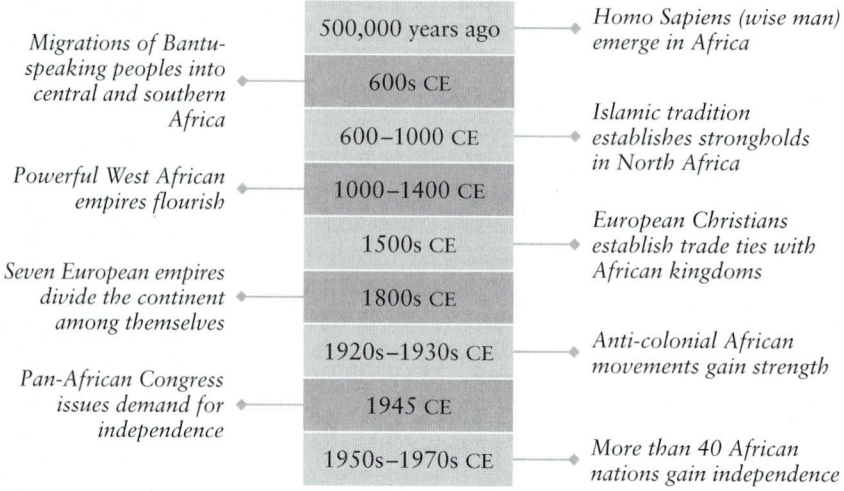

the great religions of the West. To many traditional Africans, Christianity appears to be overly compartmentalized, something that is done for two hours on Sundays but does not fill their whole lives as well as traditional African forms of religion. Others understand Christianity largely in negative terms, as disbelief in the deities and the powers of the spirit world and as the rejection of the traditional customs. Similarly, many specifics of Islamic law also are unattractive to traditional Africans. Consequently, even in those sub-Saharan regions that have embraced the classic religions of the West, the forms of Christianity and Islam that are embraced often are highly Africanized versions of indigenous and Western religious concepts. Given the mixture of traditional African and Western religions, throughout the sub-Sahara it is often difficult to demarcate the line that separates traditional customs from the classic religions of the Western world.

The Partitioning and Reopening of Africa

In the last 150 years, one obstacle to Christian "missionary" efforts in Africa has been its association with Western attempts to colonize the continent. The map of Africa was altered in the late nineteenth century as seven European colonial empires essentially divided the continent among themselves. At the Berlin Conference (1884–1885), for instance, representatives from Germany, Britain, France, Spain, Portugal, Italy, and Belgium accepted a "sphere of influence" for

each power and established protocols designed to limit conflict as each European nation maneuvered to secure control over its designated region. By the early twentieth century, only Ethiopia and Liberia enjoyed freedom from European domination. Following World War I (1914–1918), after Germany was stripped of its overseas territories, the seven colonial empires in Africa were reduced to six, but the colonial systems remained largely intact. In some areas, the Europeans ruled directly, while in other areas they maintained "indirect" control through administrative ties with traditional African kings and chiefs. In all cases, however, the objective was the same: the transfer of wealth from Africa to Europe through modernization that served the economic interests of the Europeans.[5]

During the two decades that separated the two world wars, African nations were reduced to about 50 colonies with boundaries that served the colonial powers but did not always reflect cultural divisions within the continent. Some positive things came from the colonial period. For instance, life expectancy increased in some regions of the continent, and Western-style education, thanks largely to Christian missionaries, reached previously neglected regions. The trade-off for these benefits, however, was large as colonial policies also negatively affected the environment and many of the indigenous cultures. Some

---

[5]The material in this section is discussed fully in Toyin Falola, ed. *Africa, Vol. 4: The End of Colonial Rule: Nationalism and Decolonization* (Durham, NC: Carolina Academic Press, 2003).

African rulers who derived benefits from the increase in exports that accompanied colonialism advocated accommodation with the European powers, although other Africans united in opposition to colonial rule. This debate divided Africans, sometimes along ethnic lines, and for a time the industrial powers dismissed the rising anticolonial sentiments as simply the expressions of ethnic divisions.

Before 1939, most protests of colonial rule focused on the demand that African nationals be included in legislative councils. Christian missions played a role in the protest, as many students educated in mission schools secured Western skills that enabled them to challenge the colonizers on their own terms. Their anticolonial arguments often were couched in the language of equality before God and divine justice. World War II also contributed to rising nationalism as Africans were disgusted by the white supremacy doctrines of the Axis Powers and by the lack of gratitude given by the colonial governments to the 2 million African soldiers who were recruited to fight for the Allied powers. At the war's end, Britain and France were weakened in international clout, and the new world superpower, the United States, had no incentive to promote the continuation of European colonial regimes in Africa. Moreover, the Charter of the United Nations that was ratified by the world powers appealed to African anticolonials because it invoked the rhetoric of self-determinism and human rights. In 1945, African nationalists at a Pan-African Congress in Manchester issued a demand for independence.

The transfer of power from Europeans to Africans did not take place overnight, but change did come. In the 1950s, six African nations (Libya, Morocco, Tunisia, the Sudan, Ghana, and Guinea) joined Egypt, Liberia, and Ethiopia as independent nations. The trend continued as 31 more nations won their independence in the 1960s, 5 in the 1970s, Zimbabwe in the 1980s, and Namibia in the 1990s.

musicians, and keepers of sacred places, perform specialized religious functions for the benefit of the larger community. Sacrifices of fruit, grain, cows, goats, or other precious items are presented to the ancestors at their graves or to other spirits in order to remove guilt and to avert dangers that may threaten individuals or the entire community. Specialists able to communicate with the "living-dead" practice the art of divination. Knowledge received from dream interpretation and spirit-possession trances is commonly used to find the cause of misfortune and the proper course for remedying social wrongs. Many Africans also pray for protection and health to their guardian spirits or to other deities enshrined in their hut or village.

Rites of passage also are of great importance to many Africans. Almost all tribes perform birth ceremonies that involve the naming of the child and the offering of prayers and sacrifices to the ancestors. Youth are generally introduced into adulthood through initiation rites, which may include circumcision for boys and clitoridectomy for girls. One of the most festive rites of passage is the marriage ceremony. In most tribes, everyone is expected to get married, and failure to do so often is deemed an offense against the community. Because marriage and procreation are considered communal responsibilities, polygamy is generally accepted. Unlike the attitude expressed in some of the other great world religions, in traditional African religions celibacy is not recognized as a spiritual virtue. The final rite of passage is the rite of passage from this world to the world of the departed ancestors. Most tribes perform funeral rituals with great care in order not to offend the departed spirits. Some peoples bury foodstuffs and personal belongings with the dead to assist the departed during their journey to the spirit world. In many communities, a shrine for the departed is built that serves as a contact point for communication between the surviving and the living-dead.

SACRED OBSERVANCES AND PRACTICES

Traditional African religions are largely communal traditions that place community concerns over individualistic quests for enlightenment or salvation. Spiritually gifted or designated individuals within the community, including chiefs, elders, priests, shamans,

SOURCES

The following selections are drawn from the oral traditions of more than 30 African ethnic peoples. Before reading each selection, find on the map the location of each traditional African culture. What regional similarities do you find among these diverse religious traditions?

The tribes of Africa.

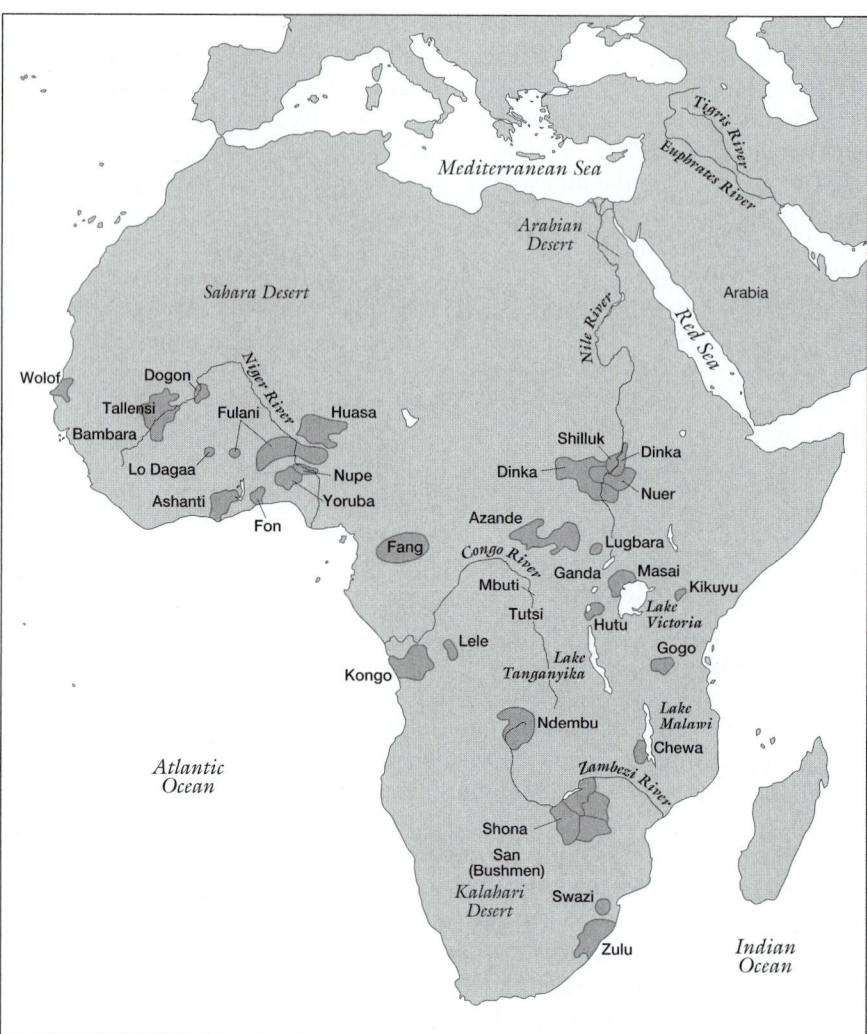

SECTION 1: Beginnings: God, Time, and the Universe

The theology of a people is often expressed in the hymns and prayers addressed to their deities. Here are two brief hymns from the Shona of Zimbabwe and the Pygmies of Zaire. Compare these expressions with other hymns to high deities included in this volume. What similarities and differences can you articulate?

THE GRANDEUR OF GOD, THE CREATOR[6]

This hymn is addressed to Mwari, God of the Shona of Zimbabwe. Mwari is the Creator of the Cosmos

_____
[6]Aylward Shorter, *Prayer in the Religious Traditions of Africa* (New York: Oxford University Press, 1975), p. 41–42.

and spirits of the deceased dwell with Him. Note how the imagery of the prayer describes the landscape of Zimbabwe.

Great Spirit,
Piler up of the rocks into towering mountains!
When thou stampest on the stone,
The dust rises and fills the land.
Hardness of the precipice;
Waters of the pool that turn
Into misty rain when stirred.
Vessel overflowing with oil!
Father of Runji,
Who seweth the heavens like cloth:
Let him knit together that which is below.
Caller forth of the branching trees:
Thou bringest forth the shoots
That they stand erect:
Thou hast filled the land with mankind,

The dust rises on high, Oh, Lord!
Wonderful One, thou livest
In the midst of the sheltering rocks.
Thou givest rain to mankind.
Hear us Lord!
Show mercy we beseech thee, Lord.
Thou art on high with the spirits of the great.
Thou raisest the grass-covered hills
About the earth, and createst the rivers,
Gracious One.

GOD, THE PAST THAT LIVES— A PYGMY HYMN (ZAIRE)[7]

In the beginning was God,
Today is God
Tomorrow will be God.
Who can make an image of God?
He has no body.
He is as a word which comes out of your mouth.
That word! It is no more,
It is past, and still it lives!
So is God.

The theology of a people also is expressed in their sacred stories. Among the most sacred stories of the LoDagaa of West Africa are the myths of the White Bagre and the Black Bagre. Longer than most African sacred stories, these stories are recited in a sacred room away from the ears of noninitiates. Both stories center on the relationship of three main characters: (1) the Younger and Elder brothers, who are the first men and ancestors of all now living; (2) the Chief God (Naangmin); and (3) the beings of the wild. The latter are dwarflike creatures of human likeness (fairies) that inhabit hills, rivers, and trees; eat wild fruits; and are like shepherds to the wild animals. As the beings that first showed humans how to cultivate land, cook food, make iron, and shoot with bow and arrow, they are the originators of human culture. They, however, also are deceiving and what they say cannot be trusted.

The storyline of the Bagre myths describes the adventures of the Younger brother who visits the beings of the wild and then, with the help of spider, climbs to heaven to meet with God himself. In heaven, God gives Younger a hoe and a child by "slender woman," who becomes pregnant after a snake shows her how to copulate. Younger returns to Earth to impart to the people the sacred knowledge of the Bagre.

Within this complex story are dialogues between the elders and the neophytes who are seeking initiation into the Bagre association. Selections from these dialogues are presented here. According to these selections, what is the theology of the LoDagaa peoples? Who and what is the nature of God?

The Nature of the High God According to the White Bagre[8]

A neophyte then asked, "Who brought Bagre?" They said, "The first people did." He asked again, "Who was that?" They said, "It was the younger brother." And he asked again, "What do they call god?" They said, "A god is here and God is there." The neophyte asked: "The one we follow in this matter, is it God we follow or is it a god?" He spoke and the elder said: "Well, we follow God. He is the senior but we can't see him. It is a god who comes down to people. That's what we call god." "Do the elders say that God's child is the one we follow?" He then said, "Yes, we follow him and so reach God." So he spoke and the neophyte asked again, "All these things, how can you know them all and be able to teach them?" They said they had performed the White Bagre up till today. . . .

Then another asked, "The beings of the wild and God, which of them brought Bagre?" They replied, "Well, God created them, put them on earth, and they sat there empty-handed. However, the younger one and his elder brother were living together when the younger one went and disappeared and they thought he was fooling. He came back and taught us all this. God created us but gave us nothing and when we were hungry, we had to find food to eat. However, the younger brother, he it was, who brought this matter and taught it to us. That is why we always say it's the ancestor's affair." So he spoke and when he'd finished, [the neophytes] said, "Now, does God know about Bagre?" They asked and he replied, "Yes. It was God who created us. Everything we say, he hears. Everything we do, he sees, because he created us and knows all about us. And God told us he would have come for all to see, but the reason was that if came here, he could not do his work. For if anyone's kinsman were about to die, he would ask, "Why does [God] kill [my] kinsman?" If someone's kinsman died, he would come and ask me to revive him. If someone was ill, they would come and

[7]*World Scripture: A Comparative Anthology of Sacred Texts* (New York: Paragon House, 1991), pp. 56–57.

[8]Jack Goody, *The Myth of the Bagre* (London: Oxford University Press, 1972), pp. 187, 197–198.

ask [me] to cure the sickness. If someone is struck by another, he will come and say, "Kill the man who struck me." That is why God doesn't want us to see him. He is near and yet far. That is why he said, "Well, he would send a person to come who is more powerful than us all." Our forefathers said that, about this person's matter, which we searched out in vain, the first men told it to our forefathers and they understood it. And we children, we have now seen it. If you're a member, the forefather's things you'll always hear them, you'll always know them. But if you're not, even if you're clever, you cannot get to know everything." They told the neophytes and they understood. You have heard the Bagre to the end. What is left? God's matter remains; the Black Bagre will come. In that they will explain these matters to you. Do you understand? That is Bagre knowledge and Bagre seeing and Bagre hearing and Bagre eating. He will eat. This is why we recite some and leave the rest. We say to the chicken-rearers and to the farmers, "Initiates, let's close the meeting."

Section 2: Humanity: The Problem of Good and Evil

Many sacred traditions have stories that explain the entrance of evil into the world. Listed in this section are several African accounts of this "loss of paradise." Note in each story who or what was to blame for the presence of evil. What do these stories tell us about traditional African attitudes toward the gods, toward each other, and toward human nature? Compare these to other sacred traditions' explanations of the emergence of evil.

The Loss of Paradise—A Dinka Account from the Sudan[9]

In the beginning God was very close to man, for the sky then lay just above the earth. There was no death, sickness, sorrow, or hunger, and men were content with one grain of millet a day granted them by God. One day, a greedy woman, who wanted to pound more than the one grain permitted, used a long-handled pestle and struck the sky. This angered God, who withdrew with the sky to its present position far above the earth. Since then the country has become spoiled, and men are now subject to death, sickness, hunger and disease.

The Price of Seeing God—A Sua Tale[10]

God had created the first human beings, two sons and one daughter. God stood on an intimate footing with his children, but without showing himself, and he had commanded them never to see him. If they did so, misfortunes would come upon them. They were then enjoying a pleasant existence. They did not need to work. God helped them with everything. All things came to them without effort on their part.

But the daughter had been entrusted with the task of placing wood in front of God's hut. One evening when she had put the pitcher of water outside the hut, she was overcome with curiosity to see her father. She hid behind a post and was able to see his arm, adorned with heavy brass rings, as he stretched it out to take the pitcher. Then God discovered her. He summoned the people, reproached them, and said that they must hereafter live alone. He himself would withdraw. But he taught them the art of forging weapons and tools and all they needed to be able to make their own way. The woman was to be the servant of the man. She was to give birth to her children with pain and carry out all the heavy work. Thus God left them. At the same time they also lost happiness and peace, and they had to work in order to live.

Death, with which they had hitherto been unacquainted, was also sent to them as a punishment. The woman's first-born child was given the name *Kukua kende*, "Death comes." The child died two days after birth. Since then no man escapes death, the avenger. Thus death came into the world.

A Woman's Bargain with Death—A Hutu Account from Rwanda and Burundi[11]

In the olden days, when Imana (God) still lived among men, Death did not live among men. Whenever he happened to stray onto the earth, God would chase it away with his hunting dogs. One day during such a chase Death was forced into a narrow space, and would have been caught and destroyed. But in his straits he found a woman, and promised her that if she would hide him he would spare her and her family. The woman opened her mouth and Death jumped inside. When God came to her and asked her if she

---

[9] *World Scripture: A Comparative Anthology of Sacred Texts* (New York: Paragon House, 1991), p. 107.

[10] Susan Feldmann, ed. *African Myths and Tales* (New York: Dell, 1963), p. 116.

[11] *World Scripture*, p. 107.

had seen Death, she denied ever seeing him. But God, the All-seeing One, knew what happened, and told the woman that since she had hidden Death, in the future Death would destroy her and all her children. From that moment death spread all over the world.

THE ORIGINS OF EVIL—A NGOMBE ACCOUNT[12]

In the beginning there were no men on earth. The people lived in the sky with Akongo and they were happy. But there was a woman named Mbokomu who bothered everybody.

One day Akongo put the woman in a basket with her son and her daughter, some cassava, maize, and sugarcane and lowered the basket down to the earth.

The family planted a garden on earth and the garden flourished thorough their care.

One day the mother said to her son: "When we die there will be no one left to tend the garden,"

"That can't be helped," the son replied.

"You must have children," the mother said.

"How?" asked the son. "We are the only people here. Where shall I find a wife?"

"Your sister is a woman," his mother replied. "Take her and have children by her." But the son recoiled from his mother's suggestion. The mother insisted, however. "That, or die childless, with nobody to continue our work. You can only get children by your sister so go and take her."

In the end the son gave in and went to his sister. The sister yielded to him quite willingly and became pregnant.

One day the sister met a creature who looked like a man except that he was completely covered by hair. She was afraid but the creature spoke so kindly to her that after a while they became friends. One day the sister took her husband's razor and went out to look for the hairy man. When she found him she made him lie down and shaved him. Now he looked like a man. His name was Ebenga meaning the beginner.

Ebenga bewitched the woman, so that when her child was born it brought witchcraft into the world. The child grew up under the spell of Ebenga. He practiced witchcraft and brought evil and sorrow to men.

In the course of time the brother and sister had other children. So the earth was peopled. But evil and witchcraft continued to the present.

---

[12]Feldmann, *African Myths and Tales* pp. 38–39.

SECTION 3: Sacred Stories: Divine Messengers, Prophets, and Priests

Among the known 250,000 African traditional tales are thousands of stories that invoke the infamous trickster theme. In Africa, Trickster inevitably is an animal of inferior size and superior cunning who uses his wits to overcome those with greater natural strength. Trickster is not an exemplary moral character, for notwithstanding his cunningness he also at times is totally selfish and ruthless. In comparison with Native American tricksters, the hero-culprit in African tales has less interest in sexual exploitations, although he is equally lustful toward food and sometimes pulls nasty pranks simply to embarrass his victims. In Western Africa, the trickster commonly is portrayed as Anansi the Spider; in the East he is the hare; while among the Yoruba, Edo, and Ibo of Nigeria, he is often Tortoise.

Here are several trickster stories. Note in each the relative size of the victim versus the trickster. Why do you think these stories were among the most popular tales in the African oral traditions?

THE TORTOISE AND THE ELEPHANT— A YORUBA STORY[13]

My *alo* [story] is about Tortoise and the elephant.

The bald-headed elf one day told the other animals that he would ride the elephant, but all the animals said: "No, you can't ride the elephant."

The bald-headed elf said: "Well, I will make a wager that I will ride the elephant into town." And the other animals agreed to the wager.

Tortoise went into the forest and met the elephant. He said to him: "My father, all the animals say you are too stout and big to come to town."

The elephant was vexed. He said: "The animals are fools. If I do not come to town it is because I prefer the forest. Besides, I do not know the way to town."

"Oh!" said the bald-headed elf, "Then come with me. I will show you the way to the town, and you can put all the animals to shame."

So the elephant followed him.

---

[13]A. B. Ellis, *Yorba-Speaking Peoples of the Slave Coast of West Africa: Their Religion, Manners, Customs, Laws, Language, Etc.* (1894). Reprint: Chicago: Benin Press, 1964. Also available from an Internet source.

When they were near the town the bald-headed elf said: "My father, I am tired. Will you kindly allow me to get, on your back."

"All right," said the elephant. He knelt down, and Tortoise climbed up on his back. Then they went on along the road.

The bald-headed elf said: "My father, when I scratch your back you must run, and when I knock my head against your back you must run faster; then you will make a fine display in the town." The elephant said: "Very well."

When they came near the town, the bald-headed elf scratched the elephant's back, and he began to run. He knocked his back with his head, and the elephant ran faster.

The animals, when they saw this, were frightened. They went into their houses, but they looked out of their windows. And Tortoise called out to them: "Did I not say I would ride my father's slave to town?"

"What do you mean by 'your father's slave'?" said the elephant, growing angry.

"I am only praising you," said Tortoise.

But the elephant saw the other animals laughing, and grew more angry. "I will throw you down on the hard stones here, and break you to pieces," he cried.

"Yes, yes, that is right," said the bald-headed elf.

"Throw me down here. That will be all right. Then I shall not die; then I shall not be hurt. If you really want to kill me, you ought to carry me to a swamp. There I shall die at once, for the mud and water will drown me."

The elephant believed the bald-headed elf. He ran to the swamp, and threw Tortoise into the mud.

Then he stretched out his foot to kick him, but the bald-headed elf dived in the mire, and came up in another place.

The other animals were there, looking on, and Tortoise called out to them, "Did I not say I would ride my father's slave to town?"

When the elephant found that he could not catch the bald-headed elf, he ran away at full speed back to the forest.

When he reached there he said to the other elephants, "Do you know what that broken-back has done to me?" And he told them the story.

The other elephants said, "You were a fool to carry that broken-back to town."

Since then the elephant has not come to town any more.

SPIDER PAYS HIS DEBT—A HAUSA STORY[14]

The Spider had contracted a number of debts, he had borrowed from every Beast of the forest, and he too counseled with himself as to what he should do, for he had no money with which to pay. When Friday had come, while it was still early in the morning, the Hen arrived to collect her debt. And when she had come the Spider said, "Good, I will pay you at once, but wait a minute or two while I prepare you some food." So the Hen was waiting inside the hut, and soon the Wildcat came. Then the Spider said, "Good, the repayment is in the hut, go and take it." So the Wildcat went and entered the hut, and seized the Hen, and twisted her neck.

Just as he was about to go off, the Dog arrived, and the Spider said, "Good, the repayment is in the hut, go and take it." So the Dog went and seized the Wildcat, and bit him, and killed him. Just as he was about to go, the Hyena arrived, and the Spider said, "Good, the repayment is in the hut, go and take it." So the Hyena ran in and seized the Dog and ate him up. Just as she was about to leave, lo! The Leopard appeared, and the Spider said, "Good, the repayment is in the hut, go and take it." So the Leopard sprang upon the Hyena, and killed her. Just as she was about to leave who should arrive but the Lion, and he came upon the Leopard.

So they began to fight, and while they were fighting and fighting, the Spider took some pepper and poured it into their eyes. When he had done this, he took up a big stick and began to beat them, and he beat them until they were dead, both of them. Then the Spider collected the meat in his house, and said that he had extinguished his debts.

THE FROG BLOWS THE TRUMPET—AN ALUR TALE FROM THE CONGO[15]

In ancient times there was a king who had two sons, the Frog and the Lizard. One day the king fell ill with a fatal disease, and he realized that he had not long to live. The king decided to name his successor. He sent word to his sons that the one who was the first to arrive at his court would become king after him. When

---

[14]Feldmann, *African Myths and Tales,* pp. 139–140.

[15]Jan Knappert, *Myths and Legends of the Congo* (Nairobi: Heinemann Educational Books, 1971), p. 10–11.

they heard this message, the two princes at once ground corn for the journey and set out on their way—the Frog from the water in which he lived, the Lizard from the rock on which he basked.

The Lizard was the first to start. He did not wait to start at the same time as the Frog, to see who could run the fastest. He thought, "I am better than that fat Frog. He is terribly ugly, and what's worse, he travels on his anus."

The Frog perceived what the Lizard thought, and saw that he had started ahead of him. He took a *yatko*, which is the branch of a certain tree known only to professional rain-makers. He pounded it into powder and strewed it in the water. At once black clouds appeared on the horizon and obscured the sun. A fierce wind began to blow, shaking the trees. Soon the first drops of rain dug holes in the dust, then a cascade of water tumbled down. The Frog was content. He traveled briskly in this nice wet weather: jump, jump, jump.

The Lizard had, up till then, been far ahead, racing along. Suddenly he felt cold: the sun disappeared, clouds collected. The Lizard looked for a place to shelter, for he did not like the rain. He found a hole in a tree and hid in it. There he waited for the rain to stop.

At last, the Frog arrived at the king's court. He told his heralds to blow their trumpets. The guardsmen at the king's gate ran to the king and announced: "His Highness the Frog has arrived. We have heard his trumpeters!" The king ordered all his men to be assembled in the hall. When the Frog entered, the king made it known that the Frog would inherit the kingdom and all that was in it.

When the sun began to shine again, the Lizard emerged from under the tree and finally arrived at court. He came just in time to hear the Frog's trumpeters announce that he would become king. The Frog said to the Lizard: "You have a skin of beautiful colors, but I have won."

Whenever frogs begin to croak, people say: "The frogs blow the trumpets of royal dignity. It will soon begin to rain."

SECTION 4: Divine Law: Justice, Reward, and Punishment

Sacred expectations can be conveyed directly through specific divine instructions like the Ten Commandments in the West and the *Law of Manu* in the East. The ethical standards of a tradition also can be presented through other forms of oral communication.

The selections in this section include a set of traditional African proverbs from the peoples of Nigeria and Ghana, some poems from Angola and Nigeria, and a popular Ashanti folktale. Identify the central message of each proverb, poem, and folktale. To what degree are the ethical standards reflected in these oral sources common to traditions outside the African continent? Which of these messages do you consider to be unique to traditional African spiritual understandings?

TRADITIONAL AFRICAN PROVERBS[16]

Igala Proverbs (Nigeria)

Where you did not sow, do not reap.
Black goats must be caught early, before it is dark.

Kanufi Proverb (Nigeria)

A noisy bird builds a bad nest.

Yoruba Proverbs (Nigeria)

Ashes fly back in the face of him who throws them.

The snail has no hands,
The snail has no feet,
Gently the snail climbs the tree.

One upon whom We bestow kindness
But will not express gratitude,
Is worse than a robber
Who carries away our belongings.

Weeping is not the answer to poverty; a lazy man who is hungry has no one to blame but himself. He who wishes to eat the honey which is under the rock should not be unduly worried about the edge of the axe. There is no place where one cannot achieve greatness; only the lazy prospers nowhere. There is no place that does not suit me, O divinity!

Igbo Proverb (Nigeria)

Where you fall, there your God pushed you down.

Buji Proverb (Nigeria)

Before you climb a tree you must start at the bottom.

Idoma Proverb (Nigeria)

The fly cannot be driven away by getting angry at it.

---

[16]*World Scripture.* The corresponding page number for each of these proverbs is as follows: 114, 513, 152, 123, 529, 556, 174, 495, 525, 655, 144, 173, 187, 654, and 198.

Akan Proverbs (Ghana)

You may not see yourself growing up, but you definitely know it when you are sinning.

If your parents take care of you up to the time you cut your teeth, you take care of them when they lose theirs.

It is because one antelope will blow the dust from the other's eye that two antelopes walk together.

However hungry you are, you do not eat with both hands.

If God gives you a cup of wine and an evil-minded person kicks it over, He fills it up for you again.

The following are traditional songs and poetry from Angola and Nigeria. What do these selections tell us about traditional attitudes regarding divine justice?

Ovambo Proverb (Angola)[17]

God is not hornless;
He is horned:
He exacts punishment for every deed.

Yoruba Song (Nigeria)[18]

God did not make the honey bee
As big as the horse.
Had he made it so big, the bee would be stinging people to
    death.
God does not elevate
People who would ridicule the unfortunate.
God does not give power
To those who would be wicked to their fellow-men.
No one gains anything through being wicked.
When the wicked are prosperous,
And the righteous are not,
If the situation continues for long
The righteous become frustrated.
Like a small needle,
That is how one first starts the act of falsehood.
The day it becomes as big as a hoe,
It kills.

An Ibo Prayer: Let Others Be Done By as They Did (Nigeria)[19]

God who created man!
My life, the lives of my relatives,
Whoever wishes me to live,
Let him live also.

Whoever wishes me to die,
Let him die.
Whoever wishes that I should have good things,
Let him have them.
Whoever says that I should not eat,
Let his mouth dry up.

IF SOMEONE DOES GOOD TO YOU, YOU SHOULD DO GOOD IN RETURN— AN ASHANTI FOLKTALE[20]

It is said that once there was a female eagle and that in her wandering she came upon a certain old woman who had a sore on her leg. And the eagle said, "Gracious me! That is an unusual kind of sore. With a sore like that, however hard you try, are you able to walk?"

The old woman said, "Oh, just a very little."

The eagle said, "You people! Nowadays, if I were to do something good for you today, tomorrow you would do something bad to thank me."

The old woman said, "Oh! I would not do that."

The eagle said, "If you will not behave like that, I will help you." After a pause the eagle commanded: "Shut your eyes, and then open them."

And the old woman shut her eyes and opened them.

The eagle then said, "Look at your sore."

And the old woman stooped to look—not a trace of it remained. Then the eagle made her close her eyes again; she opened them, and she saw that all the forest had been cleared.

The eagle said, "Close your eyes again."

The old woman closed them and then opened them, and she saw that houses were firmly built there. And the eagle made her close her eyes again. She opened them to see a town of large size. There it was—huge!

The eagle said, Old woman, it's yours."

The old woman said, "Thanks, thanks! I give you thanks! What must I give to thank you?"

The eagle said, "I do not want even a trifling thing. As for me, all that I desire is that silk-cotton tree that stands there."

The old woman said, "This thing you ask me for— it is nothing—take it."

---

[17]*World Scripture*, p. 125.

[18]*World Scripture*, p. 768.

[19]Shorter, *Prayer*, p. 106.

[20]Paul Radin, ed., *African Folktales* (New York: Princeton University Press, 1970), pp. 218–220.

Then the eagle flew off, alighted on the tree, and wove a nest and laid two eggs which she deposited in it. And she hatched the two eggs, and went off to seek for something for her children to eat.

Then the old woman's grandchild, who lived with her, began to whimper, "Ehe! Ehe!"

The old woman said, "What's the matter?"

The child said, "Let me chew an eagle's child."

The old woman said, "Where am I to get an eagle's child?"

. . . The child said, "Let me chew an eagle's child, for if I don't have one to chew I shall die."

The old woman said, "Ah! Must this my grandchild die for want of an eagle's child to chew? Go, take axes, and strike the cotton-wood tree and bring me the eagle's children.". . .

[Soon the tree was chopped down, and one of the baby eagles flew away, but the other was given to the woman's grandchild to eat.]

Not long afterward, the eagle came. When she reached the tree which they had felled, she saw one of her children sitting there. She asked it what had happened, and it told her the news. The eagle set off for the old woman's village. When she arrived there, the old woman's grandchild was eating one of her children. She said, "Old woman, I congratulate you." Then she came out from the old woman's house and commenced her magic at the outskirts of the town. She said "Sanguri!" and every person disappeared; and again she said "Sanguri!" and every house broke up at once and not a dwelling remained. "Sanguri!"—the village once again became the forest. "Sanguri!" and the old woman's sore came back. And the eagle said, "Old woman, you have seen." That is why the elders say, "If someone does good to you, thank him by doing good to him and do not return evil to thank him."

SECTION 5: Gender: Women and Men in Society

Oral traditions often express conscious or unconscious attitudes toward women. Below are three traditional African tales. The first is from the Black Bagre Myth of West Africa; the second is a cultural hero story of the Makere from the Congo; and the third is an Efik-Ibibio folktale. What insights about the status of women in society can be gleaned from these tales?

ROLE OF GENDER IN THE BLACK BAGRE[21]

[Farming] is a great boon that God gave us. Do you see that which we feed to our children and to the women too? We feed them; it's with the hope of the hoe that you feed people. And they asked, "Why is it that a girl cannot farm?" Do you know the reason why it is so, that women cannot farm?" The little old woman asked them to wait a while and keep quiet. Then she said, "This is the reason why a woman cannot hoe. She is the one who cooks. She is the one who sweeps. She is the lighter of fires. She is the fetcher of water. She is a member of another person's house. That's the reason we do not let you girls do any hoeing." The young man asked us again, "How is it that girls belong to another person's house?" And the old woman laughed softly and then said, "A young woman is unable to stay in your house," "Why is it she can't stay in your house?" "She's not a man. She gives birth and brings increase to the house; when she has given birth, for two years afterwards she sits in a room and suffers. When she finished speaking the young man laughed softly, and when he'd done so, he started off home. The great man went to his house and the little old woman took the path home and went on her way. . . .

It happened that Deri went hunting; he went to the woods and returning home, asked for water. But when he did so, he didn't get it from his wife. Anger took hold of him, so he didn't know what to do. Taking out an arrow, he shot himself and died. We saw this and we said a brave man had died. We got up and started to play with his arrow. Look at the dead now upon us. If the youth had been a man and had gone to play with a woman, he wouldn't have gone and played with arrow matters. This death that killed our children, we call it God's death." The [younger] one then said it wasn't God's death that troubled us. "What trouble comes among us?" "It is that shooting yourself with an arrow or cutting yourself with a knife, a person, who is a real man and has sense, will be much afraid of such a death. If anger seizes you and you're a real man, you go out and take your axe, and your bow, and your knife, and your arrow, and wear a quiver, and go into the woods taking your anger with you." "And what sort of thing will you do

---

[21]Goody, *The Myth of the Bagre*, pp. 263–264.

there?" "A male animal when you meet one, kill it, cut off the head and hurry home to your father's house. Then they'll know that you are indeed a real man."

THE SLAVE-GIRLS OF THE SPIRITS— A MAKERE STORY[22]

A young man called Madiango asked his father to buy him a wife, but the father said: "Are you out of your mind? Did you ever buy a wife for me? Go and find your own wives?" So the son left his father's home in pursuit of brides. He traveled through the bush until suddenly he arrived at a large compound. He could not know that he had hit upon the place where the spirits kept the women they had captured from the villages of men.

As all the women were at the riverside fishing that day, young Madiango entered through the gates unseen. He hid behind a banana tree, but he was discovered there by two slave-girls who were sweeping the compound. They stalked up to him from behind and overpowered him, until he promised them he would not try to escape. They took him to their hut, and there they made love to him.

When the other women came back and found out that the slave-girls had captured a man to make love with, they all wanted their share of him, and he had to make the round of the whole compound, which was inhabited by hundreds of women, all prisoners of the spirits.

The spirits were male but invisible, and very wicked. They wanted the women to cook great quantities of food to assuage their insatiable appetites, rather than to serve them as female companions. Each of the women, the morning after she had spent the night with Madiango, described the pleasures she had enjoyed to her best friend, who would of course claim him for the following night, and so on, until he had slept with every woman, old or young, black or white.

Then one ominous day one of the spirits arrived and challenged him to a fight. Immediately, it grasped him and threw him high up in the air, but Madiango landed on his feet, like a wild cat; Then it was his turn to seize the spirit. He took it by its belt, dragged it to the river and held it under water, until it had flown away. He later did the same with all the other spirits,

as soon as they appeared, until the women told him that every spirit had been drowned and carried away by the river. The women rejoiced and praised Madiango as a great hero, as the Conqueror of Evil Spirits.

When he had rest, Madiango had the drum beaten and announced that all the men who had been robbed of their wives by the spirits could come and fetch them back. He made each of them pay a cow to redeem his wife, which they all did without hesitation in recognition of his heroic battles. Madiango was left with forty wives and four hundred cows. He was a rich man now, and a famous chief.

THE FAT WOMAN WHO MELTED AWAY[23]

There was once a very fat woman who was made of oil. She was very beautiful and many young men applied to her parents for permission to marry her and offered a dowry; but the mother always refused. She said it was impossible for her daughter to work on a farm as she would melt in the sun. At last a stranger from a far-distant country fell in love with the fat woman, and he promised, if her mother would give her to him, that he would keep her in the shade. At last the mother agreed, and he took his wife away.

When he arrived at his house, his other wife immediately became very jealous because when there was work to be done, firewood to be collected, or water to be carried, the fat woman stayed at home and never helped, as she was frightened of the heat.

One day when the husband was absent, the jealous wife abused the fat woman so much that she finally agreed to go and work on the farm, although her little sister, whom she had brought from home with her, implored her not to go, reminding her that their mother had always told them, ever since they were born, that she would melt away if she went into the sun.

All the way to the farm the fat woman managed to keep in the shade. When they arrived at the farm the sun was very hot, so the fat woman remained in the shade of a big tree. As soon as the jealous wife saw this, she began to abuse her and asked her why she did not do her share of the work. At last she could stand the nagging no longer, and, although her little sister tried very hard to prevent her, the fat woman went

---

[22]Knappert, *Myths and Legends*, pp. 148–149.

[23]Radin, *African Folktales*, pp. 160–161.

out into the sun to work and immediately she began to melt away. Very soon there was nothing left of her but one big toe which had been covered by a leaf. This her little sister observed and, with tears in her eyes, she picked up the toe which was all that remained of the fat woman, and, having covered it carefully with leaves, she placed it in the bottom of her basket. As soon as she arrived at the house, the little sister placed the toe in an earthen pot, filled it with water, and covered the top up with clay.

When the husband returned, he said, "Where is my fat wife?" and the little sister, crying bitterly, told him that the jealous woman had made her go out into the sun and that she had melted away. She then showed him the pot with the remains of her sister and told him that her sister would come to life again in three months' time quite complete in body, but that he must send away the jealous wife, so that there should be no more trouble. If he refused to do this, the little girl said she would take the pot back to their mother, and when her sister became complete again, they would remain at home.

The husband then took the jealous wife back to her parents who sold her as a slave and paid the dowry back to the husband, so that he would get another wife. When he received the money, the husband took it home and kept it until the three months had elapsed. Then the little sister opened the pot and the fat woman emerged, quite as fat and beautiful as she had been before. The husband was so delighted that he gave a feast to all his friends and neighbors and told them the whole story of the bad behavior of his jealous wife.

Ever since that time, whenever a wife behaves very badly, the husband returns her to her parents, who sell the woman as a slave. Out of the proceeds of the sale they give the husband the amount of dowry which he paid when he married the girl.

From the insights gained in this story, how do you explain the following Yoruba poem?

YORUBA POEM (NIGERIA)[24]

Whoever has many wives will have troubles in surfeit.
He will be deceitful, he will lie, he will betray [some of them] to have them together;
It is not certain that he can have peace to pray well.

---

[24]*World Scripture*, p. 179.

SECTION 6: Daily Living: Health, Etiquette, and Holy Days

For many African peoples, to live is to transmit life. Without children, one is not considered to be fully alive. This concern for procreation is central to each of the following prayers. The first is a plea for children addressed to Imana, the Supreme God for the Hutu and Tutsi peoples.

DESPERATE PLEA FOR OFFSPRING[25]

O Imana of Urundi,
If only you would help me!
O Imana of pity,
Imana of my father's house,
If only you would help me!
O Imana of the country of the Hutu and Tutsi,
If only you would help me just this once!
O Imana, if only you would give me
A homestead and children!
I prostrate myself before you,
Imana of Urundi.
I cry to you: Give me offspring,
Give me as you give to others!
Imana, what shall I do, where shall I go?
I am in distress,
Where is there room for me?
O merciful, O Imana of mercy,
Help this once.

This same theme is expressed in the following blessing and prayer. Among the Meru of Kenya, the Mugwe is a prophet and lawmaker who controls initiation rites and warfare. The first Mugwe blessing is addressed to God on the mountain of brightness (Kirinyaga). The second is a prayer offered as a sacrifice to the God Murungu. Both express a plea to be able to transmit life.

FORMULA OF BLESSING[26]

Kirinyaga, owner of all things,
I pray thee, give me what I need,
Because I am suffering,
And also my children [are suffering]
And all things that are in this country of mine.
I beg thee for life,
The good one with things,

---

[25]Shorter, *Prayer*, p. 135.
[26]Shorter, *Prayer*, pp. 45, 53.

Healthy people with no disease,
May they bear healthy children.
And also to women who suffer because they are barren,
Open the way by which they may see children.
[Give] goats, cattle, food, honey.
And also the troubles of the other lands
That I do not know, remove.

MAY WE BEAR CHILDREN AND CATTLE

Murungu, we pray, help us,
That we may live, have strength,
May we bear children and cattle,
They too say:
Help our children.

The following selection is from an Igbo (Nigeria) Naming Ceremony.[27] What do the words to this rite tell us about child-raising practices among the Igbo?

Brethren, a new child is born,
While in the uterus it was the woman's thing;
Safely delivered, it is everybody's child, a native of Nibo, a
 Nigerian.
He shall grow under the care of his parents;
When mature he will look after his parents.
He shall listen to the good advice of his parents,
He ought not to obey wrong things.
We want truly good children, not any thing at all;
He will grow up industrious, imitating father, mother, and
 other relations.
No evil child!
Instead of a thief, may it pass away through miscarriage.
The name of the baby is "Chineney."

Along with the petitions for fertility, prayers for health and healing are abundant among traditional African religions.

DRIVE AWAY THE BLACK GOD[28]

Among the Luyia of Kenya, besides the Creator God Wele, there also is a personal source of evil, Wele Gumali or Black God. In this prayer, Wele is asked to drive away the black god from the sick victim.

Wele, you who made us walk in your country,
You who made the cattle and the things which are in it,
You may spit the medicine on your person,
He may recover and walk well,
He may plant his gardens,

Drive away the black god,
He may leave your person,
He may move into the snake
And into the abandoned homestead;
He may leave our house.

This Lugura (Tanzania) prayer for healing is addressed to both God and the ancestral spirits. Note how the petitioners are concerned with the cause of the illness. The prayer is concluded by spitting water in the four cardinal directions.

HELP US THROUGH THESE ROOTS[29]

You, Father God,
Who are in the heavens and below;
Creator of everything, and omniscient
[Of] how the earth and heaven [were made].
We are but little children
Unknowing anything evil;
If this sickness has been brought by man,
We beseech thee, help us through these roots!
In case it is inflicted by you, the Conserver,
Likewise do we entreat your mercy on your child;
Also you, our grandparents who sleep in [the dwelling place
 of the departed],
We entreat all of you, sleep on one side.
All ancestors, male and females, great and small,
Help us in this trouble, have compassion on us;
So that we can also sleep peacefully,
And hither do I spit out this mouthful of water!
Pu-pu! Pu-pu!
Please listen to our earnest request!

SECTION 7: The Human Quest: Paths to Salvation and Enlightenment

Salvation carries multiple meanings. In Western traditions, salvation often refers to overcoming sin and death. In the East, it often involves discovering the unity of all things. Among indigenous Africans, the plea to be saved is a common motif in the oral traditions, but, as in other world cultures, this hope means different things to different people. To some, the goal is to be saved from death. For others, it is the desire to be freed from evil spirits, from sorceries, from famine, and from the shame of barrenness. The first selection is a Ngbandi story from the Congo that explains the victory of the Soul over Death.

---

[27] *World Scripture*, p. 170.
[28] Shorter, *Prayer*, pp. 65–66.
[29] Shorter, *Prayer*, pp. 63–64.

THE WAR BETWEEN DEATH AND THE SOUL[30]

Death and the Soul were enemies.

Death said: "I will kill you."

The soul said: "I will not be killed."

Death collected his helpers: Lightening, Ulcers, Syphilis, Smallpox, Leprosy and Yaws.

The soul collected his helpers: Bat, Ant-eater, Owl, and Hog.

The soul and his helpers arrived in Death's village for a visit. Soul sent Bat out first to go and spy. Bat went hunting and hung in Death's hut, in a corner of the roof, and no one noticed him. Death was just saying to his soldiers: "I will raise a cloud in the sky; from it you, Lightening, will jump down on to my house, which I will give to Soul, and you will destroy it and everything in it." The soldiers of Death agreed, and dispersed.

Soul arrived in the village and was received with honor. Death vacated his own house to make sure that his guest would have every comfort. But Bat kept an eye on the sky, and suddenly he saw a cloud approaching. He shouted: "We must go now! Run!"

Soul departed hastily, with his soldiers. They had not gone far when Lightening struck Death's house and destroyed it totally.

Death exulted: "I have killed the soul!" He assembled his soldiers and had the drums beaten. "Ha! He said that he could not be killed."

At that moment they heard the drums of triumph being beaten in the village of the Soul. Death at once went out with his army, but Soul had ordered Hog and Ant-eater to dig deep pits and trenches on the way. Death and his party all fell into the pits and gave up the attack.

Since that day the Soul has been immortal.

Some tribes view life and death in fatalistic ways. What is the message of this Igbo song from Nigeria?

AN IGBO SONG[31]

We are on a market trip on earth;
Whether we fill our baskets or not,
Once the time is up, we go home.

The motif of standing before a Creator judge at the end of life is found in the oral stories of some African traditions. The following is a prayer of the Ewe of Ghana. The prayer is addressed to Mawu, the Creator who judges souls after death and then sends them back for reincarnation in accordance with their deeds done in life.

YOU WILL PASS BEFORE A SEARCHING JUDGE[32]

Life is like a hill.
Mawu, the Creator, made it sharp and slippery.
To right and to left deep waters surround it.
You cannot turn back once you start to climb.
You must climb with a load on your head,
A man's arm will not help him, for it is a trial. . . .
At the gates of the land of the dead
You will pass before a searching judge,
His justice is true and he will examine your feet,
He will know how to find every stain
Whether visible or hidden under the skin.
If you have fallen on the way he will know.
If the judge finds no stains on your feet,
Open your belly to joy, for you have overcome
And your belly is clean. . . .
Sickness is the abuse of your well-being;
You will be reminded at the gates of death,
The judge will examine your feet
And you will be punished.

The Shilluk of Sudan offer prayers and sacrifices both to God and Nyikang, their hero ancestor.

WE ARE IN YOUR HANDS[33]

We praise you, you who are God.
Protect us, we are in your hands,
And protect us, save me.
You and Nyikang, you are the ones who created.
People are in your hands
And it is you, Nyikang,
Who are accustomed to assist God to save,
And it is you who give the rain.
The sun is yours, and the river is yours,
You who are Nyikang,
You came from under the sun,
You and your father;
You two saved the earth,
And your son Dok,
You subdued all the peoples.
The cow is here for you,
And the blood will go to God and you . . .

---

[30]Knappert, *Myths and Legends*, pp. 164–165.

[31]*World Scripture*, p. 238.

[32]Shorter, *Prayer*, pp. 102–103.

[33]Shorter, *Prayer*, p. 105.

The South African Bushmen often pray to the heavenly bodies, especially to the moon, which is said to have been created by the Sky God out of his shoe. The monthly moon cycles provide the Bushman assurances of life and rebirth after death. This is a poignant prayer for the continuation of life after the pattern of the waxing and waning moon.

PRAYER TO THE MOON FOR IMMORTALITY[34]

Take my face and give me yours!
Take my face, my unhappy face.
Give me your face,
With which you return
When you have died,
When you vanished from sight.
You lie down and return—
Let me resemble you, because you have joy,
You return ever more alive,
After you vanish from sight.
Did you not promise me once
That we too should return
And be happy again after death?

SECTION 8: The Religious Life: Worship and Righteousness

A primary concern of traditional African religion is to find ways to combat the problems inflicted by witchcraft. The following selections from the Baluba and the Bakongo of the Congo sample the great volume of sacred stories that dwell on this endemic problem. What traditional African religious attitudes and customs are described in these accounts? Do you think these stories of witchcraft also serve as social control devices designed to encourage certain culturally appropriate standards of behavior?

THE WOMAN WHO ESCAPED THE WITCHES[35]

A woman was beaten by her husband. She was aggrieved, feeling humiliated and rebellious. She ran away in the middle of the night. Suddenly, at the crossroads, she heard voices but she saw nothing.

One voice said: "Take that foot, pull it this way, so that I can cut it off. Make your light shine more strongly so that I can see."

There was no light visible, but the woman knew that those were the voices of witches who were busy cutting up a human being.

Suddenly one of the voices said: "I smell a live human, where is it?" When the woman heard this, she closed her armpits by drawing her upper arms closer to her body, trying to put the witches off the scent. She withdrew quickly, and returned to her husband, to whom she told everything. He said:

"It was the powerful *buanga* [magic horn] I gave you that protected you from the evil power of those witches. It made you invisible for them; but you should never have gone to the crossroads in the middle of the night, for you know that the witches are active then. And you should never have quarreled with me, for that gave them some power over you so that they could at least smell you. Next time you run away from me, you may not be so fortunate. You may get caught in their invisible nets.

A MALE WITCH—A BAKONGO STORY[36]

A girl named Malemba had a suitor who was . . . a male member of a witches' coven and communicated with evil spirits. His girl-friend knew nothing of this.

One day the coven prepared a meal of human meat while the young man was away on a journey. After the meal there was only one human finger left and the coven decided that this would have to be sufficient for him. So they put it in a basket, added some bananas by way of garnish, and placed this in his hut on a shelf.

As it happened, that same day Malemba decided to go and visit her lover. She cooked some meat and vegetables for him and packed them nicely in a basket. When she arrived in his village, darkness had just fallen, so that she could slip into his hut without anyone seeing her. When she found that he was not at home she decided to wait for him, and sat down patiently on his bed without preparing a light to see by. Shortly after, her lover arrived and entered his hut without noticing her. . . . He did notice, however, the basket of food which the coven members had placed on his shelf. He took it down and opened

[34]Shorter, *Prayer*, p. 116.
[35]Knappert, *Myths & Legends*, p. 207.
[36]Knappert, *Myths & Legends*, pp. 64–66.

it. He found the bananas and ate them. Then he found the one finger and burst out loudly: "Those misers! They left only a finger for me! All right, when I kill my girl-friend Malemba, they will have nothing but one of her fingers!"

[When the lover lit a torch, he saw Malemba and asked]

"Malemba! Did you hear what I said?"

She said, "No! Not a word! I swear!" He took his fetish and made her swear on this sacred object. She did and, on his insistence, afterwards licked it, so that its substance would kill her if she lied. Yet her suitor still did not believe her, so he decided it would be better to eat her at once.

[When he went to assemble his fellows, she escaped, trying to outrun black magic, but they pursued her.]

They took a fetish from its pole in the village, and ordered it to find the direction the girl had taken. The fetish turned towards the mountains but found no trail, then towards the valley and there it smelled the girl. The spirit hidden in the statue was called Ngodo-mvindi. As soon as it smelled its prey, the wooden body of the spirit began to tremble and the men followed it along the path.

Before she had reached her village, the girl, Malemba, heard the voices of the men shouting behind her, so she decided to turn left towards her mother's garden. There she hid under a pile of weeds and rubble. As soon as the fetish reached that path it stopped and turned in the direction where the girl had fled. Suddenly an antelope leapt up from the fields and started running across the gardens, jumping over fences and shrubs. The fetish-spirit was misled, and followed the antelope, and so did the men. Perhaps the antelope was a good spirit who wished to help the girl. Who knows? It took the wicked men hours to pursue the running antelope in the darkness. . . . [At sunrise] the coven . . . made hastily for their own village. There they put the fetish back on its pole and sneaked into their huts, just before the ordinary people of the village began to stir.

The girl, Malemba, lay there under the weeds her mother had gathered in a heap. Before noon her mother arrived in her garden to gather some groundnuts. There she found her daughter more dead than alive, lying gasping as if she were seriously ill. "Oh, my daughter!" she cried, picked up her girl and carried her home. In the security of her mother's hut, Malemba told the story.

That evening her father came home and asked her every detail. She confessed: "I had gone to my lover's hut because I wanted his love. I never told you, please forgive me!" As soon as darkness fell the coven of evil man-eaters was on its way again. This time they made no mistake, and quickly reached the hut of Malemba's mother. When she saw her "lover" enter, the girl could not utter another word. Six wicked young men stood there, and she fell dead on the floor. The father looked each of them in the face so that he would recognize them later before the village council.

"You killed her. Wait till we have buried her. Then I will ask your reckoning."

After the funeral of Malemba, her father accused the six men before the chief's council. They were summoned and had to drink the poison of divine judgement. They all died miserably.

There are many lessons in this story. Never help anyone to do evil, for you will be killed yourself. If you are a girl and want to visit your lover, go to his mother's hut first and stay with her, so that everybody may know that you are there, and that you are his girl. His mother, if she had only known of it, would certainly have prevented him from killing his girl. Now she can only mourn her son.

Religious ritual, of course, also deals with the beautiful in life. Among the Akan of Ghana, this awakening ritual is recited before dawn on festival days. The good morning prayer promises God that the participants are learning to abide by His injunctions.

GOOD MORNING TO YOU, GOD, I AM LEARNING[37]

The heavens are wide, exceedingly wide.
The earth is wide, very, very wide.
We have lifted it and taken it away.
We have lifted it and brought it back.
From time immemorial,
The God of old bids us all
Abide by his injunctions.
Then shall we get whatever we want,
Be it white or red.
It is God, the Creator, the Gracious One.
Good morning to you, God, good morning.
I am learning, let me succeed.

---

[37]Shorter, *Prayer*, pp. 101–102.

SECTION 9: Endings: Death, Judgment, and the Afterlife

There is no single traditional African attitude toward death. This diversity of opinion is reflected in the opening selections. The first excerpt is an Edo of Nigeria funeral prayer that is addressed to the spirit of a dead man. Note the belief in a rebirth and the hope that the next incarnation may be long and happy. The second selection is a poem of the Bushmen from South Africa. Note in this poem the attitude of hopeless despair. The third excerpt, which is from the West African "Myth of the Bagre," acknowledges the great mysteries surrounding death, while the final piece, a Mali Poem of the Birago Diop, is a confident expression of the continuation of life in other forms.

EDO FUNERAL PRAYER FROM NIGERIA[38]

You came to the world and you lived to old age . . .
When you come back may you once again bring a good
    body with you.
Money, health, all the things that are used in living, you
    must bring them with you . . .
When you come again may sickness not send you back.
May you not suffer the diseases of this world in your next
    incarnation.
Great Man, you will come back!

THE GATES OF THE UNDERWORLD ARE CLOSED—A BUSHMAN POEM FROM SOUTH AFRICA[39]

The gates of the underworld are closed.
Closed are the gates.
The spirits of the dead are thronging together,
Like swarming mosquitoes.
Like swarms of mosquitoes dancing in the evening,
When the night has turned black, entirely black,
When the sun has sunk, has sunk below,
When the night has turned black,
The mosquitoes are swarming
Like whirling leaves,
Dead leaves in the wind,
They wait for him who will come,
For him who will come and will say:
"Come" to the one and "Go" to the other;

---

[38]Shorter, *Prayer*, pp. 50–51.
[39]Shorter, *Prayer*, pp. 139–140.

And God will be with his children.
And God will be with his children.

QUESTIONS AND ANSWERS CONCERNING DEATH FROM THE MYTH OF THE WHITE BAGRE[40]

One neophyte stood up and said, right, he wanted to ask how it was they know so much, and yet death still kills? He replied, "Well, knowledge came from the ancestors. And death too comes from the ancestors. The problem you pose is an old one. It is death that came first, and Bagre followed," "How then can it drive away death?" And he said, "Now, if you want the truth, Bagre is a grave matter. You grasp it with both hands, following it in the right way; watch it with your eyes, and don't let it go."

QUESTIONS AND ANSWERS CONCERNING DEATH FROM THE MYTH OF THE BLACK BAGRE[41]

One day the younger one called his children and his wives and told them to be quiet. When they were quiet, he spoke saying that they call upon God but don't know him. And he continued, "When you die you will know God." "How is it that you know God only when you die?" And he replied, "During the time when you're on earth you speak of many things. When you die, you will understand the words you speak." And he said, "About God, when you die, it's then you'll see him, like the younger one and the spider, and know God's place."

THE DEAD ARE NEVER GONE— BIRAGO DIOP, MALI POEM[42]

Those who are dead are never gone:
They are there in the thickening shadow.
The dead are not under the earth:
They are there in the tree that rustles,
They are in the wood that groans,
They are in the water that runs,
They are in the water that sleeps,
They are in the hut, they are in the crowd,
The dead are not dead.

---

[40]Goody, *The Myth of the Bagre*, p. 192.
[41]Goody, *The Myth of the Bagre*, p. 268.
[42]*World Scripture*, pp. 232–233.

Those who are dead are never gone:
They are in the breast of the woman,
They are in the child who is wailing,
and in the firebrand that flames.
The dead are not under the earth:
They are in the fire that is dying,
They are in the grasses that weep,
They are in the whimpering rocks,
They are in the forest, they are in the house,
The dead are not dead.

ORIGINS OF DEATH STORIES

Virtually every oral tradition has some story that explains the origins of death. Below are several traditional African explanations. In each story note what or who is to blame for the universality of death. What do these accounts tell us about the theology and the culture of these traditions?

Death in Exchange for Fire—A Darasa, Gaga Tale[43]

Formerly men had no fire but ate all their food raw. At that time they did not need to die for when they became old God made them young again. One day they decided to beg God for fire. They sent a messenger to God to convey their request. God replied to the messenger that he would give him fire if he was prepared to die. The man took the fire from God, but ever since then all men must die.

The End of Paradise—Basonge Tradition (Zaire)[44]

The Creator, Fidi Mukullu, made all things including man. He also planted banana trees. When the bananas were ripe he sent the sun to harvest them. The sun brought back a full basket to Fidi Mukullu, who asked him if he had eaten any. The sun answered "no" and the Creator decided to put him to a test. He made the sun go down into a hole dug in the earth, then asked him when he wanted to get out. "Tomorrow morning, early," answered the sun. "If you did not lie," the Creator told him, "you will get out early tomorrow morning." The next day the sun appeared at the desired moment, confirming his honesty. Next

the moon was ordered to gather God's bananas and was put to the same test. She also got out successfully. Then came man's turn to perform the same task. However, on his way to the Creator he ate a portion of the bananas, but denied doing so. Put to the same test as the sun and the moon, man said that he wanted to leave the hole at the end of five days. But he never got out. Fidi Mukullu said, "Man lied! That is why man will die and will never reappear."

The Origin of Death—Hottentot Story[45]

The moon, it is said, once sent an insect to men, saying, "Go to men and tell them, 'As I die, and dying live; so you shall also die, and dying live.' "

The insect started with the message, but, while on his way, was overtaken by the hare, who asked, "On what errand are you bound?"

The insect answered, "I am sent by the Moon to men, to tell them that as she died and dying lives, so shall they also die and dying live."

The hare said, "As you are an awkward runner, let me go." With these words he ran off, and when he reached men, he said, "I am sent by Moon to tell you, 'As I die and dying perish, in the same manner you shall die and come wholly to an end.' "

The hare then returned to the Moon and told her what he had said to men. The Moon reproached him angrily, saying, "Do you dare tell people a thing which I have not said?"

With these words the moon took up a piece of wood and struck the hare on the nose. Since that day the hare's nose has been slit, but men believe what Hare had told them.

PowerWeb SUPPLEMENT

1. **Veve: The Sacred Symbol of Vodoun,** Lilith Dorsey, *Parabola*, February 1999.

The "veve" is a sacred symbol of African origin that is used by Haitian Vodoun practitioners. Drawn on the ground, each veve is used as a conduit between humans and a particular spirit. In this *PowerWeb* selection taken from *Parabola*, Lilith Dorsey discusses the importance of the veve in contemporary Vodoun. Readings from *PowerWeb: Religion* are available at the McGraw-Hill *PowerWeb* website http://

[43]Feldmann, *African Myths,* p. 121.
[44]*World Scripture,* p. 306.
[45]Radin, *African Folktales,* p. 63.

www.dushkin.com/powerweb. A personal access code to *PowerWeb: Religion* is provided free with each new copy of this book. Those who purchase a used copy may buy an access code at the website.

SELECTED BIBLIOGRAPHY

Awolalu, J. Omosade. *Yoruba Beliefs and Sacrificial Rites.* London: Longman, 1979.

Barnet, Miguel. *Afro-Cuban Religions.* Princeton, NJ: Markus Wiener Publishers, 2001.

Bascom, William. *The Yoruba of Southwestern Nigeria.* New York: Holt, Rinehart and Winston, 1969.

Behrend, Heike, and Ute Long, eds. *Spirit Possession, Modernity and Power in Africa.* Madison, WI: University of Wisconsin Press, 2000.

Blakely, T. D., E. A. van B. Walter, and L. T. Dennis (eds.) *Religion in Africa: Experience and Expression.* London: James Currey, 1994.

Evans-Pritchard, Edward E. *Nuer Religion.* New York: Oxford University Press, 1956.

Falola, Toyin, ed. *Africa. 5 Volumes.* Durham, NC: Carolina Academic Press, 2003.

Feldmann, Susan, ed. *African Myths and Tales.* New York: Dell, 1963.

Goody, Jack. *The Myth of the Bagre.* London: Oxford University Press, 1972.

King, Noel. *African Cosmos: An Introduction to Religion in Africa.* Belmont, CA: Wadsworth Publishing Company, 1986.

Knappert, Jan. *Myths and Legends of the Congo.* Nairobi: Heinemann Educational Books, 1971.

Kuber, Hilda. *The Swazi: A South African Kingdom.* New York: Holt, Rinehart and Winston, 1963.

Mbiti, John S. *African Religions and Philosophy.* Garden City, NY: Doubleday, 1970.

Olupona, Jacob K., and Sulayman S. Nyang, eds. *Religious Plurality in Africa.* Berlin: Mouton de Gruyter, 1993.

Radin, Paul, ed. *African Folktales.* New York: Princeton University Press, 1970.

Ranger, T. O. and I. N. Kimambo. *The Historical Study of African Religion.* Berkeley, CA: University of California Press, 1972.

Ray, Benjamin C. *African Religions: Symbol, Ritual and Community.* Englewood Cliffs, NJ: Prentice-Hall, 1976.

Scheub, Harold, ed. *The World and the Word: Tales and Observations from the Xhosa Oral Tradition.* Madison, WI: University of Wisconsin Press, 1992.

Shorter, Aylward. *Prayer in the Religious Traditions of Africa.* New York: Oxford University Press, 1975.

Smith, Robert S. *Kingdoms of the Yoruba.* Madison, WI: University of Wisconsin Press, 1988.

Vansina, Jan. *Oral Tradition as History.* Madison, WI: University of Wisconsin Press, 1985.

Traditional Religions of Oceania 9

The indigenous traditions of Oceania, like the indigenous traditions of the Americas and Africa, are largely nonliterate oral traditions that have remained relatively isolated from both the East and the West throughout much of the historic period. In recent centuries, however, as these traditions have been discovered by other modern peoples, their influence on the course of world history has expanded. Today, some of these once-isolated indigenous traditions are no longer confined to their native boundaries but rather are located in places far removed from their origins.

SETTING

Oceania includes Australia, the world's largest island and smallest continent, plus more than 20,000 islands scattered across the vast Pacific Ocean. Most scholars believe that the first peoples to inhabit the Pacific Islands were dark-skinned Southeast Asians who migrated to islands around New Guinea about 40,000 years ago. At this far-distant time Europe was still populated with a mix of *Homo sapiens* and Neanderthals. Humans on all parts of the planet knew how to use fire and gather food, but agriculture and the use of iron tools were still far away in the distant future. The earliest migrants into the Pacific were the ancestors of the modern day Melanesians who live around Papua New Guinea, New Caledonia, the Solomon Islands, and Vanuatu. The name geographers give to these islands is *Melanesia,* which means "black islands."

A second wave of migrates journeyed into the Pacific many millennia later. This group of lighter-skinned peoples arrived a mere 4,000 years ago, at about the same time that Abraham of Ur, the father of the three great Western religions, allegedly left his ancestral homeland of Mesopotamia for Canaan. Several centuries later, around 3,600 years ago (or about the time the Aryans arrived in India), other peoples from the Philippines and Indonesia migrated into regions of the northern Pacific that geographers call *Micronesia* (which means "tiny islands"). The first settlers to this region were known as the Chamorros, a peace-loving people who often settled their disputes not with war but with tests of skill games such as canoe races or sling-throwing competitions.

Over the ensuing centuries the descendants of these peoples moved farther east into the islands of *Polynesia,* which means "many islands." Geographers generally define Polynesia as the triangular area that lies between New Zealand, Hawaii, and Easter Island. The first settlers into Polynesia came first to Samoa and Tonga, then moved north to Hawaii and Tahiti, and finally reversed course and sailed to New Zealand, arriving there only about 1,000 years ago. Although some controversy exists regarding the timing of these migrations, most would agree that large portions of Melanesia, Micronesia, and Polynesia were settled long before the time of Buddha, Jesus, or Mohammed and before the classic age of the Mayan temple builders in Meso-America.

Among many of the Pacific Islands on which these peoples still live, the highest point is only several feet above sea level. On such narrow pieces of dry earth, land is a very valuable commodity that people are compelled to keep by many means, including war, arranged marriages, and black magic. These islands also are both separated and united by the oceans. Shared sacred stories edited for the special needs of a given locale are

Oceania.

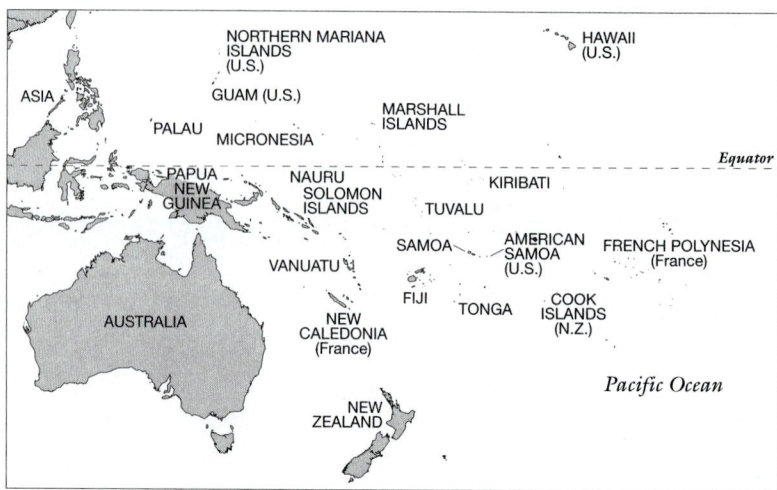

found throughout the islands. Naturally, many of these stories are about the exploits of common legendary figures—some divine, others semidivine—that these indigenous peoples remember and revere.

Although the cultures of the Pacific Islanders are ancient, the early cultures of Australia are even more ancient. The first intruders into this southern island-continent of nearly 3 million square miles arrived about 60,000 years ago, or 20,000 years before the first Southeast Asians sailed into the Pacific Islands. While the ancestors of the Australian Aborigines migrated from Asia to New Guinea to Australia, most likely they did not come by boat. At this distant time a land bridge connected Asia and Australia (or more precisely, a continental shelf called *Sahul* that included Australia, Tasmania, and New Guinea), thus making possible land travel between the two regions. Like all humans in the Pleistocene Ice Age, they lived a nomadic life and survived by hunting and gathering food. Unlike most other peoples, however, the Aborigines kept their ancient ways into modern times, choosing to sleep under the stars, go naked, and survive by hunting and gathering food rather than by agriculture.

This does not mean that all of the early inhabitants of New Guinea and Australia were alike. In New Guinea, the isolation that resulted from the rugged topography of the land led to the development of nearly 800 languages and dialects. Although topography did not restrict mobility as much in Australia as in New Guinea, linguistic diversity also was great on the southern continent. At the time of European contact with Australia, about 1 million Aborigines lived in some 500 culturolinguistic groups, some inhabiting Australia's lush eastern seaboard and others, the deserts of Central and Western Australia. For those surviving in the desert, life was never something that could be taken for granted. Unlike the Pacific Islanders who enjoyed an abundance of vegetation on limited land, these Australians enjoyed an abundance of land with scarce vegetation. Given these profound geographical differences, it is not surprising that religious customs and sacred stories of these culturally diverse people were vastly different.[1]

SACRED STORIES AND BELIEFS

Like many indigenous traditions around the globe, the religions of Oceania do not draw a distinct line between the sacred and secular. Many Oceanic cultures, although not all, accept the reality of a high God who may have once resided on or near the earth but, since primordial times, has withdrawn into the sky to a place distant from the peoples of the earth. Below this high but distant God are other supernatural beings associated with the spirit world.

---

[1]See Bo Flood, et al. *Micronesian Legends* (2002); Bo Flood, et al., *Pacific Island Legends* (1999); Roslyn Poignant, *Oceanic Mythology* (1967); James G. Cowan, *Myths of the Dreaming* (1994); and especially Tony Swain and Gary Trompf, *The Religions of Oceania* (1995).

Australian Aboriginals.

Many Pacific cultures also hold that ancestral ghosts or other primordial beings inhabit the earth. Moreover, these spirits are believed to participate actively in the daily life of the living by punishing human offenses and by assisting those who treat them with due respect. Religious specialists of various kinds understand how to communicate with the spirits through dream interpretations and divination. As in traditional African religions, divination takes many forms—inspecting and reading of entrails of birds and animals, conjuring the spirits into objects such as statues and god-catching sticks, and speaking directly with the spirits through spirit possession. The powers of spirit manipulation can work for good or evil. Native peoples throughout the Oceanic world believe that sorcery is a primary cause of misfortune, disease, and death; to protect themselves from black magic, sacred rituals and exorcisms abound.

Great religious diversity exists both between and within the regions of Oceania. Although details regarding these differentiations are beyond the scope of this volume, the following introduction paints with a broad brush some of major themes that characterize religious beliefs and practices among the Aborigines of Australia and the cultures that inhabit Melanesia, Micronesia, and Polynesia.

Place Over Time: Dreamtime and Totemism

Understanding how different people conceive time is just as critical to gaining insight into traditional Australian religion as it is to understanding traditional African religions. In Aboriginal cultures, as in indigenous African ones, there is little or no memory of events more than several generations removed. Moreover, before European contact, Aborigines did not add or count by numbers, although their languages did include concepts such as "twin" or "trinity" that expressed numerical items as quantities. Time was not measured in abstract quantifiable units. Indeed, Aboriginals used phrases such as "when the sky is aflame with red and yellow" to describe more than 30 qualitative changes during a 24-hour period, but these daily events were never associated with a moment described in numeric terms. Aborigines, instead, ordered life by reference to reoccurring events, not by the shade on a sundial or the hands of a clock. They viewed time neither linearly like the Western religions nor in measured cycles of great epochs like the Eastern religions. Rather, Aborigines held to a *rhythmic* understanding of events that required no reference to time.

The term Westerners use to describe the timelessness associated with Aboriginal religion is *Dreamtime*.

To Aborigines, all life and all things in nature are the result of the actions of shadowy spirits that acted in an era before the earth was fashioned, when all the cosmos was spirit and not physical. Plants leave their image in seeds; Aborigines believe the primordial actions of these spirit ancestors left a record of their activities through the creation of land. All places that comprise the earth are the residue of spirit events that took place in Dreamtime.

Although to Westerners it appears as if Dreamtime was in the past at the beginning of time, to Aborigines Dreamtime is not simply the past because it still exists and will always exist. Considered a timeless eternity that mixes together the past, present, and future, Dreamtime can be accessed at any moment through communion with the spirit world by way of dreams and sacred rituals. According to Aboriginal linguistic scholars, the term *Dreamtime,* in fact, is misleading because traditional Australian religion fundamentally is grounded in the ontology of place, not time. When Aborigines speak of what Westerners call Dreamtime, they are not focusing on a sacred distant time but rather on sacred events that occurred and continue to take place in sacred places. Aboriginal religion underscores the eternity of land, not time. Its cosmology assumes that something with the potential to act always existed, and, by its actions, nature and life were given order and shape. If what appears as inanimate land is in fact a manifestation of primordial spirit activities, then all natural forms that share a common site—men, women, birds, fish, animals, rain, wind—must be related in their spiritual essence. The terminology academics use to describe the belief that a kin group is related to another life form is *totemism.*

Aboriginal sacred rituals seek to maintain the link between the lands and the peoples of the land. Unlike farming cultures that have seasons of harvest and thus seasonal sacred rituals, the hunting and gathering culture of the Aborigines requires continuous rituals to ensure the continual abundance of the life essences that were deposited by the actions of the Ancestors in the land. Only someone who shares the Ancestral spirit of a site can perform the sacred cosmic balance rites. Often in the rituals the bodies of the owners of the site are decorated so that they become the Ancestors who brought forth the life essences of the land. Interestingly, the animal and plant species that allegedly are replenished by these rituals are to be avoided and not consumed by those who perform the ritual. Thus, in theory, the rituals that ensure the abundance of a commodity from the land are performed for the benefit of others outside their kin, not for the benefit of those who perform the sacred rites in a given locale. Moreover, this belief system also discourages attempts to conquer the lands of other peoples, for only those born from a site (and thus of the same spiritual essence with it) can perform the sacred rites associated with that land. In precontact times, territorial wars among the Aboriginal peoples in Australia were exceedingly rare.

The belief that all life comes from the land also carries with it important religious, gender, and economic implications. Aborigines know that sexual intercourse is necessary for procreation, but they insist that coitus itself does not produce life. Rather, they assert that the life that enters a pregnant woman comes from the Ancestral presence of the land, a presence that is maintained by the reenactments of the sacred rites. Aborigines, thus, downplay the role that individuals play in the creation of life, stressing instead the fertile powers of land alone. Moreover, because the spirit emerges from the land and belongs to the land, at death it is assumed that the spirit returns to its source to become once again a fragment of the power of the land. Divine judgment or notions of heaven or hell are foreign to Aboriginal religious thought. In addition, by asserting that humans come not from humans but from the womb of the land as a direct consequence of the sacred rituals, Aboriginal religion tends to award higher spiritual status to the men who control the sacred rites than to the women who are the bearers of the children. Finally, the Aboriginal emphasis on the link between ritual reenactment, land sites, and lifeforms and de-emphasis on the role of human involvement in the replenishing of life helps to explain their denial of biological paternity and their rejection of agriculture as a way of life.

Mana and *Tapu* in the Religions of the Pacific

Two indigenous terms commonly used to describe the religions of the Pacific islanders are *mana* and *tapu.* *Mana* has been defined both as "spirit power for success" and the experience of awe when in the presence of the sacred. In some ways similar to invisible currents of electrical power, *mana* is the supernatural energy that the supernatural beings confer on people, places, or things. *Mana* can be accumulated, stored, and then used to achieve a multitude of objectives. In some traditions it is accumulated by religious specialists and political leaders through sacred rituals and chants. In some regions, *mana* could be gained by eating the flesh of enemies. For instance, among select Melanesian peoples *mana* was stored in "skull houses" in the piles of heads won by "head-hunters" in their deadly *mana* collecting raids on neighboring tribes.

Because *mana* power can be appropriated or stolen from others, and then used for either good or evil purposes, societal rules attempt to restrict its misuse. One method of limiting the abuse of spiritual power is through *tapu*, a Polynesian word generally translated in English as "taboo." *Tapu* or taboo refers to sacred prohibitions against certain human activities or contacts that, when committed, can cause great danger both to the violators of the taboos and to their group. Individuals who violate a taboo must be avoided until purified by sacred ceremonies as contact with violators before purification threatens misfortune to the larger group. To illustrate, in many cultures taboos are associated with blood, in particular blood from menstruation and childbirth. Consequently, in these cultures menstruating women and young mothers are temporarily isolated from their communities. Anyone who associates with women at such times also must undergo purification rituals before making contact with others. One benefit of taboos is that because it is assumed that supernatural penalties come to taboo violators, there is a reduced need for human sanctions against those who commit social offenses. Consequently, indigenous cultures generally give more attention to purification rituals than to inflicting punishments on the taboo violators.

Differentiating Religious Motifs: Melanesia versus Polynesia and Micronesia

Another religious principle prevalent in many traditional cultures of Oceania is the notion of "payback" or reciprocity. Especially in Melanesia, throughout the historic period warfare has been common even among tribes within the same linguistic groupings. The prevalence of wars of revenge in Melanesia was at least in part a consequence of the religious sentiments of the peoples. The idea of reciprocity—an eye for an eye, a life for a life—is common to many world religions. In these cultures, however, death often was attributed to enemy sorcery, so an appropriate religious response to the death of a member of one com-

munity might be to launch a retaliatory raid on another village. Failure to requite the death, it was feared, might anger the Ancestral spirits, who, in turn, would bring misfortune to the community. Of course, a more positive side to retributive logic is that it also encouraged magnanimous acts and gift exchanges between the peoples of the islands.

According to Garry Trompf,[2] traditional Melanesian religions tend to share cosmologies and spiritual goals that are different from those embraced by the peoples of Polynesia and Micronesia. In Melanesia, for example, the central purpose of religion is to provide for the collective material well-being of the peoples, whereas in other regions of the Pacific, religions seek to uphold the sacred (and social) order and protect the peoples from harm. Melanesian religion is more earthbound and materialistic. Stories about a high God exist, but Melanesian cultures typically focus greater attention on place deities and warrior deities that guard each tribal zone. Female goddesses in Melanesia are rare, but masculine war gods abound. Similarly, in human society women rarely achieve leadership status and tend to be looked upon more as human property. At least among males, however, Melanesian culture tends toward egalitarianism, with each tribe led not by a hereditary king but a warrior "big-man" who gains power by competition and holds it only until replaced by a more powerful opponent.

In contrast, in Micronesia and Polynesia the gods and the structure of human society are more hierarchically ordered. Throughout the region the principal creator deity is a Sky god who dwells in the highest heavens. According to a number of their sacred stories, the creation of the earth resulted from activities that took place in the heavens, like the pulling up of an island from a rope or the dropping of a rock from the sky. Sun cults are common across the Pacific Islands, as are stories of cultural heroes who now live in the heavens, including the greatest of all Pacific heroes, Maui, the sometimes mischievous trickster who willingly defiled some of the gods and provided tools and inventions for humanity.

Outside of Melanesia, female deities are abundant among the islanders. These goddesses often unite with male gods to produce lengthy spirit world genealogies. Leadership among the mortals

---

[2]Tony Swain and Garry Trompf, *The Religions of Oceania* (New York: Routledge, 1995), pp. 121–164.

also reflects the aristocracies of the spirit world as Polynesian peoples typically are ruled by powerful dynasties of kings and queens. Notwithstanding the "vertical religion" of these Pacific cultures, projections of the afterlife are still largely earth centered. In Micronesia, the belief that a departed soul makes a journey to the west is widespread, while in many Polynesian traditions, the dead usually are said to descend into an underworld, the very gates of which are identified with some nearby sacred place. Last judgments and blissful heavenly expectations are rare throughout Oceanic cultures.

SCRIPTURES (SACRED ORAL TRADITIONS)

Like the indigenous peoples of the Americas and Africa, precontact Oceanic cultures were largely nonliterate and thus had no canonized written text of sacred writings. Unlike the other indigenous peoples, however, all the peoples of Oceania have produced material, theatrical, and verbal art forms that have been received as sacred and have been intentionally passed onward from generation to generation. Many of these peoples shared common stories of cultural heroes, although naturally their heroes often differed from place to place in name and mission. Among the Australian Aborigines, for instance, the cult heroes generally are portrayed as singers who, through their sacred songs, put power into the land. In contrast, the heroes of other Pacific Islands, particularly in Melanesia, are often warriors who gain power by the acquisition of *mana* (spirit authority) from human foes. Sometimes this involves violent means, including repaying enemies for their offenses through head-hunting raids and the capturing of human skulls.

Islanders also are less likely than the Aborigines to insist that all life is derived solely from land. This enables the island deities greater freedom to move from place to place, although it also allows these peoples to condone territorial advances and organized warfare.

Notwithstanding these differences, the sacred art and stories of all traditional Oceanic peoples support a worldview that rejects a clear line of demarcation between the sacred and the profane. The universe of traditional Oceania is a cosmos that affirms an ongoing interplay between the invisible spirit and the visible physical dimensions of reality.

THE ONGOING RELIGIOUS HISTORY OF OCEANIA

For thousands of years, the peoples of Oceania inhabited a piece of the planet that was relatively isolated from the major civilizations of the Old or the New Worlds. European records of explorers to the region first appeared in the early sixteenth century, and by the end of this century the Pacific was largely a Spanish lake. Over the ensuring centuries, other mercantile powers—Britain, France, Germany, The Netherlands, and, belatedly, the United States—also established colonial bases in the Pacific. Meanwhile, as news of "contact" with the indigenous cultures spread, European academics became increasingly infatuated with the peoples of the region. Spurring this interest was a debate that was taking place among "Enlightenment" thinkers over the nature of humankind. Some philosophers, like Thomas Hobbes (1588–1679), argued that humans were fundamentally selfish and that therefore before the ascent of civilization (and the rise of monarchy) human life was "nasty, brutish and short." Others, like John Locke (1632–1704) and Jacques Rousseau (1712–1778), understood the human condition in more favorable light and expressed higher, even romantic opinions of the "noble savages" that formed the original state of nature. The "discoveries" of the largely untouched and uncorrupted Oceanic peoples, hence, provided social philosophers with an excellent opportunity to test the various theories regarding human nature. In 1768 the Royal Society promoted an expedition to the South Seas—the last great region yet to be explored—that was undertaken by Captain James Cook. Ultimately, the reports that came from the Cook expeditions and later ones did not settle the philosophical debates, but they excited the Western academics to give serious attention to Oceanic places and peoples.

Religious Consequences of Colonization

Scholars estimate that at the beginning of the eighteenth century the population of Oceania included about 1 million in Australia and 2 million on the other islands of the Pacific. However, as a result of disease and warfare, by the mid-nineteenth century the indigenous populations in many areas of Oceania

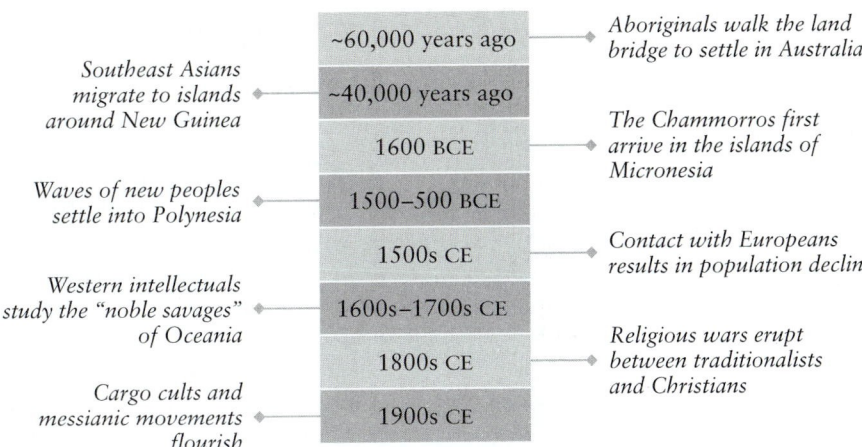

Timeline of Oceanic history.

Southeast Asians migrate to islands around New Guinea → ~40,000 years ago

~60,000 years ago ← *Aboriginals walk the land bridge to settle in Australia*

1600 BCE → *The Chammorros first arrive in the islands of Micronesia*

Waves of new peoples settle into Polynesia → 1500–500 BCE

1500s CE → *Contact with Europeans results in population decline*

Western intellectuals study the "noble savages" of Oceania → 1600s–1700s CE

1800s CE ← *Religious wars erupt between traditionalists and Christians*

Cargo cults and messianic movements flourish → 1900s CE

had been reduced by more than 95 percent. European contact did more than decimate indigenous life. It also thrust alien modes of thought into the premodern worlds of the traditional cultures, thereby altering to some extent the religious beliefs and practices of the indigenous peoples.

According to a number of Australian religious scholars, Aboriginal contact with European worldviews resulted in the appearance of beliefs in transcendent beings that were not indigenous to the southern continent.[3] Among these innovations was the belief in the All-Mother. Whereas all the other Ancestral spirits were tied to a particular land site, the All-Mother had a special relationship with all Aboriginal peoples, no matter their place of birth. Although not regarded as the creator of the cosmos, followers of the All-Mother cult looked to the All-Mother as the one who supplied a preexisting world with people. Another transcendent being honored by the Aborigines in southeastern Australia was the All-Father. The similarities between this eternal, omnipotent, and benevolent Supreme Being with the God of Christianity suggest that this cult owes its origins to Christian influences.

Elsewhere in Oceania, indigenous contact with Christian missionaries also produced changes, some beneficial and some violent. In 1828 a Tahitian prophet announced himself to be "Jesus Christ" and promised that God would send "a ship load of cloth from the skies . . . wine from heaven and cows out of the clouds." This was the first of a number of partly Christian, partly traditional Oceanic prophets who would rise to promise an imminent reordering of the cosmos. Prophetic movements both compounded and manifested the religious tensions that accompanied colonization.

Religious wars, for example, broke out in Tahiti in the 1830s when a tribal king adopted Christianity and waged war against the cult of Oro, another new religious tradition that worshiped Oro, the God of War. Several decades later the Maori Wars in New Zealand pitted religious groups against each other and culminated with the emergence of a new religion that was a mixture of Christian and traditional elements. In Samoa, after the arrival of Christian missionaries, rival chieftains competed, sometimes violently, for control of the new *mana* (spirit authority) that the Christian religion offered. Another conflict arose in Fiji in the 1880s when a traditional priest declared an approaching "Great Reversal" in which Whites would serve Blacks, and still another crisis erupted in New Guinea in the 1930s when a tribal leader invoked new rituals that promised to bring to his peoples an abundance of goods. On numerous troubled occasions during the colonial period indigenous Oceanic peoples embraced the promises spoken by "divine-human" figures to secure or reorder the cosmic order.

Cargo-Cult Religions

Western academics use the term *cargo cults* to describe the various Oceanic movements that believe in a coming age that will be initiated by the return of

---

[3]For a discussion of the impact of contact upon Aboriginal religion, see "Chapter 2: Cults of Intrusion" in Swain and Trompf, *Religions of Oceania*, pp. 48–78.

spirits from the dead who will bring with them cargoes of modern goods to be distributed to the native peoples. In some cases it is believed that this new age will be characterized by a drastic reversal in the social order, including a rearrangement of sexual mores. Although a number of these movements date to the early nineteenth century, many more appeared during and after World War II at a time when the natives witnessed massive amounts of goods and materials arriving on remote islands by Allied ships and planes.

Cargo cults express a blending of traditional and modern themes. The anticipation of a coming age when the ancestors will return and the colonial masters will depart suggests a longing for a return to former times, even as the hope that foreigners will share their wealth signals a desire to enjoy the material benefits produced by modern technologies. Some cargo cults have died out within a single generation, but others have survived and been transformed into political parties and independent churches that have struggled to achieve either reform or political independence.

SACRED OBSERVANCES AND PRACTICES

Just a little more than 150 years ago, 95 percent of the peoples on the 25,000 islands in Oceania adhered to religious practices untainted by influences from the great religions of the West. In the twenty-first century, however, the percentages have been reversed. Today 95 percent of the peoples of Oceania acknowledge some involvement with the Christian tradition.

Among some Oceanic peoples, unadulterated indigenous religious practices continue as in distant times. In Australia, some Aborigines decorate their bodies with feathers, clay, coloring, or blood and reenact the sacred myths by performing the dance rituals deemed necessary for increasing the supply of their totemic commodity. Some Aboriginal youth also observe ancient puberty rituals that may involve circumcision, teeth pulling, hair removal, scarring, or the piercing of the nasal septum. In Melanesia, ancient birth, puberty, marriage, and funeral rites are performed in communal ceremonies involving feasts and dances, and private rituals for healing, divina-

Unlike many islands within Oceania, Bali remains largely untouched by Western religious influences. Although this photograph was taken for the benefit of Western tourists, it depicts the costume and dance of an ancient Balinese culture that survives on the island to this day.

tion, success, and protection from demons and sorcery are performed by those with the specialized talents and gifts needed to conduct such rites. Many Melanesians and Australian Aborigines also continue to interpret the experience of dreaming at face value and assume that their spirits literally leave the body to converse with other spirits and return with valuable information that can help in settling troubled relationships. Moreover, across Polynesia and Micronesia some tribal peoples still gather at shrines to honor the gods and goddesses that grant *mana* in return for the ritual offerings of food and dance. These islanders also still perform rites—such as sprinkling water on newborn children, blood-stained warriors, or those contaminated by touching a dead corpse—to purify themselves from the effects of taboo.

Increasingly, however, Oceanic peoples are adopting sacred practices more compatible with Christian teachings. The type of new religious expressions appearing throughout Oceania is a function of both the local preconceptions of the islanders and the form of Christianity that has penetrated their village or region. Islanders introduced to Roman Catholic Christianity, for example, generally are more willing to participate in traditional indigenous ceremonies than those introduced to Protestant forms of Christianity. In contrast, indigenous Protestant Christians generally are less worried about eating for nourishment their own totems than indigenous Roman Catholic Christians.

Worship also is colored by the denomination of the Christian missionaries to the islands. Among tribes introduced to Christianity by Roman Catholic or Anglican missionaries, a high church liturgy often prevails, while in communities closely associated with Lutherans or Methodists, powerful singing is a central component in communal worship. Similarly, those associated with Pentecostal missions often raise their hands, pray in tongues, and share personal faith testimonies in corporate worship.

Notwithstanding these influences, indigenous Christianity also retains many precontact practices and understandings. Most islanders continue to insist that the dead have an interest in the living and that malevolent spirits roam the earth. Religion, both past and present, largely involves trying to make sense of how God, the dead, and malevolent agents interact with the living. To reach this understanding, compromises between indigenous customs and Christian traditions have been made. In the Cook Islands, for instance, islanders serve Christian communion with coconut meat and milk rather than bread and wine. Among the Trobrianders, islanders assert that the dead go first to the promised Isle of Tuma and later to the Christian heaven. In a Catholic Church among the Melpa, a picture of one of the Stations of the Cross portrays Pilate as an Australian official and Christ as a Black man. As these and countless other examples suggest, even as traditional sacred practices have been "Christianized," among many Oceanic peoples the new expressions of religiosity borrowed from Christianity also have been thoroughly "indigenized."

SOURCES

The following selections include sacred stories and descriptions of the oral traditions from the peoples of Polynesia, Micronesia, Melanesia, and Aboriginal Australia.

SECTION 1: Beginnings: God, Time, and the Universe

The Oceanic peoples of the world also have their accounts of creation. Here are selections of these stories from the indigenous peoples of the Society Islands of Polynesia, the Marshall Islands of Micronesia, and Australia. To what degree are these accounts similar to and different from the other creation stories you have read in this volume?

A POLYNESIAN CREATION STORY FROM THE SOCIETY ISLANDS[4]

In this account, Ta'aroa is the Supreme Being and Creator of the cosmos who came forth from a shell (Rumia), which later became the world.

Ta'aroa was the ancestor of all the gods; he made everything. From time immemorial was the great Ta'aroa, Tahi-tumu (The-origin). Ta'aroa developed himself in solitude; he was his own parent, having no father or mother. . . .

Ta'aroa sat in his shell in darkness from eternity. The shell was like an egg revolving in endless space, with no sky, no land, no sea, no moon, no sun, no stars. All was darkness, it was continuous thick darkness. . . . The record then proceeds to describe Ta'aroa's breaking his shell, which became the sky, his swimming in empty space and retirement into a new shell, after he had again emerged, . . . he took . . . for the great foundation of the world, for stratum rock and for soil for the world.

And the shell Rumia that he opened first, became his house, the dome of the gods' sky, which was a confined sky, enclosing the world then forming.

[4]Mircea Eliade, *Gods, Goddesses, and Myths of Creation: A Thematic Source Book of the History of Religions* (New York: Harper & Row, 1974), pp. 87–88.

A MICRONESIAN CREATION STORY FROM THE MARSHALL ISLANDS[5]

Long ago, before there was land at all and the entire world was covered with water, the creator god, Loa, made a magical sound, and all of the islands of the world were created. But they were not in their correct places, and they had no people.

Then Loa sent men to the islands. He sent one man to the north. This man was Lojibwineamen.

Another was sent to the south. This man was Lorok, which means, "man of the south."

A third was sent to the west. This was Iroijdrilil.

And the last was sent to the east. This man was Lokumuran, "the man who twists the daybreak."

Each of these men was given duties by Loa.

Iroijdrilik was the ruler of all. His job was to produce all of the living things of the earth, the plants and the animals, and all things that moved or grew.

Lorok was put in charge of the winds, which would push the clouds and fill the sails of the canoes.

And Lojibwineamen, the man in the north, was put in charge of death and dying. His call was final to all living things. Those called must set out after death to approach the Island of Nako, near Mili. Before the soul of the departed is permitted on Nako, it must first leap across a deep channel full of hungry fish. Those too heavy to make this jump, those burdened with lives full of evil or bad living, fall into the channel and are eaten by the fish. Those able to make the leap enter Nako, the spirit island, where they rest with abundant food and drink. From here the spirits will journey to join Lojibwineamen in the north. To be light enough and strong enough for this great leap requires four qualities: first, one must respect his or her mother; second, one must also respect his or her father; third, one must be brave in battle; and fourth, one must respect his or her chief.

ANKOTARINJA, THE ANCESTOR OF ANKOTA— AN AUSTRALIAN ABORIGINAL STORY[6]

In the beginning there was living at Ankota a man who had sprung from the earth without father or mother. He had been lying asleep in the bosom of the earth, and the

white ants had eaten his body hollow while the soil rested on him like a coverlet. As he was lying in the ground a thought arose in his mind: "Perhaps it would be pleasant to arise." He lay there, deep in thought. Then he arose, out of the soft soil of a little watercourse.

He looks around himself, still half asleep. Around him he see great tjatantjas waving against the sky, tnatantjas belonging to other men and women who have originated in the same way in which he has. He hesitates, "Where shall I go to?" He stands, on legs as yet weak and tottering; his body is like a skeleton, for the white ants have been feeding on him for a long while. He stands there listlessly. Then he goes to a swamp nearby, and sits down at the edge of the water.

Thoughts and wishes form in his mind. He begins to decorate himself with red down. A great tjatantja stands on his head: he has arisen out of the ground with his tjatantja on his head, and it has shot up until it hit the vault of the sky. He begins to breath heavily, and he sniffs around into the four winds: a cool breeze is blowing from the north . . . a cool breeze is blowing from the south . . . a cool breeze is blowing from the east . . . but the warm breeze is coming from the west. He draws the warm breeze in eagerly—"From the west comes the breeze that warms my heart." He returns to the spot whence he first issued forth. But his heart is now burning in anger against the west. The great tjurunga on his head falls down on the ground, and he rises and leaves it behind and sets out on his journey westward.

SECTION 2: Humanity: The Problem of Good and Evil

The following is a creation account from the peoples of Papua New Guinea in Melanesia. According to this account, how is the presence of good and evil in the world explained?

KAMBEL CREATES THE WORLD[7]

One day in the ancient time of creation, Kambel [the secret name of the creator spirit] decided to visit the earth. At that time it was an empty place, with no animals and no people. To get there, Kambel slid down to earth on a sak'r palm, a black palm that grows in

[5]Bo Flood, Beret E. Strong, and William Flood, *Micronesian Legends* (Honolulu: The Bess Press, 2002), pp. 174–175.

[6]Roland Robinson, *Aboriginal Myths and Legends* (Melbourne: Sun Books, 1977), pp. 24–26.

[7]Bo Flood, Beret E. Strong, and William Flood, *Pacific Island Legends: Tales from Micronesia, Melanesia, Polynesia, and Australia* (Honolulu: The Bess Press, 1999), pp. 101–102.

dense forest. As Kambel slid, he heard strange sounds coming from inside the bark of the palm. He listened as hard as he could, but did not recognize the sounds. The sounds seemed to change as he slid farther down the tree. He listened and listened until he was so curious he couldn't stand it any more. When he reached the bottom, he whipped out his sharp-bladed axe and hacked down the tree.

Kambel began to walk up and down beside the fallen tree. At the top of the tree, he heard only a confused and faint rumble, a murmur of sound. Something was trying to get out. Kambel chopped the tree in half where the sound was the loudest. His heart thumped in his throat! He could hardly believe what he saw. Out climbed the people who speak the Gambadi language of Papau. . . .

[Kambel continued chopping and out came the Semariji, Tandavi and the Keraki peoples].

Kambel was pleased with his new family. "You are all my children," he proclaimed. "Welcome." Then he told them which lands belong to each of them. The sky spirit sent all the tribes off in the direction of their new homes. Oh, he was tired from all that chopping! Weary, he climbed up a different tree to his resting place in the sky.

The world was not finished. There was yet much work to be done and many problems to fix. The sky and the earth were too close together. They were nearly pressing on each other. And besides, the sky was boring and empty. . . .

[Kambel then goes to work to fill and sculpt the earth and sky. The story continues:]

Kamel was very weary from all this creation. He lay down to sleep and let the earth creatures explore their new world.

Days later, he awoke and looked around, remembering all that he had done. The green valley looked the same as he remembered, but then a strange creature crawled out from under a rock. It had two heads and long fangs reaching below its chin. He hadn't made the creature! Where had it come from? How had it been born?

Kambel didn't kill the beast. Instead he sat and watched as the young earth came alive with new life, the good creatures he had created and the other ones who appeared out of nowhere. Mysterious four-footed beasts slunk out of caves and wandered off into the world. Kambel realized that life was more than his creation. It grew from other life, changing form. Most was good, but some of it was evil.

Another Melanesian story explains the presence of evil differently. In the following account, it was the murder of a divinity by human ancestors that resulted in the end of the age of paradise.

HAINUWELE AND THE "CREATIVE MURDER" (CERAM, NEW GUINEA)[8]

In mythical Times, a man named Ameta, out hunting, came on a wild boar. Trying to escape, the boar was drowned in a lake. On its tusk Ameta found a coconut and was commanded to plant it, which he did the next morning. In three days a coconut palm sprang up, and three days later it flowered. Ameta climbed it to cut some flowers and make a drink for them. But he cut his finger and the blood dropped on a flower. Nine days later he found a girl-child on the flower. Ameta took her and wrapped her in coconut fronds. In three days the child became a marriageable girl, and he named her Hainuwele ("coconut branch"). During the great Maro festival Hainuwele stood in the middle of the dancing place and for nine nights distributed gifts to the dancers. But on the ninth day the men dug a grave in the middle of the dancing place and drew Hainuwele into it during the dance. The grave was filled in and men danced on it.

The next morning, seeing that Hainuwele did not come home, Ameta divined that she had been murdered. He found the body, disinterred it, and cut it into pieces, which he buried in various places, except the arms. The buried pieces gave birth to plants previously unknown, especially to tubers, which since then are the chief food of human beings. Ameta took Hainuwele's arms to another dema-divinity, Satene. Satene drew a spiral with nine turns on a dancing ground and placed herself at the center of it. From Hainuwele's arms she made a door, and summoned the dancers. "Since you have killed," she said, "I will no longer live here. I shall leave this very day. Now you will have to come to me through this door." Those who were able to pass through it remained human beings. The others were changed into animals (pigs, birds, fish) or spirits. Satene announced that after her going men would meet her only after their death, and she vanished from the surface of the Earth.

---

[8]Eliade, *Gods, Goddesses, and Myths,* pp. 18–19.

SECTION 3: Sacred Stories: Divine Messengers, Prophets, and Priests

Oral traditions around the world also include love stories with bittersweet endings. The following selection from the Aborigines of Australia is one of these tales. What in this tale expresses themes found in all oral traditions? What specific insights about the world of the Aborigines can be found in this tale?

NERIDA AND BIRWAIN: A LOVE STORY FROM AUSTRALIA[9]

While the sun gave the stars and moon their rest, a girl and a boy met every day by a water hole. The hole was deep and dark, its bottom lost in murk. The girl, Nerida, and her friend, Birwain, loved to dig for mussels at the edge of the hole. Often they heard the distant rumble of thunder.

Nerida and Birwain loved to be together at the waterhole. They didn't know that the thunder was the angry voice of the water spirit, Wahwee. Or that they were digging at Wahwee's private water hole and he was plotting revenge. . . .

Wahwee hid in the murky water and spied on Nerida and Birwain. Day by day, they were growing older. Nerida was turning into a lovely young woman. She and Birwain were falling in love. Birwain would soon undergo initiation rites into manhood. Then he would be able to ask Nerida's family for permission to live with her.

Wahwee was jealous. He wanted the lovely Nerida for himself. In the dark hours of the night, he plotted how he would steal her. Foolish Nerida and Birwain. They wanted to be alone, away from all the eyes of the world. Little did they know that Wahwee was watching with bulging eyes as round as gourds!

One day, Nerida reached the water hole before Birwain. As she sat at the water's edge, cooling her, an old woman came by. The woman was weeping so hard the tears ran in streams down her cheeks. Nerida felt sorry for her. She offered her the warm cooked yams she had made for Birwain. . . .

"Oh no," said the woman. "I am not hungry. I am terribly sad. Your whole tribe will be killed because of you. Because of you and your lover Birwain's ignorance. . . . Over and over again, you have stolen

_____
[9]Flood, Strong, and Flood, *Pacific Island Legends,* pp. 252–257.

from Wahwee, the water spirit. He is angry. Every single mussel you cooked and ate was an insult to him. Do you not hear the thunder rumbling in the sky? But you did nothing. Then it turned into a roar, and still you did nothing. Even as the earth shook, nearly uprooting the yams, you and Birwain continued to steal."

Nerida trembled at these words. Were they true?

"Your tribe is innocent, but they will all die with you. You and Birwain are the guilty ones." She paused, and her voice softened. "I see your kind heart. You offered to share food. Too bad I can't save you."

"Dear Bargie, I am willing to die," said Nerida. "But you must save the innocent people of my tribe. Save Birwain. I will gladly die to save all of them."

"It's not that easy. Birwain stole too. He must suffer as you will suffer," said the old woman.

"Please, kind Bargie. Please save Birwain," begged Nerida.

"Come tomorrow. Alone. I will see if anything can be done. . . ."

The old woman turned into a black, slippery eel. Nerida gasped as it slid into the murky water hole. A witch! She had been tricked. She ran home without waiting for Birwain. Even as she ran, she wept. Today would be her last day alive.

The next day she returned to the water hole. How horrible the old woman looked to her. But there was no choice. "Bargie," Nerida said, trying to keep her voice from trembling, "can we save my people and save Birwain?"

"We will see. The only chance is for you to follow me into the water hole. I will dive down deep and you must follow without hesitation. Wahsee says you must ask his forgiveness. He is ready to unleash the storm of all storms. His voice will cause the clouds to collide. Thunder will break over the land. His brother the rain and winds will rage, knocking down trees. The birds will drown, the fish will drift unconscious among the coral. People will cling to their houses, but the houses will float away. Babies will drown. And then everyone else will die."

"Stop it, stop it! Cried Nerida. "Let us go. I am ready now." She knew the old woman was a witch, but there was no choice. Nerida started at the rolling black water before her. A wicked smile curled on the old woman's lip. She had stolen Nerida from Birwain!

The old woman writhed and cried out. Her back grew dark and slimy. She became a slippery eel, sliding under the water's dirty surface. Nerida looked at the sky, already darkening with Wahwee's rage, and prayed for the safety of Birwain and all people. Then she gulped air and plunged into the water.

From the forest, Birwain saw a splash. He ran to the pool, but now there were only quiet circles spreading on its surface. He found Nerida's tracks leading to the pool's edge. There they disappeared. Birwain howled with grief. Then he ran home to get his people to help him. "Wahwee, the water spirit, has her now," they said. "There is nothing to be done. If only we had known. It is strictly forbidden to go to that pool."

Birwain could think only of how to get Nerida back. Perhaps she wasn't dead yet. "I love her more than my life," he said to his tribe. "Wahwee lured her into the water. I will bring her back with the power of my love."

Every day after that, Birwain sat where Nerida's footprints disappeared into the water. Every day he chanted a love song.

Nerida, Nerida, I wait for you
Love of all time, love of my life,
I wait for you. Here on the bank
Where we fished together, I wait.

Nerida, Nerida, there is no one but you,
Come back, my Nerida, I'll lift you up.
My arms are strong for you, Nerida,
Hear my song; come, Nerida, come.

For many months Birwain sang. He didn't even notice when the greedy Wahwee poured rain on him. His tribe believed he had gone crazy. They brought him food because he would not leave the pond. But they knew he was lost to them forever, caught in Wahwee's web.

One day Birwain saw the water move. A green leaf the size of a woman's hand rose above its surface. Gently, it opened and spread, like fingers stretching in the sun. The next day another leaf appeared beside it. Birwain sang on. A flower bud unfolded next to the leaves, the face of a red water lily. He stared and stared at this unfolding beauty. Then he recognized her—the curving lip where the petals joined the stem.

He leaped to his feet and cried out, "Nerida! At last, you have come back. I am coming, my love." Birwain plunged into the dark water. He kicked in great thrusts to keep his head above water. More than anything he wanted to touch the delicate red lily, his precious Nerida.

Jealous Wahwee was watching. Just as Birwain clasped Nerida's face between his hands, Wahwee pulled him under the water, down, down, to the murky bottom of the pool. A huge and heavy weight held him by the legs and sucked him down. As his head went under, he let go of his flower Nerida. Thrashing in the rolling water, he began to choke. "I am drowning," he thought. "But at least my grave will lie near my beloved."

Then all went black inside his head. Wahwee turned him into a brown water rush. He wanted to torment the lovers. They would float near each other but never be able to embrace.

That is not how it turned out. Nerida and Birwain are together forever now. The lilies and the rushes spread until they covered the pool. The lilies live in the center, like an upturned, ruby face. The rushes surround them, lining the banks of the pool. There are so many lilies and rushes now that they rub up against one another. Tall rushes bend over the open faces of the lilies to protect them from stormy winds. If you sit quietly on the bank, you might hear the murmur of their conversation.

One of the best-known cultural heroes among the peoples of the Pacific was Maui. Stories of Maui are found in all of Polynesia and in parts of Melanesia and Micronesia. These stories portray this courageous hero and trickster as one who was willing to defile the gods and provide humans with useful inventions and tools, even as he played sometimes ruthless practical jokes on friends, foes and family. The selection presented below is a Hawaiian tale of Maui trapping the Sun.

Maui Traps the Sun[10]

Maui was a young man of strength and courage. He had a magic club, a magic spear, and a magic canoe paddle, all given to him by his grandmother. In addition to these, he had special powers because he was the son of a goddess. He was very fond of his mother, Hina, and visited her every day; for his stepfather, Aikanake-the-Wanderer, was often away from home.

The goddess Hina was known throughout the islands for her beauty and for the fine bark cloth she

---

[10]Vivian Thompson, *Hawaiian Myths of the Earth, Sea and Sky* (Honolulu: University of Hawaii Press, 1988), pp. 60–64.

made. From the time Sun came through the eastern gate until he went through the western gate, Hina worked at her tapa. She gathered the bark herself from mulberry trees. She brought sea water in which to soak it. She pounded the wet bark on her tapa log.

One time when Maui was watching her, he said, "You spend all your days making tapa!"

Hina laid aside her wooden beater, smiling in a sad way. "For those who make tapa, the day is never long enough. This piece is ready to dry but already Sun turns toward the west. My tapa will still be damp when Evening Star hangs in the sky."

"This is Sun's fault. He travels too swiftly. I shall find him and tell him so!"

"O Maui, Sun is a god!"

"We are gods, too," Maui said.

"But small ones, with small power. And you are but a half-god," his mother reminded him. "Sun has great powers. No one has ever gone close to him and lived."

"Then I shall be the first!" Maui boasted. "I shall catch Sun and make him promise to go more slowly."

Hina warned, "Take your magic club and paddle. You will surely need all the power you have."

First, Maui made snares. He gathered coconut fiber and twisted eight strong cords. At the end of each he tied a noose.

Then, as Evening Star appeared in the sky, he coiled his snares in his canoe, laid his magic club beside them, and picked up his magic paddle. One stroke carried him down the river, a second stroke to the island where Sun made his home in the crater of a dead volcano.

Maui left his canoe, took his eight snares and his magic club, and started up to House-of-Sun.

Swiftly he climbed the grassy slope. Slowly he climbed the steep side of the volcano. At the top, in the crater, Sun lay fast asleep under a blanket of clouds. Silently, Maui laid his snares. Then he hid behind a lava rock and slept through the night.

Before daybreak, Maui woke. Clouds were just beginning to roll out of the crater. Soon over its rim came Sun's longest leg, his first glittering ray of sunlight. Down the slope it came and into the center of Maui's snare it stepped.

"What is this?" roared Sun.

"You are my prisoner," said Maui.

"Let me go at once!" Sun commanded. "I have a long journey to make."

"You will journey nowhere until you promise to travel more slowly," said Maui.

"I go swiftly so my night's rest will be longer. Why should I promise such a thing?" Sun demanded.

Maui picked up his magic club before he answered. "Because my mother Hina needs more time to dry her tapas."

"Tapas! I have no time for such things!"

Maui said no more. He swung his magic club against Sun's longest leg, breaking off a piece.

Sun screamed in pain and anger. He scrambled to get three more legs over the rim of the crater. But Maui had laid his snares wisely, and each leg was caught fast. Sun thrashed about, blowing his fiery breath. Maui backed off and tied the three cords fast.

Four legs crawled over the crater's rim. Four more legs were caught. Now Sun was frightened. The more he struggled, the tighter the nooses became. One leg was broken and seven more tied fast. He began to bluster.

"You dare kill me! Without my light, plants and trees would die! Without plants, your people would die!"

Maui looked up from the cord he was tying. "Sun, let us bargain. Promise to travel more slowly for part of the time and I shall let you go."

"Ae. I promise," said Sun crossly.

With his magic club, Maui broke the cords. Sun hurried off across the sky, and Maui paddled back with the good news for Hina.

After that, for part of each year, Sun traveled at his usual speed. Days were short and darkness came early. But the rest of the year, Sun traveled more slowly. Then the days were long and filled with sunshine, and Hina was able to dry her tapas.

Sun kept his promise. If there were times when he wanted to hurry, his broken ray reminded him of the strength and courage of the young half-god, Maui.

SECTION 4: Divine Law: Justice, Reward, and Punishment

Ethical standards and the restitution required to end punishment for taboo violations also can be reflected in sacred stories. The following story is part of the sacred oral tradition of the Maori of New Zealand. What expectations were broken in this story, what were the penalties, and to what degree did the punishments fit the crimes?

THE BLOOD, THE PROMISE, AND THE TATTOO—A MAORI STORY[11]

Mataora's face was swollen and bloody. It was so swollen, he could not swallow. But his parched throat cried for water. Water! Just as his sad heart cried for his lost love, Niwareka. If he survived this torture of receiving the tattoo, then surely he would have the courage to find his wife, Niwareka, daughter of the underworld. If he found her, would she forgive him?

As Mataora lay flat on his back, the tattoo master, Uetonga, continued the peck, peck, pecking of his bone needle, piercing Mata's forehead. Piece by piece the needle broke new skin and embedded black dye made from shark oil and soot . . . the lizard lines covered Mata's face, making the tattoo, the moko. This tattoo would never come off.

Already, tattoo lines curved around and around his cheeks and chin. The mark of the lizard adorned his forehead and nose. Strange lines as crooked as lizard's legs spiraled away from his nose. Yes, he, Mata of the human world, must endure this ritual and prove he had enough courage to be a worthy husband. Then, too, he would be handsome with tattoo. Perhaps then Niwareka would forgive him. The pain of the tattoo would teach him never to cause her pain again.

Mata clenched his hands, his knuckles white and his arms trembling. . . . The pain was muddying his memory. Why had he come here? Why had he, Mataora, the proud Maori chief, traveled to this cursed underworld? This was a dreaded place where only spirits of the dead and Turehu fairy women lived. These strange but lovely, graceful women had pale skin, light eyes, and golden hair flowing to the ground like spun sunlight. Niwareka! He was searching for his beloved Niwareka.

In whispered words, he began his sad song that had given him hope during his long journey. He sang of his search for the beautiful maiden who had agreed to become his wife. He sang joyously of their happiness. Yes! Then, sadly, he sang of his jealousy, his foolish anger, an anger that had caused him to strike the very one he treasured. . . .

The daughters of Uetonga, the tattoo master, heard his singing. They listened to his sad story. . . . Quickly the daughters of the tattoo master ran to their sister.

Niwareka ceased her weeping. She walked to the tattoo house, her father's house, to see this man who sang her name. "Surely this could not be Mata, my husband. Surely no human man, not even a brave Maori warrior, would step into Rarohenga, the spirit word of darkness.

She gazed at his face, the one who lay moaning and singing. His eyes could not open because of the swelling. She touched his eyelids. Gently, gently she stopped the tears that flowed down his bleeding face. Her own tears fell on his lips. "Mata, it is I for whom you sing. Mata!"

"Niwareka," he whispered. "Forgive me."

Drop by drop she gave him water to swallow. . . .

Niwa's own sorrow till arched in her heart. She gazed at her husband. Had he learned from his pain? "The ways of your people are wicked and strange," she told him. "To hurt one another, this we cannot even imagine." Niwareka stared at her husband, "A man must never beat his woman."

Uetonga, her father, spoke now to Mata. "I feel your impatience, your desire to return with my daughter. Leave her here. Our dark world is gentle. Family does not strike family. Leave her here."

Mata hung his head in shame. "Let her come. I have learned. I will hold back my anger. My hand shall not strike her again."

Uetonga stared at the man warrior. "The tattoo I have given you will never come off." Uetonga looked a long while at Mata. "Will your words last like the lizard on your face?"

"I will give my promise. I have learned."

Uetonga looked at his daughter and then again at Mata. "Our moko does not wash off like the warrior's face paint. Wear our tattoo with honor. And with honor, remember your promise."

Niwareka returned with her warrior husband to the world of light, Te Aotuora. As a gift of parting, Uetonga gave Mata a treasured cloak called Rangi-haupapa, the cloak from which all other on earth would be designed. He gave this cloak with one warning: "As you leave our darkness, tell the gatekeeper of this treasure. Conceal nothing. Tell the truth."

But in his impatience to leave the dark world, Mata forgot.

When the gatekeeper discovered the hidden cloak, he cursed the warrior. "Never again can people return to the underworld. Never until death! Go! Take with

---

[11]Flood, Strong, and Flood, *Pacific Island Legends*, pp. 232–236.

you the owl, the bat, and the kiwi [a flightless bird]. Take them as guides. But in your world, they shall hide in the darkness. Night's black cloak will offer them safety.

With the help of the owl, the bat, and the kiwi, Mata and Niwareka returned to the light world. Because of Mata's forgetfulness, people cannot return to the spirit world until after death. But because of his courage, people has the art of tattoo, moko. . . .

Warriors—your faces bloody and your lips swollen—remember the moko! Mata's promise! Have courage, care for one another. Remember!

A creation story told in the Marshall Islands speaks of a mother figure known as Jineer ilo Kobo who gave instructions for living to her peoples. According to these instructions, what ethical values do the Marshallese peoples espouse?

THE BEGINNING OF THE WORLD— A MARSHALLESE ACCOUNT[12]

And now the woman spoke to the people and said, "It is not good to separate from each other in doing big tasks. And do not harbor trouble with one another." (Now that woman taught them that they should work together and love each other and not be separated from each other.)

Therefore they obeyed the teachings of the woman very well.

And the light of the sun was extremely great coming from the east. And they named it "raan." When it went and set in the west it became dark.

And the people were worried again. And the woman said, "Do not be worried about something we do not know about." When it was dark, stars appeared and lighted it up a little. And the people were less worried. . . .

When everything was prepared, she laid down words of testament to all the young men and women at that time that they should not separate from each other. Never mind if they have different clans. But it will be bad to separate. And she gave them another word.

She said, "Wherever you go from ocean to lagoon, no matter what lies you hear, do not obey them. That is, do not talk against people and obey lies. Do not be

like small children who tell lies. The woman taught this to the people.

And she said, "If you do great work, it will be bad if you do not help each other. It will be best if you help each other. . . . And she strongly made testament to them that they should not separate from each other. "And when you eat breadfruit (during the breadfruit season), see that you do not waste the food. But conserve it for a time when there will be no food. Also pandanus, conserve it. Also arrowroot, again conserve it. And do not waste for, for there will come a time when there will be none." . . .

And thus the woman again told them that if they did any big work, they should take time to pray. And remember, their suffering and their happiness because it came to pass.

And she said that she would go on a road, and she left her footprints. And they quickly disappeared. And the people who were there with the woman at that time died and changed into different things after death (like rocks, birds, fish and so forth). They are signs (navigation markers) to this day. (All of the people who died at that time are located in all of the areas of the Marshalls.) And the woman's footprints are still to be seen at Orjej. So that people should not forget.

SECTION 5: Gender: Women and Men in Society

Among the oral traditions of Oceania, there are numerous stories of heroines of great beauty, strength, and courage. One of these stories comes from the Solomon Islands. Tales from the Solomon Islands often are "dark" tales that involve cannibalism and black magic. In this tale, the ghosts of ancestors are overcome by the courage of Riina and the warrior women. What insights, both about the religious beliefs and the status of women on the islands, can be gleaned from this story?

THE WARRIOR WOMEN OF LUMALAO[13]

Once, in the time before, ghosts, called *gosile*, flew about the sky looking for humans to eat. They loved the taste of uncooked flesh. Especially brains. When

---

[12]Jack A. Tobin, *Stories from the Marshall Islands* (Honolulu: University of Hawaii Press, 2002), pp. 15–20.

[13]Flood, Strong, and Flood, *Pacific Island Legends*, pp. 1125–1118.

they flew, the wind rushed through their long hair, making an eerie noise—"Whooeeeiii." Those who heard this sound knew that *gosile* were nearby.

On this one day, two young women were walking near their village. They strolled together, picking flowers and talking about their husbands and their families.

Suddenly, disaster struck. Two *gosile* were flying high overhead. They were feeling a bit hungry. When the first, Otabulau, looked down, he saw the two women on the road far below. "Look at that," he said to his companion, Nuitarara. "I think I see our dinner walking down that road."

With that the two *gosile* flew down and captured the women. Now *gosile* are very strong, and it did no good for the women to resist. They cried and screamed, but the *gosile* carried them away.

The *gosile* flew to their home on Saraainonganonga, far out in the ocean. There they set the captives down while they sharpened their stone axes. When the women realized that the axes were going to be used to cut them up into little pieces, they began to cry even louder.

"Please don't eat us!" they cried. And the two *gosile*, who weren't all that hungry, decided not to eat them. Instead, they even helped the women learn to fly so that other *gosile* could not catch and eat them. They did this by cutting the women's feet and draining out all the heavy blood. But they would not let the women return to their homes. . . .

[The husbands of the women offered a reward to anyone who would rescue their wives. Many men tried, but failed.]

Word of the plight of the women, and of the huge reward offered for their rescue, spread far and wide. One day it reached the island of Lumalao. There lived a fierce group of warrior women and their leader, Riina.

"Is this true?" wondered Riina. "Is this large reward offered just for killing two *gosile*?"

Riina traveled to the island of the husbands and offered to kill the *gosile*. The villages thought she was boasting. This made Riina very angry. She stamped her feet and announced, "These are just *gosile*. And male *gosile* at that! I am stronger, and I will break their jaws!"

With that, Riina paddled back to Lumalao and gathered her large fighting group of women. Together they set out looking for the *gosile* island.

The band paddled from island to island. Finally, they neared the island of Saraainonganonga.

"Whooeeeiii."

The eerie sound floated over the waves. "This is the place," announced Riina. "Everyone hide." Riina alone stood up in the canoe. When the *gosile* saw a canoe approaching with only a single woman, they were not concerned. One of the *gosile*, Otabulau, flew down at her carrying his sharp stone axe. He intended to kill Riina and eat her for his supper!

Instead, Riina grabbed Otabulau's hair and threw him into the canoe. There all the other women tied him up in the bottom of the boat.

"Where do you get your power?" she asked. The frightened *gosile* replied, "From betel, lime, and my red stone axe." As he spoke these words, these very objects fell from his body into the bottom of the canoe.

Riina carefully and slowly stepped right over these sacred objects. It was, of course, taboo for any woman to step over sacred objects. When Riina stepped over the objects, her female essence instantly took away all of the power of Otabulau's axe, betel, and lime.

The canoe landed. The woman took the bound Otabulau and climbed to the *gosile's* cave. Nuitarara, the second *gosile*, stayed nearby. In the cave, the women found a ghastly sight. Rows and rows of skulls, some still with fresh flesh, lined the walls.

Riina was outraged. She suddenly turned on the *gosile* and drew out her special weapon. A boomerang!

With this weapon she struck the startled *gosile* and killed them both in an instant. Riina kicked down the rows of terrible skulls. Then she took the two captive women and began the long trip back to their island.

It took six days of paddling to get back to the village. The husbands and village were so happy to get their wives back and be rid of the *gosile* that they prepared a huge feast.

Thus these warrior women did what no man had been able to do. Many other tales are told of Riina and her band, but they must be kept for another time.

In the Marshall Islands there are numerous tales of supernatural malevolent beings that cause sickness and sometimes death. Often these beings are female and direct their sinister attacks on females. One of these tales is provided below. What effect would tales such as these have on the daily lives of Marshallese woman?

A *Mejenkwaad* Story from Anewetak— A Marshallese Tale[14]

Mejenkwaad are female demons. They affect (possess) women during pregnancy and after they have given birth.

There have been many cases of this in the Marshall Islands. A mouth can open up at the base of the affected person's neck. The neck can expand and stretch out to another island. And she can eat people: anyone, any sex or age, especially her husband.

Possession will take place in a pregnant woman or up until her child's *keemen* [the important celebration of the child's first birthday, and of its surviving the crucial first year of life.] And it will take place if the woman is alone.

It is worse at night. Several people of any age or sex should be with her, preferably of the age of fourteen or fifteen years upward.

The symptoms of *mejekwaad* sickness are as follows: Blood flows from between the teeth of the affected person. The eyes are wild and insane looking. The place at the back of the neck moves as if it is breathing.

If medicine is not applied, another mouth appears. Then it is too late, because the sick person goes out of her mind.

However, she may be cured by magical chants. But medicine is useless. . . .

Women who do not know the magic must be very careful. When the demon enters the woman, she is called a *mejenkwaad*. If she dies while carrying the child or after giving birth, she is called *mejenkwaad*.

Any woman who dies in childbirth is *mejenkwaad*, whether she was possessed by a demon or not. *Mejenkwaad* always try to process a pregnant woman or one with a baby. After the possessed woman dies, she is known as a *mejenkwaad*.

SECTION 6: Daily Living: Health, Etiquette, and Holy Days

To many island peoples, all that happens in life—for good or bad—is determined by the ancestral ghosts who observe and participate in the lives of the living. Among the Kwaio of the Solomon Islands, the word

for ancestral spirits is *adalo*. Kwaio oral tradition does not attempt to explain how the *adalo* control events, but it does assert that to preserve health and fortune the living must avoid the taboos of the *adalo* and provide pig, coconut, and shell offerings to them when they are angry. The following selection is a Kwaio description of the activities of these ghosts that control daily human activities.

The *Adalo* Controls Sickness and Health [Ancestral Ghosts] Among the Kwaio[15]

We refer to the *adalo* as dead. But though they're dead, it is we who are alive who make the mistakes. The *adalo* see the slightest small things. Nothing is hidden from the *adalo*. It would be hidden from us. Even the slightest pollution. Someone urinates, someone menstruates, and tries to hide it. We can't see it: only the woman who does it will know about it. But still, the *adalo* will see it. . . .

Let's say that someone is sick. Well, there's a single *adalo* causing the sickness. They'll communicate with him through divination at Larikeni's place that day. And they'll communicate with him through divination here. They'll communicate with him at Batalamo's place too. . . . If it was a living person instead of an *adalo*, it would not be possible for him to get to all those places the same day. But the *adalo* can talk to all those places at once: "I'm angry with you, so-and-so." He can tell that to all of them at six different places, or ten, on that same day. . . .

It's as though the *adalo* were a man who was in charge of us. Even though we can't see him, he's our boss. If his mind is pleased with us then we won't get sick. If the *adalo* is looking after us, what can happen to us?

But if some pollution violation—urination or menstruation—happens and the woman doesn't report it, people will die from it. The *adalo* will afflict them. Our *adalo* will abandon us . . . so that a tree someone fells will fall on us. We'll die that very day we are abandoned, or the next day, or the next. Or a snake will bite us, or we'll fall down. . . .

Anything you went out to do today could result in your death. You could die from a fall in your garden.

[14]Tobin, *Stories from the Marshall Islands*, pp. 192–193.

[15]Roger M. Keesing, *Kwaio Religion: The Living and the Dead in a Solomon Island Society* (New York: Columbia University Press, 1982), pp. 42–45.

The *adalo* might turn your mind so you would want some delicacy—a possum, say—in the top of the tree. You climb up and get to the top and you fall: that's the end of you. It's as though the *adalo* says to you, "Go and climb that tree." The *adalo* implants that idea in your mind so you'll have an irresistible urge for something up there. You say to yourself, "Oh, there's a possum on top of that tree." You climb up there, miss your handhold, and down you go to the ground.

In the Hawaiian language, the word for the spiritual ancestors who take an interest in human life, visiting people in their dreams and helping them in their troubles, is *Aumakua*. The priest who acts as a bridge between the spirit and material world is known as a *Kahuna*. Literally, this word refers to one calmed of passions and trusted by the gods with the sacred secrets. The following selection is from a twentieth-century manual that was used to instruct initiates who desired to learn the ancient ways of the Kahuna. This section in the manual deals with the "Healing Art of the Kahuna." According to this selection, what do traditional Hawaiians view as the cause of disease, and how is healing achieved?

THE HEALING ART OF THE KAHUNA[16]

The four traditional elements of life, Earth, Water, Fire, and Air denote eternity in form. They are the symbols for the presence of the Great Power in nature. . . . The Hawaiians believe that God is reflected in nature. Truth is the reality around us, and we are with God when we live in the beauty of nature.

Disease is a distortion of reality. Illness is a distortion of true perception. . . .

Each element is ruled by a special Aumakua. By focusing the mind in mediation upon these Aumakua, the power of the four elements of life can be released and brought into balance. This is the secret of kahuna healing.

A. Hina is Mother Earth and Ku is the Architect and Builder. They rule the element earth and all the Guardian Spirits of the earth. Those who wish to contact powers of earth should focus upon Hina and Ku who bring health and wealth.

B. Water has two forms, sea and fresh. Kanaloa rules the vast ocean, and Kamohalii is the male Aumakua of sea and land. Kahalopuna is the Princess of Living Water. Lono dwells in the rain clouds. These Aumakua rule the water element and all the spirits of water.

C. Pele is especially connected with fire and lives in the volcano. . . . Fire can warm and heal, but it can also burn with fierce temper. These Aumakua rule the fire elements and spirits of fire.

D. Air is considered the highest element. The most powerful Aumakua are never seen to touch the earth. They walk in the air.

All these elemental Aumakua, however, are expressions of IO [the Supreme God who is Eternal Perfection]. One God governs the world and gives mana, so that the four elements and all spirits fill nature with life.

Distortion of the four elements, overreliance on one or two of them, and false worship of them (which is another form of ego worship) lead to false psychic sight. . . .

Kahunas must not only know how to bring balance in their own lives but how to counteract against the false psychic power of others and restore balance in the sick and demented.

Example of a chant used in ritual meditation:

PRAYER FOR THE SICK

To thee, O Fiery Eye of Heaven,
From the rising of the sun to the setting of the sun,
From the higher level of heaven above
To the earth below: contact.
Arise, O Ku, the architect and builder,
And Hina, mother earth: contact.
From the sounding of time through space, blow softly the breeze of life from the four corners of heaven above and earth below so your offspring may live and enjoy life.
May the pain, swelling—the tie that binds his trouble—be unfastened, may all inflammation of the muscles and any ache in any physical organ be removed.
Remove the hate, envy, and jealousy of mankind; destroy the evil power of black magic; destroy the power of unreality in your offspring so that there will be no evil forces left in [insert name], and no force of evil surrounding [insert name] from the top of his head to the tip of his toes—either front, back or either side.
May your mana power be inside and I, Thy servant, be outside.
Now my prayer is free to wend its way to God.
May peace be with you.
Amen

---

[16]Douglas Low, ed. *The Kahuna Religion of Hawaii* by David Kaonohiokala Bray and edited by Douglas Low & David Kakuaokalani: *The Foundation of Heaven: Principles of the Hawaiian Religion* (Garberville, CA: Borderland Sciences Research Foundation, 1990), pp. 48–54.

SECTION 7: The Human Quest: Paths to Salvation and Enlightenment

The following story from Micronesia explains what happens to a people when they offend the spirits. It is, however, a story with a happy ending. In this tale, what is the transgression of the people, and how were they saved from the punishment delivered upon them by the spirits?

HOW THE WOMEN SAVED GUAM[17]

Nothing was left to eat. Children cried from hunger. Their stomachs hurt, hurt, hurt as they chewed on scraps of coconut and fish bones. The taro stopped growing. Even the banana tree hid its red flower, sad because its petals held no fingers of tasty new banana. The clouds would not drop rain. Wet winds teased, blowing through palm fronds, rattling the withered branches. But the winds only laughed and left swirls of dust, shedding no rain on the thirsty ground.

"The spirits are angry," the old woman, the maga'haga, warned. "The people no longer show respect. They take from the earth, take from the sea and give nothing in return. Nothing! No respect for the earth. No respect for the sea, the water or each other. The spirits are angry. Our punishment will come from our selfishness."

The old woman predicted correctly. The people had not taken care of the earth. Now the soil was barren and grew nothing. Water had been wasted. Wells had been emptied and now remained dry.

Suddenly a new danger, a new punishment, woke the people. A rumbling deep within the earth split the night's silence. Harder and harder the ground shook. . . . Something was eating the earth right beneath them! Rocks from the high cliffs tumbled down and crashed into the sea.

"Forgive us, Ancient Ones. Forgive us!" the people prayed.

"We will not be forgiven easily. We will not be forgiven until we show we will change our selfish ways," said the older woman. They knew they must appease their ancestral spirits, their ante, the spirit people who could stop the drought, the famine, and this island-eating monster.

The men grabbed their spears. "Run to the Men's House. Run for your lives!" they cried. The men

shoved and squeezed under the tall steep roof. . . . All the mouths were shouting, "Kill whatever is eating our land!" But no one was listening. Words were thrown like stones at each other. Spears were thrust at the darkness. Feet began stamping.

Outside, women young and old waited, shaking their heads. They listened as the men argued about what to do.

[At dawn, a monstrous parrot fish began to eat the island]

The men walked back to the village, their heads bowed in fear. "How can we capture such a giant fish? One snap and we lose our heads."

At the Weaving Pavilion, the woman gathered. They waited until all were present, from the youngest maiden . . . to the oldest auntie. . . . As the women waited, they wove long strips of plant fiber, in and out, in and out. As they wove they began chanting, praying, and thinking.

The women watched and waited, all the time weaving, weaving.
Their fingers wove ribbon of leaves.
Their voices chanted prayers of hope while their thoughts wove possibilities.

A monstrous parrot fish was eating their island. It was another punishment sent by the old ones. Their angry spirits had sent the drought and the famine. How could they appease the spirits? What sacrifice was required? . . .

They wove through the night. As the sun lifted above the straight-line horizon, they watched for signs of husbands and sons returning from the hunt. . . . Finally, sails appeared on the horizon. Soon the men were climbing out of their canoes. The women . . . asked, "Let us help you hunt the monster." . . . The men laughed, "Women cannot hunt. Women only chant and weave. What good is that?"

[The men continued against the monster, but with no success. Again the women asked to help, but were refused.]

. . . The wisest woman, the maga'haga, shook her head. She waited for the men to leave and then spoke. "Stop, rest your hands. Come with me to Agana Spring. We will wash our faces and refresh our hearts. With clear thoughts we will ask for help from our maraanan uchan, the skulls of our ancestors."

But when the women arrived at Agana Spring, they found lemon peels floating in the water. The maga'haga knew that only the women of Pago used lemons to scent their hair. This meant that already an opening had been

---

[17]Flood, Strong, and Flood, *Pacific Island Legends*, pp. 15–27.

made between Agana and Pago. If the monster keep eating, Guam would soon be gone.

"Hurry, come here to the spring. Encircle the water. I know what our sacrifice must be. Our beauty, our hair. If you are willing to help, bow your head and I shall chop off your hair."

One by one the women walked to the spring, knelt by the cool water and touched their foreheads to the black rock. The old maga'haga took out her shell knife, gave thanks, and asked for courage. Quickly she held each woman's long hair with one hand and cut with the other.

"Now we will begin a new weaving."

Again the women wove through the night, their fingers flying faster than the fluttering wings of fairy terns (a seabird). They encouraged each other with songs and stories. Their heads felt strangely light. No long tresses hung down their backs. But to everyone's surprise, their hearts also felt light and full of hope, as if a heavy burden had been cut away.

As the starlight began to fade with the morning light, the weaving was finished. "Come, quickly come." The maga'haga gathered up the black net and hurried to the shore. "Here we will wait. When the palakse', the slippery one, comes out of the tunnel, we will throw our net over its head and then everyone pull. Pull with all your strength."

The young ones looked up at their mothers, who nodded. "Yes, we can do this. We have woven our courage into one net. The strength of many has become one."

The monster fish swam out of the tunnel. It circled the women. Faster and faster, closer and closer it swam. With its great jaws wide open, it rushed right at the women!

Snap! Teeth bit into empty air. With one great throw, the women tossed the net over the monster's mouth. "Pull!" yelled the maga'haga. The women pulled as one. Giant teeth tore at the net, but the net held as if filled with magic.

"Pull! Pull up!" urged the old one. The monster's scaly body thrashed from side to side. Its tail slapped with the sea, splashing waves high into the air. The women held on. The sea became muddy with sand, murky with foam. The woman began chanting, "Be brave, be strong. Pull!"

The men heard their voices, grabbed spears and clubs and rushed to the shore. Quickly the monster was dead. Together men, women and children pulled the giant fish onto shore. They gave thanks to their ancestors and then began a chant, a new song about how the women

of Agana wove their beauty into a net of courage and saved Guam. As the people sang, they heaped coconut husks around the fish, cooked it, and ate.

At last every stomach was full. As the rain began to fall, the people knew that both the drought and the famine were over. They lifted their faces to the heavens and then nodded at each other. What happened today, how their island was saved, would be told to their children and their children's children. Remember, show respect. Take care of this island and each other. Only then will this sea and this land be yours and your children's.

Section 8: The Religious Life: Worship and Righteousness

In a number of Oceanic cultures, it is believed that everyone has a Sir Ghost or ancestral guardian that looks out for him or her. If someone offends another, then the Sir Ghost of the offended party is outraged and responds by punishing the offender by bringing sickness or ill fortune to someone in the offender's kin. To remedy the situation, divination is used to determine the identity of the offended Sir Ghost. After this identity has been determined, restitution is offered and a ceremony performed and, when the reparations are accepted by the Sir Ghost, health or good fortune will be returned to the victim of the sorcery.

The following selection is an early twentieth-century anthropologist's description of the religious activities among the Manus peoples of the Admiralty Islands. In what way is this religious resolution to personal conflicts comparable to legal litigation that is used in modern societies to resolve disagreements? Which form of restitution is more efficient and humane?

APPEASING THE SIR GHOSTS IN THE ADMIRALTY ISLANDS[18]

[T]here was a séance held in Alupwai's house. Alupwai's husband, Tunu, was ill, but not dangerously ill. The normal run of illnesses are not publicly broadcast by loud wailing, as unconsciousness is. Nor are they publicly attended by large numbers of miscellaneous people. Only some relatives and the medium attend. During this month there were probably many other séances held that were not brought to my attention. I

---

[18]R. F. Fortune, *Manus Religion: An Ethnological Study of the Manus Natives of the Admiralty Islands* (Lincoln, NE: University of Nebraska Press, no date), pp. 110–121.

went with Paliuau, Tunu's eldest brother, to this séance. Tunu had not been moved from his own house (a sign of a minor illness). The medium's whistles and oracular reports were incomprehensible to me. Paliau was attentive, grave and aloof, but I got from him a whisper or two as to the course of the séance. Paliau had commanded Tunu not to go to the white Court to bear witness that might help Tunu's wife's brother to make a new marriage and upset an old one. Tunu had gone in defiance of orders. Furthermore Tunu had not been helping Paliau in his work as he should have done. For this double offense the ghost of the father of Paliau and Tunu was making Tunu ill. . . .

A child was born to the wife of Bonyalo [a financial dependent of Paliau]. . . . Bonyalo's child seven days after its birth was treated by a magician. Sooner or later every newborn infant is treated. . . . [W]hat actually happens is that every infant has its infant troubles; it may be only to continuous crying which awakens parental anxiety. The trouble is accounted for by the theory that the infant has been affected by black magic. No oracular diagnosis from a séance is made to establish this theory. It is the general stock explanation. The kin of the ailing infant may have divination made. The question is put to the diviner whether it is not the black magic of X that is responsible. The magician, X, is always the magician with whom the kin concerned have been on bad terms. . . .

For Bonyalo's infant the magician was Korotan. . . . Paliau, over a year before, had fallen out seriously with Korotan. Korotan, although head man of the entire village, former war leader . . . and owner of the best house in Peri, was now blind, and economically backward in consequence. He had failed to meet his debts now for the first time. Paliau had dunned him for debt, until a final rupture was made by Korotan declaring publicly that he would use his black magic against Paliau. Paliua survived the black magic, but did not speak to Korotan . . . for a year. Now that avoidance was over, . . . but black magic was fully accredited . . . with causing infant troubles. So Bonyalo's infant was now to be cured by Korotan exorcising what he had caused. . . .

A fathom of shell money and ten dogs' teeth were put into a small wooden bowl and placed before Korotan. . . . A branch of betel nuts was placed on top of the bowl, and a coconut placed beside it. Korotan seated himself, took some of the betel nuts and began to chew it solemnly and silently. Then after a time he recited the customary introductory history of his magic: "This charm of black magic of green coconut

belonged to Talipale of the riverside at Ndrombut. It worked upon the infants of all. They fell ill, near to death. The diviner divined it. He exorcised it from the infants of all. They became well. . . . He gave me this charm. I work upon all infants with it."

. . . Korotan rubbed the sides of the coconut between his hands as he intoned the charm aloud. In the course of the recital he spat betel juice three times on three spots round the top of the coconut. He intoned:

"You climb on top of this green coconut, green coconut yours, this is. You are here (doing this damage) for a matter of no account I do but make, not seriously. Let it be finished.

She may eat food, she may drink water, she may drink mother's milk, she may sleep, she may wail, she may not scream, she may sleep soundly."

The infant was now put in a large wooden bowl. Korotan tipped the charmed green coconut and poured the coconut milk from it over the infant's body. . . .

Korotan now stood up, and took the infant into his arms. He crooned to it and rocked it until it stopped the vigorous crying. . . . Then he solemnly passed it between his legs from in front to behind him where it was received by a woman. He then sat down . . . took the dogs' teeth and shell money from the wooden bowl that had been placed before him at the opening of the ceremony. As he handled it, testing it by sense of touch, he said:

"Your pay, this is your pay. You come into this wooden bowl, good pay. Come and you and I will go to our house, come and guard our (mine and your) coral rubble territory; you may abandon this territory.

She may eat taro, she may drink her mother's milk, she may drink water, she may sleep, she may not wail, she may not scream, she may sleep soundly in the arms of her mother."

Korotan then put the bowl with its valuables in the house rafter (place of supernaturals) and sat beneath it silently a while. He said that it was now prohibited to wash the child for three days. Then without further speech he went. Someone took the bowl with its contents and gave it to an attendant of Korotan's to take to him.

Section 9: Endings: Death, Judgment, and the Afterlife

Origin of death stories have been told by peoples all over the world. Here are two such accounts from the oral traditions of Australia and Oceania.

THE DEATH OF JININI—AN AUSTRALIAN ABORIGINAL TALE[19]

When the world was young there was no death. This calamity was brought about by the wrongdoings of the woman Bima and her lover Japara.

Bima had a son, Jinini, of whom her husband, Purukupali, was very fond. Every morning when Bima set out to collect food she took Jinini with her, and every evening she brought him back to his doting father, together with the food she had gathered.

An unmarried man, Japara, who lived in the same camp, constantly followed Bima and persuaded her to leave Jinini under the shade of a tree while she accompanied him into the jungle. This intrigue had been going on for some time when, on one very hot day, Bima and her lover stayed away too long. When the mother returned, she saw, to her horror, that the shade of the tree had moved and Jinini was lying dead in the blazing sun.

When the father heard of the tragedy, he was demented with rage and grief. He punished his wife severely for her carelessness, then, picking up the dead body of Jinini, Purukupali walked into the sea and drowned himself. At the same time he decreed that, as his son had died, so must the whole of creation die, never to come to life again. And so it has remained from those remote times until now.

THE CIRCLE OF BIRTH AND DEATH—A SIMBANG TALE FROM PAPUA NEW GUINEA[20]

[When] the earth was new and its surface was still very hot . . . the sleeping platforms of all people were way up above the clouds. People lived forever. Time did not exist. Every day was the same as every other. Some of the people, especially the young, quick-footed ones, began to grow restless. "Please papa," begged a sky child, "Can't we just do something?"

A huge lizard lived in the sky. It was said that he was wise. But it was also said that every so often he told big, fat lies. Most of the time he was helpful. Once in a while he did something cruel. Because everyone lived forever, they needed to forgive when bad things happened.

When the earth had cooled and living things rooted and grew in its soil, the lizard told the sky people tales of amazing food and brilliant beauty. All this existed on earth! . . . The lizard told how to visit earth: slide down a long, thin bamboo pole. . . .

"But how do we get back home?" a man asked. "Yes," said another, "We can't go unless we can come back home again." "Oh, that's easy," said the giant lizard, his mouth crooked open in a smile. "Just climb back up the pole. I'll make it easy for you—I'll put notches in it like the steps of a ladder." . . .

"Thank you," said the sky people. Not everyone went. Some believed the lizard's words and some didn't. But many, oh so many, choose to go! One by one they wrapped their hands around the sturdy pole, jumped free of the clouds, and down they slid. They were so busy holding on tight they didn't see the lizard laughing at them.

Earth was gorgeous. Fresh, cool water bubbled up out of the ground. Orange-red bird-of-paradise blossoms bobbled in the breeze. Everything the lizard had said was true. . . . But then something terrible happened. One of the children stepped on an ant and crushed it. "Get up!" said the child to the ant.

The ant didn't move. It lay in flat back pieces at the child's feet. "Papa," cried the child. "Why won't it get up?" She thought all living things lived forever like the sky people. The little creature should wake up and march across the sand.

Gently the father lifted the dead ant. Other ants scurried about, frightened by his huge human shadow. He reached down and smashed another ant between his fingers. All movement stopped. The man watched and waited. Suddenly he screamed a spine-curdling yell. The tribe came running.

"What's the matter," they yelled.

"This creature." The boy's father was panting now. "It—it—it won't move. It is no more." There was no word in their language for death, so he could not even say that it had died. The people began to tremble. What kind of world had they come to?

Together they carved spears and hunted a bird, a gecko, and a pig. "We honor your spirit, living creature. May you live forever," they chanted. Then they took a heavy rock and killed the bird, the gecko, and the pig. The pig's dark blood gushed from its neck into the sand. Prayers drifted away in the evening wind. Nothing could bring these creatures back to life.

This is not what the lizard had told them! Liar! Nothing lasted here. The bees made their honey and

[19]Charles P. Mountford, *The Dreamtime: Australian Aboriginal Myths in Paintings by Ainslie Roberts* (Adelaide: Rigby Limited, 1965), p. 28.

[20]Flood, Strong, and Flood, *Pacific Island Legends*, pp. 107–110.

then they died. The flowers bloomed and their open faces shriveled. Dogs and pigs and even wives grew old and died.

Too late for the people from heaven! They had eaten the food of the earth. Now they too would experience all of earth's gifts, even the bitter ones: birth, sickness, old age, and death.

The sky people huddled together and wept. One brave woman said, "Don't give up! We must climb back to the sky. We don't need these full bellies. It is better to live forever!" The people ran to where the bamboo pole had been struck into the ground. It must still be there, waiting for them to slip their toes into the carved notches and climb hand over hand back to heaven.

But no! The evil lizard had bitten the bamboo pole clear through. It lay in pieces on the ground, splintered and still dripping with his saliva. "Look!" cried the man who had asked the lizard how they would return to the sky. "He didn't even carve the notches! All the time he was planning to leave us here!"

Sadly, the people turned away. The sound of weeping grew dimmer and dimmer as small groups wandered off by themselves. One followed the snaky curves of the river bank. Another group walked under the canopy of broad-leafed trees. A third one climbed up into the hills that lead to the mountains.

These were the ancestors of the people who live on earth today. Because of them you were born. And because our home is the earth, living things will experience forever the great cycle of birth and death.

PowerWeb SUPPLEMENT

1. **Sun Mother Wakes the World: Australian Aborigine,** Diane Wolkstein, *Parabola*, February 1999.

According to Australian Aborigines, the Sun Mother is responsible for the creation of the world by waking it at the beginning of time and by renewing creation every morning. In this *PowerWeb* supplement from *Parabola*, Diane Wolkstein describes these dreamtime beliefs that continue to be embraced by contemporary aboriginal peoples. How might an aboriginal attempt to defend the truth of this worldview to a skeptical Western audience?

Readings from *PowerWeb: Religion* are available at the McGraw-Hill *PowerWeb* website http://www.dushkin.com/powerweb. A personal access code to *PowerWeb: Religion* is provided free with each new copy of this book. Those who purchase a used copy may buy an access code at the website.

SELECTED BIBLIOGRAPHY

Beckwith, Martha Warren. *Hawaiian Mythology.* Honolulu: University of Hawaii Press, 1970.

Bellwood, Peter. *Prehistory of the Indo-Malaysian Archipelago.* Honolulu: University of Hawaii Press, 1997.

Cowan, James G. *Myths of the Dreaming: Interpreting Aboriginal Legends.* Rancho Mirage, CA: Prism House Press, 1994.

Denoon, Donald, and Philippa Mein-Smith, with Marivic Wyndham. *A History of Australia, New Zealand and the Pacific.* Malden, MA: Blackwell Publishers, 2000.

Flood, Bo, Beret E. Strong, and William Flood. *Micronesian Legends.* Honolulu: The Bess Press, 2002.

Flood, Bo, Beret E. Strong, and William Flood. *Pacific Island Legends.* Honolulu: The Bess Press, 1999.

Keen, I. *Knowledge and Secrecy in an Aboriginal Religion: Yolngu of North-East Arnhem Land.* Oxford: Oxford University Press, 1994.

Kessing, Roger M. *Kwaio Religion: The Living and the Dead in a Solomon Island Society.* New York: Columbia University Press, 1982.

Loebel-Fried, Caren. *Hawaiian Legends of the Guardian Spirits.* Honolulu: University of Hawaii Press, 2002.

Lohmann, Roger Ivar. *Dream Travelers: Sleep Experiences and Culture in the Western Pacific.* New York: Palgrave MacMillan, 2003.

Mountford, Charles P. *The Dreamtime.* Adelaide: Rigby Limited, 1965.

Parsons, Clairie D. F., ed. *Healing Practices in the South Pacific.* Honolulu: University of Hawaii Press, 1985.

Robinson, Roland. *Aboriginal Myths and Legends.* Melbourne: Sun Books, 1977.

Sahlins, Marshall. *Islands of History.* Chicago: University of Chicago Press, 1987.

Swain, Tony, and Garry Trompf. *The Religions of Oceania.* New York: Routledge, 1995.

Trompf, Garry. *Payback: The Logic of Retribution in Melanesian Religions.* Cambridge, UK: Cambridge University Press, 1994.

Thompson, Vivian. *Hawaiian Myths of the Earth, Sea and Sky.* Honolulu: University of Hawaii Press, 1988.

Tobin, Jack A. *Stories from the Marshall Islands.* Honolulu: University of Hawaii Press, 2002.

Whitehouse, Harvey. *Inside the Cult: Religious Innovation and Transmission in Papua New Guinea.* New York: Oxford University Press, 1995.

Credits

Index